# The Radio Station

*The Radio Station* offers a concise and insightful guide to all aspects of radio broadcasting, streaming, and podcasting. This book's tenth edition continues its long tradition of guiding readers to a solid understanding of who does what, when, and why in a professionally managed station. This new edition explains what "radio" in America has been, where it is today, and where it is going, covering the basics of how programming is produced, financed, delivered, and promoted via terrestrial and satellite broadcasting, streaming, and podcasting. John Allen Hendricks and Bruce Mims examine radio and its future within a framework of existing and emerging technologies. The companion website is newly revised with content for instructors, including an instructors' manual, lecture slides, and test questions. Students will discover an expanded library of audio interviews with leading industry professionals in addition to practice quizzes and links to additional resources.

**John Allen Hendricks** (Ph.D., University of Southern Mississippi) has more than 20 years of experience as a media studies educator. He currently serves as Chairman of the Department of Mass Communication and holds the rank of Professor at Stephen F. Austin State University in Nacogdoches, Texas, USA.

**Bruce Mims** (Ph.D., University of Southern Mississippi) began his career as an electronic media educator in 1977. He currently holds the rank of Professor at Southeast Missouri State University in Cape Girardeau, Missouri, USA.

# The Radio Station

## Broadcasting, Podcasting, and Streaming

**Tenth Edition**

**John Allen Hendricks**
**Bruce Mims**

Routledge
Taylor & Francis Group

NEW YORK AND LONDON

Tenth edition published 2018
by Routledge
711 Third Avenue, New York, NY 10017

and by Routledge
2 Park Square, Milton Park, Abingdon, Oxon, OX14 4RN

*Routledge is an imprint of the Taylor & Francis Group, an informa business*

© 2018 Taylor & Francis

The right of John Allen Hendricks and Bruce Mims to be identified as authors of this work has been asserted by them in accordance with sections 77 and 78 of the Copyright, Designs and Patents Act 1988.

First edition published by Focal Press 1986
Ninth edition published by Focal Press 2015

*Library of Congress Cataloging in Publication Data*
A catalog record for this book has been requested

ISBN: 978-1-138-21880-2 (hbk)
ISBN: 978-1-138-21881-9 (pbk)
ISBN: 978-1-315-21265-4 (ebk)

Typeset in Giovanni and Franklin Gothic
by Florence Production Ltd., Stoodleigh, Devon, UK

Visit the companion website: www.routledge.com/cw/Hendricks

# Contents

v

# Foreword

## *Erica Farber*

**Erica Farber** is the President and CEO of the Radio Advertising Bureau, the not-for-profit trade association representing America's broadcast radio industry, where she leads radio's advocacy efforts by helping to drive business, grow advertising revenue, and communicate radio's digital transition. A career radio broadcaster, Erica is also the host of the weekly podcast series entitled *Radio on Mainstreet*.

Source: Courtesy of Erica Farber

*

The definition of a textbook is a book used for the study of a particular subject. Now, if you are anything like I was when I was a student, the idea of reading a textbook was about as interesting as watching paint dry!

But here you are reading the opening pages of *The Radio Station* and, let me tell you, you are in luck. You are about to embark on a wonderful journey that will help you learn inside out about the incredible world of radio broadcasting and audio communications. And why is this so important? It is important because you may have just discovered the key that will open *the* door to help you decide what you want to do with the rest of your life. And that possible answer is radio!

Let me share some important facts about radio. Ninety-three percent of the population listens to radio. That's more people than watch television, use the Internet, or even use a smartphone. Radio delivers audio content to passionate and loyal listeners across multiple platforms. It's on air, online, and in the car. Radio is live and local and is the original mobile and social medium. Radio has a solid position in time spent with listening devices and captures nearly one-fifth of all weekly hours spent with media. It is the number one place people go to discover new music. Ask any singer or songwriter how they felt the first time they heard themselves or their song on the radio. Superstar Demi Lovato just said at a recent appearance, "it's a dream come true every time I hear my song on the radio."

Bringing this story to life, in the tenth edition of the *The Radio Station*, are experienced broadcasters and educators John Allen Hendricks and Bruce Mims. Through their dedication, knowledge, and expertise—coupled with their relationships with broadcasters across the country—they have organized this journey to provide you with the important details regarding the history of radio and they bring you up to date on the present state of the industry.

You will be exposed to the inner workings of a radio station from how it is programmed, researched, and produced to the individual job functions at a radio station and how they interact with each other. You will learn how radio stations promote, market, and even sell their products. You will be exposed to the technical aspects of the business and also learn about the many new technological developments and advancements helping to transform the business as it prepares for tomorrow. Plus you will have access to much more content created not only by the esteemed authors but also by many prominent and successful broadcasters.

In order to create the future it is important to understand the past. In the late 1800s Guglielmo Marconi, the father of radio, began conducting experiments with radio waves. In 1920 the first commercial aired on a radio station. Almost 100 years later radio is still the number one most listened to medium in the country. With every aspect of everything we do, we are experiencing change at lightning speed and radio broadcasting and audio communication are no different.

As you delve deeper into to this amazing communications vehicle think about your own favorite radio station. What do you like about it? Why do you listen? If you were running the radio station what would you change? What would you do differently? These questions and many more will be answered as you will discover through the pages of *The Radio Station*. It is going to be a wild ride and I hope you are as fortunate as I was and are able to find your place in this incredible world of radio.

# About the Authors

**John Allen Hendricks** (Ph.D., University of Southern Mississippi) has more than 20 years of experience as a media studies educator. He currently serves as Chairman of the Department of Mass Communication and holds the rank of professor at Stephen F. Austin State University in Nacogdoches, Texas.

Dr. Hendricks is the author/editor of more than 10 books including: *The Palgrave Handbook of Global Radio* (Palgrave, 2012); *The Twenty-First-Century Media Industry: Economic and Managerial Implications in the Age of New Media* (Lexington, 2010); *Social Media: Usage and Impact* (Lexington, 2012); and *Social Media and Strategic Communications* (Palgrave, 2012). One of his books received the 2011 National Communication Association's Applied Research Division's Distinguished Scholarly Book Award.

He is a past President of the Broadcast Education Association (BEA) (2015 to 2016) and served on the BEA Executive Committee and Board of Directors from 2009 to 2017. He is a past Chair, Vice-Chair, and Secretary of the BEA Radio and Audio Media (RAM) Division. Also, he is a past President of the Oklahoma Broadcast Education Association (OBEA).

Dr. Hendricks has experience in both commercial and noncommercial radio. From 1997 to 2009, he was responsible for the oversight of programming, budgeting, and personnel at a noncommercial, university-owned radio station at Southeastern Oklahoma State University.

**Bruce Mims** (Ph.D., University of Southern Mississippi) began his career as an electronic media educator in 1977. He currently holds the rank of Professor at Southeast Missouri State University in Cape Girardeau, Missouri.

Dr. Mims has authored articles published in the *Journal of Radio Studies*, *Journalism & Mass Communication Educator*, and *Journal of Media Education*. He was a contributor to the Michael C. Keith-authored book *Tuning In: Radio in Society Since 1945*. In addition, Dr. Mims also has published in professional trade magazines, including essays that have appeared in *Billboard*, *Broadcast Management/Engineering*, and *Radio World*.

He is an active member of the Broadcast Education Association (BEA) and served as Chairperson of its Management, Marketing and Programming Interest Division. He is a past President of the National Broadcasting Society-Alpha Epsilon Rho (NBS-AERho) and is a Charter Member and past President of the Missouri Broadcast Educators Association (MBEA).

Dr. Mims began his commercial radio broadcasting career in 1971 and transitioned to public radio broadcasting seven years later. He joined the faculty of Southeast Missouri State University in 1989.

# Preface
## Welcome to the World of Radio
*Paul McLane* Editor in Chief, Radio World

Welcome to the world of radio.

This book will open your awareness to the practices of a medium that enjoys unique power and romance. It will help you understand its career opportunities and how to pursue them.

But why, a century after revolutionizing mass communication, does radio remain so compelling? How has it thrived and reinvented itself while so many other media and electronic innovations have launched and disappeared?

Perhaps it's the unique intimacy of a voice whispering in our ear.

Paul McLane

Source: Image courtesy of Teresa Castracane Photography

Perhaps it's the skill of a curator who helps us discover songs we didn't know existed, of musicians who create soundtracks for our lives, of storytellers who create theater in our minds, of advertising professionals whose creative endeavors whet our appetite for their new products.

Maybe too it's the thrill of pleasure at the sound of the crack of a baseball bat. Or it's the "drop what we're doing" urgency of hearing a meteorologist interrupt our afternoon music to tell us about a dangerous funnel cloud forming outside of town. Or the deep satisfaction of listening to a long-form interview with our favorite author, actor, or digital innovator.

These are experiences from the listener's perspective. Radio is best when it engages, provokes, entertains, and informs us.

But who would not want to be the one *creating* those experiences?

The people who make good radio enjoy a special privilege, participating in the magic of creating intimate spaces in a very public way. I hope you'll have the opportunity to feel this yourself, and you don't have to be an air talent to do it. There are many crucial roles in creating this magic.

In their revised, expanded edition of *The Radio Station*, John Allen Hendricks and Bruce Mims have put extra emphasis on career opportunities—in music, news, sports, sales, engineering, IT, and social media.

There are other new elements. The chapter on research includes an article from Andrew Forsyth at Nielsen BDS about how to use data to identify and schedule new music, as well as an extended interview with Geoff Steadman of the Telos Alliance about its Voltair product and a discussion about changes in the influential Nielsen PPM ratings system. Cumulus Media's Mike McVay and Producer Ray Slater of *The Bobby Bones Show* provide expert insights, and veteran communications attorney David Oxenford shares expertise about regulatory issues, music, and copyright law.

This book is weighted toward commercial broadcasting operations in the United States, but will help you understand other forms including public, college, low-power FM, and U.S. government-sponsored international broadcasting. Keep in mind too that other countries have their own regulatory regimes and transmission infrastructures that differentiate broadcasting further.

If you are considering a radio career, I'd be doing you a disservice not to acknowledge that some people, particularly in U.S. commercial broadcasting, lament trends such as corporate consolidation, programming similarity, voice-tracking, and shrinking workforces. Critics also note the under-representation of women and minorities at ownership and management levels. Such factors undermine radio's quality or competitiveness, in their view. I don't dismiss these considerations, and if you enter the industry you will find debate over such issues to be a part of daily life.

But challenge anyone who tells you radio is a buggy-whip industry. We live in an exciting time to enter media careers. Not only are thousands of people making careers in radio—many doing exceptional work—but the smartest of them work for companies eager to employ and develop forward-looking multimedia professionals.

Keep in mind too that those companies are also reinventing themselves, and the term "radio" can mean something much different than it did a few years ago. People debate what exactly the word means anymore. Does it still refer strictly to over-the-air, "one to many" programs broadcast via terrestrial towers and antennas to a multitude of receivers in local listenership communities? Does it include satellite radio? How about streamed audio and online services that combine access to traditional stations with personalized or curated content?

Are we listening to radio when we plug a smartphone into a car dashboard? Is the video stream of a station's morning show part of "radio"? Why are podcasts considered different from radio? And what will come of emerging "hybrid" technologies that aim to bring an interactive, two-way aspect to our radio listening?

Radio is in a period of dramatic and accelerated evolution, as are the devices that carry our programs, as well as the very vehicles and living rooms where we want our "station" to be heard. Further, as consulting firm Research Director Inc. puts it, what was once a blind conversation is now a multidimensional relationship.

So ignore questions of definition. The listener doesn't care if words and music arrive via a land-based tower, satellite, or smart speaker. They want compelling content and experiences. Instead of asking "what is radio?" or "what is a radio station?" the question broadcasters must ask ourselves is "what business am I in?" You, the reader, have the opportunity in your career to define the answer. To me, ultimately, radio is about creating connections between us and a listener. Everything else is a tool to that end.

Radio though is unusually persistent. One learns to trust in this persistence. There's something about the inherent connection between speaker and listener, something preserved in the electronic path between microphone to eardrum, that sets radio apart. Radio succeeds because it rests on one of the earliest of our developmental experiences: sharing human emotion through sounds.

When we create meaning in the mind of fellow humans, we engage in a far older form of communication than books or moving images. It's noble. It's fundamental. And it's pretty dang cool.

# Acknowledgments

The first edition of this book was published more than 30 years ago, in 1986, and as the radio industry evolved so too did this book. Broadcast educator and radio scholar Michael C. Keith was the lead author of the first two editions and the sole author on the six subsequent editions. Broadcaster Joseph M. Krause was coauthor on the first two editions, with Michael C. Keith.

Beginning with the ninth edition of the book and now continued in the tenth edition, we enthusiastically agreed to continue the previous efforts to share the story about the radio industry in the same manner used for three decades. We have endeavored to create a practical, timely, illustrative, and accessible book on radio station operations with the focused objective of providing students of radio with the most complete account of the medium possible, from the insider's perspective.

It is presented from the perspective of the radio professional, drawing now more than ever before on the insights and observations of those who make their daily living by working in the industry. Countless radio and audio professionals have contributed to this effort to disseminate factual and relevant information about the medium in a way that captures its reality and evolution. These professionals represent the top echelons of network and corporate radio, as well as the rural daytime-only outlets spread across the country. The strategy of the book for more than three decades has been to draw upon the experience of countless broadcast and allied professionals. Again, our debt of gratitude to them is significant.

Therefore, we wish to express sincere appreciation to the many individuals and organizations that assisted in so many important ways. Foremost among them are Erica Farber and Paul McLane, who freely and frequently shared with us their assistance, guidance, and expertise. Erica was kind with her comments and support in the book's Foreword and Paul was steadfast in his support of this project with his thorough overview and comments in the Preface.

Although it goes without saying that the assistance provided by individuals in the radio industry was invaluable, we want to emphasize our appreciation to the following: John Alfonso, Matt Bailey, Dan Barron, Georgia Beasley, Gary Begin, Cherri Bell, Frank Bell, Joshua "Doc" Bennett, Gary Berkowitz, Chuck Bethea, Heather Birks, Mike Bloxham, Ted Bolton, Gordon Borrell, Brian Buckley, Ian Burns, George Capalbo, Brad Carson, Gregg Cassidy, Kevin Cassidy, Tommy Castor, Kristin Charron, Ron Chatman, Lynn Christian, Kaitlin Ciphery, Greg Clancy, Dawn Cohen, Ed Cohen, David Cole, Chuck Conrad, Randal Crow, Andrew Curran, Joe D'Angelo, John David, Glenn Davies, Tim Davis, Joel Denver, Donna Detweiler, Mike Dougherty, Dwight Douglas, Melody Dover, Rick Ducey, Bruce DuMont, Robert Dunlop, Symon Edmonds, Ashruf El-Dinary, Tripp Eldridge, Mike Engelbrecht, Doug Erickson, Erica Farber, Jim Farley, Doug Ferber, Norm Feuer, Paul Fiddick, Chuck Finney, Ellyn Fisher, Laurie Lynch Flick, Ty Ford, Andrew Forsyth, Ann M. Fotiades, Mark Fratrik, Stephanie Friedman, Ken Frommert, Radhika Gajjala, Juan Galdamez, Kevin Geary, John Gehron, Valerie Geller, Linda Conway Correll George, Josie Geuer, Thomas Gibson, Thomas Giger, Carolyn Gilbert, Paul Goldstein, Augie Grant, Matt Grasso, Jordan Groll, Rick Greenhut, Kelli Grisez, Ralph Guild, Ian Gunn, Jeff Haley, Donna Halper, Kisha Hardwick, Stephen Hartzell, Mike Henry, Juan Carlos Hidalgo, Lavonne Hill, Derrick Hinds, Libby Hiple, David Holland, Jason Insalaco, Fred Jacobs, Mike Janssen, Troy Jefferson, Haley Jones, Steve Jones, Leah Kamon, Paul Kamp, Mark Kassof, Larry Keene, Tom Kelly, Dick Kent, Deena Kimmel,

Kimberly Kissel, Robyn Knight, Valerie Komor, Wolf Korgyn, Warren Kozireski, Weezie Kramer, Michael A. Krasner, Erwin Krasnow, Warren Kurtzman, Jinny Laderer, Megan Lazovick, Stephanie Wai Lee, Lori Lewis, Guy Low, Leah Luddine, Andy Ludlum, Luke Lukefahr, John Lund, Mark Maben, Jeff Magram, Robin Martin, Andrew May, Richard May, Jr., Chea McGee, John McGrath, Steve McKiernan, Paul McLane, James McMahen, Mike McVay, Dominic Mendicino, Christine Merritt, Jon Miller, Larry Miller, Ken Mills, Charlie Morgan, Trevor Morgan, Valentina Morisoli, Allen Myers, Randi Myles, Jon Nastor, Dave Neugesser, Vicki Nichols, Kathrin Nimpsch, Clark Novak, Criss Onan, Dick Oppenheimer, Otabek, David Oxenford, Lorna Ozmon, Ben Palmer, Deborah Parenti, Norm Pattiz, Wayne Pecena, Michael Pelaia, Mathew Piccolotto, Tom Pierson, Jana Polsky, Darryl Pomicter, Sean Poole, Brittney Quarles, Robert Quicke, Joel Raab, Dick Rakovan, Mark Ramsey, Allison Reddington, Seth Resler, Skip Reynolds, B. Eric Rhoads, Nicole Ribaudo, Alice M. Rios, Jim Robertson (for his vast Rolodex), Davida Rochman, Ron Rodrigues, Sophie Rompré, John Rosso, Krissy Rushing, Luke Russert, Ed Ryan, Marty Sacks, Mark St. John, Tim Scheld, Rebecca Schnall, Dave Scott, Tom Severino, Michael Shane, Larry Shannon, Jan Shober, Glenda Shrader-Bos, Ken Sibley, Bill Siemering, Jeremy Sinon, Ray Slater, Jeff Smulyan, Geoff Steadman, Emily Stephens, Chris Sterling, Peter Stewart, Robert J. Struble, Radha Subramanyam, Dick Taylor, Marlin Taylor, Tom Taylor, Chris Thomas, Omar Thompson, Shane Toven, Jay Tyler, Martin Vacher, Dan Vallie, Dave Van Dyke, Chris Vane, Abe Velez, Rob Vining, Karen Volkman, Tom Webster, Mike Whalen, Thomas White, Leslie Whittle, Audra Wiant, Jeffrey Wilkinson, Randy Williams, Darren Willsher, Jim Wilson, Stephen Winzenburg, Ron Wittebols, Karina Wong, et al.—the list is endless and we most likely left someone off the list. For that, we apologize.

Countless companies and organizations contributed to the body of this work. They include: a2x, ABC Radio Networks, Ad Council, Air America, *All Access*, Aphex, Apple Corporation, Arrakis Systems, Associated Press, Backbone Networks Corp., Beasley Broadcast Group, The Benchmark Company, Berkowitz Broadcast Consultants, BIA/Kelsey, BMI, Bolton Research, Bonneville Broadcasting, Borrell Associates Inc., BPME, Broadcast Company of the Americas Radio San Diego, Broadcast Education Association, *Broadcasting and Cable*, Broadcasting Unlimited, Burkhart Douglas and Associates, Burli, C-SPAN Radio, CBS, CFM, CIPB, Clear Channel Sucks.com, Coleman Insights Media Research, College Broadcasters Inc., Communication Graphics, Comrex, CRN, Cumulus, David Sarnoff Library, Deer River Group, Direct Marketing Research, Donna Halper and Associates, dts/HD Radio, Edison Media Research, Electro-Voice, Emmis, Enco, Entercom Communications Corp., Erickson Media Consultants, ESPN Radio, the FCC, Finney Media, *FMQB*, FMR Associates, *The Free Beer & Hot Wings Morning Show*, Geller Media International, Global Radio News, Goldwave Inc., Greater Media, GRN-live, Harker Research, Hear2.0, Herald Media Inc., Holland Cooke Media, Hooks Unlimited, iHeartMedia, iHeartRadio, *Inside Radio*, INSOFT LLC, Integr8, Intercollegiate Broadcasting System, Interep Radio Store, International Demographics, iTunes, Jacobs Media, Jefferson Pilot Data Systems, Jelli, Joel Raab Country Radio and Media Consulting, Jones Radio News, Katz Media Group, KD Kanopy, Kelly Research, Kelton Agency, Ken Mills Agency, KHWL, KIRO, KISS-FM, KKWE, KVMA, Learfield, Library of American Broadcasting, Lund Consultants, Marketron Inc., Mediabase, Mercury Research, Metro Traffic Network, MF Digital, MMR, Moose Lake Products Company, Museum of Broadcast Communications, National Association of Broadcasters, National Radio Talent System, Nautel, NBCU, NBS-AERho, Next Media, Next Radio, Nielsen Audio, Nielsen BDS, NPR, NuVoodoo Media, O. C. White Co., Omnirax Furniture Co., Orban, Oxysys, Pandora Radio, Paragon Media Strategies, Pew Internet & American Life Project Surveys, PodcastOne Sports, Premiere Radio Networks, Public Radio International, Pure Jingles, QuikStats, Radeo, Radio Advertising Bureau, *Radio and Internet Newsletter*, *Radio Business Report*, *Radio Daily News*, *Radio Ink*, Radio-landia, Radio One, Radio SAWA, *Radio World*, RCS, *RTDNA*, SCS Unlimited, Shane Media, Shure Inc., SoCast, Specialized Data Systems Inc. (SDS), Spotify, SiriusXM Radio, Skyline Satellite Services, Society of Broadcast Engineers, Sound Exchange, Southern Arkansas University, Spanish Radio Group, Jim Steele, Annette Steiner, Strategic Radio Solutions, Sun Broadcast Group, Syndication.net, *Talkers Magazine*, Talk Radio Network, Tapscan, the Telos Alliance, 360 Systems, Tieline, TM Studios, *Tom Taylor Now*, Triton Digital, 25-Seven Systems, vCreative, WBTZ-FM, Westinghouse Broadcasting, WestwoodOne, Wheatstone, WIZN, WOR-AM, WTOP-FM, Xaxis, Xperi, Yellowtec, and Zapoleon Media Strategies.

We made every effort possible to locate industry professionals who contributed to earlier editions of this book and request updated information, and in almost every chapter you will notice that their essays are indeed new and analyze the radio industry from a fresh perspective. We express appreciation to all who assisted us in this process.

We wish to thank our Editor at Routledge/Taylor & Francis, Ross Wagenhofer, and Editorial Assistant, Nicole Salazar, who spent an enormous amount of time fielding phone calls, promptly answering emails, helping with formatting issues when our computers simply would not cooperate with us, helping to secure copyright permissions, and helping us locate lost files. Ross and Nicole provided wise and needed guidance throughout the process. We are most appreciative to Ross, and early on in the process Linda Bathgate, both of whom supported us and supported a new edition of this book.

We wish to express appreciation to Richard Sanders, of Florence Production, who served as the Project Manager of the production stage of our book, and Hugh Jackson, of Jackson Proofreading Services, for helping to clarify some of the writing. Both Sanders and Jackson were keen in their handling and oversight of our manuscript as it made its way through the final publishing stages and we thank them.

John Allen Hendricks wishes to acknowledge the diligent and conscientious assistance he received from his graduate assistant, Brody Wedgeworth. Brody's organizational and technological skills are impressive and they were key assets in helping propel this project to its completion.

Lastly, and perhaps most importantly, we wish to acknowledge and express affection and appreciation to our spouses for being patient and understanding as we worked long hours on weekends and late nights at our computers. We thank Stacy Hendricks and Mary Mims for their continued love and support.

**John Allen Hendricks**, Nacogdoches, Texas
**Bruce Mims**, Cape Girardeau, Missouri

# What's New to this Edition of *The Radio Station*

For more than 30 years *The Radio Station* has been the go-to textbook for all things in radio broadcasting education. In keeping with traditions both old and new, this edition stays the course, offering readers up-to-the-moment information about practices, issues, trends, and developments in terrestrial, Internet, and satellite radio. A new chapter introduces students to an extended discussion of career opportunities, featuring essays by accomplished Millennial professionals in the key areas of sales, promotion, programming, and engineering. Numerous industry veterans—many for the first time—share their insight and opinions in every chapter. Additional highlights include:

*Chapter 1*: This chapter has been completely restructured and retitled and is divided into nine sections that provide readers with an updated overview of the state of the radio industry. Those new sections are: Broadcasting, Profits in the Air—The Business Model Evolves, Satellite Radio, Mobile Music Services, Podcasting, Streaming, HD Radio, Public Radio/Noncommercial, and Radio Regulations and Government Oversight. There are four exciting new essay contributions. One essay from professor Larry Miller, of New York University, discusses the paradigm shift taking place in radio, while technology expert Jon Nastor discusses podcasting and its quickly growing role in the industry. Mike Englebrecht, Director of Product Engagement for TagStation and NextRadio, writes about the change in the radio industry brought on by new technologies such as streaming. Augie Grant, from the University of South Carolina, and Jeffrey Wilkinson, from the Beijing Institute of Technology, Zhuhai, China, provide an essay that proposes four interesting scenarios of how radio may evolve as a result of constantly changing competition, technology, and economic fluctuations.

*Chapter 2*: Technological advances have forced station management to continually adjust and evolve to remain financially competitive and this chapter delves deeper into that transition. The updates to the chapter includes examining strategies being implemented and challenges being faced by radio station managers as a result of the Internet and social media technologies. All essays by industry professionals have been updated, including BIA/Kelsey's Rick Ducey's radio ad revenue forecast through the year 2021. A new co-authored essay about radio economics by Augie Grant, from the University of South Carolina, and Jeffrey Wilkinson, from the Beijing Institute of Technology, Zhuhai, China, has been included in the chapter. Adding a much-needed perspective is a new essay on small-market radio management by Ken Sibley, former General Manager/Owner at KVMA-AM and KVMA-FM in Magnolia, Arkansas. Importantly, an essay by communications attorney David Oxenford, partner at Wilkinson, Barker, & Knauer, about 10 regulatory issues that all broadcast station general managers need to consider. There are updated figures and images throughout the chapter.

*Chapter 3*: Programming the music-intensive station is the subject that takes center stage in this edition. One of the industry's most widely respected and honored programmers, Mike McVay of Cumulus Media, writes about his company's return to market-based programming decision-making. Attorney David Oxenford, a widely published expert on music and copyright law, offers advice for helping programmers achieve and maintain compliance. Ray Slater, Producer of the nationally syndicated hit *The Bobby Bones Show*, weighs in on the challenges of keeping *TBBS* fresh and relevant. Michael Pelaia, President of Hooks Unlimited, explains how the use of song hooks leads to programmer success. Plus, the tenth edition features updates and insights on radio's leading music formats.

*Chapter 4*: This chapter is expanded by not only examining the importance of generating advertising revenue, with a strong focus on digital media technologies and podcasting, but also examining the responsibilities of the traffic and billing departments in radio stations. In this edition, the reader will find an expanded appendix with two offerings from SoCast media, a digital media platform that helps broadcasters make the transition to reaching and engaging their audiences in digital, especially with mobile apps and new ways to monetize on-air content through web and social media. Jason Insalaco, a Los Angeles media lawyer and talent manager representing personalities from morning show radio, talk radio, and public broadcasting, updates his essay on selling personalities. Additionally, there is an examination of strategies to generate new and additional revenue for radio stations through websites, HD radio, streaming, and podcasting. Specifcally, Jason Insalaco explores ways to monetize podcasting in his updated essay, titled "Podca$hing In." There are updated figures and images throughout the chapter.

*Chapter 5*: This chapter is significantly expanded by not only examining radio news but also examining the talk/information and all-sports formats. Prominent industry leaders share with readers their expertise of radio news, including a new industry essay from Steve Jones, Vice-President and General Manager of ABC Radio News. Jeremy Sinon, the Director of Digital Strategy for Hubbard Radio, provides an essay sharing his experience digitizing radio. New York's WCBS-AM director of news and programming, Tim Scheld, updates his essay on creating special connections between station and listener, while Andy Ludlum, former director of news programming at KNX 1070 Newsradio and KFWB News Talk 980 in Los Angeles, CA, updates his insightful essay on what makes a successful news station. Media consultant Holland Cooke authors a timely essay on new technologies and their effect on local news. Lastly, a new section on websites, podcasts, and social media is included in the tenth edition. There are updated figures, images, and content throughout the chapter.

*Chapter 6*: Multiple guest essayists appearing for the first time in *The Radio Station* address the latest developments in applied research. Consultant and broadcast innovator Andrew Forsyth offers an in-depth discussion regarding how Nielsen BDS data can be used to identify and select music for airplay. Geoff Steadman, developer of 25-Seven's Voltair processor, explores challenges associated with PPM audience measurement. Radha Subramanyam, President of Insights, Research, and Data Analytics for iHeartMedia, outlines alternative approaches to traditional, panel-based audience research. Past, present, and future techniques for music research are presented by NuVoodoo Media Services President Carolyn Gilbert.

*Chapter 7*: The updated content in this chapter examines the many ways in which radio stations promote themselves in the twenty-first century using social media technologies and traditional methods. Seth Resler, with a 20-year career in broadcasting and now a media strategist for Jacobs Media, provides two topical essays focusing on how radio stations should write social media policies and how radio stations need to establish specific goals for their website. John Lund, President of the Lund Media Group—a broadcast management and programming consulting firm in the U.S. and Canada—provides a new essay on promotions strategies for radio stations. Lauren Lynch Flick, a Washington, D.C.-based communications attorney, provides an essay about the FCC's new rules on contests and how stations need to change their existing rules to comply. Relatedly, this chapter has a new appendix, titled "Assessing the Impact on Radio and Television Stations of the Federal Trade Commission's Recently Revised Guidance on Endorsements and Testimonials." There are updated figures and images throughout the chapter.

*Chapter 8*: Award-winning copywriter, educator, and author Linda Conway Correll George draws from professional career experience to offer instruction and advice on how to write and produce copy that sells. Marty Sacks of the Telos Alliance, a leading equipment manufacturer, explains how implementing the AES67 digital audio standard across studio installations keeps station technology of the Internet Protocol (IP) forefront. Virtual consoles emerge to freshen the studio appearance, simplifying control board operation while exploiting cloud computing as the means for interconnecting studios with remote venues. Information about producing the perfect podcast or launching an Internet radio station is presented, with updated content and photos pertaining to hardware and software choices.

*Chapter 9*: Ever wondered how the game broadcast gets from the stadium to the station? Learfield Chief Engineer Randy Williams explains, taking readers through the process step by step. Editor Paul McLane of *Radio World*, the news source for radio engineers and managers, explains why broadcast engineering can be a sound career choice. Surrounding a centerpiece examination of digital transmission technologies are revised passages about FCC regulations and licensee compliance requirements. Special emphasis is directed to an examination of the future of the station engineering career, and the important role that the Society of Broadcast Engineers (SBE) performs in recruiting and educating next-generation technologists.

*Chapter 10*: This chapter—new to *The Radio Station*—examines radio broadcasting as the pathway to a successful and rewarding career. Highlights include the presentation of information about getting started and becoming involved in radio activities, beginning as early as the high school years. Positions within the station are explained and salary prospects are examined. Essayists from the four national collegiate electronic media organizations explain the multiple benefits that student members can receive by participating in chapter meetings, attending national conventions and submitting productions to student media competitions. Longtime broadcaster and consultant Dan Vallie describes the invaluable education students receive by participating in one of the National Radio Talent Institutes conducted each summer in a growing number of states.

# CHAPTER 1

# State of the Industry

## BROADCASTING

As radio enters its second century of existence, although it remains healthy, there is no denying that the AM/FM radio industry, or terrestrial radio, has entered into a time of change or a paradigm shift. The competitive landscape of terrestrial radio has changed dramatically in the last few years. Many radio insiders would argue that the industry has always been an industry that experienced change and evolved with change. Specifically, the radio industry is experiencing change in the method in which listeners consume audio and new competition from audio platforms based on the Internet. Yet, well into the second decade of this new millennium, broadcast radio—the original portable electronic medium—continues to exhibit a dominant presence in the face of these newer, very competitive audio technologies such as podcasting, streaming, satellite radio, and HD Radio side channels. Jay Williams, Jr., president of Broadcasting Unlimited, states:

> Buoyed by deregulation, consolidation and Wall Street money, then buffeted by increased competition and new technology, terrestrial radio executives are bracing for a challenging future by exploring programming and format options, more sophisticated advertiser relationships, and new digital distribution platforms to more robustly compete and grow.

A brief afternoon email discussion between the two authors of this book, one of whom lives in Texas and the other in Missouri, demonstrates how listeners navigate between different audio platforms throughout the day and, with an abundance of options, listening habits are no longer kept "local" either. During this discussion, one author casually noted:

> I only listen to either Pandora or iHeartRadio while working from my campus office and I only listen to satellite radio in my vehicle while driving (which includes terrestrial radio stations on satellite radio such as Los Angeles's KIIS-FM and New York's Z100).

Further, he shared with his colleague that he only listened to the Music Choice stations offered on cable television when at home and only listened to local terrestrial radio stations when a local sporting event was on the air and he wanted to know the score. Likewise, the other author shared, outside of the local NPR affiliate, "I too don't listen often to 'radio.' But, I do listen to quite a few 'streams' of AM and FM stations, and the occasional pureplays." As he was typing his email, he shared he was listening to WQUN, the commercial AM owned by Quinnipiac University in Hamden, Connecticut. Without dispute, the radio landscape is shifting and evolving.

Despite the shifting radio landscape, the listening numbers for terrestrial radio are very healthy and encouraging for the industry. In its *Tech Survey 13* report in 2017, Jacobs Media reports radio has the engagement of 91% of those surveyed compared to 21% engagement with podcasts, 23% engagement with satellite radio, 47% engagement with an MP3 player, and 58% engagement with streaming audio. Moreover, the *Tech Survey 13* study found that 40% of the respondents shared that they listened to less radio because there are too many commercials and repetitive music; 32% said that it was because of

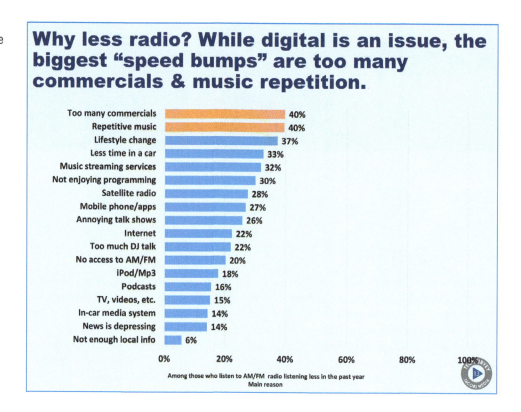

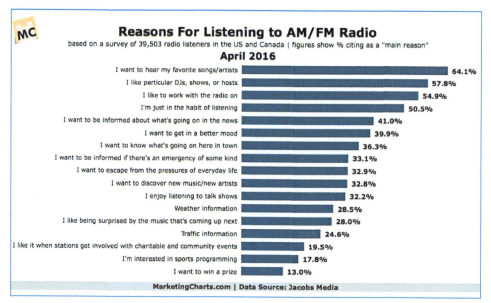

music streaming services; 28% said that it was because of satellite radio; 27% said that it was because of mobile phones/apps; and 16% said that they listened to less radio because of podcasting.

Conversely, Jacobs Media found that people listed numerous reasons for why they did listen to radio. The primary reason provided is to hear their favorite song/artists (64.1%) and because they like the deejay, show, or host. Others say they like to listen to the radio when they work (54.9%), some listen just out of habit (50.5%), some for the news (41.0%), and others to get in a better mood (39.9%), and, understandably, some just want to know what is happening in town (36.3%). Interestingly, weather (28.5%), traffic (24.6%), and sports (17.8%) rank very low as reasons why people are motivated to listen to radio.

In the *State of the Media: Audio Today 2017* study by Nielsen Audio, it was discovered that 271 million Americans aged six years old and older listened to radio on a weekly basis. Impressively, radio reaches 93% of all American adults, 92% of 18- to 34-year-olds, and 95% of 35- to 49-year-olds. Because streaming and podcasts are consumed on smartphones, tablets, and personal computers, it is worth noting the same Nielsen study found that 83% of the American population uses a smartphone, 37% uses a tablet, and 50% uses a personal computer on a weekly basis. For the coveted 25- to 54-year-old demographic, 117.8 million consumers are reached weekly by terrestrial radio, but for the most coveted demographic, 18- to 49-year-olds, 125.4 million consumers are reached on a weekly basis. Radio boasts an audience of 42.4 million Hispanics, 32.3 million blacks, and more than 175 million listeners identified as falling into other ethnic categories. Also, according to Nielsen, 18- to 24-year-olds listen to 10 hours and 15 minutes of terrestrial radio each week. Interestingly, by the end of 2016, Nielsen found that 90% of all Hispanics were reached by radio on a weekly basis. That is the highest penetration of radio reach across all demographics, ethnicities, and platforms.

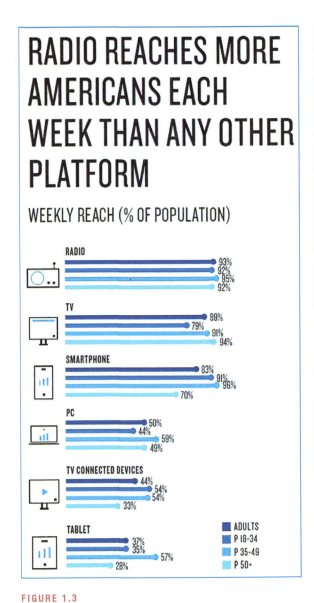

At 93% of the American population, radio is a ubiquitous medium and remains in the lead among audio listening by a good distance

Source: Courtesy of Nielsen

More than 125 million consumers who fall within the coveted 18- to 49-year-old demographic listen to radio weekly

Source: Courtesy of Nielsen

Hispanics and Blacks are a
large demographic for radio

Source: Courtesy of Nielsen

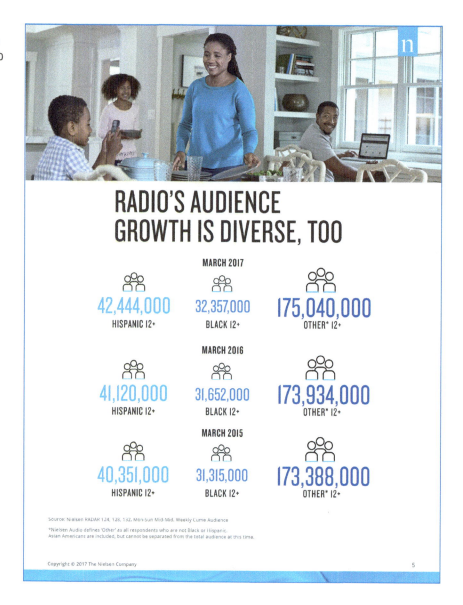

Bolstering the argument that a paradigm shift is occurring in the radio industry, Nielsen reported in 2016 that terrestrial AM/FM listening had only "inched" higher, while listening to online streaming audio with smartphones and iPads had "skyrocketed." Placing the data in context, Jon Miller, Vice-President of Audience Insights, told *Inside Radio* "With all the challenges and the new places for people to listen to music, the fact that radio usage is flat or even a little up is pretty significant. I think it speaks to the power of the medium." Data revealed that the average American adult listened to AM/FM radio for 13 hours and one minute per week. For comparative purposes, the same report revealed that adults spend 11 hours and 36 minutes per week on their smartphones and six hours and 43 minutes a week on their personal computers.

Radio—whether it be of the terrestrial, satellite, online streaming, or podcasting variety—continues to be one of the most pervasive media on earth, even more so than the Internet, which is virtually nonexistent in many parts of the world, especially in Third World countries. It is a position the commercial radio industry vigorously and aggressively promotes. The National Association of Broadcasters (NAB) is its trade organization, and it lobbies government from its Washington, D.C., headquarters. Gordon Smith, President and CEO of the NAB, speaking to *Radio Ink* in 2017, disputed the suggestion by some industry observers that terrestrial radio's future is in peril:

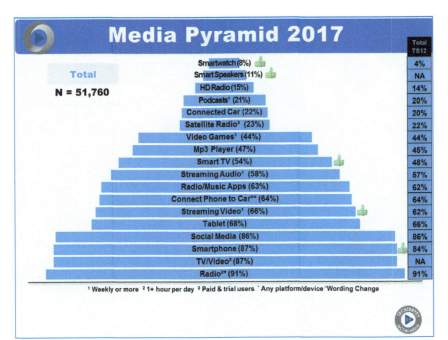

FIGURE 1.6
The media pyramid shows audience engagement with different media platforms. For now, radio reigns supreme

Source: Courtesy of Jacobs Media

There is a misperception being promoted by some that broadcast radio's influence has somehow been diminished. Advertisers sometimes lose sight of how powerful radio really is. Local radio is still the most popular place for listeners to discover new music. Every week, 262 million listeners tune into their hometown stations. Radio is a top medium for a return on advertisers' investment. These are the facts that hardly get mentioned when the future of radio is discussed. . . . In terms of attracting consumers, while we remain the most-used form of media, we can't rest on our laurels. We need to be available to listeners wherever and whenever they want. We need to continue innovating with streaming and services like NextRadio. We need to keep pushing Apple to activate radio chips on the iPhone so consumers can listen to their hometown radio stations without eating into their data plan.

Results of a 2017 study conducted by Nielsen reinforce the NAB president's claim: more adults overall consider AM/FM radio to be their number one source for learning about new music, with 66% of music listeners discovering music through AM/FM radio and 47% of the music listening audience choosing AM/FM radio. Notably, not too far behind was streaming (online audio) at 26%, online radio stations at 22%, radios that stream their signal online at 19%, satellite radio at 11%, and live streaming at 5%.

One report in 2017 showed that Pandora listening in specific media markets had declined. This decline was only discovered after Nielsen started asking the question of its survey respondents if there had been any "listenership to Pandora in the past month." Response to this question provided some parity to enable AM/FM radio stations to compare their weekly listener patterns to Pandora's listener patterns. Westwood One looked at data from nearly 40 individual markets and found that its reach was five times larger than Pandora's. Brittany Faison, a Westwood One/Cumulus Research analyst, asserts: "Pandora can't compare to AM/FM radio, America's No. 1 mass media reach."

In many ways, radio is indeed the number one mass medium. There is no patch of land, no piece of ocean surface untouched by the electromagnetic signals beamed from the more than 40,000 radio stations worldwide. The United Nations Educational, Scientific and Cultural Organization (UNESCO), sponsor of World Radio Day, recognizes on its website the pervasive nature of radio, observing:

Radio is the mass media reaching the widest audience in the world. It is also recognized as a powerful communication tool and a low cost medium. Radio is specifically suited to reach remote communities and vulnerable people: the illiterate, the disabled, women, youth and the poor, while offering a platform to intervene in the public debate, irrespective of people's educational level. Furthermore, radio has a strong and specific role in emergency communication and disaster relief.

**FIGURE 1.7**
Share of Ear Methodology: Edison Research conducted a nationally representative study of 8,000+ Americans aged 13 and older to measure their time spent listening to audio sources in 2016. Respondents completed a 24-hour diary of their audio listening on an assigned day. Diaries were completed both online and by mail using a paper diary. Diaries were completed in both English and Spanish

Source: Courtesy of Edison Research

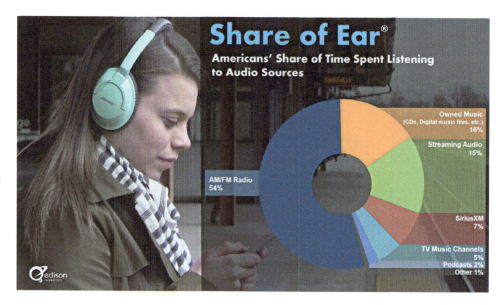

Although the number of radio receivers sold in the U.S. was at 325 million, in recent years there has been a decline in the number of receivers purchased because of other platforms for listeners to hear radio programming such as personal computers, tablets, and smartphones. In fact, a continuing debate in the radio industry with the mobile phone industry revolves around activating an FM receiver that is already built into every smartphone but not activated. If the mobile industry activated the FM receivers in the smartphones, allowing for free radio, this would reduce the amount of data they are able to sell to customers who listen to audio on their smartphones. Regarding this issue, NPR asserts:

> The smartphone has fueled a change in media consumption habits and it's a growing challenge to radio as the go-to audio source for news. To get local broadcasts, Americans increasingly download podcasts or stream from news apps where they can skip or pause our segments. As popular as this form of consumption is, these apps all suck up costly data.

Radio appeals to everyone and is available to all. Its mobility and variety of offerings have made it the most popular medium in history and, while this popularity has been on the wane in recent years, it

**FIGURE 1.8**
Radio listeners use numerous apps on their smartphones to listen to audio content, including AM/FM radio

Source: Courtesy of NextRadioApp

continues to be high. To most adults, radio is as much a part of their day as morning coffee and the ride to work. It is a companion that keeps us informed about world and local events; gives us sports scores; provides us with the latest weather and school closings and a host of other information, not to mention our favorite music; and asks for nothing in return. A Katz Radio Group study concluded that "only radio adapts to the lifestyle of its audience."

It is difficult to imagine a world without such an accommodating and amusing cohort, one that not only has enriched our lives by providing us with a nonstop source of entertainment, but has also kept us abreast of happenings during times of national and global crisis. To most Americans, radio continues to be an integral part of daily life. But, make no mistake about it: the traditional terrestrial radio landscape is indeed evolving.

## IS RADIO FACING A DIGITAL CLIFF?

### Larry Miller

Radio has been historically resilient when confronted with new competitive technology. When faced with new competition in the form of television, radio adapted and became portable, capitalizing on the invention of the transistor and an increased focus on local content.

However, that resilience is weakening. Radio, and music radio in particular, is now falling behind as audiences have begun to move on and listen to music on Spotify, Pandora, YouTube, and other digital services via smartphones at listening locations and times of day that have been radio's exclusive province for nearly a century: in the car and during drive time. Car manufacturers are transitioning vehicles to be digitally compatible. Many models now come with built-in Bluetooth technology and other easy ways to integrate handheld mobile devices, enabling drivers to listen to digital services, while other newer models are "connected cars" with built-in support for these digital services. These advances are essentially turning the car into an interactive, digital, mobile media device. Radio is facing competition of virtually unlimited choice, exactly where it has enjoyed a virtual monopoly since the first commercially successful car radio was first introduced in 1930.

AM/FM radio had been able to wait out the digital disruption that has already affected every other form of media. Now, radio is the latest industry facing massive disruption from the digital age. To survive, radio must innovate, learn from other media, and take control of its path to maintain its unique position with advertisers, audiences, and other stakeholders into the third decade of this century and beyond.

Radio has great reach, and most of what's on radio is music. Music stations comprise about three-quarters of American commercial radio stations, and music drives about three-quarters of radio's over-the-air advertising revenues.

In the past, radio along with television, print, and in-store play exposed fans to new music. However, the music industry is now less dependent on radio as a source of music discovery and exposure. As the music market accelerates its transition from a sales model to a streaming-driven access model, radio's contribution to music business revenue in the form of driving record sales in all formats has declined significantly.

Streaming now provides record labels the majority of their revenue, as well as directly impacting the *Billboard* Hot 100. Radio is now less of a tastemaker and more of a validator of the biggest hits often discovered on streaming music platforms. Younger music fans are not turning to radio first for music discovery, and the music industry is responding.

It's never been clearer. Radio has to innovate now to remain relevant as a source of music discovery.

### The Connected Car and the Smart Speaker

Radio believes the power of its strong, local brands will insulate it from digital competition. However, this may not be the case in the car as the dashboard reconfigures around connectivity with advanced digital services. The car is currently the number one location for listening to radio, and automotive is

**FIGURE 1.9**
Larry Miller

the number one revenue category for radio. As such, the connected car and its multiple audio offerings may be the greatest threat to AM/FM radio broadcasting, with 75% of new cars expected to be connected by 2020.

Radio finds itself relegated to a physical position further and further removed—several clicks away—from the center of the dashboard, notwithstanding limited use of single-station apps. In-car media screens allowing access to everything from Spotify to Pandora to iTunes are becoming the centerpiece for new models from virtually every manufacturer. AM/FM radio controls are often found below this screen, rendering them less prominent and less accessible than in the past.

Radio believes that the smart speaker will reverse the decline in the number of radios in households. But most Millennials and the younger members of Generation Z don't have a working radio where they live, so they listen to "radio" on their smartphones, tablets, and laptops. Now, we can add smart speakers to that list. But pureplay digital services have a big head start on the smart speaker platform.

Part of this issue is that, radio has not meaningfully invested in new programming or advanced digital services for smart speakers. With apologies to Curtis Mayfield, the smart speaker train is leaving the station, and it is time for radio broadcasters to get on board. AM/FM radio broadcasters need to develop a compelling digital presence in order to participate in the smart speaker revolution, but so far there are few signs that they are doing so.

Broadcasters are uniquely positioned to build on their existing customer relationships and brand identities in the new smart speaker market. But if they don't act they will quickly lose whatever advantage they may have. If radio broadcasters aim to maintain relevance if not dominance of listenership on new and rapidly evolving platforms like the connected car and smart speakers, they will have to out-innovate and out-compete digital-born disruptors for hearts, minds, and ears in a way they haven't since the birth of their industry.

## Today's Teens Have Choices When It Comes To Music Discovery

The rising "Gen Z" demographic is showing little interest in traditional media, having grown up in an on-demand environment as true digital natives. Teens have even more opportunity to engage with music than their post-baby boomer, Generation X parents. It is not only streaming that supplements radio, as teens also actively use search and social media tools and apps such as Musical.ly, Shazam, and blogs to stay on top of music trends. Radio, though still important, is being challenged by these platforms as a source of music discovery.

How teens listen to any music is important to both the music and radio industries. However, the time that teens actually invest listening to specific platforms is a better indicator of the health and prospects for those platforms. While a significant percentage of teens still listen to broadcast radio, they are far more engaged with streaming options that give them some form of control over what they hear.

In the past, radio could rely on new generations of in-demo listeners to replenish and grow its audiences. However, with the advent of music and video streaming, connected devices, and an app economy, this reliance is being challenged. Many teens are simply bypassing the medium. Even more concerning is the share of time among teens who do listen to AM/FM radio, which pales in comparison to streaming. It's worth noting that teens do not spend the same amount of time commuting in cars as their parents, but when they do enter the workforce it will likely be in cars that are much better natively enabled for streaming.

## Summary

Music is the lifeblood of the radio industry. It represents the vast majority of all content on AM/FM radio. And, although radio continues to reach, engage, and retain large audiences and generate annual revenues twice the size of the recorded music industry, the long-term trend is not radio's friend. Today's listener has access to virtually unlimited choices for audio and music consumption, of which radio is only one of a constellation of available platforms offering a galaxy of services from linear, lean-back and algorithmically driven to lean-forward, on-demand and self-curated—and everything in between.

And, while radio has consolidated over the last 20 years, the industry under-invested in advanced digital music services and failed to anticipate the emergence and scale of new competitors.

The car provided a Maginot Line of defense for radio, insulating it from competition through the early years of the digital transition. But the explosion of smartphones in the last decade and the proliferation and growth of music and audio apps and pureplay digital services have weakened AM/FM radio's dominance of in-car listening, especially among younger audiences.

What are the conditions for sustainability and growth? Unfortunately, it's easy to describe and hard to do. But, unless the industry is set to make peace with a long and inevitable decline, radio needs to invest in strong and compelling digital services. If it does, radio can look forward to a robust future built on the strong foundation it already has in the marketplace, leveraging the medium's great reach, habitual listenership, local presence, and brands. If it doesn't, radio risks becoming a thing of the past, like the wax cylinder or 78 RPM record—fondly remembered but no longer relevant to an audience that has moved on.

Adapted from *Paradigm Shift: Why Radio Must Adapt to the Rise of Digital*

**Larry Miller** is Clinical Music Associate Professor and Director of the Music Business program at NYU-Steinhardt. He is an advisor at the intersection of music, technology, and finance, and host of the Musonomics podcast.

At NYU, he teaches undergraduate and graduate courses on music analytics, strategic marketing, entrepreneurship and the business structure of the music industry. He advises music creators and rights holders on public policy and litigation, provided expert testimony before the Copyright Royalty Board and in arbitration, and supports media and technology companies and their financial sponsors on capital formation and growth strategy, digital product/service development, acquisitions, and restructuring. Previously, Larry was a Partner at L.E.K. Consulting and a senior member of the firm's media and entertainment practice. He later served as Executive Vice-President and General Manager of MediaNet.

Larry founded and operated Or Music, a Grammy Award-winning independent record label and music publisher where he signed, recorded, and published multiplatinum artists Los Lonely Boys and Matisyahu; he was Vice-President of Market Development at AT&T Labs Research, and began his career as a broadcaster at Tribune, NBC Radio Entertainment and WHTZ/Z100 New York, regarded as the most successful start-up in U.S. radio history as the station went from "worst to first" within 72 days of signing on in the country's most competitive radio market.

Larry has commented on CBS, ABC, CNBC, CNN, Fox News, and NPR; in the *Wall Street Journal*, *New York Times*, *Time*, *Business Week*, *Financial Times*, *Los Angeles Times*, and *Billboard*.

He earned an MBA at Columbia Business School and previously served as Entrepreneur-in-Residence and Adjunct Faculty Member in the music business program at NYU-Steinhardt.

## PROFITS IN THE AIR—THE BUSINESS MODEL EVOLVES

Although radio has been unable to regain the share of the national advertising dollar it attracted before the arrival of television, it does earn far more today than it did during its so-called heyday. Despite the enormous gains since WEAF first introduced the concept of broadcast advertising, FM and AM radio cannot be regarded as a get-rich-quick scheme. Many stations walk a thin line between profit and loss. Although some major-market radio stations demand and receive more than $1,000 for a one-minute commercial, an equal number sell time for the proverbial "dollar a holler."

Although the medium's earnings have maintained a progressive growth pattern, radio has also experienced periods of recession. These financial slumps or dry periods have almost all occurred since 1950, when television became mainstream. Initially, television's effect on radio's revenues was devastating. The medium began to recoup its losses when it shifted its reliance from the networks and national advertisers to local businesses.

By targeting specific audience demographics, the industry remained solvent. In the 1980s, a typical radio station earned $50,000 annually in profits. As the medium regained its footing after the staggering blow administered to it by television, it experienced both peaks and valleys financially. In 1961, for example, the FCC reported that more radio stations recorded losses than in any previous period because it began keeping records of such things. Two years later, however, the industry happily recorded its greatest profits ever. In 1963, the medium's revenues exceeded $636 million. In the next few years earnings would be up 60%, surpassing the $1.5 billion mark, and would leap another 150% between 1970 and 1980. FM profits have tripled since 1970 and have significantly contributed to the overall industry figures. The end of the twentieth century and the early part of the twenty-first century were tough financial times for the industry. By 2017, according to the Radio Advertising Bureau and Borrell Associates, radio station digital revenues alone were expected to reach a record $753 million. The same report indicated that in 2016 the average radio station generated somewhere in range of $49,159 to $602,783 in digital ad sales.

The AM daytimer segment of the industry has found it the most difficult to stay in the black. The FCC requires these radio stations to commence operating no earlier than local sunrise and to cease broadcasting around the time of local sunset so as not to interfere with other AM stations. Concerning the challenges of programming an AM daytimer, Station Manager Dan Collier observes:

> You don't have the money for staff. You don't have the budget for talented people. You don't have the resources for new equipment or to even maintain the equipment you have, which is typically in disrepair. These stations are a very tough sell to advertisers, so they lapse into decline and many eventually go silent. It doesn't have to be that way, but good management of this type of station is almost as scarce as advertising dollars.

The unique problem facing daytime-only broadcasters was further aggravated by FM's dramatic surge in popularity. The nature of the FM license gives AM daytimers subordinate status to full-time AM operations, which have found competing no easy trick, especially in the light of FM's success. Because of the lowly status of the daytimer in a marketplace that has become increasingly thick with rivals, it is extremely difficult for these stations to prosper, although some do very well. Many daytimers have opted for specialized forms of programming to attract advertisers. For example, religious and ethnic formats have proven successful.

Over the years, the FCC has considered a number of proposals to enhance the status of AM stations. One such proposal suggested that the interference problem could be reduced if certain stations shifted frequencies to the extended portion (1605–1705 kHz) of the AM band. FCC Docket 87–267, issued in the latter part of 1991, cited the preceding as a primary step in improving the AM situation. It inspired many skeptics who regarded it as nothing more than a bandage. Other elements of the plan included tax incentives for AM broadcasters who pull the plug on their ailing operations and multiple AM station ownership in the same market. In 2017, the FCC continued to study regulations and modifications to existing regulations that might serve to help revitalize the AM station. Since its inception, the radio industry has experienced significant competition through technological advancements, but it has survived and indeed thrived for the most part.

**FIGURE 1.10**
B. Eric Rhoads

## WHAT DO YOU BELIEVE?

### B. Eric Rhoads

You and I are living in perhaps the fastest-changing times in history. While much of the "old media" business still exists, the new world of media is vastly more powerful and more influential—and it's moving so fast that even the experts cannot track the rate of change.

From the perspective of my friends in Silicon Valley, you and I are employed in dinosaur media. They respect what we have done, and they want to steal our audiences and advertisers for their online audio services, but they think we're being silly when we cling to our transmitters. After all, the concept of "broadcasting" one signal to many radios is so very 1920s. They believe our model is broken, and it's just a matter of time before we lose our audiences and our advertisers—to them. What do you believe?

## Is Radio Immune to the Changes?

Many broadcasters I speak with think the radio industry is immune to the sea change that has been seen in other industries. They feel that, because it hasn't happened yet, audience loyalty has saved our industry from its digital downfall.

But maybe we've just been lucky. Many buy the argument that radio has weathered the storms of other past attacks—8-tracks, cassettes, CDs, cell phones, smartphones—so it will weather any new attacks, too.

The newspapers believed they were safe, too. And, although they pretended to embrace digital and were among the first to launch websites, the mistake they made was trying to create a "hybrid media." They should have fearlessly cannibalized the print papers and developed the next big thing so they could control it. *Newspapers* should have put newspapers out of business, rather than allowing others to launch competing services and take their businesses away.

When you live with one foot in the old world and one in the new, the tendency is to approach every decision based on the way things have always been done. For far too long, newspapers refused to allow their news to hit their websites until after it had been in print. Is radio acting the same way?

Radio always believed that the Pandoras, Spotifys, and Apples could not touch radio's business because of the high cost of streaming per person (which has now come down to almost nothing) and the high cost of licensing, which continues to plague these providers with high costs. It's radio's big advantage if they can continue to keep licensing costs low, which is an ongoing legal fight. If they lose the battle and have to pay these exorbitant rates, it threatens to crush the margins of the radio industry.

Some believe radio has lost a generation of listeners, and listening levels are in decline with people under 50, only boosted by adding younger demographics to the "total" Nielsen numbers. Yet no one knows for sure if the measured households truly represent a cross-section of what is happening in America, because these services have had a tendency to lean toward lower economic households willing to take compensation to measure listening.

The biggest "other" sea change radio faces is the perception of advertisers that radio is an older, no-longer-relevant medium. Local and national advertisers are now being controlled by the first fully digital generation, who have been seduced by the ease and effectiveness of advertising mediums such as Facebook and Google, and therefore other mediums, which still work, are being ignored. This is a giant challenge for radio to overcome. Radio continues to produce results and is a perfect medium for creating a preference in the mind of the listener before they do a search, therefore even advertisers not showing up #1 in search might get chosen because radio ads have predisposed the listener to that brand. It's a benefit radio needs to highlight rather than trying to go head–to–head against the preferences of this generation and convince them of something they may never believe.

## Are You Willing to Cannibalize?

What you believe matters now more than ever, and radio's success as an industry will rely on our willingness to cannibalize ourselves. You can try to maintain the status quo, or assume that your station digital strategy is enough of a digital insurance policy, but the real danger for all of us is ignoring facts and trends. The danger is that because we've continued to survive in spite of services such as Pandora, Spotify, Apple, etc. we're making assumptions that we will survive everything like it that comes along. It's inevitable that someone will launch something, at some point, that overcomes the issues preventing the total success of these services, overcoming things like licensing. Of course it is radio that should be considering its own alternative service, but only if it could do it well. I fear, as an industry, we are incapable of proper cannibalization and will end up like the newspaper industry, which had a shot and blew it.

## Can You Say Audio?

My passion for radio began as a kid who was fascinated by stations with entertaining personalities and my favorite music. To me, radio is entertainment, and whether it comes from a radio, a dashboard, a tablet, a mobile device, some new form of augmented reality, or an in-home device such as Alexa is irrelevant. We need to stop thinking of ourselves as being in the business of distribution by transmitter and instead be present on every device, in any possible way the consumer wants to find us. If you're clinging to your transmitter or have some silly idea that you don't want to stream to out-of-market consumers, you're missing a lot of opportunity. Radio should be investing in what we can do better than any technology. They can do playlists and "more music" as well or better than radio, but our big advantage is our knowledge of how to entertain, which goes beyond being mere playlists. Why we've forgotten this advantage is beyond me.

## Are You Admitting the Game Has Changed?

I continually hear complaints about change, about how big radio companies have cut out local personalities and changed the way they do business. Although it's sad to see so many displaced radio soldiers, the reality is that this environment, this economy, and improving technology will increase this trend. Those who are caught in the crossfire need to realize the game has changed, certain positions will never return, and you'll have to keep reinventing yourself in order to stay employable. You don't want to be an out-of work telegraph operator in a smartphone or augmented reality world. And, unlike the past, today you can invent, and compete and make a great living with your own media operated without any infrastructure. And being self-employed is a lot better than being unemployed.

## The Past Will Return?

I'm a nostalgic guy, and I love to think about the days when radio personality was at its peak and we had 15-share radio stations. They were fun times. I appreciate them, but I don't pine for their return, because there is no force in this industry big enough to make that happen. Big companies are not finally going to awaken and add back what they've cut out over the last 20 years.

## It's Time to Become Relevant Again

Every industry is facing tremendous change. Every industry is seeking efficient ways to survive through technology—and that results in jobs lost. Those of us in radio who have seen jobs eliminated, and those who have lost jobs, should not just try to shift to another station; we should realize that change will follow us all of our careers, and the only way to remain relevant and employable is to stay ahead of change.

## So What Do You Believe?

Although I embrace change personally, I also find myself fighting it daily. It's human nature, and overcoming it requires a personal plan to embrace and make change for change's sake. We cannot wait for our companies to implement change. We cannot follow everyone else. We as professionals need to step up and force ourselves to reinvent, time and again. The way you reinvent yourself today may become irrelevant in another year. Change should be in your DNA, and you need to force it to occur in your career. Avoiding it only makes you irrelevant, and that happens rapidly in today's world.

## Are You a Follower or a Leader?

I always used to think radio people were trendsetters, and some still are, but it seems that many today are no longer leading the pack. The same people who put radical music FMs on the air, spat in the face of traditional AM programming, and changed the world are now the people protecting their turf rather than inventing the next radical change. Radio today does not sound any different than it did in the 1970s. We're using the same sound effects, same lines ("the biggest hits, the best music"), and the only difference is that most of it is automated. Even though it's frightening, history tells us that someone else will reinvent us if we don't do it ourselves. It's happening all around us. You can't prevent it, but you can embrace it.

Radio—audio entertainment—will change, and if we don't each individually embrace and seek change, we will never catch up. We'll be remembered like the newspaper industry: changed, but by someone else.

**Best Advice?**

I have the benefit of a long perspective, watching the latest trends come and go. The only thing that has been consistent is change. It's always been present and always will. Nothing ever stays the same. Twenty-year-olds always reinvent what their parents and grandparents cling to. Then, when they become 50, someone reinvents them. Smart people know this and don't ever get comfortable with the status quo. They reinvent before it's necessary, because if they don't they will have it done to them. You may not get it right but trying is better than being a sitting duck. Success breeds complacency and comfort and prevents you from seeing new ways to do things. I always invest in education outside of my own industries and try to go to three or five meetings a year of industries that are reinventing the world. It keeps me fresh and helps me bring innovation to my own business. I also try to employ young innovators and listen to them. They can see things the old guard cannot see. So, embrace change. Work hard at reinvention. Try new things that make you uncomfortable. Listen and don't tell yourself all the reasons why something won't work. Your perspective and experience may be getting in your own way.

---

**B. Eric Rhoads** is a career entrepreneur with decades of launching companies and media brands, creating start-ups, and building businesses including more than 48 years' experience and leadership in the radio broadcasting field, 28 years in the publishing business, and 18 years in the art industry. Rhoads serves as Chairman of the Board of Streamline Publishing Inc., which he founded in 1985 and has been recognized by *INC* magazine as one of the fastest-growing companies in America for each of the last three years. He also has served as a consultant, advisor, or director to companies or investors in media, technology, and digital media. He has been recognized by the Broadcasters Foundation and was inducted as a "Broadcast Pioneer," one of the industry's highest honors.

In general, individual station profits have not kept pace with industry-wide profits owing to the rapid growth in the number of outlets over the past several decades. To say the least, competition is keen and in many markets downright fierce. It is common for 30 or more radio stations to vie for the same advertising dollars in large cities, and the introduction of other media in recent years, such as cable, satellite, podcasting, and streaming, intensifies the skirmish over sponsors.

In the 1990s, to counter the financial losses, many broadcasters formed local marketing (also called *management*) agreements (LMAs), whereby one radio station leases time and/or facilities from another area station. LMAs were a buzzword in the early 1990s and allowed radio stations to enter into economically advantageous, joint operating ventures, stated the editors of *Radio World*. They believed that LMAs should remain the province of the local marketplace and not be regulated by the federal government. The publication asserted that LMAs provided broadcasters with a means of functioning during tough economic times and in a ferociously competitive marketplace.

Those who opposed LMAs feared that diversity would be lost as stations combined resources (signals, staffs, and facilities). A few years later, the relaxation of the duopoly rules would raise similar concerns. Proponents argued that this was highly improbable given the vast number of frequencies. In other words, there is safety in numbers, and the public will continue to be served. However, radio station General Manager Pat McNally presciently observed that "In the long run LMAs and consolidation may cause a loss of available jobs in our business and help to continue the erosion of creative salesmanship and conceptual selling. Radio station sales staffs will become like small rep firms."

In the late 2010s, as technology advanced, the radio industry continued to adapt and evolve. In 2017, Borrell Associates reported that radio had the ability to serve the needs of local advertisers, who needed assistance with complicated platforms ranging from Facebook to Google Analytics. Local advertising remains a good source of revenue and Borrell Associates suggests that radio is poised to take advantage of that by offering services to handle both local advertising and digital advertising. *Inside Radio* reported that "For local broadcasters, such digital marketing services, which can include website design, social media marketing and digital media buying, represent a promising new revenue source. Across the radio industry, many companies are aggressively building their digital marketing offerings." Borrell found that more than $17,000 was spent annually on social media management and more than $18,000 on website maintenance by local businesses. Gordon Borrell underscores that "There is an awful lot of money in these digital services."

## SATELLITE RADIO

Radio broadcasters retain a wary eye on the satellite radio business. It is the constantly proliferating threat of increased competition from new technologies that inspires concern for the new and evolving audio options. Although broadcasters have long employed satellite programming and network services to enhance their over-the-air terrestrial signals, the idea of a direct-to-consumer alternative has not been greeted with enthusiasm. For several years, the FCC debated the question of satellite radio. In the waning years of the 1990s, the feds gave licenses to companies, such as CD Radio and XM Satellite Radio, to launch their services. During that time, the NAB vociferously argued against its introduction into the local marketplace. Despite all the brouhaha, XM Satellite launched its service in September 2001 and a year later claimed nearly a quarter of a million subscribers. Less than a year after XM Satellite rolled out its audio service, Sirius Satellite Radio debuted. It quickly became clear to terrestrial broadcasters that there was a new kid in town, one who would further accelerate the splintering of the radio listening audience. In 2008, again against the protestations of the NAB, both satellite radio services merged, with Mel Karmazin at the helm of the renamed SiriusXM.

Over-the-air broadcasters contend that their local orientation betters the services of the satellite audio companies, which are nationally based programmers. Former Infinity Broadcasting Senior Vice-President David Pearlman says,

> Broadcast radio is locally rooted and the satellite companies can't fulfill that need at the present time. This will be its saving grace and aid in its ability to withstand this frontal attack. With its selling of local news, traffic, weather, events, personalities, and services, the product differentiation will work in the industry's favor.

Satellite radio is subscription-driven and offers a wide array of program options featuring an array of famous personalities that includes channels by Garth Brooks, Bruce Springsteen, Kenny Chesney, and the service's most listened-to talent, Howard Stern. In all, satellite radio provides some 458 total channels to subscribers, which include online only channels as well as traditional satellite radio. Initially, subscribers were charged a monthly cost of $12.95 for the coast-to-coast signals (continuously in receiver range) and had to invest money for receiver equipment. Astutely, SiriusXM signed contracts with car manufacturers to install their digital receivers, predicting the acquisition of an impressive segment of the drive time listening audience in the not-too-distant future. SiriusXM reported $5 billion in revenue for 2016, which was a 10% increase from the previous year, with a net income of $1.88 billion. As of 2017, there were several subscription packages, ranging from $10.99 a month to $19.99 a month. Net subscriber growth was up by 1.75 million, bringing subscriptions to satellite radio to 32 million subscribers.

Further muddying the waters, in 2017 SiriusXM invested nearly half a billion dollars in an audio streaming service, Pandora. Like Pandora, SiriusXM can be listened to in automobiles, computers, smartphones, tablets, or homes. Because of its constant signal from a satellite, it also offers marine and aviation services as well as services for businesses. SiriusXM radios are in all of the leading automakers' vehicles including GM, Ford, Chrysler, Toyota, Mercedes-Benz, BMW, Hyundai, Honda, Nissan, Audi, and Volkswagen.

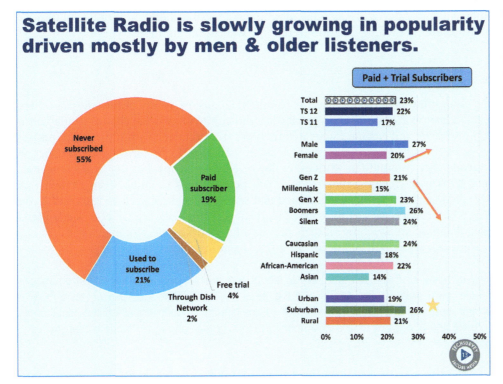

**FIGURE 1.12**
Satellite radio sees an increase in listeners that are primarily white, suburban, baby boomer, and Gen X males

Source: Courtesy of Jacobs Media

Many longtime broadcast radio listeners migrated to satellite for reasons similar to those articulated by media scholar and author Christopher H. Sterling:

> Like many older Americans, I used to listen to radio, especially in the car . . . but in the past year here in Washington, the medium has left me in the lurch. I used to listen to three stations (usually one at a time), but all have dumped friendly formats to slave after programming already available on other outlets in this market. The main public radio station dropped a decades-long classical music and talk format to rely totally on the latter—including British talk shows that keep giving me numbers I can call in London (I note with an "I told you so" feeling that their audiences and donations are down as a result). The remaining commercial classical music station got caught in a shift of Clear Channel station frequencies and now uses a fringe transmitter that can't put a decent signal into downtown. And most recently, the oldies station that had played music from the 60s and 70s "moved ahead" and now focuses on the late 70s and the 80s. Why do programmers presume nobody of 55 matters? Thank heaven for satellite radio where genuine choice thrives. I almost never turn on a radio anymore.

Former XM programming chief Lee Abrams discounted the potential impact on his medium of terrestrial HD Radio: "I'm pretty sure these guys will screw up HD. They'll add a blues channel but it'll play 200 blues songs and be run by guys who don't know much about the blues beyond Stevie Ray Vaughan." And about the potential of increased local programming on broadcast radio stations influencing the fate of his medium, Abrams said, "I doubt local radio will ever get back to the so-called 'community.' In fact, they're going the other way by cutting costs and taking on more remote voice track and syndicated programming."

To compound the competition for the listening audience, cable companies provide in-home music services for most of their subscribers. For example, Comcast cable users receive more than 45 channels of music and Suddenlink cable users receive nearly 50 channels of music that are often quite niche specific. These commercial-free channels of diverse nonstop music, replete with on-screen information about what is being played, are very attractive to subscribers and frequently result in the loss of yet another portion of traditional radio's listening audience. Despite competition from niche music programming choices such as cable radio stations, traditional terrestrial radio, and other multimedia audio choices, satcasters are in a strong position to do very well in the future.

## THE CONNECTED CAR

As emphasized, the radio industry is experiencing a prominent change in its way of life and its business model. Technological advances are occurring so quickly it is difficult to know what change or adaptation needs to be made, but change and adaptation are definitely what is occurring within the radio industry in areas that were once thought to be unquestioned—such as cars. All cars have radios and people listen to the radio while they commute to work every day or take long trips. But that is no longer the situation as technology is now changing the way in which people listen to audio, even in their cars. In fact, in late 2017, Fred Jacobs of Jacobs Media noted that several carmakers, such as Tesla and BMW, had stopped putting AM radio receivers in their new cars. Paul McLane, Editor in Chief of *Radio World*, says: "Radio people, of course, are watching all such auto dashboard design developments with concern over their future prominence—or even presence." In 2015, *Radio Ink* said:

> the radio industry is trying to figure out what to do about the dash. Radio has owned automobile listening since cars were created, but that's not the case anymore. Computer-like screens have replaced knobs and buttons, and radio can get lost in the shuffle—especially when the local car salesman is more excited about teaching a customer how to sync her phone to Pandora than to flip on the local radio station.

Moreover, the computer-like screens even have apps like smartphones.

The car dashboard is valuable real estate and all audio services want a part of that property. iHeartAudio has moved part of its digital team to Detroit to work with automakers on developing technology for the future connected car. When *Radio Ink* asked what they were doing to incorporate iHeartRadio into the dash, Darren Davis, President of iHeartRadio and iHeartMedia Networks, says:

> Everything we can think of! There's so much uncertainty about what the car dash will look like and how it will function five years from now. The best thing we can do is make sure our stations are available every possible way a station could be featured in the car.

Radio consultant Alan Burns told *Radio Ink* that in a study he conducted the consumers made it clear they were tired of too many commercials on the radio. Regarding listeners not liking all of the commercials on AM/FM radio, Burns said, "It's getting worse now because there's another point of comparison." The comparison Burns is referring to is streaming audio and podcasts in the cars received via smartphones connected directly to the radios in newer-model cars.

Consumers carry their smartphones everywhere and some even say they are "addicted" to their smartphones. *Radio Ink* astutely observed that "As devices become more a part of our daily lives, we expect those devices to follow us around seamlessly, and that includes in the car." When asked by *Radio Ink* what consumers wanted from the dash, David DiMeo, the Director for Connected-Car Innovations at Ford Direct, said: "They want access to their content. They want access to their devices. Their number one use for connected devices is still streaming audio."

By 2017, the *Infinite Dial* study conducted by Edison Research and Triton Digital found that, of the audio sources used in primary cars, 82% of users listen to AM/FM radio, 52% listen to CD players, 45% listen to digital music already owned, 26% listen to online radio, 22% listen to satellite radio, and 19% listen to podcasts. The study found that the percentage of consumers listening to AM/FM radio and CD players in the primary cars were down from the previous three years compared to the percentage of those listening to personally owned digital music, online radio, satellite radio, and podcasts, which were up from the previous three years studied. When asked which audio source consumers used most often in their primary cars, the study found that 57% most often consumed AM/FM radio, but that was less than the previous two years, while online radio (9%) and satellite radio (14%) sources had increased in use from the previous two years.

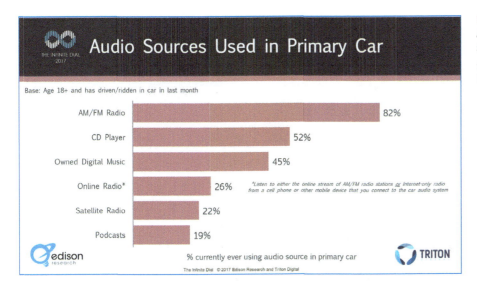

**FIGURE 1.13**

AM/FM radio listening in the primary car is still the most listened to audio service

Source: Courtesy of *The Infinite Dial 2017* from Edison Research and Triton Digital

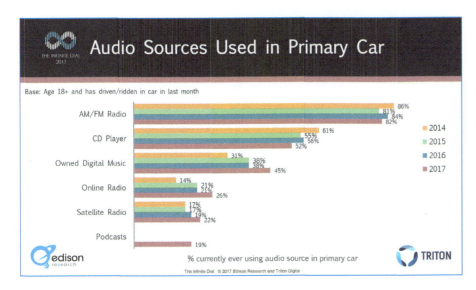

**FIGURE 1.14**

Listening to online radio, satellite radio, podcasts, and personally owned digital media was on the rise, while listening to AM/FM radio had declined

Source: Courtesy of *The Infinite Dial 2017* from Edison Research and Triton Digital

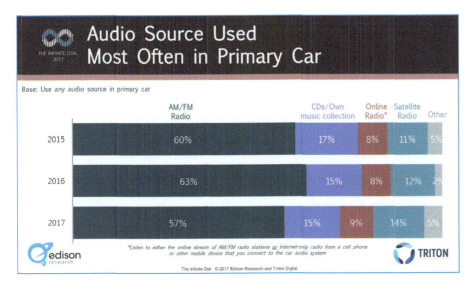

**FIGURE 1.15**

AM/FM radio continued to be the audio source used most often in cars, but online radio and satellite radio saw an increase in their percentage used most often in cars

Source: Courtesy of *The Infinite Dial 2017* from Edison Research and Triton Digital

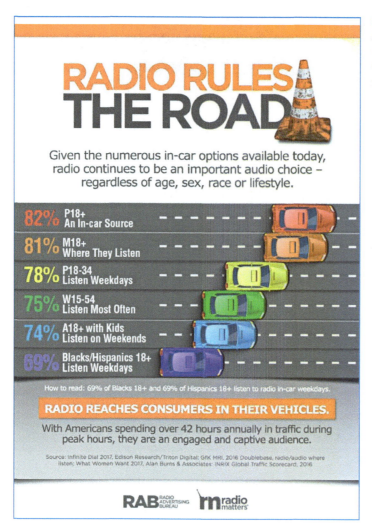

**FIGURE 1.16**

AM/FM radio remains the best option for marketers and advertisers to reach a captive audience

Source: Courtesy of the Radio Advertising Bureau

The results from the 2017 *Infinite Dial* study conducted by Edison Research and Triton Digital underscores what industry experts told *Radio Ink* in 2015: consumers want their content to follow them everywhere they go, even when they are in the car. However, in the car, even the connected car, AM/FM radio is still the leader when it comes to having the most listeners. But, if the current trends continue, it is possible that that ranking will change. Burns shared with *Radio Ink* that new cars have the new connected car systems in them, but the average age of a new car buyer is 58 years old. He predicts that eventually the younger consumers will purchase those used cars with the connected car systems and that younger consumers will eventually be able to purchase low-end priced cars that have the connected car systems installed. When that happens, Burns says, "I think the usage by the younger generation is really going to skyrocket pretty quickly." In the meantime, AM/FM radio remains the king of the road.

## FOUR VISIONS OF RADIO'S FUTURE

### Jeffrey Wilkinson and August E. Grant

Radio may have reinvented itself more than any medium over the past century. No one can predict radio's future with certainty, but it is likely that radio will again reinvent itself for the twenty-first century. Given the host of factors competing with the medium and its history of grappling with change, there are at least four general scenarios one may predict as logical paths or outcomes. The guiding principle is that technology, economics, and competition will foment change, and we must consider outcomes in terms of whether the change is positive or negative, and whether it occurs relatively quickly or slowly (relatively being itself relative). These are the underlying considerations for the four scenarios suggested here, and logically there can be hybrid outcomes combining any and all of what is offered here.

## Vision 1: Change Is Negative and Rapid—Radio Is Terminated

The harshest vision of all predicts that radio becomes the 8-track of the twenty-first century. Under this path, over the next decade, young people increasingly avoid radio. Overall listening will quickly drop, especially among the youth-oriented formats. By the year 2018, the industry approaches 90% cume, then ebbs to around 80% by 2023, 60% by 2025, and down to a rock-bottom 30% audience by 2030.

Under such conditions, advertisers will migrate to competitive media, and local advertising will follow local news to television, mobile devices, and social media. Radio station licenses would be bought and sold for a fraction of today's prices.

Media technologies are often sensitive to perceptions about them. If a technology is perceived to be old, outdated, and no longer relevant, new generations will avoid it. So a concern is that once radio listening drops below a threshold advertisers may flee to some other platform. Then it becomes a death spiral as the idea hardens that radio is an "old medium" that doesn't reach young people. Audience measures suggest that this trend is accelerating—young people are more tuned in to digital devices and services than radio.

So, at the tipping point of 89% weekly reach, some big players/investors may have their emergency plans in place. But, given that 80% of radio revenues still come from spot ads, there may yet be a niche for radio.

## Vision 2: Change Is Negative, but Slow—Radio Is Irrelevant

Conversely, there is the possibility that radio will not adapt and will instead stagnate. Radio that insists on relying on music only will find it increasingly difficult to stay relevant. Top franchises will continue to be popular, but elsewhere cracks will appear as overall listening continues to slowly erode. Eventually, radio becomes less central to people's lives and younger people drift toward sexier (and more interactive) communication platforms in America's youth-obsessed culture. Radio will play a smaller, but still significant role in entertaining the public, as radio station operators fight to attract and retain a smaller but still monetizable audience. Radio slides slowly into the sunset, casting a smaller but still perceptible shadow.

## Vision 3: Change Is Slow, but Positive—Radio Reinvents Itself

In this hopeful scenario, radio adapts and thrives. Just as it has in the past, radio meets the challenges of the marketplace, and relies upon its strengths to maintain audience and revenues. Radio is redefined as "all things audio" and embraces the digital realm to stay relevant and viable.

One important aspect of this scenario is for traditional broadcast radio to embrace localism to build community. Although Crider (2012) found localism in talk radio on the decline, there is a strong argument for stations to instead develop this core strength. Especially in the smaller markets where the decline has been the greatest, there is a need to build community. A hyperlocal focus enables broadcast radio to meet the needs of unserved audiences and thereby stay relevant. Broadcast radio can partner with community organizations to host local events and give voice to important local issues. In this way, radio can develop local personalities and keep the community engaged. In the hyperlocal scenario, music becomes secondary and serves as the bridge between the personalities and the local events. Additional text or video channels supplement audio, but the ability to start and maintain a community conversation remains primary.

## Vision 4: Change Is Positive and Rapid—Radio Is Hot!

The final possible path is a convergence of factors that would create rapid positive change for radio in all its forms. In this scenario, radio overall has no major disruptions—the hottest properties continue

**FIGURE 1.17**
Jeffrey Wilkinson

**FIGURE 1.18**
August E. Grant

to stay popular. Similar to the previous predicted path, radio adapts and becomes "all things audio," available on the phone, in the car, and on the web. But, additionally, radio enjoys moderate revenue growth (3–5%) and actively leads in community development. By once again becoming the leading local voice, social media and digital platforms enhance the local brand, which generates additional advertising revenues. This trend in turn enables stations to hire quality talent across the board, in on-air, sales, and management. In such a positive environment, the success creates an atmosphere of innovation at the fringes for communities and churches to also offer extreme hyperlocal niche programming and content.

The key to this scenario is radio's continuing role to connect local businesses with customers, who are now known as the engaged, active local audience. As long as these businesses need to target segments of the larger audience, radio will have viable target markets and revenue models.

---

**Jeffrey Wilkinson** is a Professor of Communication and the Associate Dean of Quality Assurance and International Development for the Sino-U.S. College, Beijing Institute of Technology, Zhuhai, China. His areas of teaching and research include multiplatform journalism, communication technology, media effects, and international communication.

---

**August E. ("Augie") Grant** is J. Rion McKissick Professor of Journalism at the University of South Carolina. Grant is a technology futurist who specializes in research on new media technologies and consumer behavior. His teaching and research combine the study of traditional and emerging media, with emphases on media management, organizational structure, integrated communication and consumer behavior. He has been Editor of *Communication Technology Update and Fundamentals* since 1992.

## MOBILE MUSIC SERVICES

The biggest competitive challenge to radio today is poised by a range of interactive devices such as smartphones, cell phones, tablets, and laptops with downloading and streaming capabilities for song files and podcasts as well as related but noninteractive devices such as iPods and other MP3 audio playback devices. As the Wi-Fi universe becomes ubiquitous and smartphone users have many gigs of data available for usage, observers anticipate the competition will only increase. Online radio reached a tipping point in 2013. According to Triton Digital's *Online Audio Top 20 Ranker*, the amount of online audio content consumed on mobile devices exceeded 50% for the first time. Pandora and Clear Channel's iHeartRadio are among the five most popular online services.

Recognizing the juggernaut of smartphones used daily by millions of consumers, there have been legislative attempts to mandate an FM tuner be placed in every new mobile phone. This attempt to be a part of additional audio media platforms has been embraced by the radio industry. In June 2012, radio industry officials testified before the U.S. Congress Subcommittee on Communication and Technology that having FM tuners in mobile devices is a "public safety" issue and would bring the United States into alignment with Europe and Asia. Greg Sandoval, a reporter for *CNET.com*, asserts that opponents to the FM tuner mandate "argue this is a cheap attempt by radio to piggyback on cell phones and avoid becoming more irrelevant in the digital age."

In 2013, Emmis chairman/CEO Jeff Smulyan announced that the company had partnered with Sprint to install an FM-enabled wireless app called NextRadio. This new application on Sprint phones will permit users to listen to radio stations on their smartphones. *AllAccess.com* reports that "The announcement by Sprint also marks the official launch of NEXTRADIO, the smartphone app that delivers a highly interactive artist and ad experience to FM-enabled smartphones." The software allows stations to upload branding images, call letters, slogans, and other items that will promote the station.

By 2017, the discussion and debate about FM receivers in smartphones continued. *Bloomberg* magazine notes that FCC Commissioner Ajit Pai has called on Apple, who has 40% of the smartphone market, to activate the FM chip in their phones so that in times of emergencies people could access information being broadcast from radio stations. This call to action came on the heels of a hurricane season that produced back-to-back Hurricanes Harvey, Irma, and Maria. But, at a time when the iPhone X had already been released, there was one problem: Apple had not installed the FM chip in its iPhones since the iPhone 6 was released in 2014. That is, iPhones 7, 8, and 10—there was no iPhone 9—did not even have an FM chip installed to activate or an antenna to capture FM signals. The reason that Apple may not be in a hurry to install or activate FM chips in their phones could be financially motivated. *Bloomberg* asserts that "Critics say Apple doesn't want to cannibalize its streaming service by giving iPhone owners access to free radio service."

Further, recognizing not only the growth but also the potential to generate revenue, the union that represents actors, announcers, broadcasters, journalists, dancers, deejays, news writers, news editors, program hosts, puppeteers, recording artists, singers, stunt performers, voiceover artists, and other media professionals began negotiating on its members' behalf a new pay structure for work done that is streamed online. The Screen Actors Guild and the American Federation of Television and Radio Artists (SAG-AFTRA) began the dialogue with broadcasters in 2013 and deals were agreed upon regarding various aspects of terrestrial broadcasting and online audio.

Michael A. Krasness, head of Oxysys, a mobile music networking service, expands on the virtues of his enterprise:

> For the listener, traditional music radio—both over-the-air and Internet delivery—is about listening to tracks the user already knows, plus music discovery by the radio station's playlist, driven by an ad-based revenue model. Mobile music services add to that by allowing interactive user selection of music, active participation in the music discovery process, and social networking. Similar ad-based revenue models may be augmented by e-commerce through integration of a store. Traditional radio certainly provides complementary services for our users. As a feature for our users, Oxy phling! includes simple, integrated access to a number of Internet radio stations. For the radio station, they now have access to our community of mobile users.

With Pandora, iHeartRadio and other mobile audio services likely venturing into nonmusic areas, such as talk and sports, the competitive threat to broadcast and satellite radio looms larger than ever. Mark Ramsey says, "We are fast-entering a time when 'radio' will become a feature of other things rather than simply a destination unto itself, as it has been up until now."

## THE IMPACT OF MOBILE LISTENING ON RADIO

### Glenda Shrader-Bos

The growing use of smartphones will have a profound impact on radio. Radio apps on cell phones will lead to one day nearly everyone having a radio with them at all times. Theoretically this should increase radio consumption, but research suggests that the increased accessibility of radio may not have the positive impact one might expect.

Today's smartphone is used for so many tasks that a consumer might only use it to listen to the radio during rare times or when the phone isn't tasked with a higher priority.

An analysis of Internet radio listening patterns over the current period of rapid smartphone growth gives us a glimpse of the potential impact of this phenomenon. The research shows a strong correlation between growth of mobile phone listening and a dramatic decline in listening spans. In 2010, when most Internet radio listening was done on a desktop computer, Pandora's average time spent listening was nearly one hour. By 2012, more than 70% of Pandora's listening was done on a mobile device, and average time spent listening had plunged to 46 minutes.

Broadcast groups have seen a similar decline in listening spans as more listening is done on smartphones. Broadcast radio groups have seen combined listening spans decline from 35 hours in 2010 to only 16 hours in 2012.

**FIGURE 1.19**
Glenda Shrader-Bos

Radio advertising rates are determined by the average size of a radio station's audience, traditionally measured as the number of people listening during a quarter-hour (a metric that dates back to the days when radio shows were 15 minutes long). The longer a person listens to a station, the greater the number of quarter-hours of listening. This is why radio stations make an effort to create programming that encourages longer listening spans.

The growing use of smartphones combined with multitasking is fragmenting listening into smaller and smaller periods of time, which weakens ratings and how much a radio station can charge for a commercial. Lower rates lead to lower income for a station. As a result, programming budgets are reduced. This could ultimately lead to lower-quality programming.

This is the irony of mobile Internet radio listening. Radio apps on mobile devices are leading to greater radio accessibility; however, listening spans are lower on mobile devices and virtually canceling out the advantages of greater accessibility. This ultimately causes the impact of mobile listening to negatively affect the radio industry.

The only solution is to push radio up the priority ladder for the mobile user, so that radio can successfully compete for a user's attention with emails, social media, and the like. The only way that will happen is if radio is able to create more compelling programming. This may become the single greatest challenge for radio in the coming years.

---

**Glenda Shrader-Bos** is Managing Partner and Co-Owner of Harker Bos Group, a firm that specializes in media research with companies such as CBS, Fox News, ESPN, and ABC. She joined the company in 1991 and has over 20 years of research experience. Harker Bos Group has grown from a three-person team to a full service company that specializes in Internet, radio, television, and cross-platform media research.

## PODCASTING

The ability to access audio files that contain short audio clips or fully produced programs, similar to radio programs, originated almost as quickly as the Internet became mainstream. Unlike the programming of terrestrial radio, in which station operators must secure a license from the federal government, a podcast can be created by anyone who has the desire and knowledge to do so. All it takes to listen to a podcast is a small handheld device such as a smartphone, iPad, or personal computer, all of which are almost universal and, importantly, allow listeners to timeshift their listening patterns. Timeshifting is when listeners consume audio at times that are convenient for them rather than listening to a "live" broadcast. In February 2004, Ben Hammersley, a journalist for *The Guardian*, was the first to use the term "podcasting." The website Voices.com explains,

> The term "podcast" is derived from the media player, "iPod," developed by Apple, and the term "broadcast," the traditional means of receiving information and leisure content on the radio or television. When the two words were merged, the terms podcast, podcaster, and the art of podcasting were born.

By 2005, just two years after its invention, the *New Oxford American Dictionary* declared podcasting the "word of the year." Its official definition in the dictionary is "a digital recording of a radio broadcast or similar program, made available on the Internet for downloading to a personal audio player." Despite its rapid ascension in listenership, the Pew Research Center reports that approximately half of the nation is not familiar with the term "podcasting."

According to *The Guardian*, modern-day podcasting was created in 2003 by Harvard Law School's Berkman Center for Internet & Society research fellows Christopher Lydon, a journalist and broadcaster, and Dave Winer, a software developer, with a downloadable MP3 file using an RSS feed. The RSS feed, or Really Simple Syndication, was integral to the development of podcasts and Winer, who developed RSS, says "It automates your Web surfing."

The *Guardian* reported Lydon as saying, "In the middle of the 19th century, Emerson had the idea of a global species, living in a realm of ideas, with a human universal equality in rational thought and interactive culture. . . . And suddenly, we had the tool." Today, Lydon hosts his own podcast program titled *Open Source.* The *Harvard Gazette* said:

> The podcasters of today owe a debt of gratitude to a group of Harvard scholars who revolutionized how people create and consume digital information. These scholars streamlined a method of both uploading audio files to the Internet and downloading them to a computer or mobile device.

Before arriving at Harvard as a research fellow, Winer had also worked with Adam Curry, an MTV disc jockey, who wanted to stream video on the Internet. It was that partnership that laid the foundation for what was achieved at Harvard. The very first podcast was produced in July 2003, when Lydon interviewed Winer about the technology. In an interview with the *Harvard Gazette*, John Palfrey, the co-director of the Berkman Center and member of the faculty at Harvard when Winer and Lydon were conducting the research that created modern day podcasting, says:

> People were certainly recording and putting audio files on the Web . . . the inventive genius of what this group was doing at the Berkman Center was in turning their work into a series, and into a channel. . . . The development of podcasting, of video, all of what YouTube has become, those to me are all outgrowths of that innovation. It was a confluence of things coming together and the best form of experimentation, of just trying it, of seeing what happens. And podcasting is one of those things that just stuck.

For most of its existence, podcasting had little to no revenue generating potential. According to the Interactive Advertising Bureau (IAB), that has changed. By 2017, podcasting would generate nearly a quarter of a billion dollars in revenue. The IAB estimated podcast revenue to exceed $220 million. In the Westwood One *State of Podcasting 2017* study, it was found that marketers and advertisers are keen to place ads on podcasts. Nearly 70% of marketers had "discussed investing" in podcast advertising and nearly 40% said they would "definitely consider" podcast advertising. Nearly 30% of those surveyed said they would "definitely advertise" on podcasts.

But, as of 2016, there were barriers to being able to tap the full potential of generating revenue from podcasts due to the legacy podcast download delivery model. XAPPMedia aims to change those barriers. A *Radio Ink* article explained: "XAPPMedia is a technology company that focuses on interactive audio services, and one of the goals of the company is to help radio stations generate revenue in the voice space." When asked what it was doing to generate new revenue for radio, XAPPMedia replied:

> We are helping primarily right now in the new voice space that's been created by Amazon, Alexa, and Google Home. We see this as the dawn of a new era in technology—the voice era. Like with the Web and mobile eras, there's going to be big winners and big losers. Voice will bring about profound improvements in listener convenience and content discovery, in addition to spontaneous connection with local talent. We think the radio stations and podcasters that deliver these improvements will be the winners. This is an enormous opportunity to bring radio back into the home. That's where we see a fantastic opportunity for radio right now, and we are actively engaged in that space.

For podcasts, the download delivery system does not identify the audience, it restricts listener engagement, it limits ad formats, and it conceals usage data—all of which could be insightful to advertisers and marketers. XAPPMedia says, "Podcasts were born in a download era, but we now live in a streaming world." Therefore, XAPPMedia suggests streaming, rather than downloading, podcasts provides more measurability, ad inventory, and audience engagement.

The *Infinite Dial 2017* study found that 60% of those surveyed were familiar with the term podcasting. That is estimated to be 168 million people. Forty percent, or 112 million people, said they had listened to a podcast. Twenty-seven percent of those aged 12 to 24 said they had listened to a podcast in the last month and 31% of those aged 25 to 54 had listened to a podcast within the last month. Slightly more men (27%) than women (21%) had listened to a podcast in the last month.

It's estimated 168 million are familiar with the term podcasting

Source: Courtesy of *The Infinite Dial 2017* from Edison Research and Triton Digital

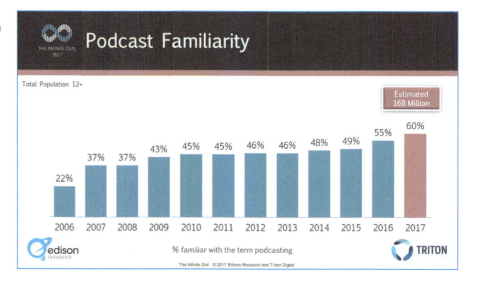

It's estimated 112 million have listened to a podcast

Source: Courtesy of *The Infinite Dial 2017* from Edison Research and Triton Digital

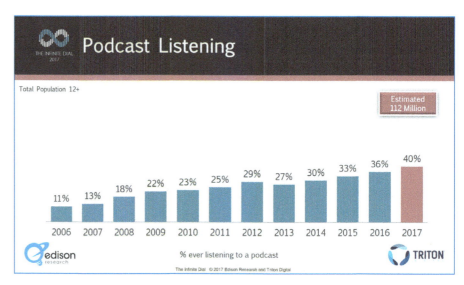

Podcast listeners are mostly between the ages of 12 and 54

Source: Courtesy of *The Infinite Dial 2017* from Edison Research and Triton Digital

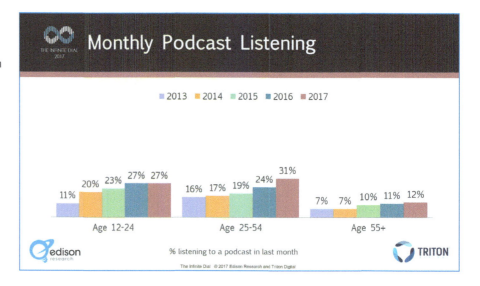

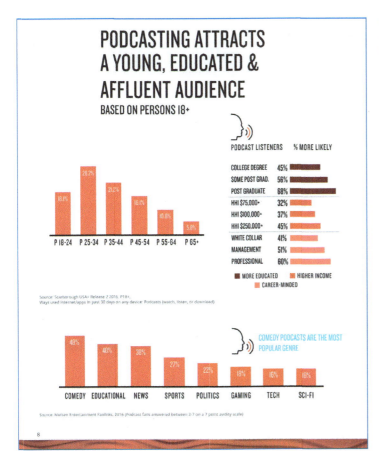

FIGURE 1.23

Highly educated professionals who earn $250,000+ and are 25 to 44 years old are the primary listeners of podcasts

Source: Courtesy of Nielsen

Advertisers and marketers have always wanted access to an audience, or a desirable demographic, so they simply follow the listeners. Edison Research reports that nearly a quarter of all Americans 12 years old and over listen to podcasts each month and 85% of that listening is occurring on a mobile device. The median age of podcast listeners is 29 years old compared to 46 years old for radio. The average listener subscribes to six podcasts weekly, notes the IAB. Edison Research describes podcast listeners as "superfans" because they spend nearly 50% more time with audio on a daily basis than average radio listeners. The study found that most podcast listening occurs in the evenings at home. Studies show podcast listeners are young, educated, affluent, and listen to podcasts on their mobile devices.

Jacobs Media reports in their *Tech Survey 13* study that one-fifth of podcast listeners (11% of the total population) reported doing so weekly, 10% reported doing so daily, and 8% reported doing so monthly. Importantly, nearly half (48%) of those surveyed had never listened to a podcast. Further, Jacobs Media found that more than half (51%) of those surveyed listened to podcasts on their smartphone, 30% listened to podcasts on their personal computers, and 11% listened on their tablets.

The IAB advertising guide explains there are different types of ads that can be embedded in podcasts that can target specific demographics. The IAB reports that

As podcast listening grows and the industry evolves, new ad formats are being developed beyond traditional ad types, the continued rise of smartphone ownership, lower data fees and the ease of consuming podcasts on the go, all provide an ideal environment for podcasts to find new listeners.

In 2017, Sirena Bergman wrote for *Mashable* that podcasting is offering gender, ethnic, and LGBTQ diversity to Millennials that terrestrial broadcasting does not. Bergman suggested that podcasting may start to solve radio's lack of diversity. Millennials view terrestrial radio as "the domain of middle-class white folks, most often of the straight male variety." Generally speaking, listeners like what they hear when consuming audio media to sound like them and they like to hear others embrace what they

Listeners consume podcasts in various locations, but mostly they are listened to at home and in vehicles

Source: Courtesy of *The Infinite Dial 2017* from Edison Research and Triton Digital

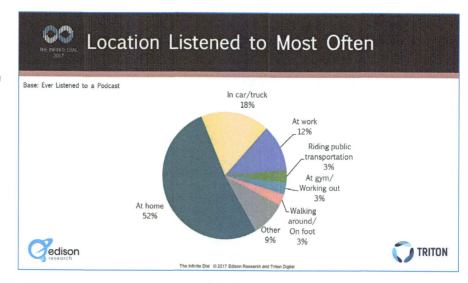

Listeners prefer to use their smartphones to listen to podcasts

Source: Courtesy of *The Infinite Dial 2017* from Edison Research and Triton Digital

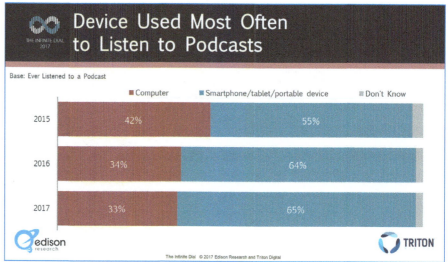

Podcast listenership is on the rise, with one-fifth of podcast listeners listening weekly and nearly a quarter listening monthly. The podcast audience is diverse in terms of ethnicity and gender and has an impressive amount of Hispanic and Asian listeners

Source: Courtesy of Jacobs Media

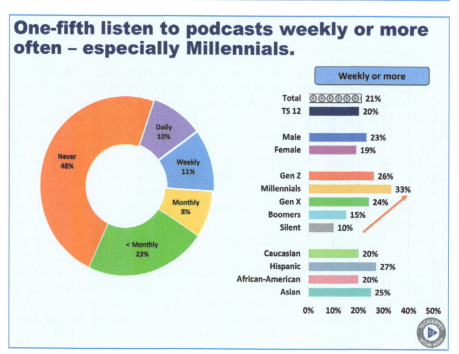

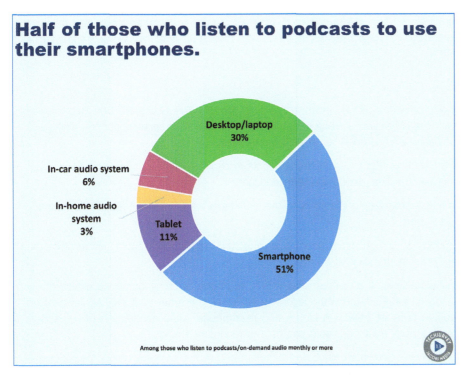

**Half of those who listen to podcasts to use their smartphones.**

Desktop/laptop
30%

In-car audio system
6%

In-home audio system
3%

Tablet
11%

Smartphone
51%

Among those who listen to podcasts/on-demand audio monthly or more

FIGURE 1.27
Listeners consume podcasts using various devices, but most consumers use their smartphones and personal computers to listen

Source: Courtesy of Jacobs Media

believe and think. Podcasts allow individuals from various backgrounds to join the dialogue. Laura Walker, President of New York Public Radio, says "There's a lower barrier to entry [with podcasting] and people from all different backgrounds can create one." Bergman suggests this explains the racially diverse audience listening to podcasts. In 2016, nearly 40% of the podcasting audience was nonwhite.

Listening to audio on the Internet has evolved into a popular pastime for millions of people around the world. In fact, September 30 is International Podcast Day. Podcast enthusiasts are encouraged to use #InternationalPodcastDay annually on their social media to spread the good word about podcasting on that day.

## THE ASTOUNDING GROWTH OF PODCASTING

### Jon Nastor

Podcasting has leveled the playing field when it comes to broadcast media. The barriers to entry have been torn down for those who have something to say.

13 years ago, the term podcast did not exist. Today, 67 million Americans are regular podcast listeners. According to the 2017 Infinite Dial survey from Edison Research, 24% of the population over age 12 are listening to podcasts on a monthly basis, and this number is increasing every year.

Under the old rules, a gatekeeper who owned the airwaves would never give a radio show to anyone without the credentials he deemed necessary. If you had the wrong sound, the wrong ideas, or simply the wrong genetics, you'd never make it behind the microphone. So, your story would go untold.

Times have changed. We now live in a time in which we can control our platforms and tell our own stories.

Today, you could create and launch a podcast in 30 days, have it build an audience of rabid fans, and—through the power of podcasting—potentially reach millions of people around the world.

FIGURE 1.28
Jon Nastor

Every day, people enjoy inspired lives built upon their art, their passions, and their ideas. Not because someone permitted them but because they decided this was their time and they weren't going to be satisfied if they missed it.

## The Birth of the Podcast

The term podcasting was coined in 2004, in an article published by *The Guardian*. Ben Hammersley wrote about a new technology that was starting to catch on: audio blogs, or episodic content that could be automatically downloaded and listened to on portable devices.

At the time, MP3 players such as iPods were allowing people to carry around an unprecedented amount of high-quality audio in their pocket. Hence the term podcast.

As blogs and websites began producing audio content, the technology was developed to make consuming the content easier and easier.

By 2005, iTunes included native podcast support. Everyone who used iTunes could now explore the world of podcasts and listen at the click of a button.

As listenership continued to swell, the number and variety of podcasts being produced exponentially increased. Producing quality audio content was becoming easier all the time. In 2006, Apple released Garageband with a built-in podcast maker. A laptop and microphone could accomplish what used to be done by professionals in fully equipped radio booths and recording studios.

This democratization has given voice to so much diverse talent and with it so many unique perspectives. With very little cost, anyone with something to say now has a platform on which to say it.

What began as a fringe medium for tech bloggers has in 2017 grown into an entire industry. There are podcast networks, production companies, and corporate sponsorships fueling growth, raising funds and allowing more and better content to continually appear.

## Who Is Listening to Podcasts?

With all the attention that podcasting has been gaining, appeal remains largely skewed toward the 18–54 age range. Podcast consumers also tend to be more educated and affluent than the average American.

One more thing we know about podcast listeners is that they dislike the interruptive, ad-heavy programming that is characteristic of mainstream radio and television. They dislike being told what to listen to and when.

That's why they are far more likely to be users of on-demand, subscription music and video services such as Spotify and Netflix. This generation wants to choose what they listen to—on-demand—and not be subjected to blatant advertising.

Advertising is very much present in the world of podcasting as well, but it differs in a few important ways. A good podcaster knows exactly who is listening, and chooses to endorse products and services that add value. The ads are typically read by the host and blend in with the rest of the show.

Listeners are willing to accept a certain amount of sponsored content when they value the information or entertainment being produced. They know it allows the show to continue running, so they can continue listening.

Advertisers are now beginning to realize the possibilities. Unlike commercial radio stations, podcasts are targeting very specific audiences. Many of the more than 60,000 shows available on iTunes are for niche markets that make it simple for companies to choose where to spend their advertising dollars.

## Podcasting Is Just Getting Started

Awareness of the term has reached more than half the population, but still less than half has ever attempted to listen to a podcast.

In the last four years, the percentage of monthly podcast listeners has doubled, from 12% in 2014 to 24% in 2017. Not to say that this explosive growth can continue indefinitely, but there are reasons to believe that it won't be over anytime soon.

There remains a large segment of the population that has never tried to download and listen to a podcast. Many people have heard of podcasting but either didn't know how to listen or didn't think there would be anything in it for them.

This means there is still huge potential for new listeners. As the medium grows, there are more listening options to draw in wider segments of the population. As production companies work with sponsors to reach new markets, the share of listening hours can only increase.

One has to assume that more hours listening to podcasts will translate to fewer hours listening to the traditional broadcast radio.

Unless they pay attention to what people want—light-ad, on-demand, diverse programming—broadcasters will continue to lose ground to those that can adapt.

**Jon Nastor** is the bestselling author of *Hack the Entrepreneur: How to Stop Procrastinating, Build a Business, and Do Work That Matters*, and the creator and host of the Hack the Entrepreneur podcast.

# STREAMING

This Nielsen headline is indicative of the change that is continuing to occur in the radio industry—"2017 is Shaping Up to be the 'Year of Music Streaming.'" Indeed, the migration of audiences toward streaming audio services has been on the rise for several years. Fluent Public Opinion Market Research reports that almost 80% of Americans state they use at least one streaming service. As a result of the increased popularity of podcast listening, Nielsen introduced enhancements to its ratings system so that broadcasters could compare their services to the services offered by podcasters.

Listening to podcasts has become so pervasive that Nielsen reported in 2016 that 404.5 billion streams were accessed by consumers. The new Nielsen features for its ratings service includes radio airplay titles ranked and then separated out by genre, format, markets, and individual stations. When speaking about the new Nielsen features, Stephanie Friedman, BDS Vice-President of Radio, says that now "[w]e can see the songs that fans are gravitating to, we can see the songs that the fans are choosing, when looking to freshen the sound of your station, both nationally and in your own market."

A 2016 Nielsen report showed there was an increase in the amount of time Americans were spending with streaming audio on iPads and smartphones. Data showed that a typical adult spent 34 minutes per week listening to audio on their smartphones, which had doubled from the previous year's report. Further, data showed that a typical adult spent 14 minutes per week listening to audio streaming on iPads or other tablets, which was an increase from only four minutes per week the previous year, and listening to streaming audio on desktop and laptop computers averaged seven minutes per week, which was down by one percentage point from the previous year's report.

For 2017, Nielsen found there was more than a 62% increase in the number of those listening to audio streams. As of mid-2017, more than 184 billion audio streams had reached listeners, compared to 113.5 billion in 2016. Ed Sheeran's song, "Shape of You," was the most-streamed song at 690 million on-demand streams. David Bakula, Senior Vice-President for Insights at Nielsen, asserts, "The first half of 2017 has seen some incredible new benchmarks for the music industry. The rapid adoption of streaming platforms by consumers has generated engagement with music on a scale that we've never seen before."

Edison Research, in its 2017 *Infinite Dial* study, looked at several aspects of consumer behavior regarding audio listening. The 2017 study did not just examine listening patterns of AM/FM terrestrial radio alone but instead combined listening to AM/FM radio stations online with listening to streamed audio content available only on the Internet. Thus, it is difficult to discern, because the data are not disaggregated,

**FIGURE 1.29**

It's estimated 170 million people listen to online radio monthly

Source: Courtesy of *The Infinite Dial 2017* from Edison Research and Triton Digital

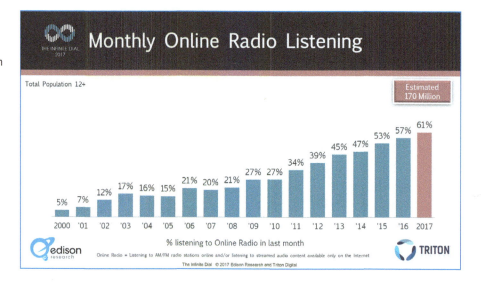

**FIGURE 1.30**

More 12- to 24-year-olds listen to online radio monthly than any other demographic

Source: Courtesy of *The Infinite Dial 2017* from Edison Research and Triton Digital

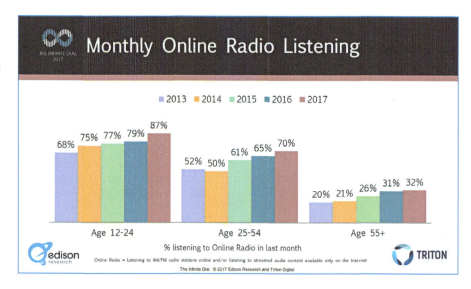

**FIGURE 1.31**

A third of those surveyed listened to Pandora within the last month

Source: Courtesy of *The Infinite Dial 2017* from Edison Research and Triton Digital

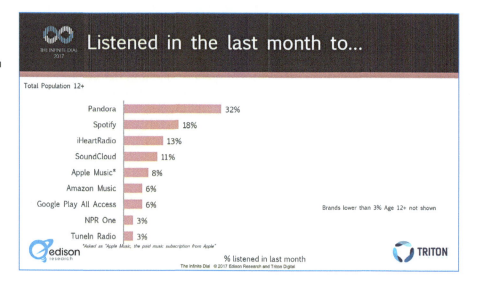

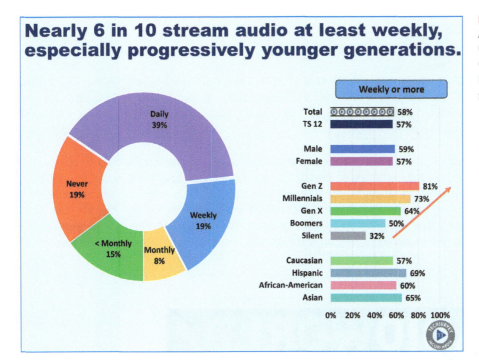

**Nearly 6 in 10 stream audio at least weekly, especially progressively younger generations.**

Daily 39%
Weekly 19%
Monthly 8%
< Monthly 15%
Never 19%

Weekly or more

| | |
|---|---|
| Total | 58% |
| TS 12 | 57% |
| Male | 59% |
| Female | 57% |
| Gen Z | 81% |
| Millennials | 73% |
| Gen X | 64% |
| Boomers | 50% |
| Silent | 32% |
| Caucasian | 57% |
| Hispanic | 69% |
| African-American | 60% |
| Asian | 65% |

0%  20%  40%  60%  80%  100%

**FIGURE 1.32**
Audio streaming is most popular among the Gen X, Millennial, and Gen Z groups; is equally popular among both genders; and has parity among all ethnicities
Source: Courtesy of Jacobs Media

whether these data represent more terrestrial AM/FM or more streaming audio such as on Pandora or Spotify. Nonetheless, the study revealed that 61% of those surveyed listened to online radio monthly. That is estimated to be 170 million people. Of those, 87% were 12 to 24 years old, 70% were 25 to 54 years old, and 32% were 55 or older. Of those surveyed, 86% were aware of Pandora, 71% were aware of iHeartRadio, and 62% were aware of Spotify. Thirty-two percent said they listened to Pandora within the last month, while 18% said they had listened to Spotify. The total of those numbers does not add up to the total listening audience, thus it is assumed the remainder of those surveyed listened to AM/FM terrestrial radio (even if it was online).

Advertisers and marketers wishing to reach the Hispanic demographic would be wise to place ads on streaming audio outlets. Hispanics average 53 minutes per week of listening to streaming audio, which was a 48% increase from the previous year's report. The streaming audience is young too. Fluent Public Opinion Market Research found that 92% of those aged 18 to 24 (Gen Z), 91% of 25- to 34-year-olds (Millennials), and 77% of those 35 years old and over listened to streaming audio. Apple Music was the most popular streaming service, with Spotify ranking second among Gen Z and Millennials. The report asserts:

Younger generations use their mobile devices extensively and are attracted to a service that allows them to listen to their favorite music on the go, online and synced across all devices. It is no surprise that these groups are much more willing to pay subscription fees for Apple Music and Spotify which offer all these benefits.

Pandora is the largest audio streaming service and describes itself accordingly:

Pandora is the world's most powerful music discovery platform—a place where artists find their fans and listeners find music they love. We are driven by a single purpose: unleashing the infinite power of music by connecting artists and fans, whether through earbuds, car speakers, live on stage or anywhere fans want to experience it. Our team of highly trained musicologists analyze hundreds of attributes for each recording which powers our proprietary Music Genome Project, delivering billions of hours of personalized music tailored to the tastes of each music listener, full of discovery, making artist/fan connections at unprecedented scale. Founded by musicians, Pandora empowers artists with valuable data and tools to help grow their careers and connect with their fans.

FIGURE 1.33

Source: Courtesy of Pandora

# pandora®

Pandora reports mid-2017 advertising revenue was at $278.2 million, which was a 5% increase on the previous year's increase. The company is diligently working to firmly position itself in the audio listening industry and creating unique ways to reach new and existing consumers. Naveen Chopra, CFO and interim CEO of Pandora, says,

> We have taken a number of steps to hone the company's strategy and position Pandora to continue to build audience and extend monetization through a combination of advertising and subscription revenue streams. In addition to exceeding our revenue expectations this quarter, we also announced several important strategic moves including a $480 million investment from Sirius XM, the sale of Ticketfly, and changes to our board and management team. We remain laser-focused on execution that attracts listeners and investments that drive the growth and monetization of our audience.

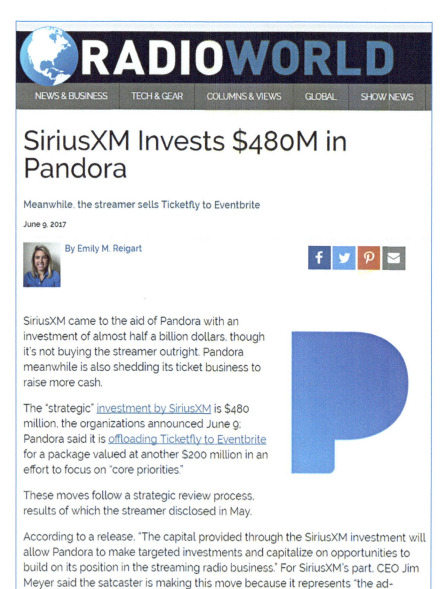

## SiriusXM Invests $480M in Pandora

Meanwhile, the streamer sells Ticketfly to Eventbrite

June 9, 2017

By Emily M. Reigart

SiriusXM came to the aid of Pandora with an investment of almost half a billion dollars, though it's not buying the streamer outright. Pandora meanwhile is also shedding its ticket business to raise more cash.

The "strategic" investment by SiriusXM is $480 million, the organizations announced June 9; Pandora said it is offloading Ticketfly to Eventbrite for a package valued at another $200 million in an effort to focus on "core priorities."

These moves follow a strategic review process, results of which the streamer disclosed in May.

According to a release, "The capital provided through the SiriusXM investment will allow Pandora to make targeted investments and capitalize on opportunities to build on its position in the streaming radio business." For SiriusXM's part, CEO Jim Meyer said the satcaster is making this move because it represents "the ad-supported digital radio business, a space where SiriusXM does not play today."

FIGURE 1.34

SiriusXM invests nearly half a billion dollars in Pandora

Source: Courtesy of *Radio World*

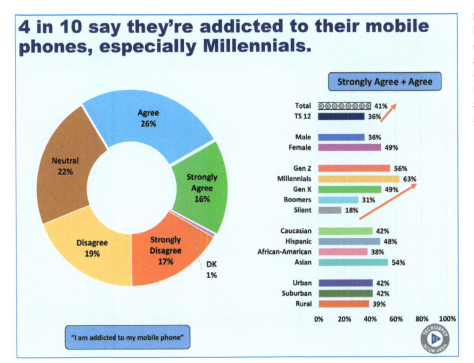

## 4 in 10 say they're addicted to their mobile phones, especially Millennials.

"I am addicted to my mobile phone"

Strongly Agree + Agree

| | Strongly Agree + Agree |
|---|---|
| Total | 41% |
| TS 12 | 36% |
| Male | 36% |
| Female | 49% |
| Gen Z | 56% |
| Millennials | 63% |
| Gen X | 49% |
| Boomers | 31% |
| Silent | 18% |
| Caucasian | 42% |
| Hispanic | 48% |
| African-American | 38% |
| Asian | 54% |
| Urban | 42% |
| Suburban | 42% |
| Rural | 39% |

Agree 26%
Neutral 22%
Strongly Agree 16%
Disagree 19%
Strongly Disagree 17%
DK 1%

**FIGURE 1.35**

Nearly half of all females surveyed, almost equally distributed across all ethnicities, among the Gen Z, Millennials, and Gen X generations report being "addicted" to their mobile phone. Mobile phones are where streaming is offered and consumed

Source: Courtesy of Jacobs Media

Younger listeners are gravitating toward alternative listening opportunities, thus helping to propel streaming to new heights. This is not surprising because young listeners are attached to their smartphones at almost all times and that is where a majority of audio streaming is consumed. Audio streaming provider Pandora reported that, at the conclusion of its second quarter in 2017, it had 76 million active listeners. Active listeners are defined as the number of distinct registered users, including subscribers, who have requested audio from a streaming service's servers within the trailing 30 days to the end of the final calendar month of the reporting period. The total listener hours for this same period was 5.22 billion, which was down slightly from the previous year's 5.66 billion total listener hours. Pandora continues to deflect criticism that its minimal reliance upon local content precludes the service from achieving "radio station" status.

In 2013, Apple announced that its iTunes Radio service had streamed to 11 million unique listeners within weeks of its launch; its most listened-to song during that period was "Hold On, We're Going Home" by Drake. Initially free to users, that soon changed. By 2016, Apple had rebranded this service to become Apple Music and it was available only to subscribers. Boasting a 40 million-song library, Apple Music subscriptions range from $4.99 month for students to a $14.99 a month ad-free service for families. *Forbes* reports as of 2017 that Apple Music had 27 million subscribers and were signing a million new subscribers a week.

Spotify leads Apple Music with its 50 million paying subscribers as of mid-2017. *Music Business Worldwide* notes that Spotify has been adding about 10 million new subscribers every six months and predicted that its subscriber base could grow to 70 million by the end of 2017. In terms of monthly unique users, Verto Analytics reports the top five audio streaming services include: Apple Music, which leads with 40.7 million, followed by Pandora Radio at 32.6 million, then Spotify at 28.5 million. iHeartRadio has 28.5 million and SoundCloud has 25.7 million monthly unique listeners.

Although traditional radio still garners a larger share of the listeners than its streaming counterparts, many listeners now indeed access their favorite radio station via their computer, smartphone, or iPad. Despite the costly copyright royalty fees imposed on Internet stations streaming music, there remain plenty of options for listeners, including all of the AM/FM stations on the iHeartRadio streaming platform. It boasts more than 850 radio stations, which deliver content such as music, news, talk, and sports. iHeartRadio defines itself thus:

FIGURE 1.36
**FIGURE 1.36**

Streaming music services are ranked based upon listenership. The ranking considers the number of sessions per user, per month to determine user engagement

Source: Courtesy of Verto Analytics

**FIGURE 1.37**

Stickiness is how likely listeners or users of a streaming service are they to return to the service day after day

Source: Courtesy of Verto Analytics

iHeartRadio is the world's largest music platform featuring terrestrial radio stations, curated streaming music channels, and incredibly exciting music events. The iHeartRadio app and desktop site is a free audio streaming service with over 200 channels of music, including some of your favorite radio stations such as Virgin, CHUM, QM FM, CJAY and many more!

These terrestrial radio stations can be listened to via personal computers or the iHeartRadio app as well as in connected cars using Apple CarPlay or Android Auto.

Pandora generates revenue from its music streaming. In 2017, Pandora released financial results that indicated that second quarter total consolidated revenue had grown to $376.8 million which was a 10% increase from the previous year. Its subscription revenue was $68.9 million, which was a 25% increase from the previous year. "The internet-radio pioneer and its brethren hope they can divert a swath of local radio ad dollars their way. But for that to happen, they have to get bigger in local markets and offer mobile ads tailored to local audiences. Kinda like radio," said *Advertising Age*. Thus, that's exactly what Pandora is doing. In its 2017 second-quarter financial report, it stated, "local revenue pushed above 30% of total ad revenue for the first time." If the strategy of going after local radio advertising dollars is successful, it could mean serious competition to the traditional radio industry. Moreover, Internet radio is experiencing growth in listenership.

**FIGURE 1.38**
The Kenwood car radio does not offer Apple CarPlay for streaming audio, but it also has Android Auto, Pandora, Spotify, and SiriusXM, as well as HD Radio. The connected car adds additional choices for consumers

Source: Courtesy of JVCKENWOOD USA Corporation

Pandora reports more than 72 million monthly listeners, while iTunes Radio is available on more than 200 million iPhones, iPods, and iPads. Unlike traditional radio, Pandora "combines users' registration data—age, gender, and ZIP code—with time, day and device as well as its so-called Music Genome Project," according to *Advertising Age*. The Genome Project's data are very attractive to advertisers to strategically target messages and therefore make ad dollars more effective. To further illustrate the potential Internet radio possesses, a 2013 *eMarketer* study estimated that there were more than 145 million digital listeners, or nearly half of the entire nation's population.

Recognizing Internet radio's ability to generate healthy advertising revenue, CBS Radio launched its Audio Ad Center in 2013, a digital platform designed for advertisers to purchase online audio advertising on CBS's 125 radio station audio streams. *Inside Radio* describes the Audio Ad Center as enabling "small businesses to buy and build audio ads for online and mobile radio listeners to run at specific times on specific station streams with frequency set by the client."

Traditional radio recognizes the potential of streaming to be a new revenue source and has made efforts to have a presence where the listeners are migrating. For example, Clear Channel introduced iHeartRadio in 2008 and has more than 30 million registered listeners to its online stations. iHeartRadio offers its listeners more than 850 radio stations from which to choose. Streaming music online has caused some distress for the industry due to music copyright royalty fees. In 2012, *The New York Times* reported that satellite and cable radio stations pay 8% of their revenue to royalty rates, while online radio stations such as Pandora pay a fraction of a cent every time a song is played, thus reducing how much music is played, considering that Pandora paid nearly 55% of its revenue that year.

Indeed, pureplay streaming and Internet radio is now big business. To illustrate just how big, in 2012, *The New York Times* reported that more than $1 billion had been collected and paid to artists and record labels. By 2016, the Copyright Royalty Board ruled that streaming stations must pay 17 cents in royalties every 100 times a song is played and song plays by subscribers will be 22 cents for every 100 times a song is played. *Rolling Stone* reported that in 2014 Pandora had paid $400 million in royalties, which was 44% of its revenue.

In spite of the formidable royalty issue confronting webcasters, the RAB determined that more than 6,000 stations were streaming their content to listeners. Meanwhile, Measure-Cast reported that streaming was continuing to grow a year later, so the practice was far from moribund. One year later, SoundExchange, the organization that collects and distributes royalties for streamed audio to recording artists and record labels, reported making the highest quarterly payment in its history. Payments distributed during the second quarter of 2013 totaled $149 million, half again as much as it paid the previous year.

As a result of rapid growth and adoption rates among consumers of streaming, SoundExchange anticipates $4.8 billion of revenue in 2017 and $8.8 billion of revenue by 2025. Mark Mulligan, of MIDiA, says:

The U.S. streaming market will be worth $4.8 billion in 2017 (in retail terms), up from $3.5 billion in 2016. Subscriptions will be the key driver of revenue growth, adding $1.2 billion compared to $0.2 billion for ad-supported. However, ad-supported is a major component of the U.S. market when factoring in revenue from semi-interactive radio services, contributing in total 30 percent to all streaming revenue, one of the highest shares globally.

Indeed, today stations continue to view the Internet, and streaming, as a viable supplement to their on-air signals, especially for promotion and audience research purposes. Streaming is a reality, as is the opportunity for everyone with the right computer and software to be a cybercaster. With an Internet encoder, the home user can transmit to an international audience. This prospect prompts a collective sigh from station managers and owners, who are losing track of the new forms of competition.

Longtime broadcaster Lynn Christian notes:

The major concern regarding the future of radio is centered on new competition from satellite, cable, and online sources. Those companies that are planning to partner with these new media choices, and develop data services, will undoubtedly be the big winners in the twenty-first century. Broadcast radio, as I have known it during the past 50 years, will not be the same in the next few years. But what American business is the same now? These are revolutionary times in radio and in the world.

Media lawyer and former general manager Jason Insalaco observes:

Radio executives programming in the rapidly changing media landscape must embrace the technological revolution that is upon them. Cell phones, the Internet, MP3 players, the iPod, and videogames are vying for the audience's attention. Programmers must heed these encroachments on terrestrial radio or else accept extinction. Rather than fear the new and evolving audio media, traditional radio needs to embrace it for its own benefit. Radio websites are great places for listeners to find out about the station's personalities, music, contests, and events. Websites are cyber-extensions of the over-the-air station brand. Station websites also enhance audience interactivity and constitute another revenue source for a station.

One of the biggest challenges confronting Internet presence continues to be fees charged to provide music. Paul Kamp of Backbone Networks, an Internet radio service provider, states:

The performance royalty rate is probably the largest obstacle. Currently, in the U.S., there are a number of different rates and laws that apply to internet performance royalty rates. This includes the Small Webcasters Settlement that requires stations of a certain size to pay a percentage of their revenue. There is also the commercial Copyright Review Board (CRB) rate that requires Internet radio stations to track performances of a particular piece. The reason this is a big challenge for Internet radio is that the rate is higher than for other broadcast media, like terrestrial and satellite broadcasts. If the rate was equal across all broadcast media we suspect there would be a rush to Internet broadcasting because of the more precise listener statistics that can be generated and the opportunity to more precisely advertise to a particular target. The royalty rate discussion masks a broader issue that needs to be confronted. The strength of the Internet is that it is worldwide. As such, an Internet broadcaster would have to pay music composition performance royalties to all of the professional performing rights organizations where a connection terminates (the country from where the listener connects).

Cognizant of the many obstacles and challenges that exist in the age of the Internet, most radio broadcasters forecast a long-term relationship between the two media—one that will benefit both. As radio heads warp speed into this "future world," it is obvious that aspiring broadcasters will have to know their way around a computer, because the audio studio will exist both over the airwaves and in cyberspace, especially when considering the amount of revenue being generated from online radio stations. BIA/Kelsey predicted that by 2017 the online radio revenue would reach more than $800 million. "As the digital marketplace continues to rise in all sectors of advertising, radio is improving

**FIGURE 1.39**
Spotify logo
Source: Courtesy of Spotify

its listener engagement online and benefitting from the value of its web and mobile assets," said Mark Fratrik, vice-president and chief economist at BIA/Kelsey, in a press release. "Overall, the industry is still recognized as an important part of the media mix as it continues to meander around, rising slightly with the rate of inflation but not keeping up with the economy."

For those interested in this aspect of the medium, the *Radio and Internet Newsletter* (*RAIN*) provides a daily update on the key issues involving radio and the Internet. In fact, *RAIN* interviewed Larry Rosin, president of Edison Research, about the study Edison Research conducted, titled *The New MainStream*, about online radio listening. Regarding the study, Rosen noted:

> The overwhelming point is this technology has brought audio to new places, new locations, and new times in people's lives that they weren't previously filling in with audio. This is the golden age of audio. If all audio were counted, people would see that never before—probably even going back to the twenties and thirties when radio had no competition—there is more audio listening going on today than ever before.

## WHEN FM MET THE INTERNET: THE WAY IT WAS, IS, AND WILL BE

### Mike Englebrecht

Like all industries, radio has its challenges.

Some are perceptual. Like the notion that "no one listens to radio anymore," or that radio, as "traditional" or "old" media, is incapable of innovation.

Some are more tangible. Like an "experience" that has not evolved as quickly as its competition, a content delivery method (broadcast) that has lost ground in consumer electronics and a lack of granular measurability for marketers living in a world of data-driven insights.

**FIGURE 1.40**
Mike Englebrecht

Despite these challenges, radio has much upon which it can capitalize.

Radio is live entertainment that's local and free, and in the worst of times it is the only available connection to life-saving information. It reaches 93% of Americans aged 18+ and accounts for 52% of all "audio consumption" among this group, which is why radio works for advertisers. Savvy marketers understand radio to be a network of geographically defined listening communities that offer the ability to target advertising messages to any number of demographically diverse audience segments.

So how can radio capitalize on its strengths and transition from its twentieth-century roots into a product experience and marketing tool that meets twenty-first-century expectations?

Radio must work together, as an industry, and *innovate*.

Until recently, the Internet (and the data networks that enable us to "connect") has been used simply as an alternate way to distribute radio content, most notably in the form of station streams. But what if radio thought differently about our ability to connect and harnessed it in a way that actually *improved* the experience for listeners, stations, and advertisers?

I believe this level of collaboration and innovation has already begun, and the key component in solving radio's biggest challenges already exists, and it is called "NextRadio."

In order to fully understand why I feel this way, let me step back and relay some history, so you can fully understand how we got here.

Beginning with the introduction of the iPhone in 2007, the smartphone became the fastest adopted technology in the history of the United States. From 2008 to 2014 its share of consumer electronics revenue jumped from 8% to nearly 50%.

The rapid rise of the smartphone resulted in an equivalent decline in sales of other electronic devices: digital cameras and video recorders, GPS devices, the MP3 player, and many of the portable devices used to tune broadcast radio.

While still the dominant choice for audio consumption in the car, radio had to find a way to make its content accessible via the smartphone. An onslaught of new competitors was readily available on the device, eroding radio's share of overall audio consumption. The only option available to radio was for stations to "stream"—repackage its over-the-air audio content and deliver it to smartphones via the Internet.

This situation put radio in a bind.

To understand why radio was in a bind, it is important to understand the most meaningful difference between the broadcast and streaming businesses: broadcast is a fixed cost way to distribute content and it is profitable; with streaming your costs rise with each listener and it is yet to be proven to be a profitable business endeavor.

And *that* was the bind: Radio's only option to be present on the mobile device—the device replacing all others—was by undertaking a method of content delivery (streaming) that loses money.

While radio had no other choice, promoting this method of consumption compounded the problem because it contributed to the slow erosion of listening taking place via radio's *profitable* over-the-air broadcasts. In turn, this led to further declines in the manufacture of devices capable of tuning the over-the-air broadcast. It was, and is, a vicious cycle.

The irony of the situation radio was in is that nearly every smartphone sold in the world has an FM chip inside of it. In other words, every smartphone *is* a radio.

But, in the United States, the device manufacturers—mostly under the direction of the wireless carriers—restrict access to the FM chip. So the capability to tune FM radio is in your smartphone. You pay for it. But you're prevented from using it for reasons I cannot explain.

And *that* little nugget—the presence of an FM chip in every smartphone—turned out to be radio's biggest opportunity: getting the FM chip activated in the smartphone.

By getting the chip activated you reverse the trend of disappearing devices capable of tuning FM *and* you make radio portable again (outside the automobile).

From there, you innovate. You merge the technologies (radio + Internet) and hardware (smartphone) in a way that capitalizes on their strengths and capabilities. In doing so you could evolve the radio experience for listeners, provide a measurable advertising solution for marketers, and ensure that radio's profitable content distribution model has a place on the most important device in a consumer's life.

On January 8, 2013, radio got its big break. That's the day Sprint announced an arrangement with the industry to unlock the FM chip on its Android devices and preload on those devices the FM tuner app, NextRadio, with a planned rollout for the fall of 2013.

## So What Is NextRadio?

NextRadio is a mobile app that enables FM-capable Android devices to tune over-the-air FM radio. It displays related visuals and actions in sync with the FM audio, transforming radio from a purely aural experience into one that is visually appealing and more engaging for the consumer.

So let me stop here for a moment, just in case you missed why NextRadio is a game-changing development for the radio industry: it's *not* streaming.

Instead, by accessing the FM chip in the smartphone, NextRadio enables *data-free* consumption of local, over-the-air broadcast radio. Translation: It turns an FM-enabled smartphone into a radio. And, while it does utilize *some* data to deliver the visual elements, on average a consumer will use 92% *less* data (versus streaming the same radio station). And because the device is not working nearly as hard (to process an audio stream via the Internet), NextRadio saves consumers 75% of their battery life (versus streaming the same station).

With NextRadio, music over FM is no longer simply "heard"—you *see* album art, song title, and artist name in sync with the audio, and songs can be purchased, liked, or disliked. When a host cracks the mic or talk programming airs, images of the personality or program are displayed, and listeners can easily engage with the content via phone, text, or social media.

The same goes for advertising. Businesses can enhance their on-air offer beyond the ear and *show* the pertinent details of their message, when the message airs, transforming the audio call to action into an opportunity for the consumer to *take* the desired action. Broadcasters generate incremental revenue by providing clients this simple, yet powerful opportunity.

NextRadio's most revolutionary development might be that it solves the measurability problem for over-the-air radio. With real-time, granular data around actual radio consumption, NextRadio takes the "one-to-many" aspect of broadcast and distills it into "one-to-one" measurement. This helps stations better understand their audience while providing advertisers with insight into the effectiveness of their campaigns and their overall return on investment (ROI)—standard expectations in the digital marketing age.

## So Where Are We Now?

NextRadio officially launched on August 16, 2013, on two devices sold by Sprint: the HTC One and HTC EVO.

As of September 2017, every wireless carrier in the United States sells FM-enabled devices and the total number of devices sold has exceeded 80 million, and continues to grow. In a matter of four years, FM-capable devices have gone from the endangered species list to 80 million+ in the United States. Amazing.

Listening via NextRadio has also increased exponentially, going from one million hours in its first full year to exceeding six million hours per month presently. Average session length on NextRadio (the amount of time people spend listening to a station) has increased from 21.1 minutes (2014) to 26.3 minutes (2015) to 30.4 minutes (2016)—blowing away the industry average of 10 minutes per listening session (according to Nielsen) and showing how an improved experience can create better results.

One other feature recently added, worth noting, is the ability to *stream* a radio station. FM is still a priority for NextRadio, but we don't want to limit access to a great local radio experience just because a device does not have an active FM chip.

It's still early, and there is plenty of work left for the industry, but all indications are that NextRadio is a success. Its impact on hardware manufacturing, its usage by consumers, and its ability to show ROI to the advertising community are evidence that FM radio has finally found a solution to its challenges, and is well positioned to thrive in the digital, mobile age.

---

**Mike Englebrecht** got his start in radio as a college intern at Chicago's iconic alt-rock station, Q101 (Emmis Communications), during the summer of 1997. A year later he was hired full-time and over the next seven years Mike held several roles within the marketing, sales, and programming departments at Q101.

In 2004, he transitioned to Emmis's newly formed Interactive division, working closely with webmasters and brand managers at Emmis-owned radio, television, and magazine properties to drive web engagement and interactive revenue.

In 2008, Emmis Interactive went worldwide—licensing its proprietary CMS to local media companies around the globe. Mike was Director of Affiliate Relations, overseeing client service, product training, and technical support. Four years later, Emmis Interactive was sold and Mike, along with eight other Emmis Interactive employees, was retained by Emmis to work on the FM smartphone initiative, NextRadio. When the initiative began in 2012, FM-enabled mobile devices were nonexistent in the United States; today there are more than 80 million in the marketplace.

Mike is currently the Director of Product Engagement for TagStation and NextRadio, working with the company's internal teams to help radio stations understand how to derive maximum value from their now playing data. He holds a BA from Loras College in Dubuque, Iowa, is a self-proclaimed "lover of radio" and resides in the far-western suburbs of Chicago with his wife and two young daughters.

# HD RADIO

A predecessor to HD Radio was AM stereo. In its hope to help AM radio out of its doldrums, in the early 1980s the FCC authorized stereocasting on the senior band. However, the commission failed to declare a technical standard, leaving that task to the marketplace. This resulted in a very sluggish conversion to the two-channel system, and by the 1990s only a few hundred AM outlets offered stereo broadcasting. Those that did were typically the more prosperous metro-market stations that ultimately featured talk and information formats.

Eventually, the FCC declared Motorola the industry standard-bearer, but by the mid-1990s the hope that stereo would provide a cure for AM's deepening malaise had dimmed considerably. By this time, many AM outlets, which may have benefited by having a stereo signal, were in a weaker financial state and unable to convert or were less than enthusiastic about any potential payback. Many were just holding on in the hope that the impending conversion of radio to digital would help level the playing field for AM. In the 2000s, the C-QUAM (Compatible—Quadrature Amplitude Modulation) system grew in popularity and allowed for HD radio to broadcast AM stereo signals.

Digital Audio Broadcasting (DAB), the generic term that describes the technology, or HD Radio, a term trademarked by developer iBiquity and owned by Xperi, makes analog AM and FM outmoded systems. With the great popularity of home and portable digital music equipment (CD, MP3s, and iPods), broadcasters have been compelled to convert their signals to remain competitive. Thus, DAB, known more popularly as HD Radio, is a solid fixture in today's radio.

At first broadcasters viewed DAB as a threat. The NAB looked at the new sound technology as an adversary. In an interview in the July 23, 1990, issue of *RadioWeek*, John Abel, NAB's Executive Vice-President of Operations, stated, "DAB is a threat and anyone who plans to stay in business for a while needs to pay careful attention."

As time went on, DAB was regarded as a *fait accompli*, something that was simply going to happen. Soon broadcasters assumed a more proactive posture regarding the technology, and then the concern shifted to where to put the new medium and how to protect existing broadcast operations.

Early on, NAB proposed locating DAB in the L-band portion of the electromagnetic spectrum. It also argued for in-band placement. Eventually the FCC saw fit to recommend that DAB be allocated room in the S-band, and it took its proposal to the World Administrative Radio Conference (WARC) held in Spain in February 1992. This spectrum designation spurred in-band terrestrial development. In-band, on-channel (IBOC) digital signaling, developed by Xperi's Glynn Walden, permits broadcasters to remain on their existing frequencies. AM/FM station operators embraced the plan out of concern that satellite DAB signal transmission represented a significant threat to the local nature of U.S. broadcasting. On the other hand, many countries are fully supportive of a satellite DAB system because they do not have the number of stations the United States possesses and thus lack the coverage and financial investment.

Several manufacturers offer HD receivers at prices that are affordable and competitive and a number of car manufacturers provide HD Radio in their latest models. Digital converters are also available at a modest price. At the 2012 NAB conference, it was reported that there are more than seven million HD Radios in the market owned by listeners. More impressively, it was reported that an HD Radio-equipped car sells every 15 seconds. The HD Radio market is clearly growing and appears to have a strong future. As of 2017, Xperi reports there are more than 3,500 digital broadcast programs and more than four billion hours of HD Radio listening annually. Overall, 78% of all radio listening is done on stations with HD Radio technology.

Considered another plus of digital radio is its capability to do other things. For example, Xperi has developed a technology that allows those stations broadcasting digitally to transmit data to portable digital devices, including smartphones. This is attractive to the station operator's bottom line. The ability to multicast (provide side-channel transmissions), which allows the medium to deliver additional program channels to the listening audience, is yet another major plus for HD Radio.

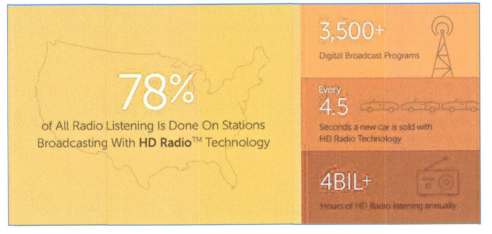

Prior to the World Administrative Radio Conference (WARC) meeting in 1992, NAB's DAB Task Force proposed a set of standards to ensure that the technology would operate effectively. The specifications included:

- CD-quality sound
- Enhanced coverage area
- Accommodation of existing AM and FM frequencies
- Immunity to multipath interference
- Immunity to stoplight fades
- No interference to existing AM and FM broadcasters
- DAB system interference immunity
- Minimization of transmission costs
- Receiver complexity
- Additional data capacity
- Reception area threshold.

After nearly a century of analog signal transmission, radio is now in the digital domain, which will keep it relevant to the demands of a technologically sophisticated listening marketplace as it embarks on its next 100 years. Hundreds of radio stations across the country became early adopters and began offering digital signals. Additionally, the majority of them are also providing expanded listening options with HD2, HD3, and HD4 services.

Clearly, HD Radio has yet to achieve widespread acceptance, but its adoption is growing in an impressive manner. Despite the technological advancement it represents, the trade press has observed that the public simply is not clamoring for a radio service that provides increased fidelity and wider dynamic range, particularly when a purchase is required in order to achieve the improvement. But recent studies show that listening to HD Radio in cars is on the rise. Rick Greenhut, Director of Broadcast Business Development at Xperi, shares that as of 2017, "there [are] 2,173 stations broadcasting in HD. They are also broadcasting an additional 1,420 HD2 channels; 464 HD3 channels, and 68 HD4 channels for a total of 4,125 separate digital channels on-air." That's an increase from the approximately 2,050 stations that were broadcasting in HD Radio at the end of 2012.

Additionally, Greenhut says:

> about 700 stations are also using part of their HD Radio digital bandwidth to send traffic and weather data in the background for the Total Traffic and Weather Network or the Broadcast Traffic Consortium. Radios in select Lexus, Honda, Mazda and Toyota vehicles display this information free of charge to the consumer.

The HD Radio technology is being used by stations as a supplement to weather and traffic alerts they broadcast over the airwaves. The digital radios provide users with visual alerts on weather and traffic and even news depending on the radio they own.

**FIGURE 1.45**
HD radios can alert users to severe weather
Source: Courtesy of Xperi

Certain industry watchdogs attribute the slow diffusion of HD Radio to the government's decision regarding whether to require broadcasters to abandon analog transmission and replace it with digital signaling. Twice in the history of television broadcasting the FCC has taken action to stimulate the adoption and spread of emerging technologies. The first of these occurred following the passage of the 1961 federal All-Channel Receiver Act. To stimulate the growth of television in the ultra high frequency (UHF) band, Congress empowered the FCC to require television receiver manufacturers to include UHF tuners in all sets manufactured in 1964 and thereafter. Decades later, the FCC required TV broadcasters in 2009 to turn off their analog broadcast and operate solely with digital (DTV) transmitters. Interestingly, neither Congress nor the FCC has imposed mandates on radio broadcasters to abandon terrestrial analog AM and FM transmissions. As the FCC observed in 2002,

> broadcasters may begin interim IBOC operations on a voluntary basis, deferring costs as they deem appropriate . . . it is important to recognize that the endorsement of the hybrid IBOC transmission systems does not compel any broadcaster to make the investments necessary to initiate digital transmissions.

More recently, proponents who support decommissioning the analog standard-band service in a process they term "AM sunset" have revived the debate. Vigorous discussion about establishing a cessation date for AM analog swirled around the 2013 convention of the NAB.

## PUBLIC RADIO/NONCOMMERCIAL RADIO

As of 2017, the FCC reports there are approximately 15,512 AM and FM radio stations in the U.S. Of that number, 4,111 stations operate without direct advertiser support and are classified by the FCC as "FM Educational." Noncommercial stations, as they are called, date back to the medium's heyday and were primarily run by colleges and universities. The first "noncoms" broadcast on the AM band but moved to the FM side in 1938. After World War II, the FCC reconstituted the FM band and reserved the first 20 channels (88.1–91.9 MHz) for noncommercial facilities. Initially, this gave rise to low-power (10-watt) stations known as Class Ds. The lower cost of such operations was a prime motivator for schools that wanted to become involved with broadcasting. Noncommercial stations can be divided into at least four categories: public, college (noncommercial educational), community, and religious.

In 1967, the Corporation for Public Broadcasting (CPB) was established as the result of the Public Broadcasting Act. The CPB website states: "CPB does not produce programming and does not own, operate or control any public broadcasting stations. Additionally, CPB, PBS, and NPR are independent of each other and of local public television and radio stations." It simply oversees the expenditures of monies set aside by Congress annually for public broadcasting. Three years after the CPB was formed, National Public Radio (NPR) was created. In 2010, it adopted a new name, shortening "National Public Radio" to just "NPR." Today, more than 900 stations use the syndication services of NPR and 95% of the U.S. population is within the area of an NPR station, which provides programming. Many NPR affiliates are licensed to colleges and universities, and a substantial number are owned by nonprofit organizations.

When NPR was created in 1970, William Siemering served as its first director of programming. In that role, he was tasked with creating the mission statement for the new radio service. NPR titled it, "National Public Radio Purposes." The document remains relevant and prescient even today and reads almost like a poem. Here is just one section of the statement in which it notes one of the editorial attitudes would be geared toward "life loving":

> It would not, however, substitute superficial blandness for genuine diversity of regions, values, and cultural and ethnic minorities, which comprise American society. It would speak with many voices and many dialects. The editorial attitude would be that of inquiry, curiosity, concern for the quality of life, critical problem solving, and life loving. The listener should come to rely upon it as a source of information of consequence, of having listened as having made a difference in his attitude toward his environment and himself.

Member stations are the primary source of funding for NPR, contributing 39% of its operating budget through station dues and fees; 24% of NPR's budget comes from corporate sponsorships and 14% is derived from grants and contributions. The remainder of NPR funding is derived from investment income and endowments. Affiliates in turn are supported by listeners, community businesses, and grants from the CPB. Program underwriting (the equivalent of sponsorships) is a primary way that public stations meet their operating budgets. These on-air announcements run approximately 15 seconds and include sponsor name and information but no direct selling message or hype. They are purchased by sponsors in much the same way that spots are sold on commercial stations. (Public radio station websites usually provide more detail on this subject.) Listener support is important and those who commit to ongoing financial contributions—sustainers—make up half of the annual local contributions to public radio.

In 2016, Nielsen ratings indicated that 37.4 million listeners tuned in to NPR on a weekly basis. Their literature states that "NPR's news and performance programming attracts an audience distinguished by its level of education, professionalism, and community involvement." Programs such as *All Things Considered* and *Morning Edition* have become the industry's premier news and information features, achieving both popular and critical acclaim, with 14.4 to 14.6 million people tuning into the programs weekly. NPR has created and made available 37 podcasts that are listened to by more than four million listeners weekly. NPR is the leader in producing podcasts and, as of 2017, held Podtrac's #1 spot. On the NPR website, Thomas Hjelm, chief digital officer at NPR, says:

> We are thrilled by the growth we have seen, NPR is a forum for robust discussion, rigorous reporting and great storytelling—and through innovations and expansion onto new devices, NPR is reaching more people on more platforms than ever before.

Research shows that NPR listeners are consumers of information from many sources and are more likely than average Americans to buy books. They are motivated citizens involved in public activities, such as voting and fundraising. They address public meetings, write letters to editors, and lead business and civic groups. In 2016, Jacobs Media found that listeners tuned in to public radio to enjoy learning new things and because they found the content more credible and objective. They also reported that the content had a deeper news perspective and they liked particular shows and hosts.

Public Radio International (PRI), known originally as American Public Radio between its 1983 debut and 1994, operates much like NPR. It provides nearly 19 million people monthly with additional

# NATIONAL PUBLIC RADIO PURPOSES

National Public Radio will serve the individual, it will promote personal growth, it will regard the individual differences with respect and joy, rather than derision and hate. It will celebrate the human experience as infinitely varied, rather than vacuous and banal. It will encourage a sense of active, constructive participation, rather than apathetic helplessness.

National Public Radio, through live interconnection and other distribution systems, will be the primary national non-commercial program service. Public radio stations will be a source for programming input as well as program dissemination. The potentials of live interconnection will be exploited; the art and enjoyment of the sound medium will be advanced.

In its cultural mode, National Public Radio will preserve and transmit the cultural past, will encourage and broadcast the work of contemporary artists, and provide listeners with an aural aesthetic experience, which enriches and gives meaning to the human spirit.

In its journalistic mode, National Public Radio will actively explore, investigate and interpret issues of national and international import. The programs will enable the individual to better understand himself, his government, his institutions, and his natural and social environment, so he can intelligently participate in affecting the process of change.

The total service should be trustworthy, enhance intellectual development, expand knowledge, deepen aural aesthetic enjoyment, increase the pleasure of living in a pluralistic society, and result in a service to listeners which makes them more responsive, informed human beings and intelligent, responsible citizens of their communities and the world.

### Implementation of Goals
Such statements of purpose are only platitudes and good intentions, unless there's a strong commitment, creative energy, and specific strategy to implement them. The detailed implementation of National Public Radio is the responsibility of the president and his staff, but some priorities and suggested approaches are necessary to help answer the how and why of NPR.

The priorities of NPR program development are to:

1. Provide an identifiable daily product, which is consistent and reflects the highest standards of broadcast journalism.
2. Provide extended coverage of public events, issues, and ideas, and acquire and produce special public affairs programs.
3. Acquire and produce cultural programs, which can be scheduled individually by stations.
4. Provide access to the intellectual and cultural resources of cities, universities and rural districts through a system of cooperative program development with member public radio stations.
5. Develop and distribute programs to specific groups, adult education and structural modular units for local productions, which meet the needs of individual regions or groups.
6. Establish liaison with foreign broadcasters for a program exchange service.
7. Produce materials specifically intended to develop the art, and technical potential of radio.

Because National Public Radio begins with no identity of its own, it is essential that a daily product of excellence be developed. This may contain some hard news, but the primary emphasis would be on interpretation, investigative reporting on public affairs, the world of ideas, and the arts. The program would be well-paced, flexible, and a service primarily for a general audience.

It would not, however, substitute superficial blandness for genuine diversity of regions, values, and cultural and ethnic minorities, which comprise American society. It would speak with many voices and many dialects. The editorial attitude would be that of inquiry, curiosity, concern for the quality of life, critical problem solving, and life loving. The listener should come to rely upon it as a source of information of consequence, of having listened as having made a difference in his attitude toward his environment and himself.

There may be regular features on consumer information, views of the world from the poets, men and women of ideas, and interpretive comments from scholars, using inputs from affiliate stations; for the first time the intellectual resources of colleges and universities will be applied to daily affairs on a national scale.

Philosophically, time is measured by the intensity of experience. Waiting for a bus and walking through an art gallery may occupy the same time duration, but not the same time experience. Listeners should feel that the time spent with NPR was among their most rewarding in media contact. National Public Radio will not regard its audience as a market, or in terms of its disposable income, but as curious, complex individuals who are looking for some understanding, meaning, and joy in the human experience.

**FIGURE 1.47**
The original National Public Radio Purposes document, or mission statement, is relevant even today

noncommercial options, airing popular programs such as *A Prairie Home Companion*, created in 1974 and hosted for the next 42 years by humorist Garrison Keillor, and many others. On its website, PRI states,

We create a more informed, empathetic and connected world by sharing powerful stories, encouraging exploration, connecting people and cultures, and creating opportunities to help people take informed action on stories that inspire them. Its mission is to serve audiences as a distinctive content source for information, insights and cultural experiences essential to living in our diverse, interconnected world.

**FIGURE 1.48**

Impressively, "sustainers" outnumber others who financially support public radio. More women and more Millennials are sustainers

Source: Courtesy of Jacobs Media

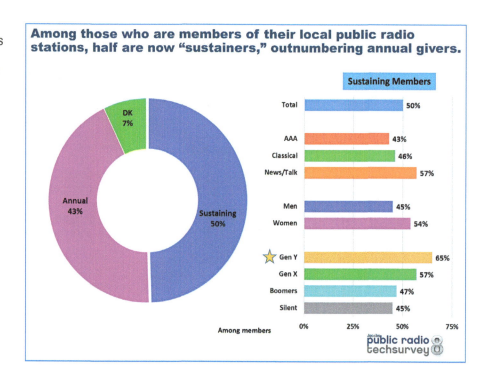

**FIGURE 1.49**

Learning new things and credible/objective programming rank high as reasons people listen to public radio

Source: Courtesy of Jacobs Media

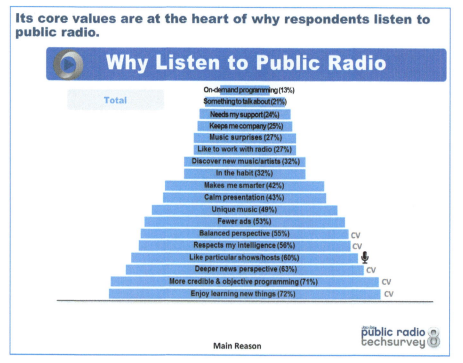

# ABOUT

## PRI Public Radio International℠

Public Radio International (PRI) is the source of more public radio programming than any other distributor in the United States. Founded in 1983 as American Public Radio, PRI is steadily moving forward with its second decade goal to "provide expanded global perspectives on world news, current events, and culture to public radio audiences."

In addition to acquiring finished programming from station-based and independent producers around the globe, PRI actively shapes and develops new programs and program formats. PRI also seeks to expand the reach, impact, and relevancy of public radio for audiences who have not traditionally been public radio listeners.

The network emphasizes programming in three general areas:

- News and information
- Classical music
- Comedy/Variety and contemporary music

PRI also distributes an average of four special programs per month.

**Keep us in mind and on file. We look forward to talking with YOU.**

 PRI Public Radio International℠

Public Radio International
100 North Sixth Street, Suite 900A
Minneapolis, Minnesota 55403
**Telephone: 612.338.5000
Facsimile: 612.330.9222**

This recycled paper is made from 50% waste paper and contains 10% postconsumer waste.

**FIGURE 1.50**
A Public Radio International
promotional piece
Source: Courtesy PRI

## ON PUBLIC RADIO

### William Siemering

Although educational radio began at the University of Wisconsin in 1917, stations were not connected by a live network nation-wide until NPR was created, with the first regular daily program, *All Things Considered* started on May 3, 1971.

I never wanted NPR to be regarded as alternative radio, but rather be considered mainstream. That's one reason I started *All Things Considered,* at 5:00 pm ET because I wanted it to be the first broadcast record of the day's events. I know it must have seemed laughable at the time as there were fewer than 100 public radio stations that were NPR members. Now it is a network of 900 stations.

Now NPR is the most respected broadcast news medium and the audience has grown by four million in the last year. NPR news programs reach 37 million a month. Now with podcasts and the ability to read transcripts of programs, it is estimated that 99 million people use some form of NRP programming

**FIGURE 1.51**
William Siemering

in a month across both broadcast and digital platforms. Programs can now be heard via live streaming, on smartphones, Google Home and Apple devices, among others.

As the largest single source of income for public radio stations is listener contributions, the programming is listener-driven and the program directors read the Arbitron ratings just as their commercial colleagues do. However, their programming must be significantly different in content and quality from commercial programs to elicit freewill contributions. (In many European countries, public service broadcasting is supported by a tax on receivers, not voluntary contributions.) Commercial stations, although sometimes involved in community service, have one goal: make a profit. Public stations have a mission to serve unmet cultural, information, and community needs.

The most listened-to programs on public radio are news and information programs: *Morning Edition*, *All Things Considered*, and *Fresh Air*. These are characterized by both the thoroughness of their coverage and the breadth of subjects. They regard news of the arts/popular culture to be as important to understanding the world as news of politicians.

No commercial network comes close to replicating these programs. While most NPR member stations carry primarily information and talk programs some also broadcast jazz, Triple A (Adult Alternative Album), bluegrass, acoustic, classical music. Some stations are directed to specific audiences such as Hispanic or Native American.

Public radio listeners tend to be educated and to include decision-makers and influentials in their communities, so their influence is great. *Publishers Weekly* said public radio is the single most important medium for the book business.

In addition to support from listeners, public radio also receives corporate and business underwriting, and grants from foundations and the CPB, which was created in 1967 to distribute federal funds and protect stations against political pressure on programming. Managing a public radio station is, therefore, more complex because its funding is so diverse. At the same time, it protects the independence of the programming from the influence of the funders.

As the audience figures show, public radio is considered more important now than ever. As public ignorance grows through social media and partisan broadcasters, the solid journalism and taking time to tell a story thoroughly are more valued and needed for our democracy.

---

**William "Bill" Siemering** was the first Director of Programming of National Public Radio where he developed the long-running and well-known radio program, *All Things Considered*. Later, at WHYY-FM in Philadelphia, he developed *Fresh Air with Terry Gross* from a local to a national program. He currently serves as president of Developing Radio Partners, an organization dedicated to supporting independent radio stations in young democracies through professional development in journalism, programming, station management, and finance.

Many public radio stations, especially those affiliated with NPR, choose to air classical music. The Intercollegiate Broadcasting System (IBS) notes that more than 800 schools and colleges hold noncommercial licenses. The majority of these stations operate at lower power, some with as little as 10 watts. Since the late 1970s, a large percentage of college stations have upgraded from Class D and now radiate signals with powers of hundreds of watts or more. Most college stations serve as training grounds for future broadcasters while providing alternative programming for their listeners.

Community noncoms are usually licensed to civic groups, foundations, school boards, and religious associations. Although the majority of these stations broadcast at low power, they manage to satisfy the programming desires of thousands of listeners. Occasionally, noncoms pose a ratings threat to commercial stations. However, this threat is usually in the area of classical music and news programming. Consequently, commercial and noncommercial radio stations manage a fairly peaceful and congenial coexistence. (See "Suggested Further Reading" at the end of this chapter for additional information on noncommercial radio.)

# RADIO REGULATIONS AND GOVERNMENT OVERSIGHT

Almost from the start it was recognized that radio could be a unique instrument for the public good. This point was never made more apparent than, in 1912, when, according to legend (which has been challenged by scholars who contend that others were involved), a young wireless operator named David Sarnoff picked up the distress signal from the sinking *Titanic* and relayed the message to ships in the vicinity, which then came to the rescue of those still alive. The survivors were the beneficiaries of the first attempt at regulating the new medium. The Wireless Ship Act of 1910 required that ships carrying 50 or more passengers have wireless equipment on board. The effective use of the medium from an experimental station in New York City's Wanamaker Building helped save 700 lives.

Radio's first practical application was as a means of communicating from ship to ship and from ship to shore. During the first decade of the twentieth century, Marconi's wireless invention was seen primarily as a way of linking the ships at sea with the rest of the world. Until that time, when ships left port they were beyond any conventional mode of communications. The wireless was a boon to the maritime services, including the Navy, which equipped each of its warships with the new device.

Coming on the heels of the *Titanic* disaster, the Radio Act of 1912 sought to expand the general control of radio on the domestic level. The Secretary of the Department of Commerce and Labor was appointed to head the implementation and monitoring of the new legislation. The primary function of the act was to license wireless stations and operators. The new regulations empowered the department to impose fines and revoke the licenses of those who operated outside the parameters set down by the communications law.

Growth of radio on the national level was curtailed by World War I, when the government saw fit to take over the medium for military purposes. However, as the war raged on, the same young wireless operator, David Sarnoff, who supposedly had been instrumental in saving the lives of passengers on the ill-fated *Titanic*, was hard at work on an idea to drastically modify the scope of the medium and convert it from an experimental and maritime communications apparatus to something that could be used by the general public. Less than five years after the war's end, receivers were being bought by the millions, and radio as we know it today was born.

The lack of government regulations dealing with interference nearly resulted in the premature end of radio (see this textbook's companion website for more information). By 1926, hundreds of stations clogged the airways, bringing pandemonium to the dial. The Radio Act of 1912 simply did not anticipate radio's new application. Thus, it was the Radio Act of 1927 that first approached radio as a mass medium. The Federal Regulatory Commission's (FRC) five commissioners quickly implemented a series of actions that restored the fledgling medium's health.

The Communications Act of 1934 charged a seven-member commission with the responsibility of ensuring the efficient use of the airways, which the government views as a limited resource that belongs to the public and is leased to broadcasters. The FCC has concentrated its efforts on maximizing the usefulness of radio for the public's benefit. Consequently, broadcasters have been required to devote a portion of their airtime to programs that address important community and national issues. In addition, broadcasters have had to promise to serve as a constant and reliable source of information, while retaining certain limits on the amount of commercial material scheduled.

The FCC has steadfastly sought to keep the medium free of political bias and special interest groups. In 1949, the commission implemented regulations making it necessary for stations that present a viewpoint to provide an equal amount of airtime to contrasting or opposing viewpoints. The Fairness Doctrine obliged broadcasters "to afford reasonable opportunity for the discussion of conflicting views of public importance." Later, it also stipulated that stations notify persons when attacks were made on them over the air. In 1987, during President Reagan's administration, the Fairness Doctrine was abolished by the FCC. The rise of conservative radio talk show hosts has been attributed to the abolishment of the Fairness Doctrine as stations were no longer required to devote airtime to cover all angles of a controversial topic.

Although broadcasters generally acknowledge the unique nature of their business, many have felt that the government's involvement has exceeded reasonable limits in a society based on a free-enterprise system. Because it is their money, time, and energy they are investing, broadcasters feel they should be afforded greater opportunity to determine their own programming. More recent justifications used by the radio industry include the fact that there is a proliferation of online and digital media choices for consumers. These additional choices for consumers, based upon traditional broadcasters' rationalization, means there is less need for the government to provide oversight to ensure the public interests and needs must be met solely via AM and FM signals. Thus, they allow the marketplace to dictate how the industry evolves.

The extensive updating of FCC rules and policy that has resulted in less regulation was based on the belief that the marketplace should serve as the primary regulator. Opponents of the deregulation feared that, with the newfound freedom broadcasters possessed, radio stations would quickly turn their backs on community concerns and concentrate their full efforts on fattening their pocketbooks.

Those who support the position that broadcasters should first serve the needs of society are concerned that deregulation (i.e., less regulatory oversight) has further reduced the medium's "good citizen" role. Robert Hilliard, former FCC Chief of Public and Educational Broadcasting, observes:

> Radio, especially the commercial sector, has long since fallen down on its "interest, convenience, and necessity" obligation born of the Radio Act of 1927. While a small segment of the industry does exert an effort to address the considerable problems facing society today, the overwhelming majority continue to be fixated on the financial bottom line. There needs to be more of a balance.

Proponents of deregulation applauded the FCC's actions, contending that the listening audience would indeed play a vital role in determining the programming of radio stations, because the medium has to meet the needs of the public to prosper.

Although the government continues to closely scrutinize the actions of the radio industry to ensure that it operates in an efficient and effective manner, it is no longer perceived as the fearsome, omnipresent Big Brother it once was. Today, broadcasters more fully enjoy the fruits of a laissez-faire system of economy, although they are not immune to commission actions.

In the spring of 1996, President Bill Clinton signed the Telecommunications Act, making it a reality and successor to the Communications Act of 1934, and ownership caps were all but eliminated. The Act opened the floodgates for those radio groups wanting to vastly expand their portfolios. For example, by 2002 Clear Channel Radio had purchased nearly 1,400 stations. Consequently, by the mid-2000s, localism had taken a substantial hit, as many of the major radio groups had replaced the indigenous broadcasts of their stations with voice-tracking and "out-of-town" programming.

In the late 2010s, the FCC initiated a Modernization of Media Regulation and solicited feedback from broadcasters during an open comment period to learn which regulations broadcasters thought were antiquated and needed modification and/or abolishment. Broadcast attorney David Oxenford noted that, in the first six months of 2017 alone, the FCC had already abolished or modified the following regulations:

> the requirements for letters from the public in the public file, allowing online recruitment to be the sole means of Equal Employment Opportunity (EEO) wide dissemination of job openings, relaxing the location restrictions on FM translators for AM stations, relaxing the limitations on noncommercial fundraising, abolishing the obligation for noncommercial stations to report the social security numbers of their board members, the rescission of FCC enforcement actions for political violations, and the revocation of a policy statement against shared services agreements.

Oxenford declared that these actions "demonstrate that this Commission is serious about deregulation."

Further, as of 2017, the FCC was studying regulations and modifications that would improve AM radio service. At the 2017 NAB/RAB Radio Show in Austin, the chairman of the FCC, Ajit Pai, promised broadcasters that the FCC would repeal an outdated or unnecessary broadcast rule every month under his term as FCC commissioner.

# CHAPTER HIGHLIGHTS

1. The radio industry is experiencing a paradigm shift as a result of technological advancements that have created new competition from other audio delivery platforms. Specifically, the radio industry is experiencing change in the method in which listeners consume audio and new competition from audio platforms based on the Internet.

2. Radio reaches 93% of all American adults, 92% of 18- to 34-year-olds, and 95% of 35- to 49-year-olds. Radio has the engagement of 91% of those surveyed compared to 21% engagement with podcasts, 23% engagement with satellite radio, 47% engagement with an MP3 player, and 58% engagement with streaming audio.

3. Although radio has been unable to regain the share of the national advertising dollar it attracted before the arrival of television, it does earn far more today than it did during its so-called heyday. By targeting specific audience demographics, the industry remained solvent.

4. Local marketing agreements (LMAs) allowed broadcasters to form contracts with one another for mutually beneficial purposes.

5. Satellite radio services are providing listeners with options besides traditional terrestrial signal reception. It is subscription driven and offers a wide array of program options featuring an array of famous personalities.

6. Cable companies provide in-home music services for most of their subscribers. These commercial-free channels of diverse nonstop music, replete with on-screen information about what is being played, are very attractive to subscribers and frequently result in the loss of yet another portion of traditional radio's listening audience.

7. Technology is changing the way people listen to audio, even in their cars. The connected car is now competing with AM/FM for audio listeners. In some newer cars, AM radio is no longer a built-in feature.

8. Consumers who have smartphones want their phone content to follow them everywhere they go, even when they are in the car.

9. Mobile music services spawned by the Internet, Wi-Fi, and smartphones draw listeners away from traditional radio, although it is anticipated that broadcast and satellite radio will become an integral part of these audio sources. Online music services such as Pandora, iHeartRadio, and Spotify are competing with traditional broadcasters not only for listeners but also for advertising revenue. Apps for smartphones, iPads, iPods, etc. are expanding the consumer's choice of music stations as well as offering an even more convenient way to listen to music.

10. Podcast listening is on the rise among Americans and offers diversity that terrestrial radio does not, which makes it attractive to Millennials and Generation Z. A podcast can be created by anyone who has the desire and knowledge to do so. All it takes to listen to a podcast is a small handheld device such as a smartphone, iPad, or personal computer, all of which are almost universal and, importantly, allows listeners to timeshift their listening patterns. Timeshifting is when listeners consume audio at times that are convenient for them rather than listening to a "live" broadcast.

11. September 30 is International Podcast Day. Podcast enthusiasts are encouraged to use #International PodcastDay annually on their social media to spread the good word about podcasting on that day.

12. The migration of audiences toward streaming audio services has been on the rise for several years. Fluent Public Opinion Market Research reports that almost 80% of Americans state they use at least one streaming service. Sixty-one percent of those surveyed listened to online radio monthly.

13. One study found that the top five audio streaming services included: Apple Music leads, with 40.7 million, followed by Pandora Radio at 32.6 million, then Spotify at 28.5 million, iHeartRadio at 28.5 million, and SoundCloud at 25.7 million monthly unique listeners.

14. Today, stations continue to view the Internet, and streaming, as a viable supplement to their on-air signals, especially for promotion and audience research purposes. Streaming is a reality, as is the opportunity for everyone with the right computer and software to be a broadcaster or cybercaster.

15. HD Radio is supplementing the conventional analog system of signal transmission and reception. There are more than 3,500 digital broadcast programs and more than four billion hours of HD Radio listening annually. Overall, 78% of all radio listening is done on stations with HD Radio technology.

16. The Corporation for Public Broadcasting was established in 1967. Three years later, National Public Radio began providing funding and programming to member stations. Today, more than 900 stations use the networked services of NPR and 95% of the U.S. population is within the area of an NPR station, which provides programming. Many NPR affiliates are licensed to colleges and universities, and a substantial number are owned by nonprofit organizations.

17. The Telecommunications Act of 1996 is the successor to the Communications Act of 1934, both acts have been the mandates given to the Federal Communications Commission to regulate the radio industry and provide government oversight.

18. In 1949, the FCC formulated the Fairness Doctrine, which obligated broadcasters to present opposing points of view. In 1987 the FCC declared the doctrine unconstitutional and eliminated it.

## SUGGESTED FURTHER READING

Aitkin, H.G.J., *Syntony and Spark*, John Wiley and Sons, New York, NY, 1976.

American Women in Radio and Television, *Making Waves: The 50 Greatest Women in Radio and Television*, Andrews McMeel, Chicago, IL, 2001.

Archer, G.L., *History of Radio to 1926*, Arno Press, New York, NY, 1971.

Aronoff, C.E. (ed.), *Business and the Media*, Goodyear, Santa Monica, CA, 1979.

Baker, W.J., *A History of the Marconi Company*, St. Martin's Press, New York, NY, 1971.

Balk, A., *The Rise of Radio, from Marconi to the Golden Age*, McFarland, Jefferson, NC, 2005.

Barlow, W., *Voice Over: The Making of Black Radio*, Temple University Press, Philadelphia, PA, 1999.

Barnouw, E., *A Tower of Babel: A History of Broadcasting in the United States to 1933*, vol. 1, Oxford University Press, New York, NY, 1966.

Barnouw, E., *The Golden Web: A History of Broadcasting in the United States 1933 to 1953*, vol. 2, Oxford University Press, New York, NY, 1968.

Barnouw, E., *The Image Empire: A History of Broadcasting in the United States from 1953*, vol. 3, Oxford University Press, New York, NY, 1970.

Barnouw, E., *The Sponsor: Notes on a Modern Potentate*, Oxford University Press, New York, NY, 1978.

Barnouw, E., *Media Marathon: A Twentieth-Century Memoir*, Duke University Press, Durham, NC, 1996.

Bergreen, L., *Look Now, Pay Later: The Rise of Network Broadcasting*, Doubleday, Garden City, NY, 1980.

Bianchi, W., *Schools of the Air*, McFarland, Jefferson, NC, 2008.

Bittner, J.R., *Broadcasting and Telecommunications*, 2nd edition, Prentice Hall, Englewood Cliffs, NJ, 1985.

Bittner, J.R., *Professional Broadcasting: A Brief Introduction*, Prentice Hall, Englewood Cliffs, NJ, 1981.

Blake, R.H. and Haroldsen, E.O., *A Taxonomy of Concepts in Communications*, Hastings House, New York, NY, 1975.

Brant, B.G., *College Radio Handbook*, Tab, Blue Ridge Summit, PA, 1981.

Brown, R.J., *Manipulating the Ether: The Power of Broadcast Radio in Thirties America*, McFarland Publishing, Jefferson, NC, 1998.

Browne, B., and Coddington (consultants), *Radio Today—and Tomorrow*, National Association of Broadcasters, Washington, D.C., 1982.

Buono, T.J. and Leibowitz, M.L., *Radio Acquisition Handbook*, Broadcasting and the Law, Miami, FL, 1988.

Campbell, R., *The Golden Years of Broadcasting*, Charles Scribner's Sons, New York, NY, 1976.

Cantril, H., *The Invasion from Mars*, Harper & Row, New York, NY, 1966.

Carpenter, S., *40 Watts from Nowhere: A Journey in Pirate Radio*, Scribner, New York, NY, 2004.

Chapple, S. and Garofalo, R., *Rock 'n' Roll Is Here to Pay*, Nelson-Hall, Chicago, IL, 1977.

Coe, L., *Wireless Radio: A History*, McFarland Publishing, Jefferson, NC, 2006.

*Cox Looks at FM Radio*, Cox Broadcasting Corporation, Atlanta, GA, 1976.

Craig, D.B., *Fireside Politics: Radio and Political Culture in the United States, 1920–1940*, Johns Hopkins University Press, Baltimore, MD, 2000.

Delong, T.A., *The Mighty Music Box*, Amber Crest, Los Angeles, CA, 1980.

Ditingo, V.M., *The Remaking of Radio*, Focal Press, Boston, MA, 1995.

Douglas, S.J., *Inventing American Broadcasting, 1899–1922*, Johns Hopkins University Press, Baltimore, MD, 1987.

Douglas, S.J., *Listening In*, Times, New York, NY, 1999.

Dreher, C., *Sarnoff: An American Success*, Quadrangle, New York, NY, 1977.

Dunning, J., *Tune in Yesterday*, Prentice Hall, Englewood Cliffs, NJ, 1976.

Edmonds, I.G., *Broadcasting for Beginners*, Holt, Rinehart and Winston, New York, NY, 1980.

Erickson, D., *Armstrong's Fight for FM Broadcasting*, University of Alabama, Birmingham, AL, 1974.

Eskanazi, G., *I Hid It Under the Pillow: Growing Up with Radio*, University of Missouri Press, Columbia, MO, 2005.

Fang, I.E., *Those Radio Commentators*, Iowa State University Press, Ames, IA, 1977.

Fisher, M., *Something in the Air: Radio, Rock, and the Revolution That Shaped a Generation*, Random House, New York, NY, 2007.

Fones-Wolf, E., *Waves of Opposition*, University of Illinois Press, Champaign-Urbana, IL, 2006.

Fornatale, P. and Mills, J.E., *Radio in the Television Age*, Overlook Press, New York, NY, 1980.

Foster, E.S., *Understanding Broadcasting*, Addison-Wesley, Reading, MA, 1978.

Fowler, G. and Crawford, B., *Border Radio*, University of Texas Press, Austin, TX, 2002.

Geller, V., *The Powerful Radio Workbook*, M Street Corporation, Washington, D.C., 2000.

Geller, V., *Beyond Powerful Radio: A Communicator's Guide to the Internet Age—News, Talk, Information & Personality for Broadcasting, Podcasting, Internet, Radio*, Focal Press, Burlington, MA, 2010.

Grant, A.E. and Meadows, J.H. (eds.), *Communication Technology Update and Fundamentals*, Waltham, MA, 2012.

Hall, C. and Hall, B., *This Business of Radio Programming*, Hastings House, New York, NY, 1978.

Halper, D., *Invisible Stars*, M.E. Sharpe, Armonk, NY, 2001.

Hasling, J., *Fundamentals of Radio Broadcasting*, McGraw-Hill, New York, NY, 1980.

Hendricks, J.A. (ed.), *The Palgrave Handbook of Global Radio*, Palgrave Macmillan, Basingstoke, 2012.

Hilliard, R.L. (ed.), *Radio Broadcasting: An Introduction to the Sound Medium*, 3rd edition, Longman, New York, NY, 1985.

Hilliard, R.L., *The Federal Communications Commission: A Primer*, Focal Press, Boston, MA, 1991.

Hilliard, R.L. and Keith, M.C., *Global Broadcasting Systems*, Focal Press, Boston, MA, 1996.

Hilliard, R.L. and Keith, M.C., *Waves of Rancor: Tuning the Radical Right*, Focal Press, Boston, MA, 1999.

Hilliard, R.L. and Keith, M.C., *Dirty Discourse: Sex and Indecency in Broadcasting*, Blackwell, Boston, MA, 2006.

Hilliard, R.L. and Keith, M.C., *The Broadcast Century: A Biography of American Broadcasting*, 5th edition, Focal Press, Boston, MA, 2010.

Hilmes, M., *Radio Voices: American Broadcasting, 1922–1952*, University of Minnesota Press, Minneapolis, MN, 1997.

Horten, G., *Radio Goes to War*, University of California Press, Berkeley, CA, 2002.

Hunn, P., *Starting and Operating Your Own FM Radio Station*, Tab, Blue Ridge Summit, PA, 1988.

Inglis, A.F., *Behind the Tube*, Focal Press, Boston, MA, 1990.

Keirstead, P.O. and Keirstead, S.K., *The World of Telecommunication*, Focal Press, Stoneham, MA, 1990.

Keith, M.C., *Signals in the Air: Native Broadcasting in America*, Praeger, Westport, CT, 1995.

Keith, M.C., *Voices in the Purple Haze: Underground Radio and the Sixties*, Praeger, Westport, CT, 1997.

Keith, M.C., *Talking Radio: An Oral History of Radio in the Television Age*, M.E. Sharpe, Armonk, NY, 2000.

Keith, M.C., *Sounds in the Dark: All Night Radio in American Life*, Iowa State University Press, Ames, IA, 2001.

Keith, M.C. (ed.), *Radio Cultures: The Sound Medium in American Life*, Peter Lang, New York, NY, 2008.

Ladd, J., *Radio Waves*, St. Martin's Press, New York, NY, 1991.

Lazarsfled, P.F. and Kendall, P.L., *Radio Listening in America*, Prentice Hall, Englewood Cliffs, NJ, 1948.

Leinwall, S., *From Spark to Satellite*, Charles Scribner's Sons, New York, NY, 1979.

Lenthall, B., *Radio America*, University of Chicago Press, Chicago, IL, 2007.

Levinson, R., *Stay Tuned*, St. Martin's Press, New York, NY, 1982.

Lewis, P. (ed.), *Radio Drama*, Longman, New York, NY, 1981.

Lewis, T., *Empire of the Air: The Men Who Made Radio*, HarperCollins, New York, NY, 1991.

Lichty, L.W. and Topping, M.C., *American Broadcasting: A Source Book on the History of Radio and Television*, Hastings House, New York, NY, 1976.

Looker, T., *The Sound and the Story*, Houghton Mifflin, Boston, MA, 1995.

Loviglio, J., *Radio's Intimate Public*, University of Minnesota, Minneapolis, MN, 2005.

MacDonald, J.F., *Don't Touch That Dial: Radio Programming in American Life, 1920–1960*, Nelson-Hall, Chicago, IL, 1979.

Matelski, M., *Vatican Radio*, Praeger, Westport, CT, 1995.

McCauley, M., *NPR: The Trials and Triumphs of National Public Radio*, Columbia University Press, New York, NY, 2005.

McGregor, M.A., Driscoll, P.D. and McDowell, W.S., *Head's Broadcasting in America: A Survey of Electronic Media*, 10th edition, Pearson, New York, NY, 2009.

McLuhan, M., *Understanding Media: The Extensions of Man*, McGraw-Hill, New York, NY, 1964.

Mitchell, J.W., *Listener Supported: The Culture and History of Public Radio*, Praeger, Westport, CT, 2005.

Morrow, B., *Cousin Brucie*, Morrow, New York, NY, 1987.

NAB, *Radio Station Salaries*, National Association of Broadcasters, Washington, D.C., 2004.

Nachman, G., *Raised on Radio*, University of California Press, Berkeley, CA, 2000.

Naughton, J., *A Brief History of the Future: From Radio Days to Internet Years in a Lifetime*, Overlook Press, Woodstock, NY, 2000.

O'Donnell, L.B., Hausman, C., and Benoit, P., *Radio Station Operations: Management and Employee Perspectives*, Wadsworth, Belmont, CA, 1989.

Orlik, P.B., *Electronic Media Criticism*, Focal Press, Boston, MA, 1994.

Paley, W.S., *As It Happened: A Memoir*, Doubleday, Garden City, NY, 1979.

Pease, E.C. and Dennis, E.E., *Radio: The Forgotten Medium*, Transaction Press, New Brunswick, NJ, 1995.

Phillips, L.A., *Public Radio: Behind the Voices*, CDS, New York, NY, 2006.

Pierce, J.R., *Signals*, W.H. Freeman, San Francisco, CA, 1981.

Podber, J., *The Electronic Front Porch*, Mercer University Press, Macon, GA, 2007.

Pusateri, C.J., *Enterprise in Radio*, University Press of America, Washington, D.C., 1980.

*Radio Facts*, Radio Advertising Bureau, New York, NY, 1988.

Ramsey, M., *Making Waves: Radio on the Verge*, iUniverse, 2008.

Rhoads, B.E., *Blast from the Past*, Streamline Press, West Palm Beach, FL, 1996.

Richter, W.A., *Radio: A Complete Guide to the Industry*, Peter Lang, New York, NY, 2006.

Routt, Ed., *The Business of Radio Broadcasting*, Tab, Blue Ridge Summit, PA, 1972.

Rudell, A., *Hello, Everybody! The Dawn of American Radio*, Harcourt, New York, NY, 2008.

Sarnoff, D., *The World of Television*, Wisdom, Agoura Hills, CA, 1958.

Schiffer, M.B., *The Portable Radio in American Life*, University of Arizona Press, Tucson, AZ, 1991.

Seidle, R.J., *Air Time*, Holbrook Press, Boston, MA, 1977.

Settle, I., *A Pictorial History of Radio*, Grosset and Dunlap, New York, NY, 1967.

Shapiro, M.E., *Radio Network Prime Time Programming, 1927–1967*, McFarland, Jefferson, NC, 2002.

Siegel, S. and Siegel, D.S., *A Resource Guide to the Golden Age of Radio*, Book Hunter Press, Yorktown Heights, NY, 2006.

Sipemann, C.A., *Radio's Second Chance*, Little, Brown, Boston, MA, 1946.

Sklar, R., *Rocking America: How the All-Hit Radio Stations Took Over*, St. Martin's Press, New York, NY, 1984.

Smith, F.L., *Perspectives on Radio and Television: An Introduction to Broadcasting in the United States*, Harper & Row, New York, NY, 1979.

Soley, L., *Free Radio*, Westview Press, Denver, CO, 1999.

Sterling, C.H. (ed.), *Encyclopedia of Radio*, Fitzroy Dearborn, New York, NY, 2003.

Sterling, C.H. and Keith, M.C., *Sounds of Change: FM Broadcasting in America*, University of North Carolina Press, Chapel Hill, NC, 2007.

Utterback, A.S., *Broadcasters Survival Guide*, Bonus, San Francisco, CA, 1997.

Vowell, S., *Radio On: A Listener's Diary*, St. Martin's Press, New York, NY, 1997.

Wertheim, A.F., *Radio Comedy*, Oxford University Press, New York, NY, 1979.

Whetmore, E.J., *The Magic Medium: An Introduction to Radio in America*, Wadsworth, Belmont, CA, 1981.

Whetmore, E.J., *MediaAmerica*, 4th edition, Wadsworth, Belmont, CA, 1989.

Winn, J.E. and Brinson, S.L. (eds.), *Transmitting the Past: Historical and Cultural Perspectives on Broadcasting*, University of Alabama Press, Tuscaloosa, AL, 2005.

Woolley, L., *The Last Great Days of Radio*, Republic of Texas Press, Dallas, TX, 1995.

Yoder, A., *Pirate Radio Stations*, McGraw-Hill, New York, NY, 2001.

# CHAPTER 2

# Station Management

## NATURE OF THE BUSINESS

Continuous technological advancements have forced radio station management to adjust and evolve to ensure that radio stations remain financially competitive. In most media markets, especially in larger ones, managers have gone from managing a single or combo station to overseeing the operations of a half dozen or more, often clustered in the same building. Additionally, the station manager must now compete with new forms of audio media, such as Internet streaming, that have quickly developed and established themselves in the radio market. Were these challenges not enough, compounding the manager's task is a host of other external factors including the constant challenges created by an economy that ebbs and flows between poor conditions and robust conditions as well as changes in the federal regulatory landscape.

As has always been the case, the medium's unique character requires the manager to deal with a broad mix of people, from on-air personalities to accountants and from sales personnel to technicians. Few other businesses can claim such an amalgam of employees. Even the station manager of the smallest outlet, with as few as four or five employees, must lead and mentor individuals with very diverse backgrounds and goals. For example, a small Maine radio group or cluster may employ three or four full-time air people, who most likely were recruited from other areas of the country. Those deejays will gain valuable experience as they begin their broadcasting careers, but some will have plans to move on to larger markets. As a result, the station will probably be looking for replacements for these individuals within a few months.

Frequent turnover of on-air personnel at small stations is a fact of life. As a consequence, members of the air staff are often regarded as transients or passers-through by not only the community but also the other members of the station's staff. Less likely to come and go are a station's managerial and technical staff. Usually, they are not looking toward the bright lights of the larger markets that provide larger salaries, since the town in which the station is located is often home to them. A small station's sales department may experience some turnover but usually not to the extent that the programming department does. Also, salespeople are likely to have been recruited from the local community, whereas air personalities more typically come from outside the community.

Running a small-market station or group presents unique challenges (and it should be noted that half of the nation's radio outlets are located in communities with fewer than 25,000 residents). Stations in larger markets, however, are faced with robust competition and jobs are kept or lost based upon ratings. Ratings provide managers with a barometer of how well the station is performing compared to its competition. In contrast to the small Maine radio group, where the closest competitors are 50 miles away, an outlet located in a metropolitan area may share the airwaves with 30 or more other stations. Competition in the larger markets is intense, and radio stations in large metro areas usually succeed or fail based on their showing in the latest listener surveys. The metro-market station manager must pay close attention to competition, while striving to maintain the best on-air product possible, to retain a competitive edge and prosper.

Meanwhile, the government's perception of the radio station's responsibility to its consumers, or listeners in the communities in which they are licensed to serve, also sets it apart from many other businesses.

57

Since its inception, terrestrial radio has been Washington, D.C.'s business. Station managers, unlike the heads of most other enterprises, have had to conform to the dictates and whims of a federal agency specifically conceived for the purpose of overseeing their activities. Failing to satisfy the expectations of the Federal Communications Commission (FCC) can result in penalties that range from large fines to the loss of an operating license; as a result, radio station managers have been obliged to stay abreast of a fairly prodigious volume of rules and regulations that are regularly changing.

The 1980s and 1990s deregulation, actions designed to unburden the broadcaster of what had been regarded by many as unreasonable government intervention, have made the life of the station manager somewhat less complicated. Nevertheless, the government continues to play an important role in American radio, and managers who value their license wisely invest time and effort in fulfilling federal mandates and regulatory requirements. After all, a radio station without a frequency is just a building with a lot of expensive equipment.

The listener's perception of the radio business, even in today's technological era when almost every community with a small business district has a radio station, is often unrealistic. Film and television's portrayal of the radio station as a hotbed of quirky characters and bizarre antics has helped foster a misconception. This is not to suggest that radio stations are the most conventional places to work, however. Because it is the station's function to provide entertainment to its listeners, it must employ creative people, and where these people congregate, whether in a small town or a large city, the atmosphere is certain to be charged. "The volatility of the air staff's emotions and the oscillating nature of radio itself actually distinguishes our business from others," observes Kentucky station manager J.G. Salter.

Faced with an audience whose needs and tastes are fickle, today's radio station has become adept at shifting gears as conditions warrant. What is currently popular in music, fashion, and leisure-time activities will be nudged aside tomorrow by something new. This, says radio show coach Randy Lane, of the Randy Lane Company, forces radio stations to stay one step ahead of all trends and fads.

Being on the leading edge of American culture makes it necessary to undergo more changes and updates than is usually the case in other businesses. Not adjusting to what is currently in vogue can put a station at a distinct disadvantage. You have to stay in touch with what is happening in your own community as well as the trends and cultural movements occurring in other parts of the country.

The complex internal and external factors that derive from the unusual nature of the radio business make managing today's station a formidable challenge. Perhaps no other business demands as much from its managers. Conversely, few other businesses provide an individual with as much to be excited about. It takes a creative person to run a radio station.

**FIGURE 2.1**
Ken Sibley

## SMALL-MARKET RADIO MANAGEMENT

### Ken Sibley

I prefer small-market radio because small-market stations should be the focus of the community. Small-market radio is uniquely able to serve each community and smaller satellite communities with coverage specific to those local areas, which make these stations invaluable.

Small-market managers must be very active in the community their stations serve. These activities range from being in the chamber of commerce to building and nurturing a personal relationship with the mayor and city council members as well as the county judge and quorum court members. These relationships assist in programming to community needs. This management requirement is something you will not find in mid-sized or major markets.

Being a general manager (GM) in a small market requires you to be creative and have programs and music the community wants to hear. You have to make programming decisions so that you are the

ONLY place for information, with the exception of a weekly or afternoon newspaper that your listeners can get on an immediate basis.

Providing the community with up-to-date weather information is one example. This includes you, or your designated employee, to come to the station during severe weather situations. We subscribe to WeatherTAP at the suggestion of the area weather service chief, telling us it was what he used at home. It provides stations weather updates quicker than any other radar and is available with a subscription to track storms and define what approximate time they will arrive in a specific area.

Importantly, during our local newscasts, at least three times per day, we read local and area obituaries. It is possible for a person to die in a small media market without anyone ever reading about it in a paper, if a newspaper is even available in that community, and never know it.

Radio is available immediately and frequently! We did local news four times daily and always provided information on an immediate basis if needed. You should also run a weekly program addressing your community and area needs. It helps to have the mayor, county judge, or local elected representatives on the station to discuss pertinent local issues to prove to the Federal Communications Commission (FCC) you are meeting requirements as a broadcaster and serving the community the station was licensed to serve.

As a GM, and later owner of a small-market station, I had to be ready to fill in at ANY job at the station when someone didn't show up or wasn't available. You're constantly looking for good part-time and full-time employees. But, in many instances, you are the *only* backup you have.

The GM of a small-market station needs to know some basic engineering to get the station back on the air in case of a technical emergency . . . not particularly the nuts and bolts of repair but basic things to get the transmitter back up to full power or back on the air as quickly as feasible. Being off the air means lost revenue.

The GM must be up to date on all FCC regulations that apply to the station. This means you must also be able to complete all the information for renewal of your license every seven years. You must be on site when an FCC inspector makes a periodic, unannounced inspection. During my many years in the business as a salesperson, general manager, and owner, I have gone through about seven such inspections and come through them with flying colors. If your state broadcast association provides the opportunity, it is prudent to participate in the Alternative Broadcast Inspection Program (ABIP), which allows an inspector to come to your station simulating a regular inspection. If the inspector finds any deficiencies, you are allowed time to correct them. After the follow-up inspection and receiving approval, your station is exempt from any future, regular FCC inspections for several years, except for inspections they might conduct where only one item is examined such as your public inspection file or Emergency Alert System (EAS) equipment and records.

You must be able to operate the station's automation system software and traffic software that handles logging, billing, and scheduling of each account as well as be able to train all new workers so they can proficiently operate the software. In a small market, you must also oversee the collection process, which is actually the responsibility of the salesperson, but the general manager/owner must also keep up with it because this is the lifeblood of a profitable station.

The GM's office serves as the human resources office. The GM is responsible for all hiring and firing at the station. As such, you must be familiar with state and national human resource laws . . . and you must DOCUMENT EVERYTHING when it comes to employee hiring, firing, and correcting. Importantly, the GM must also carry a list of accounts that the employee sells and services in case of a sudden departure. If you have five or fewer full-time employees, which we did, you are exempt from the equal employment opportunity (EEO) reporting requirements. If you have more than that, you must file annual EEO reports with the FCC. The FCC also has periodic nonnotified inspections of your EEO files that you must remain prepared for when a sudden inspection occurred.

During my years as a GM/owner, we had very little turnover of key personnel. It is important that you pay your people well and create an environment that makes them want to stay. We paid a 20% collection on sales to our salespeople, and all on-air personnel were paid by the hour. Usually we paid the sales people, who were also on-air, the time for their on-air talents and other times in addition to the commission on collections. We also provided a group insurance plan that everyone could participate in at their choice.

It is always imperative that you have a weekly staff meeting to allow all personnel to bring anything to your attention and brainstorm on sales ideas that will be coming up in the next few months.

In my role as a GM, my days began at 5 am as an on-air person during the *Morning Show*. We did a live show on both the AM and FM stations with separate on-air personalities that included a heavy emphasis on weather, school announcements, etc. Later, I was able to transition off the air and focus completely on the management of the day-to-day operations and needs of the station such as sales, staffing, engineering, FCC rules and regulations, and HR situations that constantly arose. Ultimately, my day ended whenever? Sometimes early, sometimes late. It always depended on what needed to be done on any given day.

Small-market radio is extremely rewarding. I was offered jobs at two mid–major-market stations, but after looking at the pay . . . I would have had to work two different jobs to make what I was making in my small-market station.

I was also very much involved in my state broadcast association, which was more than a two and a half hour drive away, having served on its board several times and serving as its president, just prior to my retirement. I love broadcasting and especially small-market broadcasting.

---

**Ken Sibley** began his broadcasting career in high school and continued through college before remaining at KVMA in Magnolia, Arkansas, for over 40 years before retiring on December 31, 2013. During that time, he did on-air work and sales, and later became general manager/owner. He was active in his community, having served as President of the Chamber of Commerce, President of the Magnolia Economic Development Corporation, and President of the Magnolia Rotary Club, and was appointed by Arkansas Governor Mike Beebe to the Board of Trustees at Southern Arkansas University. He has been married for 50 years to Carol Cooper Sibley, also of Magnolia, Arkansas. He currently lives in Collierville, Tennessee, after his retirement to be near his youngest grandchildren.

## THE MANAGER AS CHIEF COLLABORATOR

There are many schools of thought concerning the approach to managing a radio station. For example, there are the standard X (authoritarian), Y (collaborative), and Z (hybrid or chief collaborator) models or theories of management (which admittedly oversimplify the subject but give the neophyte a basic working model). The first theory embraces the idea that the general manager is the captain of the vessel, the primary authority, with solemn, if not absolute, control of the decision-making process. The second theory casts the manager in the role of collaborator or senior advisor. The third theory forms a hybrid of the preceding two: the manager is both a coach and a team player, or the chief collaborator. Of the three models, broadcast managers tend to favor the third approach.

Lynn Christian, of L.A. Christian and Associates, and former general manager of several major-market radio stations, preferred working for a manager who used the hybrid model rather than the purely authoritarian model:

Before I entered upper management, I found that I performed best when my boss sought my opinion and delegated responsibility to me. I believe in department head meetings and the full disclosure of projects within the top organization of the station. If you give someone the title, you should be prepared to give that person some authority, too. I respect the integrity of my people, and if I lose it, I replace them quickly. In other words, "You respect me, and I'll respect you," is the way I have always managed.

Randy Bongarten, of Bonten Media Group, and former network chief, concurs with Christian and adds:

Management styles have to be adaptive to individual situations so as to provide what is needed at the time. In general, the collaborator or team leader approach gets the job done. Of course, I don't think there is any one school of management that is right 100% of the time.

Jim Arcara, former radio network head, is also an advocate of the hybrid management style: "It's a reflection of what is more natural to me as well as my company. Employees are capable of making key decisions, and they should be given the opportunity to do so. An effective manager also delegates responsibility."

General Manager Pat McNally finds the collaborative approach suitable to his goals and temperament:

My management style is more collaborative. I believe in hiring qualified professional people, defining what I expect, and allowing them to do their job with input, support, and constructive criticism from me. My door is always open for suggestions, and I am a good listener. I consider this business something special, and I expect an extra special effort.

This also holds true for general manager Steven Woodbury:

I hire the best people as department heads and then work collaboratively with these experts. Department heads are encouraged to run their areas as if they had major ownership in the company. That instills a sense of team spirit too. Their energy level and decision-making efforts reflect this.

Charlie Morgan, SVP/Market Manager of Emmis-New York, says "a talent-focused, individualized, servant leader approach to management is always most likely to produce the best results." He adds that

There are specific moments where a command-and-control style may be required to respond to a crisis or emergency, but as a philosophy, a manager whose desire is to get the best from each individual, understanding their specific talents and motivations is going to consistently get the best results.

The manager/collaborator approach is one that allows radio to function at its full potential. "Since practically every job in the radio station is designed to support and enhance the air product, establishing a connectedness among what is usually a small band of employees tends to yield the best results," contends station manager Jane Duncklee:

I strongly believe that employees must feel that they are a valid part of what is happening and that their input has a direct bearing on those decisions which affect them and the operation as a whole. I try to hire the best people possible and then let them do their jobs with a minimum of interference and a maximum of support.

Marlin R. Taylor, Founder of Bonneville Broadcasting System and former manager of several major-market radio outlets, including WRFM, New York, and WBCN, Boston, and most recently Sirius/XM enLighten's Program Director, believes that the manager using the collaborative system of management gets the most out of employees:

When a staff member feels that his or her efforts and contributions make a difference and are appreciated, that person will remain motivated. This kind of employee works harder and delivers more. Most people, if they enjoy the job they have and like the organization they work for, are desirous of improving their level of performance and contributing to the health and well-being of the station. I really think that many station managers should devote even more time and energy to people development.

The Station General Manager and Owner of Great Plains Media Inc., Paul Aaron, believes that managers must first assert their authority, that is, make it clear to all that they are in charge, before the transition to collaborator can take place:

> It's a sort of process of evolution. Actually, when you come right down to it, any effective management approach includes a bit of both the authoritarian and collaborative concepts. The situation at the station will have a direct impact on the management style I personally deem most appropriate. As the saying goes, "different situations call for different measures." When assuming the reins at a new station, sometimes it is necessary to take a more dictatorial approach until the organization is where you feel it should be. Often a lot of cleanup and adjustments are necessary before there can be a greater degree of equanimity. Ultimately, however, there should be equanimity.

Surveys have shown that most broadcast executives view the chief collaborator or hybrid management approach as compatible with their needs. Lynn Christian contends:

> It has pretty much become the standard *modus operandi* in this industry. A radio manager must direct as well as invite input. To me it makes sense, in a business in which people are the product, to create an atmosphere that encourages self-expression, as well as personal and professional growth. After all, we are in the communications business. Everyone's voice should at least be heard.

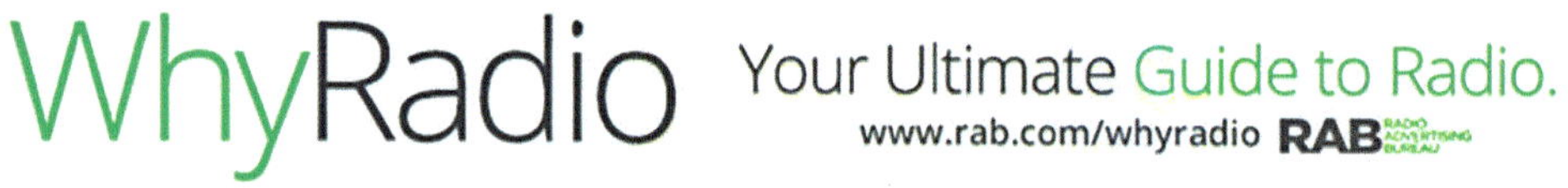
WhyRadio
Your Ultimate Guide to Radio.
www.rab.com/whyradio
RAB

**FIGURE 2.2** The Radio Advertising Bureau is a great training resource for station managers and sales staff

Source: Courtesy of RAB

## WHAT MAKES A MANAGER?

As in all professions, the trajectory to the top is seldom a short and easy one. It may take many years to get there, and dues must be paid along the way. To begin, without a genuine affection for the business, knowledge, and a strong desire to succeed it is very unlikely that the position can ever be attained. Furthermore, without the proper training and experience the top job will remain elusive. So what goes into becoming a radio station manager? According to Jim Robertson, Vice-President and General Manager of Dix Communications, the main personal and professional qualities a station manager should possess are honesty and integrity. As Robertson says:

> Everything else is moot without that to start. You must be willing to lead by example. Be a part of the process, not just an overseer. We are not a huge operation, which allows me to be much more a participant. As the size of the staff and the number of stations gets larger, the challenge of participation grows, and that brings us right back to honesty and integrity. These are core ingredients. Add to these the importance of leading a balanced life. One that allows you to share time with family, engage in leisure activities, participate in community, and so on. It is very important that a manager knows how to balance and prioritize these things.

Entercom's Dave Neugesser observes:

> A station manager has to have a complete understanding of the three legs that support the body of radio—the listener, the client, and the station. While much of what we do in programming supports the station and listener, radio is a business and the client is just as crucial. A manager must have a clear vision, tight focus, and solid strategy to succeed. He or she must have a great team to be a great leader.

Longtime broadcast executive John Gehron shares his perspective on what makes for a successful manager:

> He or she must understand what channels the audience is using and then match content to fit the channel. Deciding how to allocate resources among the many distribution sources is of utmost

importance. At the same time the manager must not pull too many resources from the primary channel and diminish its popularity.

Emmis Communications Chief, Jeff Smulyan, says that the current times require special skills:

A radio manager must be flexible. The media world is changing daily. Providing leadership that understands a rapidly changing world is the most important attribute. None of us understands how technology will change the industry. We have to provide content that can be deployed in several different ways. Content that creates a unique listening experience and provides adequate results for advertisers. Being able to adjust to the shifting market scene is crucial for any manager.

First and foremost, a prospective manager needs a good foundation, and formal education plays a strong role in this background. Hundreds of institutions of higher learning across the country offer programs in broadcast operations. The college degree has achieved great importance in radio over the past decade or two and, as in most other industries today, it has become a standard credential for those vying for management positions. Anyone entering broadcasting with aspirations to operate a radio station should acquire as much formal training as possible. Station managers with master's degrees are not uncommon. However, a bachelor's degree in communications gives the prospective station manager a good foundation from which to launch a career.

In a business that stresses the value of practical experience, seldom, if ever, does an individual land a management job directly out of college. In fact, most station managers have been in the business at least 15 years. "Once you get the theory nailed down you have to apply it. Experience is the best teacher. I've spent 30 years working in a variety of areas in the medium. In radio, in particular, hands-on experience is what matters," says former station manager Richard Bremkamp, Jr.

To radio station manager Roger Ingram, experience is what most readily opens the door to management: "While a degree is kind of like a union card in this day and age, a good track record is what wins the management job. You really must possess both."

Jane Duncklee began her ascent to station management by logging commercials for airplay and eventually moved into other areas:

For the past 17 years I have been employed by Champion Broadcasting Systems. During that time I have worked in every department of the radio station, from traffic—where I started—to sales, programming, engineering, and finally management on both the local and corporate levels.

Most radio station managers are recruited from the sales area rather than programming. Because the general manager's foremost objective is to generate a profit, often from multiple operations, station owners usually feel more confident hiring someone with a solid sales or business background. Consequently, three out of four radio managers have made their living at some point selling airtime. It is a widely held belief that sales experience best prepares an individual for the realities encountered in the manager's position. Norm Feuer, a Vice-President for Broadcast Company of Americas in San Diego, recalls that

I spent more than a decade and a half in media sales before becoming a station manager. In fact, my experience on the radio level was exclusively confined to sales and then for only eight months. After that I moved into station management. Most of my radio-related sales experience took place on the national level with station rep companies.

Station manager Carl Evans holds that a sales background is especially useful, if not necessary, to general managers: "I spent a dozen years as a station account executive, and prior to entering radio I represented various product lines to retailers. The key to financial success in radio exists in an understanding of retailing."

It is not uncommon for station managers to have backgrounds outside of radio, but invariably their experience comes out of the areas of sales, marketing, and finance. Broadcaster Paul Aaron, who worked

**FIGURE 2.3**

A job ad for a small cluster of radio stations in Arkansas is seeking a General Manager (GM). A background in sales is a desired qualification in radio management and a requirement to be involved in the local community

Source: Courtesy of AllAccess.com

## RADIO GENERAL MANAGER POSITION OPEN

Noalmark Broadcasting Corporation has a General Manager position available for its multi-station group in El Dorado, Arkansas. We are searching for a GM who leads by example in all aspects of the position. They will be expected to recruit and develop a sales staff, as well as carry their own significant sales list. They will be responsible for the overall sales as well as the bottom line for the stations. Salary consists of a base salary with the potential for earning significant commissions. This is not a "behind the desk" job, we are looking for a GM with energy and vision who is committed to local radio and who can deliver on agreed upon objectives. If you believe that you are this person, please forward your resume to the following email address: anna@noalmark.com. No phone calls please.

All replies will be strictly confidential. We are an Equal Opportunity Employer and strongly encourage women and minorities to apply.

---

as a fundraiser for the United Way of America before entering radio, contends that many managers come from other fields where they have served in positions related to sales, if not in sales itself. "Of those managers who have worked in fields other than radio, most have come to radio via the business sector. There are not many former biologists or glass blowers serving as station managers," says Aaron.

Although statistics show that the station salesperson has the best chance of being promoted to the station's head position (more general managers have held the sales manager's position than any other), a relatively small percentage of radio's managers come from the programming ranks. Station manager Randy Lane admits:

> I'm more the exception than the rule. I have spent my entire career in the programming side, first as a deejay at stations in Phoenix, Denver, and Pittsburgh, and then as program director for outlets in Kansas City and Chicago. I'll have to admit, however, that while it certainly is not impossible to become a GM [general manager] by approaching it from the programming side, resistance exists.

Many in the industry consider the programmer's role to be more an artistic function than one requiring a high degree of business savvy. However accurate or inaccurate this assessment is, the result is that fewer managers are hired with backgrounds exclusively confined to programming duties. Programmers have reason to be encouraged, however, since a trend in favor of hiring program directors (PDs) has surfaced in recent years, and predictions suggest that it will continue as new audio competition and added distribution channels for radio have put "product development" on par with sales and financial management.

Creative people may have an opportunity in radio as never before, especially if they are also able to grasp the essentials of the "other side" of the business: sales, marketing, personnel, and financial management. The reason, says Broadcasting Unlimited's Jay Williams, is that

## RADIO STATION GENERAL MANAGER

### First Media Radio—Roanoke Rapids, North Carolina & Southside Virginia

**Description**: Person to provide leadership and be responsible for revenue and profitability of First Media Radio's seven-station group in Roanoke Rapids, North Carolina and Southside Virginia.

Current General Manager has led the cluster for entire time First Media Radio has owned stations, and is willing to transition to a sales role for the right candidate. Successful candidate is expected to maximize revenues, control expenses, determine appropriate station staffing and ensure compliance with Federal Communications Commission (FCC) regulations and guidelines. Proficiency is expected in sales of local direct business, sales of regional and ad agency business, preparation of sales and programming promotions, use of social media and stations' websites, sales materials and sales events.

The Roanoke Rapids, North Carolina & Southside Virginia General Manager sets the management tone with ultimate responsibility for performance and accountability of all station personnel in the seven-station group.

The successful candidate must have four-plus years of successful radio management leadership experience. A bachelor's degree from a four-year college or university is preferred. Previous responsibility preferred. Must demonstrate both personal and team radio sales success, the ability to attract and retain top-flight talent, and inspire and build teams.

If you are looking for world-class shopping and agency orders, this is NOT for you. These are communities where radio matters and these seven stations make a real impact.

First Media Radio operates successful small-market stations in North Carolina and Virginia.

To be considered for this General Manager position, candidates must email cover letter and resume.

EOE M/F

**FIGURE 2.4**
General Manager job ad for a cluster of stations owned by First Media in North Carolina and Virginia. Multiple skill sets are needed when managing a cluster of stations

Source: Courtesy of AllAccess.com

good program managers often have great vision, can determine a solid course for the station's programming, imaging and promotion, and can get people to follow their lead. More importantly, it's the program directors who are on the cutting edge of understanding and utilizing social media, building listener interactivity, harnessing the power of listener-generated content, and adding distribution channels. And that's the future.

In reality, the most attractive candidate for a station management position is the one whose experience has involved both programming and sales responsibilities. No general manager can fully function without an understanding and appreciation of what goes into preparing and presenting the air product, nor can he or she hope for success without a keen sense of business and finance.

Today's highly competitive and complex radio market requires that the person aspiring to management have both formal training—preferably a college degree in broadcasting—and experience in all aspects of radio station operations, in particular sales and programming. Ultimately, the effort and energy an individual invests will bear directly on the dividends he or she earns, and there is not a single successful station manager who has not put in 15-hour days or longer. The station manager is expected to know more and do more than anyone else, and rightfully so, since he or she is the person who stands to gain the most.

CBS Radio Group President Dan Mason relates the qualities he sees in the most successful station managers:

A keen sense of what is "good business," humility to take the blame in bad times and to give staff credit in good times, fairness and passion for all, responsiveness to situations (not reactionary), passion for the industry, recognition and knowledge of staff (know by first names), and ability to keep personal problems out of the station.

# THE MANAGER'S DUTIES AND RESPONSIBILITIES

A primary objective of the station manager is to operate in a manner that generates the most profit, while maintaining a positive and productive attitude among station employees. This is more of a challenge than it may seem, claims radio broadcaster Cliff Shank:

> In order to meet the responsibility that you are faced with daily, you really have to be an expert in so many areas: sales, marketing, finance, legal matters, technical, governmental, and programming. It helps if you're an expert in human nature, too.

Jane Duncklee puts it this way: "Managing a radio station requires that you divide yourself equally into at least a dozen parts and be a 100% whole in each situation." The Telecommunications Act of 1996 created an environment of consolidation where managers began providing oversight of many radio stations. The late Ed Shane, a radio consultant, observed:

> The duties for station managers have changed radically. For example, at one time the manager of what became the Clear Channel cluster at Baton Rouge, had responsibility for several AM and FM stations in other parts of Louisiana and Texas. Talk about dividing yourself.

In today's consolidated environment, this is more common than not, says Jay Williams: "Mike Glickenhaus, a Clear Channel Vice-President and Market Manager, originally oversaw nine FM stations in the San Diego cluster." Station owner Bill Campbell says the theme that runs throughout the classic Tom Peters book *In Search of Excellence* is one that is relevant to the station manager's task today: "The idea in Peters's book is that you must make the customer happy, get your people involved, and get rid of departmental waste and unnecessary expenditures. A station should be a lean and healthy organism."

Station managers themselves generally must answer to a higher authority. The majority of radio stations, roughly 85%, are owned by companies and corporations that both hire the manager and help establish financial goals or projections for the station. It is the station manager's job to see that corporate expectations are met and, ideally, exceeded. Managers who fail to operate a facility in a way that satisfies the corporate hierarchy may soon find themselves looking for another job.

Few of the nation's stations are owned by individuals or partnerships. At these radio outlets, the manager still must meet the expectations of the station owner(s). In some cases, the manager may be given more latitude or responsibility in determining the station's fate, whereas in others the owner may play a more direct role in the operation of the station.

A basic function of the manager's position is to formulate station policy and see that it is implemented. To ensure against the confusion, misunderstanding, and possible unfair labor practices that typically impede operations, employees often receive a station policy manual. This manual states the station's positions on a host of issues, such as hiring, termination, salaries, raises, promotions, sick leave, vacation, benefits, and so forth. As standard practice, a station may require that each new employee read and become familiar with the contents of the policy manual before actually starting work. Job descriptions, as well as organization flowcharts, are commonly outlined to make it abundantly clear to staff members who is responsible for what. A well-conceived policy book may contain a statement of the station's programming philosophy with an explanation of the format it employs. The more comprehensive a policy book, the less likely there will be confusion and disruption.

Hiring and retaining good people are other key managerial functions. "You have some pretty delicate egos to cope with in this business. Radio attracts some very bright and highly talented people, sometimes with erratic temperaments. Keeping harmony and keeping people are among the foremost challenges facing a station manager," claims Norm Feuer.

Steve Woodbury agrees with Feuer, adding:

> You have to hire the right people and motivate them properly, and that's a challenge. You have to be capable of inspiring people. Actually, if you are unable to motivate your people, the station will fail to reach its potential. Hire the best people you can and nurture them.

Cluster Market Manager Mike Glickenhaus says:

> You make sure you have a lot of great people. You need more key people who you can give lots of responsibility to because you don't have time to micromanage them. It's important to hire the right people and then clearly lay out the vision, goals, and many of the steps that will be necessary and agree on them. You need people who understand what it takes, what they have to do, and have the direction to get there. Then as manager you have to decide what (projects or problems) you're going to apply your time to.

NAB's Executive Vice-President for Radio, John David, adds:

> There is no longer just one key to running successful radio stations. My advice would be to find as many creative people who have a real connection to the people in the audience. Hire them, treat them with respect, listen to their input, and pay them. Managers can hire people all day that agree with them. Hire people who have different ideas but are smart enough to carry out the plan with enthusiasm once the direction is determined. That goes for all departments of the team, including management. With this formula, you won't be constantly looking for people.

As mentioned earlier, managers of small-market radio stations are confronted with a unique set of problems when it comes to hiring and holding onto qualified people, especially on-air personnel. "In our case, finding and keeping a professional-sounding staff with our somewhat limited budget is an ongoing problem. This is true at most small market stations," observes station manager J.G. Salter.

The rural or small-market station is where the majority of newcomers gain their experience. Because salaries are low and the fledgling air person's ambitions are usually high, the rate of turnover is significant. Managers of small outlets spend a great deal of time training people. Salter explains:

> It is a fact of the business that radio people, particularly deejays, usually learn their trade at the 'out-of-the-way,' low-power outlet. To be a manager at a small station, you have to be a teacher, too. But it can be very rewarding despite the obvious problem of having to rehire to fill positions so often. We deal with many beginners. I find it exciting and gratifying, and no small challenge, to train newcomers in the various aspects of radio broadcasting.

Randy Lane also enjoys the instructor's role but notes that the high turnover rate affects product continuity:

> With air people coming and going all the time, it can give the listening public the impression of instability. The last thing a station wants to do is sound schizophrenic. Establishing an image of dependability is crucial to any radio station. Changing air people every other month doesn't help. As a station manager, it is up to you to do the best you can with the resources at hand. In general, I think small market managers do an incredible job with what they have to work with.

Managers of small-market stations must wrestle with the problems stemming from diminutive budgets and high employee turnover, whereas those at large stations must grapple with the difficulties inherent in managing larger budgets, bigger staffs, and facing stiffer competition. KGLD's Bremkamp observes:

> It's all relative, really. While the small town station gives the manager turnover headaches, the major-market manager usually is caught up in the ratings battle, which consumes vast amounts of time and energy. Of course, even larger stations are not immune to turnover.

It is up to the manager to control the station's finances and to do so requires knowledge of bookkeeping and accounting procedures. "You handle the station's purse-strings. An understanding of budgeting is an absolute must. Station economics is the responsibility of the GM. The idea is to control income and expenses in a way that yields a sufficient profit," says Roger Ingram.

## RADIO ECONOMICS

### August E. Grant and Jeffrey Wilkinson

### Economic Factors

Management of a radio station or cluster requires knowledge of the economics of radio. In particular, two economic factors define radio's place in today's media system and differentiate it from other media. The first is the economies of scale, which are superior for broadcast radio to almost every other mass medium. Where most media (including newspapers, magazines, and online media) have a marginal cost associated with each user, radio is like television in that virtually all costs (both technology and content) are fixed costs, with no variable cost for additional users. In simple terms, it doesn't cost the broadcaster any more to reach 100,000 listeners than it does to reach 10 listeners. The technical explanation an economist would provide is that the marginal cost of additional listeners past the first listener is zero. It is critical that managers realize that it costs your station nothing to add additional listeners to the over-the-air signal of a station.

The second economic factor that must be understood is that commercial radio has two distinct markets: First, there is the listener market, where the radio station must attract and retain individual audience members. Second, the attention of those audience members becomes the product offered for sale to advertisers, resulting in an advertising market where advertisers must be persuaded to support the station with advertising revenue.

The fastest-growing variant of radio is online radio. Although the content of your online radio stream can mirror that of terrestrial radio, there are two important differences in the economics. First, although the cost of producing content can be similar to or much less than traditional radio, online radio incurs costs of both servers and bandwidth for each audio stream delivered. On the other hand, an advantage of this type of IP-delivered radio is that each stream can be customized for each user. For the user, this means music or programming that is more directly targeted to the individual. More importantly, this means that advertisers can target specific messages at specific consumers, providing a significant increase in efficiency of advertising.

Looking ahead, a "breakeven point" will arrive when the additional value to advertisers for delivering targeted advertising is greater than the marginal cost of providing the IP stream. Until that breakeven point, traditional radio will have the economic advantage, but after that point is reached online radio will have the economic advantage.

Another economic factor to consider is the consumer's willingness to accept advertising in return for receiving the content for free. Consider the example of satellite radio, where more than 30 million households in the U.S. are willing to pay a monthly subscription fee for (mostly) commercial-free radio. In addition to satellite radio, many online radio companies (for example, Pandora, iTunes, Google Play, and Spotify) provide commercial-free streams for a monthly subscription fee. As competition increases in this market, these monthly subscription fees should fall to a point that is just above the marginal cost of the service (royalties, servers, and bandwidth).

August E. ("Augie") Grant is J. Rion McKissick Professor of Journalism at the University of South Carolina. Grant is a technology futurist who specializes in research on new media technologies and consumer behavior. His teaching and research combine the study of traditional and emerging media, with emphases on media management, organizational structure, integrated communication and consumer behavior. He has been Editor of *Communication Technology Update and Fundamentals* since 1992.

Jeffrey Wilkinson is a Professor of Communication and the Associate Dean of Quality Assurance and International Development for the Sino-U.S. College, Beijing Institute of Technology, Zhuhai, China. His areas of teaching and research include multiplatform journalism, communication technology, media effects, and international communication.

The manager allocates and approves spending in each department (in cluster operations this also means for each station). Heads of departments must work within the budgets they have helped establish. Budgets generally cover the expenses involved in the operation of a particular area within the station for a specified period, such as a six- or 12-month period. No manager wants to spend more than what is absolutely required. A solid familiarity with what is involved in running the various departments within a station prevents waste and overspending. Evans says:

> A manager has to know what is going on in programming, engineering, sales, actually every little corner of the station, in order to run a tight ship and make the most revenue possible. Of course, you should never cut corners simply for the sake of cutting corners. An operation must spend in order to make. You have to have effective cost control in all departments. That doesn't mean damaging the product through undernourishment either.

David Saperstein, President of Metro Networks, observes that, "In the early days, radio was a mom-and-pop type of business. With the huge dollars in radio today, one mistake could cost a station hundreds of thousands or even millions of dollars in revenue."

Even in large media markets such as New York, the manager must possess a broad range of expertise. Charlie Morgan says:

> A station manager/market manager must have general knowledge across all facets of the operations: sales, programming, marketing, engineering, HR, accounting, FCC regulation compliance, digital, social media, etc. You cannot be an expert in each discipline but you have to have enough understanding of each to be able to lead the experts and "conduct the orchestra" with command and confidence.

Further, Morgan shares,

> To be effective you must understand the various facets of the operation well enough to be able to recognize how they are all interlinked, what a talented leader in each discipline looks like, what questions are most important to ask to ensure your leaders are focused on the right actions, and what few priorities are most likely to improve results if delivered effectively. Time spent working at the station level and interacting with all departments is the best teacher and preparation for leading that team.

To ensure that the product the station offers is the best it can be, the station manager must keep in close touch with every department. Since the station's sound is what wins listeners, the manager must work closely with the program director and engineer. Both significantly contribute to the quality of the air product. The program director is responsible for what goes on the air, and the engineer is responsible for the way it sounds.

Meanwhile, selling the station to advertisers is vital. This falls within the province of the sales department. Traditionally, the general manager works more closely with the station's sales manager than with anyone else. In fact, in smaller stations the general manager often is the sales manager.

An excellent air product attracts listeners, and listeners attract sponsors. It is as basic as that. "The formula works when all departments in a station work in unison and up to their potential," contends Marlin R. Taylor:

> In radio our product is twofold—the programming we send over our frequency and the listening audience we deliver to advertisers. A station's success is linked to customer/listener satisfaction, just like a retail store's. If you don't have what the consumer desires, or the quality doesn't meet his standards, he'll go elsewhere and generally won't return.

In a quickly changing, dynamic industry like radio, where both cultural and technological innovations have an impact on the way a station operates, the manager must stay abreast of future trends. New technologies employed by stations compound the manager's task. For example, determining how best

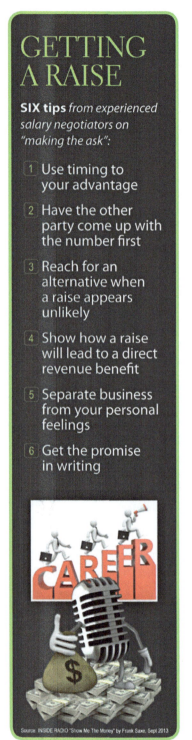

Source: INSIDE RADIO "Show Me The Money" by Frank Saxe, Sept 2013

**FIGURE 2.5**
Managers are responsible for the station's financial health including negotiating salaries with the station's staff

Source: Courtesy of *Inside Radio*

to employ a station's website and social media technologies such as Twitter and Facebook is ultimately the decision of the station manager. In terms of other new technologies, such as HD and its side channels feature also known as multicasting, former radio manager Jim Robertson says that effective strategies for the implementation of such things are a part of what is expected of station managers:

> You have to know what is going to enhance your product in the face of mounting competition. We are very excited about offering new opportunities for listening with our HD channels, and as manager you have to stay abreast of things all the time.

As of June 2017, Xperi Digital Corporation and the Radio Advertising Bureau reported there were 2,400 radio stations broadcasting in HD and more than 33 U.S. automakers placing HD radios in new automobiles. This technology approved by the FCC is designed to provide listeners with additional programming content such as real-time traffic or weather. But it is the manager's responsibility to determine how to best leverage this technology to both the station's and listener's advantage.

## THE MANAGER AND INDUSTRY ASSOCIATIONS

To stay abreast of the swiftly evolving radio landscape, managers must remain knowledgeable about industry changes and trends. Every year, the National Association of Broadcasters (NAB), the Radio Advertising Bureau (RAB), state broadcast associations, and a variety of other specialized and regional organizations conduct conferences and seminars intended to generate industry awareness and unity. At these gatherings, held at various locations throughout the country, radio managers and station personnel exchange ideas and share experiences, which they bring back to their stations.

The largest broadcast industry trade organization is the NAB, which was originally conceived out of a need to improve operating conditions in the 1920s. Initially only a lobbying organization, the NAB has maintained that focus while expanding considerably in scope. The primary objective of the organization is to support and promote the stability and development of the broadcasting industry. NAB membership dues are based on a voluntary declaration of a station's annual gross revenues. The RAB and others take a similar approach. Some organizations require individual membership fees, which are often absorbed by the radio station as well.

Produced by NAB and RAB

**FIGURE 2.6**
The NAB and RAB produce an annual conference designed to provide the radio industry with professional development and networking opportunities

Source: Courtesy of the National Association of Broadcasters and the Radio Advertising Bureau

**FIGURE 2.7**
NAB's Gordon Smith heads the nation's foremost commercial broadcasters' association

Source: Courtesy of Gorden Smith

More than 6,000 radio stations are members of the Radio Advertising Bureau (RAB), which was founded in 1951, a time when radio's fate was in serious jeopardy owing to the rise in television's popularity. Kenneth J. Costa, former RAB vice-president for marketing and the author of *History of the RAB*, explains:

> The RAB is designed to serve as the sales and marketing arm of America's commercial radio industry. Members include radio stations, broadcast groups, networks, station representatives, and associated industry organizations in every market in all 50 states.

In 2012, Erica Farber, former Publisher and CEO of *Radio and Records*, was appointed President and CEO of the RAB. In an interview with *Inside Radio* about the RAB, Farber says:

> Our commitment to the industry is unwavering and we intend to advocate and promote the medium for the long-term. Our live and local business is unique and exciting and radio matters to our advertisers and listeners. The RAB is here to serve.

The Radio Advertising Bureau is the not-for-profit trade association representing America's broadcast radio industry. Its primary objective is to drive revenue growth through advocacy, providing the tools and resources to help the industry attract new sales talent to the medium and enhance industry professionalism through training and support.

**FIGURE 2.8**
The Radio Advertising Bureau (RAB) is an excellent partner with the radio industry

Source: Courtesy of the Radio Advertising Bureau

Dozens of other broadcast trade organizations focus their attention on specific areas within the radio station, and regional and local broadcast organizations are numerous. The following list is a partial rundown of national organizations that support the efforts of radio broadcasters:

- National Association of Broadcasters, 1771 N Street, N.W., Washington, D.C. 20036
- Radio Advertising Bureau, 125 West 55th Street, 5th Fl., New York, NY 10019
- National Association of Farm Broadcasters, 1100 Platte Falls Rd., PO Box 500, Platte City, MO 64079
- Alliance for Women in Media, 8405 Greensboro Drive, Suite 800, McLean, VA 22102
- Broadcast Education Association, 1771 N Street, N.W., Washington, D.C. 20036
- Library of American Broadcasting, 6805 Douglas Legum Drive, Suite 100, Elkridge, MD 21075
- Vision Maker Media, 1800 N. 33rd St. Lincoln, NE 68503–1409
- National Association of Black Owned Broadcasters, 1201 Connecticut Avenue, N.W., Suite 200, Washington, D.C. 20036
- National Religious Broadcasters, 1 Massachusetts Avenue NW, Suite 333, Washington, D.C. 20001
- Radio Television Digital News Association, The National Press Building, 529 14th Street, NW, Suite 425, Washington, D.C. 20045
- Society of Broadcast Engineers, 9102 North Meridian Street, Suite 150, Indianapolis, IN 46260.

Financial projections for future needs must be based on data that includes the financial implications of prospective and predicted events. An effective manager anticipates change and develops appropriate plans to deal with it. Industry trade journals such as *Broadcasting and Cable*, *Radio Ink*, and *Radio and Television Business Report*, as well as online newsletters such as *Radio and Internet Newsletter*, *All Access*, and *Inside Radio*, provide managers with current information about the industry.

Regarding industry trade journals, Ed Shane observed, "Too many of the remaining trade publications are 'good news' journals, concentrating only on the most positive spin as opposed to providing balance or insight. It's as if they print news releases without vetting them."

Station consultants and "rep companies," which sell local station airtime to national advertising agencies, also support the manager in his or her efforts to keep on top of things. "A station manager must utilize all that is available to stay in touch with what's out there. Foresight is an essential ingredient for any radio manager. Hindsight is not enough in an industry that operates with one foot in the future," says Lynn Christian, who summarizes the duties and responsibilities of a station manager: "To me the challenges of running today's radio station include building and maintaining audience ratings, attracting and keeping outstanding employees, increasing gross revenues annually, and creating a positive community image for the station, not necessarily in that order." Richard Bremkamp is more laconic: "It boils down to one sentence: Protect the license and turn a profit."

**FIGURE 2.9**
Norman Feuer

## THE QUALITIES THAT MAKE A STATION MANAGER

### Norman Feuer

1. *Smart/intelligent*. This is something that I cannot teach or help someone with; they are either smart or they are not.

2. *Organized*. A GM or GSM (general sales manager) has a lot on his or her plate, especially with the limited time available to accomplish what has to be done. An unorganized person will waste that time.

3. *Good communicator*. As a group head, I also have a lot on my plate. I must rely on my managers to communicate with me quickly and efficiently. If they can do that, I have the comfort of knowing that they are able to communicate effectively with their staff on the station's missions and goals to be accomplished.

4. *Strategic thinker*. In today's world there's no such thing as a quick fix. Therefore, I need to have someone who can think through the long-term effects of each major decision that he or she makes.

5. *Motivated*. In my opinion, you cannot motivate people; they are either self-motivated or they are not. All I can do is set a work environment that motivates them to do their best.

6. *Businesslike*. I need people who understand that this is a business, not a hobby, and that every decision that they make has a return on investment and will lead to a successful business conclusion.

7. *Leader*. I want a person who is a winner, for whom people want to work, with the ability to read personnel, hire the best people, and be able to maximize the potential of all his or her people.

8. *Good track record*. Although it is nice to be able to find someone who has a winning track record on all or most of his or her previous assignments, we also understand that no one is born a GM or GSM. Therefore, it is not always a criterion.

9. *High energy level*. I've always felt that you can determine a successful person by watching the way he or she walks down the hallway. I believe a person with a high energy level tends to get his or her people to move at a higher level also.

10. *Honest and with integrity*. It is absolutely critical that you trust your manager, and trust that he or she won't try to make excuses and place blame on other people. This is a very hard ingredient to determine up front and may have to be acquired eventually.

---

**Norman Feuer** is Vice-President and Market Manager of Broadcast Company of Americas in San Diego, which owns the cluster that features XPRS, XPRS-A, and XEPE-A. Feuer has had a 50-plus year career that includes executive leadership posts at Viacom, Noble Broadcast Group, Triathlon Broadcasting, Clear Channel, and Morris Communications.

**FIGURE 2.10**

Source: Courtesy of
*AllAccess.com, Inside Radio,
Radio Ink,* and *Radio and
Television Business Report*

## MANAGING THE CLUSTER

A significant number of the nation's radio stations exist in cluster configurations, which are several stations owned by the same company and grouped together in one location. This has resulted in the downsizing of station staffs and the ultimate enhancement of the bottom line for the corporations licensed to operate these outlets. With clustering, some individuals often work for multiple stations. Thus, if there are four stations in a cluster, rather than having four separate staffs for each station, one set of staff members will do jobs at all four stations. This business model created a sweeping reorganization of the broadcast radio landscape. As a result of the Telecommunications Act of 1996, the longtime model of a single station run by a single manager is now obsolete in large and medium-sized markets and the "cluster" paradigm in which a single market manager oversees the operation of many stations—in some cases up to eight—is the standard. This creates a whole new set of challenges for radio managers. Perhaps the biggest challenge for the person responsible for the stations in a cluster is providing the appropriate amount of focus on each.

The late Tom Severino, Emmis Indianapolis Radio Market Manager, observed:

> While managing a single station or even two, you have more time to get involved with more detail in each department. When you manage a cluster of four or more, you have to stay focused on the biggest issues that move you toward goals. The right people have always been your most important asset, and that is even more critical in cluster management. You have to make sure you have the absolute right person in the right position because you have to rely on leadership at all levels more in a cluster situation. To manage this effectively everyone in the organization must know what the goals are, how they contribute to those goals, how we are doing in reaching those goals. Everyone needs to be familiar with the values of the company as well.

**FIGURE 2.11**

CBS owns radio stations in media markets around the nation. When a company owns several stations in a market, this is called a radio cluster. In this example, CBS owns six radio stations in Dallas, Texas

Source: Courtesy of CBS

**FIGURE 2.12**

BCA Radio is a cluster in San Diego, California

Source: Courtesy of Broadcast Company of the Americas

## HUMAN RESOURCES

### Dick Oppenheimer

The management of station personnel is one of the manager's greatest challenges. The following is prominent Texas-based radio executive Dick Oppenheimer's perspective on the subject.

One of the oldest sayings I can remember is that the more things change, the more they stay the same. Perhaps, but that adage certainly does not apply to the radio industry any longer.

Before there were LMAs, duopolies, and super-duopolies, you were the manager of one or, at most, two radio stations. Now the norm is to manage at least six in your market. This is an industry where the inventory is time and the commodity is people. In fact, radio is a business totally driven by people.

The typical radio station had perhaps 15 employees, and although you had middle managers you were truly "hands-on." The manager was more than just the boss; he was priest, rabbi, psychologist, big

**FIGURE 2.13**
Dick Oppenheimer

brother, confidant, and so on. Today, with upward of 100 employees, you can no longer be "hands-on." You are now a corporate figurehead. You are responsible to and for your corporation for the day-to-day operations of your slew of radio stations.

Today's radio station is far different from the one of 15 or 20 years ago. Now there's a host of considerations you as manager must keep a watchful eye on, including sexual harassment, job discrimination, hostile work environment, disabilities acts, and race, religion, and gender issues. That's just for starters.

The first thing a manager must do is learn all the rules and laws concerning areas that impact human resources. You shouldn't attempt this yourself. Hire and retain an attorney who specializes in labor law. Have the attorney write an employee manual and establish the policies that are necessary for you to be a competent personnel manager. Once you have done this, have an initial meeting with your management staff and your attorney to convey the information necessary to assist your people in their management of other people. The larger corporations have in-house counsel, as well as a human resources director who determines whether an attorney is necessary.

On an annual basis, have your employees, including managers, acknowledge that they have read and understand the company's employee handbook.

Document everything. *Remember: if it is not in writing, it did not occur.* When an employee comes to you with a complaint, have someone else present to verify the discussion and its content. Keep in mind that in a courtroom you are the defendant. All the employee has to say is that it happened. The burden of proof is yours.

Of course, one of the best ways to prevent problems is through proper hiring. It has been my experience that, often, the employee who files charges against you is a marginal or questionable employee, that is to say, an employee who should not have been hired in the first place. Unfortunately, it is not until a suit has been filed that you learn about an employee's history of filing complaints. However, there are times when a complaint is legitimate. Real problems can and do exist. You have to be mindful of this.

One of the problems is that employers are prohibited from giving recommendations on previous employees. Handling people is one of the significant challenges of any manager. It is also one of the most rewarding.

Lastly, my number one cardinal rule, whenever an employee requests to meet with you. When you do so, give that employee your full attention. Do not take phone calls and interrupt the meeting for any reason other than for a catastrophe. By giving the employee full attention, if you say no, at least the employee leaves believing you gave him/her your full attention.

---

In 2016, **Dick Oppenheimer**, one of the first broadcasters to be honored by the Austin Broadcasters Group for his outstanding contribution to the radio industry, was inducted into the Texas Radio Hall of Fame in 2012 and named the "2009 Pioneer of the Year" by the Texas Association of Broadcasters (TAB). He has had a long-running career in the radio industry including managing Houston's KYOK-AM and starting Capitol Cities Broadcasting with radio stations in Austin, Baton Rouge, Little Rock, Mobile, and Beaumont.

Capitol Cities Broadcasting was sold for one of the highest prices ever paid for a group of its size. After selling Capitol Cities Broadcasting, he started Signature Broadcasting with numerous radio station holdings. He served on the TAB Board of Directors from 1981 to 1987 and for eight years on the NAB Board of Directors. He also spent 10 years (1996 to 2006) as an Adjunct Professor at the University of Texas, College of Communications, where he was voted by the students as the #1 professor in the college. He returned to the radio business in 2008 with the acquisition of two stations in the Austin market, which he sold in 2013 and retired "for real."

Dix Communications vice-president Jim Robertson shares many of Severino's views regarding the management of a station cluster:

> The on-going balancing act of time and resources is by far top of the list from my perspective. I am fortunate to have two stations (93.7K Country/WOGK) and our three station classic rock simulcast (WNDD/WNDT/WNDN) that are capable of being number one in all of the key demographics. Each station rightfully demands and deserves equal attention. Admittedly, each station at times feels like the other is favored. I think that is good in a competitive environment. Good communication is essential in a cluster operation, especially at the department-head level. It allows each station's program director to understand why things are happening across the hall at the other station. A cluster has to function organically.

Severino offers a list of the pros and cons of the station cluster concept:

- *Pros*: As a manager, you can use each entity to cross promote each other (events, programming specials, news, formats, etc.; you can spread expenses); you can cross-utilize personnel; you can expand what is offered to advertisers; you can utilize each station's audience delivery and events to best serve the customer; you can combine resources to get better pricing from vendors (promotional items, outside marketing); and you can reduce expenses on support staff (business office, sales, and so forth).
- *Cons*: As a manager, you cannot get involved in the day-to-day detail of each entity; you cannot devote full focus on a single station; you cannot engage in long-term strategic thinking of each station enterprise.

## THE MANAGER AND THE PROFIT MOTIVE

Earlier we discussed the unique nature of the radio industry and the particular challenges station managers face as a consequence. Radio, indeed, is a form of show business, and both words of the term are particularly applicable since the medium is at once stage and store. Radio provides entertainment (and information) to the public and, in turn, sells access to the audience it attracts to advertisers.

The general manager or market manager is answerable to many: the station's owners and corporate heads, listeners, and sponsors. However, to keep his or her own job, the manager must first please the owner or corporate manager. More often than not, that person's first concern is profit. As in any business, the more money the manager generates, the happier the owner. In May 2013, Emmis's Compensation Committee restructured the way in which the company's executives and managers were paid. In a filing with the Security and Exchange Commission (SEC), Emmis proposes:

> The Committee will award a quarterly bonus to each participant based upon the extent to which the quarterly performance goal was achieved, with no quarterly bonus to be paid under the plan if less than 95% of the quarterly performance goal was achieved. The quarterly bonus, if any, will be up to 20% of the participant's annual target bonus amount.

In sum, in some situations, when managers accomplish goals they are financially rewarded and when the goals are not accomplished they see no financial rewards. Emmis owns radio stations in New York, Los Angeles, Austin, St. Louis, Indianapolis, and Terre Haute.

Profit is especially important with clustered stations owing to their potential to generate vast sums of revenue and build equity quickly. To illustrate the importance of managers building good teams to produce profits, it was reported, in 2017, that Entercom Communications purchased the struggling CBS Radio division for a price estimated by *RBR + TVBR* to be $1.49 billion. Indeed, the radio industry is big business and effective managerial oversight is imperative because so much money is at stake.

Ed Shane, radio industry consultant and former manager, observed:

> The new radio paradigm is "manager as financial expert." Pressure from corporate ownership to feed stock prices has changed the way managers think about their stations. Budgets, once an annual

FIGURE 2.14
Strategic Radio Solutions works with managers to help develop winning programming and marketing strategies for radio stations based on listener's perceptions, tastes, and media behavior
Source: Courtesy of Strategic Radio Solutions

affair, are reevaluated quarterly and even monthly. Managers now must be prepared at a moment's notice to cancel planned advertising expenditures or to move the expenditures into another quarter if the local cluster (or the company's region) is not making budgets. "Budgets" does not mean breaking even. It means achieving the percentage increase over the previous year's cash flow. Margins of 45–50% are not uncommon.

Critics have chided the medium for what they argue is an obsessive preoccupation with making money, which has resulted in a serious shortage of high-quality, innovative programming. They lament too much sameness. Meanwhile, station managers often are content to air material that draws the kind of audience that advertisers want to reach.

Marlin Taylor observes that too many managers overemphasize profit at the expense of the operation:

Not nearly enough of the radio operators in this country are truly committed to running the best possible stations they can, either because that might cost them more money or they simply don't understand or care what it means to be the best. In my opinion, probably no more than 20% of the nation's stations are striving to become the IBM of radio, that is, striving for true excellence. Many simply are being milked for what the owners and managers can take out of them.

Other detractors don't decry the "profit motive" for the problems of "sameness" as much as they do "consolidation," the result of the 1996 Telecommunications Act that allowed larger companies to buy up many smaller, individually owned and programmed radio stations in every market. Many independent stations, even in larger markets, did not have the resources to compete against group operators, and these were often the stations that provided the most eclectic programming. Conversely, group operators themselves are being challenged by other cluster operators in addition to a growing number of alternative audio sources that are taking a share of mind and dollars. Radio in its different forms such as podcasting, audio streaming, satellite radio, and digital radio is expanding, and that increases competition and puts pressure on profits. That is to say, the traditional business model is experiencing a paradigm shift and that requires managers to reevaluate their strategies.

The pursuit of profits forces the station manager to employ the programming format that will yield the best payday. In several markets certain formats, such as classical and jazz, which tend to attract small audiences, have been dropped in favor of those that draw greater numbers such as country. In some

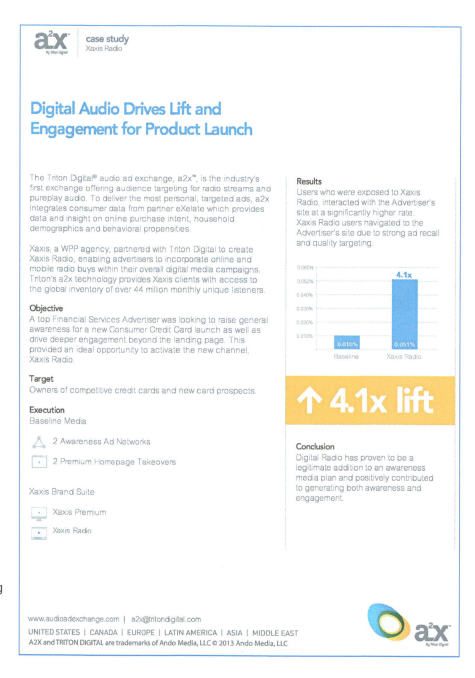

**FIGURE 2.15**

The a2x software system is used by managers to increase profits. A top financial services advertiser saw a 4.1× lift in engagement and brand awareness by running highly targeted online audio ads on Xaxis Radio, powered by Triton Digital's programmatic audio ad exchange, a2x

Source: Courtesy of Xaxis and a2x

instances, the actions of stations have caused outcries by unhappy and disenfranchised listeners who feel that their programming needs are being disregarded. Several disgruntled listener groups have gone to court in an attempt to force stations to reinstate abandoned formats. Since the government currently avoids involvement in programming decisions, leaving it up to stations to do as they see fit, little has come of their protests. However, sometimes station managers listen to the public outcry, such as in the 2005 case of WHFS in Washington, D.C. Thousands of listeners signed petitions when WHFS went off the air, prompting management to reverse its decision.

The dilemma facing today's radio station manager stems from the complexity of having to please numerous factions while earning enough money to justify his or her continued existence at the station. Marlin Taylor has suggested that stations reinvest more of their profits as a method of upgrading the overall quality of the medium.

Overcutting can have deleterious effects. A station can be too lean, even anemic. In other words, you have to put something in to get something out. Too much draining leaves the operation arid and subject to criticism by the listening public. It behooves the station manager to keep this thought in mind and, if necessary, impress it upon ownership. The really successful operations know full well that money has to be spent to nurture and develop the kind of product that delivers both impressive financial returns and listener praise.

Although it is the manager who must deal with bottom-line expectations, it is also the manager who is expected to maintain product integrity. The effective manager takes pride in the unique role that radio plays in society and does not hand it over to advertisers, notes station manager Bremkamp:

> You have to keep close tabs on your sales department. They are out to sell the station, sometimes one way or the other. Overly zealous salespeople can, on occasion, become insensitive to the station's format in their quest for ad dollars. Violating the format is like mixing fuel oil with water. You may fill your tank for less money, but you're not likely to get very far. The onus is placed on the manager to protect the integrity of the product while making a dollar. Actually, doing the former usually takes care of the latter.

Conscientious station managers are aware of the obligations confronting them and are sensitive to the criticism that crass commercialism can produce a desert or "wasteland" of bland and uninspired programming. They are also aware that, while gaps and voids may exist in radio programming and that certain segments of the population may not be getting exactly what they want, it is up to them to produce enough income to pay the bills and meet the ownership's expectations.

## WHAT MAKES A SUCCESSFUL RADIO MANAGER?

### Paul Fiddick

Here are five qualities that the most effective radio managers I've known possess.

In no particular order, one is a bias for action. Entrepreneurism is closely related, as is decisiveness. The manager must be biased toward taking the initiative.

A former boss told me on my first day in a new job: Never be afraid to make a decision for fear of making a mistake. In worst case, you're wrong and you make another decision to fix things. But that's still better than being passive and letting the "game play you."

Another quality is intelligence. There is no substitute for being bright. A manager is called upon to play many roles, and this requires an agile mind.

Related to intelligence is learning. A manager has to be more knowledgeable than ever before. S/he must be not just fluent in all the radio disciplines (programming, marketing, sales, technology) but also informed about the larger business environment. The successful manager is a lifelong learner—curious, well-read, well-rounded.

**FIGURE 2.16**
Paul Fiddick

Next is an obvious one: empathy. A manager is the voice of the station to a wide cross-section of people. The better s/he is able to communicate with these folks in their "native tongues" (of manner, culture, and vernacular), the more effective you will be. This is different from being an extrovert—it's being sensitive to "where they're coming from."

The last quality is hardest to describe. I say it this way: successful managers take things personally. This may seem counterintuitive: shouldn't managers retain a kind of cool objectivity toward their work? The job is too demanding for that kind of detachment. It's not a coincidence that successful managers are very often driven personalities!

---

**Paul Fiddick** has served as Chief Executive of four national media companies and also as a Senate-confirmed Official in the U.S. government. Throughout his career, he has negotiated the acquisition (and occasional divestiture) of scores of businesses, and built every business he managed to record levels of profitability. Paul Fiddick is President Emeritus of Emmis International, a multinational broadcasting company. During his tenure, he expanded the company's footprint into three new countries and increased its operating income exponentially. Previously, he served as Assistant Secretary of the U.S. Department of Agriculture, and during the Clinton–Bush interregnum as Acting Agriculture Secretary. Pending his confirmation to government service, Paul Fiddick was Executive Vice-Chairman and Acting President of RadioWave.com, an affiliate of Motorola. He was also a Co-Founder of Heritage Media Corporation and President of its Radio Division from 1986 through to its sale to News Corporation in 1998. He was recruited to Heritage from Multimedia Broadcasting, where he was President of the Radio Division from 1982. Paul Fiddick is a past Chairman of the Radio Advertising Bureau and Board Member of the National Association of Broadcasters. He taught at university level and is an Honors Graduate of the University of Missouri School of Journalism.

## THE MANAGER AND THE COMMUNITY

In the early 1980s, the FCC reduced the extent to which radio stations must become involved in community affairs. This deregulation process continued into the 1990s with the creation of the sweeping Telecommunications Act of 1996. Ascertainment procedures requiring that stations determine and address community issues have all but been eliminated. If a station chooses to do so, it may play musical hits 24 hours a day and virtually divorce itself from the concerns of the community. However, a station that opts to function independently of the community to which it is licensed may find itself on the outside looking in. Radio is, at its core, a local medium that relies on local audience ratings, so ignoring the needs of the public is seldom a good idea. This is especially true of small-market stations, which, for practical business reasons, have traditionally cultivated a strong connection with the community. Therefore, most stations do make an attempt to ascertain community issues and do so on a quarterly basis, maintaining the results of these surveys (often a list of the top 10 issues confronting the community of license) in their public inspection file to attest to their good citizenship and to confirm that they are serving the public interests of the communities they are licensed to serve. This looks particularly positive at license renewal time.

A station manager is aware that it is important to the welfare of his or her organization to behave as a good citizen and neighbor. Although the sheer number of stations in vast metropolitan areas makes it less crucial that a station exhibit civic-mindedness, the small-market radio outlet often finds that the level of business it generates is relative to its community involvement. Therefore, maintaining a relationship with the town leaders, civic groups, and religious leaders, among others, enhances a station's visibility and status and ultimately affects business. No small-market station can hope to operate autonomously and attract the majority of local advertisers. Stations that remain aloof in the community in which they broadcast seldom realize their full revenue potential.

One of the nation's foremost figures in broadcast management, the late Ward Quaal, President of the Ward L. Quaal Company, observed:

*A manager must not only be tied, or perhaps I should say "married" to a station, but he or she must have total involvement in the community. This is very meaningful, whether the market is Cheyenne, Cincinnati, or Chicago. The community participation builds the proper image for the station and the manager and concurrently aids, dramatically, business development and produces lasting sales strength.*

Cognizant of the importance of fostering an image of goodwill and civic-mindedness, the station manager seeks to become a member in good standing in the community. Radio managers often actively participate in groups or associations, such as the local chamber of commerce, Jaycees, Kiwanis, Rotary Club, Optimists, and others, and encourage members of their staff to become similarly involved. The station also strives to heighten its status in the community by devoting airtime to issues and events of local importance and by making its microphones available to citizens for discussions of matters pertinent to the area. In so doing, the station becomes regarded as an integral part of the community, and its value grows proportionately.

Surveys have shown that more than one-third of the managers of small-market radio stations are native to the area their signal serves. This gives them a vested interest in the quality of life in their community and motivates them to use the power of their medium to further improve living conditions.

# FCC judge moves to pull radio licenses

## By Chris McConnell

An FCC administrative law judge has decided to revoke the license of a broadcaster convicted of

**FIGURE 2.17**
Job one: "Protect the license"
Source: Courtesy of *Broadcasting and Cable*

Medium- and large-market station managers realize, as well, the benefits derived from participating in community activities. "If you don't localize and take part in the affairs of the city or town from which you draw your income, you're operating at a disadvantage. You have to tune in to your audience if you expect them to do likewise," says Bremkamp.

The manager has to work to bring the station and the community together. Neglecting this responsibility lessens the station's chance for prosperity, or even survival. Station consolidation has influenced localism across the country, but most managers continue to recognize that community involvement is a key to their success.

## THE MANAGER AND THE GOVERNMENT

Earlier in this chapter, station manager Richard Bremkamp cited protecting the license as one of the primary functions of the general manager. By "protecting" the license he meant conforming to the rules and regulations established by the Federal Communications Commission (FCC) for the operation of broadcast facilities. Since failure to fulfill the obligations of a license may result in punitive actions such as reprimands, fines, and even the revocation of the privilege to broadcast, managers have to be aware of the laws affecting station operations and see to it that they are observed by all concerned.

### TEN REGULATORY ISSUES ANY BROADCAST STATION GENERAL MANAGER NEEDS TO CONSIDER

**David Oxenford**

Operating a broadcast station is unlike operating almost any other business. The general manager of a station needs to comply not only with the usual legal obligations that apply to any business, but also to the specialized regulations that are imposed by the FCC. In today's digital world, the manager also needs to keep track of laws that apply to online content, including the often-confusing copyright laws. I've been asked to compile a list of 10 regulatory issues that a broadcast station general needs to keep in mind to stay out of trouble in his or her business operations. That list is below.

**FIGURE 2.18**
David Oxenford

This list sets out general areas of concern, not a full list of specific regulations with detailed citations to statutes and rules that can get a broadcast station into legal trouble. That list would run many pages and probably not be much help to anyone. It takes the government over 400 pages of small print just to reproduce the rules specifically applicable to broadcast stations, and that does not count the pages devoted to auxiliary licenses, tower painting and lighting, EAS operations and the many general rules that apply to all industries that the FCC regulates. Nor does it include the obligations imposed by laws adopted by Congress, or the regulations imposed by other government agencies, such as the Federal Trade Commission or the Equal Employment Opportunity Commission, or under copyright law. As it is impossible to summarize all of these many laws imposed by the federal government, as well as those imposed under state laws and municipal ordinances, we'll stick with these 10 general warnings to broadcast general managers of some of the big issues that they need to consider.

While much has been made, especially recently, about the potential deregulation of the broadcast industry, such deregulation takes time. Moreover, no deregulation will totally eliminate all regulatory concerns of the broadcaster, so our general admonitions below should continue to be good rules of the road for the broadcast general manager.

With those caveats, let's look at the 10 issues that a general manager needs to keep in mind to avoid regulatory trouble:

1. *Remember the routine filing deadlines.* Every broadcast station will have certain routine FCC filing deadlines that must be observed, or trouble will ensue. For instance, every eight years stations file their license renewal applications (all radio stations in a state file on the same day, and TV stations in that state file a year later). Don't file on time and expect a fine—and potentially even cancelation of your license. At the end of every calendar quarter, broadcasters need to place into their public file their quarterly issues programs lists, the only legally required documents where a broadcaster details how its station met the public interest needs of its community. For stations with five or more full-time employees, there is a yearly obligation to create a public file report on their EEO program compliance for the previous year. Every other year, by December 1 of odd-numbered years, all stations need to submit biennial ownership reports to the FCC. These are but some of the regular reports station managers need to remember to timely submit, or they face fines or worse.

2. *Insure that the technical operations are maintained.* Your engineer, whether he is a contractor or full-time employee, is someone that all managers need to know well, and to rely on. Even though a station may still be heard when you turn on the radio, if it is not properly maintained it can emit signals on more than just your assigned frequency, or can operate at the wrong power level. Not only may you be facing fines from the FCC if any of these problems occur, but you may be not reaching your full audience if you are under power, or you can be interfering with another broadcaster or even the communications equipment of aircraft or public safety officials if your transmitter is putting out "spurious emissions." Having a good engineer to maintain and repair all station equipment, noting it in the station log when maintenance is done or required, and seeking FCC permission for an operation that is conducted at parameters other than as specified in your license can be essential to staying out of trouble.

3. *Be prepared for emergencies.* One of a broadcaster's most important roles is to get the message out in a time of emergency. That can be simply be rebroadcasting alerts from the Emergency Alert System that are relayed over the air from another station or ones that are received online from the Federal Emergency Management Administration. Or it can be the station itself relaying critical information from local first responders or others. So be sure that your EAS system is fully functional with the ability to receive and retransmit alerts that come over that system, and be sure that first responders and others in your community know how to reach the station in the event of any local emergency. Of course, your staff should also be trained so as to be ready to respond when an emergency arises.

4. *Keep safety concerns in mind.* Whether it is loose bricks on a station's front steps that pose a hazard to visitors, a rusted broadcast tower that can fall in a storm or a station vehicle with faulty brakes, there are many hazards at a broadcast station that can cause injury and create potential

liability. FCC fines have been common for towers that have not been properly maintained or painted or whose lights are not fully operational. Other stations have had significant FCC penalties imposed when the fence surrounding an AM station is unlocked or damaged, affording people access to areas of high RF radiation. Even station contests can raise liability concerns, if you send people rushing across town to claim a prize or induce other actions likely to cause bodily harm. All these kinds of issues can cause not only FCC issues but also civil liability.

5. *Watch what you broadcast*. The FCC has all sorts of rules regulating what you can say over the air. Foul language and other indecent content can get a station in trouble when broadcast outside the "safe harbor" for such content (10 pm to 6 am). Some gambling and other lotteries (where there is prize, chance, and consideration to enter a contest) can lead to issues under federal and state law. Providing time to political candidates outside of news coverage is also subject to an extensive body of law requiring that competing candidates be treated in the same manner. For political broadcasts, there are even regulations as to how much can be charged to candidates who buy time on your station. Be sure that you are familiar with all of the FCC's content rules. Even beyond the FCC, be sure that your on-air personnel are careful with their news reporting and any entertainment content that makes fun of specific individuals. Violations of libel and slander laws can result in significant damages, if false statements are made about identifiable individuals or groups in a way likely to cause them damage to reputation or business prospects.

6. *Tell your audience when you are paid to say something*. The FCC requires that broadcasters identify when they receive anything of value, including cash or other goods or services, to say something on the air. So advertisers and sponsors need to be identified. Even online, the Federal Trade Commission imposes a similar obligation, requiring that sponsored content, even on social media, be identified. So if a station is paid for an on-air advertising schedule, and also promises that the sponsor will be mentioned on the station's Facebook page or in its Twitter feed, those online mentions need to be identified as sponsored (with an identification appropriate to the media involved—on Twitter often a "#ad").

7. *Respect the property of others*. Broadcasters need to be sure that they have the rights to the content that they use, both on the air and in a station's digital media properties. On the air, stations can't just buy DVDs of old movies and run them on the air, or take clips of those films and excerpt them to be dropped into other programs, without permission of the copyright holder. Popular music cannot be used in commercials without permission of the copyright owners. Even the melody of a song can't be used for the jingle of an advertiser without consent. And Internet content found on some social media site can't be repurposed on the air, or on station websites or social media pages, without getting permission. Numerous broadcasters have been sued, and had to settle for thousands of dollars, for taking pictures found online and using them to illustrate a story on the station's website without paying for the rights to do so. TV stations have faced similar actions for playing on the air a popular YouTube video without permission from the video's creator. Just because material has been posted online does not make it available to be used elsewhere without permission of the copyright holder.

8. *Pay for what you play*. To add to the cautions listed in the previous paragraph, radio stations playing music must pay for the content that drives their stations. For over-the-air broadcasts, stations must pay performing rights organizations ("PROs") for the public performance rights to musical compositions. Any public performance of music, when the performance is made before people who are outside an individual's family and friends, implicate a public performance right where songwriters get paid for the use of the songs that they wrote. In the US, the PROs are ASCAP, BMI, and SESAC (and an emerging group called GMR), which each represents different songwriters. Most stations that play any music, including jingles and music in commercials, need licenses from some, and most likely for music stations all, of these PROs. In the digital world (and in many countries outside the US), there is also a public performance right in the "sound recording" (the song as recorded by a particular band or singer). For noninteractive webcasts, where the listener cannot select the specific song he or she will hear, that sound recording public performance royalty is paid to an organization called SoundExchange. So even online simulcasts of over-the-air programming trigger this obligation to pay SoundExchange.

9. *Think about hiring issues*. State and federal laws prohibit hiring discrimination. So at a broadcast station, like in any other business, be careful about discriminating in the hiring at a station against anyone in a protected group. Don't make hiring decisions or run recruiting materials that suggest discrimination on the basis of race, ethnicity, gender, or age. Plus, the FCC imposes affirmative obligations on stations to reach out their communities so that all members of the community get notice of job openings at their station. The FCC even obligates stations to make efforts, even when they don't have job openings, to educate the community about jobs at broadcast stations, including the training required for broadcast positions and how to find out when such jobs are opening.

10. *Keep up with what's new*. Rules from the FCC and from other government agencies are always changing. Sometimes the changes bring opportunities that could allow you to expand or improve your operations, or to save money in regulatory compliance. Other times the developments could bring more rules that you need to observe. Be sure that you develop sources for staying on tops of these changes. Trade press reports, legal blogs and online articles, state and national broadcast associations, and a good communications attorney can all help keep you informed of the rules that you need to follow to be alert to regulatory changes.

These are just 10 broad categories of legal concerns that a broadcast general manager needs to consider as they run their stations. Many times the demands of getting programming on the air and otherwise running a business may seem overwhelming, leaving no time for consideration of the legal requirements including the matters discussed above. Don't fall into that trap, as it can lead to significant costs that can ruin any financial quarter with fines and other legal costs. Set up regular compliance plans, and enlist your staff to assist on ensure that the legal requirements are met. It is a team effort. Staying on the right side of the law is often not just required but makes good business sense.

———————————————

**David Oxenford** is an attorney who has been representing broadcasters on regulatory and transactional matters for over 35 years. He also advises broadcasters and digital media companies on copyright issues, particular dealing with music licensing. He is a Partner in the Washington, D.C., office of the law firm Wilkinson Barker Knauer LLP.

David is a regular speaker at conferences and seminars hosted by national and state broadcast associations, and is also the principal writer of the widely read Broadcast Law Blog, www.broadcast lawblog.com.

The FCC lists its fines in *47 CFR 1.80* and here are some examples of the base forfeiture amounts that can be decreased and/or increased at the commission's discretion *per incident*:

- construction or operation without authorization: $10,000
- broadcasting telephone conversations without authorization: $4,000
- unauthorized substantial transfer of control: $8,000
- violation of transmitter control and metering requirements: $3,000
- violation of broadcast hoax rule: $7,000
- failure to permit FCC inspections: $7,000
- failure to respond to FCC communications: $4,000
- exceeding power limits: $4,000
- EAS equipment broken or not installed: $8,000
- broadcasting indecent/obscene material: $32,500 (could be substantially more if the violation is really graphic)
- violation of EEO or political broadcast rules: $9,000
- violation of main studio rule: $7,000

- public file violations: $10,000

- failure to provide station ID: $1,000

- sponsor ID or lottery violations: $4,000.

Other examples of FCC fines were included in a 2013 newsletter from lawyer David Oxenford, of Washington, D.C., titled *The Cost of Little Things: FCC Fines for Regulatory Noncompliance*, which listed the following punitive amounts for rule violations:

- quarterly issues programs lists: $12,000–$15,000

- tower fencing: $4,000

- equal employment opportunity issues: $20,000.

Oxenford underscores the following: "Note that these are per occurrence too. So, in some cases where the FCC wants to make a point, each time an ad with a sponsorship ID violation (especially on a political issue) runs, the fine can be imposed."

In 2017, the FCC fined Alaskan radio station KIBH-FM $66,000 for numerous violations related to the Emergency Alert System (EAS) owing to requirements by the FCC that stations adhere to specific rules and regulations allegedly being violated. This is considered a relatively small fine compared to others that have been levied by the FCC. In 2009, Clear Channel Communication's morning radio show *Bubba the Love Sponge* was levied the largest ever fine of $715,000 for sexually explicit content that aired during the morning hours of 6:30–9 am on radio stations in Florida. CBS News reported: "One segment featured the cartoon characters Alvin the Chipmunk, George Jetson and Scooby-Doo discussing sexual activities."

The manager delegates responsibilities to department heads who are directly involved in the areas affected by the commission's regulations. For example, the program director will attend to the legal station identification (call letters and city of license), station logs, program content, and a myriad of other concerns of interest to the government. Meanwhile, the chief engineer is responsible for meeting technical standards, and the sales manager is held accountable for the observance of certain business and financial practices. Other members of the station also are assigned various responsibilities applicable to the license. Of course, ultimately, it is the manager who must guarantee that the station's license to broadcast is protected.

Although the manager may delegate regulatory responsibilities to department heads throughout the organization, it is still the ultimate responsibility of the station manager to ensure that FCC regulations are followed. Charlie Morgan shared:

> Broadcast radio in the United States is a tightly regulated industry. Unlike other audio content distribution channels, an AM or FM license is a renewable federal license granted only when licensees comply with the commission's regulations. Before Internet distribution, the regulated scarcity provided an advantage to a broadcaster. Now, the rules and regulations place broadcasters at some disadvantage to the newer, less regulated methodologies. All of that said, the day-to-day operation of a broadcast station, while clearly regulated by the FCC, is not overly encumbered and the FCC is not a large factor in operational decisions.

All rules and regulations pertaining to radio broadcast operations are contained in Title 47, Part 73, of the Code of Federal Regulations (CFR). The station manager keeps the annual update of this publication accessible to all employees involved in maintaining the license. A copy of the CFR may be obtained through the Superintendent of Documents, Government Printing Office, Washington, D.C. 20402, for a modest fee or can be accessed for free from the FCC website at www.fcc.gov/general/rules-regulations-title-47, or you can download a copy of the 47 CFR 73 file here: www.gpo.gov/fdsys/granule/CFR-2012-title47-vol4/CFR-2012-title47-vol4-part73/content-detail.html. Specific inquiries concerning the publication can be addressed to the Director, Office of the Federal Register, National Archives and Records Service, General Services Administration, Washington, D.C. 20408.

| Proposed FY 2017 RADIO STATION REGULATORY FEES | | | | | |
|---|---|---|---|---|---|
| This uses the proposed ratios for FY 2017 | | | | | |
| Population Served | AM Class A | AM Class B | AM Class C | AM Class D | FM Classes A, B1 & C3 | FM Classes B, C, C0, C1 & C2 |
| <=25,000 | $1,050 | $750 | $650 | $715 | $1,150 | $1,300 |
| 25,001 – 75,000 | $1,575 | $1,125 | $975 | $1,075 | $1,725 | $1,950 |
| 75,001 – 150,000 | $2,375 | $1,700 | $1,475 | $1,600 | $2,600 | $2,925 |
| 150,001 – 500,000 | $3,550 | $2,525 | $2,200 | $2,425 | $3,875 | $4,400 |
| 500,001 – 1,200,000 | $5,325 | $3,800 | $3,300 | $3,625 | $5,825 | $6,575 |
| 1,200,001 – 3,000,00 | $7,975 | $5,700 | $4,950 | $5,425 | $8,750 | $9,875 |
| 3,000,001 – 6,000,00 | $11,950 | $8,550 | $7,400 | $8,150 | $13,100 | $14,800 |
| >6,000,000 | $17,950 | $12,825 | $11,100 | $12,225 | $19,650 | $22,225 |

| FY 2017 RADIO STATION REGULATORY FEES, based on proposed FY 2016 fees | | | | | |
|---|---|---|---|---|---|
| This chart uses the proposed ratios in FY 2016 | | | | | |
| Population Served | AM Class A | AM Class B | AM Class C | AM Class D | FM Classes A, B1 & C3 | FM Classes B, C, C0, C1 & C2 |
| <=25,000 | $1,125 | $825 | $710 | $780 | $1,250 | $1,425 |
| 25,001 – 75,000 | $1,700 | $1,250 | $1,075 | $1,175 | $1,875 | $2,150 |
| 75,001 – 150,000 | $2,250 | $1,650 | $1,425 | $1,550 | $2,500 | $2,850 |
| 150,001 – 500,000 | $3,375 | $2,475 | $2,125 | $2,350 | $3,750 | $4,275 |
| 500,001 – 1,200,000 | $5,625 | $4,125 | $3,550 | $3,900 | $6,250 | $7,125 |
| 1,200,001 – 3,000,00 | $8,450 | $6,200 | $5,325 | $5,850 | $9,375 | $10,700 |
| 3,000,001 – 6,000,00 | $11,250 | $8,250 | $7,100 | $7,800 | $12,500 | $14,250 |
| >6,000,000 | $14,075 | $10,325 | $8,875 | $9,750 | $15,625 | $17,825 |

FIGURE 2.19
FCC's AM/FM regulatory fees document. Note that the larger a licensee's market, the higher the fee
Source: Retrieved from www.fcc.gov

To reiterate, although the station manager shares the duties involved in complying with the FCC's regulations with other staff members, he or she holds primary responsibility for keeping the station in compliance with FCC regulations and on the air.

Many of the rules and regulations pertaining to the daily operation of a radio station have been revised or rescinded. Since the CFR is published annually, certain parts may become obsolete during that period. Martha L. Girard, Director of the Office of the *Federal Register*, suggests that the *Federal Register*, from which the CFR derives its information, be consulted monthly. Subscriptions to the *Federal Register* are available; a hard copy of the publication may also be available at the local library.

Because the FCC may, without warning at any time during normal business hours, inspect a radio station to see that it is in accordance with the rules and regulations, a manager must make certain that everything is always in order. An FCC inspection checklist is contained in the CFR, and industry organizations, such as the NAB and state broadcast associations, provide member stations with similar checklists. Occasionally, managers run mock inspections in preparation for the real thing. Some stations are proactive when it comes to FCC matters and participate in the Alternate Broadcast Inspection Program (ABIP). The ABIP is a collaboration between the FCC and state broadcast associations in which the station goes through a mock inspection modeled after the one conducted by FCC field inspectors. If deficiencies are found, the station has a specific timeframe to correct the problems. Upon correction, or if no deficiencies are found, the station is issued a Certificate of Compliance and the station is exempt from random FCC inspections for three years. Essentially, the ABIP acts as an insurance policy for the station to protect itself from possible FCC compliance deficiencies. A state of preparedness prevents embarrassment and problems.

Christine H. Merritt, President of the Ohio Association of Broadcasters, explains how the ABIP works:

> The Alternative Broadcast Inspection Program (ABIP), established in cooperation with the Federal Communications Commission (FCC), helps radio and television stations ensure compliance with FCC regulations. Typically offered through state broadcasters' associations, the program provides stations with an inspection based upon the FCC Broadcast Station Self-Inspection Checklist. Inspections are conducted by a technical inspector approved by the FCC to conduct ABIP inspections. Stations certified to be in compliance with the FCC's technical rules are exempt from routine inspections by the FCC Field Office for three years.

## THE MANAGER AND UNIONS

The unions most active in radio are the Screen Actors Guild–American Federation of Television and Radio Artists (SAG-AFTRA), the National Association of Broadcast Employees and Technicians–Communications Workers of America (NABET-CWA), and the International Brotherhood of Electrical Workers (IBEW). Major-market radio stations are the ones most likely to be unionized. The overwhelming majority of American stations are nonunion and, in fact, union membership has declined in recent years.

Dissatisfaction with wages and benefits, coupled with a desire for greater security, are often motivators that prompt station employees to vote for a union. Managers seldom encourage the presence of a union since many believe that unions impede and constrict their ability to control the destiny of their operations. However, a small percentage of managers believe that the existence of a union may actually stabilize the working environment and reduce personnel turnover.

It is the function of the union to act as a bargaining agent working in good faith with station employees and management to upgrade and improve working conditions. Union efforts usually focus on salary, sick leave, vacation, promotion, hiring, termination, working hours, and retirement benefits. In 2013, SAG-AFTRA negotiated a deal on behalf of its members that was expected to generate $238 million in new salary increases for radio voiceover talent, health benefits, and retirement pensions.

A unionized station appoints or elects a shop steward, who works as a liaison between the union, which represents the employees, and the station's management. Employees may lodge complaints or grievances with the shop steward, who will then review the union's contract with the station and proceed accordingly. Station managers are obliged to work within the agreement that they, along with the union, helped formulate.

As stated, unions are a fact of life in many major markets. They are far less prevalent elsewhere, although unions do exist in some medium and even small markets. Most small operations would find it impractical, if not untenable, to function under a union contract. Union demands and work rules would quite likely cripple most marginal or small-profit operations.

Managers who extend employees every possible courtesy and operate in a fair and reasonable manner are rarely affected by unions, whose prime objective is to protect and ensure the rights of station workers.

## CHAPTER HIGHLIGHTS

1. Radio managers constantly face challenges owing to new audio competition and station consolidation. In addition, radio's unique character requires that station managers deal with a wide variety of talents and personalities.

2. The authoritarian approach to management implies that the general manager makes all of the policy decisions. The collaborative approach allows the general manager to involve other station staff in the formation of policy. The hybrid or chief collaborator approach combines elements of both the authoritarian and collaborative management models. The chief collaborator management approach is most prevalent in radio today.

3. To attain management status, an individual needs both a formal education and practical experience in many areas of station operation—especially sales.

4. Key managerial functions include operating in a manner that produces the greatest profit, meeting corporate expectations, formulating station policy and seeing to its implementation, hiring and retaining good people, inspiring staff to do their best, training new employees, maintaining communication with all departments to ensure an excellent air product, and keeping an eye toward the future, especially in terms of how new technological applications—such as websites and HD—can enhance profitability.

5. The National Association of Broadcasters (NAB), the Radio Advertising Bureau (RAB), and state broadcasting associations are among the largest radio trade industry organizations. They assist station management and other personnel to stay abreast of changes and trends in the radio industry.

6. Station clustering and consolidation have changed the personnel landscape at stations as radio groups often concentrate the operation of several stations in one central location. Some of the positions in a station cluster include a market manager, director of sales, general sales manager, director of operations, and controller.

7. In noncluster station environments, the operations manager is second only to the general manager at those outlets that have established this position. This individual supervises administrative staff, helps develop and implement station policy, handles departmental budgeting, functions as regulatory watchdog, and works as liaison with the community.

8. Managers hire individuals who possess a formal education, strong professional experience, ambition, a positive attitude, reliability, humility, honesty, self-respect, patience, enthusiasm, discipline, creativity, logic, and compassion.

9. Consultant Ed Shane: "The new radio paradigm is 'manager as financial expert.'"

10. Radio provides entertainment to the public and, in turn, sells the audience it attracts to advertisers. It is the station manager who must ensure a profit, but he or she must also maintain product integrity.

11. To foster a positive community image, the station manager becomes actively involved in the community and devotes airtime to community concerns—even though the FCC has reduced a station's obligation to do so via ascertainment.

12. Although the station manager delegates responsibility for compliance with FCC regulations to appropriate department heads, the manager is ultimately responsible for protecting the license. Title 47, Part 73, of the Code of Federal Regulations contains the rules pertaining to radio broadcast operations. Updates of regulations are listed monthly in the *Federal Register*. It can also be found online at the FCC's website at http://transition.fcc.gov/mb/audio/bickel/amfmrule.html.

13. The Screen Actors Guild–American Federation of Television and Radio Artists (SAG-AFTRA), the National Association of Broadcast Employees and Technicians–Communications Workers of America (NABET-CWA), and the International Brotherhood of Electrical Workers (IBEW) are the unions most active in radio.

14. The station manager must be aware of and comply with all federal regulations related to the operation of a radio station. The Federal Communications Commission (FCC) is the regulatory body responsible for regulating and enforcing regulations pertaining to the U.S. broadcasting industry. Violations of the regulations can be very costly to the radio station.

# SUGGESTED FURTHER READING

Agor, W.H., *Intuitive Management*, Prentice Hall, Englewood Cliffs, NJ, 1984.

Albarran, A., *Management of Electronic Media*, 5th edition, Wadsworth, Los Angeles, CA, 2013.

Appleby, R.C., *The Essential Guide to Management*, Prentice Hall, Englewood Cliffs, NJ, 1981.

Aronoff, C.E. (ed.), *Business and the Media*, Goodyear, Santa Monica, CA, 1979.

Boyatzis, R.E., *The Competent Manager*, John Wiley and Sons, New York, NY, 1983.

Brown, A., *Supermanaging*, McGraw-Hill, New York, NY, 1984.

Coleman, H.W., *Case Studies in Broadcast Management*, Hastings House, New York, NY, 1978.

Cottrell, D., *Monday Morning Leadership*, Cornerstone Leadership, New York, NY, 2002.

Creech, K.C., *Electronic Media Law and Regulation*, 5th edition, Focal Press, Boston, MA, 2007.

Czech-Beckerman, E.S., *Managing Electronic Media*, Focal Press, Boston, MA, 1991.

Elimore, R.T., *Broadcasting Law and Regulation*, Tab, Blue Ridge Summit, PA, 1982.

Goodworth, C.T., *How to Be a Super-Effective Manager: A Guide to People Management*, Business Books, London, 1984.

Hollifield, C.A., Wicks, J.L., Sylvie, G., and Lowrey, W. *Media Management: A Casebook Approach*, 5th edition. Routledge, New York, NY, 2016.

Kahn, F.J. (ed.), *Documents of American Broadcasting*, 4th edition, Prentice Hall, Englewood Cliffs, NJ, 1984.

Kobert, N., *The Aggressive Management Style*, Prentice Hall, Englewood Cliffs, NJ, 1981.

Krasnow, E.G. and Werner, E.T., *Radio Deals: A Step by Step Guide*, RBR Publications, Springfield, VA, 2002.

McCluskey, J., *Successful Broadcast Station Management and Ownership*, Pearson, Boston, MA, 1999.

McCormack, M.H., *What They Don't Teach You at Harvard Business School*, Bantam, New York, NY, 1984.

Miner, J.B., *The Management Process: Theory, Research, and Practice*, Macmillan, New York, NY, 1978.

Mogel, L., *The Business of Broadcasting*, Billboard, LA, 2004.

National Association of Broadcasters, *Political Broadcast Catechism*, 16th edition, NAB, Washington, D.C., 2007.

Pember, D.R., *Mass Media in America*, 6th edition, Macmillan, New York, NY, 1991.

Pringle, P.K., Starr, M.F. and McCavitt, W.E., *Electronic Media Management*, 5th edition, Focal Press, Boston, MA, 2005.

Quaal, W.L. and Brown, J.A., *Broadcast Management*, 2nd edition, Hastings House, New York, NY, 1976.

Rhoads, B.E., Bunzel, R., Snook, A., and McMan, W. (eds.), *Management and Sales Management*, Streamline Press, West Palm Beach, FL, 1995.

Routt, E., *The Business of Radio Broadcasting*, Tab, Blue Ridge Summit, PA, 1972.

Schneider, C., *Starting Your Career in Broadcasting*, Allworth Press, New York, NY, 2007.

Schwartz, T., *Media, the Second God*, Praeger, New York, NY, 1984.

Shane, E., *Cutting Through: Strategies and Tactics for Radio*, Shane Media, Houston, TX, 1990.

Shane, E., *Selling Electronic Media*, Focal Press, Boston, MA, 1999.

Townsend, R., *Further up the Organization*, Alfred A. Knopf, New York, NY, 1984.

# CHAPTER 3

# Music Programming and Consultancies

## PROGRAM FORMATS

"The devil is in the details," wrote famed French author Gustave Flaubert, and for our purposes in this chapter, we could say that the devil is in the *programming*. Alternately, we could opt for the observation of revered U.S. Navy Admiral Hyman Rickover, who concluded that "The Devil is in the details, but so is salvation." Indeed, designing a radio station's sound continues to be a bedeviling yet emancipating task, its intensity amplified in an environment complicated by station ownership consolidation and the resultant clustering of stations within markets. More than 15,500 AM and FM stations compete for audience attention, and additional broadcasters continue to enter the fray. Other media have emerged and proliferated to further distract and dilute radio's customary audience. The government's laissez-faire, "let the marketplace dictate" philosophy concerning commercial radio programming gives the station great freedom in deciding the nature of its air product. Yet determining what to offer the listener, who is often presented with dozens of audio alternatives, involves intricate planning. Consultant and Programmer Mike McVay of Cumulus Media underscores the role good programming plays in achieving station success:

> Radio stations are simply a platform for distribution. The content of a radio station is what makes it a success or a failure. Great programming is targeted to the largest possible audience, designed based on research that enables one to know what needs should be satisfied, easy to understand and memorable. If you are to succeed with a product, particularly in an era when mass media still dominates niche media, the most popular widespread formats (talk or music) should be what is presented. Bigger is better. It enables you to overcome rating wobbles. Without good programming you have nothing,

Tommy Castor, PD of iHeartmedia's Channel963 in Wichita, sums it up this way:

> I strongly believe that good programming on radio, in many cases, can be the ultimate deciding factor between consumers using radio and using a curated or on-demand service. While curated and on-demand services and radio share a similarity in that the consumer doesn't usually have ultimate control of the selection of the music, radio programming differs because rather than guessing what the consumer might like to listen to (based on an artist or song selection on the curated service), radio program directors use a variety or research, metrics and strategies to put together a playlist of music.

The bottom line, of course, is to air the type of format that will attract a sizable enough piece of the audience demographic to satisfy the advertiser. Once a station decides on the format it will program, it must then know how to effectively execute it. Since 1998 Edison Research has reported on radio audience demographics in its annual *Infinite Dial* studies. In its most recent study of 2,000 participants, Edison and research partner Triton Digital affirm the diversification within traditional radio and online audio services. Podcast listening continues to make double-digit percentage advancements. As a result of recent gains researchers say the platform as of 2017 qualifies for "mainstream media" status. They estimate 112 million listeners have sampled podcasts. The report reveals that 45% of respondents listen to "most of the podcast," while another 40% hear the podcast in its entirety. Terrestrial (AM and FM) stations, according to the research, remain the most popular audio medium across all respondent ages for the discovery of new music (but rank third for 12- to 24-year-old listeners, behind YouTube and "friends and family"). In the so-called "battle for the dashboard," AM and FM stations dominate, outdistancing the runner-up (CD listening) by 30 percentage points. Pandora awareness and listenership remains high. Yet, despite the inroads the pureplay has made in selling advertising in individual markets, it hasn't yet achieved granularity in terms of providing local information and entertainment—the content that attracts an audience. Thus, if "location, location, and location" are the three keys to success in selling real estate then "local, local, and local" emerges as the guiding principle for programmers at FM and AM stations to follow in creating the types of compelling radio programming that pureplays have yet offered.

Brief descriptions of several of radio's most widely adopted music formats today are presented in this chapter (for a discussion of nonmusic program formats, see Chapter 5). There are, however, more than 60 distinct music and nonmusic formats recognized by the audience research firm Nielsen Audio. The reader should keep in mind that formats morph and evolve as new trends in lifestyle and culture emerge.

Changes in audience measurement methodologies can influence programming decisions, as well as the outcomes of the research. *Inside Radio*, an industry newsletter, reported a correlation between format changes and the markets in which Nielsen Audio had implemented its Portable People Meter (PPM) system. Chapter 6 details PPM history and explains how Nielsen Audio continues its transition from a diary-based, listener-recall data collection method to an electronic, passive system for audience measurement. Most importantly, it bears observing that radio formats are dynamic and malleable, and the impetus for change is driven by various, largely economic factors.

## Adult Contemporary

In terms of the number of listeners, adult contemporary (AC, and offsprings hot AC, lite AC, modern AC, rhythmic AC, soft AC, and urban AC) continues its four-decade popularity trend. The core AC format, according to *Inside Radio*, is programmed on approximately 600 stations. When the various subformats are included in the count, the total station count springs to more than 1,400 outlets. It's radio's second most listened-to music format, trailing only contemporary hit radio (CHR). A notable characteristic of AC is its widespread appeal to women. The format attracts radio's most evenly distributed audience of listeners aged 12 to 64. AC is ethnically diverse, targeting female listeners aged 25–54 and focusing on a core of females between 30 and 45 years old. AC popularity is trending upward with teens and young adults. Almost one-third of listeners are college-educated. This programming approach is prone to fragmentation, a phenomenon ascribed to the notable population diversity across the sub-groups of the core format.

Because AC is very strong among the broader 25–54 age group it is particularly appealing to advertisers. Two core audience characteristics—above-average disposable income and the responsibility for managing day-to-day household spending—make this group a desirable advertiser target. Also, some advertisers spend money on AC stations simply because they like the format themselves. In sum, the AC format is one of the most effective in attracting female listeners.

AC outlets emphasize current and not-so-current (all the way back to the 1970s at some AC stations) pop standards, sans raucous or harsh beats. In other words, there's no hard rock, although some AC stations could be described as soft rockers. Nonetheless, the majority of stations mix in enough ballads and easy listening sounds to justify their title. The main thrust of this format's programming is the music. Programming consultant Alan Burns has studied the relationship between females and radio listening. One of the more telling pieces of information to appear in his study *Here She Comes—Insights Into Women, Radio, and New Media* underscores the importance of music to adult females. Data revealed that, for two of every three listeners surveyed, music is the primary reason for tuning in. Despite the popularity and perceived importance of the morning show to a station's success, only one in four survey respondents cited it as the principal reason for listening. More music can be aired whenever the chatter

## AMERICA'S TOP FORMATS IN 2016

RANKED BY SHARE OF TOTAL LISTENING (%)

INCLUDING THE MOST HEARD SONG IN 2016
AS CAPTURED BY NIELSEN BDSRADIO

**13.6** COUNTRY*
'SOMEWHERE ON A BEACH' BY DIERKS BENTLY

**11.1** NEWS/TALK**

**7.9** POP CONTEMPORARY HIT RADIO (CHR)
'DONT LET ME DOWN' BY CHAINSMOKERS
FEAT. DAYA

**7.8** ADULT CONTEMPORARY (AC)***
'HELLO' BY ADELE

**6.0** CLASSIC ROCK
'SWEET EMOTION' BY AEROSMITH

**5.9** CLASSIC HITS
'DON'T STOP BELIEVIN'' BY JOURNEY

**5.5** HOT ADULT CONTEMPORARY (AC)
'CAN'T STOP THE FEELING!' BY JUSTIN TIMBERLAKE

**4.2** URBAN ADULT CONTEMPORARY (AC)
'LAKE BY THE MOON' BY MAXWELL

**3.7** CONTEMPORARY CHRISTIAN
'TRUST IN YOU' BY LAUREN DAIGLE

**3.6** ALL SPORTS

**3.6** URBAN CONTEMPORARY
'NEEDED ME' BY RIHANNA

**2.7** RHYTHMIC CONTEMPORARY HIT RADIO (CHR)
'ONE DANCE' BY DRAKE FEAT. WIZKID & KYLA

**2.6** MEXICAN REGIONAL
'SOLO CON VERTE' BY BANDA SINALOENSE

**2.0** ACTIVE ROCK

**2.0** ALTERNATIVE
'FIRST' BY COLD WAR KIDS

**1.9** ADULT HITS + '80S HITS
'DON'T YOU (FORGET ABOUT ME)' BY SIMPLE MINDS

**1.8** ALBUM ORIENTED ROCK (AOR) + MAINSTREAM ROCK
'THE SOUND OF SILENCE' BY DISTURBED

**1.5** CLASSICAL

**1.4** SPANISH CONTEMPORARY + SPANISH HOT AC
'DUELE EL CORAZON' BY ENRIQUE IGLESIAS FEAT. WISIN

**1.4** ALL NEWS

Source: Nielsen National Regional Database, Spring 2016, M-SU 6AM-MID,
all listeners 12+, AQH Share
*Country = Country + New Country
**News/Talk = News/Talk/Information + Talk/Personality
***Adult Contemporary = Adult Contemporary + Soft Adult Contemporary
Nielsen BDSradio

**FIGURE 3.1**
America's top formats, ranked by share of total listening
Source: Courtesy of Nielsen Audio

is deemphasized. Songs are commonly presented in uninterrupted sweeps or blocks, perhaps 10–12 minutes in duration, followed by a brief recap of artists and titles. Despite the importance of music to the success of the format high-profile morning talent or teams remains a contributor to station popularity at certain AC stations. Commercials generally are clustered at predetermined times, and midday and evening deejay talk is minimal and is often limited to brief informational announcements. News and sports are secondary to the music. In recent years, ACs have spawned a host of format permutations, such as adult hits and adult standards. In the late 2000s, according to Arbitron, the AC subgenre showing the most growth was urban AC.

## Adult Hits/Classic Hits

Programmers seized the opportunity to meld aspects of traditional classic hits, pop, and alternative radio formats, widening the depth of the playlist to create what is popularly known as the adult hits or classic hits format. An esoteric format derivative, known variously as "Jack," "Bob," "Dave," and other names, predominantly of the male gender, evolved as one of the more successful programming approach variants. "Jack" and its masculine siblings represent attempts at humanizing a radio station, imbuing it with personality in efforts to evoke and grow listener affinity. Influenced by user experience with the iPod, and its ability to shuffle the playback of users' massive song collections in creating a randomized playback sequence, "Jack," "Bob," and "Dave" programmers thumbed their noses at radio's tightly controlled playlist approach, on occasion venturing as far back as the 1960s for music selections.

By tapping into the mindset of listeners who had grown tired of the predictability and repetition of the music presentation, "Jack" outlets have proven to be particularly successful in attracting the attention of males and females aged 35 to 44. A commonly heard positioning catchphrase, expressed in slightly different versions by stations in their on-air imaging (i.e., the airing of creative audio elements that establish and promote station personality), alludes to this approach. Buffalo's 92.9 "Jack FM," Baltimore's 102.7 "Jack fm," and Sacramento's 93.7 "Jack fm," among others, proclaim that music variety is achieved by "Playing what we want." In Nashville, 96.3 "Jack fm" asserts: "We play what we want." Despite variations in the phrasing, the approach remains the same. Classic hits popularity waned in the early 2000s but, according to industry observer and columnist Sean Ross, the format is resilient and relevant.

**FIGURE 3.2**

In the mid-2000s, radio programmers conceived a format for emulating the diversity of song choices available on an iPod

Source: Courtesy of Jack FM 105.9

## Contemporary Hit Radio

Contemporary hit radio (CHR) is the format successor to the Top 40 stations popularized during rock 'n' roll's infancy in the 1950s. Stations play only those recordings that are currently the fastest selling and most active on social media. CHR's narrow playlists are designed to draw teens and young adults. The heart of this format's demographic is 12- to 18-year-olds, although by the mid-1980s it had broadened its core audience. CHR is subject to fragmentation, the result of programmers' efforts to attract specific demographic targets. The core format takes a mainstream approach to music, focusing primarily on pop and dance tunes. Rhythmic CHR embraces R&B and hip-hop, while adult CHR's library draws from current and older chart classics.

Like AC, it too has experienced fluctuations in popularity over the decades. The broad swath of musical styles prevalent in the '90s divided listener interests and loyalties. The outcome? A number of stations abandoned the format. At one point only a couple of hundred CHR stations remained. The 1990s was a particularly troublesome decade in this regard: the sale of tangible music products (45-rpm records, cassette and CD singles) was fading and downloadable digital song files had yet to materialize. Over time, interest in the format revived and by 2010 the format resurged in popularity following the expanded implementation of Arbitron's (now Nielsen Audio's) Portable People Meter (PPM) measurement.

The format is characterized by its swift and often unrelenting pace. Silence, known as "dead air," is the enemy. The idea is to keep the sound hot and tight to keep the kids from station hopping, which is no small task in markets where two or more hit-oriented stations compete for listeners. CHR deejays have undergone several shifts in status since the inception of the chart music format in the 1950s. Initially, pop deejay personalities played an integral role in the air sound. However, in the mid-1960s, the format underwent a major change when deejay presence was significantly minimized. Programmer Bill Drake renovated the top 40 sound, tightening the deejay talk and the number of commercials in order to improve the song flow. Despite criticism that the new sound was too mechanical, Drake's technique succeeded at strengthening the format's hold on the listening audience.

In the middle and late 1970s, the deejay's role on hit stations began to regain its former prominence. The format underwent further renovation in the 1980s (initiated by legendary consultant Mike Joseph) that resulted in a narrowing of the playlist and a decrease in deejay presence. Super or hot hit (synonymous terms for the format) stations were among the most popular in the country and could be found either near or at the top of the rating charts in their markets.

Mainstream CHR has trended toward a less frenetic, more mature sound. In undergoing an image adjustment, programmers are keying in on improving overall flow of format elements. The continued preening of the playlist and the inclusion of what analyst Sean Ross terms "adult-friendly" music will keep the format viable, say the experts. In the top 40 '60s and '70s many stations enlarged listenership

## STATION FORMAT COUNT, MAY 2016

| Format | Stations | Format | Stations |
|---|---|---|---|
| Active rock | 165 | Modern adult contemporary | 16 |
| Adult contemporary | 587 | New country | 128 |
| Adult hits | 167 | News/talk/information | 1,315 |
| Adult standards/middle of the road | 129 | Nostalgia | 23 |
| Album adult alternative | 154 | Oldies | 365 |
| Album-oriented rock | 66 | Other | 36 |
| All-news | 21 | Pop contemporary hit radio | 464 |
| All-sports | 582 | Religious | 722 |
| Alternative | 163 | Rhythmic | 192 |
| Christian adult contemporary | 52 | Smooth adult contemporary | 5 |
| Classic country | 281 | Soft adult contemporary | 75 |
| Classical | 204 | Southern gospel | 116 |
| Comedy | 7 | Spanish | 371 |
| Country | 1882 | Talk/personality | 131 |
| Easy listening | 22 | Urban adult contemporary | 162 |
| Educational | 52 | Urban contemporary | 144 |
| Gospel | 296 | Urban oldies | 29 |
| Hot adult contemporary | 469 | Variety | 409 |
| Jazz | 60 | World ethnic | 46 |
| Mainstream rock | 73 | | |

**FIGURE 3.3**

Format counts, as reported by Nielsen Audio

Source: Courtesy of Nielsen Audio

by connecting not only to a primary audience of teens but secondary audiences of parents who tuned in out of curiosity about their children's musical tastes as well as adults who used radio as a means of reclaiming and preserving the feelings of their youth.

News is of secondary importance on CHR stations. In fact, many program directors (PDs) consider news programming to be a tune-out factor. "Kids don't like news," they claim. However, despite the industry deregulation that eased the requirements for broadcasting nonentertainment programming, most retain at least a modicum of news out of a sense of obligation. CHR stations remain very promotion-minded and contest-oriented.

Multiyear growth patterns in ratings and share of audience are notable. In its most recently published findings, Nielsen Audio identifies pop (mainstream) CHR as the top format for radio listeners aged six years and older—a feat the format has achieved for three years running. Slightly more than 600 stations (nearly all of them are FM) call themselves CHR, according to the industry newsletter *Inside Radio*. Many of these stations prefer the labels mainstream CHR or pop CHR. Format variants include rhythmic CHR, dance CHR, and adult CHR.

## Country

The country format has been adopted by more stations than any other and has become one of the leaders in the ratings race. Its appeal is exceptionally broad. An indication of country music's popularity is the fact that there many more full-time country stations today than in its nascent years. The estimated station count now totals more than 2,100 country, new country, and classic country AM and FM broadcasters. This format is far more prevalent in the South and Midwest, and it is not uncommon for stations in certain markets to enjoy double-digit ratings successes. Although most medium and large markets have country stations, country in the top five major markets appears on the lists of the top 10-rated stations in just two cities, Chicago and Dallas/Ft. Worth. Owing to the diversity of approaches within the format—for example, classic, Cajun, bluegrass, traditional, and so on—the country format attracts a broad age group, appealing to young and old adults alike. Listening percentages peak with persons between 45 and 54 and the demographic skews slightly to females. Fans of the format are more likely to listen to the radio at work than are listeners to other formats.

Two related and encouraging trends for proponents of the format involve younger listeners. The derivative "new country" offshoot format continues to pull in strong ratings numbers, helping to propel the genre to the second-highest rated format nationally for teens. No doubt in response to immensely popular younger artists such as Maren Morris and Kelsea Ballerini, stations are capitalizing on the promotional opportunities that young artists present, staging what former Country Radio Broadcasters president Paul Allen termed "'high school spirit'-type contests to target the next generation of listeners."

Country radio has always been particularly popular among blue-collar workers. However, the Country Music Association and the Organization of Country Radio Broadcasters report that the country music format is drawing a more upscale, better-educated audience today than it did in the past. In the 2010s, as many FM as AM stations are programming the country sound, which was not the case just a few years before. Until the 1980s, country was predominantly an AM offering. Depending on the approach they employ, country outlets may emphasize or deemphasize air personalities, include news and public affairs features, or confine their programming almost exclusively to music.

Some programming experts point to the mid-1990s as the greatest period for the country format, but its long-term history reflects periods of growth and retrenchment dating to the 1950s. The format's see-saw popularity swung from #1 in the years 2011 and 2015 but slipped to the fourth position in 2016, a downward turn possibly resulting from the resurgent popularity of the news/talk format in the hotly contested 2016 election year. Another characteristic of the format that has risen and waned over the years is its reliance on "crossovers"—songs recorded by artists who appeal to two different audiences. The practice of playing crossover hits from the Top40/CHR format is once again in programming vogue at country stations due in part to the universal appeal and popularity of acoustic pop artists.

## Soft Adult/Easy Listening/Smooth Jazz

Instrumentals and soft vocals of established songs are a mainstay at soft adult/easy listening stations, which also share a penchant for lush orchestrations featuring plenty of string orchestrations. Talk is deemphasized, and news presentation is limited to morning drive time. These stations boast a devoted audience of typically older listeners.

Efforts to draw younger persons into the easy listening fold have been moderately successful, but most of the format's primary adherents are over 50 years old. Music syndicators provide satellite-delivered, preproduced programming to approximately half of the nation's easy listening/soft adult stations. Easy listening lost some ground in the 1990s and 2000s to AC and other adult-appeal formats such as album adult alternative and new age. A more recent format variant, smooth jazz, fuses the sounds of jazz, pop, rock, and other music genres in a low-key presentation that features minimal announcer presence and interruption. Following a decade of popularity, the format declined in the mid-2000s. One reason for this, it appears, is that its core audience purchased few artist CDs or downloads. Devoted listeners were satisfied instead by whatever selections their stations offered and weren't especially interested in product ownership.

Soft adult, lite and easy, smooth jazz, adult standards, and urban AC have become replacement nomenclatures for easy listening, which, like the related moniker Beautiful Music, also began to assume a geriatric connotation.

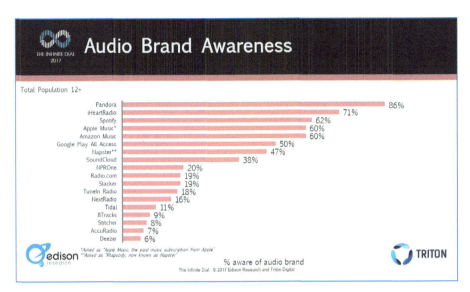

**FIGURE 3.4**
Audio Brand Awareness. From *The Infinite Dial 2017* study

Source: Courtesy of Edison Research and Triton Digital

## Classic, Active, Modern, and Alternative Rock

The birth of the album-oriented rock (AOR) format in the late 1960s (also called underground and progressive) was the result of a basic disdain by certain listeners for the highly formulaic top 40 sound that prevailed at the time. In the summer of 1966, WOR-FM, New York, introduced progressive radio, the forerunner of AOR. As an alternative to the super-hyped, ultra-commercial sound of hit song stations, WOR-FM programmed an unorthodox combination of nonchart rock, blues, folk, and jazz. In the 1970s, the format concentrated its attention almost exclusively on album rock, while becoming less freeform and more formulaic and systematic in its programming approach.

Today, AOR is often simply called rock, or more specifically modern rock or classic rock. Although it continues to do well in garnering the 18- to 34-year-old male demographic, this format has always done poorly in winning female listeners, especially when it emphasizes a heavy or hard rock playlist. This has proven to be a sore spot with certain advertisers. In the 1980s, the format lost its prominence owing, in part, to the meteoric rebirth of hit radio. However, as the decade came to an end, AOR had regained a chunk of its numbers, and in the 1990s it renamed itself modern rock. Active rock stations now adhere more faithfully to the AOR approach; as analyst Sean Ross noted, the two formats progressed lockstep in the 2000s until modern rock diverged and proponents advocated its distinction from the alt-rock enthusiasts. Ross observed in mid-2016 that both formats are enjoying a healthy existence and their outlook for success is positive. In combination they accounted for slightly more than 10% of the radio audience that year.

Generally, rock stations broadcast their music in sweeps, segueing at least two or three songs. A large song library is typical, in which 300–700 cuts may be active. Depending on the outlet, the deejay may or may not have "personality" status. In fact, the more music/less talk approach particularly common at easy listening stations is emulated by many album rockers. Consequently, news plays a very minor part in the station's programming efforts. Active rock stations are very lifestyle-oriented and invest great time and energy developing promotions relevant to the interests and attitudes of their listeners. The alternative rock format tries for distinctiveness in contrast to the other rock radio approaches. Creating this alternative sound is a challenge, says Stephanie Hindley, PD of Buzz 99.9:

> The Alternative format is a great challenge for programmers. Think of the music you liked and the things you did when you were 18. Now think of the music you liked (or will like) and the things you did (or will do) at age 34. Despite the vast differences in taste in the 18–34 demographic, we need to play music that will appeal to as many people as possible within this diverse group.

In comparison with other rock variants, alternative listeners typically are better educated (two out of three have attended a university or have earned a degree). Additionally, the format attracts the highest percentage of Hispanic and black listeners within the "rock" family of formats. As Hindley explains,

It's a constant balancing act. We have to play a lot of new music without sounding too unfamiliar. We have to be cool and hip without sounding exclusive. We have to be edgy without being offensive. Be smart without sounding condescending. Young and upbeat without sounding immature. As long as those balances are maintained on a daily basis, we will continue to have success in this format.

## Classic/Oldies/Nostalgia

These three related formats are differentiated by song choices that all enjoyed popularity decades ago. A decade ago the nostalgia station was characterized by a playlist organized around tunes popular as far back as the 1940s and 1950s, while the oldies outlet directed its focus on playing the pop hits of the late 1950s and 1960s. Today, nostalgia-formatted stations typically define their target decades as the '50s and '60s, while the oldies outlets are more attuned to the music of the 1970s and 1980s. A typical oldies quarter-hour might consist of songs by Elvis Presley, the Beatles, Fleetwood Mac, Elton John, and the Ronettes. In contrast, a nostalgia quarter-hour might consist of tunes from the pre-rock era, performed by adult-appeal artists such as Frankie Laine, Les Baxter, the Mills Brothers, Tommy Dorsey, and popular ballad singers of the mid-1900s.

"Music of your life" (MOYL), a vocal-intensive, 24-hour nostalgia presentation created in the 1970s by pop music composer and performer Al Ham, continues to be heard nationwide on a network of approximately 50 stations, freshening its playlist to include softer pop hits of the 1960s and 1970s. Stations airing nostalgia programming more likely acquire it from syndicators such as MOYL rather than attempting to program it in-house. Because much of the music predates stereo recording techniques, AM outlets are most apt to carry the nostalgia sound. Music is invariably presented in sweeps, and, for the most part, deejays maintain a low profile.

The oldies format was first introduced in the 1960s by programmers Bill Drake and Chuck Blore. Although nostalgia's audience tends to be over the age of 60, the audience for oldies skews somewhat younger. One-third of oldies listeners grew up in the turbulent, rebellious 1960s and, unsurprisingly, the music of this decade constitutes the core of the song library. Unlike nostalgia, most oldies outlets originate their own programming. In contrast with its vintage-music cousin, the oldies format features greater deejay presence. Music is rarely broadcast in sweeps, and commercials, rather than being clustered, are inserted in a random fashion between songs.

The format descriptor "oldies" is being abandoned in favor of the label "classic hits." More pop- than rock-oriented, this 1960s- to1980s-focused format has exhibited constant ratings growth in the 2000s on more than 500 outlets. Classic hits stations are favored almost equally by male and female listeners, and particularly those aged 45 to 64. Classic rock emphasizes the music of the iconic rock artists and attracts a predominantly (70%) male audience. By concentrating on tunes essentially featured by former AOR stations over the past three decades, the harder-edged classic rock format contrasts with the classic hits formula, which fills the gap between oldies and CHR outlets with playlists that draw from 1970s, 1980s, and 1990s top 40 charts.

## Urban Contemporary

Considered the "melting pot" format, urban contemporary (UC) attracts more than 31 million African-American listeners each week, a statistic that Nielsen Audio says translates to 92% of the AA population—with a near-equal mix of males and females—that radio reaches each week. Hispanic listeners, who constitute the largest minority in the nation, and whites are also in the mix; together they account for one in five audience members. As the term suggests, stations employing this format are usually located in metropolitan areas with large, heterogeneous populations. Interestingly, however, the format currently exhibits higher than national average audience shares across the deep South, which include several urban markets (although Atlanta is the only one that is considered to be a "major market"). A descendant

FIGURE 3.5
More than 80% of black Americans use radio each week
Source: Courtesy of Nielsen Audio

of the heritage black program format, UC was born in the early 1980s, the offspring of the short-lived disco format, which burst onto the scene in 1978. At its inception, the disco craze brought new listeners to the black stations, which shortly saw their fortunes change when all-disco stations began to surface. Many black outlets witnessed an exodus of their younger listeners to the disco stations. This prompted a number of black stations to abandon their more traditional playlists, which consisted of rhythm and blues, gospel, and soul tunes, for exclusively disco music. When disco perished in the early 1980s, the UC format emerged. Today, progressive black stations, such as WBLS-FM, New York, combine dance music with soulful rock and contemporary jazz, and many have transcended the color barrier by including certain white artists on their playlists. In fact, many black stations employ white air personnel in efforts to broaden their demographic base.

UC is characterized by its upbeat, danceable sound and deejays that are hip, friendly, and energetic. Stations stress danceable tunes and their playlists generally are anything but narrow. However, a particular sound may be given preference over another, depending on the demographic composition of the population in the area that the station serves. For example, UC outlets may play greater amounts of music with a Latin or rhythm and blues flavor, whereas others may air larger proportions of light jazz, reggae, new rock, or hip-hop. Some AM stations around the country have adopted the UC format; however, it is more likely to be found on the FM side, where it has taken numerous stations to the forefront of their market's ratings.

The UC influence on the formats of traditional black stations is evidenced by the swell in popularity of the urban adult contemporary (urban AC) variant and in the age alignment of audiences for the two formats. Urban AC listeners are predominantly middle-aged (35–54) African Americans who tend to stay tuned to stations for longer periods than do similarly aged listeners to other formats. This information correlates with the finding that in 2016 urban AC was the top-rated format among blacks aged 12+. UC has had an impact on urban AC stations, which have experienced erosion in their youth numbers. More than a third of listeners to the nation's 270 UC stations are aged 23 and younger and a substantial amount of listening occurs in the after-school hours. Many UC stations have countered by broadening their playlists to include artists who have not traditionally been programmed. Because of the format's high-intensity, fast-paced presentation, UC outlets can give a Top 40 impression. In contrast, they commonly segue songs or present music in sweeps and give airplay to lengthy cuts that are sometimes six to eight minutes long. Although top 40 or CHR stations seldom program cuts lasting more than four minutes, UC outlets find long cuts or remixes compatible with their programming approach. Remember, UCs are very dance-oriented. Newscasts play a minor role in this format, which caters to a target audience aged 18–34. Contests and promotions are important program elements.

A portion of urban outlets have drawn from the more mainstream CHR playlist in an attempt to expand their listener base. Several large-market stations transitioned from rhythmic CHR to hip-hop since the previous edition of this book was published. Further evidence of format splintering can be found in the recent emergence of classic hip-hop, a descriptor that consultant Harry Lyles suggests could be more fittingly termed "Old School Hip Hop." Programmer Mike McVay notes a trend that classic hip-hop stations start strong but begin to experience ratings erosion a year or so later. Meanwhile, the old-line, heritage R&B and gospel stations still exist and can be found mostly on AM stations in the South.

**Essentials**

THE AMERICAN SOCIETY OF COMPOSERS, AUTHORS AND PUBLISHERS

ASCAP is ▷

◁ a performing-rights organization whose function is to protect the rights of our members by licensing and collecting royalties for the public performance of their copyrighted musical works.

◁ the only U.S. society created and controlled by songwriters and publishers.

◁ the only U.S. society that gives writers and publishers a voice. ASCAP conducts open membership meetings, issues financial reports to its members, has writer and publisher member advisory committees.

◁ the only U.S. society that gives writers and publishers a vote. ASCAP is governed by an experienced Board of Directors composed of knowledgeable songwriters, composers and music publishers, each of whom is elected by the membership.

◁ the largest performing-rights society in the world in terms of license-fee collections and writer and publisher performance-royalty payments. 1995 income: more than $435 million.

◁ the largest performing-rights society in the world in terms of constituency. ASCAP has more than 75,000 U.S. writer and publisher members. Additionally, it represents more than 200,000 foreign-society writers and publishers.

◁ the industry leader since 1914 in negotiating license fees with the users of music.

◁ one of the most effective protectors of the rights of creators and music publishers. ASCAP lobbies in Congress and litigates in the courts, if necessary, on behalf of its constituents.

◁ the only society where writers and publishers sign identical contracts, with the right to resign every year of the contract.

◁ the only U.S. society with specific written rules covering all types of performances on all types of media, with all royalties distributed solely on that basis.

◁ the only U.S. society where payment changes have to be approved by the Board of Directors, the Department of Justice and in some cases by a U.S. Federal Court after an open court hearing. No changes are made without notice to the membership, and rates are not subject to arbitrary change at any time, as they are at other performing-rights organizations.

◁ the only U.S. society where your royalties are determined objectively over their entire copyright life and not by discretionary voluntary payments, short-term special deals or management discretion.

## Classical

Approximately 200 stations—the overwhelming majority of which are licensed as noncommercial outlets—program classical music. For the few remaining commercial stations, a loyal audience following enables owners to generate a modest to good income. Over the years, profits have remained relatively minute in comparison to other formats. However, member stations of the Concert Music Broadcasters Association reported ad revenue increases of up to 40% in the 1980s and 1990s with continued growth, albeit modest, in the 2000s. Owing to its upscale audience, blue-chip accounts find the format an effective buy. This is first and foremost an FM format insofar as the nature of the program content necessitates delivery via a high-fidelity medium.

In many markets, the performance of commercial classical stations has been affected by public radio outlets that program classical music. Because commercial classical stations must break to air the sponsor messages that keep them operating, they must adjust their playlists accordingly. This may mean shorter cuts of music during particular dayparts—in other

**FIGURE 3.6**

Radio stations pay an annual fee to music licensing services such as ASCAP, BMI, and SESAC

Source: Courtesy of ASCAP

words, less music. The noncommercial classical outlet is relatively free of such constraints and thus benefits as a result. A case in point is WCRB-FM in Boston, the city's only full-time classical station. Although it was attracting most of the area's classical listeners throughout the afternoon and evening hours, it lost many patrons to public radio WGBH's classical segments with fewer programming interruptions. In 2010 WGBH purchased WCRB-FM, relegating its classical music programming to the former commercially operated station and repositioning its programming approach to news and information.

Classical stations target the 25- to 49-year-old, higher-income, college-educated listener. News is typically presented at 60- to 90-minute intervals and generally runs from five to 10 minutes. The format is characterized by a conservative, straightforward air sound. Sensationalism and hype are avoided, and on-air contests and promotions are as rare as announcer chatter.

## Religious/Christian

Live broadcasts of religious programs began while the medium was still in its experimental stage. In 1919, the U.S. Army Signal Corps aired a service from a chapel in Washington, D.C. Not long after that, KFSG in Los Angeles and WMBI in Chicago began to devote themselves to religious programming. Soon dozens of other radio outlets were broadcasting the message of God.

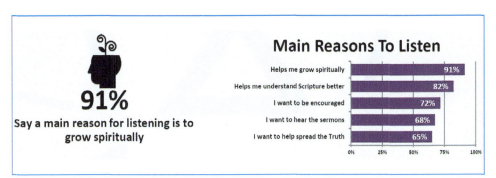

**FIGURES 3.7A AND 3.7B**
The executive summary for Christian radio stations airing both music and several hours of talk programs comes from data collected in Spring 2016, part of the Finney Media *Why Listen* national survey of Christian radio station listeners in the U.S. and Canada. Additional detail at finneymedia.com under the WHY LISTEN tab

Source: Courtesy of Finney Media

Religious broadcasters typically follow one of two programming approaches. One includes music as part of its presentation, and the other does not. Contemporary Christian-formatted stations feature music oriented toward a Christian or life-affirming perspective. Nielsen Audio estimated in 2016 that almost 900 stations representing all geographic areas attracted listeners across a wide range of ages. The typical listener is almost twice as likely to be female than male and of above-average education. Finney Media, a program consultancy specializing in service to Christian-formatted stations, says listeners to the format have two clear expectations. According to results of its 2016 *Why Listen?* survey, "77% come to Christian radio to be encouraged" and "a full 79% said that a main reason they listen is for worshipful Christian music."

A notable presence to emerge in recent years is K-Love, the contemporary Christian music service that operates a nationwide network of 400-plus FM full-power and translator stations. Operated by the California-based nonprofit Educational Media Foundation, K-Love offers a music-focused presentation with minimal interruption.

What innovation could propel the format to its next level? Consultant and talent coach Tracy Johnson told *Inside Radio*:

> Well-programmed contemporary Christian stations have the most loyal fan base I've ever seen. With the right moves, the format could greatly expand its appeal beyond the religious base, especially in a society where consumers are so stressed. How about adding more reasons to listen, like high-profile air talent?

Faith-affirming gospel stations feature music that has its origins in the black church; Southern gospel-formatted stations are mainstays of the South and Midwest; their music appeals to white listeners. Gospel programming can be heard mostly on AM stations. In all instances, music-intensive stations include the scheduling of blocks of religious features and programs. Nonmusic religious outlets concentrate on inspirational features and complementary talk and informational shows.

## Hispanic

Hispanic or Spanish-language stations constitute another large ethnic format, reaching 40 million persons weekly, an impressive 97% of Hispanic listeners. KCOR-AM, San Antonio, became the first All-Spanish station in 1947, just a matter of months after WDIA-AM in Memphis put the black format on the air. Cities with large Latin populations are able to support the format, and in some metropolitan areas with vast numbers of Spanish-speaking residents—such as New York, Los Angeles, and Miami—several radio outlets are devoted exclusively to Hispanic programming. Nielsen Audio predecessor Arbitron reported in 2008:

**FIGURE 3.8**

Hispanic listenership: Radio's fastest-growing audience. Ranking of sources listeners use to keep up to date with music

Source: Courtesy of Nielsen Audio

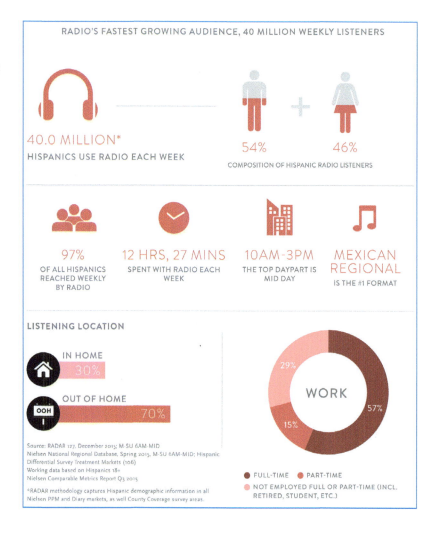

RADIO'S FASTEST GROWING AUDIENCE, 40 MILLION WEEKLY LISTENERS

**40.0 MILLION\***
HISPANICS USE RADIO EACH WEEK

54%    46%
COMPOSITION OF HISPANIC RADIO LISTENERS

**97%**
OF ALL HISPANICS REACHED WEEKLY BY RADIO

**12 HRS, 27 MINS**
SPENT WITH RADIO EACH WEEK

**10AM-3PM**
THE TOP DAYPART IS MID DAY

**MEXICAN REGIONAL**
IS THE #1 FORMAT

LISTENING LOCATION

IN HOME
30%

OUT OF HOME
70%

WORK
29%   57%   15%

Source: RADAR 127, December 2015; M-SU 6AM-MID
Nielsen National Regional Database, Spring 2015, M-SU 6AM-MID; Hispanic Differential Survey Treatment Markets (106)
Working data based on Hispanics 18+
Nielsen Comparable Metrics Report Q3 2015

\*RADAR methodology captures Hispanic demographic information in all Nielsen PPM and Diary markets, as well County Coverage survey areas.

● FULL-TIME   ● PART-TIME
● NOT EMPLOYED FULL OR PART-TIME (INCL. RETIRED, STUDENT, ETC.)

As their population continued to surge in the United States, Hispanics increased the percentage of their representation in 15 of the 20 non-Spanish language formats in our report, averaging 1.1% more in audience composition than in spring 2006. The only formats where Hispanics made up a smaller proportion of a format's listenership were UC, Oldies, Alternative and Active Rock.

Programming approaches within the format are not unlike those prevalent at Anglo stations. That is to say, Spanish-language radio stations also modify their sound to draw a specific demographic. For example, many offer contemporary music for younger listeners and more traditional music for older listeners. Talk-intensive formats parallel those popular with English-language stations and the approaches are similarly segregated by Nielsen. Thus, advertisers are able to differentiate and effectively target listeners who prefer Spanish news/talk from other Spanish-language formats including sports, religious, and variety.

Houston-based consultant Ed Shane observed in 2013 that Hispanic radio is diverse and vibrant, and reflected an impressive multiplicity of programming styles and approaches. He cited Houston as an example of market diversity, where two brands of tejano, one of exitos (hits), a lot of ranchera, and a couple of talk stations vie for listeners. Miami, by way of contrast, is a top market in which tropical is the dominant Hispanic, and is programmed on two outlets. Yet tropical is absent from the roster of formats found in Houston, where regional Mexican and Spanish contemporary occupy places within the top 10 of 12+ listeners.

Spanish media experts predicted that there would be a significant increase in the number of Hispanic stations through the 2000s, and they were right. Much of this growth occurred on the AM band but later spread rapidly on FM. Leading the station count is the Mexican regional format, found on close to 400 stations. The format ties urban contemporary (UC) for tenth place of Nielsen Audio's 2016 ranking of top formats, and is heard by an estimated one in five Hispanics. In terms of listenership, males slightly outnumber females.

## Ethnic

Hundreds of other radio stations countrywide apportion a significant piece of their schedules (more than 20 hours weekly) to foreign-language programs in Portuguese, German, Polish, Greek, Japanese, and so on. Nielsen Audio characterizes this program approach "world ethnic." Around 30 stations broadcast exclusively to American Indians and Eskimos and are licensed to Native Americans. Today, these stations are being fed programming from the AIROS Radio Network, and other indigenous media groups predict dozens more Indian-operated stations to be broadcasting by the end of the next decade. Meanwhile, the number of stations broadcasting to Asians and other nationalities is rising.

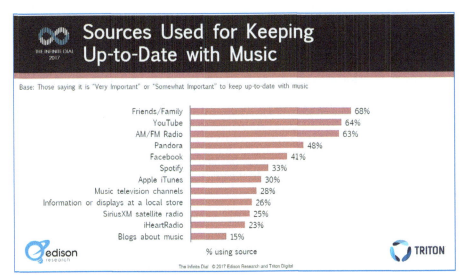

**FIGURE 3.9**

Ranking of sources listeners use to keep up to date with music

Source: Courtesy of *The Infinite Dial 2017* from Edison Research and Triton Digital

### Sources Used for Keeping Up-to-Date with Music

Base: Those saying it is "Very Important" or "Somewhat Important" to keep up-to-date with music

| Source | % using source |
| --- | --- |
| Friends/Family | 68% |
| YouTube | 64% |
| AM/FM Radio | 63% |
| Pandora | 48% |
| Facebook | 41% |
| Spotify | 33% |
| Apple iTunes | 30% |
| Music television channels | 28% |
| Information or displays at a local store | 26% |
| SiriusXM satellite radio | 25% |
| iHeartRadio | 23% |
| Blogs about music | 15% |

The Infinite Dial © 2017 Edison Research and Triton Digital

## Full Service

The full service (FS) format (also called variety, general appeal, diversified, etc.) attempts to provide its mostly middle-aged listeners a mix of all programming genres—news, sports, and information features blended with a selection of adult-oriented, pop music standards. This something-for-everyone approach initially straddled the "middle of the road" musically and subsequently became known as MOR. Over time programmers have strengthened the format's public service aspect with the inclusion of additional information programming. It is really one-stop shopping for listeners who would like a little bit of everything. Today, this type of station exists mostly in small markets where stations attempt to be good-citizen radio for everyone, although listeners tend be 40 years and above in age. It has been called the *bridge* format because of its "all things to all people" programming approach. It has lost much of its large-market appeal and effectiveness due to the diversification and rise in popularity of specialized formats. In some major markets, the format continues to do well in the ratings mainly because of strong on-air personalities. But this is not the format that it once was.

**FIGURE 3.10**

A striking visual identity for Niijii Radio

Source: Courtesy of KKWE

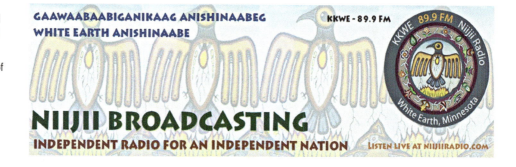

FS is the home of the on-air personality. Perhaps no other format gives its air personnel as much latitude and freedom. This is not to suggest that FS announcers may do as they please. They, like any other announcer, must abide by format and programming policy, but FS personalities often serve as the cornerstone of their station's air product. Some of the best-known deejays in the country have come from the FS (MOR) milieu. It would then follow that the music is rarely, if ever, presented in sweeps or even segued. Deejay patter occurs between each cut of music, and announcements are inserted in the same way. News and sports play another vital function at these stations. During drive periods, FS often presents lengthened blocks of news, replete with frequent traffic reports, weather updates, and the latest sports information. Many FS outlets are affiliated with professional and collegiate athletic teams. With few exceptions, FS is an AM format. Although it has endured ratings slippage in recent years, it will likely continue to bridge whatever gaps may exist in a highly specialized radio marketplace.

## Niche and HD2 Formats

When it comes to format prognostication, the term *unpredictable* takes on a whole new meaning. Indeed, there will be a rash of successful niche formats in the coming years due to the ever-increasing fragmentation of the radio audience, but exactly what they will be is anyone's guess. A common thread that weaves throughout the discussion is the almost surety that format experimentation is more active on the AM, satellite, and HD bands and less so on FM. For example, several years ago Radio Disney largely withdrew from radio station ownership, opting instead to deliver its programming via HD. Xperi, the parent of HD Radio, disseminates Radio Disney over a de facto network it created, utilizing the HD2 bands of medium- and large-market stations owned by CBS, Beasley, and Entercom.

New niche or splinter formats emerge frequently—bluegrass, Christian talk and K-Mozart classical are good examples—in an industry always on the lookout for the next big thing and competing with a myriad of other listening options. In terms of future format innovations, the rollout of HD2 and HD3 side channels (see the discussion of HD Radio in Chapter 9) has contributed somewhat to the development of new niche formats. Whether formats such as Russian American or traditional Christian

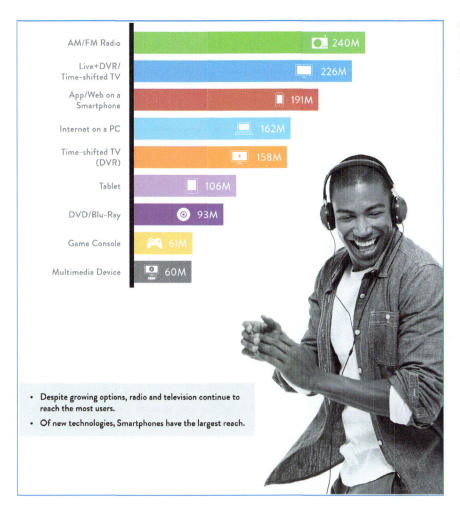

**FIGURE 3.11**
Nielsen estimates more adults use radio each month than any other media form

Source: Courtesy of Nielsen Audio

hymns could become successful as primary channel services is debatable, but a recent perusal of the HD Radio Station Directory reveals that these formats have found a home on HD2 side channels. Experts remain divided in their opinions about the role that HD Radio plays in enlarging format diversity. Experimentation with an even wider variety of listening choices is evident with online radio, where many formats are streamed exclusively by the pureplays. A useful portal for discovering the variety of programming available from Internet-only radio stations is maintained by Grace Digital, a manufacturer of Internet radio tuners, at https://myradio.gracedigital.com.

As far as the future goes: who knows? Radio is hardly a static industry, but it is one that is subject to the whims of popular taste. When something new captures the imagination of the American public, radio responds, and often a new format is conceived.

## Public Radio

Like numerous college stations, most public radio outlets are noncommercial in operation and program in a block fashion. That is to say, few employ a primary (single) format, but instead offer a mix of program ingredients, such as news/information and entertainment features. National Public Radio (referenced nowadays as "NPR" during the network's on-air identifications), American Public Media, Public Radio International, and Public Radio Exchange, along with state public radio systems, provide a myriad of features for the hundreds of public radio facilities around the country. Topping the list of prominent music genres are classical and jazz. Public radio news broadcasts, among them NPR's *Morning Edition* and *All Things Considered* and PRI's *The Takeaway*, lead all radio in audience popularity for information focused on national and world events.

The popularity of NPR and its programming is reflected by a shift in the way that listeners access the network's content. Pew Research Center statistics indicate that for the period 2010–16 NPR's audience held relatively steady, fluctuating between 26 and 27 million weekly listeners. NPR continues to be a vanguard in the spread of podcast popularity, growing its weekly unique podcast total in 2015 to 2.5 million users—a 25% increase over the previous year.

**FIGURE 3.12**
Mike Janssen

## ON PUBLIC RADIO

### Mike Janssen

Public radio continues to be defined by the service's hallmarks for decades: in-depth news and public affairs programming, along with genres of music that commercial radio largely ignores. But with digital platforms continuing to draw an ever-growing share of listeners' time and attention, public radio stations and networks are putting more and more effort into reaching their audiences in earbuds, on smartphones and wherever the fractured media landscape is taking us next.

Despite these trends, traditional broadcast radio is far from obsolete. NPR has been touting recent gains in its radio audience, possibly bolstered in part by the intense news cycle of an election year and the ongoing aftermath of Donald Trump's move into the White House. Anchored by NPR's newsmagazines, *Morning Edition* and *All Things Considered*, the news format remains a staple of public radio. In 2015, nearly a quarter of public radio stations aired mostly news, according to an analysis by the Station Resource Group using NPR data. Meanwhile, public radio music formats such as classical, jazz and adult album alternative maintain a presence on hundreds of stations across the country.

But this relatively unchanging mix of programming on public radio's FM stations belies the creative explosion taking place off air, with a good deal of that energy focused on podcasts. With origins in the early 2000s, podcasting is hardly a new technology. But the smash success of the 2014 podcast *Serial*—itself a spinoff of public radio's *This American Life*—changed everything. The in-depth examination of the mysterious death of a Baltimore high school student riveted listeners, in turn reigniting the interest of program producers in exploring the potential of the intimate, episodic medium. Suddenly, it seemed that everyone wanted to emulate whatever it was that made *Serial*—and 2017 successor series *S-Town*—so addictive.

So far, few have cleared that bar. But NPR, American Public Media, and public radio stations have redoubled production and promotion of podcasts. Some have borrowed from *Serial*'s playbook to present localized variations of the cold-case inquiry. (One, American Public Media's *In the Dark*, won a Peabody award in 2017.) But other station-produced podcasts are content to explore various local and regional issues while enjoying the relative freedom afforded by the podcast medium—a less formal tone, variable episode length (no pesky newscasts to work around or time posts to hit), and more flexibility with advertising than FCC limitations allow for broadcast programming. That latter factor is no small consideration. NPR in particular has enjoyed strong growth in ad revenue in recent years, thanks largely to podcast sales. No wonder the network is continuing to unveil new podcasts on a regular basis— recent popular additions include *Invisibilia*, *Embedded*, and *Hidden Brain*.

Given this growing split between public radio's broadcast and digital activities, where will the medium go from here? It seems difficult to imagine a time when FM stations are no longer important to the system—they draw large audiences and still drive much of public radio's fundraising from listeners. But some observers wonder whether the advent of self-driving cars, crazy as it may seem, could be a cloud on the horizon. If your "drive" to work someday frees you to read news on your smartphone or listen to a podcast, will you still tune into your local NPR station?

These innovations stem from the realization that today's media consumers are getting news from a growing array of platforms and devices. Radio remains a popular medium on its own, but consumption on digital platforms continues to grow, particularly on portable devices such as smartphones and tablets. The emergence of a new platform demands that station and network leaders once again consider how to allocate resources to best take advantage of the opportunities presented. Managers often speak of the importance of being agile, innovative, and flexible as the system strives to remain relevant. Some stations paired with public television stations have responded by consolidating their newsrooms among all media, assigning their producers and reporters to create content for radio, TV, and online all at once. KPBS, a joint licensee in San Diego, was a trailblazer in this trend of "convergence." It has had such success that it now offers "boot camps" to other stations that seek to follow its example.

What kinds of programming are filling up all of these new platforms and broadcast schedules? NPR news programming has continued to expand its reach and popularity, while news stations that can afford the expense are developing their own midday news and talk shows to complement and extend the news offerings from NPR and its competitors, Public Radio International and American Public Media. In attempts to appeal to younger listeners and ethnically diverse audiences and keep pace with the growing diversity of the American public, stations and networks have also launched shows that aim for a fresher sound or take advantage of social and mobile media.

Public radio's traditional music formats of classical and jazz persist on many stations, while adult album alternative (also known as triple A) music has become a staple as well. But classical has lost ground on a number of stations as they have acquired or started to produce more news and talk programming. Regardless of format, for listeners seeking thoughtful, in-depth news and musical genres that get little airplay elsewhere, the lower end of the dial remains a go-to spot on FM radio and is likely to remain so for years to come.

---

**Mike Janssen** is Digital Editor for *Current*, the trade publication covering public and nonprofit media in the U.S. He is also Supervising Producer of *The Pub*, *Current*'s biweekly podcast about all things public media. Mike's writing has appeared in the *Washingtonian*, the *Washington City Paper*, the *LA Weekly* and *In These Times*, among other publications. Mike lives in Washington, D.C., where he enjoys biking, cooking, and playing his banjo.

## THE PROGRAMMER

PDs are radiophiles. They live the medium. Most admit to having been smitten by radio at an early age. "It's something that is in your blood and grows to consuming proportions," admits programmer Peter Falconi. Entercom Program Manager (PM) Brad Carson confesses to this ulterior motive: "I was always glued to (hometown station) WSMI (Litchfield, Illinois) to find out on 'snow days' if my school was cancelled or not. (I always rooted for cancellations.)" As a teen, Carson prepped for his first real job by producing "a series of 'fake' radio shows on a cassette player mixing music, announcing, and incorporating various entertaining 'impressions' of my high school teachers." What was the response? "My friends seemed to think they were hilarious," he says, "so I continued." The customary route to the programmer's job involves deejaying and participation in other on-air-related areas, such as copywriting, production, music, and news. Success largely depends on the individual and where he or she happens to be. In some instances, newcomers have gone into programming within their first year in the business. When this happens, it is most likely to occur in a small market where turnover may be high. On the other hand, it is far more common to spend years working toward this goal, even in the best of situations. "Although my father owned the station," recounts longtime PD Brian Mitchell, "I spent a long time in a series of jobs before my appointment to programmer. Along the way, I worked as station janitor, and then got into announcing, production, and eventually programming."

Experience contributes most toward the making of the station's programmer. However, individuals entering the field with hopes of becoming a PD do well to acquire as much formal training as possible. The programmer's job has become an increasingly demanding one as a result of expanding competition. "A good knowledge of research methodology, analysis, and application is crucial. Programming is both an art and a science today," observes general manager Jim Murphy. Programmer Andy Bloom concurs with Murphy, adding, "A would-be PD needs to school himself or herself in marketing research particularly. Little is done anymore that is not based on careful analysis."

*Radio Ink* publisher B. Eric Rhoads echoes this stance: "The role has changed. The PD used to be a glorified music director with some background in talent development. Today the PD must be a marketing expert." The complexity of radio marketing has increased, due in particular to the juggernaut of social media, which, along with database marketing activities, have helped elevate the PD to the role of brand manager. "Radio itself is changing," Rhoads added, "and the PD must adapt. No longer will records and deejays make the big difference. Stations are at parity in music, so better ways must be found to set stations apart." In *Radio Ink*, the industry newsmagazine he publishes, Rhoads reported that Saga Communications, a corporate operator of 90 AM and FM stations, adopts the "brand manager" title, applying it to personnel formerly known as "program directors." The charge to the brand manager: take ownership of all delivery platforms and extend your oversight of content beyond the air signal by proactively managing your online presence as well as your social media activities.

The concept of "brand management," when applied to a day in the life of programmer Brad Carson's world, means taking on multiple responsibilities:

> My normal day includes writing and producing promotional announcements and station "imaging", creating marketing plans/promotions with clients and creative partners, logistical planning for talent who are traveling around the country covering sports, deejaying, and even voice tracking a radio show in another city. In the last three years creative planning and marketing have become more important. If you don't understand the nuts and bolts of what talent do and put into the best shows, you're not going to be a strong programmer. There are some obvious "tricks of the trade" that we use to create the secret sauce just like every brand. Talent coaching and creativity are at a premium.

Cognizant of this change, schools with curricula in radio broadcasting emphasize courses in audience and marketing research, as well as other programming-related areas. An important fact for the aspiring PD to keep in mind is that more persons than ever before who enter broadcasting possess college degrees. Even though a degree is not necessarily a prerequisite for the position of PD, it is clearly regarded as an asset by upper management. Joe Cortese, syndicated air personality, contends that:

> It used to be that a college degree didn't mean so much. A PD came up through the ranks of programming, proved his ability, and was hired. Not that that doesn't still happen. It does. But more and more the new PD has a degree or, at the very least, several years of college. . . . I majored in

**FIGURE 3.13**
Program directors' cubicles inside the programming bullpen at SiriusXM offices in Washington, D.C.

Source: Courtesy of SiriusXM and Marlin Taylor

communication arts at a junior college and then transferred to a four-year school. There are many colleges offering communications courses here in the Boston area, so I'll probably take some more as a way of further preparing for the day when I'll be programming or managing a station. That's what I eventually want to do.

Cortese adds that experience in the trenches is also vital to success. His point is well taken. Work experience does head the list on which a station manager bases his or her selection for PD. Meanwhile, college training, at the very least, has become a criterion to the extent that, if an applicant does not have any, the prospective employer takes notice.

## THE PD'S DUTIES AND RESPONSIBILITIES

Where to begin this discussion poses a problem because the PD's responsibilities and duties are so numerous and wide-ranging. Tommy Castor views it this way: "I don't have a large staff, but large expectations, and so it can be very easy for me to fall into the mentality that I need to always do everything I possibly can to improve my radio station." Second in responsibility to the general manager (in station clusters, the individual station programmer reports to the director of operations, who oversees all programming for the various stations), the PD is the person responsible for everything that goes over the air. This involves working with the station manager or director of operations in establishing programming format policy and overseeing its effective execution. In addition, he or she hires, mentors, and supervises music and production personnel, plans various schedules, manages the programming budget, develops promotions (in conjunction with the promotion or marketing director, if there is such a person in this role), monitors the station and its competition, assesses research, and may even pull a daily air shift. The PD also is accountable for the presentation of news, public affairs, and sports features, although a news director is often appointed to help oversee these areas.

The PD alone does not determine a station's format. This is an upper management decision. The PD may be involved in the selection process, but, more often than not, the format has been chosen before the programmer has been hired. For example, the ownership and management of fictitious station WYYY has decided on the basis of declining revenues that the station must switch formats from country to CHR to attract a more marketable demographic. After an in-depth examination of its own market, research on the effectiveness of CHR nationally, and advice from a program consultant and national advertising rep company, the format change is deemed appropriate. Reluctantly, the station manager concludes that he must bring in a CHR specialist, which means that he must terminate the services of his present programmer, whose experience is limited to the country format. The station manager advertises the position availability in various industry trade publications and their websites, interviews several candidates, and hires the person he or she feels will take the station to the top of the ratings. When the new PD arrives, he or she is charged with the task of preparing the new format for its debut. Among other things, this may involve hiring new air talent, acquiring a new music library or updating the existing one, creating and producing promos and purchasing jingles, developing external promotions and a social media presence, and working in league with the sales, traffic, and engineering departments for maximum results.

On these points, Corinne Baldasano, Senior Vice-President of Programming and Marketing for Take On The Day LLC, observes:

> First of all, of course, you must be sure that the station you are programming fills a market void, i.e., that there is an opportunity for you to succeed in your geographic area with the format you are programming. For example, a young adult alternative Rock station may not have much chance for success in an area that is mostly populated by retirees. Once you have determined that the format fills an audience need, you need to focus on building your station. The basic ingredients are making sure your music mix is correct (if you are programming a music station) and that you've hired the on-air talent that conveys the attitude and image of the station you wish to build. At this stage, it is far more important to focus inward than outward. Many stations have failed because they've paid more attention to the competition's product than they have their own.

Once the format is implemented, the PD must work at refining and maintaining the sound. The deejay staff must be monitored and mentored to ensure the cohesiveness of the on-air product. Speaking about the importance of good mentoring, Leslie Whittle, PD of Houston's 104.1 KRBE, says, "It's absolutely necessary to the future of any business to mentor." Named "One of the Best Program Directors in America" by *Radio Ink* in 2016, Whittle explains that mentoring is an activity that can extend beyond on-air performance review and coaching:

> This doesn't only take time, it takes understanding of the goals and capabilities of those you mentor. What do they REALLY want? A career as a Program Director? To be a DJ? To produce audio? Do they want to hear their music on the radio? Put together great events for clients? And most importantly, CAN you help them accomplish these goals with the right guidance? Today's technology means less chances to get on-air experience, so it's more important than ever now to know the potential of those you mentor.

After a short time, the programmer may feel compelled to modify air schedules either by shifting deejays around or by replacing those who do not enhance the format. Efforts to maintain consistency between the weekday and weekend "sound" of the station also have to be made. The PD prepares weekend and holiday schedules as well and this generally requires the hiring of part-time announcers. A station may employ as few as one or two part-timers or fill-in people or as many as eight to 10. This largely depends on whether deejays are on a five- or six-day schedule, as well as the extent to which the station utilizes automation and voice-tracking (see Chapter 8). Air personnel often are hired to work a six-day week. The objective of scheduling is not merely to fill slots but to maintain the continuity and consistency of sound. A PD prefers to tamper with shifts as little as possible and fervently hopes that he has filled weekend slots with individuals who are reliable. Brian Mitchell says:

> The importance of dependable, trustworthy air people cannot be overemphasized. It's great to have talented deejays, but if they don't show up when they are supposed to because of one reason or another, they don't do you a lot of good. You need people who are cooperative. I have no patience with individuals who try to deceive me or fail to live up to their responsibilities.

A station that is constantly introducing new air personnel has a difficult time establishing listener habit. The PD knows that to succeed he or she must present a stable and dependable sound, and this is a significant programming challenge, albeit one that has been mitigated somewhat by the practice of voice-tracking "unstaffed" overnight and weekend air shifts. The techniques of voice-tracking assist the PD in maintaining a consistent 24/7 on-air sound.

Programmer Brad Carson defends the practice: "Talent-sharing from station to station," he says, "using voice-tracking and other methods (networks, for example) has helped many stations, regardless of market size or format, put the best voices and talent in radio markets across America." Detractors of voice-tracking criticize the practice, claiming that owners' primary objective in eliminating local talent is the reduction of expenses. Carson, however, believes that this viewpoint can be inconsistent with a PD's objectives:

> While many have demonized voicetrackings and network radio because of cost reduction (which is not always the case when using these tools) radio groups want to put the very best content on the air. Content is still king. High quality content and entertaining content are always the goal.

Marlin R. Taylor, Founder of Bonneville Broadcasting System and veteran major-market station programmer and manager, underscores the need for station personnel to support their nonlocal air talent:

> In most cases, if a station is to truly stay connected to the listener, "local" is an element that must be factored in. If you're talking about a voice-tracker from outside the market, he/she needs to be provided with information that enables the person to include content relevant to the local community. If it's a network music show, there should be timely local information included in the local breaks

beyond just commercial spots. Otherwise, a properly run station that utilizes either of these extensively on weekends and even overnight hours needs to have someone available to communicate information should an emergency or other major newsworthy event occur in the community or region that the listener should be aware of.

PD/midday air personality Randi Myles of Detroit's Praise 102.7 notes not only that successful programming must be local, but that the programmer should be sensitive to the innate needs of listeners. She explains:

Programming radio is a way to cater to the overall 'needs' for the market you work in. In my case, Inspirational music caters to those who love gospel music, who go to church (mostly) or for the person who needs to be lifted up after a hard day or unfortunate situation. That is a small group of people in some areas, but in a larger market like Detroit . . . it's a bigger group of listeners. The same goes for any format really. You look for the need and then program the station accordingly.

## MARKET-BASED PROGRAMMING DECISION-MAKING

### Mike McVay

The decision to shift programming decision-making authority and control from the corporate level to that of the markets was less about a strategy and more about a tactic. We at Cumulus needed to do it if we were to turn around the ratings of our company. Our CEO, Mary Berner, assigned us the task of "fixing" programming in order that we could improve the ratings, thus improving our advertising sales efforts and growing revenue. This meant a restructuring of how we approached the product side of the business and the quality or level of the individuals we would retain or hire to program our stations.

**FIGURE 3.14**
Mike McVay

Our company was out of step with what our competitors were doing. There was some good and some bad with that. The way in which many stations in North America were programmed had gone full circle. Many USA broadcast companies, prederegulation, owned only seven AM and seven FM stations. That was the maximum permitted by the Federal Communications Commission. Stations operated very much unto themselves and were specifically tailored to their markets. Like with anything, there were exceptions, but stations tended to operate independent of each other beyond carrying specific group products like the news. When the ownership cap was extended, radio started to become much more systematized, and while systems are necessary some companies took it to the extreme. They eliminated the ability to focus closely on the uniqueness of an individual market. It eliminated the individuality among programmers and talent, and stifled creativity.

The good in how the company previously operated was that the highest-ranked programmer in the company, my then-director, is a creative person who wasn't afraid to develop new products and "throw them against the wall to see if they'd stick." What was bad about it was that we didn't allow time or provide resources for research and development. A new product was thought of and the program was launched. In some cases it was in a massive fashion across multiple stations and network channels. The level of success varied greatly as these individual markets were so different from one another. In some cases we changed the format and/or name of a heritage radio station and launched a new product without marketing or promotional support. That's 180 degrees off of what one should do when preparing to launch a new product.

We began the programming turnaround when the CEO announced the decentralization of programming at Cumulus. Her statement to the company was "Programming is the oxygen of Cumulus." There it was. The focus on having the best product and the importance of programming to turn around the business. We began by creating the Office of Programming (OP). I am the creative side of that office. My team, and ultimately me, is responsible for everything that comes out of the speakers. The administrative side rests with my partner in the OP, Bob Walker. He handles the sales interface, works with market managers and is business and operationally focused.

Giving the power to program back to the program directors, and enabling the market managers to be involved in programming decisions has created a collaborative spirit within the company. It also has heightened the awareness of the need for individuals to accept responsibility for the ratings. To that end we evaluate our programmers' performances twice yearly. We provide them with tools to improve should there be such a need. We created a structure that enables them to be creative.

We are employing many of the philosophies, systems and tactics that my former programming consulting company (McVay Media) used in improving the product on client stations. That is, to focus on music or talk (sports and/or news talk) content that provides instant gratification. Every time I hit the button for your station I hear a topic I am attracted to or a song that I like. It's information that satisfies one's need for survival information and answers the question "what's happening today?" Personalities that are relatable people. They live in the listeners' world. They must work hard to be better prepared and better informed than their competition. Building day-to-day tune-in. If I don't listen, I will miss something. Great experiential contests that make the winning experience shared as we live through the fantasy of that one person who won. Marketing tactics designed to accomplish your rating goal and satisfy a specific need of the audience. We preach these philosophies on our weekly sharing conference programming calls.

A focus on opportunity development, providing resources like research, and launching an ongoing education program that shares "best practices" for multiple facets of programming. Our focus is on music, content, information, personality, promotion, and marketing. We've enabled programmers to select and air the music that they feel is proper for their audiences. We've enabled programmers to select the talent that they want for their stations, develop contests and promotions that can attract an audience, and we've allowed them to decide how best to image their radio stations. They are responsible for the success or failure of their stations and as such must be prepared to accept such responsibility.

What we do not do is abandon our programmers. Our structure is that there are three individuals who are vice-president/Programming Operations that oversee "buckets" of markets. Their job is to look at an entire cluster of stations in a market, determine how they best fit together versus the competition, and provide a more global view. We have three researchers who provide us with insight into the ratings, the content and lead us in SWAT analysis when a station is underperforming or showing poor performance. We have two individuals who focus on training. Their role is to look at what works in what situations and share that information as well as teach "best practices." We also have VP/formats who serve as consultants. They are experts in music and talk formats. They're the support that a programmer has available to use when they desire a different perspective or are simply looking for guidance. These systems are designed to allow a program director to conduct daily business without eliminating the time to be creative.

The significance of this shift is that programmers can now develop and create content that is attractive to their specific markets. The decentralization of programming has enabled PDs to be more reactive to the competition, to be proactive in creating new concepts and programs and to work more closely with sales in designing advertiser-friendly programming that is not detrimental to the ratings.

Our focus is beyond the FM and AM bands. We're developing content for online, on-demand and podcasting. We're creating new and unique programming for our HD2 channels. These blank canvasses require new thinking, new perspectives and the type of no-boundaries thinking that comes from youth. Our success, 15 months of continual rating increases (as of this writing), will lead other companies to adopt our decentralized approach. That means more opportunities for individuals who possess the vision to be creative while not losing the discipline to be responsible.

---

**Mike McVay** is Executive Vice-President/Content and Programming for Cumulus Media and Westwood One. He oversees the programming of 450 radio stations and two radio networks. He is a veteran 40-year programmer with consulting, management, ownership, sales, programming and on-air experience. In addition he has developed and launched several nationally syndicated programs. As an international consultant he has programmed more than 300 stations. McVay has received numerous awards and acknowledgments, and is the recipient of the prestigious Rockwell Award. *Radio Ink* ranked him #4 among America's top programmers and he was named one of the titans of talk by *NTS* magazine every year 2012–16.

Production schedules also are prepared by the programmer. Deejays are usually tapped for production duties before or after their airshifts. For example, the morning person who is on the air 6–10 am may be assigned production and copy (commercial scriptwriting) chores from 10 am until noon. Meanwhile, the midday deejay who is on the air from 10 am until 3 pm is given production assignments for 3–5 pm, and so on. Large radio stations frequently employ a full-time production person. If so, this individual handles all production responsibilities and is supervised by the PD.

A PD traditionally handles the department's budget, which generally constitutes 30–40% of the station's operating budget. Working with the station manager, the PD ascertains the financial needs of the programming area. The size and scope of the budget vary from station to station. Most programming budgets include funds for the acquisition of program materials, such as subscription music services, network and syndicated program features, and contest paraphernalia. A separate promotional budget usually exists and this too may be managed by the PD. The programmer's budgetary responsibilities range from monumental at some outlets to minuscule at others. Personnel salaries and even equipment purchases may fall within the province of the program department's budget. Thus, Brian Mitchell believes that "an understanding of the total financial structure of the company or corporation and how programming fits into the scheme of things is a real asset to a programmer."

Devising station promotions and contests also places demands on the PD's time. While large stations often can afford to appoint a promotion director, the same cannot necessarily be said of situations in the smaller markets. In instances where full-time promotions directors are employed, the PD and promotion director work together in the planning, development, and execution of the promotional campaign. The PD, however, retains final veto power should he or she feel that the promotion or contest fails to complement the station's format. When the PD alone handles promotions and contests, he or she may involve other members of the programming or sales department in brainstorming sessions designed to come up with original and interesting concepts. The programmer is aware that the right promotion or contest can have a major impact on ratings. Thus, he or she is constantly on the lookout for an appropriate event partner or sponsor. In the quest to find the promotion that will launch the station on the path to a larger audience, the PD may seek assistance from one of dozens of companies that offer promotional services.

The PD's major objective is to program for results. If the station's programming fails to attract a sufficient following, the ratings will reflect that unhappy fact. All medium and larger markets are surveyed by ratings companies, primarily Nielsen Audio. Very few small, rural markets, with perhaps one or two stations, are surveyed. If a small-market station is poorly programmed, the results will be apparent in the negative reactions of the local retailers. Simply put, the station will not be bought by enough advertisers to make the operation a profitable venture. In the bigger markets, where several stations compete for advertising dollars, the ratings are used to determine which is the most effective or cost-efficient station to buy. PDs constantly monitor the competition by analyzing the ratings and by listening. However, rather than contrast with each other, pop stations tend to reflect one another. This, in fact, has been the basis of arguments by critics who object to the so-called mirroring effect. What happens is easily understood. If a station does well by presenting a particular format, other stations are going to exploit the sound in the hopes of doing well also. WYYY promotes commercial-free sweeps of music and captures big ratings, and soon its competitor programs likewise. PD Myles cautions against becoming a "reactionary" programmer. One of the principal challenges she faces is

worrying too much about what other stations are doing. If you focus on your station, the listeners' needs and being in the community, you win. Yes, ratings are important, but you can't achieve them if you are not in touch with your audience.

Keeping in step with, or rather one step ahead of, the competition requires that the PD knows what is happening around him or her at all times.

Jingles are an imaging element used as a means of establishing a station's position in the minds of listeners. Greg Clancy, GM and Vice-President, Creative, at TM Studios in Dallas, recounts the history of jingle pioneer and programming icon Gordon McLendon in the late 1950s:

A jingle recording session. Clustering around studio microphones enhances vocalists' performances

Source: Courtesy of TM Studios/WestwoodOne

Gordon pioneered the Top 40 format on the Mighty 7–90, KLIF in Dallas. He thought if people heard the station name put to a melody, they would have more top-of-mind recall of the station name. This was important when listeners filled out ratings sheets. It turns out Gordon was correct in his assumptions, and a cottage industry was born.

Decades later, "jingling" continues to be a viable approach for creating and building station identity and position with audiences.

Thomas Giger, of the Netherlands-based production studio Pure Jingles, concurs. Giger adds that Pure Jingles, whose work is heard on numerous U.S. outlets, "help[s] radio stations to put their brand out to the listener in an auditory way that captures attention and brands the logo melody of the station into the listener's mind." Whether Nielsen Audio measures radio listening with the traditional diary or the newer, electronic Portable People Meter (PPM), the end result, Giger says, is the same. "It's important to make your brand memorable in listeners' heads." "Jingles are heard on all formats," Clancy notes, and says that "the music styles vary greatly. For example, we might use orchestral music for a news imaging package and use a full synthetic composition with effects for a CHR station. We use different vocal configurations for different formats as well."

Probably 60% of the nation's PDs pull an airshift (go on the air themselves) on either a full-time or part-time basis. A difference of opinion exists among programmers concerning their on-air participation. Many feel that being on the air gives them a true sense of the station's sound, which aids them in their programming efforts. As PM Brad Carson sees it, being an on-air personality enables him to stay on top of a station's performance. "How could it not?" he questions. "Your colleagues you work closely with respect you more. Being 'hands on' helps with understanding. You know what is going on. I think there are obvious benefits." Others contend that the three or four hours that they spend on the air take them away from important programming duties. Major-market PDs are less likely to be heard on the air than their peers in smaller markets because of additional duties created by the size and status of the station. Meanwhile, small- and medium-market stations often expect their PDs to be seasoned air personalities capable of filling a key shift. "It has been my experience when applying for programming jobs that managers are looking for PDs with excellent announcing skills. It is pretty rare to find a small-market PD who does not have a daily airshift. It comes with the territory," says consultant and voiceover talent Gary Begin.

purejingles.com

Pure Jingles logo

Source: Courtesy of Thomas Giger and Pure Jingles

Whether or not PDs are involved in actual airshifts, almost all participate in the production of commercials, public service announcements (PSAs), and promos. In lieu of an airshift, a PD may spend several hours each day in the station's production facilities. The programmer may, in fact, serve as the primary copywriter and spot producer. This is especially true at non-major-market outlets that do not employ a full-time production person.

## MULTITASKING PROGRAM DIRECTORS AND THEIR NEED FOR AIR-PERSONALITY COACHES

### Lorna Ozmon

**FIGURE 3.17**
Lorna Ozmon

When large groups of radio stations began being bought up by a handful of big companies the role of the program director in America began to change dramatically. Add to that the economic recession beginning in 2008 and the multitasking program director became the state of the industry. In today's radio environment it is not uncommon for a program director to be responsible for the day-to-day operations of two or more radio stations and pull an air shift as well, making complete attention to every programming detail an almost physical impossibility. Today most program directors' days are filled with obligatory meetings having little or nothing to do with the actual programming of the station and dealing with whatever problems and issues arise at any given moment.

One of the most disturbing results of this seismic shift in the roles of radio program directors is a lack of time to be proactive as it relates to coaching and developing their air personalities. A radio station's air personalities can be its most unique and valuable asset. But, because they are so time-challenged, program directors today tend to devote the little time they might find to spend with their air personalities on performance correction and no time on coaching and performance development.

It is for this reason now more than ever before that radio stations are employing an outside radio air-personality coach. An air-personality coach provides radio stations with a service that the program director once performed but no longer can. An outside air-personality or morning show coach has the time to dedicate hours or, as in my case, even days to just one morning show or other radio project. No program director today has even a spare hour much less a spare day to listen to, analyze and prepare a thorough air-personality coaching plan to execute with the air talent in this day and age.

Beyond the issue of time, great air-personality coaches also bring a unique set of specific performance skills to a radio station. These skills include improvisational technique, comedy and creative thinking training, episodic radio content execution tactics, how to build a successful ensemble cast, and character and role development. Most of today's program directors have little or no experience in any of these creative disciplines so the air-personality coach also provides them with a brand-new set of skills that increase their value to their radio stations and in the industry in general.

---

**Lorna Ozmon** is President of Ozmon Media Inc., a radio air-personality and morning show development company founded in 1990. She is one of America's leading radio air-personality development specialists working in every format in both commercial and public radio. She holds a BA in theater arts with an emphasis on theatrical direction and was a major-market radio air personality, program director, and general manager before establishing Ozmon Media Inc. Her client list includes stations owned by Alpha Broadcasting, CBS, iHeartMedia, Cox Broadcasting, Emmis, Entercom, and NPR.

The PD must possess an imposing list of skills to perform effectively the countless tasks confronting him or her daily. There is no one person, other than the general manager, whose responsibilities outweigh the programmer's. The PD can make or break the radio station. Summing things up, Chief Programmer Jimmy Steal states:

A programmer must possess balance and understanding of both the science and art of show business. A station needs someone who understands that strategies and tactics are for the conference room, and fun, engagement, buzz, innovation, and exceeding listener's expectations are for over the air and online.

Of course, programming "magic" does not create itself. It is, rather, the product of careful, attentive show preparation activities, or "show prep." The PD must prep not only for his or her on-air appearance but also lead by example in assisting the airstaff in the choices of appropriate content in order to achieve consistency in the station's sound and position.

Air personnel typically prep for their shows by one or more of three methods: (1) conducting their own research, (2) subscribing to syndicated show-prep services, and (3) relying on the assistance of the station programming consultant. Seth Resler is a former major-market air personality who now serves as consultant for Jacobs Media's Digital Dot Connector. In-house show-prep activities, in his opinion, are excellent supplements to consultants' services to clients in the major markets. But what about on-air talent in the smaller markets that are just beginning to get a foothold in the business? Resler views the in-house research as a viable, standalone activity, one that clusters around the use of RSS (really simple syndication) feeds. "It doesn't cost anything" to use feed-aggregating software, Resler observes, and it can be extremely helpful in monitoring the activities of what he terms the local-market "influencers." Such persons, he says, are

> Big enough that they have their own following—their own audience—in your market but at the same time are small enough that they're still impressed when the station or its deejay re-Tweets them or shares their content on Facebook.

He explains, "The idea here is that if we can reach that 'Influencer,' then they can turn around and they can reach their audiences . . . and they can share and expose you, and that helps expose you to their audiences." He recommends that PDs convene a meeting of the staff and brainstorm to identify "Influencers" within the market and then enter their social media contact information into the aggregation software. He suggests Feedly (www.feedly.com) as one example of free, easy-to-use software.

**FIGURE 3.18**
A model of a station's competitive environment as conceived by Arbitron

Source: Courtesy of Arbitron/Nielsen Audio

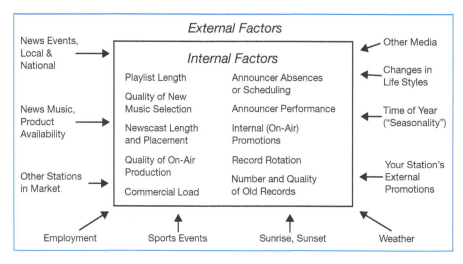

## PROGRAMMING A CLUSTER OPERATION

The widespread ownership consolidation of the radio industry that began in the late 1990s has resulted in a paradigm shift in programming responsibilities. Radio clusters may consist of as many as eight stations. In this situation, one individual is usually assigned to perform the function of general supervisor of all cluster programming, and each of the stations within the cluster has a designated PD, who reports to this person—typically referred to as the director of operations. Radio corporations see it as a macrocosm/microcosm overseer design and arrangement.

As might be imagined, the challenges of programming a cluster are compounded by the very number of the stations involved. Gregg Cassidy, who programmed stations in Chicago, Denver and Milwaukee, observes:

> Programming a single station is very simple versus programming a cluster. In programming a single station you have all the time necessary to evaluate all areas of your station daily. You can check

## DAY-BY-DAY PROGRAM MANAGEMENT AT A STATION CLUSTER

### Brad Carson

*Editor's Note: Brad Carson's workday is one that exemplifies the typical routine of a cluster PD. Carson is responsible for managing programming for the two sports stations in Entercom's Memphis cluster and for producing a weekday sports talk show. He also voice-tracks weekly shows in Memphis and Indianapolis. The key to his success, he believes, is to establish strong local ties and keep up to date with all aspects of his assignments.*

**FIGURE 3.19**
Brad Carson

Program directors must stay organized and take advantage of the national and local opportunities presented to them. Technology has certainly helped. For example, 20 years ago we were using paper Rolodexes to manage our contacts lists to book interviews. Today you can DM (direct message) a potential guest on social media then save their phone number on your smartphone. Smartphones have changed the game for the audio/radio business.

We have video, audio, guest booking, and all these capabilities at our disposal now, in an easy-to-use smartphone format. But we still must keep tabs on all of the basic radio/media things, make the music or programming sound perfect, partner with clients to effectively create ratings and revenue, hire and manage talent, perform an on-air shift in many cases, learn new ways of creating great radio and working with new technology. We must create fun and magic using storytelling.

A glimpse at the list of typical day-in-the-life events of Brad Carson reflects these activities:

- Write voiceover scripts and schedule sessions for station voice talents.
- Conduct telephone voiceover talent review sessions, coaching them on the sound of the scripts.
- Write lines that on-air talent will voice for upcoming promotions/events.
- Record commercials and personal voice elements with a production person. Discuss the situation that we can't voice a certain advertiser's script because it conflicts with another advertiser we already endorse.
- Conduct an aircheck meeting with morning show talent.
- Manage email correspondence with network representatives of one of the stations regarding a technical issue.
- Participate in client meeting with station account executive; meet with a client we endorse.
- Schedule studio time for a sports talk talent (who also writes for a national website) traveling to another city.
- Send lineup of guests and "benchmarks" for talk lineup for the following day.
- Design marketing pieces to be used online.
- Review websites and social media elements; correspond about Twitter and Facebook content with Entercom social media content manager.
- Participate in format-specific conference call with other Entercom program directors.
- Program meeting with the general manager.
- Visit with each member of the staff.
- Prepare BMI and ASCAP affidavits.
- Produce afternoon talk show in real time on sports station.
- Upload podcast from that show and prep for next day's show.
- And, last but not least, make a list for the next day's activities.

**Brad Carson** is the Director of Branding/Sports Programming at Entercom-Memphis' WMFS-FM/AM and WMC-AM, executive producer of *The Gary Parrish Show*, and host on WMC-FM 100, WLFP (94.1 The Wolf), and WNTR (107.9 The Mix-Indy). Brad voices commercials for GCV Productions in New Jersey. He is a graduate of North Central College in Naperville, IL (BA) and the University of Nevada, Las Vegas (MA), and has been on air in Illinois, Las Vegas, and Atlantic City.

your air talent each week, reevaluate your music and music rotations, be very creative with your on-air promotions, and take the necessary time to create clever and compelling production. Programming a cluster is like being a father of many children rather than one or two. Time becomes very valuable. In the simplest form, I would devote all my energy to one station per week.

The twin activities of listing and prioritizing are part and parcel of Tommy Castor's workday. The iHeartmedia programmer observes:

I only have so many hours in one day and it's so important to me to prioritize and work smart while working hard. I have to have a daily to-do list where not only do I list all of my tasks for that day, but I always prioritize them so I know what the most important duties that day will be. Usually these are items that I believe may make the most difference in improving the sound of my radio station, gaining (and sustaining) listeners, improving revenue opportunities, maximizing our digital and social media brands and managing my staff so they are achieving success at a high level. Not all of these are possible to accomplish all of the time, so I just need to be realistic with what I can improve and change.

According to WIZN/WBTZ's Matt Grasso, consolidation has created other problems for programmers:

Ironically, if not paradoxically, many quality radio pros making top dollars were cut out in the downsizing and consolidation frenzy. This often left lesser talent in markets with clusters. Worse yet, with many passionate, quality pros out of work, no one has been minding the store and developing new talent. This has become today's major challenge—finding and developing new talent. There used to be a line out the door of people wanting to be on the radio, but the perception that consolidation and downsizing have killed the job market has dramatically changed that.

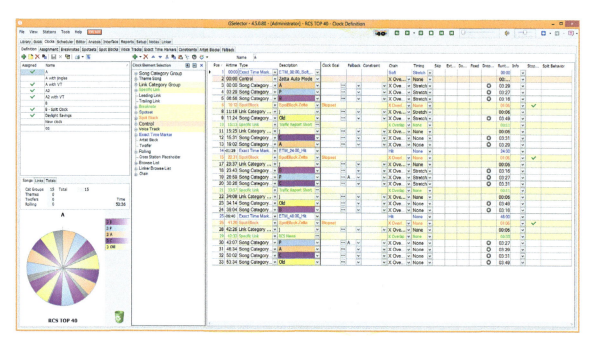

**FIGURE 3.20**

Music cataloging and scheduling is managed by apps such as RCS GSelector

Source: Courtesy of RCS

# SATELLITE RADIO PROGRAMMING

In laying the foundation of satellite radio with the creation of the Digital Audio Radio Service (DARS) by the FCC in 1992, almost another decade would pass before the first signals would bounce down from space to listeners. XM Radio came first, in late 2001, with the successful launch of its two satellites, appropriately named "rock" and "roll." Competitor Sirius followed several months later. What follows is a brief sketch of the original concept for the organizational structure that was put into place at the time of the creation of XM Satellite Radio in the early 2000s. XM's Chief Creative Officer, the legendary programmer and consultant Lee Abrams, served XM as its original Chief Creative Officer. In recounting the early days of the satcaster, Abrams described his role in the launch of digital radio broadcasting:

> I was the head overseer of programming. For original content, we had a senior vice-president of music. We had a vice-president of Talk, who handled the day-to-day operations of the nonmusic channels. Original Talk programming, such as Take 5 and XM Traffic, had a PD along with a staff of talent and producers. The vice-president of Talk also spearheaded the relations with third-party providers. Every cluster had a senior PD, and each channel had a PD. Channels often had music directors and deejays. A vice-president also oversaw the pure operational aspects, like computer systems and production. There was a staff of senior production directors who supervised a group of producers, aka audio animators. Supporting the animators were production assistants, who often came from the internship ranks at XM. The programming department also had a music librarian and staff that oversaw the ingestion of music into the system. Keep in mind things changed as they were tweaked to enhance the efficiency of the department. As they say, it was a work in progress.

Indeed. By early 2009 the two competitors had merged, and in the years since the combined company's fortunes have fallen and risen. In the company's most recent assessment, announced in early 2017, SiriusXM reported a record-setting roster of more than 31 million subscribers. CEO James Meyer, in describing the programming advancements of calendar year 2016, informed investors, "Once again, we raised our game. More live programming, one-of-a-kind concerts, new music channels, and must-hear sporting events. No one else can match our easy-to-use content bundle." He continued:

> We made some major moves in our sports programming also by adding two of the biggest brands in sports. We created a new exclusive 24x7 channel, FOX Sports on SiriusXM, showcasing some of FOX's biggest talent such as Colin Cowherd, Skip Bayless and Shannon Sharpe.

# ELEMENTS OF PROGRAMMING

Programming has become a very complex undertaking, observes Andy Bloom. Few programmers entrust the selection and scheduling of music and other sound elements to deejays. There is simply too much at stake and too many variables, both internal and external, that must be considered to achieve maximum results within a chosen format. "For instance, all of our music is tested via callout," Bloom says. This important implement in the programmer's toolbox is a survey procedure for determining music preferences. So-termed because of its origins as a telephone *call-out* technique to query survey respondents, similar results today can be more efficiently obtained by using online methodologies. In any instance, the use of *song hooks* is the key to collecting usable information about listeners' interests in songs. Hooks are simply snippets edited from full-length recordings that preserve the most-recognizable or attention-grabbing portions of songs—the parts that "catch the ear" of listeners. In many instances, that portion is located in the chorus between the verses. While it's possible to create the hooks in-house, it's also common for programmers to rely on the services of a company that specializes in the creation and syndication of hooks. One such company, Hooks Unlimited, curates a library of almost 150,000 hooks readily available for use in music testing situations, including call-out, online, auditorium, and focus group settings.

**FIGURE 3.21**
Michael Pelaia

# HOW A SONG HOOK CAN "HOOK" A LISTENER

## Michael Pelaia

Music research has been used as a tool by programmers to identify opportunities and fine-tune their brands for more than 30 years. It is critical for radio stations to know what keeps the audience listening and why listeners may tune away. Research helps them stay on course.

The hook in a song is the repetitive lyric phrase or musical notes that "stay in people's minds" and help them recall the song. In simple terms . . . the hook is what the song is selling to your ears.

Music hooks are used in several areas of the digital music landscape today. The sample you see in a digital music platform (such as iTunes or Google Music) is usually one to two minutes long. This helps you get a feel for the song, likely because you are unfamiliar with it. It is usually used to help you decide if you like the song enough to buy (or stream) it.

In radio music research, song hooks used in market research are usually only six to eight seconds in length. Why so short? When you test segments with listeners, a researcher is hoping to capture the listener's reaction to a song they know and have heard before. If a person is not familiar with a song, they are asked not to rate it. Song hooks are used in current music testing (known as call-out), library music testing (tested in-person or online), and perceptual research (clustered together to help define formats). Assuming the listener knows the song, a shorter hook is all that is needed to capture their opinion. This can evoke either a positive or negative response.

Programmers often use a mix of methods to decide how to play a song. Current-based stations usually have a music meeting or listening session where they sample songs they consider introducing to their audience. Some stations do this live on the air and get listeners to vote on the station's web page or ask listeners to call in to the deejay. The programmer likely also looks at chart data (*Billboard*), airplay data (Mediabase, BDS), and secondary data from market competitors or other stations owned by the same company as their own station. Without these resources, a programmer must add a song based on keen knowledge of their audience and their gut telling them if it's a hit. Some do just that, but it is dangerous to rely solely on your gut.

**FIGURE 3.22**
Hooks Unlimited logo
Source: Courtesy of Hooks Unlimited

Once the song is established, it becomes important to test it to ensure it (1) is still popular, (2) fits the texture of the music being played, and (3) has not fatigued in the minds of listeners. An example of this is "Tears in Heaven" by Eric Clapton. During its heyday, this song was played on a very high rotation and tested well in the research. It was played so much that, while it garnered a 4.75 on a five-point scale, it also had 60% or more of listeners saying they were "tired" of hearing it. In current-based formats this is commonplace. More recently, Adele's "Hello" reflected this listener sentiment. The songs are played so frequently (sometimes once an hour) they "burn out." Bad songs don't last long. Good songs played in such a high frequency sometimes need to be rested (taken out of regular airplay rotation) for a while. The station can then make room for new hits and brings the song back as "gold," where it might be played once or twice a day or week.

The 1994 song "Hook" by Blues Traveler is a brilliantly written song that is both a hit song and a satire of a hit song. The song's lyrics, aimed directly at the listener, assert that the lyrical content of any song is effectively meaningless, insofar as the song's musical hook will keep listeners coming back, even if they are unaware of the reason. In the introduction, John Popper sings:

It doesn't matter what I say / So long as I sing with inflection / That makes you feel that I'll convey / Some inner truth of vast reflection.

Further on in the song, however, he uses more blatant lyrics, claiming that formulaic music is an easy way to make money:

When I'm feeling stuck and need a buck / I don't rely on luck, because / the hook brings you back . . .

In this song . . . the hook is about a hook!

Radio is the leading reach platform, as 93% of people listen to AM/FM radio. Most stations broadcast or stream some type of music format. Music is universal, ingrained in our lives from an early age. Most everyone at some point in their lives has listened to music, and likely it was from the radio.

So . . . why is the hook so important? The familiarity and repetition is easy to latch on to, and it hopefully evokes a response. That reaction keeps you listening. . . and it keeps you coming back for more!

---

**Michael Pelaia** is President of Hooks Unlimited, located in Decatur, GA, just outside of Atlanta. He received his BS in Telecommunications Management from Ithaca College before starting in local radio sales in suburban New York. In 1988, Michael joined Arbitron (now Nielsen Audio), providing customer service to radio rep firms and agencies. From there he joined Coleman Insights near Raleigh, NC, as Research Analyst, eventually assuming the role of Vice-President, Operations. Michael then relocated to Atlanta, GA, in 1996 and joined Eagle Research, a division of Cox Media, in the roles of Project Director, VP Operations and eventually EVP/COO of the Eagle Group. In 2002, Michael joined Hooks Unlimited as President.

Hooks Unlimited provides music research materials to radio stations, research firms, and consultants worldwide to help them adjust and improve their programming. He recently became a volunteer guide with Musicians on Call, a nationwide organization that provides live, in-room music performances in health-care facilities to patients unable to leave their room. He currently resides in Atlanta, Georgia, and in his free time enjoys music, cycling, hiking, and cooking.

Music research takes other forms. Bloom continues: "At least one or two perceptual studies are done every year, depending on what questions we need answered. Usually a couple of sets of focus groups per year, too. Everything is researched, and nothing is left to chance." In most cases, the PD determines how much music is programmed hourly and in what rotation and when news, public affairs features, and commercials are slotted. Program clocks (also known variously as sound hours, wheels, and format disks) are simply diagrams depicting the sequence of presentation of music, commercials, and other programming elements. Clocks are carefully designed by the PD to ensure the effective presentation of on-air ingredients. In the days prior to the computerization of the on-air presentation, program clock diagrams would be posted in the control studio to inform and guide air talent as to what is to be broadcast and at what point in the hour.

Today, while the concept of the clock and the various program elements are internalized within the software that manages the audio playout, the decisions about what is to be broadcast and in what order are made by the PD. Although not every station provides deejays with such specific programming schemata, today very few stations leave things up to chance since the inappropriate scheduling and sequencing of sound elements may drive listeners to a competitor. Radio programming has become that much of an exacting science. With few exceptions, stations use some kind of software-assisted formula in conveying their programming material.

According to Entercom's Brad Carson,

Music stations that want to maximize rotations and use sound strategy to play the right songs the "right" amount of times use music scheduling software programs like RCS Selector or Music Master. Each of these programs use a virtual "clock" with songs positioned around imaging elements, commercials, and talk positions where talent/personalities either talk over song intros, between songs into cold intros or before/after commercials within a given hour.

In explaining how station personnel manage the process of song scheduling, Carson says the process begins by determining the appropriate number of songs to be scheduled within the hour. A certain total number of songs (this ideal number is often based off what similarly formatted stations that the station monitors from around the country use) is selected; the scheduler then assigns codes to the various songs' attributes. Music schedulers are able to code almost every characteristic of their songs including genre, era, gender, tempo, mood, and even research-score ranks. Songs considered "powers" play more than various other identifiable categories. But after songs are "auto-scheduled" most program managers/music directors choose to review the entire playlist log by hand to "massage" it. For example, maybe the computer places a "power" song by Ariana Grande in spot #1 and the next song slotted to play is by Bruno Mars in spot #2, owing to the circumstances of that particular clock. The music scheduler then might see that and just simply "juggle" the #2-spot song by Mars with the #3-spot song from the Chainsmokers. It would then go (#1) Grande, (#2) Chainsmokers and then (#3) Mars vs. (#1) Grande, (#2) Mars then (#3) Chainsmokers.

Carson cautions that a programmer can become too prescriptive in designing the selection "rules." He explains,

> With some of these music scheduling programs (like RCS Selector) it's possible to set up so many "rules" that the program won't place songs in every slot. I think it's valuable to at the very least take a few minutes to review the log and see if there's anything out of sorts that you don't like for the brand. In today's radio, most music programmers also are doing another pass through their log to hand place imaging elements that go perfectly with the scheduled music log.

**FIGURE 3.23**

Software assists programmers with clock construction

Source: Courtesy of Impressive Interfaces

In the instance of RCS software, the Selector companion program Linker integrates the station imaging content into the music schedule.

Indeed, program clocks are set up with the competition and market factors in mind. For example, programmers will devise a clock that reflects morning and afternoon drive periods in their market. Not all markets have identical commuter hours. In some cities morning drive may start as early as 5:30 am; in others it may begin at 7 am. The programmer sets up clocks accordingly. The clock structure parallels the activities of the community in which the station operates.

Program clocks keep a station on a preordained path and prevent deejays from deviating from the program-execution philosophy. As stated, each programming element—commercial, news, promo, weather, and so on—is strategically located in the sound hour to enhance flow and optimize impact. Balance is imperative: with too much deejay patter on a station promoting more music and less talk, listeners become disenchanted; with too little news and information on a station targeting the over-30 male commuter, the competition benefits. Radio executive Lorna Ozmon observes:

> When constructing or arranging the program clock, you have to work forward and backward to make sure that everything fits and is positioned correctly. One element out of place can become that proverbial hole in the dam. Spots, jock breaks, music—it all must be weighed before clocking. A lot of experimentation, not to mention research, goes into this.

It was previously pointed out that a station with a "more music" approach minimizes deejay talk in order to have time for scheduling additional tunes. Nothing is left to chance. This is true of stations airing the super-tight hit music format. Deejays say what appears on their monitors and move the music. At stations where deejays are given more control, program clocks play a less crucial function. Outlets where a particular personality has ruled the ratings for years often let that person have more input as to what music is aired. However, even in these cases, playlists generally are provided and followed.

## TOP 10 RADIO FORMATS OF 2016

| | Persons 6+ Share | Persons 18-34 Share | Persons 25-54 Share |
|---|---|---|---|

| Rank | Format | 2016 |
|---|---|---|
| 1 | News Talk Information | 9.60% |
| 2 | Pop Contemporary Hit Radio (CHR) | 8.10% |
| 3 | Adult Contemporary (AC) | 7.50% |
| 4 | Country* | 7.40% |
| 5 | Hot Adult Contemporary (AC) | 6.40% |
| 6 | Classic Hits | 5.30% |
| 7 | Classic Rock | 5.10% |
| 8 | Urban Adult Contemporary (AC) | 4.80% |
| 9 | All Sports | 4.70% |
| t10 | Mexican Regional | 3.70% |
| t10 | Urban Contemporary | 3.70% |

Source: Nielsen January-November 2014, 2015 and 2016. AQH Share across 45 non-embedded PPM markets. Mon-Sun 6am-Midnight.
Read as: From January-November 2016, 9.6% of U.S. radio listeners in PPM markets aged 6+ were turned to a News/Talk station during any 15-minutes period during the day.
*Country is a combination of Country and New Country formats
t—Tie for rank.

**FIGURE 3.24**
Tracking the trends: Top formats in Nielsen-rated markets
Source: Courtesy of Nielsen Audio

On the subject of on-air talent, Lynn Christian observes:

> Requirements have changed in the past few years. Stations are not just looking for a "pretty voice." Today's radio management looks for talent with facile minds who are great observers—people who can listen as well as speak, plus possess the ability to demonstrate a warm and always interesting personality.

On the other side of the coin, talent wants their managers to operate in a manner that makes for a positive atmosphere and experience, says PD Jimmy Steal: "The keys to managing talent are (1) honesty, (2) inspiration, (3) creativity, and (4) empathy."

In addition to concentrating on the role deejays play in the sound hour, the PD pays careful attention to the general nature and quality of other ingredients. Music is, of course, of paramount importance. Songs must fit the format to begin with, but, beyond the obvious, the quality of the artistry and the audio mix must meet certain criteria. A substandard musical arrangement or a disc with poor fidelity detracts from the station's sound. Station imaging must integrate effectively with other programming features to establish the tone and tenor of the format. Otherwise they might have the reverse effect of their intended purpose, which is to attract and hold listeners. Commercials, too, must be compatible with the program elements that surround them.

In all, the PD scrutinizes every component of the program clock to keep the station true to form. Adherence to the clock structure helps maintain consistency, without which a station cannot hope to cultivate a following. Erratic programming in today's highly competitive marketplace is tantamount to directing listeners to other stations or the multitude of audio listening opportunities. At one time, top 40 stations were the unrivaled leaders of formula programming. Today, however, even full service (FS) and classic rock outlets, which once were the least formulaic, have become more sensitive to form. The age of freeform commercial radio has long since passed, and it is doubtful, given the state of the marketplace, that it will return. Of course, stranger things have happened in radio.

**FIGURE 3.25**
Peter Stewart

## A RADIO STATION ISN'T JUST A RADIO STATION ANY MORE

### Peter Stewart

"The business you are in is so much more than a linear stream of in-the-moment 'info-tainment' from one person to many." That's how I started my contribution to the previous edition of this book, before I went on to talk about websites and apps. What I wrote then (that a successful radio station is one which helps an audience in more ways that just with auditory entertainment) is more true than ever.

When Chuck Berry wanted to hear a song, he had to write a letter and mail it to his local deejay. Years later, in "Calling Occupants," brother and sister pop duo The Carpenters told us how listeners to all-hit radio could phone the all-request line. Now everyone has a jukebox in their pocket: their favorite songs downloaded onto their phone, or streamed live via services such as Spotify and Pandora. You have to provide something different. It's the songs that'll attract people to your station, but it's the other content that'll keep them listening.

But nowadays it's not just on air that you need to have distinctive difference, you need to be in other places too. After all, you don't just have a radio station, you have a multimedia publishing empire: on the radio, online, on smartphones, and yes, on TV. And that means more ways to connect with your community, build your brand and, let's face it, make money.

On your website and app you may include a feed of local news, perhaps with the scripts, audio of the most recent bulletin, longer interviews or background information with the newsmakers, links to other sites with in-depth information and statistics; weather reports, almanacs, moving radar forecasts and webcams for local towns; live traffic news with feeds from cameras at major junctions; and local events that can be filtered according to location, date, price and theme.

You can provide background details of the songs you play, with affiliate links to download them (so you make a bit of money), information on concert dates and album reviews; added background on the guests you have spoken with, how they can be contacted, affiliate links to download their book; and more information on your advertisers, their location, and online discount vouchers.

And through social media platforms you can have a conversation with your community through the use of text, links, still images, and recorded or live video. Yes, that's the "TV" part. With live video streaming such as Facebook Live, you can show behind the scenes at your remote broadcast, give an insight into a playlist or news meeting, have the presenters take part in a weekly challenge, break news, interview decision-makers... But don't just "broadcast." Watch the comments, read and reply. Converse. Communicate! Build a relationship.

And above all promote your on-air content. Drive listeners back to the real estate that you own: your frequency and your website. Don't have so much of a presence on Facebook that you are giving Zuckerberg all your listeners' eyes, so they buy from advertisers there. You need to drive them back to your back yard, so you can capture their contact details, their demographics, their eyeballs and their wallets.

Having a multiplatform presence will deepen their experience and engagement with your station, show and staff, and turn the relatively-passive radio listener into a participator. Along the way you will learn more about them so you can create more of the content that they like.

Wherever they come across your brand.

**Peter Stewart** has been a radio presenter, producer, and news editor in the UK, for BBC and commercial stations, for 30 years. A winner of a New York International Radio Award, he has trained staff and university students in all aspects of radio and TV presentation and production, face-to-face and via his books: *Essential Radio Skills* (2nd edition, Methuen Drama), *Essential Radio Journalism* (Methuen Drama), and *Broadcast Journalism* (7th edition, Focal Press).

Now a "digital producer," he trains staff at places such as the BBC and Oxfam in social media and mobile journalism skills. In 2015 he was the author of the world's first book on "how to live-stream," which has now been published as *The Live-Streaming Handbook* (Focal Press, 2017).

www.PeteStewart.co.uk
@TweeterStewart

## THE PD AND THE AUDIENCE

The programmer, regardless of whether he or she works for a broadcast, satellite, or Internet radio station, must possess a clear perception of the type of listener the station management wants to attract. Initially, a station decides on a given format because it is convinced that it will make money with the newfound audience, meaning that the people who tune in to the station will look good to prospective advertisers. The purpose of any format is to attract a desirable segment of the radio audience whose attention can be marketed to advertisers. Just who these people are and what makes them tick are questions that the PD must constantly address to achieve reach and retention. An informed programmer is aware that different types of music appeal to different types of people. For example, surveys have long concluded that heavy rock appeals more to men than it does to women, and that rock music, in general, is more popular among teens and young adults than it is with individuals over 40. This is no guarded secret, and certainly the programmer who is out to gain the over-40 crowd is doing themselves and their station a disservice by programming even an occasional hard rock tune. This should be obvious.

A station's demographics refer to the characteristics of those who tune in: age, gender, income, and so forth. Within its demographic profile, a station may exhibit particular strength in specific areas, or *cells* as they have come to be termed. For example, an AC station targeting the 25- to 49-year-old group

**FIGURE 3.26**
Leslie Whittle

### FOMO: THE FEAR OF MISSING OUT

#### Leslie Whittle

Never forget: Programming IS the product. Without a strong product, the chance for success is exponentially decreased. Possible, but it rarely happens, and certainly isn't earned or deserved. "Good programming" includes all aspects of a radio station: on-air, digital, station and talent brand, market presence, community service, and more. All must be constantly evaluated within the context of your market and to the expectations of your listener. It doesn't matter how good the product is if you don't deliver to expectations.

The ability to meet these expectations is just the starting point. In order to be truly "good" and be able to differentiate yourself from other entertainment options, radio stations need to become *destinations*. Instill in your audience "Fear of Missing Out," or "FOMO." The opportunities for doing this are endless, but it's not just about the artists you play or what's happening in your city (remember listeners can get this "information" in any number of ways). It's about HOW you present what's happening. Did your morning show make your listeners CARE about bullying at a local high school? Did your promo make your listeners LAUGH because sometimes it's fun to make fun of Justin Bieber? Did your afternoon drive deejay make your listeners THINK when he relayed a story about the police chief? Is your night deejay KNOWN for debuting the biggest records as soon as they debut on iTunes? Instilling "Fear of Missing Out" in your audience is what separates radio from other music services.

---

**Leslie Whittle** is Program Director of Cumulus CHR 104.1 KRBE in Houston, Texas. She works with on-air talent and develops marketing, music, and research strategies. Prior to her work in Houston, Whittle was the Research Director of iHeart Austin, Texas, and the day-to-day program director of KHFI iHeart/Austin.

may have a prominent cell in women over 30. The general information provided by the major ratings surveys indicate to the station the age and sex of those listening, but little beyond that. To find out more, the PD may conduct an in-house survey or employ the services of a research firm.

Because radio accompanies listeners practically everywhere, broadcasters pay particular attention to the lifestyle activities of their target audience. Social media platforms can be helpful in assisting PDs in developing deeper understanding of and insight into the listener. Facebook, the dominant service, continues to extend its reach into the populace. *The Infinite Dial*, the Edison Research/Triton Media annual study, estimated in its 2017 study that Facebook usage among persons aged 12 and older has increased nine percentage points since this text's previous edition, rising from 58% to 67%. Three of every four persons aged 12–24 have Facebook profiles.

A station's geographic locale often dictates its program offerings. For example, hoping to capture the attention of the 35-year-old men, a radio outlet located in a small coastal city along the Gulf of Mexico might decide to air a series of one-minute informational tips on outdoor activities, such as tennis, golf, and deep-sea fishing, which are exceptionally popular in the area. Stations have always catered to the interests of their listeners, but, beginning in the 1970s, audience research became much more oriented to lifestyle.

In the 1990s, broadcasters delved further into audience behavior through psychographic research, which, by examining motivational factors, provides programmers with information beyond the purely quantitative. Perhaps one of the best examples of a station's efforts to conform to its listeners' lifestyle is *dayparting*, a topic briefly touched on in the discussion of program clocks. For the sake of illustration, let us discuss how a classic hits-formatted station may daypart (segmentalize) its broadcast day. To begin with, the station is targeting an over-40 audience, somewhat skewed toward men. The PD concludes that the station's biggest listening hours are mornings between 7 and 9 am and afternoons between 4 and 6 pm, and that most of those tuned in during these periods are in their cars commuting to or from work. It is evident to the programmer that the station's programming approach must be modified during drive time to reflect the needs of the audience. Obviously, traffic reports, news and sports updates, weather forecasts, and frequent time checks are suitable fare for the station's morning audience. The interests of homebound commuters contrast slightly with those of work-bound commuters. Weather and time are less important, and most sports information from the previous night is old hat by the time the listener heads for home. The presentation should elicit a mood of relaxation, and the diversion of thought away from the drudgery of that day's work experience. Stock market reports and information about upcoming games and activities take up the slack. Midday and evening hours call for further modification, because the lifestyle and entertainment desires of the station's audience is different. Any programming adjustments the PD makes should have the objective of attracting and retaining audience interest.

The PD relies on survey information and research data to better gauge and understand the station's audience. However, as a member of the community that the station serves, the programmer knows that not everything is contained in formal documentation. He or she gains unique insight into the mood and mentality of the area within the station's signal simply by taking part in the activities of day-to-day life. Entercom Programmer Brad Carson immerses himself in work with Memphis-area nonprofit organizations. Not only does he make a valuable contribution to the community; he also is able to make and sustain connections with audience members. Carson says, "I like helping local charities like St. Jude Children's Research Hospital and Special Kids and Families. I enjoy meeting listeners." A programmer with a real feel for the area in which the station is located, as well as a fundamental grasp of research methodology and its application, is in the best possible position to direct the on-air efforts of a radio station. Concerning the role of audience research, Peter Falconi says, "You can't run a station on research alone. Yes, research helps to an extent, but it can't replace your own observations and instincts." Brian Mitchell agrees with Falconi:

> I feel research is important, but how you react to research is more important. A PD also has to heed his gut feelings. Gaps exist in research, too. If I can't figure out what to do without data to point the way every time I make a move, I should get out of radio. Success comes from taking chances once in a while, too. Sometimes it's wiser to turn your back on the tried and tested. Of course, you had better know who's out there before you try anything. A PD who doesn't study his audience and community is like a racecar driver who doesn't familiarize himself with the track. Both can end up off the road and out of the race.

## THE PD AND THE MUSIC

Not all radio stations have a music director. The larger the station, the more likely it is to have such a person. In any case, it is the PD who is ultimately responsible for the music that goes over the air, even when the position of music director exists. The duties of the music director vary from station to station. Although the title suggests that the individual performing this function would supervise the station's music programming from the selection and acquisition of records to the preparation of playlists, this is not always the case. At some stations, the position is primarily administrative or clerical in nature, leaving the PD to make the major decisions concerning airplay. In this instance, one of the primary duties of the music director might be to improve service from distributors representing the recorded music industry to keep the station well supplied with the latest releases.

Stations in smaller markets historically haven't been adequately serviced by record labels with new music releases and thus rely on subscription services such as HitDisc from TM Studios or Top Hits U.S.A. from RPM Inc. to fill in the gaps in their music libraries. TM Studio's Greg Clancy explains:

> As new songs break on the charts, stations require the audio to put these songs on the air. Our HitDisc service is a delivery vehicle that assists the labels and artists by getting the music to the stations for play.

Over the years the music industry and the radio medium have formed a mutually beneficial alliance. It's been said that "politics makes strange bedfellows." That sentiment also has been often applied in describing the symbiotic, love/hate relationship that exists between the radio broadcasting and recorded music industries. Without the product provided by the recording companies, radio would find itself with little in the way of programming material, insofar as 90% of U.S. stations feature recorded music. At the same time, radio serves as the principal means by which the recording industry gets word of its new releases to the general public. Succinctly put, radio sells recorded music.

Radio stations seldom pay for their music (CDs or audio files). Recording companies at no charge offer download links or send demos of their new product to most stations in return for the publicity that stations provide by playing the tunes. But stations must pay annual licensing fees to performing rights organizations (PROs) to broadcast the copyrighted compositions of the organizations' members. Terrestrial, satellite, and online radio stations almost universally contract with as many as four PROs to manage licensing and payments for the legal public performance of copyrighted compositions: the American Society of Composers, Authors, and Publishers (ASCAP), Broadcast Music Incorporated (BMI), and SESAC (known formerly as the Society of European Stage Authors and Composers; the organization's website says this full name is no longer in use) represent the legal interests of thousands of composers and publishers whose works are performed on stations. In the time since the previous edition of this book went to press, a fourth PRO, Global Music Rights (GMR), emerged, attracting into its fold an impressive number of copyright holders of some of pop music's most noteworthy compositions.

Stations collectively negotiate through the industry's Radio Music Licensing Committee (RMLC) with the PROs to establish fair and just licensing fees. ASCAP and BMI, the organizations with the largest membership rosters, are fee-based, with payments determined according to station revenue. Both PROs offer a "blanket" license for music stations that "covers" stations' usage of all compositions within the organizations' catalogs. In the case of ASCAP, the amount paid by AM and FM stations at this writing was 1.7% of annual gross income. According to ASCAP, noncommercial radio stations "pay an annual fee determined by the U.S. Copyright Office."

**FIGURE 3.27**
BMI is one of four prominent performing rights organizations (PROs)
Source: Courtesy of BMI

Licensing fees range from a few hundred dollars at small, noncommercial, educational stations to tens of thousands of dollars at large, commercial, metro-market stations. The payments made by stations are then distributed to the composers and publishers of the songs that were broadcast in accordance with formulas established by each PRO. *Inside Radio* cites results of an academic study that estimated that terrestrial stations in 2014 paid a collective sum of $382 million in royalties to ASCAP, BMI, and SESAC. Contrary to public perception, financial compensation for performing artists and musicians is available only to those who also compose and publish songs that receive "public performance" credit via airplay on terrestrial stations. In fact, for almost seven decades broadcasters have regarded the publicity for performers and their record labels generated by airplay as equitable compensation.

When framing the Digital Millennium Copyright Act (DMCA), Congress moved in a new direction with respect to the matter of artist compensation. Passed in 1998, the DMCA requires owners of online music streaming websites, including those of broadcast stations and pureplays such as Pandora, to obtain licenses for the legal permission to disseminate copyrighted compositions and recordings. Permission was required not only for the right to stream copyrighted music recordings but also for commercials in which the vocal talents of union members was utilized. Securing these rights necessitated the payment of fees additional to the amounts paid to the PROs for the performance rights associated with the streaming of copyrighted compositions. In sum, the obligation of stations to compensate composers, publishers, and, now, performers and record labels, was one that many of the pioneer online webcasters was not prepared to meet. The unforeseen financial burden produced a chilling effect on the nascent online radio industry. As a result, operators of numerous stations who were unable or unwilling to pay up elected instead to shutter their webstreams.

Since 2007 the recorded music industry has advocated passage of legislation that would levy what has been termed a "performance tax" on stations that would be collected and distributed to the community of musicians and record labels. Passage of this legislation would bring about a sea change in the industry, obligating station owners for the first time in the 80-plus-year history of the medium to pay

# EIGHT THINGS BROADCASTERS SHOULD KNOW ABOUT MUSIC ROYALTIES

## David Oxenford

While broadcasters are familiar with the rules set up by the FCC, many are far less comfortable with the copyright laws that deal with the use of music in their over-the-air broadcasts and on their digital platforms, including any webcast services that they offer or any podcasts that they produce. Here are eight things that any broadcaster should know about music royalties.

**1.** The royalties you pay to ASCAP, BMI, and SESAC cover only your normal programming uses of musical compositions—and do not cover the inclusion of recorded music in commercials, promos or online services other than simulcasts.

The royalties that a broadcaster pays to ASCAP, BMI, and SESAC cover only the public performance of musical compositions—the words and musical notes of a song. For commercial broadcasters, the licenses that you obtain from these organizations also cover playing your over-the-air programming in your studio building and on your telephone lines for people who are on hold, and simulcast Internet streams. But these licenses are only for the words and music—the actual recording of a song by a particular singer or band (the "sound recording") is not covered by these royalties. At the time that this article was written, broadcasters do not have to pay royalties for the public performance of the sound recording when it is broadcast over the air or when playing in their studios, but they do when their programming is delivered to the public by Internet streaming or through other digital delivery methods (see #3 below).

However, as these royalties give you only the public performance rights and only to the musical compositions, these rights do not give a station the right to make copies of a song linked up with spoken words (like in an advertising commercial produced by a station), and they do not give you the rights to take the tune of a popular song and create new lyrics for that song to use in a commercial or station promotion. Nor do they give you the rights to take the sound recording of that song and use it in any commercial or other recorded program not meant for immediate onetime airing on the station. So using a popular song in a commercial or promotion, especially if it will be provided to other stations or redistributed on the Internet or through other communications channels, needs rights that are usually obtained directly from the composers (or their publishing companies) and the performers (or their record companies).

**2.** ASCAP, BMI, and SESAC may not be the only collection societies you'll have to pay for the public performance of musical compositions.

For decades, ASCAP, BMI, and SESAC have been the only organizations that collect royalties for the public performance of musical compositions in the United States. Most stations, especially music-intensive stations, need rights from all three collection societies, as each of these societies holds the rights to license the public performance of different songs, and most music stations will play music from each of these organizations. Some stations will try to eliminate SESAC music (as it is the smallest of the three organizations) to avoid paying their royalties, but they need to be careful that their music does not appear in commercials, production music, or syndicated programming airing on the station.

There is nothing that legally precludes the creation of new licensing societies. In 2017, radio broadcasters heard from a new society asking for royalties for the public performance of musical compositions— Global Music Rights ("GMR"). GMR was formed by a music industry veteran, who convinced a number of major composers to withdraw their songs from ASCAP and BMI and license them through GMR. Stations that play GMR music, and many will, need to pay GMR royalties as well as those of the other three collection societies. As GMR has signed major artists in many formats, especially classic rock and contemporary hit radio, stations need to look at paying GMR royalties to avoid legal issues.

Nothing precludes the formation of new collection organizations in the future. Some publishing companies (the companies that deal with most of the business and legal issues for composers) with large catalogs of music have suggested that they might, at some point, attempt to license the music to which they hold the rights themselves, withdrawing from ASCAP or BMI. Watch trade press reports carefully for news of these changes.

**3.** All stations that stream music must pay royalties to SoundExchange in addition to the royalties that are paid to ASCAP, BMI, and SESAC.

I am always surprised that there are still broadcasters who don't realize that, when they stream their music, they need to pay SoundExchange in addition to ASCAP, BMI, and SESAC. SoundExchange is paid for the digital performance of sound recordings. The royalties that they collect are split between the performers themselves and the copyright holder in the sound recording (typically the record label). Once a station makes an Internet transmission, the station needs to pay not only ASCAP, BMI, and SESAC but also SoundExchange.

In the United States, at this time, broadcasters pay SoundExchange royalties only in connection with nonbroadcast digital transmissions of sound recordings. Other digital music providers, such as SiriusXM and webcasters, also pay these royalties. In much of the rest of the world, broadcasters do pay these royalties for their over-the-air programming. SoundExchange and the record companies have been pushing Congress to change the laws to require that broadcasters also pay these royalties. At the time that this article was written, those efforts have not been successful, but watch for future actions in this area.

**4.** There are limits on the music that you can play under the SoundExchange license.

To be able to pay under the license that is administered by SoundExchange, you need to observe certain rules that limit the music that you play. These rules were set up to make it difficult for listeners to record music by knowing what artists were coming up, and also to prevent digital services from setting up single-artist channels that could substitute for music sales.

The rules, called the "performance complement," prohibit a webcaster from playing more than two songs from the same album consecutively. A webcaster also cannot play more than three songs from the same album in a three-hour period, nor can it play more than four songs from any artist (or even from different artists featured in the same collection, e.g., a box set) in a three-hour period. You also cannot preannounce when a song will be played, nor publish a program guide that sets that out when particular songs will be aired (except for classical music stations that were publishing program guides 20 years ago when these rules were adopted).

The National Association of Broadcasters (NAB) has negotiated waivers from two of the major record labels for broadcasters who simulcast their over-the-air signal, as long as such stations observe a conventional radio format. So, if you are covered by these waivers (and one requires a specific opt-in notification to the label), you could stream a broadcast containing a feature on a band where you exceed the performance complement. But you probably could not go an all-Beatles format or another format that is not typically what is aired by a broadcast station. In any such feature that has performances that exceed the performance complement, you need to be sure that the music comes from one of the labels that has agreed to the NAB waiver. Technically, if you can't abide by these rules, you must either stop streaming the portion of your programming that does not comply or get direct licenses from the record labels to use their music in a manner different than permitted under the SoundExchange license— and such negotiations are not an easy task.

**5.** You need to report what you play and how many people heard each song.

As part of the SoundExchange royalty obligations, stations need to report monthly on the songs that they have streamed, and how many people heard some or all of each track. Payments due for such streaming must also be made monthly, within 45 days of the end of a month. Some noncommercial stations and some stations with very small streaming audiences may have more limited reporting requirements. Check with an attorney to make sure that your station fits these limited exemptions.

Most stations work with a streaming service provider that measures the station's online audience on a constant basis, and generates reports of music use by correlating the listening numbers with the songs that are scheduled in the station's music scheduling software. SoundExchange can audit webcasters—and they usually conduct a number of audits each year to make sure that the monthly reports accurately depict the music that was played. ASCAP, BMI, and SESAC also require reporting, though usually for broadcasters it requires only the submission of playlist information for a few weeks each quarter. These organizations also have the rights under their agreements to audit broadcasters to ensure their compliance with their royalty obligations.

**6.** SoundExchange royalties apply only to "noninteractive" streams—and not to podcasts or any on-demand music service.

A SoundExchange license only gives you the right to stream music in a noninteractive manner—one where the listener does not know and cannot control the specific song that is coming up next. Essentially, when Congress created the license that is paid to SoundExchange, they made it easy for online stations to write one monthly check and get rights to all of the music they wanted to use, but the license is restricted to services that essentially act like radio—the listener can pick the kind of music that they want to hear, but he or she never knows for sure what the next song will be. So, using the SoundExchange license the listener can pick a rock station, or a jazz stream or a classical site, and they can even have a webcaster create a channel of music that sounds like a particular artist. But, for the service to qualify to pay SoundExchange, the listener can't be in a position to know what the next song will be.

For any other online offering where the listener knows what he or she will be hearing, or where they can figure it out because the same songs are always played in the same order—downloads, music services such as Spotify or Rhapsody where you can pick a song and hear it on demand, on-demand streams where the same songs are streamed in the same order every time you click on the stream, or podcasts that contain music—the service needs to get the rights to use the music directly from the copyright owner. Broadcasters need to be careful about the ways that they may use music, for instance in podcasts—as SoundExchange, ASCAP, BMI, and SESAC do not cover that kind of use—so the station will need to get permission directly from the artist or record label to use music in this manner.

**7.** SoundExchange rates are paid on a per-performance basis, while ASCAP, BMI, SESAC, and GMR seek royalties based on a percentage of revenue.

Because, when streaming, a broadcaster (or any other webcaster) can count exactly how many people are listening at any time, royalties are paid on a per song, per listener basis. That means that each time a song is played, broadcasters need to count how many people are listening to that song, and pay royalties based on the total number of songs listened to by each listener. In 2017, when this article was written, nonsubscription webcasters paid at the rate of $.0017 per song per listener. These rates will be adjusted each year to take into account increases in the cost of living, and will be reviewed in 2020, with potentially different rates to take effect in 2021 (see below). Noncommercial stations (except those that receive Corporation for Public Broadcasting [CPB] money as CPB has negotiated a separate music license) pay a flat $500 per year for up to 159,140 aggregate tuning hours per month. If a noncommercial webcaster streams more than that on any stream, most pay at the commercial rates.

ASCAP, BMI, and SESAC royalties are paid as a percentage of the revenue of a broadcaster, and also include revenues that the broadcaster receives from its over-the-air simulcast streaming. Webcast streams originated by a broadcaster which are not a simulcast of a broadcast station or HD stream are subject to different royalties that these organizations charge webcasters. If you do not pay the royalties or otherwise get the rights to the music that you use, you are subject to a lawsuit for copyright infringement. Such suits can result in huge damages, as much as $150,000 per song used without permission.

**8.** How are these royalties set?

Royalties for SoundExchange are set by the Copyright Royalty Board every five years. The Copyright Royalty Board is a three-judge panel appointed by the Librarian of Congress. They conduct hearings to determine commercially reasonable royalties to be paid by digital services (unless parties representing the services can reach a settlement with SoundExchange as to what the royalties should be). The current royalties for webcasting expire at the end of 2020, so a proceeding will begin in 2019 and be finalized in 2020 to set rates that go into effect in 2021 unless royalties are voluntarily negotiated by groups representing different types of webcasters before then.

ASCAP and BMI royalties are negotiated between groups representing various industry segments and these performing rights organizations. Commercial radio is usually represented by the Radio Music License Committee. TV has a similar organization. Another organization represents religious broadcasters. Other groups represent various noncommercial broadcasters. If no agreement can be reached with any group of similarly situated broadcasters, a trial to set reasonable royalties is held by US District Court Judges who oversee antitrust consent decrees that govern these organizations. SESAC, while not subject to an antitrust consent decree, has agreed in settlements of antitrust lawsuits with the radio and TV industries to arbitrate the royalties that will be paid by commercial broadcasters. These rates will be reviewed every three years, unless rates are voluntarily negotiated. Other music rights, like those to be paid by GMR, are still under review. At the time that this article was written (in mid-2017), there is litigation between RMLC and GMR to determine if they too should be subject to some sort of arbitration process, or whether the rates that are charged by GMR can be freely set by that organization.

\*

These points just scratch the surface on these questions, as the whole area of music rights is incredibly complicated. For more information about music rights and the SoundExchange royalty, you can check out my blog—www.broadcastlawblog.com (under the internet radio or music rights topics), or look at the websites of the various collection organizations under the "service provider" tab. But, if you are looking to use music in any broadcast or digital setting, it is always best to consult a lawyer familiar with these issues.

---

**David Oxenford** is an attorney who has been representing broadcasters on regulatory and transactional matters for over 35 years. He also advises broadcasters and digital media companies on copyright issues, particularly those dealing with music licensing. He is a Partner in the Washington DC office of the law firm Wilkinson Barker Knauer LLP. David is a regular speaker at conferences and seminars hosted by national and state broadcast associations, and is also the principal writer of the widely read Broadcast Law Blog, www.broadcastlawblog.com.

**FIGURE 3.28**

Protecting artists' income and rights

Source: Courtesy of SoundExchange

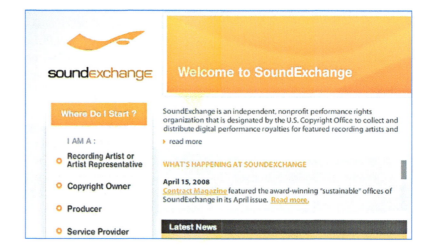

royalties to artists for terrestrial broadcasts of copyrighted recordings. The National Association of Broadcasters (NAB) as of this writing has successfully lobbied against the measure, citing the promotional value that radio broadcasting afforded the recorded music industry as sufficient compensation and hinting to the potential for job cutbacks at the local station level if the legislation passes.

In a move that attracted industry attention, Clear Channel Communications (known today as iHeartMedia) announced in 2012 that it had agreed to share a percentage of its broadcast revenues with Nashville record label Big Machine in return for label consideration. Clear Channel said it anticipated the deal with the label, and its roster of high-profile artists including Taylor Swift, Tim McGraw, and Rascal Flatts, would propel the growth of its online content aggregator app. The company subsequently struck deals with other labels. Other prominent corporate owners, notably Entercom, Greater Media, and Beasley Broadcast Group Inc., followed suit, negotiating sharing agreements with record labels. CBS Radio created the position director/music initiatives, whose responsibilities include creating partnerships with labels for the purpose of promoting established and developing artists. These relationship-development announcements are strong indicators that the two industries were interested in discovering the mutual benefits that can accrue as a result of partnership agreements.

## MANAGING THE MUSIC LIBRARY

When music arrives at the station, whether it is in physical or electronic form, the music director (sometimes more appropriately called the music librarian or music assistant) processes the recordings through the system. This may take place after the PD has screened them. The following passage describes the processes for storing and retrieving songs. For a detailed description of how music directors identify and evaluate newly released and recurrent recordings see Chapter 6. After the decision is made to add a tune to the library, the song is categorized and indexed, typically in accordance with station-defined parameters. Programmer Jon Lutes suggests this approach to the classifications of songs, designating music categories in the following manner: new music, medium current, hot current, hot recurrent, medium recurrent, bulk recurrent, power gold, secondary gold, tertiary gold, and so forth. It must be emphasized that each station approaches cataloging in its own fashion as there are no FCC rules that speak to this activity.

Here is a simple example. An AC outlet receives an album by a popular female vocalist whose last name begins with an L. The PD auditions the album and decides to place three cuts into regular on-air rotation. The music director then assigns the cuts the following catalog numbers: L106/U/F, L106/D/F, and L106/M/F. L106 indicates where the album may be located in the library, either in a physical storage location or in a software database. In this case, the library is set up alphabetically and then numerically within the given letter that represents the artist's last name. In other words, this would be the 106th album found in the section reserved for female vocalists whose names begin with an L. The next symbol indicates the pace (termed "tempo") of the cut: U(p) tempo, D(own) tempo, and M(edium) tempo. Subcategorizing songs by tempo enables the programmer to adjust the pacing of the presentation. The F that follows the tempo symbol indicates the artist's gender: female. Playlists are then assembled and stored as a log file for playout in automated or live-assist facilities or printed for use in stations operated manually by the deejays. Software executes the playout of songs, selecting them from an internal music-rotation database.

The number of companies selling both hardware and software designed for playout offers great choice to programmers. Among the computerized music systems, RCS GSelector Micropower Corporation's Powergold, MusicMaster, Music 1, and Natural Music from Broadcast Software International are some of the most successful and widely used. *Billboard,* in both its print and online versions, and *Mediabase* remain valued sources of music industry information. Format-specific chart and artist information can be found on the All Access Music Group website and in its emailed newsletters.

**FIGURE 3.29**
RCS Selector2Go, mobile program scheduling software for use across all web platforms and devices

Source: Courtesy of RCS

## ADVICE TO PROGRAMMERS

**Frank Bell**

### Rule 1: Follow the Listeners, Not the Format

So many people in radio get caught up in terms such as CHR, hot AC, alternative, and active rock that they lose track of their goal: finding listeners. Consumers of radio think in terms of "what I like" and "what I don't like." By researching your listeners' tastes and giving them what they want (as opposed to what fits the industry's definition of what they should have), you'll maximize your chances for success.

### Rule 2: Think Outside In, Not Inside Out

The fact that one company may now own several stations in a market and is capable, for example, of skewing one FM toward younger females and the other toward older females does not mean that you will automatically "dominate females." The only reality that counts is that of the listener. If listeners feel your station serves a meaningful purpose for them, they will happily consume your product and cast their vote in your favor if approached by a ratings company. If they believe you are simply duplicating what is already available elsewhere on the dial, you will be doomed to ratings obscurity.

### Rule 3: Early to Bed, Early to Rise, Advertise, Advertise, Advertise

In the ratings game, the dominant issue is "top-of-mindness," regardless of whether Nielsen is measuring unaided recall with diaries or actual behavior with Personal People Meters. The best way to get that is through advertising your name and your station's benefits on your own air and on any other medium you can afford. Just for fun, here's a diagram I sometimes use to show first-time PDs the various factors that influence their station's ratings:

$$\frac{X - Y}{A} \times B = \text{ Your Ratings}$$

$X$ is what your station does. $Y$ is what your direct competitors do. $A$ represents "environmental" factors in the market, such as what's on TV during the survey, riots, floods, earthquakes, and major sporting events. $B$ is what the rating service does. In the case of Nielsen, this would include the response rate, editing procedures, and distribution of respondents by race, age, and sex. The most important thing to understand is that, as PD, the only part of the equation you can control is $X$. Do the best you can to keep your station sounding compelling, entertaining, and focused on its target audience, and don't get an ulcer over those elements you can't control.

---

After graduating from American University in 1977, **Frank Bell** embarked on a radio adventure covering 33 years and hundreds of successful stations. Beginning as an on-air talent, he bought his first radio station with some friends at age 25 and later applied those programming, research and marketing skills as a corporate executive on behalf of privately owned companies such as Keymarket Communications and publicly traded Sinclair Communications and Cumulus Media. In 2010, he joined 13 Management in Nashville to oversee radio station and record label relations for international superstar Taylor Swift.

## THE PD AND THE FCC

The government is especially interested in the way a station conducts itself on the air. For instance, the PD makes certain that his or her station is properly identified once an hour, as close to the top of the hour as possible. The ID must include the station's call letters and the town in which it has been authorized to broadcast. Failure to properly identify the station is a violation of FCC rules.

Other on-air rules that the PD must address have to do with program content and certain types of features. For example, profane language, obscenity, sex- and drug-related statements, and even innuendos in announcements, conversations, or music lyrics can jeopardize the station's license. The FCC prohibits indecent broadcasts during certain hours of the day, and the cost for violating this rule can cost the station dearly. For example, in 2006, the Commission raised the maximum charge for offenses in this category from $32,500 to $325,000 per violation. Adjustments for inflation are made periodically, and as a result the penalty increased to approximately $383,000 in 2016. Complaints from the public about indecency on TV outnumber those lodged against radio broadcasters and the FCC tends not to impose the penalty maximum amount. Political messages and station editorials are carefully scrutinized by the programmer. On-air contests and promotions must not resemble lotteries in which the audience must invest to win. A station that gets something in return for awarding prizes is subject to punitive actions. Contest rules must be clearly delineated and publicized, although in 2015 the FCC began permitting stations to disclose rule information on their websites instead of over their airwaves, provided that stations announced to listeners the web URL where the information had been published. PD eyes and ears must be attentive to station promotions that create hoaxes, which could endanger public safety.

No one associated with the station may receive payment for plugging a song or album on the air. This constitutes "payola" or "plugola" and was the cause of great industry upheaval in the late 1950s. Today, PDs and station managers continue to be particularly careful to guard against any recurrence, although there have been charges that such practices still exist. In fact, in the mid-2000s the FCC began a formal investigation into payola allegations against four major radio groups: CBS Radio, Clear Channel, Entercom, and Citadel. It was the largest federal inquiry since the payola scandals prompted congressional hearings in 1960. Indeed, PDs must be vigilant of this illegal practice, which seems impervious to eradication.

The PD must monitor both commercial and noncommercial messages to ensure that no false, misleading, or deceptive statements are aired, and that sponsors and endorsers are properly identified, including

so-called "pay-for-play" arrangements. Additionally, it is the PD's responsibility to ensure that the content of station promotional messages excludes any distortion of the station's ratings survey results. A station that is not number one and claims to be is lying to the public as far as the FCC is concerned, and such behavior is not condoned. The PD should uphold the public interest standard, maintaining a proportion of entertainment to nonentertainment (news and public affairs features) programming. The PD helps maintain the station's Emergency Alert System (EAS), making certain that proper announcements are made on the air and that the testing protocol is followed. PDs also instruct personnel in the proper procedures used when conducting on-air telephone conversations to guarantee that the rights of callers are not violated.

The station log (which ultimately is the chief engineer's responsibility) and program log (no longer required by the FCC but maintained, at least for a brief period of time, by most stations anyway) are examined by the PD for accuracy. In addition, the station manager may assign the PD the responsibility for maintaining records in the station's public inspection file. If so, the PD must be fully aware of what documents the file is required to contain, and where to preserve them. In 2017 the FCC voted to eliminate its requirement that stations maintain in the PI file paper copies of letters and emails received from the public. The FCC and many state broadcast associations will provide station operators with a public inspection file checklist upon request. This information is available in the Code of Federal Regulations (47CFR73.3526) as well.

Additional programming areas of interest to the FCC include procedures governing rebroadcasts and subcarrier activities. The PD also must be aware that the government is keenly interested in employment practices. The programmer, station manager, and other

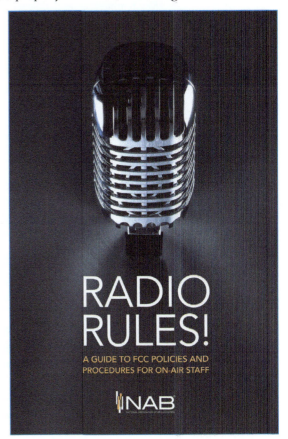

**FIGURE 3.31**
Cover image of *Radio Rules!*
Source: Courtesy of National Association of Broadcasters

department heads are under an obligation to familiarize themselves with equal employment opportunity (EEO) and affirmative action rules. An annual employment report must be sent to the FCC. Personnel associated with noncommercial stations have the additional responsibility of complying with "underwriting" regulations and the on-air acknowledgments of contributors. The FCC draws a line between announcements that merely acknowledge contributing businesses from those that cross the line and promote them.

Detailed information about FCC regulations and practices of specific interests to programmers and air talent employed by commercial radio stations may be found in the publication *Radio Rules! A Guide to FCC Policies and Procedures for On-Air Staff*. Published by the National Association of Broadcasters (NAB) and available from the NAB Store at nabstore.com, *Radio Rules!* is a concise reference document that examines more than two dozen topics related to programming and internal operations of commercial radio stations.

## THE PD AND UPPER MANAGEMENT

The pressures of the PD's position should be apparent by now. The station or cluster programmer knows well that his or her job entails satisfying the desires of many—the audience, government, air staff, and, of course, management. The relationship between the PD and the station or corporation's upper echelon is not always serene or without incident. Although their alliance is usually mutually fulfilling and productive, difficulties can and do occur when philosophies or practices clash. Radio legend Dick Fatherly summarized the delicate nature of the PD–GM relationship:

> Most inhibiting and detrimental to the PD is the GM who lacks a broad base of experience but imposes his opinions on you anyway. The guy who has come up through sales and has never spent a minute in the studio can be a real thorn in the side. Without a thorough knowledge of programming, management should rely on the expertise of that person hired who does. I don't mean, "Hey, GM, get out of the way!" what I'm saying is, don't impose programming ideas and policies without at least conferring with that individual who ends up taking the heat if the air product fails to bring in the listeners.

Station manager Chuck Ducoty contends that managers can enhance as well as inhibit the programmer's style:

> I've worked for some managers who give their PDs a great deal of space and others who attempt to control every aspect of programming. From the station manager's perspective, I think the key to a good experience with those who work for you is to find excellent people from the start and then have enough confidence in your judgment to let them do their job with minimal interference. Breathing down the neck of the PD is just going to create tension and resentment.

Programmer Peter Falconi believes that both the PD and the manager should make a sincere effort to get to know and understand one another:

> You have to be on the same wavelength, and there has to be an excellent line of communication. When a manager has confidence and trust in his PD, he'll generally let him run with the ball. It's a two-way street. Most problems can be resolved when there is honesty and openness.

Programmer Andy Bloom offers this observation: "Great upper management hires the best players, gives them the tools to do their job, and then leaves them alone. A winning formula." An adversarial relationship between the station's PD and upper management does not have to exist. The station that cultivates an atmosphere of cooperation and mutual respect seldom becomes embroiled in skirmishes that deplete energy—energy better spent raising revenues and ratings.

# PROGRAM CONSULTANTS AND SYNDICATORS

Radio programming consultants have been around almost from the start, but it was not until the medium set a new course following the advent of television that the field grew to real prominence. By the 1960s, consultants were directing the programming efforts of hundreds of stations. In the 1970s, more than one-third of the nation's stations enlisted the services of consultants. The number of stations increased from 2,000 in the 1950s to more than 18,000 in the 2010s. As formats emerged and splintered, the number of consultants initially rose, too; their duties enlarged to include providing counsel about music selection, audience research, and marketing. Independent consultancies experienced a reversal of fortunes in the aftermath of the 1996 ownership rules changes as several large group owners relocated the responsibilities to in-house advisors. Today, the field of radio consultancy has shrunk substantially due to the corporatization of the radio industry.

Longtime pro Mark St. John, Co-Founder with Guy Zapoleon of Zapoleon Media Strategies, comments on the changes consolidation have visited upon the consultancies, saying: "Consolidation has definitely had a major impact on our business. The two major chains, iHeartmedia and Cumulus, do not hire outside consultants for the most part. They have highly evolved internal structures to oversee programming efforts." Joel Raab, of Joel Raab Associates, is another consultant who sees opportunities for growth. Regarding the impact of corporatization on his consultancy, which specializes in servicing country-formatted stations, Raab observes, "From my perspective, I could argue that it has helped. My business is as strong as ever." Millennials, according to successful consultant and educator Donna Halper, typically

> find radio boring, with too many commercials and the same songs over and over. To get these people back (and I do believe it can be done) radio needs to return to its roots and get involved with the community again. As a consultant and someone who loves radio, I hope we will see more local personalities and more local programming. Radio needs to get back to being a friend again.

"Professionals running radio stations want to win," Mark St. John observes, "and that is why we are hired in the first place." Reluctance by managers to pursue new approaches and ideas *can* be overcome, says Raab:

> My experience with GMs is that they *will* take risks, as long as you can show them that those risks have a good chance of paying off. It helps if you can give a real-life example in which a certain idea has worked. It's all about dollars and cents.

Calling upon her considerable experience enables consultant Valerie Geller to reconcile the risk-aversion mentality philosophically:

> Risk is always a challenge. Radio is a creative process. While the fear of failure can loom even larger in a tight economy, if you want to win, you have to try new things. Risk is part of the game.

She concedes the uncertainty by analogizing the radio business with a social institution: "Yes, radio is a risky business, but so is getting married (which statistically has a 50% failure rate) but that doesn't stop people from getting married." She notes in her seminal text *Beyond Powerful Radio—A Communicator's Guide to the Internet Age* that

> the emphasis is on taking those risks in a very calculated way. The book specifically shows you how to maximize your creative risk to achieve potential success. Often my job as a consultant is to help clients get to the place where they can appreciate the benefits of risking and succeeding. But it's harder for some than for others.

Whether the radio consultancy function will be completely absorbed by corporations remains to be seen. However, consultants continue to play an important role in the shaping and management of the medium today.

Stations use consultants for various reasons, says Fred Jacobs, president of Jacobs Media:

> Stations realize that they need an experienced, objective ear to make intelligent evaluations. Consultants are also exposed to ideas and innovations from around the country that they can bring to their client stations. As radio has become more competitive, stations understand that their need for up-to-date information about current trends in programming and marketing has increased.

Fewer than 100 broadcast consultants are listed in the various media directories around the country. Joel Raab views the shift from independency to corporate employment as beneficial to both parties, serving to make programming at the owner level stronger. St. John views the moves to corporate employment by these former independents as good for his business. As he sees it,

> some of the top programming minds in America from Mike McVay to Steve Smith to Guy Zapoleon are now working inside companies. That trend is likely to continue and has to be viewed as a positive for those of us remaining as independent consultants!

Again, in the age of station consolidation and massive radio groups, consultancy often originates in-house. One of the distinct benefits that major corporations accrue, according to Valerie Geller, is exclusivity. She explains, "One advantage from the corporate perspective: When you hire somebody to work for you, he or she won't be available to be hired by your competitors to work against you." She regards the impact of corporate hiring on the profession as minimal, reasoning that "hiring a company in-house 'group' consultant has solved some problems for certain station groups, it has not fundamentally changed the nature of the work we do."

The stations Joel Raab consults that operate outside the larger markets tend to need basic programming and audience-relationship guidance: "In smaller markets, we are doing more music scheduling than ever for stations, as staff cutbacks and quality control issues have necessitated more involvement on our part. More time is spent advising clients regarding social media usage and concerns." Among other services, Fred Jacobs says his company offers

> in-market visits for monitoring and strategizing; ongoing monitors of client competition from airchecks or station "listen lines"; critiques of on-air talent, assistance/design of music scheduling and selection; computer programs that assist with promo scheduling, database marketing, and morning show preparation; design of off-air advertising and coordination with production; and design/implementation of market research for programming, image, and music.

Following an extensive assessment of a station's programming, a consultant may suggest a major change:

> After an in-depth evaluation and analysis, we may conclude that a station is improperly positioned in its particular market and recommend a format switch. Sometimes station management disagrees. Today, the majority of stations in major and medium markets switching formats do so with the aid of a consultant (or an in-house programming executive in cluster situations).

According to the National Association of Broadcasters (NAB), 3–5% of the nation's stations change formats each year. Consultants' fees range from hundreds to thousands of dollars per day, depending on the complexity of the services rendered and the size of the station and its market.

## PROGRAM SUPPLIERS

One part art, one part technology: what the glib, personality-driven, deejay approach did to revolutionize program presentation in the 1950s, so did the emergence of "automated" radio during the 1960s. In a triumph of technology, automation systems enabled station operators to minimize the need for human intervention by storing music, commercials, weather announcements, and other program elements on magnetic recording tape and then schedule and sequentially play back the recordings at a later date. Because the process for automating the broadcast was technically sophisticated the circumstances motivated station management to seek out syndicator services that could, for a fee, provide the station with libraries of prerecorded music and instructions for format execution. Today, digital storage devices have displaced the analog tape playback systems of yesteryear. When properly executed, the automated format of today can sound so lifelike as to be virtually indistinguishable from live programming. In addition to numerous independent syndicators many of the large radio corporations create programming for distribution to their own stations, relaying real-time program content by satellite and Internet. As a result, fewer independent 24-hour format suppliers exist today. As Jay Williams observes:

> Consolidation changed the syndication business; two of the largest syndicators are now owned by the biggest station groups. Perhaps because their own stations are now clients, or perhaps because individual stations are reluctant to rehire staff after the recession, or maybe it's because national advertisers are increasing their support, but syndicated programming and products have improved and become more popular. Once relegated to late nights and weekends, syndicated shows have found their way to every daypart including morning drive. And as syndicators have become more adept at creating flexible, customized original programming, that trend will continue.

It has been estimated that over half of the country's radio outlets have purchased syndicated programming of some type, which may consist of as little as a series of one- or two-minute features or as much as a 24-hour, year-round station format. Both economics and service motivate radio stations to contract syndicators. Equally as prominent are the providers of the 24-hour automated formats, companies that specialize in dayparted and occasional special-event programming to meet specific broadcaster needs. For smaller-market stations, syndicated programs offer several distinct advantages, as Jay Williams explains. According to him:

> The advantages of airing outside programming are compelling especially for small and medium-market radio stations. It might cost $30,000 or more for a local operator to create a home-grown morning show with two people, but that includes risks. The local morning show may not be successful, the talent may not get along, or perhaps worse, the local show is so successful the talent is lured away to a larger market. Yet for that same amount of money, a station can choose a successful syndicated morning show and eliminate their management worries. That alone makes syndication an appealing option especially for non-programming oriented station owners and managers.

## SYNDICATOR SERVICES

The name "Drake–Chenault" was synonymous with the 24/7, tape-based program syndication business in the late 1960s. Founded by legendary programmer Bill Drake and business partner Gene Chenault, D–C distinguished itself from the various instrumental music format syndicators of the day, notably Schulke Radio Productions and Bonneville, by incorporating recorded song-and-artist deejay intro and outro announcements into the music presentation. Embellishing an automated music format with deejay announcements is commonplace today, but it was quite a technological achievement for D–C, whose signature automated format, "HitParade," predated today's digitized voice-tracking technique by several decades.

The major program syndicators of the tape-based era prospered in the 1970s through the 1990s, usually marketing several distinctive, fully packaged radio formats. "In its heyday, Peters Productions made available a complete format service with each of their format blends. They were not merely a music service. Their programming goal was the emotional gratification of the type of person attracted to a particular format," says Dick Ellis, whose former company offered a dozen different formats, including beautiful music, easy listening, standard country, modern country, adult contemporary, standard MOR, super hits, easy contemporary, and a country and contemporary hybrid called natural sound. Century 21 Programming also was a leader in format diversity, explains Dave Scott. "Our inventory included everything from the most contemporary super hits sound to several Christian formats. We even offered a full-time Jazz format. We had programming to fit any need in any market."

The demand for syndicator product has paralleled, if not exceeded, the increase in the number of radio outlets since the 1960s. Again, the new millennium has brought a change in the field of program

syndication with the large radio corporations often assuming the responsibilities for program production in-house. Syndication of the personality-driven programs in the contemporary marketplace is dominated by only a handful of companies, led by Premiere Networks. Premiere is a subsidiary of iHeartmedia, the largest owner/operator of radio stations in the U.S. According to its website, Premiere Networks:

> syndicates 90 radio programs and services to more than 5,500 radio affiliations and reaches over 245 million listeners monthly. Premiere offers the best in talk, entertainment and sports programming featuring the following personalities: Rush Limbaugh, Ryan Seacrest, Glenn Beck, Delilah, Steve Harvey, George Noory, John Boy and Billy, Sean Hannity, Elvis Duran, Dan Patrick, Nikki Sixx, Kane, Mario Lopez, Bobby Bones, Cody Alan, Johnjay & Rich, Jay Mohr and others.

Today, WestwoodOne, United Stations Radio Network, Salem Music Network, Radio Disney, Compass Media Networks, Learfield Communications, and other firms serve the industry with specialized programming features ranging from 24/7 format delivery to rock concerts to play-by-play sports coverage.

**FIGURE 3.33**
Ray Slater

### PRODUCING *THE BOBBY BONES SHOW*

#### Ray Slater

I've produced *The Bobby Bones Show* for about four years. I started as an intern and did that for a couple of years before eventually being hired full-time in Austin, Texas. The show then moved to Nashville, Tennessee, where the show originates and where I currently live. As producer I am Bobby's right-hand man. Using a private communication system I'm the only one who talks into his ear during the show. Bobby and I both run the control board using the RCS NexGen program automation playout software. I load keys to various audio clips onto his button-bar wall that enable Bobby to select and play clips during the show.

I also send in my own personal content before the show. Here's a few examples: like this:

1. Wait till you hear what Ray wants to write off . . .

   I was drinking with a guy from the company this weekend and ended up spending $100 on booze. I want to write it off. I can't remember if we talked business but we definitely talked about the show so i think that is a write-off. You guys are lucky I didn't have the company card or I would have been swiping that thing like crazy.

ANGLE: TBBS cast member Lunchbox submitted a strip club receipt to get reimbursed because he had a meal there.

2.   Ray noticed something from *House of Cards* that nobody else did: the Underwood lady said "vote your conscience." That's the exact thing Ted Cruz said: "Vote your conscience." He ripped that line from *House of Cards*!!!!!!

ANGLE: is anyone excited about the show's upcoming season?

The entire show cast sends Bobby about 30 news stories that are interesting, all with different angles/ideas for the show. Again, this is just to help Bobby with some brainstorming. But he's the personality, so usually he comes up with about 60% of the material used on the show. During the show I also email customized content to the show's affiliated stations. This is material that airs exclusively in their market. Our show uploads to a satellite in Los Angeles for delivery to the affiliates so I communicate with people in L.A. to make sure our signal is strong and everything is running smoothly. Our conversations are usually less than 10 seconds.

My final task is to prepare a couple of segment starters for Bobby. Here's an example:

Who's the first actor to hit 100 million "likes" on Facebook? Vin Diesel. "The Fast and the Furious" star. Diesel is the third person to achieve this major milestone, following predecessors Shakira and Cristiano Ronaldo. (Source: *Entertainment Weekly*, 7/31/16)

What's America's favorite summer Olympics sport to watch on TV? We like swimming the best, followed by gymnastics, basketball, track and field, and soccer. (Source: Statista, Statistics and studies from more than 18,000 sources)

Krispy Kreme donut-flavored soda is now a thing . . . thanks to a partnership between Krispy Kreme and Cheerwine. The soda reportedly smells like a cross between cherries and Dr. Pepper, but it doesn't taste exactly like donuts.

As a producer my responsibility is to make Bobby's job as easy as possible. When he Snapchats pictures of him chilling with his dog, and not stressing about the show, that's when I know I'm doing a good job. I do have a lot of grunt work (spots/station liners/emails with program directors across America) but I genuinely enjoy the on-air/creative things I bring to the show. Last but not least I must tell you that I wake up every morning at 1 am. Because of that I am always ahead of major news stories, and, most importantly, Bobby himself! Thanks for reading!!

---

**Ray Slater** is producer of *The Bobby Bones Show*. He likes to wear cut-off shirts, works out more than anyone on the show, and is the go-to for "Could Ray Do This" with crazy web trends and challenges.

Also playing a prominent role in the program syndication marketplace are the producers of full-time music formats. Using satellites and the Internet to distribute programming to client stations, syndicators of these 24/7 formats typically provide a near-turnkey entertainment package that includes real-time delivery of deejay-hosted music and custom-tailored station imaging elements such as IDs, liners, breaks, and sweepers. Top-caliber deejay talent ensures that the overall presentation has a major-market "sound." WestwoodOne, a leading provider, makes available a variety of program formats, including country, adult contemporary, rock, classic hits, adult standards and Hispanic. The network structures the presentation in such a way as to make it equally suitable for "round-the-clock" or dayparted (nights and weekends) use. In addition to the satellite-delivered formats, which target the needs of smaller-market stations, the company offers two services for stations in larger, more competitive markets. In both instances, WestwoodOne provides tested music and imaging services, customized to the specific market.

**FIGURE 3.34**

Trade publication ad for the syndicated *Free Beer and Hot Wings Morning Show*

As far as the on-air personalities are concerned, it's up to each station to decide whether to employ local announcers or utilize out-of-market talent operating from the company's centralized studio. In the latter instance, WestwoodOne personalities utilize station-supplied, localized information about events, promotions, and weather in recording station-specific voice tracks. Relayed individually to each client station over the Internet and automatically integrated into the station's customized digital automation system, the voice tracks impart a major-market feel to broadcasts in locations where the talent-employment expense would otherwise be cost-prohibitive. Syndicators assist stations during the installation and implementation stage of a format and provide training for operators and other station personnel. Comprehensive operations manuals are left with subscribers as a source of further assistance.

Syndicators offer programs on a barter basis, for a fee without presold spots (commercial announcements) or for a fee containing spots. Leasing agreements generally stipulate a minimum two-year term and assure the subscriber that the syndicator will not lease a similar format to another station in the same market. Should a station choose not to renew its agreement with the syndicator, all material must be returned unless otherwise stipulated. The majority of format syndicators also market production libraries, jingles, and special features for general market consumption.

## CHAPTER HIGHLIGHTS

1. Radio station success is determined by programming. Program format descriptors for music-intensive stations typically are drawn from the style of music offered.

2. The AC format, in its variations, features older pop hits (since the 1970s) and more recent songs to supplement a library of current pop standards. It appeals particularly to 25–49-year-old females, which attracts advertisers. It often utilizes music sweeps and clustered commercials. AC has spawned a variety of subgenres, including adult hits, adult standards, and iPod imitators Jack and Mike.

3. CHR features current, fast-selling hits from the top 40 charts. It targets teens, broadcasts minimal news, and is very promotion/contest-oriented. The introduction of Arbitron's PPM audience measurement technology suggests renewed audience interest in the format.

4. Country is the fastest-growing format since the 1970s. More prevalent in the South and Midwest, it attracts a broad age group and offers a variety of subformats. Recently it has become the second-highest rated format nationally for teen listeners.

5. Easy listening/smooth jazz stations feature mostly instrumentals and minimal talk. The primary audience is over 50. Their popularity has dwindled in recent years owing to myriad softer AC formats.

6. The nostalgia playlist emphasizes popular tunes from the 1940s and pre-rock 1950s, presenting its music in sweeps with a relatively low deejay profile.

7. Rock or AOR stations began in the mid-1960s to counter top 40 stations. They featured music sweeps with a large airplay library, and they played rock album cuts. News was minimal. The format attracted a predominantly male audience aged 18–34. Classic rock, modern rock and alternative rock are format variants.

8. The oldies playlist includes hits between the 1950s and 1960s, relying on veteran air personalities. Commercials are placed randomly and songs are spaced to allow deejay patter.

9. UC is the "melting pot" format, attracting a heterogeneous audience. Its upbeat, danceable sound, and hip, friendly deejays attract the 18–34 age group. Contests and promotions are important.

10. Classical commercial outlets are few, but they have a loyal audience. Primarily an FM format appealing to a higher-income, college-educated (upscale, 25–49 years old) audience, classical features a conservative, straightforward air sound.

11. Religious stations are prevalent on both the FM and AM bands. Religious broadcasters usually approach programming in one of two ways. One includes music as a primary part of its presentation, whereas the other does not.

12. Ethnic stations serve the listening needs of minority groups. Black and Hispanic listeners constitute the largest ethnic audiences; Hispanic listeners constitute America's fastest-growing audience.

13. Full service (FS) stations (formerly MOR) rely on the strength of air personalities and features. Mostly an AM format, FS attempts to be all things to all people, attracting an over-40 audience.

14. Niche formats, like all-children, business, and tourist radio, are popping up all over the dial as the listening audience becomes more diffused. Radio Disney is tapping into interest in HD2 stations to deliver programming.

15. Public and noncommercial stations typically employ a block format promoting diversity rather than a single form of programming. NPR is proactively developing its online presence and podcast library.

16. PDs are hired to fit whatever format the station management has selected. They are chosen primarily for their experience, although education level is important.

17. The PD is responsible for everything that is aired. Second in responsibility for in-house operations to the general manager (except in a cluster arrangement with a director of operations), the PD establishes programming and format policy; hires and supervises on-air, music, and production personnel; handles the programming budget; develops promotions; monitors the station and its competitors and assesses research; is accountable for news, public affairs, and sports features; and may even pull an airshift.

18. The PD's effectiveness is measured by ratings in large markets and by sales in smaller markets.

19. The PD determines the content of each sound hour, utilizing program clocks to ensure that each element—commercial, news, promo, weather, music, and so on—is strategically located to enhance flow and optimize impact.

20. PDs must adjust programming to the lifestyle activities of the target audience. They must develop a feel for the area in which the station is located, as well as an understanding of survey information and research data. PDs rely on established research procedures and techniques to ascertain listeners' music preferences. Social media presence is a necessity.

21. The PD must also ensure that the station adheres to all FCC regulations pertaining to programming practices, anticipating problems before they occur. Indecent programming has resulted in huge fines, so PDs must be especially vigilant in this area.

22. Payola (plugola) has plagued the medium since the 1950s and continues to this day. The illegal pay-for-play practice requires careful monitoring by the station's PD and manager to ensure it does not occur. Large fines have been dealt to those stations violating the FCC laws governing this practice.

23. Stations must pay an annual music licensing fee to ASCAP, BMI, and/or SESAC for the privilege of broadcasting and webstreaming the copyrighted compositions of these organizations' members.

24. In the 2000s, the recording industry required that radio stations streaming music on their websites had to compensate it for such use. SoundExchange collects royalties paid by stations and distributes the proceeds to record labels and performers.

25. The significant increase in stations and formats created a market for consultants. Today, the ranks of radio consultants have been reduced due to consolidation and major radio companies typically have their own in-house consultant in the form of an experienced programming executive.

26. Consultants provide various services, including market research, programming and format design, hiring and training of staff, staff motivation, advertising and public relations campaigns, news and public affairs restructuring, social media strategies, and technical evaluation (periodic airchecks of sound quality).

27. Aspiring consultants should acquire background experience in the medium, solid educational preparation, and strong interpersonal skills.

28. Station executives opposed to using consultants fear losing the station's local flavor, becoming a clone of other stations, and having to justify the substantial expense.

29. Investments by stations in research have fallen off markedly.

30. Statistically, stations using programming consultants more often than not experience improved ratings.

31. Increased use of programming syndication is related to the increased use of computers and satellites. Most of the nation's stations purchase some form of syndicated programming.

32. Syndicated programs are generally cost-effective, of high quality, and reliable, thus allowing smaller stations to achieve a metro-station sound.

33. Program syndicators provide a variety of test-marketed, satellite- and Internet-delivered radio formats—from country to top 40 to religious. Services may include music, breaks, promos, customized IDs, and even promotions.

34. While some program syndicators charge fees for their programs, others barter (swap) programming in return for access to a station's commercial airtime inventory.

## SUGGESTED FURTHER READING

Adams, M.H. and Massey, K.K., *Introduction to Radio: Production and Programming*, Brown and Benchmark, Madison, WI, 1995.

All Access Group, *Industry Directory*, www.allaccess.com.

Armstrong, B., *The Electronic Church*, J. Nelson, Nashville, TN, 1979.

Bender, G., *Call of the Game: What Really Goes On in the Broadcast Booth*, Bonus, Chicago, IL, 1994.

Broady, J., *On Air: The Guidebook to Starting a Career as a Radio Personality*, BVI, San Bernardino, CA, 2007.

Busby, L. and Parker, D., *The Art and Science of Radio*, Allyn & Bacon, Boston, MA, 1984.

Carroll, R.L. and Davis, D.M., *Electronic Media Programming: Strategies and Decision Making*, McGraw-Hill, New York, NY, 1993.

Chapple, S. and Garofalo, R., *Rock 'n' Roll Is Here to Pay*, Nelson-Hall, Chicago, IL, 1977.

Cliff, C. and Greer, A., *Broadcasting Programming: The Current Perspective*, University Press of America, Washington, D.C., 1974 to date, revised annually.

Coddington, R.H., *Modern Radio Programming*, Tab, Blue Ridge Summit, PA, 1970.

DeLong, T.A., *The Mighty Music Box*, Amber Crest, Los Angeles, CA, 1980.

Denisoff, R.S., *Solid Gold: The Popular Record Industry*, Transaction, New York, NY, 1976.

Deweese, S.B., *Radio Syndication: How to Create, Produce, and Distribute Your Own Show*, Elfin Cove Press, Bellevue, WA, 2001.

Dingle, J.L., *Essential Radio*, Peregrine, Marblehead, MA, 1995.

Eastman, S.T., *Broadcast/Cable Programming: Strategies and Practices*, 6th edition, Wadsworth, Belmont, CA, 2001.

Geller, V., *Beyond Powerful Radio: A Communicator's Guide to the Internet Age—News, Talk, Information & Personality for Broadcasting, Podcasting, Internet, Radio*, Focal Press, Boston, MA, 2011.

Hall, C. and Hall, B., *This Business of Radio Programming*, Billboard, New York, NY, 1977.

Halper, D., *Full-Service Radio*, Focal Press, Boston, MA, 1991.

Halper, D., *Radio Music Directing*, Focal Press, Boston, MA, 1991.

Hilliard, R. and Keith, M., *Dirty Discourse: Sex and Indecency in American Radio*, Iowa State Press, Ames, IA, 2003.

Hutchby, I., *Confrontation Talk: Arguments, Asymmetries, and Power on Talk Radio*, L. Erlbaum, Mahwah, NJ, 1996.

Hutchings, W., *Radio on the Road*, 8th edition, Aslan, Fairfield, CT, 2006.

Inglis, A.F., *Satellite Technology*, Focal Press, Boston, MA, 1991.

James, J., *The PD Chronicles: Blatant Confessions of a Radio Guy*, Xlibris, Bloomington, IN, 2001.

Johnson, T. and Burns, A., *Morning Radio*, Johnson, Washington, D.C., 1999.

Keith, M.C., *Radio Programming: Consultancy and Formatics*, Focal Press, Stoneham, MA, 1987.

Keith, M.C., *Signals in the Air: Native Broadcasting in America*, Praeger, Westport, CT, 1995.

Keith, M.C., *Sounds in the Dark: All Night Radio in American Life*, Iowa State Press, Ames, IA, 2001.

Keith, M.C., *Radio Cultures: The Sound Medium in American Life*, Peter Lang, New York, NY, 2008.

Kempner, M.A., *Can't Wait Til Monday Morning: Syndication in Broadcasting*, Rivercross, Orlando, FL, 1998.

Land, J., *Active Radio: Pacifica's Brash Experiment*, University of Minnesota Press, Minneapolis, MN, 1999.

Lochte, B., *Christian Radio: The Growth of a Mainstream Force*, McFarland, Jefferson, NC, 2006.

Lujack, L. and Jedlicka, D.A., *Superjock: The Loud, Frantic, NonStop World of Rock Radio Deejays*, Regnery, Chicago, IL, 1975.

Lynch, J. and Gillispie, G., *Process and Practice of Radio Programming*, University Press of America, Lanham, MD, 1998.

MacFarland, D.T., *The Development of the Top 40 Format*, Arno Press, New York, NY, 1979.

MacFarland, D.T., *Contemporary Radio Programming Strategies*, Lawrence Erlbaum Associates, Hillsdale, NJ, 1990.

Maki, V. and Pederson, J., *The Radio Playbook*, Globe Mack, St. Louis, MO, 1991.

Matelski, M.J., *Broadcast Programming and Promotion Worktext*, Focal Press, Boston, MA, 1989.

McCoy, Q., *No Static: A Guide to Creative Programming*, Miller Freeman, Chicago, IL, 1999.

Mirabito, M.M. and Morgenstern, B.L., *New Communication Technologies: Applications, Policy, and Impact*, 4th edition, Focal Press, Boston, MA, 2000.

Morrow, B., *Cousin Brucie*, Morrow and Company, New York, NY, 1987.

NAB, *The New Media Law Handbook for Radio Broadcasters*, National Association of Broadcasters, Washington, D.C., 2007.

Norberg, E., *Radio Programming: Tactics and Strategies*, Focal Press, Boston, MA, 1996.

Passman, A., *The Deejays*, Macmillan, New York, NY, 1971.

Pierce, D., *Riding the Ether Express*, University Center for Louisiana Studies, Siana, LA, 2008.

Rhoads, B.E., Bunzel, R., Snook, A., and McMan, W. (eds.), *Programming and Promotion*, Streamline Press, West Palm Beach, FL, 1995.

Routt, E., McGrath, J.B., and Weiss, F.A., *The Radio Format Conundrum*, Hastings House, New York, NY, 1978.

Sauls, S.J., *The Culture of American College Radio*, Iowa State University Press, Ames, IA, 2000.

Shane, E., *Selling Electronic Media*, Focal Press, Boston, MA, 1999.

Sklar, R., *Rocking America: How the All-Hit Radio Stations Took Over*, St. Martin's Press, New York, NY, 1984.

Utterback, A.S., *Broadcaster's Survival Guide: Staying Alive in the Business*, Bonus, Chicago, IL, 1997.

Utterback, A.S. and Michael, G.F., *Voice Handbook: How to Polish Your On-Air Delivery*, Bonus, Santa Monica, CA, 2005.

Vane, E.T. and Gross, L.S., *Programming for TV, Radio, and Cable*, Focal Press, Boston, MA, 1994.

Warren, S., *Radio: The Book*, 3rd edition, NAB, Washington, D.C., 1999.

Wilcox, J., *Voiceovers: Techniques and Tactics for Success*, Allworth Press, New York, NY, 2007.

# CHAPTER 4

# Sales

## COMMERCIALIZATION: A RETROSPECTIVE

As of 2017, BIA/Kelsey, an advisory firm that studies trends in local advertising and marketing, reported that overall radio revenue was on the rise from previous years. The increase in advertising revenue is attributed to the maturation of digital technologies such as apps, websites, and social media platforms. The overall health of advertising generated revenue is important because selling commercials is what keeps the majority of radio stations on the air. Because of digital media firmly gaining its foothold, now radio salespeople or account executives (AE), not only sell airtime on traditional terrestrial radio but also sell advertising on digital platforms such as Internet, mobile, social media, and apps.

147

### OUTLOOK FOR LOCAL BROADCAST RADIO'S COMPETITIVENESS

**Rick Ducey**

Even with the high growth of digital listening to streaming services ranging from Spotify to Stitcher, BIA/Kelsey is forecasting a relatively stable outlook for local radio station advertising revenues in the 2016–21 period. We do see the digital portion of local radio stations' revenue becoming a more significant share of those revenues in both absolute and relative terms, rising from $1.2 billion (7.8% of total revenue) to $2.1 billion (12.5% of total revenues). Most of the digital revenues comes from selling display advertising on stations' owned and operated digital assets (e.g., web pages, mobile apps, streaming services). Some radio operators, iHeart in particular, have committed to building out digital ad platforms that leverage the incursion of programmatic ad exchanges into linear media such as broadcast radio.

**FIGURE 4.1**
Rick Ducey

Over the next five years, there are several trends that local radio broadcasters will face in the marketplace.

1. *Data-driven advertising*: Marketers have developed a strong affinity for the kinds of data-infusion they can enjoy when targeting digital listening audiences. While broadcast radio buying and selling trades primarily on Nielsen's gender and age demographics, marketers using a variety of data sources can access literally thousands of consumer attributes to target their digital buying. Linear media must develop an effective competitive response to this in cross-platform selling (i.e., broadcast and digital packages) to achieve higher growth in the advertising market.

2. *Smartphones*: Initiatives such as NextRadio that bridge the mobile app and live radio experience and iHeart Radio's My Music to link local stations with more personalized song, album, and artist choices on digital platforms including mobile phones are essential innovations for local radio's efforts to be relevant in the smartphone age.

3. *Connected cars*: As we read more about autonomous and connected cars, we may wonder about the timelines for commercial deployments and market impacts. But we do see increasing collaboration and innovation among media, auto, and tech companies when it comes to the connected car as

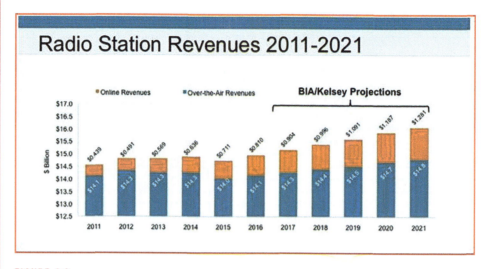

**FIGURE 4.2**
Radio's ad revenue forecast through 2021
Source: Courtesy of BIA/Kelsey

a new platform for information and entertainment. Radio used to "own the car" but it's been getting crowded out by an increasing array of infotainment options in the head unit ranging from GPS location intelligence services (location targeted ads for local and contextually relevant points of interest) to digital signage that can offer personalized messaging based on data exchanges with connected cars and mobile devices. Consumers spend a significant amount of time in the car and it's a new opportunity—and battleground—for local radio broadcasters seeking to maintain dominance in the "mobile infotainment cabin" formerly known as "the car."

4.  *Radio station valuations*: Major radio group operators continue to be frustrated by how Wall Street values their often-profitable companies versus digital pure plays that are money-losing propositions. Radio stations are typically valued by their EBITDA multiples and these have steadily declined from 11.2 in 2009 to as low as 6.5 to 7.5 in mid-2017. The explanation provided by equity analysts tracking broadcast and Internet stocks is that Wall Street values companies on future expectations or current values. Radio stocks typically aren't seen as either value or growth stocks and so don't get the same favorable treatment of digital pure play stocks that get that digital growth premium. This is the case even though broadcast radio companies can generate substantial cash flow and profitability. Broadcast radio owners and management need to develop and execute on credible growth scenarios if they wish to convert their huge listening bases into not only revenue growth but also higher corporate valuations.

**Rick Ducey** is Managing Director at BIA/Kelsey. He oversees the advisory services, strategy, and financial consulting practice areas. He is an expert in digital media innovations, competitive strategies, new product development, and new business models, including digital ecosystem collaboration strategies. Prior to joining BIA in 2000, Rick Ducey was Senior Vice-President of NAB's Research and Information Group. Before joining NAB in 1983, he was a Faculty Member in the Department of Telecommunication at Michigan State University, where he taught and researched in the areas of emerging telecommunication technologies and strategic market research. He also served on the Graduate Management Faculties of George Mason University and George Washington University in telecommunications management, and the University of Maryland, where he taught strategic market management and research methodologies. Rick Ducey received his Ph.D. from Michigan State University.

# SELLING AIRTIME

The account executive sells a radio station's audience to companies that wish to reach those listeners attracted to the station's programming. Airtime is intangible. You cannot see it or hold it in your hand; it is not like any other form of advertising. Compared to advertising in other media outlets, an effective radio commercial can make a stronger and more lasting impression on the mind of the listener in much the same way that a popular song tends to permeate the gray matter, which makes radio one of the most effective means of advertising when used correctly.

As noted, digital sales are increasing and this technology is providing radio with a fertile new area to generate revenue. According to BIA/Kelsey, at the close of 2016 digital ad revenue generated $811 million. And, in 2017, a Bridge Ratings study found that 46% of businesses include digital as a normal and regular aspect of their overall advertising strategy. In that regard, GroupM Next, the division of ad giant WPP, found that online listeners of Internet radio are more likely to buy products that have been advertised on Internet radio and less likely to jump past ads to avoid hearing them. The same study found that the average age for Internet radio listeners is 34, while the average age for terrestrial radio is 47. Further, the study predicts that Internet radio listening will increase as more automobiles are built with digital dashboards. In 2017, Pandora—the automated online music streaming service—reported that it had earned $223.3 million in the first quarter of that year alone. To compete directly with terrestrial radio, Pandora opened sales offices in 25 U.S. media markets. Pandora is becoming a fierce competitor for radio advertising dollars considering it has nearly 76.7 million listeners and 5.21 billion total listener hours for just the first quarter of 2017.

In terms of chasing advertising dollars, the radio industry is increasing its profits from local media advertising. A BIA/Kelsey study finds that local media advertising will compound annually by a rate of 4.2%, which equates to $172.2 billion by the year 2020. Mark Fratrik, BIA Senior VP and Chief Economist, told *Inside Radio* that the radio industry will rank fifth out of the 12 media outlets they tracked.

Digital advertising will account for some of radio's increased advertising revenue. BIA/Kelsey finds that in 2016 digital ad revenue rose by 14% and accounted for $811 million of the radio industry's online platforms such as apps, websites, and social media. Traditional over-the-air advertising revenue is also forecast to increase. Fratrik says:

**FIGURE 4.3**

NextMedia explains the advantages of radio advertising to clients

Source: Courtesy of NextMedia

In an age where consumers have many entertainment choices, local radio maintains its strength and popularity in the marketplace among national and local advertisers. Going from sixth to fifth is encouraging, despite the fact that there are other media growing faster than radio. It's still a very relevant part of media mixes for many advertisers, even after the onslaught of satellite radio and streaming services.

FIGURE 4.4
Radio retains through commercials (even for in-car music!) better than TV

Source: Courtesy of NuVoodoo Media and All Access.com

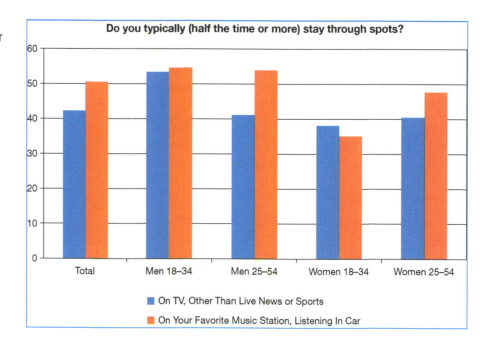

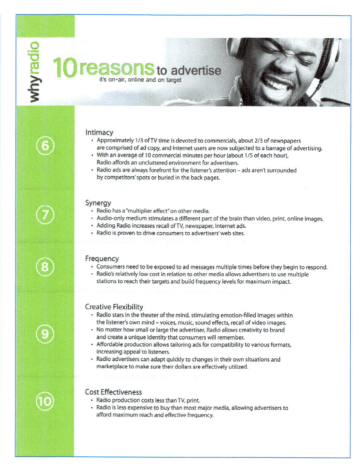

FIGURE 4.5
The Radio Advertising Bureau explains 10 reasons to advertise on radio

Source: Courtesy of the Radio Advertising Bureau

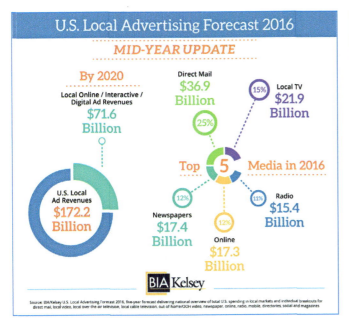

FIGURE 4.6
The local media advertising forecasts through 2020 look good for the radio industry

Source: Courtesy of BIA/Kelsey

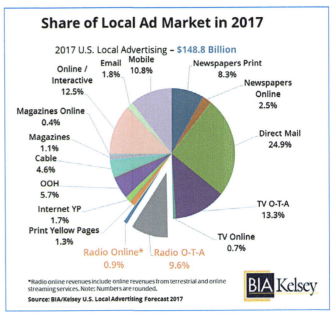

FIGURE 4.7
The share of local ad market is diversified across many media outlets. The competition for ad dollars is strong

Source: Courtesy of BIA/Kelsey

# BECOMING AN ACCOUNT EXECUTIVE

The majority of newly hired account executives have college training because a formal understanding of research, marketing, and finance is important. Broadcast sales is a familiar course at many colleges and universities with programs in mass communication. Research and marketing courses designed for the broadcast major are prevalent. Former general manager Richard Bremkamp asserts:

A degree indicates a certain amount of tenacity and perseverance, which are important qualities in anyone wanting to sell radio. Not only that, but the candidate with a degree often is more articulate and self-assured. As in most other areas of radio, ten or 15 years ago fewer people had college diplomas, but the business has become so much more sophisticated and complex because of the greater competition and emphasis on research that managers actually look for salespeople with college training.

Whether a candidate for a sales position has extensive formal training or not, he or she must possess knowledge of the product in order to be hired. The late Bob Turley, who was a general sales manager in West Virginia, said:

To begin with, an applicant must show me that they know something about radio; after all, that is what we're selling. The individual doesn't necessarily have to have a consummate understanding of the medium, although that would be nice, but they must have some product knowledge. Most stations are willing to train to an extent. I suppose you always look for someone with some sales experience, whether in radio or in some other field.

Although not an absolute requirement, stations do prefer a candidate with prior sales experience. General manager Wolf Korgyn, of KHWL-FM in Oklahoma, says:

It always makes the hiring process easier when the applicant has prior sales experience, but honestly a trained monkey can be taught to sell. What you can't teach is personality and attitude. Those are the most important traits. Everything else, I can teach them.

Weezie Kramer, Entercom's Chief Operations Officer (COO), notes that experience is necessary "sometimes but not always." Kramer explains,

Particularly today as it is sometimes easier to train someone with no experience than to un-train someone's bad experience. I would also suggest that even using the term "radio sales" does not encompass what we do. Our job is marketing solutions—and that is a relationship that is driven by understanding a client's needs and developing solutions that meet their needs (not just a sale).

Hiring inexperienced salespeople is a gamble that a small media market radio station generally must take. In larger media markets, radio sales credentials are required but that is a luxury that smaller stations cannot afford. Thus, they must hire salespeople without experience and the station must provide at least a modicum of training. Unfortunately, many stations fail to provide adequate training and this contributes to the high rate of turnover. New salespeople are commonly given two to three months to display their talents and exhibit their potential. If they prove themselves to the sales manager by generating new business, they are allowed to stay. Conversely, if the sales manager is not convinced that the apprentice salesperson has the ability to bring in new accounts, he or she is terminated.

According to RAB figures, 70% of the radio salespeople hired by stations are gone within three years; another study shows that 73% of new radio salespeople leave the business within a year. Although this sounds less than encouraging, it needs to be emphasized that to succeed in broadcast sales invariably means substantial earnings and rapid advancement. The battle can be a tough one and the dropout rate is high, but the rewards of success are great.

Radio account executives have the potential to earn a salary much larger than anyone else who works for a radio station. Contrary to popular opinion, the salesperson's salary generally exceeds the deejay's, especially in the smaller markets. In the larger markets, certain air personalities' salaries are astronomical and even surpass the general manager's income, but major-market sales salaries are commonly in the five- and even six-figure range. *Inside Radio* conducted a study which found that the average annual salary for radio salespeople in media markets 200 and smaller is $60,500, while the average annual salary in media markets one through 10 is $136,700.

Kramer explains that "most stations remain commission-based but there is a trend towards base salary plus (either commission or commission and bonus)." But the percentage of commission paid to salespeople varies from station size to market size. In a small media market, Korgyn says,

For us, since we're a brand new station and poor as hell, we're commission-only. We pay a flat 20% of gross sale when paid by the client. I think that is probably the norm for small market and "owner-operator" scenarios. Two of the other local stations here in Altus, Oklahoma pay 15% commission only as well.

Characteristics that managers most often look for in prospective salespeople include ambition, confidence, energy, determination, honesty, and intelligence. Korgyn says,

To me, the most important quality in a salesperson is the perception of being genuine and honest. If a customer trusts your salesperson, they will openly spend advertising dollars when they have them to spend. Add to that some passion, belief in the station, a touch of friendliness and a good firm handshake, and you've got the perfect salesperson.

Kramer asserts that "the following talent themes are usually found in successful radio sellers: Command, Activator, Charisma/woo, and Strategic Communication." When hiring a salesperson, Kramer adds, "self-discipline, initiative, tenacity, goal orientation, competitiveness, and self-confidence" are characteristics that are all desired qualities.

| | |
|---|---|
| 1. | Discipline |
| 2. | Attention to detail |
| 3. | Follow-through |
| 4. | Honesty |
| 5. | Listening |
| 6. | Timeliness, promptness |
| 7. | Determination |
| 8. | Thoroughness |
| 9. | Always prospecting |
| 10. | Creativeness |
| 11. | Consistently rediscovering and fulfilling prospect/client needs |
| 12. | Flexibility |
| 13. | Love the business |
| 14. | Sincerely want their clients to succeed |
| 15. | Knowledge |
| 16. | Strong work ethic |
| 17. | 50-plus-hour work week |
| 18. | Organized |
| 19. | Effective time/territory management |
| 20. | Priority management/crisis avoidance techniques |
| 21. | Accessible to clients/peers/management |
| 22. | Faith in God, self, product |
| 23. | Unwavering enthusiasm |
| 24. | Total personal acceptance of successes and failures |
| 25. | Focus-focus-focus. Know what you want, what you need to do, do it |
| 26. | Understanding and application of the basics of selling |
| 27 | Persistence |

| | |
|---|---|
| 28. | Insistence on doing the best possible job—not just "good enough" |
| 29. | Deliver on promises |
| 30. | Very presentable personal appearance |
| 31. | Open-minded—never stop growing |
| 32. | Advance preparation—no winging it |
| 33. | Rarely forget to ask for the order (as opposed to rarely remembering) |
| 34. | Regular self-improvement. Read a lot, listen to tapes. Attend seminars. |
| 35. | Strong communication skills: intra-office and with clients mail/phone/in-person |
| 36. | Aggressiveness—stay with prospect/client until the job is done right |
| 37. | Empathy/sincere caring for client's results |
| 38. | Results oriented |
| 39. | Do-it-now attitude |
| 40. | Keep good records |
| 41. | In office/on street early and stay late |
| 42. | Under-promise and over-deliver |
| 43. | Get into the client's shoes, view things from client's perspective |
| 44. | Anticipate and eliminate problems before they develop |
| 45. | Don't make assumptions |
| 46. | Don't take anything for granted, especially your station's place in the buy |
| 47. | Loyalty to company, clients, self |
| 48. | Keep in touch with clients, especially during their schedules |
| 49. | Don't take rejection personally |
| 50. | Sell ideas and solutions, not spots, flights, or packages |

**FIGURE 4.8**
The attributes, habits, and characteristics America's top local radio salespeople say make them winners
Source: Courtesy of *Radio Ink*

Jason Insalaco, a media lawyer and former general manager, says the qualities that make a good salesperson include:

- appreciation and genuine enthusiasm for the media brand
- reliability
- good reputation.

Insalaco asserts:

> A successful salesperson works at establishing strong relationships with clients, but also maintains solid relationships with the on-air production staff, the station's on-air personalities, and the traffic department (commercial-announcement scheduling department). These fellow staff members are integral for creating an engaging sales package. If an AE works well with these other team members, then the AE will be able to deliver successfully for their clients.

Korgyn says:

> When I hire someone, regardless of position, I look for a few key elements: promptness to the interview, neatness in attire (not suits and ties, just neat, attractive, and clean), a great smile that lights up the room and makes me want to smile, positive energy, and good eye-contact. If these things are there, there's a good chance everything else will fall right in line.

Friedman believes that it is important for a salesperson to have insight into human nature and behavior:

> You really must be adept at psychology. Selling really is a matter of anticipating what the prospect is thinking and knowing how best to address his concerns. It's not so much a matter of outthinking the prospective client, but rather being cognizant of the things that play a significant role in his life. Empathy requires the ability to appreciate the experiences of others. A salesperson who is insensitive to a client's moods or states of mind usually will come away empty-handed.

When hiring a salesperson, Insalaco says, "Seeking someone who has established relationships in the business and who genuinely enjoys meeting new people and forming new relationships" are important qualities.

Sales managers recruit heavily from within the radio station itself rather than immediately looking elsewhere for salespeople. For decades, it was believed that programming people were not suited for sales. An inexplicable barrier seemed to separate the two areas. This attitude has changed, and sales managers now give serious consideration to on-air staff who desire to make the transition into sales. For example, the morning deejay has the opportunity to become an afternoon salesperson. Regarding whether deejays make successful salespeople, Korgyn says:

> That depends entirely on the deejay and their personality. If they are hugely popular in the area, they might be able to ride that wave into a sale, but outside of that, if they are odd, abrasive, or weird— as many good deejays are, they will fall flat in sales. Radio deejays and salespeople just have a need for different skillsets.

The main advantage of hiring programming people to sell the station is that they have a practical understanding of the product. Affirming that deejays can make good salespeople, Kramer keenly observes:

> While most on air talent do not want to be a sales rep they are very effective "sellers." They are selling the stationality, the brand, the music, the lifestyle, the vibe of what they do every day to their audience. They create emotional connections to their fans and that makes them terrific ambassadors for advertisers' products. They also can help build relationships and bonds with clients by making calls with our account representatives. Think about it. Our talent are our stars. Why wouldn't our clients want to mingle and connect with them like any fan?

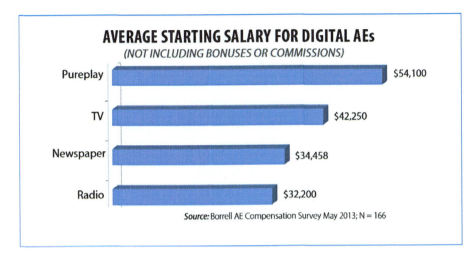

FIGURE 4.9
Starting salaries for digital account executives
Source: Courtesy of Borrell Associates Inc.

Realizing, too, that sales is the most direct path into station management, programming people often are eager to make the shift. The trend has been greater than ever to recruit managers from the programming department; however, a background with sales experience is still preferred.

Borrell Associates found that the average starting salary for a digital account executive in radio is $32,200, and notes that 11% of the nation's radio stations have dedicated digital sales teams and, of those, 60% offer special incentive rates to increase a salesperson's salary. *Inside Radio* says, "Among those radio stations that do have digital-only reps, the team remains small with an average of fewer than three salespeople. The typical combined sales force has ten sales reps selling both on-air and online ads."

## THE SALES MANAGER

The general sales manager (also called director of sales [DOS] in cluster operations) supervises the marketing of a station's or cluster's airtime. This person is responsible for moving inventory, which, in the case of the radio outlet, constitutes the selling of spot and feature schedules to advertisers. To achieve this end, the sales manager directs the daily efforts of the station's account executives, establishes sales department policies, develops sales plans and materials, conceives of sales and marketing campaigns and promotions, sets quotas, and in most cases sells.

A station's sales department customarily includes an emphasis on national, regional, and local sales. The station's, or the cluster's, general sales manager usually handles national responsibilities. This includes working with the station's rep company to stimulate business from national advertisers. The regional sales manager is given the responsibility of exploring sales possibilities in a broad geographical area surrounding the station(s). For example, the regional person for an outlet in New York City may be assigned portions of Connecticut, New Jersey, and Long Island. The local sales manager at the same station would concentrate on advertisers within the city proper. The general sales manager oversees the efforts of each of these individuals.

For cluster operations, Kramer explains:

The majority of our stations are cluster sold. However some, particularly markets where we have five or more stations, may have separate teams. For example, a "spoken word" team and a "music team." In a pure cluster, account executives represent all brands. We do this so that we can honestly present ourselves as marketing solutions experts who listen, discover, and solve clients' problems. If one represents the entire brand portfolio (including all of our platforms) vs. a "slice" of it, then they can solve client problems with the assets that best fit the clients' needs vs. just selling what we have.

The size of a station's sales staff varies according to its location and reach. A typical small-market radio station employs between two and four account executives, and the medium-market station averages about five. Large, top-ranked metropolitan outlets employ as many as eight to 10 salespeople, although it is more typical for the major-market station to have approximately half a dozen account executives. Of course, in cluster operations where team selling often exists, these numbers will vary, as a salesperson may be selling the airtime of several stations. It is not uncommon for there to be dozens of sales personnel in cluster operations. Kramer explains that Entercom Communications Corp., a cluster operation, has "radio stations in 23 markets that range from medium to large. Smaller markets have around ten account executives. Larger markets can have upwards of 40."

The general sales manager/DOS reports directly to the station or station cluster's general manager and works closely with the programming department in developing saleable features. Daily and weekly sales meetings are scheduled and headed by the sales manager where goals are set and problems addressed. The sales manager also assigns account lists to the staff and helps coordinate trade and cooperative advertising (co-op) deals.

As mentioned earlier, the head of the sales department is usually responsible for maintaining close contact with the station's rep company as a way of generating income from national advertisers who are handled by advertising agencies. The relationship of the sales manager and rep company is a particularly important one and will be discussed in greater detail later in this chapter. Also, the sales manager must be adept at working ratings figures to the station's advantage for inclusion in sales promotional material that is used at both the national and local levels.

All sales come under the scrutiny of the sales manager, who determines whether an account is appropriate for the station and that conditions of the sale meet established standards. In addition, the sales manager may have a policy that requires credit checks to be made on every new account and that new clients pay for a portion of their spot schedule up front as a show of good faith. Again, policies vary from station to station.

**FIGURE 4.10**
The Radio Advertising Bureau is the sales and marketing arm of the radio industry
Source: Courtesy of the RAB

It is up to the head of sales to keep abreast of local and national sales and marketing trends that can be used to the station's advantage. This requires the sales manager to constantly survey trade magazines such as *Radio Ink*, *Radio Business Report*, and *ADWEEK*, and attend industry seminars such as those conducted by the Radio Advertising Bureau (RAB). No sales department can operate in a vacuum and hope to succeed in today's dynamic radio marketplace.

Statistics continue to show that sales managers are most often recruited to fill the position of general manager and are paid lucrative salaries. It is also becoming more commonplace for sales managers to have experience in other areas of a station's operations, such as programming and production, a factor that has become increasingly important to the person who hires the chief account executive. An *Inside Radio* study found that the average salary for the DOS in radio media markets 101+ was $91,000, while the average salary for the DOS in radio media markets one through 10 was $210,000.

## RADIO SALES TOOLS

Rates for airtime depend on the size of a station's listenership—the bigger the audience, the more expensive the rates. At the same time, the unit cost for a spot or a feature is affected by the quantity or amount purchased—the bigger the "buy," the cheaper the unit price. Clients also receive discounts for consecutive week purchases over a prescribed period of time—say, 26 or 52 weeks. Although rare, a few stations publicly publish the fees that they charge for airtime in a rate card.

Owing to increased competition, stations do not always publish their rate cards since the rates might be constantly changing based upon economic and market demands. John Potter, of the Radio Advertising Bureau, says:

Few stations use published rate cards. Many are using computers with Yield Management software that automatically adjusts the rates. Some use computer spreadsheets to communicate rates internally to

FIGURE 4.11
KHWL-FM, Altus, Oklahoma, rate card. Although a rarity, some stations still use them

Source: Courtesy of Wolfpack Media LLC

salespeople who write custom proposals based on the advertiser's needs. A handful that use internal rate cards are using grids so they can adjust rates by nothing more than an announcement in a sales meeting or a quick email to the sales staff. The few stations that are publishing fixed rate cards are generally small markets that have little competition other than from their local newspaper that publishes a fixed rate card.

Radio marketing expert Jay Williams, Jr., agreeing with Potter, contends that the station rate card is on its way to obsolescence:

> some stations do use grid cards—but only internally—to let sellers know what grid/rates they should be quoting in their presentations. Rate cards are decreasingly shown to clients because they distract the account executive's focus from helping the client solve advertising and promotional problems and often force them into a negotiation with the client about spot rates.

FIGURE 4.12
Radio San Diego's
rate card with the
account
executive's sales
expectations, or
expected goals,
listed

Source: Courtesy of
Broadcast Company
of the Americas Radio
San Diego

## Planning rates for Christal
As of                5/15/13

**KPRI**

| Dayparts | 60's 5/15 - 6/2/13 | 6/3/13 forward :60's | :30's | May :15's | 6/3 - forward :15's |
|---|---|---|---|---|---|
| M-F 6-10a | 250 | 150 | 120 | 100 | 70 |
| M-F 10a-3p | 250 | 150 | 120 | 100 | 70 |
| M-F 3-7p | 250 | 150 | 120 | 100 | 70 |
| M-Sun 6am-12mid | 75 | 25 | 15 | 25 | 25 |
| Sa / Su 10a-7p | 140 | 40 | 25 | 35 | 35 |

**Walrus**

| Dayparts | 60's 5/15 - 6/2/13 | 6/3/13 forward :60's | :30's | :15's | :15's |
|---|---|---|---|---|---|
| M-F 6-10a | 125 | 90 | 75 | 80 | 40 |
| M-F 10a-3p | 125 | 90 | 75 | 80 | 40 |
| M-F 3-7p | 125 | 90 | 75 | 80 | 40 |
| M-Sun 6am-12mid | 50 | 20 | 10 | 30 | 30 |
| Sa / Su 10a-7p | 100 | 30 | 25 | 80 | 40 |

| Padres | N/A or $500 | | $200 | $150 | $150 |
|---|---|---|---|---|---|

**Mighty 1090**

| Dayparts | 60's 5/15 - 6/2/13 | 6/3/13 forward :60's | :30's | :15's | :15's |
|---|---|---|---|---|---|
| M-F 6-10a | 180 | 140 | 100 | 100 | 40 |
| M-F 10a-3p | 180 | 140 | 100 | 100 | 40 |
| M-F 3-7p | 180 | 140 | 100 | 100 | 40 |
| M-Sun 6am-12mid | 50 | 20 | 20 | 25 | 25 |
| Sa / Su 10a-7p | 100 | 30 | 40 | 100 | 70 |

Furthermore, WIZN's Matt Grasso observes:

> We never let salespeople show rate cards to clients. Rate cards force the client to try to figure out our business, radio, when radio reps should be learning about their businesses and creating customized presentations for them. Worse, clients always try to find the lowest rates on a rate card and then want to apply those rates to prime time, forcing the radio salesperson to negotiate with himself. By using computerized internal rate cards, sales management can quickly and easily adjust rates to meet demand and ensure proper inventory control.

The sales manager and station manager (DOS and market manager in cluster setups) work together to determine advertising rates, basing their decisions on ratings and what their market can support.

Some of the day's best times for purchasing ads is during feature programs. Among the most prevalent features that stations offer are traffic, sports, weather, and business reports during different dayparts. Newscasts also are available to advertisers. Features generally include an open (introduction) and a 30- or 60- second announcement. They are particularly effective advertising vehicles because listeners tend to pay greater attention during these times. A station wants to establish credibility with its features and therefore prefers to maintain continuity among its sponsors. A feature with a regular sponsor conveys stability, and that is what a station seeks.

Because the size of a radio station's audience generally varies depending on the time of day, rates for spots (commercials) or features must reflect that fact. Thus, the broadcast day is divided into time classifications: 6–10 am weekdays is typically a station's prime selling period and therefore may be designated AAA; afternoon drive time, usually 3–7 pm, may be called AA because of its secondary drawing power. Under this system, the midday segment, 10–3 pm, would be given a single A designation, and evenings, 7–midnight, as B. Overnights, midnight–6 am, may be classified as C time. Obviously, the fees charged for spots are established on an ascending scale from C to AAA. A station may charge $300 for an announcement aired at 8 am and $45 for one aired at 2 am. The difference in the size of the station's audience at those hours warrants the contrast.

As previously mentioned, the more airtime a client purchases, the less expensive the cost for an individual commercial or unit. For instance, if an advertiser buys 10 spots a week during AAA time, the cost of each spot would be slightly less than if the sponsor purchased two spots a week. A client must buy a specified number of spots to benefit from the frequency discount. "I always advise my clients to buy the shortest unit of commercial time possible without compromising their message," says Bob Adams, vice-president and market manager for the Cumulus stations in York, Lancaster, and Reading, PA, whose stations sell 30-second spots for 25% less than 60-second spots. He adds:

> You can say the "Pledge of Allegiance" in 20 seconds. So think of what you can say if you have the right words strung together. By buying shorter, better scripted commercials, advertisers can use the extra money to buy more frequency and get their message to more potential customers.

Many stations use a grid structure, as Potter explained. This gives stations a considerable degree of rate flexibility. For example, if a station has five rate-level grids it may have a range between $20 and $50 for a 60-second spot. Clients would then be given rates at the lower grid if the station had few sponsors on the air, thus creating many availabilities (places to insert commercial messages). As business increased at the station and availabilities became scarcer, the station would ask for rates reflected in the upper grids. Gridding is based on the age-old concept of supply and demand. When availabilities are tight and airtime is at a premium, that time costs more.

Grids are inventory-sensitive; they allow a station to remain viable when business is at a low ebb. Certainly, when inventory prices reach a bargain level, this encourages business. For instance, during a period when advertiser activity is sluggish, a station that can offer spots at a considerable reduction stands a chance of stimulating buyer interest.

When business at a station is brisk, because of holiday buying, for example, the situation may be exploited in a manner positive to the revenue column. Again, the supply and demand concept (one idea on which capitalism is based) is at work.

Clients are offered several spot schedule plans suited for their advertising and budgetary needs. For advertisers with limited funds, run-of-station (ROS) or best-time-available (BTA) plans are usually an option. Rates are lower under these plans because no guarantee is given as to what times the spots will be aired. However, most stations make a concerted effort to rotate ROS and BTA spots as equitably as possible, and during periods when commercial loads are light they frequently are scheduled during premium times. Of course, when a station is loaded down with spot schedules, especially around holidays or elections, ROS and BTA spots may find themselves buried. In the long run, advertisers using these plans receive a more than fair amount of choice times and at rates considerably lower than those clients who buy specific dayparts.

In *Radio Advertising's Missing Ingredient: The Optimum Effective Scheduling System*, by Pierre Bouvard and Steve Marx, an innovative system is presented that improves the power of a spot schedule. According to the authors, "Optimum effective scheduling ensures that the effective reach, those hit three or more times, is at least 50% of the total reach." The idea behind optimum effective scheduling (OES) is to strengthen the impact of client buys. The OES formula is designed to heighten the efficiency of a spot buy through a system of scheduling based on ratings performance. This is accomplished by factoring a station's turnover ratio and cume.

Total audience plan (TAP) is another popular package offered to clients by many stations. It is designed to distribute a client's spots among the various dayparts for maximum audience penetration, while costing less than an exclusive primetime schedule. The rate for a TAP spot is arrived at by averaging

FIGURE 4.13
Once ads are sold, a sales order and contract are completed and signed. At most stations, this process is done electronically using computer software

Source: Courtesy of Wolfpack Media LLC

## 98.7 FM LONE WOLF KHOWL
### Oklahoma's Radio Revolution!

## Advertising Sales Order

| Business Name | | Contact Name | |
|---|---|---|---|
| Address | | | |
| City | | State | Zip |
| Phone | Website | Email | |

| Primary Conflict | Secondary Conflict (Optional) |
|---|---|

**Spot Length**

☐ 30-Second Spot _____ Spots @ $_____ each
☐ 60-Second Spot _____ Spots @ $_____ each

**Run _____ Spots Per Day**

☐ Weather Sponsorship @ $_____ month
☐ Live On-Site Remote for _____ Hours @ $100/hr

**Production**

☐ Client-Produced Spot
  ☐ Received From Client
☐ KHWL-Produced Spot
  ☐ Client Approved Copy
  ☐ Produced and Ready
☐ Agency-Produced Spot
  ☐ Client Approved Copy
  ☐ Received From Agency

**Package Specials**

☐ Full Blitz 30 • 300 Spots @ **$1,500**
☐ Full Blitz 60 • 300 Spots @ **$2,250**
(Approximately 10 Per Day)

☐ Strafing Run 30 • 100 Spots @ **$500**
☐ Strafing Run 60 • 100 Spots @ **$750**
(Approximately 3 Per Day)

**Order Notes and Special Instructions**

| Salesperson | Cash Amount This Sales Order | Trade Amount This Sales Order |
|---|---|---|
| Authorized Client Signature | Date | |

Wolfpack Media LLC • 102 W Broadway Street • Altus, Oklahoma 73521 • 580-482-KHWL • www.khowl.fm

the cost for spots in several time classifications—for example, if AAA is $80, AA $70, A $58, and B $31, the TAP rate per spot is thus $59. The advantages are obvious. The advertiser is receiving a significant discount on the spots scheduled during morning and afternoon drive periods. At the same time, the advertiser is paying more for airtime during evenings. TAP is very attractive because it exposes a client's message to every possible segment of a station's listening audience with a measure of cost-effectiveness.

Bulk or annual discounts are available to advertisers who buy a heavy schedule of commercials over the course of a year. Large companies in particular take advantage of volume discounts because the savings are significant.

Stations present their clients with rates for their specific schedule or with a package price for the entire schedule. Jennifer McCann, former GM of Burlington Broadcasters, shares that "While some small market stations still rely on rate cards, stations in major markets do not." Using systems similar to "yield management" systems first introduced by the airline industry, medium and larger stations often use programs such as Marketron to manage and price their spot inventory to ensure their sales goals. A radio station is constantly faced with uneven and ever-changing demands on a limited amount of commercial time. Certain dayparts near the end-of-the-week, special programming, and drive-times near holidays might easily sell out, yet other time periods might have plenty of "avails." Using an inventory management system enables stations to continuously price their inventory by day, or daypart, and even by the hour, months in advance. This knowledge gives the sales department the up-to-the-minute pricing and "avail" information it needs to serve the client and allows the station to maintain the maximum control of its inventory and revenue.

**FIGURE 4.14**
David Gleason

## HISPANIC RADIO: BIAS IN THE BUYING PROCESS

### David Gleason

In the 1970s, Spanish-language radio moved into an era of rapid growth, with many new stations in an increasing number of markets. As such stations began to proliferate and to register good, saleable numbers in the ratings, success was tempered by what was referred to as the "Spanish discount." This term refers to a conscious undervaluation of audience deliverability, and thus desirability, when those audiences were Hispanics.

Such pricing pressures had long affected African-American-targeted stations. That market, dating back to its initial growth in the 1950s was the victim of similar "no buy" or "buy cheap" restrictions by advertisers. These buying practices came to include "no Hispanic" and "no urban" dictates because some advertisers simply excluded ethnic media from buying consideration, while others bought ethnic radio but exerted downward pressure on rates.

Discriminatory practices that had long existed in the buying of broadcast media targeted at African-Americans and Hispanics were addressed by the FCC following a formal inquiry. In 2011, an FCC action required stations to include nondiscrimination clauses in all sales contracts and the certification of compliance at the time of license renewal.

The FCC said in its Enforcement Advisory of March, 2011:

> In adopting this requirement, the Commission addressed reports that some advertising contracts contain 'no urban/no Spanish' dictates that are intended to minimize the proportion of African American or Hispanic customers patronizing an advertiser's venue—or dictates that presume that African Americans or Hispanics cannot be persuaded to buy an advertiser's product or service.
>
> (FCC Advisory 2011–06)

While discriminatory buying practices are predominantly an internal decision of ad buyers, the FCC showed by this action that it was aware of such practices and that it would not tolerate them. For the ethnic-targeted broadcaster, the FCC attention was welcome. The more recent actions by the Commission reflect that agency's awareness that the practice existed and dated back many decades. In the case of Hispanic broadcasters, the "Spanish discount" is the earliest manifestation of ungrounded advertiser attitudes to the effect that listeners to Spanish-language stations have lower incomes and thus "buy less," or that Hispanics are otherwise not desirable targets for advertising. This stereotype caused advertisers to apply pressure on Spanish-language station rates. This is evidenced by the lower ratings to revenue conversions of Spanish-language stations in nearly every market in the US. The discount mentality is not unique to Hispanic radio or to ethnic radio; "old timers" recall the "country discount" seen many, many decades ago when country stations were thought to bring low-income consumers to advertisers.

---

**David Gleason** is a radio programming consultant and former EVP of Univision Radio, as well as a former owner and group manager. His website is www.americanradiohistory.com.

## POINTS OF THE PITCH

Not all sales are made on the first call; nonetheless, the salesperson always goes in with the hope of closing an account. Generally, the first call is designed to introduce the station to the prospective sponsor and to determine the sponsor's needs. However, the salesperson should always be prepared to propose a buy that is suitable for the account. This means that some homework on the business must be done relative to the business before an approach is made. "First determine the client's needs, as best as possible. Then address those needs with a schedule built to reach the client's customers. Don't walk into a business cold or without some sense of what the place is about," advises Charles Friedman.

If all goes smoothly during the initial call, the salesperson may opt to secure an order at that time. If the account obliges, fine. In the event that the prospective advertiser is not prepared to make an immediate decision, a follow-up appointment must be made. The callback should be accomplished as close to the initial presentation as possible to prevent the impression from fading or growing cold. The primary objective of the return call is to close the deal and the order. To strengthen the odds, the salesperson must review and assess any objections or reservations that may have arisen during the first call and devise a plan to overcome them. Meanwhile, the initial proposal may be beefed up to appear even more attractive to the client, and a "spec" tape (see the later section "Spec Spots") for the business can be prepared as further enticement.

**FIGURE 4.15**

This KHWL-FM account executive business card is used to capture the attention of the client with its creative design. In small radio media markets, the general manager is also a salesperson

Source: Courtesy of Wolfpack Media LLC

Should the salesperson's efforts fail the second time out, third and even fourth calls are made. Perseverance does pay off, and many salespeople admit that, just when they reckoned a situation was hopeless, an account said yes. Retired general sales manager Ronald Piro says,

> Of course, beating your head against the wall accomplishes nothing. You have to know when your time is being wasted. Never give up entirely on an account; just approach it more sensibly. A phone call or a drop-in every so often keeps you in their thoughts.

What follows are two checklists. The "Do" list contains some suggestions conducive to a positive sales experience, and the "Don't" list contains things that will have a negative or counterproductive effect.

## Do

- research the advertiser; be prepared; have a relevant plan in mind;
- be enthusiastic; think positive;
- display self-confidence; believe in yourself and the product;
- smile; exude friendliness, warmth, and sincerity;
- listen; be polite, sympathetic, and interested;
- tell of the station's successes; provide testimonial material;
- think creatively;
- know your competition;
- maintain integrity and poise;
- look your best; check your appearance;
- be objective and keep proper perspective;
- pitch the decision-maker;
- ask for the order that will do the job;
- service the account after the sale.

## Don't

- pitch without a plan;
- criticize or demean the client's previous advertising efforts;
- argue with the client – this just creates greater resistance;
- bad-mouth the competition;
- talk too much;
- brag or be overly aggressive;
- lie, exaggerate, or make unrealistic promises;
- smoke or chew gum in front of the client;
- procrastinate or put things off;
- be intimidated or kept waiting an unreasonable amount of time;
- make a presentation unless you have the client's undivided attention;
- lose your temper;
- ask for too little; never undersell a client;
- fail to follow-up;
- accept a "no" as final.

Checklists like the preceding ones can serve only as basic guidelines. Anyone who has spent time "on the street" as a station account executive can expand on this or any other such checklist. For the positive-thinking radio salesperson, every call gives something back, whether a sale is made or not.

Overcoming common objections is a necessary step toward achieving the sale. Here are some typical "put-offs" presented to radio sales reps:

1. Nobody listens to radio commercials.
2. Newspaper ads are more effective.
3. Radio costs too much.
4. Nobody listens to your station.
5. We tried radio and it didn't work.
6. We don't need any more business.
7. We've already allocated our advertising budget.
8. We can get another station for less.

9. Business is off and we haven't got the money.

10. My partner doesn't like radio.

There are countless rebuttals for each of these statements, and a knowledgeable and skilled radio salesperson can turn such objections into positives.

### TAPSCAN™
#### LOCAL MARKET RADIO RATINGS SOFTWARE SUITE

**See How We've Improved TAPSCAN!**

TAPSCAN 11.2 offers a new NTR Schedule tab, enhanced research reports and more browser support.

Radio salespeople know TAPSCAN as the software that makes it easy to tell their station's story and generate more revenue. The intuitive design is easy to use and master—if your sellers can use a mouse, they will be able to use TAPSCAN from their very first day on the job.

The next planned release offers a new NTR Schedule tab, enhanced research reports and more browser support.

Powered with exclusive Maximi$er®-level data, TAPSCAN gives you access to customized demos, geographies, dayparts and multibook averages. TAPSCAN gives you an edge by making almost every part of the sale easier, from the initial presentation all the way to the hand-off to traffic.

Contact your Nielsen Audio representative for a demo today.

**With TAPSCAN, you can:**

• Demonstrate the sales potential of your audience with more than 80 categories of RETAIL SPENDING POWER qualitative information

• Show advertisers the number of listeners they can reach only through your station

• See what you—and your competition—can charge to hit a requested CPP

• Find out how many spots you need to run to reach a certain frequency, based on a demo and daypart

• Determine your reach and frequency by specific demo, daypart and spot level

• Demonstrate your power against newspapers, magazines, television, cable and outdoor

• Get proposals to clients faster with e-mail-friendly PDF output

• Streamline order approval and automate the transfer to your traffic system

**Data used in system:**

Respondent-Level Radio Data, Summary-Level Radio Data, Black Radio Data, Hispanic Radio Data, Eastlan Radio Data

The TAPSCAN Suite may include TAPSCAN, TrafficLink®, RETAIL SPENDING POWER℠, MEDIAMASTER℠ and pdfFactory®

Want more info? Contact your account manager now!

Maximi$er®, MEDIAMASTER℠, RETAIL SPENDING POWER℠ and TrafficLink® are marks of Arbitron Inc.
TAPSCAN™ is a mark used under license.
pdfFactory® is a registered mark of FinePrint Software, LLC.

Copyright © 2013 Nielsen

**FIGURE 4.16**
Software designed to help ad agencies make a buy
Source: Courtesy of Nielsen

# LEVELS OF SALES

There are three levels from which the medium draws its sales: retail, local, and national. Retail accounts for the biggest percentage of the industry's income: more than 70%. Retail sales—also referred to as *direct sales*—involve the radio station salespeople directly interacting with advertisers within its signal area.

In this case, a station's account executive works directly with the client and earns a commission of approximately 15% on the airtime he or she sells. An advertiser who spent $1,000 would benefit the salesperson to the tune of $150. A newly hired salesperson without previous experience often will work on a direct retail basis and will not be assigned advertising agencies until he or she has become more seasoned and has displayed some ability. Generally speaking, the smaller the radio station, the more dependent it is on retail sales, although most medium- and metro-market stations would be in trouble without strong business on this level. All stations, regardless of size, have some contact with advertising agencies. Here again, however, the larger a market, the more a station will derive its business from ad agencies. This level of station sales generally is classified as local. The number of advertising agencies in a market will vary depending on its size. A sales manager will divide the market's agencies among his reps as equitably as possible, sometimes using a merit system. In this way, an account executive who has worked hard and produced results will be rewarded for his efforts by being given an agency to work. The top billers—that is, those salespeople who bring in the most business—often possess the greatest number of agencies, or at least the most active ones. Although the percentage of commission a salesperson is accorded, typically 6–8%, is less than that derived from retail sales, the size of the agency buys usually is far more substantial.

The third category of station sales comes from the national level. In most cases, it is the general sales manager who works with the station's rep company to secure buys from advertising agencies that handle

---

## RESOLUTIONS FOR SELLERS

(Now a perennial first-of-the-year *tactics* topic, these resolutions are designed to inspire and motivate the sales staff.)

* I will have breakfast at 7:30 AM with at least two clients a week.
* Each week, I will read a trade magazine from three client businesses.
* I will set aside one hour a day to prepare written presentations.
* One Saturday morning per month will be set aside to call on retailers.
* I will read at least one book on selling and one book on advertising each month.
* I'll carry a list of my top 10 prospects and call on at least one each day.
* I'll follow each sales presentation with a hand-written thank-you note.
* I will remind myself each day that 8% of sales are made after the fifth call.
* I will demonstrate to my prospects that I am willing to work for their business.
* I will always ask, "Is there something else you'd like to hear about?"
* I will remind myself each day that I am not selling time—my business is creating opportunities, processing ideas, and distributing information.

**FIGURE 4.17**
Advice to Salespeople
Source: Courtesy of Shane Media

national accounts. Again, national business is greater for the metro station than it is for the rural. Agencies justify a buy on numbers and little else, although it is not uncommon for small-market stations, which do not even appear in ratings surveys, to be bought by major accounts interested in maintaining a strong local or community image.

Producer Ty Ford observes that agency involvement has decreased in recent years because of intensified competition among the different media and the unpredictable national economy:

> Increased competition from cable, television, radio, and print has forced many ad agencies out of business. Stations now frequently offer "agency discounts" to direct retail clients just to close the sale. Also, more retail companies are forming their own in-house agencies.

Although this may be true, the ad agency is still an important factor in station revenues. Each level of sales—retail, local, or national—must be sufficiently cultivated if a station is to enjoy maximum prosperity. Neglecting any one of these levels would result in a loss of station revenue.

**FIGURE 4.18**
Wolf Korgyn

## PROFIT SHOULD NOT BE THE *SOLE* REASON WE ARE IN BUSINESS

### Wolf Korgyn

I'd like to say that we as radio executives MUST remember that, while profit is important, it should not be the sole reason we are in the business. The conglomerates have ruined radio in pursuit of the almighty dollar.

Radio today is a mere shadow of what it once was. I have listeners every day who come into the station and marvel at how different we are and that they haven't listened to FM radio in YEARS—only to accidentally find us on the dial and never return to their smartphone. This hasn't happened just once or twice but dozens of times per month over the past year. The modern listener has forgotten about music radio and has moved on to satellite, Internet, Pandora, Spotify, and, of course, their smartphone devices.

Radio is in danger of going the way of the dinosaur. The only way to avoid that is to give listeners live content, live deejays, interactive shows, and, most of all, passion . . . because radio is magic. No other broadcast medium touches its audience like radio. You may be broadcasting to thousands, but as a listener that deejay is talking to you. For the time that you are listening, you are not alone. That deejay is your friend, a voice you can count on being there, a reminder that you are part of something larger than yourself.

When a station voice-tracks or employs a jukebox format like Jack or Bob or John or any of the dozen or so jockless formats now popular in the industry, it strips the one thing that radio has over the alternative digital formats . . . it strips away the personality. It strips away the soul.

The best advice I can give to a radio executive in today's world—regardless of whether you are in sales, in production, or in the air-studio—is to share your *passion* with the listeners. Without passion, radio is nothing more than a jukebox with commercials, and in today's world of the Internet, satellite radio, and smartphone, why would someone choose a jukebox with commercials over their own personal jukebox *without* commercials? They wouldn't. They don't.

Give listeners what Pandora, Spotify, and their smartphone will never give them . . . a warm, friendly voice sharing a song, a story, a laugh, or a tear. Because *that* is what makes radio magic.

---

**Wolf Korgyn** is Owner and General Manager of KHWL-FM in Altus, Oklahoma.

# SPEC SPOTS

One of the most effective ways to convince an advertiser to purchase an ad is to provide a fully produced sample commercial, or "spec spot." If prepared properly and imaginatively, a client will find it difficult to deny its potential. Spec spots are often used in callbacks when a salesperson needs to break down a client's resistance. More than once, a clever spec spot has converted an adamant "no" into an "okay, let's give it a shot." Spec spots are also used to reactivate the interest of former accounts who may not have spent money on the station for a while and who need some justification to do so.

## RAB Guide to Writing Great Radio Copy

Developing a great creative Radio campaign is crucial to getting results for your client but the big question is how do you do it? On the following pages you will find a 10 step plan that will help guide you through the challenges, demands and pitfalls of the copywriting process. Don't be afraid to use Radio's creative potential to the fullest and take the time needed to create great-sounding and brilliant campaigns.

### STEP 1: FIND OUT WHAT THE CLIENT WANTS

I know it sounds simple and obvious but so many stations and agencies make the mistake of not listening to what their clients really want and hope to achieve with their campaign. And without understanding the real reasons behind why a potential client wants to go on the air, the commercial campaign — no matter how humorous or clever — is doomed.

### STEP 2: ASK THE RIGHT QUESTIONS

So to find out what the client wants, you have to ask some questions. Some call it a Client Needs Analysis. And even though this isn't the most exciting part of the creative process, it is crucial to your success. Here are some samples:

1. Is there anything you would like to feature?
   Maybe your clients just got in a huge load of widgets and they need to sell them fast! Or maybe a certain item has a higher profit margin and it would make sense to push that product.

2. Who is your best prospect?
   This question will allow you to get into demographics and find out who they are targeting. Is it male or female or both? What percentage? Average age? Income? Profession and education level? If you represent more than one station, then these questions can help steer your client to the right "position on the dial."

3. Why do customers come to you?
   This question and others below that are similar, allow the client to tell you their story. Keep in mind that perception is reality and you should consider getting different viewpoints from co-workers, family and friends.

4. What is your single greatest competitive advantage?

5. Do you have a positioning statement?

6. What do you feel is your unique selling position?
   The USP or unique selling position (or point) is a marketing concept that allows a company to differentiate themselves from their competition.

7. What is your primary business image?

8. What's the biggest misperception you feel people have about your business?
   Sometimes this misperception can be used in the commercial to help overcome objections. For example, perhaps customers think a popular brand will automatically be too expensive. Or perhaps the potential customers feel that the location is too far away when in reality it's only a 10 or 15 minute drive.

1 of 7

**FIGURE 4.19**

The RAB's guidelines for salespeople to use to write effective and engaging radio spots. Please see this chapter's Appendix 4A for more of this guide

Source: Courtesy of the Radio Advertising Bureau

Specs also are effective tools for motivating clients to "heavy-up" or increase their current spot schedules. A good idea can move a mountain, and salespeople are encouraged by the sales manager to develop spec tape ideas. Many sales managers require that account executives make at least one spec tape presentation each week. The sales manager may even choose to critique spec spots during regularly scheduled meetings.

The information needed to prepare a spec spot is acquired in several ways. If a salesperson has already called on a prospective client, he should have a very good idea of what the business is about as well as the attitude of the retailer toward the enterprise. The station sales rep is then in a very good position to prepare a spot that directly appeals to the needs and perceptions of the would-be advertiser. If a salesperson decides that the first call on a client warrants preparing a spec tape, then he or she may collect information on the business by actually browsing through the store or perusing the business's website as a customer might. This gives the salesperson an accurate, firsthand impression of the store's environment and merchandise. An idea of how the store perceives itself, and specific information, such as address and hours, can be derived by checking its website or by examining any ads it may have run in the local newspaper. Flyers that the business may have distributed also provide useful information for the formulation of the copy used in the spec spot. Listening to commercials the advertiser may be running on another station can also give the salesperson an idea of the direction in which to move.

Again, the primary purpose of a spec spot is to motivate a possible advertiser to buy time. A spec spot that fails to capture the interest and appreciation of the individual for which it has been prepared may be lacking the necessary ingredients. It is generally a good rule of thumb to avoid humor in a spec spot, unless the salesperson has had some firsthand experience with the advertiser. Nothing fails as abysmally as a commercial that attempts to be funny and does not come across as such to the client—thus, the saying "What is funny to one person may be silly or offensive to another."

Although spec spots are, to some extent, a gamble, they should be prepared in such a way that the odds are not too great. Of course, a salesperson who believes in an idea must have the gumption to go with it. Great sales are often inspired by unconventional concepts.

## OBJECTIVES OF THE BUY

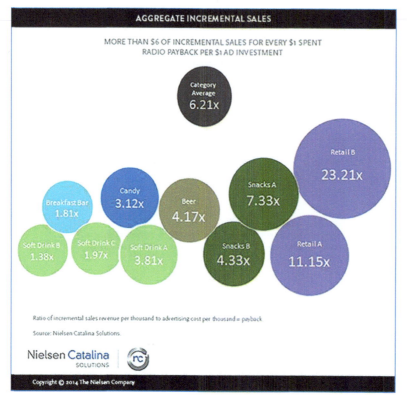

**FIGURE 4.20**
Each dollar of ad spend generated an average sales return of $6 from listeners

Source: Courtesy of Nielsen

A single spot on a radio station seldom brings instant riches to an advertiser. However, contends former general manager John Gregory, a thoughtfully devised plan based on a formula of frequency and consistency will achieve impressive results:

> It has to be made clear from the start what a client hopes to accomplish by advertising on your station. Then a schedule that realistically corresponds with the client's goals must be put together. This means selling the advertiser a sufficient number of commercials spread over a specific period of time. An occasional spot here and there doesn't do much in this medium. There's a right way to sell radio, and that isn't it.

Our "Do" and "Don't" lists of selling suggested that the salesperson "ask for the order that will do the job." They also said not to undersell an account. Implicit in the first point is the idea that the salesperson has determined what kind of schedule the advertiser should buy to achieve the expected results. Too often salespeople fail to ask for what they need for fear the client will balk. Thus, they settle for what they can obtain without much resistance. This, in fact, may be doing the advertiser a disservice, because the buy that the salesperson settles for may not fulfill declared objectives. Former sales manager Piro says:

> It takes a little courage to persist until you get what you think will do the job. There is the temptation just to take what the client hands you and run, but that technique usually backfires when the client doesn't get what he expected. As a radio sales rep, you should know how best to sell the medium. Don't be apologetic or easily compromised. Sell the medium the way it should be sold. Write enough of an order to get the job done.

To potentially increase sales, the salesperson can provide statistics to the client that show the effectiveness of radio advertising and its ability to reach large audiences at certain times of the day. In 2014, a Nielsen Catalina Solutions study found that radio advertising was the best return on the investment (ROI) than any other medium. The study found "that each dollar of ad spend generated an average sales return of $6 from the listeners in the 28 days after they heard the ads."

Inflated claims and unrealistic promises should never be a part of a sales presentation. Avoid claims such as, "If you buy spots on my station, you'll have to hire additional salespeople to handle the huge crowds." Salespeople must be honest in their projections and in what a client may expect from the spot schedule they purchase. One effective strategy is to share with clients past successes and data that support the effectiveness of radio advertising.

## Local Celebrity Endorsement Drove Young Adults to Test Drive the Chevy Cruze

**OBJECTIVE**
Milwaukee Chevrolet Dealers wanted to create buzz around the launch of the Chevy Cruze with 18-34 year olds.

**SOLUTION**
Entercom Milwaukee developed an integrated marketing campaign that centered around a local radio celebrity, Kraig Karson. The endorsement campaign educated fans about the inherent benefits and compelling features of the Chevy Cruze. Kraig's endorsement brought the campaign to life with social media and digital integration including blogging and video.

**TESTIMONIAL**
"We have been very pleased with the results of the Kraig Karson endorsement of the Chevy Cruze and look forward to another year-long program."
— George H. Gibbs, Agency Account Director

http://bcove.me/pt33nmv4 • http://bcove.me/8k8e05dn • http://bcove.me/yg8xwhnz

## Entercom Created Social Media Buzz and Sales Results for the Rocky Mountain Ford Dealers

**OBJECTIVE**
The Rocky Mountain Ford Dealers wanted to drive qualified traffic into 10 local Ford Dealers during their national "Swap Your Ride" program.

**SOLUTION**
Entercom Denver worked with the Rocky Mountain Ford Dealers to localize the national "Swap my Ride" campaign. Over 4 weeks local DJs "swapped" their rides and shared their driving experiences with their listeners. The campaign encouraged listener engagement by encouraging people to submit a video entry to "Win a Ride" from their local Ford dealers. Each video was viewed by the general public to create additional buzz and "votes."

**RESULTS**
Over the course of the campaign, the promotion created buzz in the market reaching over 1 million people and the Rocky Mountain Ford Dealers recorded a 12% sales increase over the previous year.

## Online Radio Campaign Helped Jewel's "Sweet and Wild" Album Debut on Billboard's Top 10

**OBJECTIVE**
Jewel's record label, Big Machine Records, wanted to create heightened awareness and immediate sales for Jewel's new CD release, "Sweet and Wild".

**SOLUTION**
Entercom worked with Big Machine Records to develop a two-week online radio campaign to air prior to the launch of Jewel's "Sweet and Wild" CD. The online radio campaign aired across six Entercom country music radio stations.

**TESTIMONIAL**
"The launch was a huge success! The album debuted at #10 on Billboard Charts. We are convinced that the online radio campaign gave us the opportunity to expose this new album to the most passionate country music listeners in the U.S."
— John Zarling, Sr.
Director, New Media & National Promotion Strategy, Big Machine Records

**FIGURES 4.21, 4.22, AND 4.23**
Entercom uses case studies as a means to demonstrate to clients how well-planned and well-executed advertising strategies have been successful

Source: Courtesy of Entercom Communications Corp.

# PROSPECTING AND LIST BUILDING

When a salesperson is hired by a radio station, he or she is customarily provided with a list of accounts to which airtime may be sold. For an inexperienced salesperson, this list may consist of essentially inactive or dormant accounts, that is, businesses that either have been on the air in the past or those that have never purchased airtime on the station. The new sales rep is expected to breathe life into the list by selling spot schedules to those accounts listed, as well as by adding to the list by bringing in new business. This is called *list building*, and it is the primary challenge facing the new account executive.

A more active list, one that generates commissions, is given to the more experienced radio salesperson. A salesperson may be persuaded to leave one station in favor of another based on the contents of a list, which may include large accounts and prominent advertising agencies. Lists held by a station's top billers invariably contain the most enthusiastic radio users. Salespeople cultivate their lists as a farmer does his fields. The more the account list yields, the more commissions in the salesperson's pocket.

New accounts are added to a sales rep's list in several ways. Once the status of the list's existing accounts is determined, which is accomplished through a series of in-person calls and presentations, a salesperson must begin prospecting for additional business. Area newspapers are a common source. When a salesperson finds an account that he wishes to add to his or her list, the account must be "declared." This involves consulting the sales manager for approval to add the account to the salesperson's existing list. In some cases, the account declared may already belong to another salesperson. If it is an open account, the individual who comes forward first is usually allowed to add it to his or her list.

Other sources for new accounts include the Internet, Yellow Pages, television stations, and competing radio outlets. Every business in the area is listed in the Yellow Pages, which contains many display ads that provide useful information. Local television stations are viewed with an eye toward their advertisers. Television can be an expensive proposition, even in smaller markets, and businesses that currently spend money on it may find radio's rates more palatable. On the other hand, if a business can afford to buy television, it often can afford to embellish its advertising campaign with radio spots. Many advertisers place money in several media—newspaper, radio, television—simultaneously. This is called a *mixed media* buy and is a proven advertising formula for the obvious reason that the client is reaching all possible audiences. Finally, businesses that are currently advertising on other stations constitute good prospects because they have obviously already been sold on the medium.

In the course of an average workday, a salesperson will pass hundreds of businesses, some of which may have just opened their doors or are about to do so. Sales reps must keep their eyes open and be prepared to make an impromptu call. The old saying "the early bird gets the worm" is particularly relevant in radio sales. The first account executive into a newly launched business often is the one who gets the sale.

A list containing dozens of accounts does not necessarily ensure a good income. If those businesses listed are small spenders or inactive, little in the way of commissions will be generated and billing will be low. The objective of list building is not merely to increase the number of accounts, but rather to raise the level of commissions it produces. In other words, a list that contains 30 accounts, of which 22 are active, is preferable to one with 50 accounts containing only 12 that are doing business with the station. A salesperson does not get points for having a lot of names on his list.

It is the sales manager's prerogative to shift an account from one salesperson's list to another's if he or she believes the account is being neglected or handled incorrectly. At the same time, certain in-house accounts, those handled by the sales manager, may be added to a sales rep's list as a reward for performing well. A salesperson's account list may also be pared down if the sales manager concludes that it is disproportional with the others at the station. The attempt to more equitably distribute the wealth may cause a brouhaha with the account person whose list is being trimmed. The sales manager attempting this feat may lose a top biller; thus, he or she must consider the ramifications of such a move and proceed accordingly. This may even mean letting things remain as they are. The top biller often is responsible for as much as 30–40% of the station's earnings.

# PLANNING THE SALES DAY

An effective radio salesperson is very busy each week making in-person calls to existing and new clients and uses a daily call sheet and calendar for effective time management. Kramer says,

> A typical day/week includes prospecting, cold calling, researching client categories or info to use in presentations, going on client discovery or initial idea calls, developing creative ideas, writing presentations, making presentations, admin work related to closed business or customer service, sales training or sales meetings, a coaching one-on-one with the direct manager, and driving to appointments. A good rep will make between 12–15 face calls a week.

When preparing a daily call sheet, a salesperson, especially one whose station covers a vast area, attempts to centralize, as much as possible, the businesses to be contacted. Time, energy, and gas are needlessly expended through poor planning. A sales rep who is traveling 10 miles between each presentation can get to only half as many clients as the person with a consolidated call sheet. Of course, there are days when a salesperson must spend more time traveling. Not every day can be ideally plotted. It may be necessary to make a call in one part of the city at 9 am and be in another part at 10 am. A salesperson must be where he or she feels the buys are going to be made. "Go first to those businesses likeliest to buy. The tone of the day will be sweetened by an early sale," contends Ronald Piro.

---

## SELLING PERSONALITY

### Jason Insalaco

Radio account executives can benefit from this source by selling additional exposure to advertisers. Another thing to keep in mind is that podcasting and streaming allow local advertisers with smaller budgets who previously could not afford a conventional broadcast schedule the opportunity to purchase less expensive online advertising. Account executives can attest to the difficulty of selling radio's intangible and sightless nature. Online advertising helps overcome this challenge. Visual banner ads allow streaming listeners to click on ads directly to take them to a client's website. Furthermore, radio programmers now have access to immediate data to provide their advertisers with the number of streaming listeners and podcast downloads. Nielsen Digital Audio Ratings provide real-time data on digital consumption and clarify returns on digital investment for advertisers. Online digital content is a win–win for advertisers, programmers, and the listener.

---

Jason Insalaco has more than 20 years of experience in the radio industry. Throughout his tenure, he has worked as a station manager, program director, and executive producer, and in other programming and production roles at radio stations in Los Angeles, San Francisco, and Boston. In addition, Jason is a media lawyer and has worked as a talent manager representing personalities from morning show radio, talk radio, and public broadcasting. He currently develops content and new media initiatives for commercial and public radio. He earned an undergraduate degree from Boston College and obtained a law degree from Loyola Law School in Los Angeles.

**FIGURE 4.24**
Jason Insalaco

Sales managers advise their reps to list more prospects than they expect to contact. In doing so, they are not likely to run out of places to go should those prospects they had planned to see become unavailable. "You have to make the calls to make the sales. The more calls you make, the more the odds favor a sale," points out Gene Etheridge.

The telephone is one of the salesperson's best tools. Although it is true that a client cannot sign a contract over the phone, much time and energy can be saved through its effective use. Appointments can be made and a client can be qualified via the telephone. That is to say, a salesperson can ascertain when the decision-maker will be available Charles Friedman says:

Rather than travel 20 miles without knowing if the person who has the authority to make a buy will be around, take a couple of minutes and make a phone call. As they say, "time is money." In the time spent finding out that the store manager or owner is not on the premises when you get there, other, more productive calls can be made.

If a client is not available when the salesperson appears, a callback should be arranged for either later the same day or soon thereafter. The prospective advertiser should never be forgotten or relegated to a call three months later. The sales rep should try to rearrange his or her schedule to accommodate a return visit the same day, if the client will be available. However, it is futile to make a presentation to someone who cannot give their full attention. The sales rep who arrives at a business only to find the decision-maker overwhelmed by distractions is wise to ask for another appointment. In fact, the client will perceive this as an act of kindness and consideration. Timing is important.

A record of each call should be kept for follow-up purposes. When calling on a myriad of accounts, it is easy to lose track of what transpired during a particular call. Maintaining a record of a call requires little more than a brief notation after it is made. Notes may then be periodically reviewed to help determine what action should be taken on the account. Follow-ups are crucial. There is nothing more embarrassing and disheartening than to discover a client, who was pitched and then forgotten, advertising on another station. Sales managers usually require that salespeople turn in copies of their call sheets on a daily or weekly basis for review purposes.

## SELLING WITH AND WITHOUT NUMBERS

Not all stations can claim to be number one or two in the ratings. In fact, not all stations appear in any formal ratings survey such as Nielsen's ratings. Very small markets are not visited by Nielsen or other rating services for the simple reason that there may be only one station broadcasting in the area. An outlet in a nonsurvey area relies on its good reputation in the community to attract advertisers. In small markets, salespeople do not work out of a ratings book and clients are not concerned with cumes and shares. In the truest sense of the word, an account person must sell the station. Local businesses often account for more than 95% of a small-market station's revenue. Thus, the stronger the ties with the community, the better. Broadcasters in rural markets must foster an image of good citizenship to make a living.

Civic-mindedness is not as marketable a commodity in the larger markets as are ratings points. In the sophisticated multi-station urban market, the ratings book is the Bible. A station without numbers in the highly competitive environment finds the task of earning an income a difficult one, although there are numerous examples of low-rated stations that do very well. However, "no numbers" pretty much puts a metro area station out of the running for agency business. Agencies almost invariably "buy by the book."

FIGURE 4.25
Nielsen (NYSE: NLSN) is an international media and marketing research firm serving the media—radio, television, and cable—and the mobile industry as well as advertising agencies and advertisers around the world. Nielsen businesses include measuring network and local market radio audiences across the United States. Specifically for radio, its goal is to measure audio and provide data for advertisers to effectively value the radio medium and help determine its rightful place in the media planning mix

Source: Courtesy of Nielsen

A station without numbers "works the street," to use the popular phrase, focusing its sales efforts on direct business.

An obvious difference in approaches exists between selling for a station with ratings and selling for a station without ratings. In the first case, a station centers its entire presentation around its high ratings: "According to the latest Nielsen ratings, WXXX-FM is number one with adults 24 to 39." The station's ratings are never out of the sales pitch for very long, and at advertising agencies the station's standing speaks for itself: "We'll buy WXXX because the book shows that they have the largest audience in the demos we're after."

The station without rating numbers sells itself on a more personal level, perhaps focusing on its unique features and special blend of music and personalities, and so forth. In an effort to attract advertisers, nonrated outlets often develop programs with a targeted retail market in mind, for example a home "how to" show designed to interest hardware and interior decor stores, or a cooking feature aimed at food and appliance stores.

## MARKET SURVEY RANKINGS, FREQUENCY, TYPE AND POPULATION

**BY RANKING**

| MKT CODE | RANK | TYPE | FREQ | MARKET | DST | METRO 12+ POPULATION | HISPANIC 12+ POPULATION* | BLACK 12+ POPULATION** |
|---|---|---|---|---|---|---|---|---|
| 001 | 1 | PPM | 13 | New York | BH | 16,350,800 | 3,982,200 | 2,771,300 |
| 003 | 2 | PPM | 13 | Los Angeles | BH | 11,497,600 | 4,917,600 | 822,400 |
| 005 | 3 | PPM | 13 | Chicago | BH | 7,980,800 | 1,632,400 | 1,347,300 |
| 009 | 4 | PPM | 13 | San Francisco | BH | 6,694,200 | 1,482,100 | 449,300 |
| 024 | 5 | PPM | 13 | Dallas-Ft. Worth | BH | 5,950,300 | 1,566,400 | 960,100 |
| 033 | 6 | PPM | 13 | Houston-Galveston | BH | 5,718,100 | 1,948,100 | 992,500 |
| 015 | 7 | PPM | 13 | Washington, DC | BH | 4,899,700 | 752,000 | 1,306,400 |
| 047 | 8 | PPM | 13 | Atlanta | BH | 4,747,700 | 465,100 | 1,618,500 |
| 007 | 9 | PPM | 13 | Philadelphia | BH | 4,593,300 | 388,300 | 945,400 |
| 013 | 10 | PPM | 13 | Boston | BH | 4,280,100 | 446,800 | 331,600 |
| 429 | 11 | PPM | 13 | Miami-Ft. Lauderdale-Hollywood | BH | 4,035,200 | 2,084,800 | 835,200 |
| 011 | 12 | PPM | 13 | Detroit | B | 3,818,800 | 148,300 | 839,700 |
| 039 | 13 | PPM | 13 | Seattle-Tacoma | BH | 3,779,500 | 324,400 | 246,600 |
| 057 | 14 | PPM | 13 | Phoenix | BH | 3,586,100 | 994,300 | 210,000 |
| 540 | 15 | 4S | 4 | Puerto Rico | | 2,980,300 | * | * |
| 027 | 16 | PPM | 13 | Minneapolis-St. Paul | BH | 2,935,000 | 148,400 | 245,600 |
| 063 | 17 | PPM | 13 | San Diego | BH | 2,843,600 | 891,800 | 157,200 |
| 035 | 18 | PPM | 13 | Denver-Boulder | BH | 2,680,800 | 539,700 | 152,300 |
| 087 | 19 | PPM | 13 | Tampa-St. Petersburg-Clearwater | BH | 2,650,100 | 458,200 | 313,700 |
| 321 | 20 | PPM | 13 | Nassau-Suffolk (Long Island) | BH | 2,481,000 | 424,200 | 241,800 |
| 021 | 21 | PPM | 13 | Baltimore | BH | 2,408,600 | 127,000 | 697,100 |
| 017 | 22 | PPM | 13 | St. Louis | B | 2,348,100 | 66,300 | 436,500 |
| 051 | 23 | PPM | 13 | Portland, OR | H | 2,308,900 | 275,500 | 75,200 |
| 093 | 24 | PPM | 13 | Charlotte-Gastonia-Rock Hill | BH | 2,254,800 | 192,600 | 512,100 |
| 379 | 25 | PPM | 13 | Riverside-San Bernardino | BH | 2,073,700 | 1,078,700 | 181,900 |
| 059 | 26 | PPM | 13 | San Antonio | BH | 2,043,700 | 1,076,800 | 148,600 |
| 023 | 27 | PPM | 13 | Pittsburgh, PA | B | 2,001,500 | 33,400 | 178,000 |
| 065 | 28 | PPM | 13 | Sacramento | BH | 1,992,700 | 379,900 | 158,600 |
| 101 | 29 | PPM | 13 | Salt Lake City-Ogden-Provo | H | 1,885,700 | 264,400 | 30,500 |
| 257 | 30 | PPM | 13 | Las Vegas | BH | 1,838,300 | 519,800 | 219,900 |
| 031 | 31 | PPM | 13 | Cincinnati | B | 1,820,300 | 50,900 | 230,800 |
| 131 | 32 | PPM | 13 | Orlando | BH | 1,817,100 | 557,400 | 303,600 |
| 019 | 33 | PPM | 13 | Cleveland | BH | 1,774,700 | 89,600 | 354,400 |
| 135 | 34 | PPM | 13 | Austin | BH | 1,745,300 | 522,200 | 133,400 |
| 041 | 35 | PPM | 13 | Kansas City | BH | 1,720,900 | 139,200 | 229,700 |
| 215 | 36 | PPM | 13 | San Jose | H | 1,655,000 | 407,000 | 48,400 |
| 045 | 37 | PPM | 13 | Columbus, OH | B | 1,647,400 | 60,800 | 268,700 |
| 115 | 38 | PPM | 13 | Raleigh-Durham | BH | 1,546,600 | 148,400 | 349,200 |
| 049 | 39 | PPM | 13 | Indianapolis | BH | 1,528,300 | 91,000 | 247,400 |
| 393 | 40 | 2S | 2 | Hudson Valley | BH | 1,518,500 | 317,600 | 193,600 |
| 043 | 41 | PPM | 13 | Milwaukee-Racine | BH | 1,502,500 | 142,300 | 233,600 |
| 413 | 42 | PPM | 13 | Middlesex-Somerset-Union | BH | 1,489,800 | 328,600 | 203,800 |
| 073 | 43 | PPM | 13 | Nashville | BH | 1,437,400 | 92,600 | 236,600 |
| 077 | 44 | PPM | 13 | Providence-Warwick-Pawtucket | BH | 1,410,100 | 155,500 | 78,800 |
| 109 | 45 | PPM | 13 | Norfolk-Virginia Beach-Newport News | BH | 1,409,100 | 90,300 | 439,700 |
| 166 | 46 | PPM | 13 | Greensboro-Winston-Salem-High Point | BH | 1,276,500 | 106,400 | 290,200 |
| 299 | 47 | PPM | 13 | West Palm Beach-Boca Raton | BH | 1,269,200 | 260,500 | 224,700 |
| 107 | 48 | PPM | 13 | Jacksonville | BH | 1,267,300 | 101,200 | 267,100 |
| 053 | 49 | 4S | 4 | New Orleans | BH | 1,260,100 | 101,500 | 396,700 |
| 083 | 50 | 4S | 4 | Oklahoma City | BH | 1,251,000 | 134,400 | 135,800 |
| 075 | 51 | PPM | 13 | Memphis | B | 1,120,600 | 54,500 | 516,800 |
| 061 | 52 | PPM | 13 | Hartford-New Britain-Middletown | BH | 1,080,100 | 156,300 | 124,700 |
| 516 | 53 | 2S | 2 | Monmouth-Ocean | H | 1,042,900 | 97,000 | 57,400 |
| 105 | 54 | 4S | 4 | Richmond | B | 1,041,400 | 59,700 | 313,500 |
| 055 | 55 | 4S | 4 | Louisville | B | 1,038,700 | 42,900 | 159,300 |
| 269 | 56 | 2S | 2 | McAllen-Brownsville-Harlingen | H | 1,012,400 | 904,500 | 6,000 |
| 037 | 57 | 4S | 4 | Buffalo-Niagara Falls | B | 987,000 | 43,100 | 120,300 |
| 079 | 58 | 4S | 4 | Rochester, NY | B | 966,200 | 61,500 | 107,700 |
| 191 | 59 | 4S | 4 | Greenville-Spartanburg | B | 958,300 | 58,900 | 168,700 |
| 515 | 60 | 2S | 2 | Ft. Myers-Naples-Marco Island | H | 958,100 | 194,900 | 72,700 |
| 095 | 61 | 4S | 4 | Birmingham | B | 919,400 | 34,900 | 272,400 |
| 207 | 62 | 4S | 4 | Tucson | H | 872,500 | 295,700 | 34,800 |
| 099 | 63 | 4S | 4 | Honolulu | | 858,400 | 76,600 | 44,600 |
| 067 | 64 | 4S | 4 | Dayton | B | 836,500 | 20,300 | 122,100 |
| 103 | 65 | 4S | 4 | Tulsa | | 818,500 | 68,000 | 72,500 |
| 069 | 66 | 4S | 4 | Albany-Schenectady-Troy | | 813,900 | 41,400 | 65,500 |
| 089 | 67 | 4S | 4 | Fresno | H | 800,100 | 397,800 | 41,600 |
| 127 | 68 | 4S | 4 | Grand Rapids | | 779,000 | 68,400 | 59,900 |
| 141 | 69 | 4S | 4 | Albuquerque | H | 760,500 | 351,500 | 21,700 |
| 145 | 70 | 4S | 4 | Allentown-Bethlehem | H | 724,000 | 104,300 | 39,400 |
| 071 | 71 | 4S | 4 | Des Moines | | 722,700 | 39,400 | 34,300 |

**FIGURE 4.26**

Nielsen's top radio media markets ranked in the U.S. Ratings are obtained in these markets and used by radio stations and clients to effectively plan radio buys

Source: Courtesy of Nielsen

The salesperson working for the station with the cherished "good book" must be especially adept at talking numbers, because they are the key subject of the presentation in most situations. "Selling a top-rated metro station requires more than a pedestrian knowledge of numbers, especially when dealing with agencies. In big cities, retailers have plenty of book savvy, too," contends Piro.

Selling without numbers demands its own unique set of skills, notes WNRI's Gregory:

> There are really two different types of radio selling—with numbers and without. In the former instance, you'd better know your math, whereas in the latter, you've got to be really effective at molding your station to suit the desires of the individual advertiser. Without the numbers to speak for you, you have to do all the selling yourself. Flexibility and ingenuity are the keys to the sale.

## ADVERTISING AGENCIES

Advertising agencies came into existence more than a century ago and have played an integral role in broadcasting since its inception. Their presence continues to be felt today, but not to the extent that it was prior to the advent of television.

Agencies annually account for hundreds of millions in radio ad dollars. The long, and at times turbulent, marriage of radio and advertising agencies was, and continues to be, based on the need of national companies to convey their messages on the local level and the need of the local broadcaster for national business. It is a two-way street. From the perspective of a radio station's sales department, Kramer asserts,

*The best agencies are a total advocate for the client and work with different media to create campaigns with the best possible chance for success. A great agency also listens to new ideas and presents the best of those ideas to the client. Agencies play a significant role in creating, planning, negotiating, placing, posting, and determining the ROI (return on investment) of the media placed.*

Today, hundreds of advertising agencies use the radio medium. They range in size from mammoth to minute. Agencies such as McCann Erickson, Young & Rubicam (Y&R), J. Walter Thompson (JWT) Global Advertising Agency, Saatchi & Saatchi, and Leo Burnett bill in the hundreds of millions annually and employ hundreds. An executive report from eMarketer estimated that 2017 would see a total of $206 billion spent on all advertising in the U.S. More specifically, media observer Jack Myer, in his *29th Annual Marketing & Advertising Data and Spending Forecast*, predicts that radio advertising revenue will increase from 2.8% in 2017 to 3.0% in 2020, which is a jump from $15.9 billion to $17.8 billion; ad agencies handle a vast portion of those dollars. More typical, however, are the agencies scattered throughout the country that bill between $500,000 and $2.5 million each year and employ anywhere from half a dozen to 20 people. Agencies come in all shapes and sizes and provide various services depending on their scope and dimensions.

The process of getting national business onto a local station is an involved one. The major agencies must compete against dozens of others to win the right to handle the advertising of large companies. This usually involves elaborate presentations and substantial investments by agencies. When and if the account is secured, the agency must then prepare the materials—audio, video, print—for the campaign and see to it that the advertiser's money is spent in the most effective way possible. Little is done without extensive marketing research and planning. The agency's media buyer oversees the placement of dollars in the various media. Media buyers at national agencies deal with station and network reps rather than directly with the stations themselves. It would be impossible for an agency placing a buy on 400 stations to personally transact with each.

There are basically three types of agencies: *full service agencies*, which provide clients with a complete range of services, including research, marketing, and production; *modular agencies*, which provide specific services to advertisers; and *in-house agencies*, which handle the advertising needs of their own business.

The standard commission that an agency receives for its service is 15% on billing. For example, if an agency places $100,000 on radio, it earns $15,000 for its efforts. Agencies often charge clients additional fees to cover production costs and some agencies receive a retainer from clients.

The business generated by agencies constitutes an important percentage of radio's revenues, especially for medium- and large-market stations. However, compared to other media, such as television, radio's allocation is diminutive. The nation's top three agencies invest more than 80% of their broadcast budgets in television. Nonetheless, hundreds of millions of dollars are channeled into radio by agencies that recognize the effectiveness of the medium.

## REP COMPANIES

Rep companies are the industry's middlemen. Rep companies are given the task of convincing national agency media buyers to place money on the stations they represent. Without rep companies, radio stations would have to find a way to reach a myriad of agencies on their own—an impossible feat.

With a few exceptions, radio outlets contract the services of a station rep company. Even the smallest station wants to be included in buys at the national level. Basically, the rep company is an extension of a station's sales department. The rep and the station's sales manager work together closely. Information about a station and its market are crucial to the rep. The burden of keeping the rep fully aware of what is happening back at the station rests on the sales manager's shoulders. Because a rep company based in New York or Chicago would have no way of knowing that its client station in Arkansas has decided to carry the local college's basketball games, it is the station's responsibility to make the information available. A rep cannot sell what it does not know exists. Of course, a good rep will keep in contact with a station on a regular basis simply to keep up on station changes.

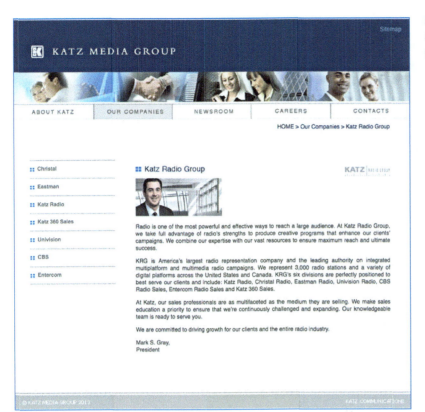

**FIGURE 4.27**
A rep company explains itself
Source: Courtesy of Katz Media Group

There are far fewer radio station reps than ad agencies, and with the clustering of stations by radio corporations the number of rep companies has dwindled dramatically as broadcasters assume the burden of representing themselves. Today, there are just a handful of major rep companies handling the 9,000-plus commercial stations around the country because the huge radio companies assume this function in-house.

Major rep firms pitch agencies on behalf of hundreds of client stations. The large and very successful reps often refuse to act as the envoy for small-market stations because of their lack of earning potential. A rep company typically receives a commission of between 5 and 12% on the spot purchases made by agencies, and because the national advertising money is usually directed first to the medium and large markets, the bigger commissions are not made from handling small-market outlets. Many rep companies specialize in small-market stations, however, especially in the age of consolidation.

Although a small rep company may work for the agencies on behalf of numerous stations, it will seldom handle two radio outlets in the same market. Doing so could result in a rep company being placed in the untenable position of competing with itself for a buy, thus creating an obvious conflict of interest. In the past few years, many larger rep firms have taken on multiple stations in the same market owing to the clustering approach of their clients.

The majority of station reps provide additional services. In recent years many have expanded into the areas of programming and management consultancy, and almost all offer clients audience research data, as well as aid in developing station promotions and designing sales materials such as rate cards.

## NEW REVENUE SOURCES: WEBSITES, HD RADIO, STREAMING, DIGITAL, AND PODCASTING

Websites, high-definition (HD) channels, streaming audio, and digital (e.g., apps) have become additional sources of revenue for most stations. Stations use the Internet (i.e., websites, streaming, apps, etc.) as a secondary means of generating revenue and communicating with their listeners. Indeed, a prominent

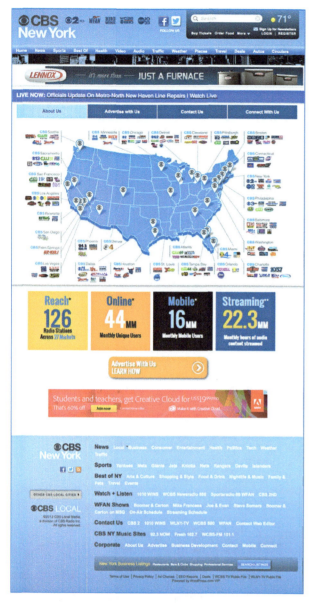

presence on the Internet is a twenty-first-century requirement and another way to add value to traditional commercial buys that have been sluggish at best in years past. Korgyn asserts:

> Websites can generate significant revenue from "banner ads" if the station has an active website. The success of a station's website and social media presence depends entirely on how tech savvy the staff is. For a website to generate any revenue, it must be updated often, offer contests and other "draws" for listeners to keep coming back, and provide a fun and interactive interface. HD Radio (which we haven't implemented yet due to the robber-baron, monopolistic license pricing from Xperi) has a great opportunity to present additional revenue streams through its "Artist Experience (AE)" screen displays. This could be used to display client ads during the commercials themselves, sponsored weather updates, sponsored contests, etc. The AE is a great tool for marketing.

As of 2017, a new business model for webpages and radio stations emerged that did not necessarily involve the radio station itself. That is, stations create websites designed to serve the interests of local communities and then sell advertising on those websites intended to reach a local, specific demographic. *Inside Radio* reports:

> To unlock the potential of digital, some radio broadcasters are looking beyond their airwaves and formats, and building digital destinations that stand apart from their core radio businesses. Such efforts include hyper-local news websites, online restaurant and travel guides, e-newsletters and local event listings.

An example of this new business model includes a Tyler, Texas, website that focuses on local sports—the East Texas Sports Network—that Townsquare Media created to meet local needs.

Other radio companies, such as Radio One, are buying existing websites, such as Bossip.com, which focuses on black celebrity news. It, along with other websites Radio One has purchased, feeds content back to the stations and also delivers an instant digital audience to deliver to advertisers. Gordon Borrell, President of Borrell Associates, says, "Too many media companies are looking at the opportunities in digital media as a product extension as opposed to a new business. Look at it as a new program, format or section and leverage existing resources to do that." This new business model is an important and growing revenue stream for radio stations as both Borrell Associates and the Radio Advertising Bureau report that digital revenue was expected to reach $753 million in 2017. Borrell suggests, "Every market is known for something, whether it is something grown there or an aspect of tourism. Those are the opportunities to develop something that is inherent and exclusive to your region."

Regarding online selling opportunities, Jason Insalaco says:

> Radio account executives can benefit from this source by selling additional exposure to advertisers. Another thing to keep in mind is that podcasting and streaming allow local clients of lesser means, who previously could not afford a conventional broadcast schedule, the chance to purchase less expensive Web commercials. Account executives can attest to the difficulty of selling the intangible

(sightless) nature of radio. Web advertising helps overcome this objection. Visual banner ads allow streaming listeners to click on ads that will take them directly to a client's website. Furthermore, radio programmers now have access to immediate data that provides advertisers with the number of users streaming their station and downloading specific podcasts. The current Nielsen ratings system provides audience data four weeks after the measurement was taken and is arguably arbitrary due to sampling inconsistencies and often erratic results. However, streaming and podcasting is a win-win for programmers who strive to retain the fickle listener and garner additional income.

**FIGURE 4.29**
Nielsen ratings provide stations with data showing how many listeners and what type of demographics are tuning in during different dayparts. The more listeners a station has, the more money it can charge for advertisements

Source: Courtesy of Nielsen

Importantly, one thing for broadcasters to keep in mind is that consumers do not always find online advertising welcoming or effective. A study conducted by Adobe in 2012 found that nearly a third of consumers thought that online advertising was ineffective and more than half of those surveyed thought that banner ads were ineffective. The same study found that, in terms of capturing a consumer's attention, radio ads were 15% more likely to capture a consumer's attention compared to online ads at 7%.

Meanwhile, HD side channels (HD channels) provide additional revenue streams for stations. While HD adoption is relatively slow, but growing, expectations indicate that advertiser interest in the innovative formats emerging will increase. In several major markets, HD formats have already attracted sponsors seeking a more niche clientele. An example of a new format emerging on HD side channels that attract niche demographics includes iHeartRadio's Pride Radio, targeting the LGBT community. To maximize HD Radio's revenue potential, Kevin McNamara of RadioMagOnline.com says:

> Let's get back to the fundamentals that worked years ago, serving the community. How about instead of putting some regurgitated music channel on the multicast channels, utilize them for providing public access to the communities within the station's service area. What I am suggesting here is not necessarily selling time to local businesses, rather giving time (and perhaps equipment and resources) to the communities to broadcast local events, particularly high school sports events or anything else that has relevant interest to the residents of that area. . . . Would I also put this content on my streaming site? Absolutely not . . . make this content special and exclusive to the local HD Radio audience.

Xperi Corporation helps stations generate revenue on their multicast channels—HD2, HD3, and HD4. There are almost 4,200 of these individual HD side channels, from which consumers can choose and marketers can advertise. A team of sales people is based in New York and operates the HD Radio Ad Network in more than 60 media markets. This is an expanding market as there are more than 25 million HD receivers in automobiles and over 2,500 primary HD stations in North America.

Rick Greenhut, Director of Broadcast Business development at Xperi, says that digital radio adds value to radio stations in terms of new revenue streams: "Perhaps the most telling detail supporting the added value case is the fact that today over $9 billion of the $16 billion generated annually by the U.S. radio industry comes from stations using HD Radio technology."

Not to be overlooked is the fact that, in the U.S., more than 36 million cars are equipped with an HD Radio and Xperi Corporation reports 37 auto manufacturers are offering 230 different car models with digital radios. The connected car, with digital radio and its special features, even provides users with the ability to interact with apps by using Apple CarPlay. When describing CarPlay, Apple says it

> takes the things you want to do with your iPhone while driving and puts them right on your car's built-in display. You can get directions, make calls, send and receive messages, and listen to music, all in a way that allows you to stay focused on the road. Just connect your iPhone and go.

FIGURE 4.30
The connected car offers additional
revenue streams for radio stations
ranging from digital radio to Apple
CarPlay

Source: Courtesy of *Iphonedigital*

Again, both digital radio and the ability to connect smartphones to auto radios adds additional ways stations can reach consumers.

Audio streaming and pure play stations have not yet developed an effective business model to generate advertising revenue. Despite having more than 78 million listeners, newer audio media outlets such as Spotify, Apple Music, and Pandora have not been as fortunate when it comes to generating revenue from digital ad sales. As of 2017, Spotify, Apple Music, and Pandora reported losses. In 2016, Pandora reported a loss of $76 million, while Spotify reported a $194 million loss. Adding to the complexity of the situation, research indicates that consumers are annoyed by advertising interruptions on audio streaming services.

FIGURE 4.31
HD Radio transmits both audio and
data to receivers providing more
options for listeners and creating
options for revenue streams

Source: Reproduced with permission from
Xperi

**Digital Sound**

HD Radio broadcasts deliver crystal clear, CD-like digital audio quality to consumers.

**HD2/HD3**

Adjacent to traditional main stations are HD2/HD3 Channels, providing new original formats on the FM dial.

**PSD**

Program Service Data provides song name, artist, station ID, and other relevant data streams.

**Active Alerts**

Delivers critical and life saving messages during emergency situations.

**Artist Experience**

Visual images, such as album art of over-the -air broadcasts from HD Radio stations.

**iTunes· Tagging**

iTunes Tagging provides users the means to "tag" broadcast radio content for later review and purchase from the iTunes Store.

**Traffic**

HD Radio Digital Traffic delivers more in-depth traffic data and travel conditions – as much as 10x faster than other broadcast methods.

**Instant Info**

News, sports, weather and more, useful information at the touch of a button.

**Bookmark**

Bookmark enables users to store information about content on the radio and delivers interactive information via QR codes.

**FIGURE 4.32**
Research indicates that listeners are annoyed by advertising on Pandora
Source: Courtesy of Jacobs Media

Although social media networks have not proven to be tools for generating revenue for stations yet, they are indeed getting closer to that goal. Jim Fox, Operations Manager and Station Manager for Entercom/Sacramento, stated in an interview with All Access Music Group:

> I view social media as I did our old bumper sticker campaigns: I know they are of value to the brand even if I can't produce any data to quantify it. KRXQ approaches social media with more than 25 years of heritage and very clearly defined personalities. KKDO tends to speak with one collective voice since it boasts "no annoying DJs."

The business model for online radio stations is evolving and, since listeners have been accustomed to having ad-free music, the introduction of ads on Pandora has not been embraced enthusiastically by consumers.

It is not just streaming audio listeners who are frustrated with advertising. The Jacobs Media Techsurvey13, conducted in 2017, found that four in 10 terrestrial radio listeners noted too many commercials (tied with repetitive music) was their reason for spending less time with the medium. When compared to advertising in other media platforms such as television and newspapers, radio fared much worse. Fred Jacobs says, "the bad news is that radio ads leave much to be desired. In fact, consumers are more likely to negatively rate commercials on the radio compared to those who generally like them." Elaborating further, Jacobs asserts,

> it's hard not to conclude that when it comes to its commercial monetization efforts, radio has its challenges. This isn't anything new, but as commercial stop-sets have become more cluttered with even poorer quality ads in recent years, these conditions take their toll on both those listening, as well as those advertising on the medium.

In an attempt to harness the potential of all platforms that might generate new and additional revenue streams, the radio industry has not overlooked the massive smartphone industry and all of those consumers. In 2017, *Inside Radio* reports that mobile revenue was expected to grow by 34% to generate $48 billion. That's a 58% share of digital media advertising revenue. *Inside Radio* explains:

> Through their apps, radio can deliver mobile ads targeted by location, demographics such as gender and age, and behavioral and contextual targets. By capturing device IDs and gathering information on users from registration, radio stations can direct ads to very specific—and valuable—advertising targets.

Further, when interviewed by *Inside Radio* about radio stations using mobile apps to generate ad revenue, Steve Meyers, the Executive Vice-President of Digital for the Beasley Broadcast Group, says,

> Mobile apps have the power to not only restrict content based on time, geographic location and interests, but to show direct attribution of our audiences' attendance at a specific time and place. The days of mobile display banner are over.

The Techsurvey 13 found that 40% of AM/FM radio listeners decreased listening time as a result of too many commercials

Source: Courtesy of Jacobs Media

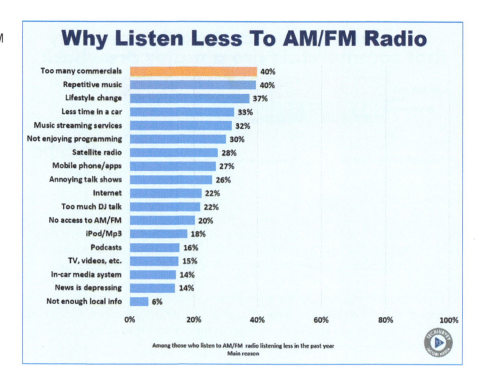

**Why Listen Less To AM/FM Radio**

| | |
|---|---|
| Too many commercials | 40% |
| Repetitive music | 40% |
| Lifestyle change | 37% |
| Less time in a car | 33% |
| Music streaming services | 32% |
| Not enjoying programming | 30% |
| Satellite radio | 28% |
| Mobile phone/apps | 27% |
| Annoying talk shows | 26% |
| Internet | 22% |
| Too much DJ talk | 22% |
| No access to AM/FM | 20% |
| iPod/Mp3 | 18% |
| Podcasts | 16% |
| TV, videos, etc. | 15% |
| In-car media system | 14% |
| News is depressing | 14% |
| Not enough local info | 6% |

Among those who listen to AM/FM radio listening less in the past year
Main reason

SoCast is a leader in the radio industry in helping radio stations transition to reach a digital audience

Source: Courtesy of SoCast

Beasley Broadcasting is using beacon technology and geo-targeting to gain a better understanding of their listener's behavior to provide data to potential advertisers as evidence of their effectiveness at reaching specific demographics.

In 2016, CBS Radio released its mobile app, which provided access to more than 200 of its radio stations, ranging from news and sports to music and talk. The mobile app was downloaded more than 17 million times. CBS Radio recognized the app's ability to generate revenue and created numerous functions for ad placement. According to CBS Radio, it boasts the app provides users with many functions, ranging from full screen ad units, to banners on the now playing display, and including rich media creative, all advertiser messages are clickable and interactive and refreshed upon user interaction with the apps. Clients can tailor their message based on station, genre or location.

The mobile apps not only allow for the streaming of terrestrial radio stations; they also allow for podcasts to be downloaded by users.

As the Internet becomes ubiquitous and consumers continue to migrate to all the features the web can offer, there are companies who specialize in helping radio stations transition from purely traditional broadcasting into the digital, social media world to reach all audiences, especially those using mobile apps. Importantly, this provides stations with a wide array of opportunities to generate new revenue and promote their stations. SoCast, founded in 2009, aimed to "harness their experience in social media dynamics, audience-facing platforms, and live event engagement, and give it to someone with greater reach and brand awareness, the results would be potentially game-changing." As the company websites notes, "That someone turned out to be Radio." SoCast offers many informative resources and services to radio stations such as (1) *Digital 101: An Essential Checklist for Radio in the Digital Age*, (2) *Managing Technology to Drive Growth*, and (3) *How can your Radio Stations Increase Digital Revenue?* to name only a few.

**FIGURE 4.35**
SoCast logo

Source: Courtesy of SoCast

Indeed, SoCast, and similar companies, seem to be moving in a financially wise direction. Data from the Pew Research Center show that 77% of Americans own a smartphone. A comScore study indicates 87% of the time spent by consumers on a smartphone is spent using apps, not the Internet. Further, the study shows that smartphone users spend more than two hours a day using smartphone apps, with music apps ranking among the most popular, particularly iHeartRadio and Spotify.

## PODCA$HING IN

### Jason Insalaco

With the explosion of portable, on-demand media, content creators are presented with a unique opportunity to create and monetize podcasts. Podcasting was originally introduced in the early 2000s to coincide with the release of the iPod and has achieved critical mass in less than two decades. According to a 2017 study by Edison Research and Triton Digital, Podcasting consumption continues to expand, as 40% of Americans aged 12+ said that they had listened to a podcast, while 24% said that they had listened to one in the past month, up from 21% only one year before.

Audio professionals are monetizing podcasts in nontraditional ways beyond broadcasting's staple of the 30-second commercial.

Whether a major broadcast operator or an independent podcast pioneer, a sustainable one-size-fits-all revenue model has not yet surfaced for the digital download. The podcast frontier is populated with a "wild west" mentality—anything goes, and anything is worth a shot.

Adam Carolla is one of those digital pioneers who has developed a multifaceted approach to podcast monetization with the launch of his podcast in 2009 after a 15-year career on terrestrial radio. His daily 90-minute podcast, *The Adam Carolla Show*, features topical news discussions, celebrity guests, and comedy at AdamCarolla.com. The Adam Carolla podcast officially broke the Guinness World Record for the "Most Downloaded Podcast," receiving 59,574,843 unique downloads from March 2009 to March 2011.

Carolla is a podcast trailblazer who ventured into the medium after a successful run hosting the nationally syndicated program *Loveline* and a morning show for CBS Radio. He launched his podcast venture only a few days after his syndicated morning program ended in February 2009, and he has not looked back.

Carolla explains his seamless transition: "I never actually missed a day of the show. I ended my morning show on a Friday. And on Monday, I launched my podcast and have been doing it ever since."

Surpassing 2,000 podcast episodes, Carolla has tested podcasting's monetization potential through trial and error. He monetizes his podcast using traditional host-endorsed commercials interspersed throughout the show along with innovative revenue methods—live shows, book sales, subscriptions, revenue shares, listener cruises, podcast courses, documentaries, and speeches on college campuses. Carolla has even launched his brand of beer and liquors, which he promotes on his podcast and during live appearances.

Adam Carolla's live performances deliver steady revenue. Carolla takes his program on the road several times a month to large venues and hosts his live podcast in front of an eager audience. Typically, the Carolla live podcasts attract thousands of paying fans. Nearly every show is a sellout. In addition, he has embarked on Carolla cruises with hundreds of listeners who pay a healthy sum to spend four days with Carolla and his content collaborators for podcasts, live shows, and interactive games.

Through an innovative, revenue arrangement, Carolla promotes his documentaries, books, and liquor brands on his podcast and sells them through his site. While utilizing the podcast as a powerful venue to promote his books and films, Carolla also receives revenue share for all merchandise purchased from Amazon.com and dozens of other companies when accessed through AdamCarolla.com. As a result of the deal, he receives a percentage of a purchase every time one clicks through the sponsor's link on his site and buys something. The relationship is a financial boon to his podcast operation. In fact, Carolla has turned down lucrative offers to take his program back to traditional radio. He credits this decision largely on the success of the revenue-share arrangement along with his other income generators.

"Podcast listeners are loyal," Carolla said. "Initially, I suggested that if they were going to buy something, they could click through our Amazon link to help us out. 'Wet our beaks' a bit." Listener response drastically exceeded the show's expectations and has thus expanded to other advertisers who want a piece of his growing audience. "The response has been overwhelming. The podcast listeners are driving huge numbers and the result is amazing," Carolla said.

Adam Carolla has expanded beyond his own podcast and now hosts and produces 12 weekly shows on his Carolla network. These spinoff podcasts focus on topics geared to a different target audience: car repair to home improvement. The niche audiences for these programs provide advertisers with listeners more likely to engage with their products and services.

Not one to leave any stone unturned, Carolla offers a paid subscription for program archives and premium subscriptions for some specialty podcasts. The idea behind it is that only a very small percentage of people pay, but they will more than make up for the folks who are listening for free. The more dedicated fans pay a subscription for access to thousands of hours of content.

Although inventive in his approach, Carolla admits that, in the end, it's all about the audience. "Sponsors care about how many ears and/or eyes you are selling," Carolla said:

> Whether it's a banner being dragged by a plane over a beach or someone listening to the radio, Madison Avenue cares about the number of impressions. Whether you are selling podcast downloads or selling impressions of stadium attendees beholden to the blimp ad flying overhead with an advertisement, numbers are still the most important.

---

**Jason Insalaco** has more than 20 years of experience in the radio industry. Throughout his tenure, he has worked as a station manager, program director, and executive producer, and in other programming and production roles at radio stations in Los Angeles, San Francisco, and Boston. In addition, Jason is a media lawyer and has worked as a talent manager representing personalities from morning show radio, talk radio, and public broadcasting. He currently develops content and new media initiatives for commercial and public radio. He earned an undergraduate degree from Boston College and he obtained a law degree from Loyola Law School in Los Angeles.

Although audio technology for podcasting has been around since the early 2000s, radio stations have failed to find a definitive way to generate revenue from podcasting. However, that seems to be changing as podcasting popularity is on the rise. Edison Research found that, as of 2016, nearly 40% of U.S. adults age 12 years and older had downloaded and listened to a podcast. That is an estimated 98 million listeners. Twenty-one percent, or 57 million people, reported listening to a podcast on a monthly basis. With a monthly listenership averaging 57 million people, that's attractive for advertisers who want to reach consumers. Studies show that podcast users are educated, young, and have full-time jobs and are willing to engage with the ads in podcasts. For the year of 2017 alone, *Inside Radio* reports revenue from podcasts was expected to exceed $220 million.

With the increase in listeners, marketers and advertisers are changing their opinions about buying time on advertising on podcasts. In fact, podcasts are likely to become a very profitable venture for the radio industry and broadcasting industry if their popularity continues on its upward trajectory. In 2017, Westwood One found that 68% of advertisers had discussed placing ads in podcasts, an increase from 41% in 2015. The study found that 37% were likely to consider advertising in podcasts within a six-month period, an increase from only 18% in 2015. Further, the Westwood One study found that almost a third (29% of those surveyed) were already advertising in podcasts, up from only 15% in 2015. Also, the study found the median age of podcast listeners was 29, compared to 46 years old for terrestrial radio listeners. Overall, this offers a very desirable demographic to advertisers.

Regarding the change in attitude toward podcasts by advertisers, Suzanne Grimes, Executive Vice-President for Corporate Marketing for Cumulus Media and President of Westwood One told *Inside Radio*, "We knew that advertiser sentiment for podcast advertising was growing, as we have seen a significant increase in advertising spend on the Westwood One podcast network." Further, she adds, the *State of Podcasting 2017* study "quantifies the conversation, consideration, and intention among marketers to place their brands in the expansive podcast programming environment. It's great news for all of us in the fast-tracking on-demand space."

Interestingly, the competition to traditional AM/FM radio has created an environment that has made the industry sensitive to the negative connotation that "terrestrial radio" has among some listeners and

## RADIO 2.0: TODAY'S LOCAL INTEGRATED SOLUTION PROVIDER

### Weezie Kramer

Radio today integrates multiple on-air, online, and digital assets to create dynamic and solution-oriented, integrated campaigns for clients. Campaigns coordinate multiple marketing assets to engage consumers and motivate action and response from fans.

Our goal is to create great content, provide terrific entertainment and talent, and deliver it to consumers on any platform that they want to access it, whenever they want to access it. With all of these platforms we have new ad and sponsorship opportunities that offer audio and video and display and direct-to-consumer revenue opportunities. We bring these elements together to create response for our clients and amplify a client's campaign to better resonate and connect with our listeners and drive results for our clients. It's interesting to note that combining multiple elements almost always increases our results for clients.

Some of radio's integrated and digital assets include:

### Internet Radio

- The fastest-growing segment of the radio industry, Internet radio today represents up to 15% of the total listening audience.
- Online listeners across desktop, laptop, and mobile applications tend to be among the most loyal, tech-savvy, and responsive.
- Internet radio is consumed at the "point of purchase" as consumers are just a mouse click away from a client's website, a search engine, or their favorite social media site.

**FIGURE 4.36**
Weezie Kramer

Internet radio is delivered on dynamic players that enhance music discovery, provide video and pictures, streaming, podcasts, and blogs, as well as contesting and e-commerce. We also have apps for iPhones and Androids and mobile websites.

### Display Ads and Banner Ads

- Rich media display ads add color and ROI to a traditional campaign.
- Display ads run throughout our websites in a variety of universal sizes including 728 x 90, 300 x 100, and 300 x 250.

### Video Pre-Rolls

- "Must-see" video pre-roll and video ads provide visuals and motion that serve our most ardent fans as they opt in to their favorite content (300 x 250 "video ads" are our most popular assets).
- Video pre-rolls provide an online roadblock that requires a user to view a commercial message before they can progress on the site.

### Rich Media/Walk-On Video

- Rich media video ads, such as "walk-on" or "disruptive" video ads, launch on a radio station website page and bring additional attention and excitement to an advertiser's message.
- Rich media walk-on videos are interactive and clickable and can include people, station personalities, vehicles, or more to engage the audience and encourage consumers to click to find out more.

### Microsites/Landing Pages

Creative, client-branded websites and web pages enhance an advertiser's marketing message by providing information, videos, and content specifically designed to activate the targeted demographic for the campaign.

### Website Takeovers

- Daily and hourly takeovers of radio station websites can include static banner ads, visual takeovers, side bars, and more to powerfully reinforce an advertiser's message.
- Website takeovers provide an online roadblock that literally "take over" a web page. Visitors are inundated with an advertisers company's marketing message during a specific timeframe reinforcing an advertiser's campaign and motivating them to take action.

### Social Media Activation

- Incorporating an integrated approach to promote an advertiser's social media strategy drives consumer interest for an advertiser's company, resulting in more followers involved in an advertisers social media extensions (i.e., Facebook, Twitter, etc.).

### Mobile/Text Programs

- Combining an on-air campaign with texting can dynamically build an advertiser's brands' database.
- Text-to-win programs drive consumers into retail locations to pick up a text code and enter to win prizes and redeem special offers.
- Text alerts can be used to build a text database to share information and send daily/weekly/monthly information, tips, special offers or coupons and create an ongoing dialogue with consumers.

### Loyalty Programs

- Loyalty programs give consumers an opportunity to earn points to be used toward prizes from an advertiser's business, station prizes, special incentives, and more.
- Loyalty programs help create additional listener engagement by facilitating an interactive relationship, which, by extension, benefits the advertiser.

### Contests and Promotions

- On-air giveaways and contesting are a proven staple of radio marketing, reinforcing an advertiser's objective to a highly engaged listener.

- Contests are a great way to create additional exposure and excitement for advertisers' products or offerings.

### HD Radio

HD Radio offers an enhanced user experience and better fidelity. Benefits of HD Radio include:

- FM radio that sounds almost as good as a CD.
- AM radio that sounds as good as traditional FM.
- Increased listening options with multicasting.
- Tagging a song for later purchase through the iTunes Store.

### And more . . .

---

Since 2000, **Weezie Kramer** has served as a Member of Entercom's Operating Committee and has been responsible for operations in 10 Entercom markets (Boston, Seattle, Denver, Portland, Kansas City, Milwaukee, Providence, Springfield, Madison and Norfolk), as well as spearheading the company's reinvention efforts, where she has focused on developing enhancements to drive the company's future growth. Kramer is also a past Chair of the RAB Board of Directors. She was the first woman to chair the RAB Board, and currently serves on the RAB Executive Committee. She was elevated to station Group President in 2013 and to Chief Operating Officer in May 2015.

whether online competition should be called "radio" or "audio." Thus, *Inside Radio* reports that the CEO of one major radio corporation encourages the corporation's radio sales team to not use the term "radio" when referring to online radio stations. "We tell our salespeople to call the webcasters 'Internet audio'—not 'Internet radio,'" said the CEO. Radio stations will continue experimenting with revenue models to determine what is most effective.

## NONTRADITIONAL REVENUE

One way to generate nontraditional revenue is via co-op advertising. It has been estimated that more than $600 million in radio revenue comes from co-op advertising—no small piece of change, indeed. Kramer explains Entercom's definition of "nontraditional" revenue as

> primarily generating revenue through nonad channels or by monetizing our audience. Our connection between our fans (listeners) and our stations enables us to monetize events, experiences and assets (from concerts to bridal fairs to joining our air talent and artists we play in away destinations).

Specifically regarding co-op advertising, Kramer says

> We also have an e-commerce channel where we directly sell coupons and items to our audience. Likewise, due to the natural fluctuations in the nation's economy, co-op opportunities remain available, but account executives have to dig deeper to find them. . . . Co-op represents a nice opportunity but is often underutilized by sellers. I would estimate that the total percent of co-op would be low single digits.

Co-op advertising involves the cooperation of three parties: the retailer whose business is being promoted, the manufacturer whose product is being promoted, and the medium used for the promotion. In other words, a retailer and manufacturer get together to share advertising expenses. For example, Smith's Sporting Goods is informed by the Converse Running Shoes representative that the company will match, dollar for dollar, up to $5,000, the money that the retailer invests in radio advertising. The only stipulation of the deal is that Converse be promoted in the commercials on which the money is spent. This means that no competitive product can be mentioned. Converse demands exclusivity for its contribution.

Manufacturers of practically every conceivable type of product, from lawn mowers to mobile homes, establish co-op advertising budgets. A radio salesperson can use co-op to great advantage. First, the station account executive must determine the extent of co-op subsidy a client is entitled to receive. Most of the time the retailer knows the answer to this. Frequently, however, retailers do not take full advantage of the co-op funds that manufacturers make available. In some instances, retailers are not aware that a particular manufacturer will share radio advertising expenses. Many potential advertisers have been motivated to go on the air after discovering the existence of co-op dollars. Mid-sized retailers account for the biggest chunk of the industry's co-op revenues. However, even the smallest retailer is likely eligible for some subsidy, and a salesperson can make this fact known for everyone's mutual advantage.

The sales manager generally directs a station's co-op efforts. Large stations often employ a full-time co-op specialist. The individual responsible for stimulating co-op revenue will survey retail trade journals for pertinent information about available dollars. Retail associations are also a good source of information, because they generally possess manufacturer co-op advertising lists. The importance of taking advantage of co-op opportunities cannot be overstressed. Some stations, especially metro-market outlets, earn hundreds of thousands of dollars in additional ad revenue through their co-op efforts.

From the retailer's perspective, co-op advertising is not always a great bargain. This usually stems from copy constraints imposed by certain manufacturers, which give the retailer a 10-second tag-out in a 30- or 60-second commercial. Obviously, this does not please the retailer who has split the cost of advertising 50/50. In recent years, this type of copy domination by the manufacturer has decreased somewhat, and a more equitable approach, whereby both parties share evenly the exposure and the expense, is more commonplace.

Co-op is also appealing to radio stations because they do not have to modify their billing practices to accommodate the third party. Stations simply bill the retailer and provide an affidavit attesting to the time commercials aired. The retailer, in turn, bills the manufacturer for its share of the airtime. For its part, the manufacturer requires receipt of an affidavit before making payment. In certain cases, the station is asked to mail affidavits directly to the manufacturer. Some manufacturers stipulate that bills be sent to audit houses, which inspect the materials before authorizing payment.

Event marketing is another key form of nontraditional revenue generation. This involves the creation of a popular event, such as a food or arts festival, wherein merchants pay to be associated with it. This has become a very common and successful way for stations to make income without adding to their on-air spot loads. Jay Williams, Jr. says, "Stations are going outside the traditional spot load box and engaging in different ways to generate income." In 2012, Clear Channel collaborated with country music superstar Toby Keith to give away a Ford F-150 pickup truck. Radio listeners were required to listen to Clear Channel radio stations as well as the Clear Channel-owned iHeartRadio and were prompted to text messages using their cell phones in order to win the vehicle. Cleverly, the truck had a custom-designed Toby Keith iHeartRadio channel.

With the rapid adoption of new media technologies by consumers, nontraditional revenue potential and new opportunities have expanded. Jason Insalaco says, "What once was considered non-traditional revenue has become expected bottom-line revenue such as advertising from streaming, podcasting, and Web impressions." Further, Insalaco asserts:

> There are still opportunities for major non-traditional revenue in creating specific brand monetization opportunities with effective merchandising, licensing, and taking the program "on the road." Ironically, public radio has demonstrated the most successful examples of non-traditional revenue. For example, American Public Media's *A Prairie Home Companion* hits the road several times a month and plays to large, sold-out crowds that pay healthy ticket prices. Chicago Public Radio's *This American Life* successfully generates revenue with radio swag such as T-shirts, mugs, and posters along with creative tchotchkes including custom USB drives with 35-plus hours of content and even an original *This American Life* comic book.

Korgyn adds,

> This one is a tough one really. Much of the non-traditional revenue in today's radio world is dependent on having technically savvy staff who embrace social media and the new "digital age." Sales opportunities exist in website banner ads, Facebook and Twitter mentions, RDS text ads and HD Radio display ads, and of course the ubiquitous "Live Remote."

## TRADE-OUTS

Stations commonly exchange airtime for goods, although top-rated outlets, whose time is sold at a premium, are less likely to swap spots for anything other than cash. Rather than pay for needed items, such as office supplies and furnishings, studio equipment, meals for clients and listeners, new cars, and so forth, a station may choose to strike a deal with merchants in which airtime is traded for merchandise. There are advertisers who use radio only on a trade basis. A station may start out in a relationship that is exclusively trade with a client in the hope of eventually converting him to cash. Split contracts also are written when a client agrees to provide both money and merchandise. For example, WXXX-FM needs two new office desks. The total cost of the desks is $800. An agreement is made whereby the client receives a $1,400 ROS spot schedule and $600 cash in exchange for the desks. Trade-outs are not always this equitable. Stations often provide trade clients with airtime worth two or three times the merchandise value to get what is needed. Thus, the saying "need inspires deals."

Many sales managers also feel that it makes good business sense to write radio trade contracts to fill available and unsold airtime, rather than let it pass unused. Once airtime is gone, it cannot be retrieved, and yesterday's unfilled availability is a lost opportunity.

## TRAFFIC AND BILLING

### The Air Supply and Program Logs

The job of the sales department, and that of the account executives, is incomplete without considering traffic and billing. A station sells airtime—that is its inventory, its product. The volume or size of a given station's inventory depends chiefly on the amount of time it allocates for commercial matter. For example, some stations with adult contemporary and easy listening formats deliberately restrict or limit commercial loads as a method of enhancing overall sound and fostering a "more music, less talk" image.

A full-time station has more than 10,000 minutes to fill each week. This computes to approximately 3,000 minutes for commercials, based on an 18-minute commercial load ceiling per hour. In the eyes of the sales manager, this means anywhere from 3,000 to 6,000 availabilities or slots—assuming that a station sells 60- and 30-second spot units—in which commercial announcements are inserted.

Inventory control and accountability at a radio station are no small jobs. They are the primary duties of the traffic manager, and this position is pivotal enough in a radio station that it has its own professional association, the Traffic Directors Guild of America (TDGA). The guild's mission is "To foster pride in our unique profession, and to promote the contributions we provide to the Radio and Television Broadcasting Industry. The Traffic Directors Guild seeks to enhance our member careers through information, cooperative services and education." It is a nonunion organization whose goal is to serve revenue management scheduling professionals, accounts receivable, continuity, operations and business management personnel.

### The Traffic Manager

Vicki Nichols, Traffic Manager for Emmis Indianapolis, says the traffic manager's responsibility is, in its simplest form, "to manage inventory in a way that maximizes revenue." A daily log is prepared by the traffic manager (also referred to as the traffic director). This document is a schedule of programming elements (commercials, features, and public service announcements [PSAs]) to be aired and a record of what was actually aired. It serves to inform the on-air operator of what to broadcast and at what time, and it provides a record for, among other things, billing purposes.

Let us examine the process involved in logging a commercial for broadcast beginning at the point at which the salesperson writes an order for a spot schedule:

1. The salesperson writes an order and returns it to the station.
2. The sales manager then checks and approves the order.
3. The sales secretary enters the order into the computer software.
4. Copies of the formalized order are distributed to the traffic manager, sales manager, billing, salesperson, and client and/or accessed by these individuals via the station's software database.
5. The order is placed in the traffic scheduling book or entered into the computer for posting to the log by the traffic manager using highly specialized programming software.
6. The order is logged commencing on the start date stipulated by the buy.

Although the above list is both a simplification and generalization of the actual process, it does convey the basic idea. Keep in mind that not all stations operate in exactly the same manner. The actual method for preparing a log will differ from station to station depending on whether it is in a large or a small market. Station program logs are computer-generated and there are a number of companies available to broadcasters who offer traffic and billing software such as Marketron.

**FIGURE 4.37**
Marketron logo

Source: Courtesy of
Marketron

Deborah Esayian, Chief Revenue Officer for Marketron, one of the nation's leading traffic and billing software companies, says "The era of manual log preparation is in the past. With the availability of simple and sophisticated cloud-based traffic software, most all stations have switched to a more reliable platform like Marketron Traffic."

There are many benefits to using computer software to schedule commercial traffic and generate billing invoices. The technological growth of stations and their advertisers has led to the use of sophisticated computer software for traffic and billing purposes. Particularly, Esayian says the following are benefits:

- Many advertisers and agencies now require the ability to view and pay their invoices online from radio stations. Also, the need for proof of performance for spot times and copy running necessitates the use of sophisticated software to keep up with demand in an automated fashion with an online presence.

- Proper placement of advertisements to maximize the available schedule while maintaining competitive separation and fair spot distribution is important. Traffic software allows for insertion of competitive codes and spot separation rules to automatically alert the traffic manager if placement is violating any of these advertiser requirements.

- Special programming (sporting events or holiday schedules) will disrupt the normal log layout for a day or event. Where spot breaks are, the length of time between, and available placement will need to be altered for these time periods. Traffic software allows for the easy creation of temporary logs that can be laid over existing logs for the time the special programming is running, and then removed when it is complete.

Esayian says that the primary benefit for radio stations to use traffic and billing software is that

> The traffic and billing systems allow for the fast, accurate, and secure revenue workflow from insertion to invoicing. In addition, it puts all data into one area where management can pull and review reports to help them better manage their sales and revenue for the station.

It is the traffic manager's responsibility to see that an order placed by an account executive is logged as specified and that each client is treated fairly and equitably. A sponsor who purchases two spots,

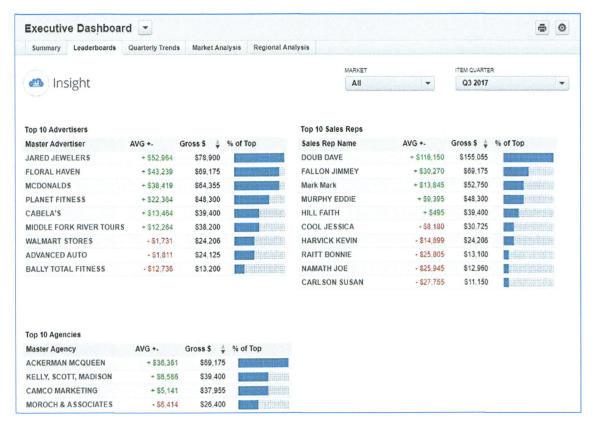

**FIGURE 4.38**

Insight is Marketron's reporting service that allows for customizable ad hoc reporting. This screenshot is of an executive dashboard that was customized to the executive's specific needs. Dashboards can include performance reports, pacing to financial goals, and trends at the station and market level

Source: Courtesy of Marketron

five days a week, during morning drive time can expect to receive good rotation for maximum reach. It is up to the traffic manager to schedule the client's commercials in as many quarter-hour segments of the daypart as possible. The effectiveness of a spot schedule is reduced if the spots are logged in the same quarter-hour each day. If a spot is logged at 6:45 am daily, it is only reaching those people tuned at that hour each day. However, if on one day it is logged at 7:15 am and then at 8:45 am on another, and so on, it is reaching a different audience each day. It also would be unfair to the advertiser who purchased drive time to have spots logged only prior to 7:00 am, the beginning of the prime audience period. Most stations have a rotation chart that indicates when commercial breaks will be taken so that the traffic software can schedule the commercials.

## WHAT IS TRAFFIC? (NO, WE MEAN THE *OTHER* TRAFFIC)

### Larry Keene

No, this broadcast traffic person doesn't go up in the chopper to report on drive time gridlock on the freeway, interstate, or high volume arteries. Broadcasting actually has two areas involving the word "traffic." We are the "other one," although, in a way, we do control what goes where, when, and under what conditions.

Our traffic is the revenue management specialist. And the truly successful managers will confirm you should never underestimate the value of the traffic professional when the campaigns are handed off from sales and creative for insertion into the financial funnel controlled by the revenue management specialists of traffic.

We're guessing about how we got so lucky to be stuck with the name "traffic" in our titles, but possibly because we are the incoming receiver of placement duties from sales, programming, technicians, promotion, marketing, production, and management. The incoming is like a major freeway intersection in Los Angeles all transitioning to directed streams of . . . well, traffic seems the most appropriate word to describe it—we are the traffic cop, traffic controller, traffic director, or manager that directs it to its proper destination.

Please realize that air traffic controllers, highway traffic officers, and broadcast traffic personnel all function in a similar manner . . . hundreds of planes heading for the airport terminal, hundreds of vehicles on the highways headed for different destinations, and hundreds of programs and commercials trying to find their "avails" on the program log.

Our key employees in "traffic" involve the scheduling of programs, commercial content, program teasers, promotional announcements, and all the other components that comprise what is heard on the audio of your favorite stations, website, or wireless-delivered content.

It seems fairly simple to us, but it's confusing to others, especially when someone in an elevator asks you what you do. Be prepared for a blank stare when you say, "I'm the traffic director or traffic manager. At WXXX."

It's easy to say that you schedule the programs and commercials on your favorite radio stations—but that inevitable moment or two of silence from the person that had asked you what you do always feels slightly awkward. The truth is you're in charge of a multitasking highly complex revenue center that links all of the program segments for the station audience.

You may have heard of the buzzword "STEM," which is an acronym for science, technology, engineering, and mathematics. Traffic is a little of each, rather than a reliance on just one of the four. However, those of us involved in the profession tend to think it's a little more of science and math, and then blended with computer technology and engineering.

From the outside, many will say, you have limited amounts of inventory made up of "spaces" or avails for commercials, promos, and items precommitted to networks or required legal items such as required station identifications, etc. Your job, outsiders believe, is to put the inventory into the available spaces and your job is done. If only it was that easy.

You and your tools must calculate which items have the priorities over others. You must try to avoid having competitors running back-to-back; most days there are more items than there are spaces.

The program director has given instructions that the commercial sets cannot be longer than $x$ number of minutes, so you must decide how to combine the varying lengths of 10-, 15-, 20-, 30- and 60-second announcements can be combined before a "clutter" factor causes audience tune-out.

Another consideration is avoiding having the same announcer's voice of several announcements in a row. Scientifically speaking, you lose listener credibility if it's the same voice telling you what to buy three or four times in a row. All of the foregoing items blend together. Fortunately, computer software helps immeasurably—but the "human factor" is alive and well and comes into play more often than nontraffic personnel realize.

When it's all over, you also need to confirm that all commercials or revenue-producing items ran within the time frames that were dictated by the original orders received from agencies and a wide host of sales personnel. (That's continuity, but it's crucial to your tasks, too.) Stations need to promote themselves and their programs—you're the person that verifies that the "promos" are ready to roll at the right time.

Next day, the traffic staff does it all over again. Actually, you're the key multitasker that maximizes the revenue for the sales department, confirms that all the commercial, promotional, legal, and programming segments are not only properly scheduled but that they are all in-house and in-place for on-demand playback. While every duty is important, maximizing the revenue takes the number one priority position.

And, in today's world, that entire procedure is usually needed for not just one, but multiple stations including subchannels (such as HD2, HD3, etc.), website audio streaming, display ads, banners and boxes on your stations' websites, mobile feeds, and—as the disc jockeys like to say—the list goes on and on.

And, if you think that's confusing, consider the many titled positions within the traffic department (although traffic director and traffic manager seem to be the more commonly used): TDGA tends to prefer the all-inclusive title of traffic professional. There are at least 30 different titles in traffic; all could be summarized as "traffic." That's like saying Baskin-Robbins and Ben & Jerry's have so many flavors from which to choose. To most of us, simply put—they're all "ice cream." And to our colleagues in management, sales, creative, talent, and technical, they think all of our titles are all just "traffic."

---

**Larry Keene** is a 56-year veteran of the radio business, ranging from on-air personality to program manager, producer of the *Joe Pyne Show* and the Miss America Radio Network for 25 years, sales manager, traffic manager, general manager, owner of two radio groups, Executive Board Member of NAFMB, NRBA, President of NJBA for three terms, national sales manager of a major traffic software vendor, Founder of TDGA. He is the author of the *TDGA Radio-TV Glossary of Broadcast Terms*, a 100-plus page volume of approximately 1,250 terms and definitions, etc. (considered by many to be the "back-office Bible" of broadcasting terms).

Using traffic and billing software, the traffic manager maintains a record of when a client's spots are aired to ensure effective rotation. Another concern of the traffic manager is to maintain adequate space between accounts of a competitive nature. Running two restaurants back-to-back, or within the same spot set, would likely result in having to reschedule both at different times at no cost to the client. In addition to using traffic software, the traffic manager designates certain times within the hour in which commercial breaks will occur. It also falls within the traffic manager's purview to make sure that copy and the production of the commercial(s) are in on time. Most stations have a policy requiring that commercial material be on hand at least 48 hours before it is scheduled for broadcast.

Station traffic manager Jan Hildreth says that holiday and political campaign periods can place added pressure on not only the traffic person, but also the salesperson:

> The fourth quarter is the big money time in radio. The logs usually are jammed, and availabilities are in short supply. The workload in the traffic department doubles. Things also get pretty chaotic around elections. It can become a real test for the nerves. Of course, there's always the late order that arrives at 5 pm on Friday that gets the adrenaline going.

Traffic and billing software enables a salesperson, along with station management, to constantly monitor the amount of sales being made and whether financial targets are being met for both the station and the individual salesperson.

There are few station relationships closer than that of the traffic department with programming and sales. Programming relies on the traffic manager for the logs that function as scheduling guides for on-air personnel and the logs need to be uploaded into the automation systems that are used by many stations to broadcast both commercials and music. Sales depends on the traffic department to inform them of existing availabilities and to process orders onto the air. Radio station traffic manager Barbara Kalulas observes that:

> It is crucial to the operation that traffic has a good relationship with sales and programming. When it doesn't, things begin to happen. The program director (PD) has to let traffic know when something changes; if not, the system breaks down. This is equally true of sales. Traffic is kind of the heart of things. Everything passes through the traffic department. Cooperation is very important.

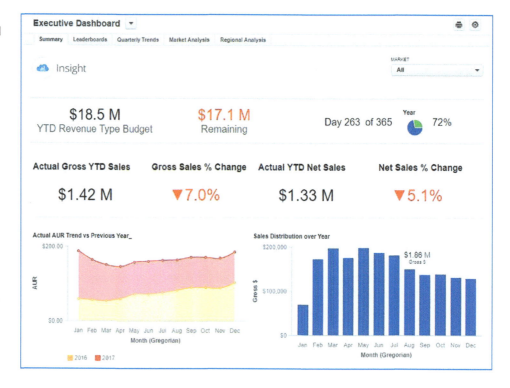

## Directing Traffic

Although the initial financial expenditure for computers is substantive and the hardware is expensive to maintain, computers, nonetheless, are a required investment for radio stations, according to Nichols:

> Fewer employees are needed to produce the same volume of work. What used to be the responsibility of many is now pared down to smaller staffs. Although some companies have pared it down *too* small, expecting unrealistic volume of work from too few employees. I won't name the companies (but Emmis is not one of them).

Stations across the nation utilize software to manage their traffic and billing procedures. In a 2013 interview with *Talkers*, Jeff Haley, the CEO of Marketron, a leading provider of traffic and billing software for radio stations, explained how his company helps stations:

> While technology like ours can enable radio stations to streamline their operations, when it comes to sales, it still needs a human touch to make the deal. With Marketron on board, a station's sales reps are able to save time on data keeping and management, and pull together more sophisticated packages to suit each advertiser, leveraging all available platforms, and markets.

The traffic software can increase a station's efficiency. Haley says:

> For example, Mediascape customers who take advantage of our Network Connect service routinely save between two and eight hours of work time per station per week through the benefit of integrations with network providers such as Dial Global, Premiere, Cumulus, and others which replace what was once a very labor-intensive and manual process with an automated workflow. We can demonstrate the same efficiencies in a variety of areas of our customers' operations such as digital sales, billing activities, and reporting where once highly manual and complex processes are becoming automated and simplified, freeing time to focus on truly critical functions and unlocking tremendous value for our customers.

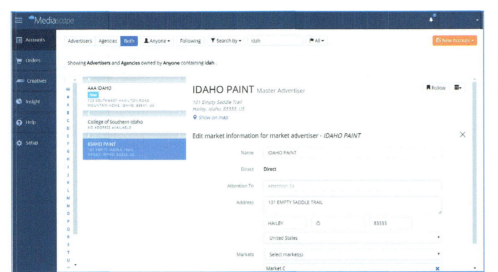

FIGURE 4.40
Mediascape Accounts: Manage the contact details for all of the accounts, corporate wide or follow only those accounts that are of interest

Source: Courtesy of Marketron

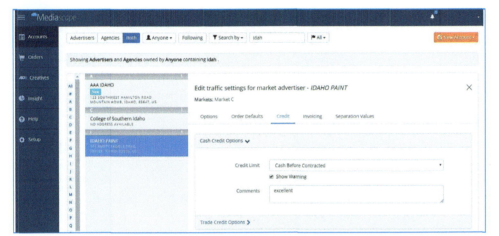

FIGURE 4.41
Mediascape Accounts: The traffic system settings for all markets are centrally controlled from one location for maximum stability

Source: Courtesy of Marketron

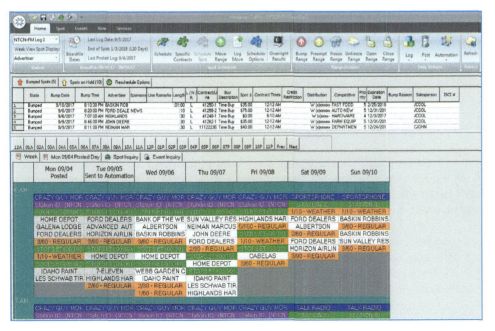

FIGURE 4.42
The Boardfile is the area in which Marketron traffic managers manage their logs. This screenshot is in weekly view which allows spots to be moved across hours, days, or weeks, along with other features geared to maximize the revenue for every log

Source: Courtesy of Marketron

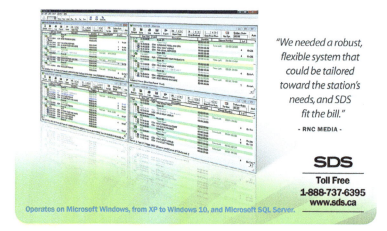
In an interview with *Radio Ink*, WPOC-FM's Jim Dolan observed that "The move right now is toward putting your sales force in the field armed with laptops and instantaneous online access to inventory, availability, and contract information." Traffic software will continue to improve the efficiency of the station's traffic and billing department. Various types of traffic and billing software are available. Several companies, most notably Marketron, Harris Osi-Traffic, Wide Orbit, Natural Broadcast Systems, and ACI Media, specialize in providing broadcasters with software packages. Prices for computer software vary depending on the nature and complexity of the software program.

## Billing

At most stations, advertisers are billed for the airtime they have purchased after a portion or all of it has run. Few stations require that sponsors pay in advance. It is the job of the billing department to notify the advertiser when payment is due. Al Rozanski, former Business Manager of WMJX-FM, Boston, explains the process involved once a contract has been logged by the traffic department:

> We send invoices out twice monthly. Many stations bill weekly, but we find doing it every two weeks cuts down on the paperwork considerably. The first thing my billing person does is check the logs to verify that the client's spots ran. We don't bill them for something that wasn't aired. Occasionally a spot will be missed for one reason or another, say a technical problem. This will be reflected on the log because the on-air person will indicate this fact.

Nichols explains the process in Indianapolis:

I generate logs for the next day. On the next day, I reconcile and post the previous day's logs. On Mondays, the accounting department invoices all orders that have expired during the previous week (after all logs are posted). On the Monday following the end of broadcast calendar month, [the individual responsible for billing] invoices everything that ran in the month. Then [the individual in the billing department] and the business manager run tons of revenue reports, balancing the receivables (payments from advertisers) against the invoices. I think at some point during the month they send statements to clients who have not remitted checks in a timely manner.

Although some stations still send invoices via traditional mail, the radio industry has also utilized email as a means to deliver invoices. "Local merchants are now more accustomed to receiving invoices by email, rather than waiting for a bill to come in the mail," says Scott.

Not all radio stations have a full-time business manager on the payroll. Thus, the person who handles billing is commonly responsible for maintaining the station's financial records or books as well. In this case, the services of a professional accountant may be contracted on a regular basis to perform the more complex bookkeeping tasks and provide consultation on other financial matters.

Accounts that fail to pay when due are turned over to the appropriate salesperson for collections. If this does not result in payment, a station may use the services of a collection agency. Should its attempt also fail, the station likely would write the business off as a loss at tax time. The standard payment policy for radio stations is "payable net thirty (30) days from receipt of invoice." Late charges, collection action, and ultimately litigation could ensue if payment is not made for the messages advertised. Nichols states, "It's the salesperson's responsibility to collect past due amounts from their accounts, I believe, until it gets so past due it needs the attention of a collections agent."

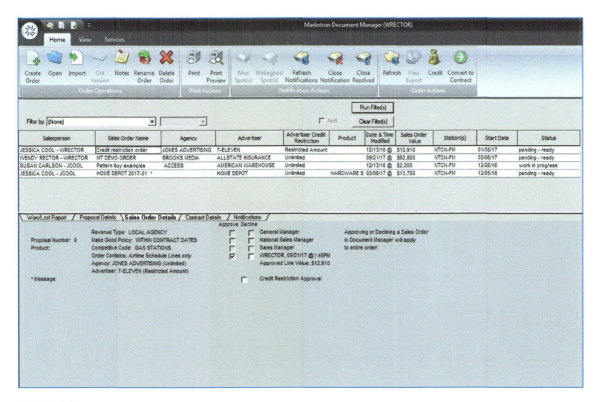

**FIGURE 4.44**
Marketron's Document Manager serves as an electronic desktop and approval queue for all contracts in the system from a status of pending through historical

Source: Courtesy of Marketron

## STANDARD TERMS AND CONDITIONS

1 Approvals. Station reserves the right to approve all advertising, which approval shall not be unreasonably withheld. Advertiser agrees that advertisements and promotions which it runs in accordance with this Agreement shall be in accordance with applicable rules and policies established from time to time by Station.

2. Commercial Content. Station assumes no responsibility, obligation or liability with respect to the content or style of the advertising provided by the Advertiser and Advertiser agrees to indemnify Station for any liability which may result from broadcasting said commercial. In an effort to provide the community with wholesome entertainment, Station reviews all programming and commercials which it places for broadcast, and reserves the right to reject any particular advertisement provided by Advertiser. See station's production guidelines for a thorough detail of stations commercial policies.

3. Additional Requested Broadcasts. Except as otherwise agreed to in writing, if Advertiser continues to request that Station broadcast advertising beyond that specified herein, additional broadcasts shall be considered a part of this contract, at the rate established by the Station from time to time, and otherwise subject to these terms and conditions, until otherwise agreed to in writing.

4. Confirmations and Cancellations. All contracts and revisions are scrutinized for accuracy prior to mailing. Upon receipt of station contracts by Advertiser, it is Advertiser's responsibility to notify Station of any possible discrepancy. If Station receives no notice within seven (7) days of issue, the contract or revision will be considered correct and Advertiser will be responsible for payment. Station requires two (2) weeks notice of cancellation.

5. Trademarks and Non-Exclusivity. This Agreement does not grant Advertiser the rights to use tradenames, trademarks or service marks of Station. No merchandising, promotional or other special consideration, nor any product category exclusivity or other protection regarding any broadcast, will be provided by Station in connection with the scheduled advertising unless specifically set forth in this Agreement.

6. Failure to Broadcast Commercials. Advertiser acknowledges that commercials occasionally may not be broadcast when scheduled due to events beyond the reasonable control of Station. in the event scheduled advertising is not broadcast when scheduled. Station shall be entitled to place advertising on a subsequent, comparable broadcast, on a "make good" basis. In no event shall Station be liable for any consequential or incidental damages relating to its failure to air scheduled advertising.

7. Execution by Agency. If this Agreement is entered into by an Advertising Agency on behalf of an Advertiser, said Agency jointly and severally undertakes the obligations of Advertiser hereunder.

8. Massachusetts Law. This Agreement is made and entered into in Massachusetts and shall be interpreted, construed and enforced in accordance with the laws of the Commonwealth of Massachusetts.

### CREDIT POLICY

1. Extension of Credit. Standard Station credit policy is cash in advance for Advertiser's first order, pending approval of credit, and said credit will not be extended without a completed and signed credit application from Advertiser on file.

2. Credit limits. Individual credit limits are established at the sole discretion of Station and are subject to review from time to time.

### COMMISSIONS AND DISCOUNTS

1. Agency Commissions. Commissions will be paid by Station only to established Advertising Agencies in good standing.

### PAYMENTS

1. Payments. Standard Station payment policy is that all invoices are due and payable net thirty (30) days from receipt of invoice.

2. Late Charges. Any amounts due Station from Advertiser not paid within (30) days of receipt of invoice are subject to a five percent (5%) late payment charge.

3. Collections. In the event of any collection action or litigation to collect amounts due from Advertiser, Station shall be entitled to reasonable cost of collection and attorneys fees as determined by the Court.

**FIGURE 4.45**
Terms and conditions of an advertising buy
Source: Courtesy of WXLO-FM

**FIGURE 4.46**
SDS CRM software keeps the station personnel abreast of accounts receivables (or billing), revenue, inventory, and the station's budget

Source: Courtesy of SDS

## The FCC and Traffic

Because of its efforts to deregulate the broadcasting industry in the 1980s, the FCC no longer requires radio stations to retain copies of a program log. However, under existing rules, some sort of document is still necessary to inform programming personnel of what is scheduled for broadcast and to provide information for both the traffic and billing departments pertaining to their particular functions. A program log creates accountability. It is both a programming guide and a document of verification. There are no stipulations regarding the length of time that logs must be retained. As a general practice, most stations hold onto physical copies of logs for approximately two years for the sake of accountability, but, with computers and hard drive space serving as archive sources, logs may be kept indefinitely without creating physical space issues.

# CHAPTER HIGHLIGHTS

1. Selling commercials keeps radio stations on the air.

2. An effective radio commercial makes a strong and lasting impression on the mind of the listener.

3. A successful account executive needs: an understanding of research methods, marketing, finance; some form of sales experience; and such personal traits as ambition, confidence, honesty, energy, determination, intelligence, and good grooming.

4. Individuals from the programming department have made successful job transitions to sales because they have a practical understanding of the product they are selling.

5. Although an increasing number of station managers are being drawn from programming people, a sales background is still preferred.

6. The sales manager, who reports directly to the station or cluster's general manager, oversees the account executives, establishes departmental policies, develops sales plans and materials, conceives campaigns and promotions, sets quotas, works closely with the program director (PD) to develop saleable features, and sometimes sells.

7. Rates for selling airtime vary according to listenership.

8. Station listenership varies according to time of day, so rate card daypart classifications range from the highest costing AAA (typically 6–10 am weekdays) to C (usually midnight–6 am). Fixed-position drive time spots are usually among the most expensive to purchase.

9. Computerized rate cards allow rates to be quickly adjusted, while using a grid structure allows for considerable rate flexibility. Grids are inventory-sensitive and they let a station remain viable when business is slow.

10. For advertisers with limited funds, ROS, BTA, or TAP are cost-effective alternatives.

11. Because few sales are made on the first visit, it is used to introduce the station to the client and determine the client's needs. Follow-up calls are made to offset reservations and, if necessary, to improve the proposal. Perseverance is essential.

12. Radio sales are drawn from three levels: retail, local, and national. Retail sales are direct sales to advertisers within the station's signal area. Local sales are obtained from advertising agencies representing businesses in the market area. National sales are obtained by the station's rep company from agencies representing national accounts.

13. A fully produced sample commercial (spec spot) is an effective selling tool. It is used to break down client resistance on callbacks, to interest former clients who have not bought time recently, and to encourage clients to increase their schedules.

14. The salesperson should commit the advertiser to sufficient commercials, placed properly, to ensure that the advertiser achieves his or her objectives. Underselling is as self-defeating as overselling.

15. New accounts are added to a salesperson's list by "prospecting" searching newspapers, Yellow Pages, television ads, competing radio station ads, and new store openings. Only open accounts may be added (those not already declared by another salesperson at the same station).

16. A good salesperson averages 12—15 face calls a week and when preparing a daily call sheet it is important to logically sequence and centralize the businesses to be contacted. Also, advance telephone contacts can eliminate much wasted time.

17. Station websites, HD channels, new media technologies, and podcasts are additional opportunities for revenue at stations. The Internet is a very useful sales and prospecting tool for account executives.

18. A salesperson at a station with a high rating has a decided advantage when contacting advertisers. Stations with low or no numbers must focus on retail sales (work the street), developing programs and programming to attract targeted clients. Stations in nonsurvey areas must rely on their image of good citizenship and strong community ties.

19. Ad agencies annually supply hundreds of millions of dollars in advertising revenue to stations with good ratings. Media buyers at the agencies deal directly with station and network reps.

20. A station's rep company must convince national agency media buyers to select their station as their advertising outlet for the area. Therefore, the station's sales manager and the rep must work together closely.

21. Among nontraditional revenue sources are co-op advertising—which involves the sharing of advertising expenses by the retailer of the business being promoted and the manufacturer of the product being promoted—and events marketing, wherein stations create events in which merchants invest their promotional dollars.

22. Rather than pay for needed items, or to obtain something of value for unsold time, a station may trade (trade-out) advertising airtime with a merchant in exchange for specific merchandise.

23. Each commercial slot on a station is called an *availability*. Availabilities constitute a station's saleable inventory.

24. The traffic manager (or traffic director) controls and is accountable for the broadcast time inventory.

25. The traffic manager prepares a log to inform the deejays and board operators of what to broadcast and at what time.

26. The traffic manager is also responsible for ensuring that an ad order is logged as specified, that a record of when each client's spots are aired is maintained, and that copy and production commercials are in on time.

27. Programming relies on the traffic manager for the logs that function as scheduling guides for on-air personnel; the sales department depends on the traffic manager to inform them of existing availabilities and to process orders onto the air.

28. Although most traffic people are trained in-house and are drawn from the administrative or clerical ranks, they must possess patience, an eye for detail, the ability to work under pressure, and keyboarding skills.

29. Traffic departments use computers and scheduling and billing software to enhance speed and efficiency. Therefore, traffic managers must be computer-knowledgeable.

30. In many instances, station ownership consolidation (clustering) has eliminated individual station traffic and billing departments and a single traffic hub within the cluster prepares logs and sponsor invoices for all the stations. In some cases, outside companies have assumed the task.

31. Based on the spots aired and depending upon each station's preference, as recorded and verified by the traffic department, the billing department sends invoices weekly or via email to each client. Invoices are sometimes notarized for clients with co-op contracts.

## SUGGESTED FURTHER READING

Aitchison, J., *Cutting Edge Radio: How to Create the World's Best Radio Ads*, Prentice Hall, Englewood Cliffs, NJ, 2002.

Astor, B. and Small, J., *Direct Response Radio: The Way to Greater Profit with Measurable Advertising*, Book Surge, New York, NY, 2008.

Barnouw, E., *The Sponsor: Notes on a Modern Potentate*, Oxford University Press, New York, NY, 1978.

Baron, R. and Sissors, J., *Advertising Media Planning*, 7th edition, McGraw-Hill, Columbus, OH, 2010.

Bergendort, F., *Broadcast Advertising*, Hastings House, New York, NY, 1983.

Bouvard, P. and Marx, S., *Radio Advertising's Missing Ingredient: The Optimum Effective Scheduling System*, NAB, Washington, D.C., 1991.

Bovee, C. and Arena, W.F., *Contemporary Advertising*, Irwin, Homewood, IL, 1982.

Broadcast Marketing Company, *Building Store Traffic with Broadcast Advertising*, Broadcast Marketing Company, San Francisco, 1978.

Brown, D.E., *Selling Time: How to Sell Small Market Radio Advertising*, self-published by CreateSpace Independent Publishing Platform, 2009.

Burton, P.W. and Sandhusen, R., *Cases in Advertising*, Grid, Columbus, OH, 1981.

Cox, J., *Sold on Radio: Advertising in the Golden Age of Broadcasting*, McFarland, Jefferson, NC, 2008.

Culligan, M.J., *Getting Back to the Basics of Selling*, Crown, New York, NY, 1981.

Cundiff, E.W., Still, R.R. and Govoni, N.A.P., *Fundamentals of Modern Marketing*, 3rd edition, Prentice Hall, Englewood Cliffs, NJ, 1980.

Delmar, K., *Winning Moves: The Body Language of Selling*, Warner, New York, NY, 1984.

Diamond, B. and Frost, J., *Selling Air: How to Jump Start Your Career in Radio Sales*, iUniverse, 2008.

Diamond, S. Z., *Records Management: A Practical Guide*, AMACOM, New York, NY, 1983.

Doyle, D.M., *Efficient Accounting and Record Keeping*, Wiley Small Business Series, New York, NY, 1978.

Dunn, W.W. and Barban, A.M., *Advertising: Its Role in Modern Marketing*, 4th edition, Dryden Press, Hinsdale, IL, 1978.

Gardner, H.S., Jr., *The Advertising Agency Business*, Crain, Chicago, IL, 1976.

Geskey, R., *Media Planning and Buying in the 21st Century*, 2nd edition, 20/20 Communications, Ann Arbor, MI, 2013.

Gilson, C. and Berkman, H.W., *Advertising Concepts and Strategies*, Random House, New York, NY, 1980.

Heighton, E.J. and Cunningham, D.R., *Advertising in the Broadcast and Cable Media*, 2nd edition, Wadsworth, Belmont, CA, 1984.

Herweg, G.W. and Herweg, A.P., *Making More Money Selling Radio Advertising without Numbers*, NAB, Washington, D.C., 1995.

Hoffer, J. and McRae, J., *The Complete Broadcast Sales Guide for Stations, Reps, and Ad Agencies*, Tab, Blue Ridge Summit, PA, 1981.

Hunter, J. and Thiebaud, M., *Telecommunications Billing Systems*, McGraw-Hill, New York, NY, 2002.

Johnson, J.D., *Advertising Today*, SRA, Chicago, IL, 1978.

Jugenheimer, D.W. and Turk, P.B., *Advertising Media*, Grid, Columbus, OH, 1980.

Keith, M.C., *Selling Radio Direct*, Focal Press, Boston, MA, 1992.

Kelley, L.D., Jugenheimer, D.W., and Sheehan, K.B., *Advertising Media Planning: A Brand Management Approach*, 3rd edition, M.E. Sharpe, Armonk, NY, 2012.

Lane, R., King, K. and Reichert, T., *Kleppner's Advertising Procedure*, 18th edition, Prentice Hall, Upper Saddle River, NJ, 2010.

Lipsky, M., *Radio Tips*, RDR, Muskegon, MI, 2005.

McGee, W.L., *Broadcast Co-Op, the Untapped Goldmine*, Broadcast Marketing Company, San Francisco, CA, 1975.

Montgomery, R.L., *How to Sell in the 1980s*, Prentice Hall, Englewood Cliffs, NJ, 1980.

Muller, M., *Essentials of Inventory Management*, American Management Association, New York, NY, 2011.

Murphy, J., *Handbook of Radio Advertising*, Chilton, Radnor, PA, 1980.

National Association of Broadcasters, *Think Big: Event Marketing for Radio*, NAB, Washington, D.C., 1994.

Prooth, V., *"Radio Advertising Doesn't Work." Says Who!*, American Mass Media Corporation, New York, NY, 2006.

Rhoads, B.E., Bunzel, R., Snook, A., and McMan, W. (eds.), *Sales and Marketing*, Streamline Press, West Palm Beach, FL, 1995.

Schreibfeder, J., *Achieving Effective Inventory Management*, Effective Inventory Management, Dallas, TX, 2005.

Sell, D., *How to Make Your Radio Advertising Work for You*, self-published by David Sell, 2011.

Shane, E., *Selling Electronic Media*, Focal Press, Boston, MA, 1999.

Shaver, M.A., *Make the Sale: How to Sell Media with Marketing*, Copy Workshop, New York, NY, 1995.

Slater, J., *Simplifying Accounting Language*, Kendall-Hall, Dubuque, IA, 1975.

*Standard Rate and Data Service: Spot Radio*, SRDS, Skokie, IL, published annually.

Warner, C. and Buchman, J., *Media Selling: Broadcast, Cable, Print, and Interactive*, 3rd edition, Iowa State University Press, Ames, IA, 2004.

Weyland, P., *Successful Local Broadcast Sales*, Amacom, New York, NY, 2007.

Wild, T., *Best Practice in Inventory Management*, John Wiley & Sons, New York, NY, 1998.

Zeigler, S.K. and Howard, H.H., *Broadcast Advertising: A Comprehensive Working Textbook*, 2nd edition, Grid, Columbus, OH, 1990.

# APPENDIX 4A: RAB GUIDE TO WRITING GREAT RADIO COPY

Source: Courtesy of the Radio Advertising Bureau

## RAB Guide to Writing Great Radio Copy

Developing a great creative Radio campaign is crucial to getting results for your client but the big question is how do you do it? On the following pages you will find a 10 step plan that will help guide you through the challenges, demands and pitfalls of the copywriting process. Don't be afraid to use Radio's creative potential to the fullest and take the time needed to create great-sounding and brilliant campaigns.

### STEP 1:  FIND OUT WHAT THE CLIENT WANTS

I know it sounds simple and obvious but so many stations and agencies make the mistake of not listening to what their clients really want and hope to achieve with their campaign. And without understanding the real reasons behind why a potential client wants to go on the air, the commercial campaign — no matter how humorous or clever — is doomed.

### STEP 2:  ASK THE RIGHT QUESTIONS

So to find out what the client wants, you have to ask some questions. Some call it a Client Needs Analysis. And even though this isn't the most exciting part of the creative process, it is crucial to your success. Here are some samples:

1.  Is there anything you would like to feature?
    Maybe your clients just got in a huge load of widgets and they need to sell them fast! Or maybe a certain item has a higher profit margin and it would make sense to push that product.

2.  Who is your best prospect?
    This question will allow you to get into demographics and find out who they are targeting. Is it male or female or both? What percentage? Average age? Income? Profession and education level? If you represent more than one station, then these questions can help steer your client to the right "position on the dial."

3.  Why do customers come to you?
    This question and others below that are similar, allow the client to tell you their story. Keep in mind that perception is reality and you should consider getting different viewpoints from co-workers, family and friends.

4.  What is your single greatest competitive advantage?

5.  Do you have a positioning statement?

6.  What do you feel is your unique selling position?
    The USP or unique selling position (or point) is a marketing concept that allows a company to differentiate themselves from their competition.

7.  What is your primary business image?

8.  What's the biggest misperception you feel people have about your business?
    Sometimes this misperception can be used in the commercial to help overcome objections. For example, perhaps customers think a popular brand will automatically be too expensive. Or perhaps the potential customers feel that the location is too far away when in reality it's only a 10 or 15 minute drive.

1 of 7

## STEP 3:  HELP POSITION YOUR CLIENT

Most clients on local Radio expect a measurable response from their investment on your station. Whether it's an increase in phone calls, more traffic to their store or simply more hits on their website, advertisers want something to happen. Now that you have already done your Client Needs Analysis, use that information to effectively help your client separate themselves from the competition with proper positioning.

1.  Know the competition

    Who truly competes for your client's business? There may be 3 women's shoe stores in town, but if each is targeted at a different group of customers (teens, discount and upscale) then, except for some minor overlapping, they can be said to be non-competitive.

    However, if there are 3 athletic shoe stores and each carries the same brands of shoes, then all three compete directly with one another.

    Write down each competitor and a list of their perceived "strengths" or selling points such as:
    - Discount or competitive prices
    - Excellent service
    - Superior quality/variety of goods
    - Convenient locations/hours

2.  Know Thyself

    Apply the same criteria when evaluating the perceived position and strengths of your client — just as you did for competitors. Remember that it may be difficult to get an accurate description of the perceived position of your client from your client. So do an informal survey with your friends, family and co-workers. Try to get a good sense of how the client is already received by customers to help you determine how you can change or enhance that image.

3.  Define the Differences

    Most successful products or stores have established a very definite, easily explained and easily recognized position in the marketplace.  By writing down crucial differences between competitors, you can arrive at a focal point for a commercial. After all, sometimes it's the little differences that can make a person choose one store or product over another.

## STEP 4:  GETTING IT ALL TOGETHER

There are several "style" categories of commercials. Don't get bogged down by always using one style for your client. Get creative by varying the elements and determining what works best for the advertiser.

1.  Straightforward

    Sometimes the simplest approach works best. Imagine one effective voice delivering a well-written narrative message.  This direct approach works particularly well when a positive image has previously been established and a specific event is being promoted, like a sale. In these cases, you can simply expand on or enhance the positive feelings that are already in place.

2.  Music

    The use of music in commercials can be powerful since music can evoke an emotional response and create a positive feeling that transfers to the product or service.  Music can also be used to tie together a mixed media campaign (TV or Internet) while aiding in recall.  Music also means jingles and when done right, jingles can cut through the clutter and stick in the mind for years.

NOTE: *Remember that copyrighted music that plays on your station may not be used for a recorded commercial for your client unless they pay the publisher for the rights to use that music. (That means even though that trampoline client would love to use Van Halen's "Jump" as an intro to their spot, they need to acquire the rights to that song before the commercial airs. See BMI.com for more information.)*

3. Slice of Life

The "slice of life" approach allows the audience to relate personally to the commercial elements. Overhearing bits of real life conversation — between lovers, spouses, parents, neighbors — make the potential customers an active albeit silent participant instead of just a passive listener.

If the actors in the spot strike a responsive chord, the listener is much more apt to be open to the client's offering.

The major drawback in writing and producing slice of life spots is that they must be done extremely well to be effective. Talent must be believable and likeable or you lose credibility with the listener. Poorly written dialogue or wooden delivery will turn off the audience and have them reaching for the dial.

4. Humor

Humor engages the listener, creates emotional responses and provides entertainment. But there are pitfalls in trying to be funny. Have you ever heard a really funny commercial that you enjoyed and when you went to tell a friend about it, you couldn't remember the product being advertised? Make humor part of the selling point.

Also, what's funny to you, may not work for your target audience. Try to stick with universals- situations that revolve around family or intimate relationships work because these problems have the same human elements. Don't be afraid to exaggerate for comic effect. A precise true to life retelling may not be that funny but exaggeration can make people laugh and identify with the situation.

5. Testimonial

The testimonial can be very effective in persuading a customer to try a new product or service. Affirmation by other customers can be a convincing argument and Radio is the best media for "word of mouth" advertising. Testimonials are fairly easy to produce but make sure you get your talent to relax and take their time in telling about their experience. Also, remember that a testimonial from a personality on your station is a premium spot and should always cost extra to the client.

## STEP 5: OVERCOMING WRITER'S BLOCK

It's every writer's nightmare and every deadline's biggest obstacle. But there are several techniques that you can employ to overcome this looming monster. In fact, one of the first things that you can do is go back to Step 1 in this article and do your homework, ask the right questions, find out the clients wants and needs, etc. The commercial could possibly write itself once you are done. However, for those times when you can't get out of the starting gate, Jeffery Hedquist from Hedquist Productions offers these tips and tricks:

1. Sound Effects

Randomly choose a sound effect from the production library and give yourself 2 minutes to write a commercial for your client using that effect even if it doesn't seem appropriate. Try another and do it again. Limber up your imagination and make connections between ideas that might not seem related at first. If you don't have commercial gold at this point, purposely choose a sound effect that would not normally be associated with the advertiser. For example, if the client sells office products, don't go with keyboards clicking or copy machines humming, try something different like a fire engine or a baby crying. Then, working

APPENDIX 4A-4

with a 2 minute deadline, force yourself to come up with some copy using that sound effect along. Once again, your mind will stretch to connect those two disparate parts of the equation and start stringing words and ideas together to bridge that gap. If you work at it, a commercial will emerge usually built around an analogy or metaphor. For example, the sound of a baby crying can represent the way we all turn into out of control babies when the office equipment doesn't work and we can't fix it. Or the fire engine could be an example of what it's like when emergencies arise in the office. Sound effects can quickly communicate and reinforce problems and solutions and create a shortcut to the minds of your audience.

2. Silence is golden
   Don't overlook the power of silence and quieter sounds. Silence can grab your attention and serve as powerful contrast to bombastic sound effects. It can also be used to highlight a solution or relieve tension.

## STEP 6:  GET DOWN TO BASICS — FOLLOW THESE COPYWRITING TIPS

Here is a basic list of tips to get you started:

1. Goal – Start by writing down the goal and one main point you want to get across. This step will be a huge help in deciding how you will create the commercial and what form or style it will take.

2. Elements – Next, write down the elements or information that must be in the commercial.  For example, store name, address (physical and/or web), image to convey, description of merchandise, benefits to consumer.

3. Approach – Decide on how your main points and information will be communicated; how will the ideas be strung together into a coherent work of creative art?

4. Opening – Grab their attention or lose them forever. Entertain, enlighten, amuse or cause anticipation. Don't temp the listener to tune out.

5. Simplicity – Don't use extremely complex language. Keep dialogue conversational, not stilted. Write for the ear, not for the eye. Read copy out loud.

6. Clarity – At the end of the commercial, your audience will understand exactly what you've tried to say. Don't be overly clever or you might lose your clarity. Limit the big idea to ONE per spot. No clutter.

7. Active Language – Stay away from passive verbs. If you want people to act on your commercial, choose action words.

8. Credibility – Listeners tend to follow your advice when they believe you and identify with the circumstances presented in your commercial. Write in a realistic manner, unless you are employing exaggeration or fantasy.  Keep the voices credible and the talent believable.

9. Product Mention – There is no rule concerning how many times the client's name must be mentioned. Make the spot and selling process memorable.

10. Editing – You have a limited amount of time (usually 60 or 30 seconds). Write the copy and then edit it once, deleting all unnecessary words. Then, go through it again and edit even more tightly.  An economy of words is essential in the commercial.

11. Group Efforts — Get a group together and try some brainstorming. Even useless ideas can spur successful attempts. Group thought can overcome any writer's block.

Another good checklist you can go through includes:
- Define the advertising objective — the goal of the campaign
- Define the commercial objective — the goal of the commercial
- State specific benefits — what's in it for the customer
- Make a specific offer — to get measurable results focus on one offer
- Issue a call to action — explain how/when to take advantage of the offer
- Support material — extra details needed about the product or client
- Closure — tie up loose ends and include a strong last impression

## STEP 7:  MAKE SURE YOUR MASTERPIECE PASSES THIS TEST

Before you do a final production of that work of art you've just produced, run through this checklist of "Copywriting Deadly Sins" provided by creative consultant, Dan O'Day.

1.  SIN 1: Did you fail to attract the listener's attention?
    Think of how many commercials you hear on the Radio that do not command the listener's attention. Now make sure that your commercial isn't one of them. Just think of it this way: the most important part of a print ad is the headline. In a Radio commercial, the opening line IS the headline.

2.  SIN 2: Did you fail to appeal to the listener's self-interest?
    The listener doesn't care about the advertiser. The listener cares about what the advertiser can do for him or her. Most copywriters make the mistake of writing about the advertiser instead of the potential customer. Make sure you have identified a need or a problem that will be filled or solved by the advertiser.

3)  SIN 3: Did you fail to paint a picture?
    If you think about it, Radio is actually a visual medium. Listeners convert the sound of your commercial into a mental picture that can inspire and motivate them to act upon your words. Choose those words carefully to paint a picture that will get results for your client.

4.  SIN 4: Were you so clever or creative that you forgot to sell?
    It happens to the best of us. A good commercial is not one that makes people laugh; it's one that motivates them to act. Make your message clear. Don't bury it in a clever idea.

5.  SIN 5: Did you forget to give the listener a reason to act now?
    As mentioned before, most local Radio clients are expecting tangible, measurable results from their campaigns. The copy should reach active customers who are looking for that particular product or service as well as passive customers who might be in the market soon. "Hurry to the sale soon" just doesn't cut it.  Be creative and find a new way to express the offer.

6. SIN 6: Did you use cliché-ridden copy?

Commercial clichés are trite and empty and don't communicate anything to the listener – don't use them. Find a way to say it fresher. It may take a little bit of time, but it's worth it to keep people from tuning out. Some common ones to avoid:

- "Now is the time."
- "They won't last long..."
- "Savings throughout the store..."
- "The sale you've been waiting for..."
- "Conveniently located..."

7. SIN 7: Did you write too much copy?

Avoid this common pitfall by getting in the habit of reading your copy aloud and timing yourself. The trick is to read it in a normal conversational pace. If it takes YOU seventy-five seconds to read it aloud, what makes you think your production person can do a good job with the same copy in just sixty seconds? Remember, too many words crammed into one fragile minute can be fatal.

## STEP 8:   LEARN HOW TO SELL YOUR IDEAS AND WIN SUPPORT

Now it's time to share your brilliant ideas with your client but there are few things to keep in mind when selling the creative and promoting the unique marketing abilities of your staff and station.

1. Don't produce a lousy spec spot.

Sure you can hear how great it's going to sound in your head but the client is going to have a hard time hearing that "leap". In other words, don't produce a "speculative" spot unless you are certain it can sound great. Instead, present copy only and describe the commercial. If it's based on an already proven idea, play that commercial as an example of what you would like to accomplish.

2. Explain your assumptions and manage their expectations.

Present the rationale behind your ideas. Explain why you picked that music or that announcer or that approach because you have the client's goals and expectations in mind.

3. Sell a marketing strategy, not a commercial

This may involve the production of a campaign instead of one spot. It's important that your client understand that you are interested in increasing their sales, not just yours. By presenting a complete plan, in which creative plays an important part, you become a member of their staff and are perceived as a hard-working player on their team.

4. Use testimonials before and after a sale.

Provide stories of satisfied customers. These are most often in print form but you can also interview advertisers in your studio asking how the campaign or spot worked. These interviews can be edited (with permission) into great audio success stories that can be used on sales calls, presentations or possibly on air!

5. Involve production people in sales.

Everyone benefits by seeing how the other side works.  Take a production person on a sales call. Get their input and reward their productivity. In these days of consolidation, many production people can feel overworked and underappreciated. Some restaurant trade, concert tickets or even a handwritten thank you note can go a long way.

## STEP 9: TIPS AND TRICKS IN TECHNICAL PRODUCTION

Technically speaking, the days of reel to reel and razor blade splicing are gone. Today's computers and audio programs are helping production directors create more spots in a shorter amount time with sound effects that would be virtually impossible a few years ago. However, faster is not necessarily better and Production Director Robert Diaz offers these tips:

1. Don't Skimp On Tools

   A great read full of emotion and enthusiasm can become lousy with a bad microphone. The good thing is that most Radio stations have decent equipment because the quality of sound is the key aspect of being "on-the-air."

2. Musical Choices

   A varied production library is a key component in creating great Radio commercials. "Sound-alike" music keeps you out of trouble when that sub sandwich client wants to use "Yellow Submarine" as their theme song. Also a library of sound effects will be handy when trying to create the right atmosphere. Keep in mind that single royalty-free tracks can now be downloaded over the Internet and all those production music files can be stored on a hard drive for easy access.

3. Stay Focused

   Finally, remember to encourage production people to stay focused and really understand what you want to convey. If they don't understand the effect you're listening for or the message you want to convey, the commercial or campaign will go nowhere- communication is essential.

## STEP 10: TAKE PRIDE IN YOUR WORK AND SELL COMPETIVELY

By now, you've put in the time researching your client, learned about his or her needs, determined the message that needs to be expressed in the commercial and thought of the perfect way to do it. So now it's time to present your masterpiece.

Why not present it that way to the client?

   Someone once said that a sale is a transfer of ideas. Present your idea in an exciting way and get the client excited about the sale! Position it as an answer to the client's problems or goals. Remember the creative work that you have done can literally determine the success of an account and reinforce your relationship with a client.

Nobody said it was going to be easy.

   This one you know already. The challenges of developing, writing and producing great creative are many – but you can do it! There's no doubt that the key to successful creative is doing your homework and the RAB is here to help. As a member, you can check out RAB.com for more great information like Instant Backgrounds, recent articles, even "Gold Digger" reports that allow you to dig deep into demographic and lifestyle groups. Plus, there are great creative examples in our MP3 audio archive and over 2000 scripts in our commercial library just waiting to get your creative juices flowing. And the newly revised Creative Resource Directory has nearly 100 professional RAB-recommended agencies or production houses that are ready to help you get your client's commercial to the next level.

If you are not a member of RAB, visit rab.com for more information or call 1-800-232-3131!

## APPENDIX 4B: SOCAST MEDIA: WHY MOBILE APPS ARE ESSENTIAL FOR DIGITAL SUCCESS

Source: Courtesy of SoCast Media

> **The average time spent consuming digital media per adult in the USA is 2.8 hours per day.**

# Why Mobile Apps are Essential for Digital Success

In today's digital landscape, there is nothing more important than keeping your brand top of mind. Understanding  an effective mobile strategy is predicated on more than just a mobile-friendly website is what differentiates  Radio brands destined to win in the long-run. Staying connected to the people who love your brand, namely your audience, is the only way to stay relevant and grow market share.

Whether they are a single station or cluster, Radio groups are investing in Mobile Apps for Radio because they understand that the attention of consumers is literally in the palm of their hand. Today the average time spent consuming mobile media per adult in the USA is 2.8 hours per day, surpassing desktop and other connected devices.

If your Radio station is vying for the attention of your listeners on their smartphone, you'll have to consider building a Mobile App so they have access to what they want: your brand on their screen. This placement will make your brand available for convenient consumption of your content and prepared for the connected car and other technologies in the coming years.

Apps are effective ways of further extending your Radio brand into the digital space. They build brand recognition, encourage listener loyalty, boost engagement, and most importantly provide you with additional revenue possibilities. Read on to learn why your Radio station needs a Mobile App and why a Mobile App for Radio should be part of your marketing strategy.

 SoCast

> **Today, listeners expect brands to have a mobile presence. 80% of time spent in smartphones is spent in App.**

## Access to Brand

A Mobile App for Radio is a great way to grow brand awareness and strengthen loyalty among your fans. It is an extension of your brand, and today's content consumers expect brands to have an easily accessible mobile presence. The average consumer spends 80% of their smartphone time in-app, so having your Radio brand's logo on the phone screen is not only a valuable piece of real-estate for your brand, but imperative to staying relevant with your listener in the modern digital landscape.

While being mobile web friendly ensures consumers have a fluid experience on their mobile devices, listeners rarely use browsers especially when an app is available. In fact, browser usage and mobile site navigation is predominantly a result of in-app behavior.

With Mobile Apps providing one click access to listeners, your audience has a simple and familiar platform to navigate your content, promotions, and features. Apps also deliver access to your live stream which is convenient for listeners and especially P1's as they can access their favourite station on their terms, wherever they are, at the palm of their hand, and most importantly on their time.

The constant connection to your station via an app means that listeners can take you anywhere. As it stands, 46% of terrestrial Radio Apps are used outside of terrestrial broadcast range. Audiences are even willing to consume their valuable phone data to stay connected to your station.

By providing a Mobile App experience to your audience, you retain your best listeners, gain new ones and increase digital tune-ins for your station while redistributing your content digitally.

**KEEP IN MIND:** *A good looking App, with a seamless experience, and access to your stream, is the best way to grow awareness and extend your brand offering in the digital space.*

 SoCast

" **Providing a Radio App for listeners is a way of** rewarding listener loyalty **in itself.**

## Grow Loyalty and Membership

With all the noise in the digital ecosystem, it's difficult to provide listeners with the value and sense of connection that they crave. Providing a Mobile App can effectively streamline their attention, retain their focus and provide them with the feeling that one of their favourite brands is just a fingertip away.

Providing a user-friendly, engaging, and versatile app for listeners, is a great way of saying "Thank you" to loyal listeners. An app is another opportunity to sign up new and existing listeners to become new members. By offering sign-ups on your app you can offer a unified experience for listeners that spans from on-air to digital.

A Mobile App for your Radio station is unique as it provides listeners with exclusive app content. Listeners love turning to apps to satisfy their need for dedicated content and services they can't find on your website. They want something interactive and engaging that they can respond to quickly. By creating completely exclusive app offerings, your brand is spurring direct action to strategic content, further molding the bond with your listeners. Like all stations in the app market, downloading the app is half the battle. The rest of the time is ensuring they come back, and regularly engage, creating a stronger relationship with listeners, growing the lifetime value of your customer, and ultimately gaining strength to your brand.

The more often you can get your members involved with your Radio station's app, the sooner they will tune in to your stream, interact with your brand, and engage with your contests and promotions.

**KEEP IN MIND:** *In the end, listeners will spend significantly more time online using an app for streaming activities, exclusive content, and deals than they would on a mobile site.*

> ❝ **Listeners** who **opt-in to push messages** average **3x more app launches** than those who didn't.

## Interaction and Engagement

A modern Mobile App uniquely allows a station to create **1 on 1 interactions** with their listeners. Listeners can reach out to their favorite DJ in real time, ask them questions, request songs, or engage with a program on social channels. Having a platform that spurs this kind of interaction is key to creating stronger bonds with the audience and loyalty with your brand.

Sending out updated information and using **push notifications** are the primary reasons why an app is better than a mobile site. While push notifications are sometimes regarded as noisy, they are actually non-intrusive as app users have opted-in to the service. Your best biggest fans will opt-in to notifications as a way to be in the loop with your brand's content. Push notifications can remind listeners about contests, weather updates, concert listings and event promotions. Listeners who opt-in to push messages average roughly 3x more app launches than those who opted out. Mobile Apps for Radio have the opportunity to tap listeners on the shoulder and engage them in real-time, giving them the option to interact with their favourite brand as the information goes live.

Other ways brands can grow engagement with their listeners are with Radio specific features. An in-app song rating system, live commenting to blog posts and real-time social feeds foster interaction with your brand and amongst listeners.

Radio always has been about two-way conversations, compelling storytelling, and crowd sourcing. A Mobile App for your station makes it so much easier to get feedback on local stories, personalize the connection with on-air personalities, and offer more value to ambassadors of your brand.

**KEEP IN MIND:** *Push notifications are a great way to connect with your listeners in real-time as your content goes live.*

SoCast

APPENDIX 4B-6

> By investing in a mobile app for your radio station, you have access to the most valuable ad inventories in the digital marketplace.

## Generate Revenue

The most efficient way for Radio brands to generate revenue through a Mobile App is sponsorship. Sponsored apps allow advertisers to become partners with your Radio brand. In return the Radio brand will provide advertising inventory in the app that will reach the advertisers target demographics. It also allows potential customers to be reached wherever they are instead of having to wait until they log on to their computer or jump in their car.

Sponsorship opportunities and packages can include splash ads, promoted posts, and contests. Splash Ads are some of the finest sponsorships as they appear instantly when the app is opened, can be changed often and guarantees that the user will see it. These ads work best in conjunction with other sponsored content such as: contests, events, shows, special guests etc.

Promoted posts are native to the SoCast App and are embedded in social media streams (similar to a promoted Tweet or Facebook post). These ads allow for mass outreach at a low cost, and increased brand recognition. They are frequent, easy to set-up and can coincide with the app's splash ad, and other sponsored content.

In-app contests allow advertisers to sponsor contests that are specific to the app's target demographic. Advertisers can also sponsor app navigation and menu items. This approach works great when paired with other advertising inventories, or as part of a larger package deal, adding additional value.

Mobile Apps for Radio also have access to the highest paying pre-roll adverts which include both video and audio formats. These can be placed before listeners listen to your stream, when the app loads, or throughout the navigation of the app.

By investing in a Mobile App for your Radio station, you have access to the most valuable ad inventories in the digital marketplace. The problem with so many content based apps, is that they can never produce enough content for the user to consume, which spurs app burnout. Radio, which has content embedded in their DNA, doesn't see this problem. This leaves listeners coming back to the app while growing impressions that keep advertisers coming back.

## Key Takeaways

**Mobile Apps for Radio brands...**

- Build Brand Recognition
- Drive Listener Engagement
- Grow Listener Loyalty
- Generate Digital Revenue
- Provide Value to Advertisers
- Create a Modern Marketing Channel

Radio brands that expect to compete for attention in the digital era  should consider expanding their brand to where consumers can access it all the time: the app market. A Mobile App for Radio offers so much more than a stream to your station. It provides a content rich experience with listeners where they can interact, share, and stay connected with their favorite station.

**Speak with our Specialists on Growing Digital Revenue and Engagement for your Radio Station.**

**Talk to a Specialist**

SoCast   T: 416.635.6678   E: info@socastdigital.com   socastdigital.com

# APPENDIX 4C: SOCAST MEDIA: HOW TO MONETIZE ON-AIR CONTENT THROUGH THE WEB AND SOCIAL MEDIA

Source: Courtesy of SoCast Media

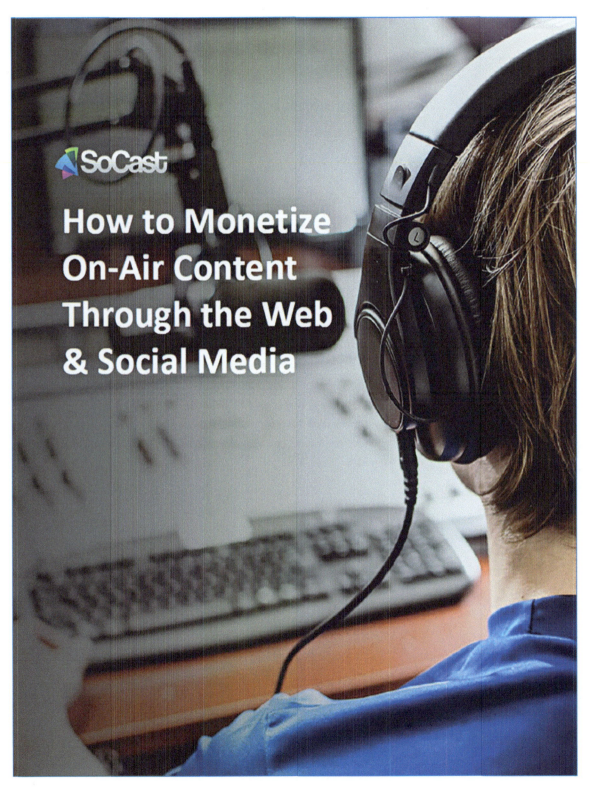

> **Today, Radio has an incredible opportunity to extend the reach, shelf life, and value of on-air content by taking advantage of new technology.**

# How to Monetize On-Air Content Through the Web & Social Media

The amount of original content your station produces each day is one of your greatest and most valuable assets. Before websites and social media were around, that content would expire immediately after it airs. Today, Radio has an incredible opportunity to extend the reach, shelf life, and value of on-air content by taking advantage of new technology.

Opportunities to increase digital revenue are directly correlated to the quantity and quality of content your station puts online. Simply put, any station that ignores digital media is flushing dollars straight down the digital drain. Read on to learn more about how you can monetize your on-air content through your website and social media.

> **If you're not extending the life of your content past the airwaves, you're wasting your digital assets and lowering your station's overall online value and search rank.**

## Re-Package On-Air Content for Online Publishing

What does your website look like? On top of advertising, show times, displaying the weather, and embedding your Radio stream, does your site mirror all of the original, engaging, informing, and entertaining content you create, day in and day out? Is it optimized for digital consumption? If you're not extending the life of your content past the airwaves, you're missing out on digital assets and lowering your station's overall online value and search rank.

Regardless of whether it's a news piece, entertainment gossip, listener survey, guest interview, opinion piece, or local initiative, there are ways to re-package and re-purpose your content online. Here is a laundry list of ways you can re-package your on-air content for online publishing:

- Audio clips of show highlights/memorable moments
- Photo galleries from live remotes and events
- Video clips or photos from guest speakers and interviews
- Polls and surveys about popular topics
- Local concerts & events calendars
- Studio and behind-the-scenes footage and photos

You can also enhance or extend on-air content that is otherwise restricted by time limits by publishing online. For example, your jocks may only have a minute or two to share their thoughts on a particular subject, but they can later expand on that topic by writing a short blog about it. Blogs are among the highest ranked and most popular form of online content because they are fresh, original, and relevant to the interests of their audience. Sound familiar? That's right, blogs are just a digital form of what your jocks have been doing on-air for decades. Make it last.

**KEEP IN MIND:** *Don't fill your site with generic, irrelevant content that simply clutters your pages without adding value to your brand.*

Remember, what makes your Radio brand unique is your local involvement and original personalities. Quality and consistency is key both on-air and online, so use your best assets to your advantage.

So how does doing all this add value to your digital assets?

| You're constantly updating your website, which improves search rank | → | You're adding depth (pages) to your website, which provides additional ad inventory | → | You're driving more traffic and extending the duration of page visits, which adds value to your ad inventory |

**"** People are spending more time finding news and entertainment items via Facebook and Twitter, than sourcing it from search engines.

# Use Social Media to Extend Content Reach & Site Traffic

Once you've begun populating your website with fresh content, you can (and should) extend its reach even further through the use of social media. There are a few ways you can do this:

1. Post links to your content in social media yourself (remember to use attention-grabbing, network-appropriate headlines!)
2. Embed sharing buttons to every piece of share-worthy content on your site so your audience can share it to their networks.
3. Enable comments so that your readers can start a discussion (comments are a form of social media even if they live on your website!)
4. Include a link back to your website or Listen Live player in every post.

The reason why it's so crucial to incorporate social media into your digital content strategy is because social networks have become primary hubs for content discovery. This means that people are spending more time finding news and entertainment items via Social, rather than sourcing it from search engines. And who has all the best local news and entertainment? That's right, you do. Make it visible.

In addition to the above, search engines including Google are crawling social networks for content just as much as they are websites. So having your content present in both spaces increases its search rank and relevance when people search for information on certain topics. The easier it is for people to find and share your content, the more traffic you'll have flowing through your site; and the more traffic, the more valuable your inventory will be.

**KEEP IN MIND:** *Social media is a two-way platform, not an online bulletin board. Don't spam your audience with links — use your content to inspire and engage people in conversation.*

"
**Your ad partners will see more value in your audience if you're able to segment and advertise to their target markets.**

## Get Creative with Digital Ad Inventory

Once you have plenty of fresh online content and a significant amount of website traffic, it's time to monetize. Banners and big box ads are the most obvious and straightforward ways to generate revenue online, whether you're packaging it with on-air spots or creating an entirely separate digital campaign, but there are so many other ways you can use digital space to provide more value to your advertisers and generate more revenue, such as:

- Sponsored contests
- Sponsored streams (i.e. player wraps)
- Inserting audio & video pre-rolls into content galleries
- Coupons and promo codes from partners
- Sponsored traffic and weather feeds
- Cross Promotional Social Campaigns

**KEEP IN MIND:** *Going overboard with display ads, pre-rolls, and wraps all over the page will clutter your site and drown out your station's brand.*

Another creative way to monetize online content is by exploring opportunities outside of your website. For instance, your listener clubs and social audiences can also give you a competitive advantage by gathering demographic information through listener club sign-ups and Facebook contests. Your clients will see more value in your audience if you're able to segment and advertise to their target markets, whether it's on your site or through email marketing. Third-party contesting, analytics and geo-targeting tools can be extremely helpful for this purpose.

APPENDIX 4C-7

It will take some time and investment to maximize your station's digital revenue, but you don't need a huge budget or a separate digital sales team to turn your website and social properties into a revenue-generating engine. You've already invested in a website and social media is a virtually cost-free marketing resource, so there is no excuse not to take advantage of every opportunity available to maximize on-air content.

For more information and assistance in executing your digital content strategy, get in touch with a SoCast expert today. SoCast is the only Radio website and Mobile App solution that drives social engagement into tune-ins and ad revenue.

**The SoCast Platform is the only Radio Website and Mobile App solution that drives social engagement into tune-ins and ad revenue.**

**Request a Demo**

 SoCast  T: 416.635.6678  E: info@socastsrm.com  socastdigital.com

# CHAPTER 5

# News, Talk, and Sports

## INTRODUCTION

People claim to listen to radio more for music than for any other reason, although studies are clearly showing that this is changing owing to a growing reliance on other audio media sources. The Pew Research Center's Project for Excellence in Journalism's *State of the News Media 2016* study found that news/talk/information was the most listened-to format on radio. The study indicated that 9.6% of U.S. radio listeners chose the news/talk/information format over all others including pop contemporary hit music, adult contemporary music, and even country music. The study also noted there were 29 terrestrial radio stations broadcasting with the all-news format.

The 2016 Pew *State of the Media* study found that 25% of American adults get their news from radio. That compares to 57% getting their news from television and 38% getting their news from digital/social media sources. Further, of the 38% who get their news from digital sources, 28% obtained their news specifically from websites or news apps. Newspapers trailed all media, with only 20% of all Americans getting their news from print. Interestingly, Nielsen reports that young listeners are contributing to the increase in radio news audiences. The number of Millennials, those aged 18 to 34 and born between 1982 and 2004, listening to radio has increased faster than any other demographic. Studies also indicate that Americans get their news from radio or logging onto a radio station's website, especially to obtain information about politics. The Pew Research Center found that 44% of those surveyed got their news about the 2016 presidential election from radio. However, it is worth noting that local TV news, at 57%, and cable TV news, at 54%, beat out radio news.

| MOST LISTENED-TO RADIO FORMATS | |
|---|---|
| *Percentage of Americans Aged 6 or Older Who Turned to Each Format During Any 15-Minute Period During the Day* | |
|  | % |
| News/talk/information | 9.6 |
| Pop contemporary hit radio | 8.1 |
| Adult contemporary | 7.5 |
| Country | 7.4 |
| Hot adult contemporary | 6.4 |
| Classic hits | 5.3 |
| Classic rock | 5.1 |
| Urban adult contemporary | 4.8 |
| All-sports | 4.7 |
| Mexican regional | 3.7 |
| Urban contemporary | 3.7 |

**FIGURE 5.1**
News/talk/information radio is the most listened-to format

Source: Courtesy of Nielsen Media Research publicly available data

**FIGURE 5.2**
Steve Jones

## GREAT JOURNALISTS ARE TERRIFIC STORYTELLERS

### Steve Jones

Great journalists are terrific storytellers. They gather facts, identify relevance, and create narratives that connect these stories to their audiences. Storytellers know that, when it comes to impacting listeners, if they don't engage them they can't inform them. And few mediums have allowed storytellers to engage audiences more effectively and more intimately than broadcast radio. Radio is your companion. It entertains and enlightens. It connects you to your community. It creates new experiences and helps you discover your next favorite music artist. And it's free! It's also an industry that is deeply disrupted by technology. As I write this, I've just asked my Alexa-enabled "smart thermostat" to deliver my ABC News Radio update. Yes, my "radio newscast" is coming out of a tiny speaker built in to the thermostat on my wall. That same ABC News report is being heard across the country on smartphones, through connected consumer devices and, very importantly, on broadcast radio stations. And, while it's the technology that creates multiple points of distribution, it's the resilience of radio people who continually adapt and find ways to reach these listeners. This "listening" is on a sharp upward trend. Every day, more consumer devices become voice-activated. In this universe of increasingly ubiquitous audio, the need grows for talented storytellers who understand how to craft language and produce audio effectively. If you have a passion for journalism and understand how to effectively use audio to tell stories, there are many exciting and rewarding opportunities that await you!

---

**Steve Jones** is Vice-President and General Manager of ABC News Radio and is in charge of strategic planning, business development, programming, and operations for ABC-branded audio content covering news, entertainment, lifestyle and sports. The ABC audio brands include America's most listened-to network, ABC News Radio, along with iconic brands ABC Radio, ABC Sports Radio, and a growing suite of digital audio and text businesses marketed as ABC Radio Digital.

ABC News Radio reaches more than 73 million listeners each week and is affiliated on approximately 1,650 radio stations. Beyond broadcast radio, ABC produces content for digital radio companies, satellite radio, wireless carriers, websites, and radio partners around the globe. ABC Radio Digital syndicates written news, entertainment, and lifestyle stories to over 600 radio websites and major brand portals.

Under Jones's leadership, ABC News Radio has received some of the highest honors in broadcasting including more than a dozen Edward R. Murrow Awards, 10 International Radio Festival Awards, five National Headliner Awards and three New York Festivals Awards. Jones was twice named by the readers of *Radio & Records* as "News Executive of the Year." In 2017, he was voted by readers of *Radio Ink* as one of "Radio's Best Managers" and also was named on its annual "Forty Most Powerful People in Radio" list.

Prior to leading ABC News Radio, Jones was the Vice-President for Programming and Operations for ABCNews.com, during which time he oversaw all content and production. Under his leadership, the ABCNews.com team won multiple awards, including an Edward R. Murrow Award for Best Network News website and a Peabody Award for ABCNews.com's coverage of the 2001 terror attacks. Jones also launched the first regularly scheduled webcast by a network, oversaw the launch of interactive web programming, and co-produced ABC's online millennium coverage and other special event programming.

Jones joined ABC News Radio in 1986 as a writer and assumed increasing responsibility. During this period his work won two Writers Guild of America (WGA) Awards and an Overseas Press Club Award.

Prior to joining ABC News, Jones was a radio newscaster and disc jockey on several stations, including WXRK-FM (K-Rock), New York, WLIR/Long Island, and WPIX/New York. He also has worked as television reporter for Cablevision's News 12/Long Island.

Jones was a 2010 Columbia University Graduate School of Journalism Fellow in the Sulzberger Executive Leadership Program. He has an undergraduate degree from Adelphi University. He lives in Armonk, New York, with his wife and two children.

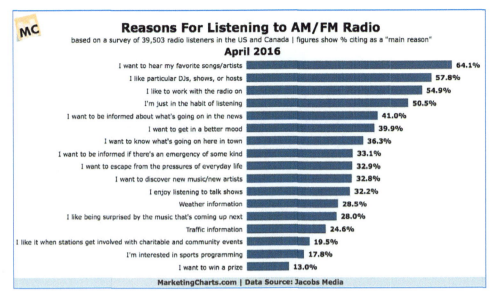

**Reasons For Listening to AM/FM Radio**
based on a survey of 39,503 radio listeners in the US and Canada | figures show % citing as a "main reason"
**April 2016**

| Reason | % |
|---|---|
| I want to hear my favorite songs/artists | 64.1% |
| I like particular DJs, shows, or hosts | 57.8% |
| I like to work with the radio on | 54.9% |
| I'm just in the habit of listening | 50.5% |
| I want to be informed about what's going on in the news | 41.0% |
| I want to get in a better mood | 39.9% |
| I want to know what's going on here in town | 36.3% |
| I want to be informed if there's an emergency of some kind | 33.1% |
| I want to escape from the pressures of everyday life | 32.9% |
| I want to discover new music/new artists | 32.8% |
| I enjoy listening to talk shows | 32.2% |
| Weather information | 28.5% |
| I like being surprised by the music that's coming up next | 28.0% |
| Traffic information | 24.6% |
| I like it when stations get involved with charitable and community events | 19.5% |
| I'm interested in sports programming | 17.8% |
| I want to win a prize | 13.0% |

MarketingCharts.com | Data Source: Jacobs Media

**FIGURE 5.3**
Almost half of radio listeners state that news is the reason they tune in to radio and a third state they listen to radio for information such as being informed in times of an emergency. Other reasons cited for listening to radio is to get updated weather, listen to talk shows, traffic reports, and sports programming

Source: Courtesy of Jacobs Media

According to Nielsen, the news/talk/information audience is highly educated and consists of high-income earners. Practically all the nation's more than 11,000 commercial stations (4,646 AM stations and 6,755 FM stations) program news to some extent—with CBS and ABC being the primary deliverers of the news. Radio's tremendous mobility and pervasiveness has made it an instant and reliable news source for millions of Americans.

**FIGURE 5.4**
CBS Radio News logo

Source: Courtesy of CBS News

Says former WBZ General Manager (GM) Ted Jordan:

> In one sense we suffered from the same market compression as everyone else. But in other ways, it's easier today as there was more AM competition. All things considered, the news quality is as good, but now the systems in place are better, the networks we use (ABC and CBS) are better and more responsive, and the stringers are better. We used to have our own Washington, D.C., bureau because we didn't trust the networks to deliver the story. Now we can. They have really become responsive to the needs of the local stations. There is now a greater sharing of resources at our operations. We have a dotted-line relationship with WBZ TV. Their newspeople give updates on our air and our anchors appear on television. We are able to co-brand the stations and get a larger share of mind.

Adds Jay Williams,

> Radio stations have been able to cut costs by reallocating resources, partnering with a TV affiliate or a local newspaper, making use of portable, easy-to-use digital technology to report from the scene, and working more closely with networks and outside stringers to get follow-up reports on key stories. As to the talk that there are fewer real news sources today, I know Ted Jordan, of WBZ, believes that isn't the case. Just the opposite, in fact.

A Radio Television Digital News Association (RTDNA) study in 2017 found that 75.2% of AM stations and 65.6% of FM stations broadcast news daily. Overall, nearly 70% of stations broadcast news daily and that is an increase of three percentage points from the previous year's survey. The good news about these findings is that the numbers are up from what the previous year's study revealed. Logically, the RTDNA study revealed that the larger the radio newsroom, the greater the amount of locally produced news.

Ethnic news radio has suffered in both news coverage and listenership numbers in past years, for instance when Disney purchased New York City's KISS and WBLS in 2012 and began simulcasting the

Most all radio formats broadcast news throughout the day. Aside from the stations whose formats are news/talk/information, country and adult contemporary stations broadcast the most news for listeners

Source: Courtesy of the Radio Television Digital News Association

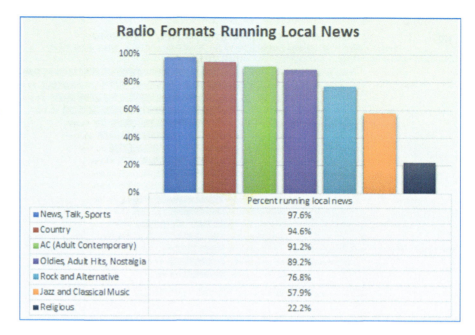

**Radio Formats Running Local News**

| | Percent running local news |
|---|---|
| News, Talk, Sports | 97.6% |
| Country | 94.6% |
| AC (Adult Contemporary) | 91.2% |
| Oldies, Adult Hits, Nostalgia | 89.2% |
| Rock and Alternative | 76.8% |
| Jazz and Classical Music | 57.9% |
| Religious | 22.2% |

Changes in the amount of news provided by stations across markets in 2017

Source: Courtesy of the Radio Television Digital News Association

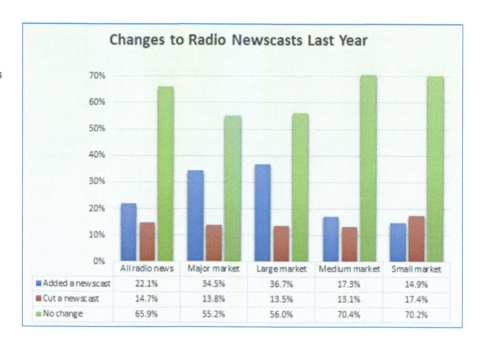

**Changes to Radio Newscasts Last Year**

| | All radio news | Major market | Large market | Medium market | Small market |
|---|---|---|---|---|---|
| Added a newscast | 22.1% | 34.5% | 36.7% | 17.3% | 14.9% |
| Cut a newscast | 14.7% | 13.8% | 13.5% | 13.1% | 17.4% |
| No change | 65.9% | 55.2% | 56.0% | 70.4% | 70.2% |

two stations. As a result of the two stations' merger, *The Tom Joyner Morning Show* and *The Michael Baisden Show*, the most listened to news and talk shows among African-Americans in New York City, were canceled.

In Boston, the nation's tenth largest media market, iconic WBZ NewsRadio 1030 continues to dominate. Mark W. Hannon, Senior Vice-President and Market Manager for CBS Radio, Boston, says:

> There's no secret sauce, other than being completely reflective of your marketplace as WBZ has been for 90-plus years. During horrific circumstances like the Boston Massacre, WBZ is the go-to place to get news and information, and when people face difficulties and tragedies, they turn to things that they can trust, and in our case, that's WBZ Radio.

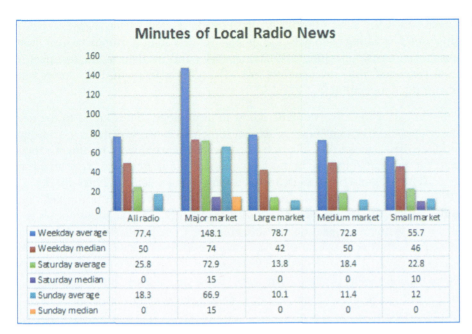

**Minutes of Local Radio News**

| | All radio | Major market | Large market | Medium market | Small market |
|---|---|---|---|---|---|
| ■ Weekday average | 77.4 | 148.1 | 78.7 | 72.8 | 55.7 |
| ■ Weekday median | 50 | 74 | 42 | 50 | 46 |
| ■ Saturday average | 25.8 | 72.9 | 13.8 | 18.4 | 22.8 |
| ■ Saturday median | 0 | 15 | 0 | 0 | 10 |
| ■ Sunday average | 18.3 | 66.9 | 10.1 | 11.4 | 12 |
| ■ Sunday median | 0 | 15 | 0 | 0 | 0 |

**FIGURE 5.7**

Radio stations broadcast almost 80 minutes of news per day. Based upon the size of the station's market, the amount of news broadcast per day ranges from 55 minutes in small markets to nearly 80 minutes in large markets. Stations in larger media markets can afford to devote more resources to delivering news for listeners

Source: Courtesy of the Radio Television Digital News Association

## LOCAL RADIO NEWS

### Holland Cooke

What would continue to differentiate and value local radio stations to listeners—and advertisers that support them—is the local content that is unavailable from iTunes, satellite radio, and the plethora of Internet-related content. Smartphones made these non-AM/FM audio competitors as portable as broadcast radio, including in-car, where users connect smartphones to dashboard audio systems by cord or Bluetooth.

Then came so-called "smart speakers" such as Amazon's Echo and Dot ("Alexa") and Google's similar Home device and Apple's iHome. These changed the in-home listening experience, and for traditional radio it's a good news/bad news situation. The good news: AM/FM receivers are now missing from many homes, so these "digital concierge" devices that perform so many tasks reintroduce local broadcasts via station streams easily available by voice command. The bad news: Alexa will serve up lots of other audio too, literally millions of song titles to Amazon Prime members; and podcasts, the audio version of on-demand consumption that has redefined "television" in the Netflix era. So local broadcasters who continue to invest in relevant, useful local content will continue to be unique. But, as a practical matter, debt prohibits most radio station owners from doing so since "a perfect storm" in the 1990s: Just as deregulation triggered a trading frenzy that inflated station sale prices, digital automation enabled consolidated corporate owners to pay their hefty mortgages by reducing payroll. Today, broadcasters who continue to invest in local programming are conspicuous by comparison.

Holland Cooke is a media consultant who works at the intersection of radio and the Internet. Previously, he managed all-news WTOP Radio, Washington D.C., and was Vice-President of a *USA Today* new media unit. He publishes a monthly newsletter for broadcasters and digital content creators. His website is www.HollandCooke.com and he is @HollandCooke on Twitter.

**FIGURE 5.8**
Holland Cooke

While WBZ may have been somewhat slow adjusting to the Portable People Meter (PPM) world in 2009, it quickly made up ground, "creating content blocks, giving listeners an opportunity to hear more content without it being broken up, simulcasting *CBS Evening News* and we deploy our reporters in ways we can optimize our resources" with sister station, WBZ-TV. "Our assignment desks speak with each other. This is a time of full cooperation."

Hannon suggests that "the struggle is to deliver content, adjust to technology, and respond to the new ways people are consuming news," noting that "how we get that content to consumers needs to continue to evolve . . . Twitter, social media . . . to get the content to them where they reside vs. waiting for them to come to us." The focus on "strengthening the brand is to embrace the technology. We're trying to get a foothold in Twitter so WBZ lives and breathes in a space where younger demographics are living." That plan is working. WBZ won the 2013 NAB Marconi Award for News Talk Station of the Year and Mark Hannon garnered the 2013 Radio Wayne award as Market Manager of the Year. The station's two networks, "ABC and CBS, have maintained great quality and continue to be great resources," Hannon says, and predicts that

> the future is bright. We're back to sharing resources with WBZ-TV and the Sports Hub FM, and we're good at migrating our content to the website and online. If we stay local, reflect the market, and have great content, we'll be fine.

## THE NEWSROOM

The number of individuals working in a radio station newsroom will vary depending on the size of a station, whether it is part of a cluster operation or a single outlet, and its format. While some stations have huge news operations that employ large numbers of individuals, on average a station in a small market employs one or two full-time newspeople. Of course, some outlets find it financially unfeasible to hire newspeople. These stations do not necessarily ignore news, rather they delegate responsibilities to their deejays to deliver brief newscasts at specified times, often at the top of the hour. Stations approaching news in this manner make it necessary for the on-air person to collect news from the wire service while music is playing and broadcast it nearly verbatim—a practice known as "rip 'n' read." Little, if any, rewriting is done because the deejay simply does not have the time to do it. The only thing that persons at "rip 'n' read" outlets can and must do is examine wire copy before going on the air. This eliminates the likelihood of mistakes. Again, all this is accomplished while the music is playing. NPR reporter Corey Flintoff warns against neglecting to examine wire copy before airtime. "We've all been caught with stuff that appears to scan at first sight but turns out to be incomprehensible when you read it."

In larger markets, music-oriented stations rarely allow their deejays to do news. Occasionally, the person jockeying the overnight shift will be expected to give a brief newscast every hour or two, but in metro markets this is fairly uncommon. There is generally a newsperson on duty around the clock. A top-rated station in a medium market typically employs four full-time newspeople; again, this varies depending on the status of the outlet (one of a cluster of stations) and the type of programming it airs. For example, easy listening stations that stress music and de-emphasize talk may employ only one or two newspeople. Meanwhile, an AC station in the same market may have five people on its news staff in an attempt to promote itself as a heavy news and information outlet, even though its primary product is music. Certainly some music stations in major markets hire as many as a dozen news employees. This figure may include not only on-air newscasters but also writers, street reporters, and technical people. Stringers and interns also swell the figure.

During the prime listening periods, when a station's audience is at its maximum, newscasts are programmed with greater frequency, sometimes twice as often as during other dayparts. The newsroom is a hub of activity as newspeople prepare for newscasts scheduled every 20–30 minutes. Half a dozen people may be involved in assembling news but only two may actually enter the broadcast booth. A primetime newscast schedule may look something like this:

| Drive Coverage, am | Drive Coverage, pm |
|---|---|
| Smith 6:25 am | Lopez 3:25 pm |
| Bernard 7:00 am | Gardner 4:00 pm |
| Smith 7:25 am | Lopez 4:25 pm |
| Bernard 8:00 am | Gardner 5:00 pm |
| Smith 8:25 am | Lopez 5:25 pm |
| Bernard 9:00 am | Gardner 6:00 pm |
| Smith 9:25 am | Lopez 6:25 pm |

Midday and evening are far less frenetic in the newsroom, and one person per shift may be considered sufficient.

A standard-size newsroom in a medium market will contain several pieces of audio equipment, not to mention office furniture such as desks, computers, file cabinets, and so on. The standard audio production equipment that is found in all radio station studios is used by the newsperson. Also, the modern radio newsroom will also be equipped with various monitors to keep newspeople on top of what is happening at the local police and fire departments and weather bureau. Various wire service machines provide the latest news, sports, stock, and weather information, as well as a host of other data. Depending on the station's budget, two or more news services may be used. Stations with a genuine commitment to news create work areas that are designed for maximum efficiency and productivity. Jim Farley, Vice-President of News and Programming at WTOP, says news stations have "Lots of computers, video monitors, and smartphones. Many of our reporters use their iPhones for reporting from the field. Oh, and a working coffee pot!"

New equipment and technology continue to streamline news coverage for radio journalists. Tim Scheld, WCBS-AM's Director of News and Programming, stated that new technology has been an exciting addition to radio news. In an interview with *Radio Ink*, he said:

**FIGURE 5.9**
The WTOP newsroom and editors' desk. From left to right: film critic Jason Fraley, *Morning Drive* Editor Mike Jakaitis, and Editor Desiree Smith
Source: Courtesy of WTOP-FM, Washington, D.C.

First off, the equipment we use out on the street has changed significantly in the past ten years. Smartphones are smarter. They allow reporters to take photos, tweet, post onto Facebook, record audio, and connect via broadband to deliver high quality live audio. The technical developments in the past few years have been breathtaking, and we continue to test new avenues all the time. We are also now seeing social media play a larger role in the delivery of news to consumers. While some might consider it competition to the traditional media, I actually view it as an opportunity for us to expose our reporting and newsgathering to an audience that may not normally consider radio news as a source of information. It's an exciting time for us. Challenging, but exciting.

## SIRIUSXM NEWS/ ISSUES FULL CHANNEL LINEUP

CNBC

FOX Business

FOX News Channel

FOX News Headlines 24/7

CNN

HLN

MSNBC

Bloomberg Radio

BBC World Service

SiriusXM Insight

NPR Now

PRX Public Radio

POTUS Politics

SiriusXM Patriot

SiriusXM Urban View

SiriusXM Progress

FOX News Talk

CNN International

C-SPAN Radio

**FIGURE 5.10**
The SiriusXM channel lineup boasts nearly 20 news/issues radio stations from which its subscribers may choose

Source: Retrieved from www.siriusxm. com/channellineup

Indeed, a visit to WCBS-AM's website allows listeners to not only listen to the station but also "like" its Facebook page and follow its news updates on Twitter.

In situations where newsrooms have been combined and consolidated, more personnel, equipment, and space may be in evidence since it may be serving a myriad of stations. Cluster operation newsrooms accommodate reporters and newsreaders assigned to the various stations under the one roof.

News in satellite radio originates from a host of outside sources. Originally operating as two independent satellite radio entities, XM and Sirius, the two companies merged to become SiriusXM in 2007. SiriusXM provides feeds (channels) from Fox News, CNN, MSNBC, CNBC, Bloomberg Radio, BBC World Service, NPR Now, and others. Satellite radio is not in the business of generating news itself, so the "newsroom" (as we have been referring to it) does not exist at SiriusXM, although this may change in the future.

## THE ALL-NEWS STATION

Stations devoted entirely to news programming arrived on the scene in the mid-1960s. Program innovator Gordon McLendon, who had been a key figure in the development of two music formats, beautiful music and top 40, implemented all-news at WNUS-AM (NEWS) in Chicago. In 1965, Group W, Westinghouse Broadcasting, changed WINS-AM in New York to all-news and soon did the same at more of its metro outlets: KYW-AM, Philadelphia, and KFWB-AM, Los Angeles. While Group W was converting several of its outlets to nonmusic programming, CBS decided that all-news was the way to go at WCBS-AM, New York, KCBS-AM, San Francisco, and KNX-AM, Los Angeles. Other stations that migrated to an all-news format in the 1960s were WTOP-FM in Washington, D.C., and KNX 1070 in Los Angeles.

**FIGURE 5.11**
The nation's top 10 revenue generating stations in 2016

Source: Courtesy of BIA/Kelsey

### Top Ten Highest Revenue Radio Stations in 2016

| CALLS | AM or FM | Format | Owner | Rank | Market Name | Est. Revenue-Station 2016 ($000) |
|-------|----------|--------|-------|------|-------------|----------------------------------|
| WTOP | FM | News | Hubbard Radio LLC | 7 | Washington, DC | $67,500 |
| KIIS | FM | CHR | iHeartMedia | 2 | Los Angeles, CA | $65,900 |
| WHTZ | FM | CHR | iHeartMedia | 1 | New York, NY | $48,000 |
| WFAN | FM | Sports/Talk | Entercom | 1 | New York, NY | $46,500 |
| WBBM | AM | News | Entercom | 3 | Chicago, IL | $45,000 |
| KBIG | FM | Hot AC | iHeartMedia | 2 | Los Angeles, CA | $44,000 |
| WCBS | AM | News | Entercom | 1 | New York, NY | $44,000 |
| WLTW | FM | Lite AC | iHeartMedia | 1 | New York, NY | $42,000 |
| WINS | AM | News | Entercom | 1 | New York, NY | $40,000 |
| KFI | AM | News/Talk | iHeartMedia | 2 | Los Angeles, CA | $38,000 |

BIA Kelsey                                    Source: BIA/Kelsey

Since its inception, radio news has become quite profitable too. WTOP-FM in Washington, D.C., was the nation's top revenue generating station, bringing in a whopping $67.5 million in advertising revenue for the 2016 fiscal year. Of the top 10 highest revenue grossing stations in 2016, half of them were news and/or news/talk formats. The fourth highest grossing radio station in 2016 was WFAN-FM, a sports/talk format.

Because of the exorbitant cost of running a news-only operation, it has remained a primarily metro-market endeavor. It often costs several times as much to run an effective all-news station as it does to run one music station. This usually keeps small-market outlets out of the business. Staff numbers in all-news stations far exceed that of formats that primarily serve up music. Although a lone deejay is needed at an adult contemporary or top 40 station, all-news requires the involvement of several people to keep the air sound credible. In large markets, the newsroom staff can be a large operation, with many people contributing to the daily gathering and delivery of news.

Even though the cost of running a news station is high, the payback can more than justify expenditures. However, this is one format that requires a sizable initial investment, as well as the financial wherewithal and patience to last until it becomes an established and viable entity. Considerable planning takes place before a station decides to convert to all-news, since it is not simply a matter of hiring new jocks and updating the music library. Switching from a music format to all-news is dramatic and anything but cosmetic.

AM has always been the home of the all-news station. There are only a handful of FM news and information outlets. The format's prevalence on AM has grown considerably since the late 1970s, when FM took the lead in listeners. The percentage of all-news and news/talk formats on AM continued to increase in the 1980s as the band lost more and more of its music listeners to FM. However, all-news stations in a handful of metro markets keep AM at the top of the ratings charts. In the early 1990s, it was common to find one AM outlet among the leaders, and almost invariably it programmed nonmusic. This has changed little in the late 2010s. Some media observers predict that all-news will make inroads into FM as that band gives over large segments of its music audience to digital technologies. At the start of 2016, BIA/Kelsey reports there are 32 radio stations throughout the U.S. that identify themselves as having an all-news format.

All-news stations are keeping pace with technological advancements. Tim Scheld, Director of News/Programming at WCBS Newsradio 880, says, "The biggest, most successful radio news operations in America embraced digital long ago. They have full service, active websites and are delivering radio news via digital platforms like *TuneIn* and *Radio.com*. All of the traditional news operations are expanding their brands to the digital space. The next frontier is social media."

**FIGURE 5.12**

WTOP logo

Source: Courtesy of WTOP-FM, Washington, D.C.

**Number of all-news stations at close of 2015 stood at 32**

| Calls | AM or FM | City of license | State of license | Parent |
|---|---|---|---|---|
| WBBR | AM | New York | NY | Bloomberg Communications Inc. |
| KQV | AM | Pittsburgh | PA | Calvary Inc. |
| KCBS | AM | San Francisco | CA | CBS Corporation |
| KFRC | FM | San Francisco | CA | CBS Corporation |
| KNX | AM | Los Angeles | CA | CBS Corporation |
| KYW | AM | Philadelphia | PA | CBS Corporation |
| WBBM | AM | Chicago | IL | CBS Corporation |
| WCBS | AM | New York | NY | CBS Corporation |
| WCCO | AM | Minneapolis | MN | CBS Corporation |
| WCFS | FM | Elmwood Park | IL | CBS Corporation |
| WINS | AM | New York | NY | CBS Corporation |
| WWJ | AM | Detroit | MI | CBS Corporation |
| WJDY | AM | Salisbury | MD | CC Media Holdings Inc. |
| WOKV | AM | Jacksonville | FL | Cox Media Group |
| WOKV | FM | Atlantic Beach | FL | Cox Media Group |
| KGO | AM | San Francisco | CA | Cumulus Media Inc. |
| WYAY | FM | Gainesville | GA | Cumulus Media Inc. |
| KLIV | AM | San Jose | CA | Empire Broadcasting Corp |
| WAMT | AM | Pine Castle Sky Lake | FL | Genesis Communications |
| WIXC | AM | Titusville | FL | Genesis Communications |
| WTLP | FM | Braddock Heights | MD | Hubbard Broadcasting Inc. |
| WTOP | FM | Washington | DC | Hubbard Broadcasting Inc. |
| WWWT | FM | Manassas | VA | Hubbard Broadcasting Inc. |
| WMEA | FM | Portland | ME | Maine Public Broadcasting Corporation |
| WMCD | FM | Claxton | GA | Neal Ardman |
| WWNS | AM | Statesboro | GA | Neal Ardman |
| KPMI | AM | Bemidji | MN | Paskvan Media Inc. |
| KRFP | FM | Moscow | ID | Radio Free Moscow Inc. |
| KOMO | AM | Seattle | WA | Sinclair Broadcast Group Incorporated |
| KOMO | FM | Oakville | WA | Sinclair Broadcast Group Incorporated |
| WRSW | AM | Warsaw | IN | Talking Stick Communications LLC |
| KNEZ | FM | Fernley | NV | Times-Shamrock Communications Inc. |

Source: BIA/Kelsey.
"State of the News Media 2016"

**PEW RESEARCH CENTER**

**FIGURE 5.13**

Number of all-news stations around the nation

Source: Courtesy of BIA/Kelsey and *State of the News Media 2016*, Pew Research Center

FIGURE 5.14
WTOP-FM is in a major radio market and has a very large group of individuals working to deliver the news

Source: Courtesy of WTOP-FM, Washington, D.C.

FIGURE 5.15
Andy Ludlum

## WHAT MAKES A SUCCESSFUL NEWS RADIO STATION?

### Andy Ludlum

Great radio news of the future has to be about one thing, it must be *local*. Radio is personal and intimate. Look at any successful radio personality and you'll see someone who has a strong, personal connection with his or her local audience.

But then listen to a couple of hours of all-news radio. Probably the only time you'll hear the word "you" is in the commercials.

I believe the key to success in the news business is your ability to tell compelling stories to your local audience.

Storytelling is an essential and ancient part of what makes us human. Before most people could read or write our culture and religion was passed on through storytelling.

Through storytelling we not only learn what matters, but why it matters. Sounds like Journalism 101 doesn't it? We remember stories far better than a list of facts because our brains perceive little distinction between a story we are told and something that is actually happening to us.

Quite likely the radio we know today will become a thing of the past. If you consider the technological explosion of just the last few years, you see the methods of delivery and platforms for consuming news are constantly changing. That change will increase exponentially and we'll soon have tools and devices we can't even imagine today.

Deregulation and consolidation have left many small communities without any significant local news. We hear of terrible incidents where storms or tornadoes have swept through unsuspecting towns without warning. We've also heard of courageous and dedicated deejays, without any formal news training, going on the air and informing and comforting their communities.

I tell young people who are just starting out now in radio news to expect that they absolutely won't be ending their careers in radio news. Instead, as media technologies converge, I see the journalist of the future working in an exciting, multimedia, multiplatform environment where they are delivering their message in many ways and many formats daily. From audio podcasts to handheld video productions, from blogging to short-form messaging such as tweeting and texting, all will have direct and regular interaction with the audience. It won't be easy: more than ever broadcast job security is a flimsy thing. I've had a very successful 40-year career, yet I was laid off four times, twice by the same company!

The need for specific local information will not disappear. We need to know about traffic. We need to know why there's smoke in the sky. We need to know why potholes are not being fixed. We need to know why the local sales tax is so high. We need to know how elected officials are spending our tax money. We need to know where the jobs are. We need to know if a dangerous storm is bearing down on us. The communicator who remembers it is "all about local" will succeed in the future.

With the 2016 presidential election, we were reminded of the tremendous power of social media and nontraditional sources of news. If traditional sources of news do not meet the needs of the local consumer, they will be discarded as irrelevant. That's not to say accuracy and truth have gone out of style. They are essential in cementing the listener's personal connection with the stories we tell. New digital tools will help us be interactive and collaborative with our audience.

The secret to great information communication in the future is that it be immediate, interactive, intimate, and *local*.

---

**Andy Ludlum** spent 40 years in broadcasting news and information on radio and television. He's been the news and program director of great radio stations in Los Angeles, Seattle, and Kansas City, including KNX, KFWB, KABC, and KMPC in Los Angeles, KIRO and KING in Seattle, and KMBZ in Kansas City. Ludlum started in radio in the 1970s as a traffic reporter in San Jose, CA. He had the opportunity to broadcast from all over the world and cover some exceptional events, from the 1981 assassination of Anwar Sadat in Egypt to the economic emergence of China and the rebirth of democracy in the former Soviet Union. While working in Washington State he covered the 1980 eruption of Mount St. Helens. Ludlum's stations have frequently been recognized for excellence in news broadcasting, receiving three national RTDNA Edward R. Murrow Awards for Overall Excellence and local Emmys and Golden Mikes from the Radio Television News Association of Southern California. The Greater Los Angeles Chapter of the Society of Professional Journalists honored Ludlum in 2012 as a Distinguished Journalist in Radio. You can follow Andy Ludlum on Twitter at @aludlum.

## TRAFFIC REPORTS

Traffic reports are an integral part of drive time news programming at many metropolitan radio stations. Although providing listeners with traffic condition updates can be costly, especially air-to-ground reports that require the use of a helicopter or small plane, they can help strengthen a station's community service image and also generate substantial revenue. To avoid the cost involved in airborne observation, stations sometimes employ the services of local auto clubs or put their own mobile units out on the roads. A station in Providence, Rhode Island, broadcasts traffic conditions from atop a 20-story hotel that overlooks the city's key arteries. Fixed cameras at key traffic locations are also used.

**FIGURE 5.16**
KNX 1070 Newsradio logo
Source: Courtesy of KNX 1070 Newsradio, Los Angeles, CA

David Saperstein says, "Companies like Metro Network provide stations with outside traffic reporting services in a manner that is more cost- and quality-effective than a station handling it themselves."

Traffic reports are scheduled several times an hour throughout the prime commuter periods on stations primarily catering to adults, and they range in length from 30–90 seconds. The actual reports may be done by a station employee who works in other areas of programming when not surveying the roads, or a member of the local police department or auto club may be hired for the job. Obviously, the prime criterion for such a position is a thorough knowledge of the streets and highways of the area being reported.

## THE ELECTRONIC NEWSROOM

The combined use of computers, online resources, and smartphones is the norm. Computers linked to the various wire and Internet information services are used to access primary and background data on fast-breaking stories and features. Many stations have installed touch screen computer monitors and traditional flat-screen, high-definition television sets in on-air studios to have instant access to breaking news and weather. Instead of handheld copy, newscasters simply read from the studio monitors. The speed and agility with which news copy can be produced and edited makes a computer the perfect tool for broadcast journalists.

Radio newsrooms have fully embraced technological advances such as the Internet and smartphones. Scheld describes the WCBS Newsradio 880 newsroom: "Our newsroom has telephones, televisions, Internet, and computers that can record and edit audio. We also have equipment that keeps us connected to news resources like CBS News and the *Wall Street Journal*." However, some very technologically advanced radio newsrooms still have and use very traditional broadcasting equipment. At KRLD-AM, in the Dallas/Ft. Worth radio media market in the United States, Alice Rios, former co-anchor of the KRLD-AM *Morning News* in Dallas, says the following pieces of equipment are regularly used:

> An edit station where there's a computer, microphone, and a phone. Scanners, still. (Gotta love the sound of scanners in the background of old school newsrooms.) Reporters use small Marantz recorders when they go out on stories and actually many of them now have software on their phones that allow them to get interviews/audio on their smartphones. *Very* handy so that if anyone on the news staff happens to live near the scene of a breaking news story, they can go on air with audio clips, within minutes.

Stations use news services such as the Burli Newsroom and Burli NE, both of which are software products designed for radio stations to: (1) gather news from all parts of the world from sources such as newswires, Tweets, emails, RSS feeds, and internal stories; (2) edit stories from within the software itself to align with the station and announcer style; (3) share stories across multiple platforms including social media as well as share stories between workstations within the same newsroom; and (4) customize text and audio directly from a prompter to tailor the news being delivered to meet a station's style and format. Burli boasts international customers ranging from WINS 1010 AM in New York, Colorado Public Radio, Global Radio in London, and 93.7 JR FM in Vancouver, Canada. Burli was founded in 1996 in Vancouver and has steadily expanded since that time.

The Internet, email, smartphone, and social media connect radio station newsrooms with the information super highway to keep its listening public informed and up to date. The Internet has become the best resource for information on every conceivable topic. "It is in constant use. Our brand is WTOP. Our distribution channels are radio, TV, streaming audio, wtop.com, email, text and Twitter alerts, Facebook and mobile," says Farley. As a search medium, there is none better. Data of every variety are at the fingertips of all newspeople today. The world of cyberspace has revolutionized newsgathering. Says broadcaster and academic Larry Miller, "The evolution has been from old-fashioned teletype 'wire' by landlines, to satellites, to computers and the Internet. Even audio is accessed online."

According to broadcast scholar David Reese, "Today, newsrooms use station websites to deliver news, and consumer usage patterns indicate that acquiring information this way is growing in popularity." Jason Insalaco adds,

> The listener is no longer going to remain captive to a news station to learn the day's headlines. An added plus is that many station websites offer live information on traffic flow and so forth. Station websites give outlets needed additional cache in the multimedia environment.

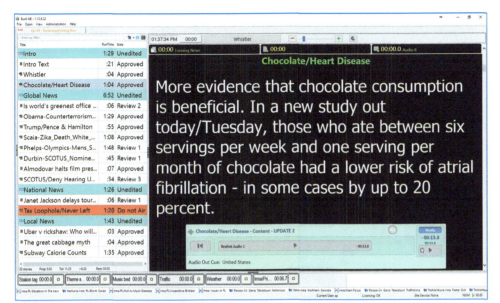

FIGURE 5.17

Burli NE's main screen allows for a dense and powerful view of incoming news and editing tools. Publishing and dispatch is only a click or two away

Source: Courtesy of Burli

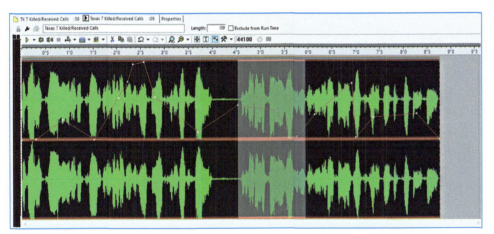

FIGURE 5.18

For radio customers, the built-in Prompter allows for easy reading and audio playback to air, along with on-the-fly, newsroom-wide live editing

Source: Courtesy of Burli

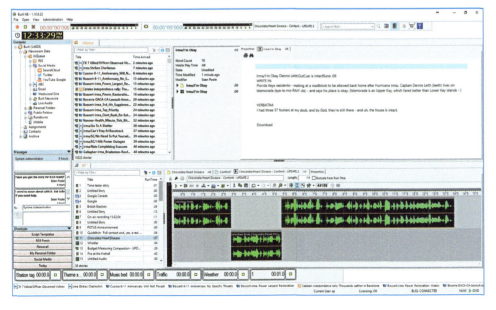

FIGURE 5.19

Burli's custom multi-track editor was designed from the ground up with newsroom workflow and toolsets in mind. Burli NE's main screen allows for a dense and powerful view of incoming news and editing tools. Publishing and dispatch are only a click or two away

Source: Courtesy of Burli

**FIGURE 5.20**

As noted, companies provide specifically tailored software for newsrooms. "There are computer software packages these days that a newsroom can buy. In my day we used the old file and cards and Rolodex, but today news rooms that can afford it use software to file stories, keep archives of copy, record and play actualities, and so forth," says radio consultant Donna Halper

Source: Courtesy of Burli

**FIGURE 5.21**
WTOP Twitter site
Source: Courtesy of WTOP-FM, Washington, D.C.

Not all stations are effectively competing with digital news on various websites. Jim Farley, of WTOP-FM in Washington, D.C., says, "Some stations and groups are, others are not. Here at WTOP, we don't consider ourselves a radio station. We are a digital news organization."

The Internet has made information gathering much faster and efficient. Scheld shares:

> The Internet has replaced the research department. We used to have thick books called "reverse directories" that would provide us phone numbers in every neighborhood in our listening area so we could track down witnesses to breaking news. The Internet has revolutionized our business. It puts important information at our fingertips and allows us to check facts and figures important to our stories. The Internet also connects us to our listeners better than ever.

Other technology has contributed greatly to the efficiency and performance of the electronic newsroom. For instance, ISDN (integrated services digital network) significantly improved the quality of phone interviews. With ISDN technology, newsrooms can create seamless reports (in terms of audio fidelity), thus creating the impression (or illusion) that all the voices on the air come from the same studio and even from the same microphone. When asked if radio newsrooms utilize ISDN, Andy Ludlum, then the Director of News Programming at Los Angeles's KNX 1070 Newsradio and KFWB News Talk 980, said

> Yes we still use ISDN daily. We are beginning to run into problems in some parts of the country where phone companies will not install ISDN circuits, much as they have moved away from installing 8kc or higher audio circuits from point to point.

Although ISDN installation is becoming problematic, Ludlum says,

> There are a number of alternatives, most using high bandwidth Internet connections such as Verizon's Fios. Using a codec, such as a Comrex Access device, you can get high quality, ISDN or studio-quality audio from remote to station. Many news operations are also using VoIP applications (Voice-over Internet Protocol)—such as Skype or broadcast applications such as LiveReportPro.

Further, he notes that,

**FIGURE 5.22**
Facebook is used as a way to disseminate news by most stations

Source: Courtesy of WTOP-FM, Washington, D.C.

## BOSTON HERALD RADIO

### Jay Williams, Jr.

Boston's second largest daily newspaper created its own radio station—Boston Herald Radio. "We looked at buying stations in 2005 but the cost was too high [even for] limited signals. . . . Now you can start a Web station for less than $50,000," says Jeff Magram, COO and CFO of Herald Media Inc.

Faced with declining circulations, newspapers are scrambling to add platforms and extend reach, but Herald Radio firmly establishes the paper as a direct competitor for Boston's traditional radio news, talk, and sports stations. Boston Herald Radio started with 12 hours a day of live, local programming

**FIGURE 5.23**
Jay Williams, Jr.

featuring well-known radio hosts, but often broadcasts late for events such as the last mayoral contest, delivering political analysis and live on-scene reports as the story developed.

Magram explains the *Herald*'s rationale:

> For years our columnists have been on the radio... then you have radio stations that rip and read *Boston Herald* stories. We talked for years about taking advantage of our own talent on our own radio station ... and leveraging our own resources. With the explosion in smartphones, it was the right time to try a radio platform.

Boston Herald Radio can be accessed from bostonherald.com, TuneIn, *Herald* news and sports apps, iTunes Radio, and even Wi-Fi Connect in commuter trains.

"WBZ and WRKO? I think we can compete 100%; the challenge is getting people to find us and figure out how to connect to Boston Herald Radio," Magram notes.

> But in terms of product and resources, we'll be just as good if not better; our depth of reporting resources is so much greater. If we were running Boston Herald Radio during the bombings, we could have had our reporters calling in, in the field on the phone, and giving information live,

He adds that greater listenership will happen over time as manufacturers put more web access in cars.

**FIGURE 5.24**
Boston Herald Radio Studio—host's station
Source: Courtesy of Herald Media Inc.

**FIGURE 5.25**
Boston Herald Radio Studio. *Morning Meeting* show with hosts Jaclyn Cashman and Hillary Chabot and guests former Boston Mayor Ray Flynn and Democratic Strategist Scott Ferson. Executive Producer Tom Shattuck with his back to the camera in the producer's booth. (Left to right: Hillary Chabot, Ray Flynn, Scott Ferson, and Jaclyn Cashman)
Source: Courtesy of Herald Media Inc.

And what about the future? Magram says the relatively low-cost infrastructure—producers and hosts, the streaming vendor relationship, and a terrific software program—should allow the station to operate for a long time as it also can tap the existing news gathering, reporting and marketing resources of the *Boston Herald*:

> We're no longer just a newspaper, we're a multimedia organization with 440,000 daily readers and 2.3 million unique visitors to our website. Our mission is to extend the brand beyond the existing walls, move more into digital, more into the Web, more into video both prerecorded and live streaming. There is an audience that wants our content and we need to give it to them in any fashion that they want it. We'll be driven by demand.

## THE NEWS DIRECTOR

News directors, like other department heads, are responsible for developing and implementing policies pertaining to their area, supervising staff members, and handling budgetary concerns. These are basic to any managerial position.

At WTOP in Washington, D.C., the news director's responsibilities are "Day-to-day news coverage, quality control, hiring, training, managing people," says Farley. At WCBS Newsradio 880 in New York City, says Scheld:

> The news director is like the coach of a team. The news director is responsible for setting up his or her staff to succeed. The news director sets the tone, provides editorial direction, and coordinates news coverage for the radio station. The most important function of any news manager is to solicit ideas, and harness the potential of an entire staff.

The news department poses its own unique challenges to the individual who oversees its operation. These challenges must be met with a considerable degree of skill and know-how. Education and training are important. Surveys have concluded that station managers look for college degrees when hiring news directors. In addition, most news directors have, on average, five years of experience in radio news before advancement to the managerial level. In a 2013 RTDNA study, it was discovered that the average radio news director is responsible for the oversight of 2.6 stations, not just one station. Moreover, today's news directors have responsibilities beyond just overseeing the newsroom, with announcing, sports, general manager and/or program director being the most likely responsibilities and titles held at the same time.

The news director and program director (PD) work together closely. At most stations, the PD has authority over the news department, since everything going over the air or affecting the air product is his or her direct concern and responsibility. Any changes in the format of the news or in the scheduling of newscasts or newscasters may, in fact, have to be approved by the station's programmer. For example, if the PD is opposed to the news director's plans to include two or more recorded reports (actualities) per newscast, he may withhold approval. Although the news director may feel that the reports enhance the newscasts, the PD may argue that they create congestion and clutter. In terms of establishing the on-air news schedule, the PD works with the news director to ensure that the sound of a given newsperson is suitably matched with the time slot he or she is assigned.

Getting the news out rapidly and accurately is a top priority of the news director. Judy Smith, who functions as a one-person newsroom at a San Antonio station, says:

> People tune to radio news to find out what is happening right now. That's what makes the medium such a key source for most people. While it is important to get news on the air as fast as possible, it is more important that the stories broadcast be factual and correct. You can't sacrifice accuracy for the sake of speed. As a radio news director, my first responsibility is to inform our audience about breaking events on the local level. That's what our listeners want to hear. . . . Because I'm the only newsperson on duty, I have to spend a lot of time verifying facts on the phone and recording actualities. I don't have the luxury of assigning that work to someone else, but it has to be done.

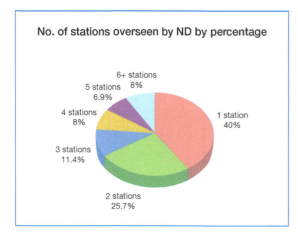

No. of stations overseen by ND by percentage

**FIGURE 5.26**
Number of stations per news director
Source: Courtesy of the Radio Television Digital News Association

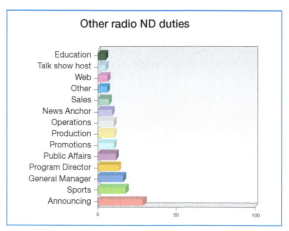

Other radio ND duties

**FIGURE 5.27**
Other radio news director duties
Source: Courtesy of the Radio Television Digital News Association

Larry Jewett perceives his responsibilities similarly:

First and foremost, the news director's job is to keep the listener informed of what is happening in the world around him. A newsperson is a gatherer and conveyor of information. News is a serious business. A jock can be wacky and outrageous on the air and be a great success. On the other hand, a newsperson must communicate credibly or find another occupation.

Gathering local news is the most time-consuming task facing a radio news director, according to former news director Cecilia Mason:

To do the job well you have to keep moving. All kinds of meetings—governmental, civic, business—have to be covered if you intend on being a primary source of local news. A station with a news commitment must have the resources to be where the stories are, too. A news director has to be a logistical engineer at times. You have to be good at prioritizing and making the most out of what you have at hand. All too often, there are just too many events unfolding for a news department to effectively cover, so you call the shots the best way that you can. If you know your business, your best shot is usually more than adequate.

**FIGURE 5.28**
WCBS Newsradio 880 logo celebrating 50 years of serving New York

Source: Courtesy of WCBS-AM Newsradio, New York, NY

In addition to the gathering and reporting of news, public affairs programming is often the responsibility of the news director. This generally includes the planning and preparation of local information features, such as interviews, debates, and even documentaries. Ultimately, the news director's primary goal is to ensure the credibility of the station's news operation. For the well-schooled and conscientious news director, this means avoiding advocacy and emphasizing objectivity. Says media scholar Indra de Silva:

So much of broadcast news today is opinion and commentary—infotainment—rather than dispassionate and unbiased reporting. That is a corruption of the long-held ideal that news should be fair and balanced. Editorializing a newscast essentially misleads the audience, which ultimately is a violation of the broadcaster's public trustee role.

## WHAT MAKES A NEWSPERSON?

College training is an important criterion to the radio news director when hiring personnel. It is not impossible to land a news job without a degree, but formal education is a definite asset. In terms of a formal education, "We want people who know a lot. Smart people. A college degree helps but it alone is not a determinant of quality of work or career success," says Farley. In order to move into management, a formal education is a requirement. However, while a strong desire to be in the radio industry sometimes suffices, a formal education is always the best choice for individuals desiring a career in radio. When asked if a formal education was absolutely required to work in radio news, Rios stated:

Not necessarily. There are several on-air personalities in our CBS Radio cluster in Dallas, who did not go to or finish college. I'd almost say half have college degrees, half do not. The thing is, those who did not get a degree in communications/RTV or journalism or political science are the people who . . . at the age of 14 and 15 started hanging out at radio stations while in high school; making copies, making coffee, etc. They just knew at an early age working in radio was their destiny. Having said that, the reason I personally believe getting a formal education is important is twofold. It's not only crucial for the experience one receives at a campus radio station (getting an internship is especially important as 90% of the time if you are a total team player and yes-(wo)man it leads to land a job at the station you intern for), but in this business—and hear me now—you *need to have a backup plan*. There is a very high turnover rate in this industry. If you are a good writer, you can always be a producer or editor in either radio or TV really. But . . . for those who think they have what it takes to be an on air reporter, or talent like the late Kidd Kraddick, I have this to say: You can have the best voice in the land. But when ratings are not good and there are changes in management . . . the person who hired you may've thought you were a rock star but the next manager might think you are mediocre at best. It would be wise to have a backup plan and consider getting a teaching certificate or . . . getting into public relations. Anything. Getting a job has a lot to do with timing and talent level. When it comes to writing though, if you are a good writer you will likely not have a hard time finding a job.

**FIGURE 5.29**
The radio news reporter does not just stay in the studio, he or she goes to where the news is happening to cover fires, severe weather, rioting, or any other type of breaking news

Source: © 2017 American Broadcasting Companies Inc.

Specifically, an individual planning to enter the radio news profession should consider pursuing a broadcasting, journalism, or liberal arts degree. Courses in political science, history, economics, and literature give the aspiring newsperson the kind of well-rounded background that is most useful. As Cecilia Mason says:

> Coming into this shrinking field today, a college degree is an attractive, if not essential, credential. There's so much that a newsperson has to know. I think an education makes the kind of difference you can hear, and that's what our business is about. It's a fact that most people are more cognizant of the world and write better after attending college. Credibility is crucial in this business, and college training provides some of that. A degree is something that I would look for in prospective newspeople.

Even though education ranks high, most news directors still look for experience first. Jewett notes:

> As far as I'm concerned, experience counts the most. I'm not suggesting that education isn't important. It is. Most news directors want the person that they are hiring to have a college background, but experience impresses them more. I believe a person should have a good understanding of the basics before attempting to make a living at something. Whereas a college education is useful, a person should not lean back and point to a degree. Mine hasn't gotten me a job yet, though I wouldn't trade it for the world.

Newsman Smith agrees that

> The first thing I think most news directors really look for is experience. Although I have a Bachelor of Arts degree myself, I wouldn't hold out for a person with a college diploma. I think if it came down to hiring a person with a degree versus someone with solid experience, I'd go for the latter.

Scheld also acknowledges prior experience is important:

> Prior experience is helpful and does prepare an individual to work in the major market newsroom. Some people come into the newsroom with little news experience but they must bring in other valuable tools such as computer and audio editing skills.

**FIGURE 5.30**
A typical radio station news studio

Source: Courtesy of WTOP-FM, Washington, D.C.

Gaining news experience can be somewhat difficult in the age of downsizing and consolidation, at least more so than acquiring deejay experience, which itself is more of a challenge today than it was a decade ago. Small stations, where the beginner is most likely to break into the business, have slots for several deejays but seldom more than one for a newsperson. It becomes even more problematic when employers at small stations want the one person that they hire for news to bring some experience to the job. Larger stations place even greater emphasis on experience. Thus, the aspiring newsperson is faced with a sort of "Catch-22" situation, in which a job cannot be acquired without experience and experience cannot be acquired without a job.

One way to gain experience is through internships. WTOP-FM's Farley says, "It helps, but there's not much of a farm system out there anymore. We use a lot of interns, and their internship is in many cases an audition." Scheld agrees with Farley about the value of internships:

> You do not need a college degree to work in a newsroom but it sure does help. You don't need postgraduate experience to contribute in the newsroom but any experience you bring makes you a more valuable player in the operation. The single best experience that candidates can bring to a newsroom is the internship. Internships expose you to the professional environment and are invaluable.

Agreeing with Farley about the importance of on-the-job experience and internships, Rios asserts:

> An experienced reporter or editor will nine times out of ten get a job before a recent college graduate. I'm talking about this being the case in a major market like New York, Los Angeles, Chicago, or Dallas. Out of college you *must* be willing to do, and take, any job you are offered in a small(er) market. Getting that experience while you are young and single and don't have a family to consider, if only for half a year, will be the gateway into a bigger market, thus more money. Paying your dues, they call it. I just can't stress enough how important it is to be realistic, and not expect to be a news anchor in radio or TV, right out of college. Most important though, is being a good writer.

Former news director Frank Titus says that there are ways of gaining experience that will lead to a news job:

> Working in news at high school and college stations is very valid experience. That's how Dan Rather and a hundred other newsmen got started. Also working as an intern at a commercial radio station fattens out the resume. If someone comes to me with this kind of background and a strong desire to do news, I'm interested.

Among the personal qualities that most appeal to news directors are enthusiasm, assertiveness, energy, and inquisitiveness. Mason contends:

> I want someone with a strong news sense and unflagging desire to get a story and get it right. A person either wants to do news or doesn't. Someone with a pedestrian interest in radio journalism is more of a hindrance to an operation than a help.

Titus wants someone who is totally devoted to the profession: "When you get right down to it, I want someone on my staff who eats, drinks, and sleeps news." Other needed qualities to succeed in the radio newsroom include the "ability to think on your feet, great storyteller, multimedia skills, and an incredible energy and drive," according to Farley.

On the practical side of the ledger, WCRN newsman Sherman Whitman says that good typing skills are essential:

> If you can't type, you can't work in a newsroom. It's an essential ability, and the more accuracy and speed the better. It's one of those skills basic to the job. A candidate for a news job can come in here with two degrees, but if that person can't type, that person won't be hired. Broadcast students should learn to type.

Meanwhile, Jewett stresses the value of possessing a firm command of the English language:

> Proper punctuation, spelling, and syntax make a news story intelligible. A newsperson doesn't have to be a grammarian, but he or she had better know where to put a comma and a period and how to compose a good clean sentence. A copy of Strunk and White's *Elements of Style* is good to have around.

WCBS Newsradio's Tim Scheld agrees that writing skills are a must: "A successful radio news reporter must be a good writer. There is no substitute for good writing skills. You must be skeptical, cynical, and curious. Reporters must also be great storytellers."

An individual who is knowledgeable about the area in which a station is located has a major advantage over those who are not, says Whitman:

> A news-person has to know the town or city inside out. I'd advise anybody about to be interviewed for a news position to find out as much as possible about the station's coverage area. Read back issues of newspapers, get socioeconomic stats from the library or chamber of commerce, and study street directories and maps of the town or city in which the station is located. Go into the job interview well-informed, and you'll make a strong impression.

**FIGURE 5.31**
Radio news salaries

Note. * = No data.
Source: Courtesy of the Radio Television Digital News Association

### MEDIAN RADIO NEWS SALARIES BY MARKET SIZE

| Position | Average ($) | Median ($) | Minimum ($) | Maximum ($) |
|---|---|---|---|---|
| News Director | 43,400 | 37,000 | 12,000 | 130,000 |
| News Reporter | 38,800 | 40,000 | 12,000 | 95,000 |
| News Producer | 41,100 | 42,500 | 15,000 | 61,000 |
| News Anchor | 49,300 | 44,000 | 20,000 | 110,000 |
| Sports Anchor | 33,000 | 30,000 | 18,000 | 55,000 |
| Sports Reporter | 25,300 | 26,500 | 15,000 | 38,000 |
| Web Prod/Ed | 41,100 | 39,000 | 20,000 | 75,000 |

### RADIO NEWS STARTING SALARIES

| Position | Major ($) | Large ($) | Medium ($) | Small ($) |
|---|---|---|---|---|
| News Director | 80,000 | 50,000 | 37,000 | 28,000 |
| News Reporter | 50,000 | 41,000 | 30,000 | 33,000 |
| News Producer | 44,000 | 45,000 | 36,500 | * |
| News Anchor | 60,800 | 43,000 | 35,000 | 27,500 |
| Sports Anchor | * | 30,000 | 32,500 | 30,000 |
| Sports Reporter | * | * | 25,000 | 28,000 |
| Web Prod/Ed | 36,000 | 49,000 | 37,500 | 29,500 |

### SALARIES FOR RADIO NEWS PERSONNEL

| Position | Average ($) | Median ($) | Minimum ($) | Maximum ($) |
|---|---|---|---|---|
| All Radio News | 28,100 | 27,000 | 15,000 | 45,000 |
| News Reporter | 29,900 | 28,000 | 15,000 | 45,000 |
| General News | 25,800 | 25,000 | 18,000 | 35,000 |
| News Anchor | 26,400 | 26,000 | 20,000 | 35,000 |
| News Director | 25,600 | 25,000 | 18,000 | 35,000 |
| Producer | 32,000 | 28,500 | 25,000 | 42,000 |

Unlike a print journalist, a radio newsperson must also be a performer. In addition to good writing and newsgathering skills, the newsperson in radio must have announcing abilities. Again, training is usually essential, says Smith:

> Not only must a radio newsperson be able to write a story, but he or she has to be able to present it on the air. You have to be an announcer, too. It takes both training and experience to become a really effective newscaster. Voice performance courses can provide a foundation.

Most colleges with broadcasting programs offer announcing and newscasting instruction.

Entry-level news positions pay modestly, whereas newspeople at metro-market stations earn impressive incomes. With experience come the better-paying jobs. Finding that first full-time news position often takes patience and determination. Several options are available for individuals searching for jobs in the industry such as *Broadcasting & Cable* or the RTDNA's website, which offers daily feature content along with a daily newsletter for members. Also, sites such as YouTube serve as fertile places for advice on how to get a job in broadcasting. Tim Scheld's advice can be found on YouTube.

Radio station websites are the primary places that stations post job openings, but networking is important to secure the next job. Scheld says:

> All of our jobs are posted on our websites but the importance of networking cannot be overemphasized. If you are looking for work in a major market as a reporter you need to be talking to people who work in that market now and see what kind of help and advice they can provide you in terms of job possibilities. News openings are rare and most managers need to have a good idea of the top candidates for any openings at any given time.

## WHAT IT TAKES TO WORK AT THE BOSTON HERALD CORPORATION

### Jeff Magram

Want to know what it takes to work at the Boston Herald Corporation? "We don't hire many 'just reporters' anymore," said Jeff Magram, COO and CFO of Herald Media Inc:

> You have to write, take pictures, create video, know social media and be able to promote yourself. It's about the quality of the video; do people care if it's not thoroughly edited, or is it about getting the content up? Maybe you could have TV that's a little bit "rougher," maybe you don't need to have those highly polished TV anchors.

Magram hints that "Herald TV" might happen someday. And, "yes, writing is very important—what we stress is credibility and accuracy; it's paramount to us as a company. So you have to have credible sources and vet those sources."

**FIGURE 5.32**
Jeff Magram

---

**Jeff Magram** has more than 20 years of experience in the newspaper and media industry and has been the chief operating officer and CFO of Herald Media since 2001. He oversees the operations of the company and is responsible for the execution of corporate strategy. Magram is also responsible for strategic planning and has led the company through a period of organic and acquisitive growth. During Magram's tenure, Herald Media, once known exclusively as a newspaper company, has developed into a multimedia platform distributing content and providing advertising solutions in print, online, on video, and on radio. Herald Media is a multimedia company that owns and operates the *Boston Herald* newspaper, the second largest newspaper in terms of circulation in New England, bostonherald.com, a suite of online classified advertising websites (jobfind.com, homefind.com, and carfind.com), and Boston Herald Radio.

# ORGANIZING THE NEWSCAST AND OTHER PROGRAMMING ELEMENTS

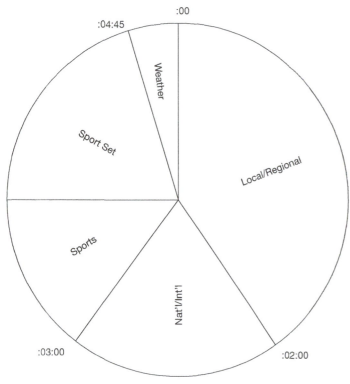

**FIGURE 5.33**
Five-minute newscast format clock

News on music-oriented radio stations is commonly presented in five-minute blocks and aired at the top or bottom of the hour. During drive time periods, stations often increase the length and/or frequency of newscasts. The five minutes allotted to news is generally divided into segments to accommodate the presentation of specific information. A station may establish a format that allows for two minutes of local and regional stories, one minute for key national and international stories, one minute for sports, and 15 seconds for weather information. A 30- or 60-second commercial break will be counted as part of the five-minute newscast.

The number of stories in a newscast may be preordained by program management or may vary depending on the significance and scope of the stories being reported. News policy may require that no stories, except in particular cases, exceed 15 seconds. Here, the idea is to deliver as many stories as possible in the limited time available, the underlying sentiment being that more is better. In five minutes, 15–20 items may be covered. In contrast, other stations prefer that key stories be addressed in greater detail. As few as five to 10 news items may be broadcast at stations taking this approach.

Stories are arranged according to their rank of importance, the most significant story of the hour topping the news. An informed newsperson will know what stories deserve the most attention. Wire services weigh each story and position them accordingly in news roundups. The local radio newsperson decides what wire stories will be aired and in what order.

News and talk formats rely on program clocks to impose structure on program elements and establish pacing. News stations use key format elements to maintain ratings through the hour. Many all-news stations work their clocks in 20-minute cycles. During this segment, news is arranged according to its degree of importance and geographic relevance, such as local, regional, national, and international. Most news stations lead with their top local stories. News stories of particular interest are repeated during the segment. Sports, weather, and other news-related information, such as traffic and stock market reports, constitute a part of the segment. Elements may be juggled around or different ones inserted during successive 20-minute blocks to keep things from sounding repetitious.

Assembling a five-minute newscast takes skill, speed, and accuracy. Stories must be updated and rewritten to keep news broadcasts from sounding stale. This often requires that telephone calls be made for late-breaking information. Meanwhile, on-the-scene voicers (actualities) originating from audio news services such as Associated Press or fed by local reporters must be recorded and slotted in the newscast. "Preparing a fresh newscast each hour can put you in mind of what it must have been like to be a contestant on the old game show *Beat the Clock*. A conscientious newsperson is a vision of perpetual motion," observes Cecilia Mason.

In the talk format, two-way conversation and interviews fill the space generally allotted to songs in the music format. Therefore, talk wheels often resemble music wheels in their structure. For example, news is offered at the top of the hour, followed by a talk sweep that precedes a spot set. This is done in a fashion that is reminiscent of the easy listening format presentation. Of course, not all stations arrange their sound hours as depicted in these pages. Many news and talk format variations exist.

FIGURE 5.34
A top market news station offers a profile of itself
Source: Courtesy of Infinity

**WBZ NEWS RADIO 1030**

1170 SOLDIERS FIELD ROAD  BOSTON  MASSACHUSETTS  02134   TELEPHONE (617) 787-7000

## WBZ NewsRadio 1030

**A BRIEF DESCRIPTION**

*WBZ NewsRadio, the first commercially licensed station in the country, has been broadcasting to New Englanders for almost 80 years. Our award winning coverage has earned WBZ many honors including 2000's "News Station of the Year," from the Associated Press, and three recent Marconi Awards, "The Most Prestigious Radio Award Available."*

 WBZ has close to a million listeners weekly. The exclusive all news format creates a foreground listening environment, that delivers results for our advertisers.

 Our award winning news anchors and reporters have an aggregate experience level of over 100+ years in broadcasting!

 Our combined resources of both radio and television make up the largest news gathering organization in New England. Many of our radio anchors gain exposure daily on WBZ-TV 4 adding to their tremendous popularity.

 WBZ highlights advertisers' messages by airing commercials as islands surrounded by news, traffic, weather or business reports. During our news, your commercial is always the first and only sixty second commercial in a commercial break.

 WBZ's 50,000 watt clear channel signal reaches all of New England, and at night 38 states and six Canadian Providences. Our reach is unparalleled!

 We maintain a 52 week marketing campaign promoting ourselves on TV, print, web, and at countless on-site events throughout New England.

 WBZ is a leader in community involvement spearheading many events including Children's Hospital Telethon and fundraising, Call for Action, Domestic Violence and StormCenter.

 WBZ is the flagship station for the Boston Bruins and the Boston Bruins Radio Network and the only place fans can catch every game every time they play.

## HOW DO YOU CREATE THAT SPECIAL CONNECTION BETWEEN STATION AND LISTENER?

### Tim Scheld

The bond between listener and radio station is something that takes years, even decades to develop. The foundation of that bond is trust developed over time with consistent performance. The goal is to deliver a product or service that will keep them coming back for more. For a news radio brand, it's not just about having what people need; it's about how the information is conveyed. There needs to be honesty and authenticity. That comes with having news personalities who can connect with listeners. We don't put on any airs—we are real people. We laugh at a good joke, we get mad at higher tolls, we hurt when communities we cover see pain and violence. We are not just providing news to our

FIGURE 5.35
Tim Scheld

community; we are members of the community delivering news, and hopefully that comes through in what we say, how we say it, even in the questions we ask.

Part of our mission is also staying connected to the community, and understanding the responsibility of being a voice for the people in that community. First and foremost, I think it's important to have a presence in the places you cover, and not just visit them in times of tragedy. That can be a challenge when you consider that in our Tri-State area we have hundreds of municipalities. We also take seriously our responsibility to tell stories about the tremendous good going on across our listening area. These stories are the ones that provoke the most reaction and lead to new connections and new story ideas. It's also important to build partnerships with local organizations such as the Tunnel to Towers Foundation, the New York March of Dimes, WHY Hunger, the Special Olympics, and the 9/11 National Museum. We partner with these organizations to help them have a positive impact on our community.

Over five decades of delivering all-news at WCBS 880 in New York our radio has built a loyal following where listeners have passed on the radio station experience to their children and children's children. But we are also mindful that to stay relevant we need to make sure we serve the needs of these new generations of listeners and part of that mission is to make sure our content is available everywhere they are. These days if we are not delivering our news on multiple platforms including; on air, online, and on social media in audio, video, and photos we cannot hope to be successful going forward. Our on-air slogans sum it all up—"When you need to know, we've got you covered," and "Everywhere you are, we are."

---

**Tim Scheld** is Director of News and Programming at New York's WCBS Newsradio 880, a job he has held since October 2003. Prior to becoming a news manager, Scheld spent 20 years working as a local radio reporter in New York City at both WOR-710AM and then WCBS Newsradio 880. In 1994, Scheld was hired as a national correspondent for ABC News Radio, where he worked until he left to take the News Director position at WCBS-AM. He was part of the 2001 Peabody Award–winning coverage from ABC News of the September 11 attacks and has won numerous awards for his reporting from organizations such as the RTDNA, the New York Press Club, and the New York State Associated Press Broadcasters. Scheld is a Member of the Board of Directors of the RTDNA representing the NY–NJ–PA region. WCBS Newsradio 880 was the winner of the NAB's 2017 Marconi Award for Legendary Radio Station.

**FIGURE 5.36**
The WCBS 880 studio in New York

Source: Courtesy of WCBS-AM, New York. Photo Credit Martin Untrojb

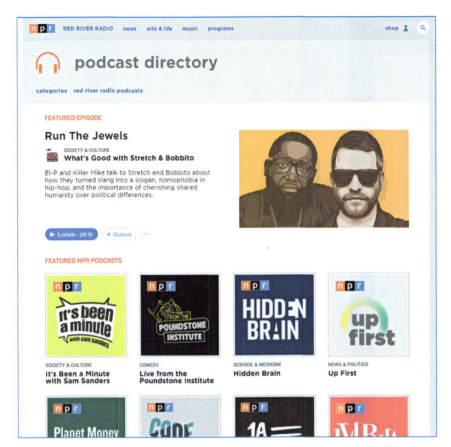

FIGURE 5.37
The use of podcasts continues to grow
Source: Courtesy of NPR

Finally, most newspeople read their news copy before going on the air. "Reading stories cold is foolhardy and invites trouble. Even the most seasoned newscasters at metro market stations take the time to read over their copy before going on," comments Whitman. Many newspeople read copy aloud in the news studio before airtime. This gives them a chance to get a feel for their copy. Proper preparation prevents unpleasant surprises from occurring while on the air.

## WIRE SERVICES—AUDIO AND INTERNET

Without the aid of the major broadcast news wire service (Associated Press), blogs, social media (Twitter, Facebook), and the inestimable number of news-oriented websites and television network news channels that exist (CNN, MSNBC, Fox, Drudge Report, Politico, Huffington Post, etc.), radio stations would find it almost impossible to cover news on national and international levels. Indeed, wire service, Internet, and television are vital sources of news information to nearly all of the nation's commercial radio stations.

Both large and small stations rely on the news copy fed to them by the Associated Press (AP), considered by many in the industry to be a well-respected news wire service. In the AP's *2016 Annual Report*, it was noted that the AP received its fifty-second Pulitzer Prize and had a global reach of 106 countries. It staffed news bureaus in all 50 U.S. state houses and more than 263 locations worldwide. Impressively, it provides more than 2,000 news stories a day, with 9.4 million Twitter followers, 456,200 Facebook likes, and 2.6 million YouTube views. Farley says:

> I believe you need at least some of the resources from Associated Press to compete well. There are plenty of online and social media outlets from which to get news, but (a) which ones can you trust and (b) are you stealing somebody else's intellectual property?

The AP offers digital news packages that can be uploaded to radio station websites or shared via social media such as Twitter and Facebook. Associated Press's website states:

> AP can provide breaking news and information directly to your audiences via your internal and external websites, desktops, wireless services and other interactive applications. Our extensive suite of services spans more than 30 categories of industry-targeted content to fit your digital needs.

In 2012, the Spanish Broadcasting System (SBS) announced that 10 of its Spanish-language stations would offer Associated Press's Spanish Online Newsfeed on their websites. "Our partnership brings the most trusted news source to our U.S. Hispanic online audience in Spanish. Multiple content verticals, like news, sports, entertainment, etc., are great additions to our network of sites," said SBS vice-president of digital sales Andrew Polsky, in an *All Access* interview.

The audio cuts provided by the AP news service are an integral part of many station newscasts. Radio scholar Larry Miller observes:

> When these audio clips are sent to subscribing stations, they will also send along a menu which will list the type of cut (A-actuality, V-voicer, or W-wrap), who it is, what it's about, how long it runs, and the outcue.

Miller cautions that audio cuts should be used sparingly:

> They should not be overused to pad out a newscast. Relevance, audio quality, and length should rule the decisions regarding how much audio to use. With the proper application of these sources, even a one-person news operation can sound like a big city newsroom.

The wire service is only one means of news gathering for radio stations. Scheld asserts:

> Wire services are just part of the equation in the modern newsroom. The Internet has become an enormous and invaluable resource providing quick access to everything from maps to public records. Social media has also emerged as an important resource with many newsrooms using tools like TweetDeck to develop news tips into news stories. TweetDeck has become more important than the police scanner in our newsroom.

**FIGURE 5.38**

Associated Press web page listing services to its radio affiliates

Source: Courtesy of the Associated Press

FIGURE 5.39
Twitter is used by most radio news stations to disseminate information

Source: Courtesy of Twitter.com

**FIGURE 5.40**
TweetDeck is a common tool used by news stations to disseminate information

Source: Courtesy of Twitter.com

From 1958 to 1999, United Press International (UPI) also provided wire service and audio to radio stations via the UPI Radio Network, but it ceased its operation in 1999. Broadcast wire services came into existence in the mid-1930s, when UP (which became UPI in 1958 after merging with INS) began providing broadcasters with news copy.

# RADIO NETWORK NEWS AND SYNDICATOR SERVICES

During the medium's first three decades, the terms *networks* and *news* were virtually synonymous. Most of the news broadcast over America's radio stations emanated from the networks. The public's dependence on network radio news reached its height during World War II. As television succeeded radio as the mainstay for entertainment programming in the 1950s and 1960s, the networks concentrated their efforts on supplying affiliates with news and information feeds. This approach helped the networks regain their footing in radio after a period of substantial decline. By the mid-1960s, the majority of the nation's stations used one of the four major networks for news programming.

In 1968, ABC decided to make available four distinct news formats designed for compatibility with the dominant sounds of the day. American Contemporary Radio Network, American FM Radio Network, American Entertainment Radio Network, and American Information Network each offered a unique style and method of news presentation. ABC's venture proved enormously successful. In the 1970s,

**FIGURE 5.41**
ABC Radio offers its subscribers a wide array of services to deliver news, music, website content, photos, and live streaming

Source: © 2017 American Broadcasting Companies Inc.

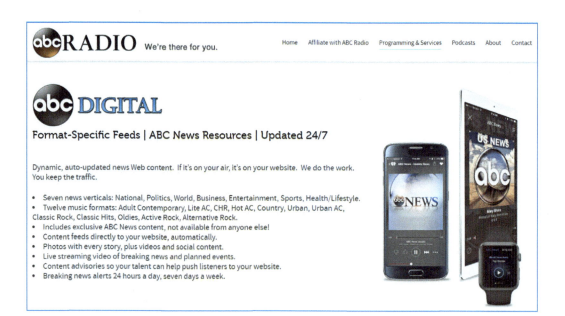

more than 1,500 stations subscribed to one of ABC's four news networks. To this day, ABC News Radio remains one of the largest radio news services in the United States and offers multiple services to its affiliates and subscribers.

In addition to the national radio news services, several state and regional news networks do well, but the big three, ABC, NBC, and CBS, continue to dominate. Meanwhile, independent satellite news and information networks and the cable news services, such as CNN, have joined the field.

According to Metro Network President David Saperstein, today

> more and more stations are realizing the benefits that exist in outside news services, which provide the information that listeners would otherwise seek elsewhere. This allows the station to focus its marketing dollars, thus directing resources toward optimizing and maintaining what draws and keeps listeners.

Of course, this latter trend has raised additional concerns about the decline in local news coverage as cited in recent RTDNA surveys. Station consolidations have resulted in the erosion of local news operations.

The popularity in radio news listening can be attributed to a number of things, but the fact that radio news does it so thoroughly and professionally at the global, national, and local levels is among the primary reasons that Steve Jones, Vice-President and General Manager of ABC Radio News, thinks new listeners are flocking to the format. Jones says:

> 93% of Americans listen to broadcast radio each week and news radio is a key driver of that listening. The most successful news and talk stations have local news departments that cover their communities. These stations turn to network news providers such as ABC News for national and international coverage, context and insight.

ABC News Radio has a dedicated team of reporters in New York City, Washington, D.C., Chicago, Dallas, Los Angeles, and London and all journalists hired by ABC News are trained to report for radio and ensure that ABC News Radio is covered on each assignment. Jones adds:

> Beyond the ABC News staff, our affiliate reporters at both the 1,650 radio stations and over 200 TV stations contribute to ABC News Radio each day. This results in over 400 pieces of audio created daily. Our most important service to these stations is crisis coverage.

ABC News Radio is on the scene for breaking news wherever it may occur. In this regard, Jones also says,

> When major news breaks, ABC News Radio provides ongoing coverage. For example, when hurricanes Irma and Harvey hit the U.S. in 2017, ABC News Radio provided up to 14-hours of continuous coverage so that radio stations could pre-empt their local programming and take ABC News coverage to fit their individual program needs. Our coverage is led by a radio anchor with reporters in the field. This coverage includes live interviews with officials, experts and eyewitnesses. We use social media to identify people making news and then find those people and interview them live.

Further, Jones shares,

> ABC Radio produces news, entertainment and sports audio programming for radio stations. As of late 2017, ABC Radio's content was heard on more than 1,650 U.S. stations as well as across Canada and globally through the Armed Forces Radio Network. You also can hear ABC News Radio on multiple digital audio apps and platforms. ABC Radio's primary service is ABC News.

News coverage is another form of program content to which the syndication model of distribution has been applied with success. GRNlive was initially established as Global Radio News in the late 1990s. The organization embraced the Internet as a marketplace for news audio collection and distribution. CEO Henry Peirse described its early days in terms of its approach, which differed from similar organizations. GRN, he explained, was "more than rip and read with clips on subscription." Rather, it was:

> a pay as you use international news service with content supplied by a vast network of freelance reporters all over the world. The idea was to give radio stations freedom to create news bulletins to suit their audience and use the Internet as the marketing, delivery and sales tool.

Peirse continues:

> When the first Internet bubble burst in the early 2000s, GRN reconstituted itself to act as a management network for freelance reporters globally. Over the years they used the technology they pioneered as a distributor for a wide variety of radio and audio clients. But the business now is the network of reporters who can provide live interviews, audio, research, video, stills, fixing and anything else a news publisher or broadcaster (radio and TV) might need in an age of depleted newsroom resources.

He describes GRNlive as an organization that achieves the efficiencies of networked newsgathering operations yet requires no agency subscription in order to participate. "Arguably," he says, this approach is "still ahead of its time but the model fits into the existing schematic of newsrooms and is growing into the new world of information publishers, be they brand name broadcasters or influential websites."

What is the difference between a network and a syndicator? Phil Barry explains:

> There's no practical difference between the two, at least not as far as the public is concerned. The "network" designation stems from the old, what we used to call "wired" networks like ABC, CBS, (full service offerings, etc.) of the day, as opposed to standalone shows, or services. Nowadays, within the industry, the differentiation is more likely a reference to whether the commercial inventory is sold inside, or outside of RADAR [the Nielsen-provided network radio measurement service]. . . . From an advertising sales perspective, "network" often refers to inventory sold as part of a RADAR grouping, and inventory not part of RADAR is referred to as sold in "syndication." Nonetheless, there isn't a hard and fast definition that applies in every case. WestwoodOne, for example, refers to itself as a "network," but some of the shows are sold in "syndication."

**FIGURE 5.42**

GRNlive: A nonsubscription, alternative approach to the network-distribution model for gathering and distributing news internationally

Source: Courtesy of Henry Peirse and GRNlive

## NEWS IN MUSIC RADIO

In the 1980s, the FCC saw fit to eliminate the requirement that all radio stations devote a percentage of their broadcast day to news and public affairs programming. Opponents of the decision argued that such a move would mark the decline of news on radio. In contrast, proponents of the deregulation commended the FCC's actions that allowed for the marketplace to determine the extent to which nonentertainment features are broadcast. In the late 1980s, RTDNA expressed the concern that local news coverage had declined. This, they said, had resulted in a decrease in the number of news positions around the country. Supporting their contention they pointed out that several major stations, such as KDKA, WOWO, and WIND, had cut back their news budgets.

But WCRN News Director Sherman Whitman believes that the radio audience wants news even when a station's primary product is music: "The public has come to depend on the medium to keep it informed. It's a volatile world and certain events affect us all. Stations that aim to be full service cannot do so without a solid news schedule."

"Responsible broadcasters know that it is the inherent duty of the medium to keep the public apprised of what is going on," claims Larry Jewett:

> While radio is primarily an entertainment medium, it is still one of the country's foremost sources of information. Responsible broadcasters—and most of us are—realize that we have a special obligation to fulfill. The tremendous reach and immediacy that is unique to radio forces the medium to be something more than just a jukebox.

News Director Frank Titus believes that stations will continue to broadcast news in the future:

> There might be a tendency to invest less in news operations, especially at more music-oriented outlets, as the result of the regulation change and rampant consolidations, but news is as much a part of what radio is as are the deejays and songs. What it comes right down to is people want news broadcasts, so they're going to get them. That's the whole idea behind the commission's actions. There's no doubt in my mind that the marketplace will continue to dictate the programming of radio news.

News Director Roger Nadel concurs:

> As the age of the average listener increases, even people tuning in to "music" stations find themselves in need of at least minimal doses of news. So long as those stations are doing well financially, owners can be content to maintain some kind of a news operation. News is not likely to disappear; not even at music stations.

Competition from the wave of new audio services has also influenced the role of news in terrestrial radio.

## NEWS/TALK/INFORMATION

Not long after KCBS in San Francisco began its all-news programming, another Bay City station, KGO-AM, introduced the hybrid news/talk/information format in which news shares the microphone with conversation and interview features. Over the years, this hybrid format has caught on and leads the pure all-news format in popularity. According to Nielsen, the news/talk/information format is the fifth most listened to format among 25- to 54-year-olds, it is the tenth most listened to format for 18- to 34-year-olds, and it is the number one most listened to format when looking at the demographics of all listeners aged six years old and older.

The news/talk/information format combines extensive news coverage with blocks of programming devoted to the airing of telephone and studio interviews. These stations commonly "daypart" or segmentalize their programming by presenting lengthened newscasts during morning and afternoon

### Top 10 Radio Formats

read as: from January-November 2016, 9.6% of US radio listeners in PPM markets aged 6+
were tuned to a News/Talk station during any 15-minute period during the day

#### in 2016

| | Persons 6+ share | | | Persons 18-34 Share | | | Persons 25-54 Share | |
|---|---|---|---|---|---|---|---|---|
| Rank | Format | Share | Rank | Format | Share | Rank | Format | Share |
| 1 | News Talk Information | 9.6% | 1 | Pop Contemporary Hit Radio (CHR) | 12.2% | 1 | Pop Contemporary Hit Radio (CHR) | 8.8% |
| 2 | Pop Contemporary Hit Radio (CHR) | 8.1% | 2 | Country* | 8.6% | 2 | Country* | 7.3% |
| 3 | Adult Contemporary (AC) | 7.5% | 3 | Hot Adult Contemporary (AC) | 7.3% | 3 | Adult Contemporary (AC) | 7.1% |
| 4 | Country* | 7.4% | 4 | Urban Contemporary | 6.6% | 4 | Hot Adult Contemporary (AC) | 7.0% |
| 5 | Hot Adult Contemporary (AC) | 6.4% | 5 | Adult Contemporary (AC) | 6.5% | 5 | News Talk Information | 6.9% |
| 6 | Classic Hits | 5.3% | 6 | Rhythmic Contemporary Hit Radio (CHR) | 5.1% | 6 | Classic Rock | 5.4% |
| 7 | Classic Rock | 5.1% | t7 | Mexican Regional | 5.0% | 7 | All Sports | 5.3% |
| 8 | Urban Adult Contemporary (AC) | 4.8% | t7 | Alternative | 5.0% | 8 | Classic Hits | 4.7% |
| 9 | All Sports | 4.7% | 9 | Classic Rock | 4.5% | 9 | Urban Adult Contemporary (AC) | 4.6% |
| t10 | Mexican Regional | 3.7% | 10 | News Talk Information | 4.1% | 10 | Mexican Regional | 4.5% |
| t10 | Urban Contemporary | 3.7% | | | | | | |

*\* Country is a combination of Country and New Country formats*

**MarketingCharts.com | Data Source: Nielsen**

**FIGURE 5.43**

The news/talk/
information format
is very popular
among all age
groups

Source: Courtesy of
Nielsen

drive time hours and conversation in the midday and evening periods. The format's core base of listeners is better educated; today, three of every four listeners is university-educated. In markets measured by Nielsen's Portable People Meters (PPM), news/talk/information is one of the leading formats and is in the top 10 most listened-to formats.

Thanks in part to the fragmentation of the "news" and "talk" franchises, the number of outlets has grown consistently for more than three decades. In the late 1990s, over 1,000 stations offered the information and/or news format. This was up nearly 300% since the late 1980s. In 2011, it was estimated that almost 1,800 stations specialized in the talk format. More than 100 stations alone concentrated on sports exclusively, and dozens of others were beginning to splinter and compartmentalize into news/info niches, such as auto, health, computer, food, business, tourism, and entertainment.

National talk networks and syndicated talk shows, mostly of a conservative nature, continued to draw huge audiences in the new millennium, as more and more baby boomers became engaged in the political and social dialogues of the day. Despite the fact that a liberal talk radio network (Air America) debuted in the 2000s, the service faltered; its reception was anything but stellar. Right-wing hosts (Rush Limbaugh being king among them) continued to rule the genre.

An indication that the news/talk/information format is achieving equality in the balance of conservative and liberal viewpoints in the new media environment emerged during the 2012 presidential election campaign. During that campaign, one report about a study of listener patterns concluded that users streamed content labeled "liberal" almost two-to-one over "conservative" programming.

The news/talk/information format has expanded to satellite radio, too. SiriusXM offers almost 10 stations from which subscribers can choose. They range from entertainment information that focuses on pop culture with Bravo TV's Andy Cohen to medical information covering topics that range from sexual health to sports medicine to psychiatry. The SiriusXM channel lineup is impressive.

---

**SIRIUSXM TALK/
ENTERTAINMENT FULL
CHANNEL LINEUP**

Radio Andy

Faction Talk

Entertainment Weekly Radio

VOLUME

TODAY Radio Show

SiriusXM Stars

Doctor Radio

Business Radio

**FIGURE 5.44**

The SiriusXM channel lineup boasts
eight talk/entertainment radio stations
from which its 32 million subscribers
may choose

Source: Retrieved from www.siriusxm.com/
channellineup

## FM TALK

Although it is not recognized within the industry as a format descriptor per se, the approach adopted by FM stations to the presentation of information differs significantly enough from AM news/talk to warrant its own discussion. The growing presence of FM talk is perhaps the most unique manifestation in nonmusic radio. This approach reflects industry awareness of the Millennial and Gen Z generation audience, persons who likely came of age as radio listeners after music formats had migrated from the AM band to FM and Internet streaming. The exchange of music for talk on FM dispels the long-held belief that the high-fidelity requirements for music reproduction necessitated its placement on FM, relegating talk programming to AM radio with its low-fidelity performance capabilities. Talent consultant Jason Insalaco gives his perspective on the rise of the *discourse* format on what has always been the dial for music:

> While traditional AM talk has been profiled in recent years for its explosion onto the radio landscape, FM talk radio has become a popular format for an audience previously ignored by talk programmers. FM talk's primary audience is 25–44 years old. This demographic likely did not grow up listening to AM talk radio. In fact, the FM talk audience has very likely tuned to AM very little during its lifetime. FM talk does not program itself like a traditional full-service AM talk outlet. There is not the emphasis on news and traffic, which is a staple of the AM talkers.

FM talk is inherently personality-driven both by nationally syndicated talkers such as Glenn Beck, Stephanie Miller, and Michael Smerconish and by a host of local talents. News and political discussion find their way into FM talk but the main focus is on entertainment and lifestyle. Insalaco adds:

> FM talk programs itself more like an FM music station than an AM talk station. It features shorter segments covering a variety of issues in contrast to the one-hour AM talk sweep. Issues discussed typically come from sources like *Rolling Stone* and *People* magazine and the local sports and entertainment sections of the newspaper. Topics are not necessarily caller intensive as with most AM talkers. Listener participation is a part of FM talk radio; however, there is not the typical topic-monologue-caller participation cycle of AM talkers. Moreover, the "bumper music" played to intro segments of FM talk comes from the latest alternative and rock artists found on the competing music stations. This gives the station a youthful sound and grabs the potential talk listener who is scanning the dial. FM talk's competition comes from Alternative/Modern Rock/AOR and Classic Rock stations. The future of FM talk looks bright. Expect the format to become more widespread in the coming years.

Clearly, the number of FM talk outlets in major markets is on the increase. While ratings for stations in the top 10 markets typically amount to about half of those earned by heritage AM talkers, FM talkers continue to trend upward and attract saleable and typically younger listeners.

**FIGURE 5.45**
98.7 FM ESPN is an all-sports radio station in New York

Source: Courtesy of 98.7 FM ESPN, New York

## RADIO SPORTSCASTS AND ALL-SPORTS FORMAT

Sports is most commonly presented as an element within newscasts. Although many stations air sports as programming features unto themselves, most stations insert information, such as scores and schedules of upcoming games, at a designated point in a newscast and call it sports. Whether a station emphasizes sports largely depends on its audience. Stations gearing their format for younger demographics or women often all but ignore sports. Adult-oriented stations will frequently offer a greater abundance of sports information, especially when the station is located in an area that has a major league team.

Stations that hire individuals to do sports—and invariably these are larger outlets since few small stations can afford a full-time sportsperson—look for someone who is well-versed in the subject. Former radio sports director John Colletto contends:

To be good at radio sports, you have to have been involved as a participant somewhere along the line. That's for starters, in my opinion. This doesn't mean that you have to be a former major leaguer before doing radio sports but to have a feel for what you're talking about, it certainly helps to have been on the field or court yourself. A good sportscaster must have the ability to accurately analyze a sport through the eyes and body of the athlete.

Unlike news, which requires an impartial and somewhat austere presentation, sportscasts are frequently delivered in a casual and even opinionated manner. Colletto says:

Let's face it, there's a big difference between nuclear arms talks between the United States and the Soviets and last night's Red Sox/Yankees score. I don't think sports reports should be treated in a style that's too solemn. It's entertainment, and sportscasters should exercise their license to comment and analyze.

Although sports is presented in a less heavy-handed way than news, credibility is an important factor, contends Colletto:

There is a need for radio sportscasters to establish credibility just as there is for newspeople to do so. If you're not believable, you're not listened to. The best way to win the respect of your audience is by demonstrating a thorough knowledge of the game and by sounding like an insider, not just a guy reading the wire copy. Remember, sports fans can be as loyal to a sportscaster as they are to their favorite team. They want to hear the stories and scores from a person they feel comfortable with.

The style of a news story and a sports story may differ considerably. Although news is written in a no-frills, straightforward way, sports stories often contain colorful colloquialisms and even popular slang. Here is an example by radio sportswriter Roger Crosley:

The Dean College Red Demon football team rode the strong running of fullback Bill Palazollo yesterday to an 18–16 come-from-behind victory over the American International College Junior Varsity Yellow Jackets. Palazollo churned out a team high 93 yards on 25 carries and scored all three touchdowns on blasts of 7, 2, and 6 yards. The demons trailed the hard-hitting contest 16–6 entering the final quarter. Palazollo capped a 12-play 81-yard drive with his second six-pointer early in the stanza and scored the clincher with 4:34 remaining. The demons will put their 1 and 0 record on the line next Sunday at 1:30 against the always tough holy cross jayvees in Worcester.

**FIGURE 5.46**
An inside look at the 98.7 ESPN studio during The Michael Kay Show as Don La Greca (center) and Peter Rosenberg (left) speak with NY baseball great Darryl Strawberry

Source: Courtesy of ESPN 98.7 FM

**FIGURE 5.47**
One of the ESPN 98.7 New York studios from the perspective of the host. The computer (center left) uses a program called Wide Orbit to control the mic and facilitate communication between the talent and the studio as well as allows the talent to choose from a library of sound bites also known as "drops" to add some fun to the show. The mini-mixer to the left is used by the host to communicate with the studio during network shows

Source: Courtesy of ESPN 98.7 FM

Sportscasters are personalities, says Colletto, and as such must be able to communicate on a different level than newscasters. "You're expected to have a sense of humor. Most successful sportscasters can make an audience smile or laugh. You have to be able to ad-lib, also."

The wire services, networks, and Internet are the primary source for sports news at local stations. On the other hand, information about the outcome of local games, such as high school football and so forth, must be acquired firsthand. This usually entails a call to the team's coach or a direct report from a stringer or reporter.

## SIRIUSXM ALL-SPORTS FULL CHANNEL LINEUP

ESPN Radio

ESPN Xtra

Mad Dog Sports Radio

FOX Sports

ESPNU

SiriusXM FC

SiriusXM NFL Radio

SiriusXM Nascar Radio

SiriusXM NHL Network Radio

SiriusXM Rush

**FIGURE 5.48**
The SiriusXM channel lineup boasts 10 all-sports radio stations from which its subscribers may choose

Source: Retrieved from www.siriusxm.com/channellineup

In addition to radio stations that broadcast sportscasts throughout the day, there are stations that have adopted an all-sports format. The trend in the last few years in the proliferation of the all-sports format has boosted the popularity of nonmusic radio and significantly contributed to the dominance of "chatter" radio in the ratings. Propelling the trend are the new entrants into sports radio networking, including the 2013 launches of "major league" broadcasters CBS Sports Network and NBC Sports Radio. ESPN, the dominant brand in sports media content, distributes programming to more than 700 stations, including more than 350 full-time affiliates. Fox Sports Radio and Yahoo!/Gow (formerly Sporting News Radio) also make the starter's list, ensuring that the 2010s is the format's most competitive decade.

In fact, AM radio is able to claim a younger demographic because men aged 18 to 29 years are big fans of sports radio. Overall listenership is well-distributed across all demographics, helping the format to become one of radio's top 10 most listened-to format in 2016, coming in at the ninth most listened to format. Among listeners who are 25 to 54 years old, all-sports is the seventh most listened-to format. Male listeners outnumber females and they tend to be more affluent and better educated than radio audiences in general. Meanwhile, all-sports has begun to migrate to both FM and satellite radio in significant numbers. The SiriusXM channel lineup provides its 32 million subscribers with a varied selection of all-sports stations for listeners to hear information/updates about the sport of their choice or simply listen to games that range from hockey to football to auto racing.

A 2015 *Sports Illustrated* article about sports radio formats notes that podcasts are swiftly gaining listeners. ESPN Audio, also offered on TuneIn (which expands its reach), is the nation's largest sports network and attracts 60% of sports listeners.

ESPN Audio averages more than 20 million listeners a week, with 80% being males. The all-sports format and, especially ESPN Audio, is also attempting to increase its share of female listeners.

Traug Keller, ESPN Senior Vice-President, notes that audio streaming is becoming much more popular among all listeners:

> I will tell you that the report card, which are the numbers, is very good. What is particularly good is our growth in streaming. You cannot just look at Arbitron and now Nielsen numbers. You need to look at the streaming numbers as well and that as a report card is we are doing well. I'd say given what we are getting back in terms of demo information and audio information, it is good. The weekend is a place for us to kind of bring people in and give them a chance and hopefully that is our bench. Honestly, there is a lack of female on-air talent. It's a market issue. We are really doubling down on that. Women are increasingly more and more sports fans and they are underserved. There is growth there. Hispanics are underserved. There is a real opportunity there.

In terms of audio streaming, to which Keller alludes, PodcastOne Sports, which debuted in September 2017, was the latest sports programming venture to be offered up for listeners. In *Talkers* magazine, Norm Pattiz, who is the Executive Chairman of PodcastOne, said, "This network demonstrates PodcastOne's interest in dramatically expanding our already successful portfolio of sports-related programming to build a singular hub for sports fans and brands." Sports programming definitely has a solid base of very loyal, mostly male, listeners. The late Ed Shane, a radio consultant, makes this observation regarding the success of the format:

**FIGURE 5.49**
PodcastOne
Sports logo

Source: Courtesy
of PodcastOne and
Norm Pattiz

> The element of "guy talk" is an important factor and one of the central ingredients that gives this format its special appeal. For our client stations, I define sports radio as "beer, babes, and ball," and not always in that order.

## STATION WEBSITES, PODCASTS, AND SOCIAL MEDIA

Every radio station maintains a website and social media platforms such as Twitter and Facebook, and almost all provide podcasts for listeners to have access to constant programming. Websites and podcasts also expand revenue generating opportunities. Each are additional marketing tools and they provide listeners with a digital extension of their on-air signals, because so many people sit in front of their computers at work and at home for countless hours. Indeed, a station website is not only for listening but it is also a visual component of a radio station, a means of giving more sight to a once-sightless medium. As consultant Ed Shane said it,

> Social networks add an element radio has long coveted: a screen. Posting pictures via Instagram or videos via YouTube allows the audience to share the experience of an event, a live broadcast or a celebrity interview. YouTube expands from the station's network of "followers" to the world.

Says Ressen Design/Radeo Internet Radio's Darryl Pomicter: "Websites complement all terrestrial broadcast systems, supplementing and expanding content. They give stations reach they never had before—locally, nationally, and globally."

Station websites hold great value for program directors (PDs) for three vastly different reasons, contends Matt Grasso, WIZN/WBTZ Operations Manager:

> First off, P1s [*first preference*, the dedicated listeners] spend a lot of time with your radio station, and the website is a way to keep things fresh and exciting for them. Games, exclusive Web-only promotions, staff blogs and bios all provide an exclusive, behind the scenes look at the product. Next, time spent listening (TSL) drives the ratings bus and your online broadcast boosts it. There are a lot of people who are procrastinating at work. Plug them into your station. Give them lifestyle news and information and watch your TSL rise. And finally, the website constitutes new inventory. You can clutter your airwaves with so much stuff. Your website is a new place to do business.

Station websites come in all shapes and sizes. That is to say, they can be simple, offering a limited number of links, or they can be highly interactive and multi-tiered with dozens of links. Not all sites are constructed as income streams, but more and more radio stations are viewing them as another good source of nontraditional revenue. Adding the iTunes Music Store link to their sites to allow their listeners to purchase the tunes they heard on-air was one of the first attempts to monetize the Internet presence. Emmis was the first station group to do so on its stations in Chicago, Indianapolis, Austin, and St. Louis. In a more recent development, the products of Radio2Video represent the extension of traditional radio activities into nontraditional areas. In this instance, the company notes on its website that it specializes in creating "broadcast quality, high definition video advertising from radio commercials" to assist stations in taking full advantage of the enhancements that color picture and motion lend to advertising messages on stations' sites.

Larger stations and cluster operations typically hire an individual to maintain a station's web presence. This person usually holds a title such as director of digital strategy, services, and/or sales. Content responsibilities are the province of other specialists (digital solutions coordinator or similar title), but they are usually working closely with or under the direction of this individual; together these employees share responsibilities for maintaining the appearance, relevance, and revenue-generating potential of the website, social media, and overall digital plan for the station or the cluster of stations. The growing digital role for radio stations has made it another potential career option for those interested in entering the radio field. Clearly, an applicant for this position should possess a knowledge of graphic arts, social media, and web page design. Additionally, an overall knowledge of radio programming and marketing would be of special value.

**FIGURE 5.50**
Jeremy Sinon

## TURNING THE TITANIC: ONE MAN'S TALE OF DIGITIZING RADIO

### Jeremy Sinon

Radio . . . it's funny, most days I forget I work in radio. In a world full of endless ways to produce, distribute, and consume content, good old-fashioned radio can get lost in the shuffle. Even though I work for a radio company.

Don't get me wrong, radio is the undercurrent of everything we do; it's the reason why we are here at all. But, when I'm in my world, I'm focused on apps, websites, social media, smart speakers, digital dashboards, smart TVs, smart watches and more. I'm looking at all of these things trying to make the best decisions to make sure we are available to our consumers in all the ways they want to consume us.

Radio is how we got here, but where we are going is some place completely different.

As director of digital strategy for Hubbard Radio, I oversee our digital products and initiatives and try to guide the company in the right direction to help keep our brands vibrant and viable in an ever-changing media landscape.

I've worked in radio for over 15 years. It's almost hard for me to believe as I write that. I originally came from a digital background. My career started as a designer in the agency world. I designed websites and software applications for all sorts of different businesses for five years before falling into radio. I came into the industry as someone who knew way more about the digital space than most traditional radio employees. But I knew nothing about radio.

I spent the early years of my radio career butting heads against program directors and marketing directors, begging them to try the things I was talking about. Back then, these were simple things like keeping our websites up to date, building our email databases, and promoting our websites and online streams on the air. Bit-by-bit, month-by-month I would watch as these concepts caught on.

As the years went by the digital mission got more and more complicated and diverse. Things like podcasting, social media, mobile apps, and more came in to play.

There were always naysayers and folks that either didn't want to buy-in, or were too busy focusing elsewhere to worry about our digital growth. After all, the large bulk of our revenue still came from the traditional model (and still does to this day). Fortunately, I was lucky to be in groups with strong, forward thinking management that helped push the digital charge.

As our digital growth continued, so did my professional growth. When I started at Hubbard Radio, running our local digital department in Minneapolis, I was in charge of a two-man department wearing more hats than I could count. When I did eventually move to my new position in corporate, 10 years later, I left my Minneapolis digital department, which had grown to 14 employees. These people consisted of designers, web developers, project managers, social media strategists, videographers and more.

Over my decade in my Minneapolis role we built new products, initiatives, and even a very successful social media services business. We probably redesigned our websites four or five times. We tried different streaming techniques, different social media strategies, standalone web sites, station apps, and more. We tried a lot of things. We succeeded a lot but we had our failures as well. When we failed, we learned and we moved on.

The thing is, we could afford to fail. Thanks to radio, we had a steady business model that was fueling everything we were trying to do. The revenue came in from traditional revenue channels and we invested what we could into our digital growth, even if we couldn't see an immediate payoff.

Sometimes, I think radio people forget what a great advantage we have over the people and companies out there that are trying to disrupt our business. It's hard for a start-up to try things and fail, if they fail they lose money and the sting hurts a lot more. Plus, they don't have built-in audiences that they can motivate to consume whatever the new initiative is. We will succeed if we use these things to our advantage. Basically, just try stuff. Make your best guess and promote the heck out of it.

Now in my corporate role I get to do just that, but on a bigger scale. I'm focused on distribution and consumption of audio in our apps, on smart speakers and beyond. Things that affect all of our stations.

One project that I am most proud of is our streaming platform, a concept that I came up with many years ago while I was still working for the local market. I looked around and saw what a terrible user experience we had in our web-based stream players and mobile apps. Traditionally we had worked with outside vendors to spin up a stream web player and launch a mobile app that we didn't think too much about after it was launched. We basically just checked a box, "Mobile app, done." But, for the end user, the experience was not good. I noticed the opportunity and campaigned aggressively internally for us to take charge of our own destiny. I wanted us to build our own platform, start with web players then design a mobile app that looked, felt, and acted the same. That way, no matter how the listener chose to consume us, the experience would feel the same. We could build in registration and offer up "listener rewards" that rewarded people for how long they listen (kind of like frequent flyer miles).

I pushed this idea for four years; I mocked up interfaces and continually tweaked them and re-presented them to anybody who would listen. Leadership was liking what I was selling but I think the concept was just too big to wrap our heads around. We had never built anything that big before. Hubbard eventually decided to put their faith in me and they gave us a budget to turn the vision into reality.

Long story short, we now have a streaming platform that we are proud of. We have killer apps and our usage numbers are growing by leaps and bounds. I would put our solution up against anybody else's in the industry. But, most importantly, we now have something that we OWN and we can build on top of it.

But just when we think we have everything figured out, along comes the next thing. Podcasting, smart speakers, and digital dashboards pose a threat to fragment audio consumption even more than it currently is. But, where some see threat, the forward thinkers need to see opportunity. The way people consume us may change, but change is ok as long as we are still being consumed.

So, what is "radio" anyway? For me, "radio" is an audio-based business model that reaches consumers through a myriad of different platforms. Whether it's an audio stream on mobile apps, smart speakers, or web sites, entertaining/informative posts on Facebook, Twitter, Snapchat, Instagram, and more, or great content, articles, and blogs on web sites, it's a place that people can consume together as a community and laugh and share and be connected.

Oh yeah, and we have that FM signal thing too . . . I always forget about that.

———————————

**Jeremy Sinon** is the Director of Digital Media strategy for Hubbard Radio, a family-owned broadcasting company based out of Minneapolis/St. Paul. Hubbard Radio owns and operates 41 stations in seven different markets across the United States. Jeremy has led digital for Hubbard Radio for the past 11 years. Before that, Jeremy worked at the Minnespolia iHeartRadio/Clear Channel offices.

Although podcasts were originally designed for downloading content to iPods and MP3 players, radio stations have found them to be a value-added programming feature. Thousands of podcasts are available on the Internet, and most radio stations now offer podcasts of their on-air features on their websites. Some stations have created exclusive, podcast-only programs. Says consultant Jason Insalaco:

Podcasting "exclusives" can drive Internet traffic and increase the time listeners spend on the website. For example, website-exclusive interviews with newsmakers, musical artists, entire unedited press conferences, or even the local high school football game can provide supplemental content for station podcasts. It's a good community service, too.

Matt Grasso adds, "Podcasts are useful to station programming because it's a way to take the station with you." Grasso asserts that programmers generally were skeptical about the value of podcasting. Now, he says, "they realize that they are just another way to get even closer to the listener."

Regarding podcasts, Tim Scheld, News Director of WCBS radio in New York, says:

While podcasting seems to be the shiny new penny of audio content, in reality it has been around for years. So much of what we do gets edited from our over the air pieces that our ability to play or deliver the full interviews we conduct and do so as an on demand extra product makes us more valuable. All of our reporters and anchors participate in this content as on demand audio. We also deliver weekly podcasts on Author Talks, Small Business Interviews, and News on the Rocks. Audio of Demand or longer form interviews appear regularly in a podcast category called 880 Extras. We are fully engaged in podcasting.

**FIGURE 5.51**

The amount of consumers listening to podcasts is quickly growing. ABC Radio created the ABC Podcast Network and offers multiple podcasts for listeners to consume at their leisure

Source: © 2017 American Broadcasting Companies Inc.

Indicating the importance of Facebook and Twitter as prominent elements in the engagement of listeners, NPR Digital issued social media guidelines for its member stations. Shane says, "Be specific about what you want from your audience" and give the audience "a heads up on tomorrow's topics" are examples of NPR directives. The outline reminded hosts that "Your show is on the radio for one or two hours a day; it's online 24/7." Regarding social media and news coverage, Jones says:

[R]adio has embraced social media and is using it to build news brands, expand audience and deepen listener engagement. For ABC News Radio, there is significant demand for our breaking news coverage. When stories are unfolding live on radio, stations build currency with their audience and reaffirm to listeners that radio is the place to turn for immediacy and relevancy. Our affiliates are much more inclined to pre-empt their local programs or syndicated talk shows and run our wall-to-wall coverage when a major news event occurs.

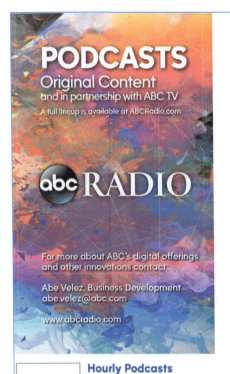

### Everybody's Got Something
Season 2 debuted June 2017 • 1 episode per week

"Regardless of how much money you have, your race, where you live, what religion you follow, you are going through something," wrote *GMA* host Robin Roberts.

The *Everybody's Got Something* podcast explores her journey and features intimate conversations with newsmakers such as India Arie, Delilah, Tig Notaro, Tony Robbins and Giada De Laurentiis.

### No Limits with Rebecca Jarvis
Launched Jan 2017 • 1 episode per week

ABC News Rebecca Jarvis, hosts weekly conversations with the world's most influential and successful women, as they reveal how they built their empires — from their earliest mistakes to their riskiest decisions — to the day that finally changed everything.

### 10% Happier with Dan Harris
1 episode per week

Dan Harris is a fidgety, skeptical ABC newsman who had a panic attack live on *GMA*, which led him to something he thought was ridiculous: meditation. He wrote the *New York Times* best-seller, *10% Happier*. In this podcast, Dan talks with celebrities, scientists, meditation teachers, experts and gurus about whether there's anything beyond 10%.

### Hourly Podcasts
Updated and available 24/7

Never miss the news with the ABC News' podcast, *Information Network Hourly Newscast*. With leading stories updated right at your fingertips, you can listen daily to stay informed with your most trusted news source.

### This Week with George Stephanopoulos
1 episode per week (Sun)

Brought to you by George Stephanopoulos and the ABC News Team, this podcast features a Sunday morning discussion program with newsmaker interviews, panel discussions, debates and commentary on a wide range of global issues.

### Nightline
5 episodes per week (Tue-Sat)

Late night television's award-winning news program brings you a podcast with in-depth reporting on the major stories of that day, combined with the most relevant topics in pop culture and entertainment.

### World News Tonight with David Muir
7 episodes per week (Mon-Sun)

The ABC News team brings popular television broadcast, *World News with David Muir* to a podcast, where he hosts discussions of the most compelling news from around the world, including interviews with today's top newsmakers.

### Powerhouse Politics
1 episode per week

Hosted by ABC News' Chief White House Correspondent, Jonathan Karl; Political Director, Rick Klein; and Chief Political Analyst, Matthew Dowd; this podcast features headliner interviews and in-depth looks at the people and events shaping US politics.

**FIGURE 5.52**
The ABC Radio Podcast Network offers many podcasts for listeners including hourly updates, *Nightline*, *Power House Politics*, *This Week with George Stephanopoulos*, and *World News Tonight with David Muir* to name a few

Source: © 2017 American Broadcasting Companies Inc.

Shane says he advises his broadcast clients to "be where the listeners are" when they choose social media platforms:

> If your listeners are on Facebook, that's where you engage them. If they follow news on Twitter, you want to be there, too. Post traffic information, news about celebrities—whatever they're interested in. Today, information moves at the real-time speed of Twitter, a very current content experience.

He adds that watching trends on Facebook and Twitter constitutes a form of show prep. And he cautions that all social media activity should point back to the station and its website.

## RADIO NEWS/INFORMATION/SPORTS AND THE FCC

The government takes a greater role in regulating broadcast journalism than it does print. Although it usually maintains a hands-off position when it comes to newspapers, the government keeps a watchful eye on radio to ensure that it meets certain operating criteria. Since the FCC perceives the airways as public domain, it expects broadcasters to operate in the public's interest.

In 2013, the FCC began an initiative called Critical Information Needs (CIN). RBR.com reports that "The FCC has a research model to study this topic with an eye toward ensuring that Americans are getting the news and information they need, regardless of location, ethnicity or any other factor." The CIN study will focus its radio study on stations with news/talk formats.

The FCC requires that radio reporters present news factually and in good faith. Stories that defame citizens through reckless or false statements may not only bring a libel suit from the injured party but action from the FCC, which views such behavior on the part of broadcasters as contrary to the public's interest. Broadcasters are protected under the First Amendment and therefore have certain rights, but as public trustees they are charged with the additional responsibility of acting in a manner that benefits rather than harms members of society.

Although the FCC tends to take a hands-off approach, broadcasters still believe there are things the FCC can do to create an environment that is conducive to radio stations covering the news: "I believe the FCC should allow more cross-ownership of radio, TV and newspaper as a means of sharing news resources and costs. Exemptions should be made to keep newspaper and broadcast news organizations viable," says Farley.

Broadcasters are free to express opinions and sentiments on issues through editorials. However, to avoid controversy, many radio stations choose not to editorialize even though the FCC encourages them to do so.

## NEWS ETHICS

The highly competitive nature of radio places unusual pressure on newspeople. In a business where being first with the story is often equated with being the best, certain dangers exist. Being first at all costs can be costly indeed, if information and facts are not adequately verified. As previously mentioned, it is the radio journalist's obligation to get the story straight and accurate before putting it on the air. Anything short of this is unprofessional. Rios says:

> I'd have to say the state of radio these days is very good. As always, the beauty of news radio is whether you are listening at home or in your car when there's breaking news, we can get the information on air instantly, once confirmed. That is the advantage we will always have over television news. What is happening though because of the Internet is . . . stories are out there that you see and want to run with, but as always you *have* to verify any story before running it. Have we been burned before? Yes, especially with sensational, pop culture stories. We are much more careful and thorough with stories that are important to our local audience.

Steve Jones, Vice-President and General Manager of ABC Radio News, emphasizes that:

> [At] ABC News Radio, nothing is more important to us than accuracy; being right is always more important than being first. From our newsroom in New York, we produce up to six unique news reports per hour every day. The news content of these reports is similar but the length of the content differs to allow radio stations programming flexibility based on whether they are news stations, talk stations or music stations.

The pressures of the clock, if allowed, can result in haphazard reporting. If a story cannot be sufficiently prepared in time for the upcoming news broadcast, it should be withheld. Getting it on air is not as important as getting it on air correctly. Accuracy is the newsperson's first criterion. News accounts should never be fudged. It is tantamount to deceiving and misleading the public. Scheld, of WCBS in New York, says:

> It's the responsibility of everyone who we hire from producers to reporters, to understand the mission of getting the facts straight before putting something on the air. It is part of the culture of the radio station to verify the facts of a story before putting it on the air to the best of our ability.

News reporters must exhibit discretion not only in the newsroom but also when on the scene of a story. It is commendable to assiduously pursue the facts and details of a story, but it is inconsiderate and insensitive to ignore the suffering and pain of those involved. For example, to press for comments from a grief-stricken parent whose child has just been seriously injured in an accident is callous and cruel and a disservice to all concerned, including the station the newsperson represents. Of course, a newsperson wants as much information as possible about an incident, but the public's right to privacy must be respected. As Rios says:

> You can learn to become a good reporter, but instinct has a lot to do with it. Instinct in knowing what questions to ask in an interview. Sensitivity as well. You will inevitably cover a funeral. Tough assignment, trying to get an interview with a friend or loved one about the death of a toddler or teen, for example. It's all in the approach and genuine sincerity. And knowing when and when *not* to push for an interview. Schmoozing with police on the scene of a story or police communications liaison is never a bad thing. Make friends with police. Most importantly though is being able to *paint a picture*, through words and sound. Radio is theatre of the mind. The listeners have to imagine the story while they're driving or washing dishes at home.

Objectivity is the cornerstone of good reporting. A newsperson who has lost his or her capacity to see the whole picture is handicapped. At the same time, the newsperson's job is to report the news and not create it. Although maintaining objectivity is the goal, it is not always possible. Scheld asserts that:

> Reporters do have to maintain objectivity in delivering the facts of a story but there is no way we can completely divorce ourselves from the emotions that come from some stories. If our baseball team wins the championship, and our city celebrates, we get caught up in the excitement. If we witness tragedy such as the terrible shootings in Newtown, we cannot help but deliver this news with a sense of personal trauma. There is no way around it. Our listeners want us to be authentic.

Agreeing with Scheld, Rios states:

> Objectivity, is critical. You have to present both sides of controversial stories and *never* let your personal stance on any topic be obvious. And never run a controversial story without getting both sides. We actually had a news anchor who would literally skip a story that had anything to do with the political party opposite to the one he sided with. He would always use the excuse that he simply ran out of time to do the opposing view story. He ultimately got fired.

The mere presence of a member of the media can inspire a disturbance or agitate a volatile situation. Staging an event for the sake of increasing the "newsiness" of a story is not only unprofessional but

# CODE OF ETHICS

## PREAMBLE

Professional electronic journalists should operate as trustees of the public, seek the truth, report it fairly and with integrity and independence, and stand accountable for their actions.

## PUBLIC TRUST

Professional electronic journalists should recognize that their first obligation is to the public.

Professional electronic journalists should:

- Understand that any commitment other than service to the public undermines trust and credibility.
- Recognize that service in the public interest creates an obligation to reflect the diversity of the community and guard against oversimplification of issues or events.
- Provide a full range of information to enable the public to make enlightened decisions.
- Fight to ensure that the public's business is conducted in public.

## FAIRNESS

Professional electronic journalists should present the news fairly and impartially, placing primary value on significance and relevance.

Professional electronic journalists should:

- Treat all subjects of news coverage with respect and dignity, showing particular compassion to victims of crime or tragedy.
- Exercise special care when children are involved in a story and give children greater privacy protection than adults.
- Seek to understand the diversity of their community and inform the public without bias or stereotype.
- Present a diversity of expressions, opinions, and ideas in context.
- Present analytical reporting based on professional perspective, not personal bias.
- Respect the right to a fair trial.

## INDEPENDENCE

Professional electronic journalists should defend the independence of all journalists from those seeking influence or control over news content.

Professional electronic journalists should:

- Gather and report news without fear or favor, and vigorously resist undue influence from any outside forces, including advertisers, sources, story subjects, powerful individuals, and special interest groups.
- Resist those who would seek to buy or politically influence news content or who would seek to intimidate those who gather and disseminate the news.
- Determine news content solely through editorial judgment and not as the result of outside influence.
- Resist any self-interest or peer pressure that might erode journalistic duty and service to the public.
- Recognize that sponsorship of the news will not be used in any way to determine, restrict, or manipulate content.
- Refuse to allow the interests of ownership or management to influence news judgment and content inappropriately.
- Defend the rights of the free press for all journalists, recognizing that any professional or government licensing of journalists is a violation of that freedom.

## TRUTH

Professional electronic journalists should pursue truth aggressively and present the news accurately, in context, and as completely as possible.

Professional electronic journalists should:

- Continuously seek the truth.
- Resist distortions that obscure the importance of events.
- Clearly disclose the origin of information and label all material provided by outsiders.

Professional electronic journalists should not:

- Report anything known to be false.
- Manipulate images or sounds in any way that is misleading.
- Plagiarize.
- Present images or sounds that are reenacted without informing the public.

## INTEGRITY

Professional electronic journalists should present the news with integrity and decency, avoiding real or perceived conflicts of interest, and respect the dignity and intelligence of the audience as well as the subjects of news.

Professional electronic journalists should:

- Identify sources whenever possible. Confidential sources should be used only when it is clearly in the public interest to gather or convey important information or when a person providing information might be harmed. Journalists should keep all commitments to protect a confidential source.
- Clearly label opinion and commentary.
- Guard against extended coverage of events or individuals that fails to significantly advance a story, place the event in context, or add to the public knowledge.
- Refrain from contacting participants in violent situations while the situation is in progress.
- Use technological tools with skill and thoughtfulness, avoiding techniques that skew facts, distort reality, or sensationalize events.
- Use surreptitious newsgathering techniques, including hidden cameras or microphones, only if there is no other way to obtain stories of significant public importance and only if the technique is explained to the audience.
- Disseminate the private transmissions of other news organizations only with permission.

Professional electronic journalists should not:

- Pay news sources who have a vested interest in a story.
- Accept gifts, favors, or compensation from those who might seek to influence coverage.
- Engage in activities that may compromise their integrity or independence.

## ACCOUNTABILITY

Professional electronic journalists should recognize that they are accountable for their actions to the public, the profession, and themselves.

Professional electronic journalists should:

- Actively encourage adherence to these standards by all journalists and their employers.
- Respond to public concerns. Investigate complaints and correct errors promptly and with as much prominence as the original report.
- Explain journalistic processes to the public, especially when practices spark questions or controversy.
- Recognize that professional electronic journalists are duty-bound to conduct themselves ethically.
- Refrain from ordering or encouraging courses of action that would force employees to commit an unethical act.
- Carefully listen to employees who raise ethical objections and create environments in which such objections and discussions are encouraged.
- Seek support for and provide opportunities to train employees in ethical decision-making.

*In meeting its responsibility to the profession of electronic journalism, RTDNA has created this code to identify important issues, to serve as a guide for its members, to facilitate self-scrutiny, and to shape future debate.*

**FIGURE 5.53**
RTDNA Code of Ethics

Source: Reproduced by permission of the Radio Television Digital News Association

illegal. Groups have been known to await the arrival of reporters before initiating a disturbance for the sake of gaining publicity. It is the duty of reporters to remain as innocuous and uninvolved as possible when on an assignment. Recall Indra de Silva's comment earlier about the need for news to be presented in a thoughtful and conscientious way.

Several industry associations, such as RTDNA and the Society of Professional Journalists, have established codes pertaining to the ethics and conduct of broadcast reporters. Scheld says:

> The codes of professional conduct are important for an organization. The idea is for our work to benefit the public good. We need to do our jobs in a fair minded way motivated by a pursuit of the truth. Any reminder of those pillars is a good thing.

## CHAPTER HIGHLIGHTS

1. The Pew Research Center's Project for Excellence in Journalism's *State of the News Media 2016* study found that news/talk/information was the most listened-to format on radio. The study indicated that 9.6% of U.S. radio listeners chose the news/talk/information format over all others including pop contemporary hit music, adult contemporary music, and even country music.

2. The news/talk/information audience includes highly educated and high-income earners.

3. If the station is in a major media market, the radio newsroom is composed of many people with varying roles. Large news staffs may consist of newscasters, writers, street reporters, and tech people, as well as stringers and interns.

4. News stories must be legible, intelligible, and designed for effortless reading. They should sound conversational, informal, simple, direct, concise, and organized.

5. Actualities (on-the-scene voicers) are obtained from news service feeds, online sources, and station personnel at the scene.

6. Traffic reports are an integral part of drive time news programming at many metropolitan radio stations and can help strengthen a station's community service image and also generate substantial revenue.

7. Computers, online resources, and smartphones connected to the various wire and Internet information services are used by radio newsrooms to report on fast-breaking stories and features. Many stations have installed touch screen computer monitors and traditional flat-screen, high-definition television monitors with access to the cable news networks in the on-air studio to have instant access to breaking news.

8. The news director, who works with and for the PD, supervises news staff, develops and implements policy, handles the budget, ensures the gathering of local news, is responsible for getting out breaking news stories rapidly and accurately, and plans public affairs programming. News directors also hold multiple jobs at some stations depending on the size of the market in which the station is located.

9. News directors seek personnel with both college education and experience. However, finding a news slot at a small station is difficult since its news staffs are small, so internships and experience at high school and college stations are important. In addition, such personal qualities as enthusiasm, aggressiveness, energy, inquisitiveness, typing skills, a knowledge of the area where the station is located, announcing abilities, and a command of the English language are assets.

10. The size of a station's news staff depends on the degree to which the station's format emphasizes news, the station's market size, the emphasis of its competition, and station consolidations. Small stations often have no newspeople and require deejays to use "rip 'n' read" wire service copy.

11. In the newsgathering process, the wire service, Internet, and television are important sources of information to nearly all of the nation's commercial radio stations.

12. Even though the FCC no longer mandates that radio stations provide news for listeners, all responsible broadcasters do so regardless.

13. The all-news, news/talk/information, and all-sports formats are popular among radio listeners. All-news formats attracts all demographics, while all-sports formats attract primarily the male demographic.

14. All-news stations rotate time blocks of local, regional, and national news and features to avoid repetition. The format requires three to four times the staff and budget of most music operations and, owing to the operating expense, the format is heard only on a few major-market stations.

15. The news/talk/information format combines extensive news coverage with blocks of programming devoted to the airing of telephone and studio interviews.

16. All-talk combines discussion and call-in shows. It is primarily a medium- and major-market format. Like all-news, all-talk is mostly found on AM (and is the domain of conservative talkers) but is now finding a home on the FM band.

17. All-sports has boosted the nonmusic format's numbers and now is offered by several networks, including CBS, NBC, and ESPN.

18. Stations maintain a website and social media platforms such as Twitter and Facebook, and almost all provide podcasts for listeners to provide constant programming. Websites and podcasts expand revenue generating opportunities. Websites, podcasts, and social media represent a way to strengthen a station's ties to its audience.

19. The FCC expects broadcasters to report the news in a balanced and impartial manner. Although protected under the First Amendment, broadcasters making reckless or false statements are subject to both civil and FCC charges.

20. Ethically, newspersons must maintain objectivity, discretion, and sensitivity.

## SUGGESTED FURTHER READING

Anderson, B., *News Flash: Journalism, Infotainment, and the Bottom-Line Business of Broadcast News*, Jossey-Bass, San Francisco, CA, 2004.

Barnas, F. and White, T., *Broadcast News Writing, Reporting, and Producing*, 6th edition, Focal Press, Burlington, MA, 2013.

Bartlett, J. (ed.), *The First Amendment in a Free Society*, H.W. Wilson, New York, NY, 1979.

Bittner, J.R. and Bittner, D.A., *Radio Journalism*, Prentice Hall, Englewood Cliffs, NJ, 1977.

Bliss, E.J., *Now the News*, Oxford Press, New York, NY, 1991.

Bliss, E.J. and Hoyt, J.L., *Writing News for Broadcast*, 3rd edition, Columbia University Press, New York, NY, 1994.

Block, M., *Broadcast News Writing for Professionals*, Marion Street Press, Oak Park, IL, 2005.

Block, M. and Durso, J., *Writing News for TV and Radio: The New Way to Learn Broadcast Newswriting*, CQ Press, Washington, D.C., 2010.

Boyd, A., *Broadcast Journalism*, 5th edition, Focal Press, Boston, MA, 2008.

Boyer, P.J., *Who Killed CBS?*, Random House, New York, NY, 1988.

Chantler, P. and Stewart, P., *Essential Radio Journalism: How to Produce and Present Radio News (Professional Media Practice)*, Bloomsbury Methuen Drama, New York, NY, 2009.

Charnley, M., *News by Radio*, Macmillan, New York, NY, 1948.

Cox, J., *Radio Journalism in America: Telling the News in the Golden Age and Beyond*, McFarland, Jefferson, NC, 2013.

Culbert, D.H., *News for Everyman: Radio and Foreign Affairs in Thirties America*, Greenwood Press, Westport, CT, 1976.

Day, L.A., *Ethics in Media Communications*, Wadsworth, Belmont, CA, 1991.

Fang, I., *Those Radio Commentators*, Iowa State University Press, Ames, IA, 1977.

Fang, I., *Radio News/Television News*, 2nd edition, Rada Press, St. Paul, MN, 1985.

Friendly, F.W., *The Good Guys, The Bad Guys, and the First Amendment: Free Speech vs. Fairness in Broadcasting*, Random House, New York, NY, 1976.

Frost, C., *Reporting for Journalists*, Routledge, New York, NY, 2002.

Garvey, D.E., *News Writing for the Electronic Media*, Wadsworth, Belmont, CA, 1982.

Geller, V., *Beyond Powerful Radio: A Communicator's Guide to the Internet Age—News, Talk, Information & Personality for Broadcasting, Podcasting, Internet, Radio*, Focal Press, Burlington, MA, 2011.

Gibson, R., *Radio and Television Reporting*, Allyn & Bacon, Boston, MA, 1991.

Gilbert, B., *Perry's Broadcast News Handbook*, Perry, Knoxville, TN, 1982.

Hall, M.W., *Broadcast Journalism: An Introduction to News Writing*, Hastings House, New York, NY, 1978.

Halper, D., *Icons of Talk Radio*, Greenwood, Westport, CT, 2008.

Hilliard, R.L., *Writing for Television, Radio, and New Media (Broadcast and Production)*, Wadsworth, Boston, MA, 2011.

Hitchcock, J.R., *Sportscasting*, Focal Press, Boston, MA, 1991.

Hood, J.R. and Kalbfeld, B. (eds.), *The Associated Press Handbook*, Associated Press, New York, NY, 1982.

Hunter, J.K., *Broadcast News*, C.V. Mosby, St. Louis, MO, 1980.

Johnston, C., *Election Coverage: Blueprint for Broadcasters*, Focal Press, Boston, MA, 1991.

Kalbfeld, B., *Associated Press Broadcast News Handbook*, McGraw-Hill, New York, NY, 2001.

Keirstead, P.A., *All-News Radio*, Tab, Blue Ridge Summit, PA, 1980.

Keirstead, P.A., *Computers in Broadcast and Cable Newsrooms*, Erlbaum, Mahwah, NJ, 2005.

Mayeux, P., *Broadcast News Writing and Reporting*, Waveland Press, Chicago, IL, 2000.

Nelson, H.L., *Laws of Mass Communication*, Foundation Press, Mineola, NY, 1982.

Raiteri, C., *Writing for Broadcast News*, Rowman & Littlefield, Lanham, MD, 2005.

Shrivastava, K.M., *Broadcast Journalism in the 21st Century*, New Dawn Press, Elgin, IL, 2004.

Simmons, S.J., *The Fairness Doctrine and the Media*, University of California Press, Berkeley, CA, 1978.

Stephens, M., *Broadcast News: Radio Journalism and an Introduction to Television*, Holt, Rinehart and Winston, New York, NY, 1980.

Wenger, D. and Potter, D., *Advancing the Story: Broadcast Journalism in a Multimedia World*, CQ Press, Washington, D.C., 2007.

Wulfemeyer, K.T., *Broadcast Newswriting*, 2nd edition, Iowa State University Press, Ames, IA, 2003.

# CHAPTER 6

# Research

## WHO IS LISTENING?

As early as 1929, the question of listenership was of interest to broadcasters and advertisers alike. That year, Cooperative Analysis of Broadcasting (CAB), headed by Archibald M. Crossley, undertook a study to determine how many people were tuned to certain network radio programs. Information was gathered by phoning a preselected sample of homes. On the local station level, researchers employed various methods to collect audience data, including telephone interviews and mail-out questionnaires.

In 1938, C.E. Hooper Inc. began the most formidable attempt up to that time to provide radio broadcasters with audience information. Like Crossley's service, Hooper also used the telephone to accumulate listener data. CAB relied on listener recall; Hooper, however, required that interviewers make calls until they reached someone who was actually listening to the radio. This approach became known as the "coincidental" telephone method. Both survey services found their efforts limited by the fact that 40% of the radio-listening homes in the 1930s were without a telephone.

As World War II approached, another major ratings service, known as Pulse, began to measure radio audience size. Unlike its competitors, Pulse collected information by conducting face-to-face interviews. Pulse and Hooper were the prevailing radio station rating services in the 1950s as the medium worked at regaining its footing following the meteoric rise of television. In 1965, the American Research Bureau (later to be known as Arbitron) began measuring radio audience size through the use of a diary, which required respondents to document their listening habits over a seven-day period. By the 1970s, Arbitron reigned as the leading radio measurement company, whereas Hooper and Pulse faded from the scene.

To provide the radio networks and their affiliates and advertisers with much-needed ratings information, Statistical Research Inc., of New Jersey, introduced Radio's All Dimension Audience Research (RADAR) in 1968. The company gathered its information through telephone interviews with more than 6,000 household respondents. In the 1990s, Arbitron retained its hold on first place among services measuring radio audiences, especially following the demise of competitor Birch/Scarborough, which gained considerable acceptance following its debut in the late 1970s. In 1991, this audience measurement company became yet another victim of the economic malaise. Arbitron's supremacy in the business carried forward into the new millennium, owing in large part to advancements the company made in measuring listenership across multiple platforms. In September, 2013 Nielsen Holdings N.V. finalized its acquisition of Arbitron in a deal reported by the *Wall Street Journal* to be valued at $1.3 billion. Nielsen was widely known for its television audience measurement service and, according to information made public at the time of the announcement, regarded Arbitron as a viable business partner, capable of assisting the company in extending its services to the measurement of out-of-home electronic media consumption. Arbitron has since been rebranded as Nielsen Audio, although vestiges of the "Arbitron" brand may be found online in Nielsen Audio web pages and in certain print products.

Ratings companies must be reliable, and credibility is crucial to success. Therefore, measurement techniques must be tried and true. Information must be accurate, because millions of dollars in advertising revenues are at stake. In 1963, the Broadcast Rating Council was established to monitor, audit, and accredit the various ratings companies. The Council created performance standards to which rating services are expected to adhere. Those that fail to meet the Council's operating criteria are not accredited. A nonaccredited ratings service will seldom succeed. In 1982, the Broadcast Rating Council was renamed the Electronic Media Planning Council to reflect a connection with the ratings services dealing with the cable television industry. Renamed the Media Rating Council (MRC) in 1997 to include Internet constituencies, the MRC's declared purposes are:

1. To secure for the media industry and related users audience measurement services that are valid, reliable, and effective.

2. To evolve and determine minimum disclosure and ethical criteria for media audience measurement services.

3. To provide and administer an audit system designed to inform users as to whether such audience measurements are conducted in conformance with the criteria and procedures developed.

**FIGURE 6.1**
Ed Cohen

## ON AUDIENCE RESEARCH

### Ed Cohen

Commercial radio is different from the typical business. We can't measure directly who is "buying" our on-air product (referring to listening) or how much listeners "buy," requiring the use of a proxy, the ratings. Ratings are surveys of a (hopefully) representative sample of the population that allow us to get an approximation of our audiences so that buyer and seller can place a dollar value on our audiences, facilitating advertising transactions.

In the U.S., the primary supplier of ratings data is Nielsen. Their system uses the electronic Portable People Meter (PPM) in the largest markets with reports issued every four weeks, and a seven-day paper diary in the smaller markets with reports covering 12 weeks, released at specific intervals. In the U.S., radio is a local medium, but national data are available as well. While the primary use of the information is for the buy/sell process, we intensively analyze the information for programming purposes as well, looking for any possible edge over the competition. Every station's goal is to improve their ratings because higher ratings equate to higher revenue and profits. Improved ratings should also reflect listener satisfaction because, if individuals choose to listen longer, that should mean they're enjoying what they hear on our stations.

Broadcast radio faces major competitive challenges today with the ubiquity of the Internet, specifically more options for the time that people spend with audio entertainment and information, whether from streaming, podcasts, or other digital options including our own online offerings. Those of us in the industry believe we're well positioned to take on this new competition with our advantages of expertise in music curation, localism, air talent, and promotion.

When it comes to measurement, we're less sanguine about the prospects. More choices mean more strain on the survey-based PPM and diary services resulting in large and sometimes inexplicable swings in reported audience sizes. Over the last few years, we've seen the advent of "big data" in media measurement—for example, set-top box data for television and census-level measurement for digital media. While these innovations have their own issues that will be resolved over time, users generally have greater confidence in measurement that utilizes big data. The radio industry needs a similar boost and may get one from automotive infotainment systems, which may supply the "big data" for audio in the relatively near future.

We've also seen some recent progress in cross-platform data, which is measurement of how consumers use media across all electronic platforms with the need to count all the impressions—in other words, one number for the audience across multiple platforms. Further, advertisers are constantly developing more sophisticated ways to evaluate their purchases, using "media-mix models" that attempt to determine the contribution of each medium to the return on their advertising spend.

The next few years may reveal some of the biggest changes we've ever seen in audience measurement, not only for radio but broadly across all media. The measurement of radio audiences will have to evolve quickly for the medium to not only survive but prosper in the future.

**Ed Cohen**, PhD, is Vice-President, Ratings and Research, Cumulus Media.

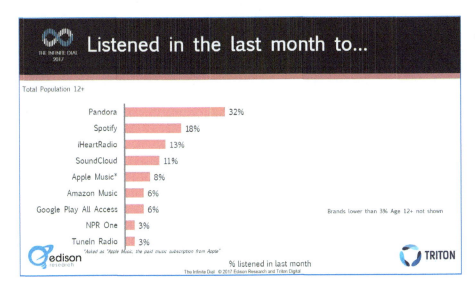

**FIGURE 6.2**

Audience fragmentation: top competitors to traditional AM/FM radio

Source: *The Infinite Dial 2017* study, courtesy of Edison Research and Triton Digital

## THE RATINGS AND SURVEY SERVICES

The extreme fragmentation of today's listening audience, created by the almost inestimable number of stations and formats, makes the job of research a complex but necessary one. All stations, regardless of size, must put forth an effort to acquaint themselves with the characteristics of the audience, says Edward J. Noonan, who served as Co-Director of Survey Research Associates: "A station cannot operate in a vacuum. It has to know who is listening and why before making any serious programming changes." Today, this information is made available through several ratings services and research companies. More stations depend on Nielsen Audio audience measurement data than any other.

Since the cessation of Birch/Scarborough services, broadcasters have had little choice but to subscribe to Nielsen Audio—that or go without the listening estimates on which so many agencies and advertisers rely. One alternative service to Nielsen Audio is Eastlan Ratings, which began in 1999. This privately held company specializes in serving the smaller-market broadcaster. It provides audience estimates to approximately 450 client stations located in 90 markets nationwide, ranging from Alaska to Florida. Whereas Nielsen Audio relies on electronic measuring devices and diaries to gather data from listeners, Eastlan employs the recall methodology, conducting its surveys principally by landline telephone and cellphone. Nielsen Audio covers more than 270 markets, ranging in classification from major to small. All markets are measured at least once a year during the spring; however, larger markets are measured on a year-round, ongoing basis.

To determine a station's ranking, Nielsen Audio follows an elaborate procedure. First, the parameters of the area to be surveyed are established. The firm sees fit to measure listening both in the city or urban center, which it refers to as the metro survey area (MSA), and in the surrounding communities or suburbs, which it classifies as the total survey area (TSA). MSAs are organized mostly along the boundaries established by the federal government as metropolitan statistical areas; TSAs define geographic areas that subsume the metro survey area and include additional counties or parishes. These areas are further delineated into designated market areas (DMAs), a geographic subdivision scheme developed by Nielsen Media Research for the purpose of identifying county and parish placements within markets. Once the areas to be measured have been ascertained, Nielsen Audio selects a sample base composed of individuals to be queried regarding their listening activities. The following paragraphs describe procedures Nielsen Audio has used for many years to gather listening information using a paper, pamphlet-styled diary it supplies to panelists; information about its passive electronic measurement system, the Portable People Meter (PPM), appears later in this chapter. Nielsen Audio conducts its surveys over a 12-week period, during which time new panelists are selected weekly.

Initial contact with potential participants is made by phone call, either to household landlines or individual cellphones. For purposes of bias avoidance, eligible panelists must not be affiliated with any radio station, TV station, newspaper, or advertising agency serving the market and must be at least 12 years of age. When the sample has been established, a letter is sent to targeted households informing prospective panelists that they have been selected to participate in a radio listening survey and asking for their cooperation. Within a couple of days of the letter being received, a Nielsen Audio interviewer calls to describe the purpose of the survey as well as to determine how many individuals aged 12 or older reside in the household. Nielsen Audio places more than four million telephone calls annually in its effort to recruit survey panelists. Upon receiving the go-ahead, Nielsen Audio mails its seven-day survey diary, which requires respondents to log their listening activities. A monetary premium, consisting of an incentive stipend of a dollar or two, accompanies the document. The diary is simple to deal with, and the information it requests is quite basic: the amount of time (daypart) tuned to a station, station call letters, program name, personality name or dial setting; whether AM or FM; and where listening occurred—car, home, work or elsewhere. In advance of the survey participating stations provide the company with key information about their facilities (call letters, frequency, identifying slogans and the names of personalities and specialty programs) to assist Nielsen Audio personnel in ensuring that the respondent data can be accurately credited to the appropriate station, Although the diary asks for information pertaining to age, sex, and residence, the actual identity or name of those participating is not requested.

**FIGURE 6.3**

Page from an Arbitron/Nielsen Audio Radio Market Report defining parameters of the survey area

Source: Courtesy of Nielsen Audio

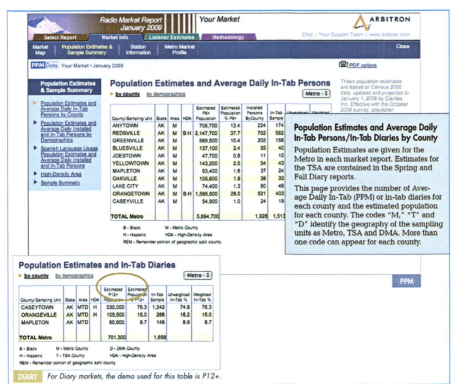

FIGURE 6.4
Diary/population correlations
Source: Courtesy of Nielsen Audio

Prior to the start of the survey, a representative of Nielsen Audio makes a presurvey follow-up telephone call to those who have agreed to participate. This is done to make certain that the diary has been received and that everyone involved understands how to maintain it. Another follow-up call is made during the middle of the survey week to ascertain if the diary is being kept and to remind each participant to return it promptly upon completion of the survey. Panelists are provided with toll-free telephone and online assistance to help them should questions about the process arise. Outside the metro area, follow-ups take the form of a letter. The diaries are returned to Nielsen Audio offices, where optical character readers (OCRs) scan the diaries and prepare the data for processing and computation.

Nielsen Audio claims that 65 of every 100 diaries it receives are usable, a remarkable compliance percentage considering that the company mails almost two million diaries each year. Upon arriving at company headquarters, diaries are examined by editors and rejected if they fail to meet criteria. Diaries that are inadequately or inaccurately filled out are not used. Any diary received before the conclusion of the survey period is immediately voided, as are those that arrive more than 12 days after the end of the survey period. Diaries with blank or ambiguous entries also are rejected. Those diaries that survive the editors' scrutiny are then computer-processed, and their information is tabulated. Prior to 2006, subscribing stations received a printed *Radio Market Report* (the "book") within a few weeks after the last day of the survey. Today, Arbitron disseminates the information electronically, preserving the "look" of the "book" while shortening the time between data processing and delivery.

Nielsen Arbitrends is a computerized data service has been made available to subscribers since the 1990s. Information regarding a station's past and current performances and those of competitors is available at the touch of a finger. Breakouts and tailor-made reports are provided on an ongoing basis by Arbitrends to assist stations in the planning of sales and marketing strategies.

Nielsen Audio's most formidable rival in recent years was Birch/Scarborough, headquartered in New Jersey. As a radio audience measurement service, Birch provided clients with both quantitative and qualitative data on local listening patterns, audience size, and demographics. Birch interviewers telephoned a prebalanced sample of households during the evening hours, seven days a week, to acquire the information. "Respondents aged 12 or older were randomly selected from both listed and nonlisted telephone households. These calls were made from highly supervised company toll-free long-distance

Instructions for filling out a diary to document AM, FM, and satellite radio listening. Accuracy is important

Source: Courtesy of Nielsen Audio

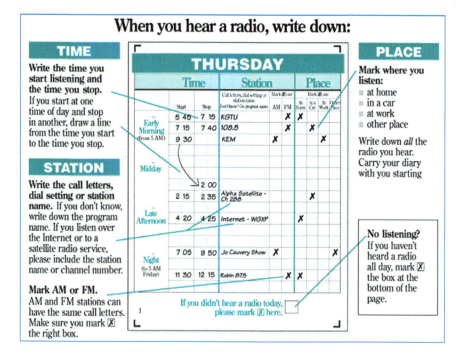

Audio listening occurs across a variety of delivery platforms

Source: Courtesy of Nielsen Audio

facilities," noted Phil Beswick, Vice-President of the defunct Birch/Scarborough Broadcast Services. The sample sizes varied depending on the size of the market being surveyed. For example, Birch/Scarborough contacted approximately 1,100 households in a medium market and between 2,000 and 8,000 households in major metro markets.

Dozens of other research companies throughout the country (among them Coleman Insights, Bolton Research Corporation, Mark Kassof & Company, Frank N. Magid Associates Inc., Paragon Media Strategies, International Demographics Inc./The Media Audit, Media Psychology Research Center, Gallup Inc., Ipsos MediaCT, Mediabase, TAPSCAN, and others cited in this chapter) provide broadcasters with a broad range of useful audience information. While some of them use approaches similar to Nielsen Audio (and the former Birch) to collect data, others use different methods to provide the broadcast, satellite, and online radio industries with an array of both qualitative and quantitative research information. In the hyperactive radio industry arena, both traditional and novel audience survey techniques must ultimately prove themselves by assisting stations in their unrelenting quest for stronger ratings numbers.

## QUALITATIVE AND QUANTITATIVE DATA

Since their inception in the 1930s, ratings services primarily have provided broadcasters with information pertaining to the number of listeners of a certain age and gender tuned to a station at a given time. It was on the basis of these quantitative data that stations chose a format and advertisers made a buy.

Owing to the explosive growth of the electronic media in recent years, the audience is presented with many more options, and the radio broadcaster, especially in larger markets, must know more about the station's intended listeners to attract and retain them. Subsequently, the need for more detailed information has arisen. TroyResearch is an example of a research firm that focuses on qualitative rather than quantitative audience information. Since the late 1990s this company has assisted stations, gathering data about audiences and music preferences, conducting its inquiries online. Not so long ago, a station that was shooting for a top spot in the ratings surveys had to be concerned with more than simply the age and sex of its target audience. Competitive programming strategies were being built around an understanding and appreciation of the lifestyles, values, and behavior of those listeners sought by a station. CEO Mike Henry of Paragon Media Strategies says the industry has undergone "seismic change" in the ways that research is performed and utilized. The rules by which stations operated at the turn of the millennium, he believes, are today either different or nonexistent. He summarizes the changes in a series of seven observations:

1. There has been a major reduction in the amount of primary research used by radio for programming purposes. Most stations get no primary research for programming in the average year.
2. A major increase in the amount of secondary research used by radio has occurred. For instance, polling monitors have replaced music testing procedures for most stations.
3. There is new reliance on using Nielsen Audio (and Media Monitors Mscore) for research and not just for ratings.
4. There is an increasing reliance on the utilization of "in-house" and "self-selected sample" research tools (e.g., online studies among the station database, new music testing panels, etc., resulting in as much marketing as research).
5. Reliance on social media feedback mechanisms, led by Facebook and Twitter.
6. Increased reliance on consultants who tell radio stations what to do rather than having the stations invest more money on researching the thoughts of listeners.
7. Research today in radio is focused squarely on sales research and its use for driving sales rather than on programming research and its use in driving ratings.

How have the changes Henry enumerated affected day-to-day life inside the radio station? He expressed the opinion that in most instances the program director (PD) is now the station's "programming research director" and all the responsibility for gathering research depends upon the PD's best judgment. This situation, he asserts, is a budgetary issue. "As you can imagine," he says, "the quality and reliability of station programming research has fallen off the cliff."

## FROM PAPER TO ELECTRONIC MEASUREMENT: THE PORTABLE PEOPLE METER

Another approach to measuring station listenership has emerged in the form of the Portable People Meter (PPM). Initially developed by Arbitron and introduced in 2006 as an alternative to the conventional paper diary method of collecting audience listening data, successor Nielsen Audio has continued making strides in migrating to passive, electronic audience measurement. In a statement issued in the months following the rollout of PPM technology Emmis Communications leader Jeff Smulyan characterized it as "long overdue." He added,

> We are finally getting credit for the huge audience we felt we had all along in Arbitron's previous methodology. In Los Angeles, for example, one of our Emmis station's cume was up 70% and our other Emmis station cume has almost quadrupled. That's a lot of people listening to us that we were not getting credit for.

No longer must PPM survey panelists take an active role in recording their listening activities. The PPM does it by detecting electronically coded, inaudible tones, termed *watermarks*, embedded into the signal transmissions by radio stations. Nielsen supplies stations with encoding devices that watermark their broadcasts. Special circuitry "masks" the tones in such a way as to make them imperceptible to listeners yet recognizable by the PPM receiver. Differentiation among stations within markets occurs without misidentification because each station transmits its own unique tone. Think of it as a station's individualized "fingerprint"—no two stations within a given market utilize the same watermark.

Portable meters are cellphone-sized devices that are worn or carried by survey panelists for an agreed-upon period of time. PPM technology approximates human hearing in the sense that reproduced sound from stations must be of sufficient volume in order to be "heard" by humans and "sampled" by the unit. PPM devices acquire station codes, storing the information. Nielsen retrieves the data electronically, and when panelists dock the meters for the night on their charging stands data get uploaded. Older docking systems used telephone modems to communicate back to the mothership; newer technology uses the Internet.

The company then creates timely reports for distribution to radio stations, advertising agencies, consulting firms, and other paying subscribers. Stations do not have to subscribe to PPM in order to encode their signals. Nielsen (and Arbitron before it) made certain to provide encoders to a broad section of broadcasters, including college stations and religious and other noncommercial entities, in order to represent a comprehensive set of stations in PPM measurement. While any station may encode PPM, the use of ratings data is strictly limited to paid service subscribers.

Within a year of the 2006 launch, however, members of the radio broadcasting community, along with industry observers, criticized PPM, citing problems with methodology and sample sizes. Arbitron proceeded in 2008 with PPM rollout experiments in other major markets. Following its New York City test, Arbitron elicited additional criticism over its method for recruiting panelists. Insufficient representation of certain racial and ethnic minorities, claimed New York attorney general Andrew Cuomo, led to inaccurate ratings and a subsequent reduction in advertising revenue for stations that programmed to Hispanics and African-Americans. Dissatisfaction with PPM in other markets led to the formation of the PPM Coalition, an industry group whose membership consisted of the National Association of Black Owned Broadcasters (NABOB), the Spanish Radio Association, Univision, and others. The Coalition appealed to the FCC for assistance in resolving its dissatisfactions with PPM. Arbitron and the Coalition, with the assistance of the U.S. House of Representatives Oversight and Government Reform Committee, mended their relationship, pledging to work collaboratively in the future.

Following its 2013 acquisition of Arbitron, Nielsen Audio announced its intention to enlarge its sample sizes in PPM markets, increasing the number of panelists by 6%. Additionally, the firm escalated its efforts to empanel sufficiently representative pools of African-American and Hispanic listeners. Historically, these panelists have proved difficult to recruit.

Geoff Steadman of equipment manufacturer the Telos Alliance observed that Arbitron's multiple-year investment in PPM research and development culminated in its widespread adoption when market leaders Clear Channel (now iHeartRadio) and CBS contracted for the use of the device their major markets. ABC, Citadel, Entercom, Cumulus, Beasley Broadcast Group, and the Spanish Broadcasting System soon followed suit. On the heels of these agreements, four other major radio groups—Bonneville International Corporation, Emmis Communications Corporation, Greater Media Inc., and Lincoln Financial Media—signed multiyear contracts for PPM radio ratings. When the Media Ratings Council accredited PPM in certain markets the announcement signaled to the industry that the device was likely here to stay. While Nielsen strives for each of its 48 PPM markets to gain accreditation, many markets remain "under review" by the MRC. At this writing, the split between accredited/under-review markets is approximately 60/40.

Tripp Eldredge, President and CEO of DMR/Interactive, offers his views as to why the PPM is superior to the paper method of gathering audience data:

> The PPM is both passive and longitudinal. Both qualities lead to a superior methodology. Because it's passive, it doesn't rely on the memory or consciousness of the respondent to gather data and more importantly report it correctly. The diary relies on proper station identification as well as proper reporting of behavior on a quarter-hour by quarter-hour basis. Because it's longitudinal, it provides much more stable results for the time periods most relevant to advertisers and broadcasters. Much of the differences in the diary methodology can be a result of sampling error, depending on the time period in question. The meter eliminates much of the instability due to randomness because it's kept for an average of six months. Also, the long-term nature of the meter may serve to eliminate the survey bias inherent in the diary process.

Longitudinal measurement should yield some important new audience insight. One important new PPM benefit is the ability to track loyalty and brand-switching over time. Diary data-gathering identifies the preferred station during the week-long measurement. The First Preference (P1) is the station that gets the majority of a consumer's listening. P1 drives the majority of a station's AQH (average quarter-hour) listening. However, the diary could not track the changes in P1 from week to week or month to month. The meter can because it tracks the same consumers from day to day, etc. This new metric will provide new and better feedback to programmers and potentially to advertisers as they begin to understand how loyalty impacts listening and how it is impacted by programming and marketing components.

One of the challenges of administering a system like PPM, according to Steadman, is the curation of panels. Nielsen attempts to recruit and maintain panelists who represent a statistically representative cross-section of the population. Panels vary in size by market, so New York City and Los Angeles have the largest panels. A single meter can represent hundreds or thousands of listeners, so each panelist matters. PPMs don't work if panelists don't carry them, so Nielsen often recruits multiple members of a single household to reinforce meter-wearing behavior by members of the household. Meters contain a motion-sensing device called an accelerometer, and information about movement (or lack thereof) is recorded along with PPM tones. This mechanism helps ensure that panelists are actually carrying their meters, and not just "parking" them next to a radio or leaving them in a drawer. Nielsen Audio staff maintains contact via texts, emails, and calls with panelists. Panelist terms typically last six to 18 months. Panelists are minimally compensated or "thanked" for their involvement in the program with

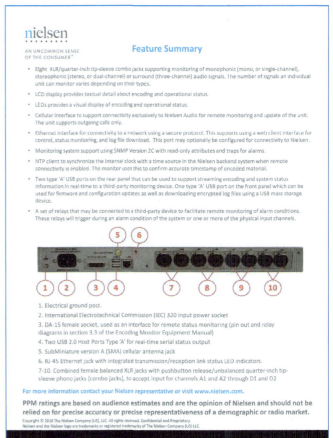

**FIGURE 6.7**

Nielsen Audio's Portable People Meter encoder monitor. This device detects the presence or absence of the PPM watermarking tones transmitted by stations and received by listeners' PPM devices. Alarm circuitry in the monitor alerts a station engineer in the event of PPM encoder malfunction

Source: Courtesy of Nielsen Audio

small cash awards and other incentives. Panelists are also obligated not to disclose their participation in the program. Stations that seek to defraud the system by influencing panelist behavior run the risk of being delisted from the market report, sued, or both.

Two PPM-related developments have occurred since the publication of the previous edition of this text. Broadcasters leveled criticism about PPM performance, citing as problematic the technology's inadequate recognition of watermarked content in certain Nielsen-termed "difficult to encode" formats. Smooth jazz, classical and certain talk formats have been cited as examples in the trade press of formats that are difficult to encode.

In 2015, broadcast equipment innovator the Telos Alliance's 25-Seven Systems division introduced the Voltair watermark monitor and enhancer. This device saw widespread and rapid adoption in the 48 PPM markets in the USA, garnering fans and creating controversy about PPM technology. According to Geoff Steadman, founder of 25-Seven Systems,

> Voltair laid bare some questions and concerns that program directors around the country had about PPM since it was introduced in 2006. Basically, we examined the technical properties of the system, explored what we saw as challenges in audio encoding behavior, and proved the premise that not all audio encodes equally well. We created a box that gave broadcasters control of the inherent trade-off between watermark encoding robustness and audibility.

The Voltair system attaches to the PPM encoder unit, wrapping around it in the program equipment signal chain. Where formerly stations had a rudimentary green light, red light "go/no-go" monitoring system to tell them if the system was working, Voltair offered a quality of service metric, a new way for stations to measure the encodability of audio, and control over encoding levels where formerly there was none. According to Steadman,

> Voltair provided visibility into a process that had been a hidden "black box." Program directors started correlating meter count data that they got as part of their subscription to Nielsen Audio with Voltair's data output, and began drawing their own conclusions. On the technical side, this introspection led to optimizations in audio processing and airchain device order. In programming terms, we saw PDs rearrange quarter-hour content, saw stopsets and song orders re-sorted, and watched as savvy operators put fresh insights to use.

Steadman continues,

> Watermark systems like PPM use the actual program audio as the source material to generate watermark tones. A system like PPM attempts to hide the tone "payload" in the audio stream so that listeners don't perceive the tones but meters can pick them up. It should come as no surprise that silence doesn't encode because there are no places for watermarks to hide, while dense rock music with lots of sonic energy between 1 kHz and 3 kHz tends to encode great. Environmental factors, such as a panelist's acoustic environment, further impact the reception of tones by meters. To the human listener, tones are noise. To PPM meters, talk and music are noise, and the watermark tones are the program.

About a year after the introduction of Voltair and, by some accounts, in response to it, Nielsen reformulated PPM encoding, rolling out E-CBET or "enhanced-critical band encoding technology" and updating their encoders. While Nielsen cast this change as "keeping a level playing field," radio stations did not turn their Voltairs off, although many appear to have dialed back Voltair enhancement levels. In 2016, Nielsen Audio also introduced new watermark-monitoring equipment to address requests from station engineering. The newer generation of Nielsen monitors offers more of a "quality of service" indication than the simple green/red light monitors they replace. "PPM is a game of inches, and the difference between being number three vs. number four in a major market can mean millions in revenue," continues Steadman. "Audio encodability is one factor in a complex eco-system.

# DEVELOPER PROFILE: GEOFF STEADMAN

Geoff Steadman is the Founder of 25-Seven Systems and one of the principal innovators behind the industry-changing Voltair processor. A lifelong broadcaster, he got his first taste of radio in high school, ran his college station, worked in small-market commercial radio in the Midwest, and eventually moved to public radio in Boston. In 1990, he joined AKG Acoustics in a job that would lead him into the product development and management side of the broadcast industry.

In 2004, Steadman started 25-Seven Systems, putting a product dream team together with longtime colleagues and ushering in award-winning products such as Audio Time Manager and profanity delay Program Delay Manager. In 2013, 25-Seven became part of the Telos Alliance, where he continues his work as leader of the brand he created.

**FIGURE 6.8**
Geoff Steadman

Source: Courtesy of the Telos Alliance

**FIGURE 6.9**
The Voltair watermark enhancement processor saw wide and rapid adoption by commercial broadcasters in PPM markets during 2015–2016. Over 950 units were shipped

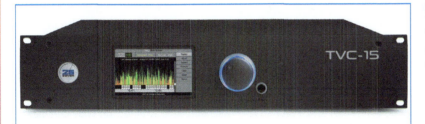

Source: Courtesy of the Telos Alliance

**FIGURE 6.10**
Telos/25-Seven Systems's TVC-15 analyzer and monitor can monitor PPM watermarks directly off air

Nielsen has announced, but had yet to implement at press time, its Digital Audio Ratings service. In recognition of the widespread delivery of FM and AM radio broadcasts across a variety of online platforms, Nielsen revealed in early 2016 that station listenership measurement in 48 PPM markets would be extended to smartphones, tablets, and computers. According to a company news release,

> Nielsen Digital Audio Ratings employs Nielsen's proprietary software development kit (SDK), which is integrated into mobile apps and web players. This method uses big data, a census-style measurement approach and demographic information from third-party data providers, which is calibrated with Nielsen's PPM panel. The product combines digital audio measurement with clear, industry-standard methodology, allowing clients to measure the total reach of radio listening.

Triton Digital offers another approach to quantifying online listenership. Its proprietary product is Webcast Metrics, and it captures listening data of the online "pureplays," such as Spotify and Pandora, in addition to broadcast station streams. President of Market Development John Rosso says Triton Digital "produces a set of tools, products and services, including Webcast Metrics for online audience measurement." Rosso cites this product as "the standard basis for most advertising transactions in online audio today." One similarity between the Nielsen and Triton approaches to measurement: both are census-based, and thus do not utilize samples and surveys to drive the measurement process.

"The Voltair story continues," Steadman states,

and we've introduced new means to detect and measure encoding in the form of our TVC-15 Watermark Analyzer and Monitor. This device was initially created to give stations a new tool to better monitor their watermarking. TVC-15 uses a completely different algorithm from Voltair, and can pick up watermarks directly off air, or from any recorded source. Midway through the development, we realized we could also use the device to connect directly to a Voltair unit, providing what we call "adaptive enhancement." This process can push Voltair processing higher when encoding is weak, but also back it off when encoding is robust, helping prevent audible artifacts, which can be more pronounced with E-CBET. Currently we are doing special research to help spoken word audio encode better, and to provide stations solutions to insure that their audio watermarking is performing as optimally as possible.

**FIGURE 6.11**
Radha Subramanyam
Source: Courtesy of iHeartMedia

## AUDIO AND RADIO MEASUREMENT

### Radha Subramanyam

Radio is the number one mass reach medium in America, reaching 93% of adults every week. The smartphone extends radio reach even further, as now consumers can take the radio with them wherever they are. We are at an interesting inflection point in the history of media measurement, including but not limited to radio. Historically, media measurement has always been highly dependent on panels—a collection of individuals and households recruited by a measurement company. The type of panel can vary by medium. In radio, this panel-based approach is represented by the PPM panel, or "Personal People Meter" panel, as well as a "diary panel" often utilized by smaller markets that incorporates people logging their listening. Though they may be just a small sample of a population, those recruited are statistically representative of the entire population and their listening habits are measured 24/7. In short, their media consumption is meant to represent all Americans and that consumption becomes the metric the radio industry uses to both program channels and work with advertisers.

However, as people consume media in more ways across devices and platforms, the limits of the panel-based approach have become more apparent. Panels have not been able to keep up with changes in consumer behavior and, as a result, they have become less representative of media consumption as a whole. These older methods struggle to adequately measure each platform and our new ways of listening challenge existing technologies. One such example is how the PPM does not capture the true extent of listening via headphones. Another concern is panel recruitment, which is challenged by fundamental shifts in how we live and work. The traditional phone-based methodologies are not as effective when a large chunk of American households only have cell phones.

There are more critical concerns with the traditional panel approach related to demographics and technology. As the country becomes increasingly diverse, panel recruitment is simply not keeping up with the changing population. As media producers and advertisers, we have always cared about broad demographics. However, it's also imperative that we focus on the various "tribes" who consume different kinds of content and the diversity of listenership in America. A ranker based on the adults 18–49 demographic doesn't tell us about the Millennial woman, who might be the core target of a station. Panel size and stability as they relate to specific groups have become critical questions in assessing media quality. There's also a technology concern. With the advent of digital methods of "targeting" and the ongoing innovation in advertising technologies commonly known as "ad tech," the need for more granular views takes on additional momentum. The traditionally small panel sample size is unable to provide these views.

So how do we best address these issues? Ideally, we'd incorporate larger panels for audience measurement. While measurement companies should certainly double down on making panels more representative and more stable, it has become increasingly apparent that we need fresh approaches. The media world has largely aligned around the concept of the "hybrid" approach that brings together different kinds of data, which we'll call big data and panel data.

With this new hybrid approach, big data on media delivered from servers, SDKs, tags, and other digital methods are calibrated with panel data particularly centered on demographics to provide a more holistic look at what is truly being consumed. In simpler terms, think of this as getting who is listening and how long they're listening from a range of sources and mathematically arriving at a fuller view of media consumption. These hybrid approaches allow more granular looks at audience groups and have the potential to help us optimize advertising to make sure it is reaching the right target. The investment in big data is crucial because it has the potential to unlock what is called "return path" data—data that not only tell us what was delivered but tell us potential actions taken by the consumer as a result of this.

At iHeartMedia, which has the largest national reach of any radio or television outlet in America, we're focused on driving innovation in this hybrid and return path approaches to media measurement. iHeartMedia collaborates with various companies to expand media measurement. The measurement space is ripe for innovation and we will see continued action and approaches over the next five years.

---

**Radha Subramanyam**, Ph.D., is President of Insights, Research and Data Analytics for iHeartMedia, where she develops and manages an expansive range of data and research efforts involving digital analytics, ratings and measurement, programmatic projections, ad sales research, mobile measurement, programming analysis, music research, campaign measurement/attribution and marketing research. She is one of a select group of media and entertainment executives with extensive experience in all areas of industry–television, digital, radio, and social media. Prior to joining iHeartMedia, Subramanyam held senior executive roles at Yahoo! and MTV Networks and was one of the founding leaders of a new analytics and consulting practice at Nielsen. She began her media career at NBCUniversal after having previously taught media and entertainment courses at Vassar College and New York University. Subramanyam has been widely recognized by the industry and her peers through several awards, including being named one of the Most Influential Women in Radio by *Radio Ink* in 2013, 2014, 2015, and 2016. She holds a Ph.D. in radio, television, and film from Northwestern University.

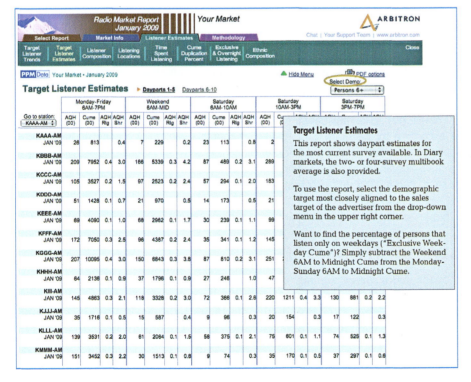

**FIGURE 6.12**

List of hypothetical stations reflects their market ratings positions

Source: Courtesy of Nielsen Audio

PPM encoding and decoding hardware

Source: Courtesy of Nielsen Audio

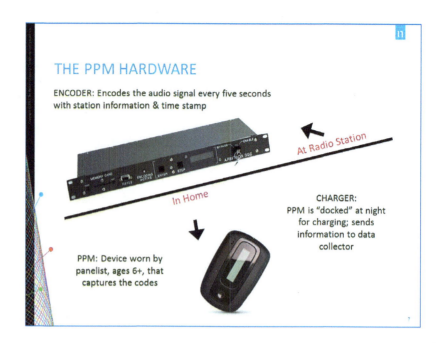

Other devices have challenged the PPM. Smartphones were being touted in the mid-2000s as potential audience measurement devices given their ubiquity and expanding service capabilities. In 2006, The Media Audit, an operational division of International Demographics Inc., teamed with Ipsos, a multinational research company, to explore the feasibility of using a smartphone for such purposes. Houston, Texas, was the location chosen for the test. Stations in the nation's sixth-largest radio market began prepping for the test. Later that year, Arbitron took legal steps to keep The Media Audit/Ipsos from entering the ratings business, citing their smartphone technology as an infringement on its patented PPM technology. In separate agreements, The Media Audit and Ipsos both agreed to withdraw from efforts to engage in smartphone audience measurement for the next three years and, as of this writing, have not announced intentions to return.

In terms of what the PPM means to on-air personnel, Jason Insalaco posits this view:

> Music is winning over deejay patter. Consequently, programmers of struggling morning shows are pulling back their personalities from the usual bits, interviews, and banter and offering more music-intensive morning programming. However, PPM data also indicates that strong morning show personalities are continuing to exhibit success equal to, if not greater than, AQH compared to the old diary methodology. The new measurement device highlights the strengths and weaknesses of the station. If a morning show was underperforming according to the diaries, it will likely become even more glaring under PPM. Programmers have a large amount of weekly data at their fingertips with PPM. It also is showing that midday and afternoon drive listening is reaching audience levels sometimes equal to morning drive. As programmers become more comfortable with PPM, they will take more risks on the air. If the early data shows that something new is not working, programmers can quickly change course without having to wait months to discern a trend as they did under the previous diary system.

## IN-HOUSE RESEARCH TECHNIQUES

Research data provided by the major survey companies can be costly. For this reason and others, stations conduct their own audience studies. Although stations seldom have the professional wherewithal and expertise of the research companies, they can derive useful information through do-it-yourself surveys, creating questionnaires for landline telephone, online, face-to-face, and mail surveys.

Telephone surveying has traditionally been a commonly used method of deriving audience data on the station level. It is generally less costly than the other forms of in-house research, and sample selection is less complicated and not as prone to bias. It also is the most expedient method. There are, however, a few things that must be kept in mind when conducting call-out surveys via landline telephones. One is the increasing number of telephone subscribers who have "cut the cord" and relinquished landline phone service. Additionally, many landline numbers are unlisted, although this shortcoming can be easily overcome through the use of software capable of generating lists of randomized telephone numbers. Another limitation of this method is the public's wariness of phone solicitations for interviews, the result of the fear that the ultimate objective of the caller is to sell something. The public is inundated by phone solicitors (of both the human and computerized varieties). Finally, extensive interviews are difficult to conduct over the phone. Five to 10 minutes usually is the extent to which an interviewee will submit to questioning.

Internet and email services provide another valuable means for those radio stations that survey their audiences. Many stations employ computers for call-out research purposes. There are many obvious benefits; interactivity and archiving are foremost among them. The face-to-face or personal interview is also a popular research approach at stations, although the cost can be higher than call-out, especially if a vast number of individuals are being surveyed in an auditorium setting. The primary advantages of the in-person interview are that questions can be more substantive and greater time can be spent with the respondents. Of course, more detailed interviews are time-consuming and usually require refined interviewing skills, both of which can be cost factors.

Mail surveys, in both paper and electronic forms, can be useful for a host of reasons. To begin with, they eliminate the need to hire and train interviewers. This alone can mean a great deal in terms of money and time. Because no interviewers are involved, one source of potential bias also is eliminated. Perhaps most important is that individuals questioned through the mail are somewhat more inclined toward candor because they enjoy greater anonymity. The major problem with the mail survey approach stems from the usually low rate of response. One in every five questionnaires distributed may actually find its way back to the station. The length of the questionnaire must be kept relatively short and the questions succinct and direct. Complex questions create resistance and may result in the survey being ignored or discarded.

Large- and major-market outlets usually employ someone to direct the research and survey efforts. This person works closely with upper management and department heads, especially the program director and sales manager. These two areas require data on which to base programming and marketing decisions. At smaller outlets, area directors are generally responsible for conducting surveys relevant to their department's needs. A case in point would be the PD who plans a phone survey during a special broadcast to help ascertain whether it should become a permanent program offering. To accomplish this task, the programmer enlists the aid of a secretary and two interns from a local college. Calls are made, and data are collected and analyzed.

The objective of a survey must be clear from the start, and the methodology used to acquire data should be as uncomplicated as possible. Do-it-yourself surveys are limited in nature, and overly ambitious goals and expectations are seldom realized. However, in-house research can produce valuable information that can give a station a competitive edge. Today, no radio station can operate in a detached way and expect to prosper.

Every station has numerous sources of information available to it. Directories containing all manner of data, such as population statistics and demographics, manufacturing and retailing trends, and so on, are available online, at the public library, city hall, chamber of commerce, and various business associations. The American Marketing Association and American Research Foundation also possess information designed to guide stations with their in-house survey efforts.

## MUSIC RESEARCH

The processes by which music programmers identify and select songs for airplay have evolved over the seven-decade history of formatic radio. Initially it was a fly-by-the-seat-of-your-pants approach in which deejays relied on gut instincts in deciding what to play. It has since become a sophisticated, organized activity that employs recognized research techniques. What follows below is a description of how the process works. Note that this information correlates with the Chapter 3 discussion about how station personnel manage the music library.

# MUSIC RESEARCH

## Carolyn Gilbert

The history of music research for radio goes back to the late 1970s. Using push-button phones, pages out of phone books and pencil hashmarks on paper grids, data were generated and processed using Radio Shack TRS 80s. High school and college girls came to work to make annoying phone calls at dinner time to find out which songs qualified radio listeners liked and didn't like.

Radio stations all over the country started testing "hooks," the five to seven seconds of songs that are the catchiest. The word "burn" came into use to express that phenomenon when radio stations played a song so much that it was beaten into the ground and listeners were ready to scream. Unfamiliarity, dislike, neutral, and passion scores were recorded. The samples included about 100 respondents. The test included between 30 and 40 songs. And it was called "callout research." It gave stations a strategic advantage. Eventually, just about every major music station used this type of data.

Auditorium music tests (AMTs) were a different form of hook testing. This was an event. Qualified respondents arrived at a central location and listened to upwards of 600 hooks. There was a break. Dinner was served. Respondents could earn up to $100 for three hours of their time. Sometimes recruiting companies posted signs at universities to recruit. Or brought in a church group on a bus. Everyone lived within 10 miles of the hotel—even in markets where the metro was 100 square miles. Yes, there were flaws. Both methodologies had their flaws (as does every methodology). But it was what we had.

Research, by definition, should be conducted scientifically. Respondents should be recruited randomly. All surveys should be administered in the identical way, during a proscribed period of time. Because, as an industry, radio people don't necessarily understand what comprises research, some things have been passed off as research that really aren't.

- Online opt-in services have been sold as barter[1] products. While it's been sold as such, it's not really a research product. Respondents here are recruited from radio station databases, or via channels that tell the participants for whom the survey is being done. It's been referred to as a "request line on steroids" because no station uses the request line as an indicator of what to play.

- There are national surveys conducted every year that are recruited directly from databases that contain names of people who have deliberately opted in to receive information about radio stations. Using that as an indicator of passion for the medium is like filling Giants Stadium on a football Sunday and asking how many people like football. If you use that as your base, you're going to come away thinking that 95% of Americans love football.

- Some companies are still using telephone methodology and delivering half samples and rolling the results. Their pitch is "stability." But if you refresh half a sample this week and use data from last, of course your data will be stable.

- Today, you see "crowdsourcing" used to generate data from large numbers of people for hardly any money. Large numbers aren't necessarily better (see the football reference, above). The expression "You get what you pay for" is nowhere more appropriate than when considering the corner-cutters in radio data collection.

In 1990, we used telephone research for two reasons: First, everyone had a landline and answered their phones.[2] And, second, Arbitron[3] used telephone recruiting exclusively; if you weren't going to talk to us, you weren't going to talk to them. So we didn't care about you. The company I ran until 2008 had 700 employees using 400 telephone stations and CATI[4] technology to make over 10,000 phone calls a week. A lot of data. A lot of employee turnover. A lot of close calls in terms of reaching sample goals and meeting deadlines. In 1981, you could make 5.7 complete music calls per man-hour on the phones. In 2008, when I left the company I ran, that completion rate was 0.3 completions per man-hour on the phones.

The world has changed a lot since then. Media have become pull instead of push. TV viewers decide when they will watch what they want to watch. Radio listeners are accessing podcasts that they can listen to at will. National Public Radio makes everything available at the listener's will—not the stations'. So too have the research and marketing worlds changed. Interruption research has been replaced by interactive research. Respondents participate when they want to. They use their computers. They use their tablets. They use their mobile phones.

In 2017, our company and others are conducting online music research the right way: using nonradio databases from myriad companies (mine uses over 60 companies) to generate fresh samples every week. The contact is push (not opt-in). The access is pull, where respondents do it when they have time. We pay respondents to participate[5] instead of paying telephone operators. We do the work that 700 people did with five people. Our samples are qualified. Our samples are full. Our data are cleaned and perfect.[6] Every time.

**FIGURE 6.15**
NuVoodoo logo

We have renamed "call-out" as OMR (online music research). AMTs have become OMTs. Hooks are randomized (something that couldn't be done in the predigital days of analog tape playback). Participants can start an OMT and take a break at their convenience and come back later.

Stations are still using music research to determine what to play and how often it should be played. Technology has changed, but top stations in top markets still want to know what their listeners want to hear. And it's fairly amazing that most people don't know that. Many people still believe that disc jockeys play what they want, or that the record companies decide, or that there's some corporate edict on what to play when. Not true. Research is done because it works. Techniques change, but the interest in an accurate read on what listeners want is a mainstay at radio stations that win.

---

**Carolyn Gilbert** is President/Owner of NuVoodoo Media Services LLC, formed in 2010 to provide innovative products to the industry that work within limited budgets and deliver results. A broadcast journalism major at Penn State University, Gilbert has served in leadership positions at Jacor, Clear Channel, and the Tribune Company.

---

### Notes

1   In barter, commercials are played by the station in exchange for a product or service; no cash exchanges hands.

2   The Centers for Disease Control in Atlanta (which for some strange reason is the keeper of these data) indicates that about half of the population no longer has a landline telephone. Our own proprietary research tells us that when you factor in both cell phone–only households and those who prescreen their calls using caller ID, about 16% of those 14–54 will actually take a call from a stranger.

3   The radio ratings currency. They were sold to Nielsen and still hold a virtual monopoly on radio ratings information in the US.

4   Computer-assisted telephone interviewing.

5   Just like Nielsen Audio pays their respondents.

6   Using this methodology, we always have extra respondents, so that our staff actually deletes respondents that don't "look right." This is a luxury we never had in the Callout and AMT worlds. We'd just pray that enough people participated or showed up.

Regardless of whether the song selection responsibilities fall to the music director or program director, this individual will actually audition and select what songs are to be designated for airplay. It bears noting, however, that in instances where the decisions are made by a music director they are based on criteria established by the station's programmer. Obviously, a music director must work within the station's prescribed format. If the PD feels that a particular song does not fit the station's sound, he will instruct the music director to remove the cut from rotation. Since the PD and music director work closely together, this seldom occurs.

Historically, a song's rotation usually is relative to its popularity, as determined by its position on national charts. For instance, songs that enjoy top ranking, say those in the top 10, will get the most airplay on hit-oriented stations. When songs descend the charts, their rotation decreases proportionately. Former chart-toppers are then assigned another rotation configuration that initially may result in one-tenth of their former airplay, and eventually even less. In addition to the trade publicatons, PDs and music directors derive information pertaining to a record's popularity from social media, song download information, and numerous other sources. Stations that do not program from the current charts compose their playlists with songs that were popular in years gone by. In nonhit formats, there are no "power-rotation" categories or hit-positioning schemata; a song's rotation tends to be more random.

In 1989, *Billboard* became the first trade publication to track radio airplay as it happened and to count "spins," or plays, in compiling charts. *Billboard* and its companion publication, *Airplay Monitor*, used Broadcast Data Systems (BDS) to electronically detect airplay by matching segments of songs called "footprints" to actual play on stations monitored over the air. This system served helped to bring an end to a deceitful practice termed the "paper add." MDs falsified reports to the national music trade magazines, indicating the addition of songs to their playlists but not giving them actual airplay. The practice of reporting "paper adds" decreased because a song reported to the (now defunct) trade publication *R&R* could be tracked in BDS detections. In mid-1999 both *R&R* and *The Gavin Report* (also defunct) began using charts based on airplay detection with information compiled by Mediabase, a monitoring service owned by Premiere Radio Networks.

Constructing a station playlist is the single most important duty of the music programmer. What to play, when to play it, and how often to do so are some of the key questions confronting this individual. The music director relies on a number of sources, both internal and external, to provide the answers but also must cultivate an ear for the kind of sound the station is after. Some people are blessed with an almost innate capacity to detect a hit, but most must develop this skill over a period of time. The ability to spot a "hit" is more important today than in the past. Programmers, according to music technology blogger Paul Lamere, can take a cue from his "deep dive" research into the data pertaining to the behaviors of Spotify listeners. How important is it to pick the right songs? Consider this: the data suggest that listeners skip a quarter of all songs they select; half of the songs are skipped before they finish. Thus, putting the "wrong" song into the playlist rotation causes tune-out more quickly today. For a primer on applying basic research practices to identifying and selecting music, read on.

**FIGURE 6.16**
Andrew Forsyth

## MUSIC SELECTION

### Andrew Forsyth

Selecting new music for commercial radio airplay is a complex process requiring a sense of market needs, cultural trends, and target audience musical appetite, based on a keen understanding of the music programming plans and policies of the station and, of course, good ears.

Today's program director (often referred to as brand manager) and music director draw their musical choices from a combination of resources. In the past the weekly published charts from the likes of *Billboard*, *Radio and Records (R&R)*, *The Gavin Report*, etc. gave programmers insight into the consensus of their colleagues. Sales reports garnered by calls to local record stores tracked the popularity of titles with the music consumer. By the late 1960s to early 1970s, many of the successful stations in large markets instigated call-out research to assist in determining audience reaction to new and current material. The outcomes of these tactics would assist programmers in making their choices. The rule of thumb has remained: subjective personal choice is only a good attribute if it is measured against objective data from credible sources.

Services such as Nielsen's BDSradio roll the data required for the music selection process into one dashboard. BDSradio merges airplay and sales data as well as song appeal metrics in a presentation that is specifically designed for music programmers. The physical layout of BDSradio allows the user to view data from a series of default reports (format charts, station reports, and title and artist data, as well as SoundScan sales and coalesced on-demand streaming data from the top streaming suppliers). There is an option for customized charts detailing airplay over any specified period of time from any combination of monitored services. These reports explore current, recurrent and gold allocations, daypart usage, head-to-head music log comparisons, station-to-market, format or selected station, sales, and on-demand usage on an hourly, daily, weekly, or any time frame within a calendar year.

These data aid programmers in determining music choices based on information driven by airplay, the commitment of purchases, and the appeal of on-demand streaming selection. The data provide programmers with strategic information as to how the music product is scheduled and rotated over its current, recurrent, or gold life cycle. In this section we will focus on the selection of new music to the current categories.

*Charts*: Traditionally, in a weekly review of new music activity the programmer will look to charts that are specific to their station's format. This helps them understand what is radio-friendly and has been chosen by similar stations targeting a similar audience. Charts are also used by the labels and promoters to track airplay nationally, by market and at the station level. The labels invest heavily in supporting artists and radio airplay with social media, retail advertising, concert promotion, and tour support. This outside "buzz" creates demand for the artist, which is satiated in part by radio. Conversely radio aligns itself with the interest generated by the labels by giving the titles mass exposure. This leverages radio's greatest asset: reach and frequency. Radio reaches more people in the United States every day than any other medium and has the ability to deliver the message often. Charts map the life cycle of a song at the format. The chart demonstrates which titles are moving up with increased airplay exposure, those that have attained a plateau and those that are receding over time as the music industry moves on to newer releases.

Following this cycle, when radio decides to add a new selection that decision creates a domino effect: the new replaces the old, which replaces that which is even older. In the simplest terms, the station's active library is broken into three overarching categories: current, recurrent, and gold, giving a framework for the music cycle. Nielsen BDS identifies current, recurrent, and gold (CRG) titles in its reports. This provides quick insights into playlists. Typically, CRG categorization is subjective and each PD has his/her own rules for defining the allocation. BDS applies its rules consistently across each format based on song history in the *Billboard* charts. Although BDS's rules may differ from that of an individual station, this consistent approach facilitates an accurate assessment of stations' song rotation patterns over many formats.

Nielsen BDS classifies a song as current, recurrent, or gold based on that song's spin activity separately in each format. This is an advanced feature and not available in other products. In this way, a song may be a current in AC and a recurrent in top 40 because the song's movement from current to recurrent is based on the date it falls off each individual chart.

*Current*: A song that has recently been released or rereleased by a label.

*Recurrent*: A song that recently appeared on a *Billboard* chart then dropped off.

*Gold*: A song that either has been a recurrent for one year or, if it has never been on a chart, has a release date older than two years.

Nielsen BDS also includes on-demand streaming rankings for the titles as it pertains to the chart. This information is derived by compiling on-demand—active decisions made by the listener—from a wide range of service providers such as Spotify, Apple Music, YouTube, Tidal, etc. Over the course of a week

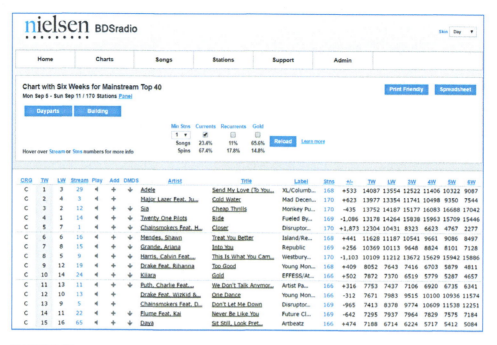

FIGURE 6.17
Mainstream top 40 report excerpt

FIGURE 6.17
Mainstream top 40 report excerpt

over eight billion streams are captured on these services. This coalesced data represents the choice made by listeners. The ranking of the top titles gives a metric indicating appeal.

## Reading the Chart

This sample shows the listing of the top 20 ranking at the date posted for mainstream top 40 (also known as CHR [contemporary hit radio]). The charts show the number of individual plays (spins) for these titles from stations on the top 40 panel, composed of 170 stations from markets across the country over the past seven days. From left to right the "C" under the CRG column indicates the report is for current titles. This week's (TW) #1 title is Adele's "Send My Love (To Your New Lover)." The song has moved up from the #3 position last week (LW). The title ranks #29 at on-demand streaming and is airing at 168 of the 170 panel stations. It has added 533 spins to total 14,087 in the past seven days. Six weeks ago the song garnered only 9,087 spins.

FIGURE 6.18
Inset detail of streaming info for Adele's "Send My Love (To Your New Lover)"

Hovering over the streaming rank shows that the title has been losing appeal with on-demand consumers for the past six weeks, peaking at the #22 position six weeks ago and dropping to #29 this week. This indicates that appeal for this song is waning as listeners are moving their choices to other titles.

Song trends are documented in the sample of the chart shown below. Chainsmokers' "Closer" is seeing an increase of over 1,800 spins this week moving this song into the #5 spot in terms of airplay. Streaming shows this song is already #1 with on-demand listeners. Their previous #1 top 40 title "Don't

Let Me Down" lost 965 spins in the past seven days and has dropped out of the top 10 to #13, with a #5 ranking at streaming.

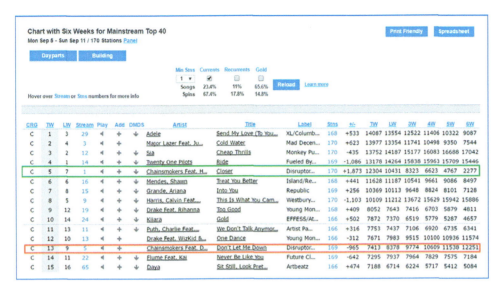

FIGURE 6.19

Chart performance of two Chainsmokers recordings

That "Don't Let Me Down" has made way for the new release does not necessarily mean that radio will completely drop airplay.

FIGURE 6.20

Detail inset of chart performance of Chainsmokers' "Don't Let Me Down"

This decision would be supported by the continuing strength of the song at on-demand streaming, where it has been in the #4 or #5 position for the past six weeks, indicating sustained appeal for "Don't Let Me Down."

*Station airplay* is identified by clicking on the title, which opens up a frame showing other format usage and Top 40 radio airplay by market. "Closer" is seen to be #2 on the dance chart and falling while it gains momentum at other formats. The detection list shows the stations that have played the title in the past seven days, with each station rank of play and the total number of spins over the latest 24/7 period.

The same view can be seen for recurrent and gold titles. This aids programmers in their decisions to add and move songs within their library inventory. Over and above station profile and comparative reports, there is a multitude of custom chart functions, which allow users to create reports on a variety of airplay and streaming metrics.

*Breaking Music*

Services such as SHAZAM and Nielsen BDS provide data on breaking new music. This information gives programmers a heads-up on the new material attracting attention before it breaks at radio. SHAZAM tracks look up requests or inquiries for song titles. As new songs are played and are searched by

**Chainsmokers Feat. Halsey / Closer / Disruptor/Columbia / 2016**      `Print Friendly`   `Spreadsheet`
Appeared on these 7-Day Rolling Charts

| TW | LW | Chart | Stations | +/- | TW | LW | 3W | 4W | 5W | 6W |
|---|---|---|---|---|---|---|---|---|---|---|
| 3 | 1 | Dance | 6 of 7 | -18 | 352 | 370 | 321 | 249 | 158 | 68 |
| 5 | 7 | Mainstream Top 40 | 170 of 170 | 1873 | 12304 | 10431 | 8323 | 6623 | 4767 | 2277 |
| 11 | 15 | Rhythmic | 44 of 58 | 395 | 2307 | 1912 | 1512 | 1129 | 729 | 405 |
| 31 | 45 | Adult Top 40 | 57 of 93 | 367 | 1253 | 886 | 638 | 305 | 175 | 81 |
| 46 | 55 | Latin Pop | 6 of 32 | 33 | 213 | 180 | 136 | 96 | 52 | 15 |
| 231 | 280 | Latin | 6 of 144 | 33 | 213 | 180 | 136 | 96 | 52 | 15 |
| 890 | 1203 | Adult Contemporary | 5 of 85 | 17 | 24 | 7 | 6 | 0 | 1 | 0 |
| 2027 | 1801 | Alternative | 1 of 57 | 1 | 2 | 1 | 3 | 3 | 0 | 0 |
| 2321 | 1451 | Mainstream R&B/Hip-Hop | 2 of 71 | -1 | 2 | 3 | 0 | 0 | 0 | 0 |
| 2681 | 0 | Triple A | 1 of 32 | 1 | 1 | 0 | 1 | 0 | 0 | 0 |

. . . and detected on these stations between Mon Sep 5 - Sun Sep 11

| Calls | Format | Metro | Market | Owner | Stn Rank | Spins | Spin Hist |
|---|---|---|---|---|---|---|---|
| WBMP - FM | Mainstream Top 40 | 1 | New York | CBS Radio | 2 | 110 | Show History |
| WHTZ - FM | Mainstream Top 40 | 1 | New York | iHeartMedia | 13 | 48 | Show History |
| WKTU - FM | Mainstream Top 40 | 1 | New York | iHeartMedia | 24 | 24 | Show History |
| WNEW - FM | Adult Top 40 | 1 | New York | CBS Radio | 148 | 2 | Show History |
| WSOU - FM | Mainstream Rock | 1 | New York | Seton Hall U... | 366 | 1 | Show History |
| KAMP - FM | Mainstream Top 40 | 2 | Los Angeles | CBS Radio | 2 | 122 | Show History |
| KIIS - FM | Mainstream Top 40 | 2 | Los Angeles | iHeartMedia | 13 | 46 | Show History |
| WBBM - FM | Mainstream Top 40 | 3 | Chicago | CBS Radio | 5 | 116 | Show History |
| WKSC - FM | Mainstream Top 40 | 3 | Chicago | iHeartMedia | 7 | 78 | Show History |
| WTMX - FM | Adult Top 40 | 3 | Chicago | Hubbard Broa... | 24 | 23 | Show History |
| KLLC - FM | Adult Top 40 | 4 | San Francisco | CBS Radio | 40 | 15 | Show History |
| KMVQ - FM | Mainstream Top 40 | 4 | San Francisco | CBS Radio | 2 | 126 | Show History |
| KREV - FM | Mainstream Top 40 | 4 | San Francisco | Royce Intern... | 2 | 112 | Show History |
| KVVF - FM | Rhythmic | 4 | San Francisco | Univision Ra... | 13 | 63 | Show History |
| KYLD - FM | Mainstream Top 40 | 4 | San Francisco | iHeartMedia | 1 | 125 | Show History |

**FIGURE 6.21**
Station airplay info for Chainsmokers' "Closer"

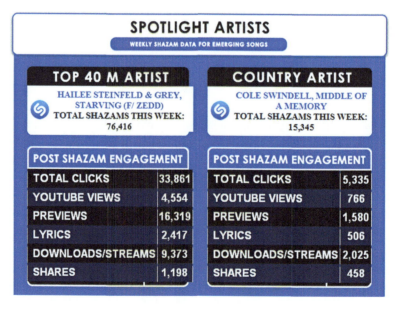

**FIGURE 6.22**
This chart reflects info about breaking music

inquisitive listeners looking to identify the title, data are compiled into a chart highlighting these queries. This registers initial interest.

Nielsen BDS presents the on-demand data in a manner that complements and is linked to airplay and digital sales from its sale-tracking platform, SoundScan. This sample chart retains the same functionality of the airplay charts, combining total national airplay, digital sales, and streaming usage. On the chart below, Ariana Grande's "Side To Side" is already ranked #8 at on-demand, with over 13 million streams, ranks #11 in digital sales but has yet to find traction on radio, ranking #1,374. Attentive programmers will see this as an indicator of audience appeal for this track. Streaming also indicates the shelf life of hit songs. Sia's "Cheap Thrills" is still the most played song on radio but streaming listeners have moved away from the song with it slowly diminishing over the past six weeks to the #13 most-streamed song. Market specific data are being tested as this is written. That focused data will provide insight into local and regional trending.

**FIGURE 6.23**
Highlighted details of chart performances of recordings by two popular vocalists

All of these tools are in use to provide programmers with a series of inputs to assist in adding an objective point of view to their own inherent musical knowledge. Music programming is truly an area where art meets science. Through careful determination commercial radio curates the country's over-the-air playlist.

Andrew Forsyth consults Nielsen BDSradio for operations, research and market development. He has performed, programmed, managed, and consulted in a variety of formats. From the Communications Arts Program at Loyola College he started in radio at Canadian Marconi's CFCF/CFQR-FM and the legendary CHOM-FM in Montreal. Over the years, he launched stations across Canada including OZ-FM Newfoundland, CJFI-FM for Rogers, CKIK Calgary, KX Country in Toronto and Hamilton and K-Rock Kingston. He is a co-founder of TSC (The Shopping Channel) and the Canadian Satellite Users Association. Associated with Bohn Media/SparkNet Communications for over 15 years, he used his expertise in regulatory affairs, music research, and product design to help meet the needs of various clients including Rogers, Corus, Cogeco, Rawlco, Harvard, Blackburn, and Goldenwest. Forsyth managed affiliate relations at start-up for SparkNetworks radio syndication. He has headed key research projects for CBC, SOCAN, CAB, and the CRTC including music usage and emerging artist policy studies. He is a tenured Professor of Communication Arts for Seneca College at York University.

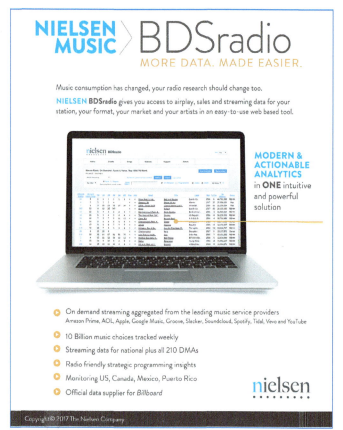

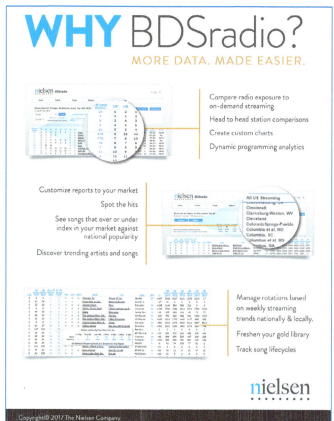

**FIGURE 6.24**
Nielsen BDS promotional brochure

## RESEARCH DEFICITS

Although broadcasters refer deferentially to the ratings surveys as the "book" or "bible," the stats they contain are audience listening estimates—no more and, it is hoped, no less. Since their inception, research companies have been criticized for the methods they employ in collecting audience listening statistics. The most prevalent complaint has had to do with the selection of samples. Critics have charged that they invariably are limited and exclusionary. Questions have persisted as to whether those surveyed are truly representative of an area's total listenership. Can 1% of the radio universe accurately reflect general listening habits? The research companies defend their tactics and have established a strong case for their methodology.

In the 1970s, one criticism directed to ratings companies at a time when the wired, landline telephone was the primary means of contact was their neglect in recruiting minorities to participate in surveys. In efforts to rectify this deficiency, both Arbitron and Birch established special sampling procedures. The survey companies also had to deal with the problem of measuring Spanish-speaking people. Arbitron found that using the personal retrieval technique significantly increased the response rate in the Spanish community, especially when bilingual interviewers were used. The personal retrieval technique did not work as well with blacks, since it was difficult to recruit interviewers to work in many of the sample areas. Thus, Arbitron used a telephone retrieval procedure that involved callbacks to selected households over a seven-day period to document listening habits. In essence, the interviewer filled out the diaries for those being surveyed. In the 1980s, Arbitron implemented differential survey treatment (DST), a technique designed to increase the response rate among blacks and, later, among Hispanic listeners, who, historically, were underrepresented ethnicities in Arbitron's surveys. The company became more intensive and proactive in its telephone-recruitment efforts to induce minorities into participating on

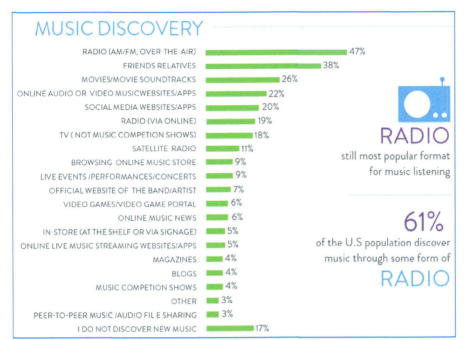

FIGURE 6.25
FM and AM radio stations serve a vital role in new music discovery
Source: Courtesy of Nielsen Audio

panels. Another incentive tactic was to increase the amount of the premium (financial compensation) that Arbitron offered its panelists. The survey company provided incentives over the customary $1–2 compensation. Up to $5 is paid to some respondents of certain black households. DST employs follow-up calls to retrieve diaries.

During its years of operation, Birch/Scarborough Research employed special sampling procedures and bilingual interviewers to collect data from the Hispanic population. According to the company, its samples yielded a high response rate among blacks. Thus, Birch did not use other special sampling controls. Ethnic listening reports containing average quarter-hour and cume estimates for Hispanics, blacks, and others were available from the company in a format similar to that of its Capsule Market Report.

Both survey companies employed additional procedures to survey other nontelephone households, especially in markets that have a large student or transient population. In the late 1970s, a Boston station targeting young people complained that Arbitron failed to acknowledge the existence of more than 200,000 college students who did not have personal phone listings. The station, which was rated among the top five in the market at the time, contended that a comprehensive survey of the city's listening audience would bear out the fact that they were, in fact, number one.

Similar complaints of skewed or inconclusive surveys persist today, but the procedures and methods used by the major radio audience research companies, although far from perfect, are more effective than ever. Christopher Porter says the greatest misconception about research data is that they are absolutes etched in granite:

The greatest fallacy is that research findings are gospel. This goes not only for the quantitative studies but for focus groups as well. Regardless of the methodology, any findings should be used as a "gut adjuster," rather than a "gut replacer." Sampling error is often ignored in a quantitative study.... When we report that 25% of a sample feels some way about something, or when a station with a 4.1 beats one with a 3.8 in a book, most station managers and PDs take all these statistics at face value.

Former station manager Lorna Ozmon, Founder of Ozmon Media Inc., concurs with Porter and warns that research should help direct rather than dictate what a station does:

I use research, rather than letting it use me. The thing to remember is that no methodology is without a significant margin of error. To treat the results of a survey as gospel is dangerous. I rely on research to provide me with the black-and-white answers and depend on myself to make determinations on the gray areas. Research never provided a radio station with the glitter to make it sparkle.

Station general manager (GM) Richard Bremkamp also expresses concern over what he perceives as an almost obsessive emphasis on survey statistics:

The concern for numbers gets out of hand. There are some really good-sounding stations out there that don't do good book, but the money is in the numbers. Kurt Vonnegut talks about the "Universal Will to Become" in his books. In radio that can be expanded to the Universal Will to Become Number One. This is good if it means the best, but that's not always what it means today.

The proliferation of data services has drawn criticism from broadcasters who feel that they are being oversurveyed and overresearched. When Arbitron introduced its computerized monthly ratings service (Arbitrends), the chairman of its own radio advisory council opposed the venture on the grounds that it would cause more confusion and create more work for broadcasters. He further contended that the monthly service would encourage short-term buying by advertisers. Similar criticism was lodged against Birch/Scarborough's own computerized service, BirchPlus. However, both services experienced steady growth.

Compounding the task of audience surveying is the challenge of achieving statistically viable response rates, regardless of whether the methodology is telephone- or Internet-based, David Pearlman observes: "Audience research is increasingly hard to acquire. Response rates are the foremost issue facing . . . anyone . . . measuring listening or consumer habits." The temporal nature of research results also helps to illustrate the story of the difficulties of acquiring meaningful, correct information. It is a situation, as Dave Van Dyke, President and CEO of Bridge Ratings LLC says, that dictates the strategy adopted by his company. Bridge Ratings LLC, he explains,

was founded on and continues to pursue the most accurate consumer media consumption data possible. We have invented some new matrixes while combining them with tried and true research methodologies. Our research is revolutionary in the sense that it truly captures media consumption at a moment in time. That is why we do constant, ongoing field work for many of the world's largest and most influential media companies and investment firms.

**FIGURE 6.26**
Consultants use strategic marketing techniques in developing campaigns for improving station performance

Source: Courtesy of DMR/Interactive

The accelerated pace of technological change makes it difficult to pinpoint listener response at any given moment. Van Dyke elaborates:

One of the benefits of our methodologies is its ability to recognize how fast-changing technology is impacting entertainment media. That ability to capture behaviors as a snapshot is why our clients are consistently asking for more studies because they know how quickly behaviors change.

Adds consultant Gary Begin: "Until PPM or some other methodology is fully realized, getting diary-keepers to make accurate entries will largely depend on their remembering a station's name or frequency, and that, as we well know, is a dubious business." The status of radio research is that certain former practices are continuing to decline, the victims of rising costs.

# HOW AGENCIES BUY RADIO

The primacy of numbers perhaps is best illustrated through a discussion of how advertising agencies invest money with radio stations. It is the media buyer's job to effectively and efficiently invest the advertiser's money—in other words, to reach the most listeners with the budget allotted for radio use. According to media buyer Lynne Price, the most commonly employed method determines the cost per point (CPP) of a given station. Price explains the procedure:

> A media buyer is given a budget and a gross rating point (GRP) goal. Our job is to buy to our GRP goal, without going over budget, against a predetermined target audience, i.e., adults 25 to 54, teens, men 18 to 34, etc. Our CPP is derived by taking the total budget and dividing by the GRP goal, or total number of rating points we would like to amass against our target audience. Now, using the CPP as a guideline, we take the cost per spot on a given station, and divide by the rating it has to see how close to the total CPP the station is. This is where the negotiation comes in. If the station is way off, you can threaten not to place advertising until they come closer to what you want to spend.

The other method used to justify station buys is cost per thousand (CPM). Using this technique, the buyer determines the cost of reaching 1,000 people at a given station. The CPM of one station is then compared with that of another's to ascertain efficiency. To determine a station's CPM, the buyer must know the station's average quarter-hour audience (AQH persons) estimate in the daypart targeted and the cost of a commercial during that time frame. The following computation will provide the station's CPM: by dividing the number of people reached into the cost of the commercial, the CPM is deduced. Thus, the lower the CPM, the more efficient the buy. Of course, this assumes that the station selected delivers the target audience sought. Again, this is the responsibility of the individual buying media for an agency. It should be apparent by now that many things are taken into consideration before airtime is purchased.

## WHAT A RESEARCH COMPANY DOES

### Ted Bolton

Bolton Research is a quantitative research company—our main objective is to get the opinions of radio listeners on virtually anything having to do with the programming and marketing of a given station (or future station). There are several methods we use to get the info:

*Perceptual studies.* These are in-depth surveys that gather opinions on issues such as music preferences, station personalities, and competitors. All respondents are included based on their age, listening habits (e.g., favorite station), favorite music types, ethnicity, county of residence, and anything else of importance to the station (client). These surveys run 15–20 minutes. Respondents are selected at random. We also do tracking studies, which include respondents from the original survey and which measure changes in opinion (usually six months out from the original survey). Perceptual studies are the foundation of research because they provide overall market information: perceptions of the client's station and its competitors, which the station uses to make programming, marketing, and sales decisions. The information gathered also aids us in designing a research program for the station.

*Music and program testing.* There are several commonly used methods for testing music and program elements.

1.  *Auditorium testing.* This is the industry standard for testing music that may be aired on the station. Respondents are screened according to station listenership, and paid an incentive between $35 and $50, depending on the market size. The typical test involves 100–150 respondents; they are usually split into two groups. Each group gathers at a hotel, where they listen on speakers to 350–400 hooks (five to 10 seconds of a song, the most memorable part). In total, 700–800 hooks will be tested. The respondents score each hook, using a 1–5 (or similar) scale. They also note if they are familiar with the song, and give it a "burn score" if they're tired of hearing the song.

Bolton Research does "Personalized Music Tests" (PMT) instead of auditorium tests. Respondents in a PMT come to a facility at a time of their choice, and they test the hooks on portable music players with headphones. We've found that we have a better turnout than the auditorium tests and that the results are better because each respondent hears the hooks the same way (in an auditorium, respondents are at different distances from the speakers) without distractions from other listeners. Auditorium tests are still the industry standard, however.

2. *Perceptual analyzer tests.* In both of the previous methods, responders typically score hooks with paper and pencil. The data then must be coded and tabulated before the client sees the results. A recent development, perceptual analyzer tests, gives a client instant information. As the scores are given, the computer produces an instant, continuous EKG-like graph that shows averages for different groups—a station's "core" listeners and its competitors' listeners, for instance. We've found this method (we call the test "BoltScan") to be most useful in testing music in the original order that it actually aired, thereby showing us both popular songs that keep listeners tuned in, and the stuff that causes tune-out. It works the same way for testing morning shows, comedy bits, and so on.

3. *Call-out music research.* This is a staple of radio programming. Respondents of a specific age and listening group—typically core listeners in a tight age range—are called at home and asked to score 25–30 hooks. The test is obviously short and can be conducted biweekly or even weekly. This information is most useful for trending the familiarity, popularity, and burnout of songs (usually new songs) over time. Call-out is a task often assigned to station interns, but a number of research companies offer the service as well.

4. *Focus groups and listener panels.* Focus groups are, of course, used for all kinds of consumer product testing, and radio is no exception. Again, respondents are screened for age and listenership. Participants are paid a small incentive and come to a focus group facility or hotel room in groups of eight to 12. Station staff observe while the moderator asks respondents about their likes and dislikes of station attributes, including music preferences, personalities, competing stations, etc. Listener panels are more informal and are usually done in-house by the station. Respondents are recruited on the air or from the station's database. Again, respondents are asked for their opinions about the station.

4a. *Web-based research.* Listeners can be recruited via the web to participate in perceptual and music testing research. In some cases respondents are offered incentives. This vastly improves upon the quality of the sample base. However, many stations make use of the optional opt-in type study, where listeners are asked to become part of a "Listener VIP Club." The quality of any sample is highly dependent upon the incentives that, in turn, have an impact on response rates.

5. *Statistics.* Although some complicated statistical methods are sometimes used, the vast majority of data analysis involves "descriptive" statistics: frequency and average scores. Frequency is a computation of how many people fit into a category or choose a given response to a question. Averages (mean, median, and mode) are measures of average or typical performance. For most research reports, these basic statistics are enough. Some more sophisticated statistics are used to look for relationships and differences between groups: correlation ANOVA (analysis of variance), t-tests, chi-square, and cluster and factor analysis. For instance, we often use cluster analysis to separate respondents into distinct groups, such as modern rock and classic rock lovers. This helps a station to determine which artists are unique elements in a specific audience's tastes.

Why do research? Not every radio programmer is a convert to the gospel of research. It is expensive, and stations are always on a tight budget. Many programmers have done just fine using experience and their gut to get them through. In addition, as people become more guarded with their privacy, both in terms of personal information and home invasion with the telephone, research becomes a more difficult and expensive proposition. Yet, the market intelligence research provides is vital to the stations. Research provides information that can make the gut feeling more of a sure thing or tell you that your gut is all wrong. Even the best research is useless if it's not studied and properly applied. Also, shoddy research *can* do a lot more harm than good. As is the case with most things in life, you frequently get what you pay for.

Ted Bolton, Ph.D., has more than 25 years of experience in helping companies create marketing strategies that accelerate the acceptance and diffusion of entertainment content and new media technologies for a wide range of applications. He founded Bolton Research Corporation and it has grown to become one of the leading media/technology research firms in the U.S., serving AT&T, Time Warner, CBS, NBC, ABC, Comcast, Banc One, Clear Channel Communications, and others.

Dr. Bolton's dissertation invented a predictive modeling algorithm for new technology adoption and diffusion that is still in use today. At Bolton Research he led the industry in new media product testing, predictive modeling, consumer ethnography, and a wide assortment of seminal music and artist testing techniques. His passion for media, advertising, music, and information technologies is based on the premise that technologies only work if people integrate them into their existing way of life.

## THE FUTURE OF RESEARCH IN RADIO

Most experts agree that the role of research in radio will continue to grow despite the trend toward downsizing and clustering. They base their predictions on the ever-increasing fragmentation and niching of the listening audience, which makes the jobs of targeting and positioning more complex. The field of broadcast research has grown considerably in the past two decades, and there is every reason to suspect that the growth will continue. As demographic targets and formats splinter, there will be an increasingly greater need to know. Christopher Porter sees the fragmentation and niching as creating a greater demand for research: "With the inevitability of more competition in already overcrowded markets, the need to stay abreast of market developments is critical. Yes, the role of research will continue to grow."

WGAO Station Manager Vic Michaels contends:

Cost-effective ways to perform and utilize sophisticated psychographic data have made the computer standard equipment at most stations, small and large alike. Research is becoming a way of life everywhere, and computers and station websites are an integral part of the information age. Computers encourage more do-it-yourself research at stations, as well, and websites allow for the collection of data and the interaction with audience.

Gary Begin contends that advances in research technology also will continue to improve the nature and quality of research: "As with the portable ratings devices now being touted, we'll see more improvement in methodology and a greater diversity of applicable data as the result of high-tech innovations."

## THE ROLE OF RESEARCH

### Warren Kurtzman

Research plays a more vital role in the success of radio stations than at perhaps any other time since our firm's founding nearly 35 years ago. Globalization and the increased diversification of nearly every country we work in have created greater fragmentation in listener tastes. These developments, coupled with the technology-fueled explosion in media choices available to consumers, have increased the complexity of the marketplaces most radio stations compete in exponentially.

When markets are more complex it makes the tasks of successfully programming, positioning, and marketing of radio stations harder. Our experience is that stations are most successful at attracting large audiences when they are well known, possess brand attributes with which listeners want to affiliate, and are strongly associated with types of content for which large appetites exist. That is where research comes in—it helps radio managers objectively understand the tastes of audiences and the degree to which their stations and their competitors are associated with the brand attributes and content listeners desire the most.

**FIGURE 6.28**
Warren Kurtzman

In recent years, this complex environment has become even more challenging to navigate due to the introduction of electronic audience measurement in many markets, such as the Portable People Meter (PPM) system utilized in the largest markets in the United States and Canada. Prior efforts to measure audience sizes through written diaries and telephone interviews generally meant that stations that were well known and positively branded could count on regularly finishing atop the ratings. Electronic audience measurement has taught us that building a strong brand is not enough; to be a ratings leader, a radio station must be strongly branded *and* must deliver content on a moment-by-moment basis that is as compelling as possible.

It is not enough, however, to do more research in response to these factors. Research must adapt to the changing habits of consumers and must focus on delivering insights that are customized to the needs and objectives of each radio station. That has resulted in the development of many more tools than radio stations had at their disposal as recently as a decade ago. For example, the PPM measurement system has led to the development of more sophisticated research services for evaluating content on the minute-by-minute—and, in some cases, the second-by-second—level.

Thus, research's role in radio remains vital. It is a key "science" that complements the "art" of creative programmers and managers and produces successful radio stations around the world.

---

**Warren Kurtzman** was named President and Chief Operating Officer of Coleman Insights in August 2008 after serving as a Vice-President since joining the firm in May 1995. He works directly with dozens of clients and oversees the day-to-day operations of the company, which helps media companies in North America, South America, Europe, and Asia build strong brands and develop great content through consumer research. His background includes 11 years in radio station management and media research with Strategic Radio Research, Arbitron Inc., WUUU/Utica, New York, and WVBR/Ithaca, New York. Kurtzman holds a Bachelor of Science degree in Policy Analysis from Cornell University in Ithaca, New York, and a Master's in Business Administration from New York University. He resides in Raleigh, North Carolina, with his wife, two children, and two dogs.

**FIGURE 6.29**
Online services play an important role in the selection of new music

Source: Courtesy of Matt Bailey and Integr8 Research

# Guide to New Music Tools

**How to use these tools in concert with new music research to select the best new music:**

 **Spotify**
Use it to spot when listeners still love a song, but no longer want to hear it as often.

 **SHAZAM**
Use it to help see which new songs you're playing are sparking interest with your listeners.

**Expect contemporary hit songs to be:**
**Developing in** weeks **1** to **8**
**At their peak in** weeks **9** to **20**
**Declining after** week **20**

 iTunes
Song Sales: Don't look for songs that are top sellers today, look for songs that stay top sellers week after week.

 YouTube
Watch out for songs with videos that go viral overnight—they tend to disappear almost as quickly. The real hits tend to develop slowly over several weeks.

For more information about **INTEGR8** new music research, visit www.integr8research.com

| Custom Local Callout Song | Sample Report Artist | Grade | | | | Mean | | | | Burn | | | | Unfamiliar | | | | Total Grade | Total Mean | Total Burn | Total Unfam |
|---|---|---|---|---|---|---|---|---|---|---|---|---|---|---|---|---|---|---|---|---|---|
| | | Male | Female | 25-34 | 35-44 | Male | Female | 25-34 | 35-44 | Male | Female | 25-34 | 35-44 | Male | Female | 25-34 | 35-44 | | | | |
| 1 Boys Round Here | Blake Shelton | 86 | 90 | 87 | 89 | 4.00 | 4.10 | 4.04 | 4.07 | 21% | 17% | 21% | 17% | 3% | 0% | 4% | 0% | 88 | 4.05 | 19% | 2% |
| 2 Runnin' Outta Moonlight | Randy Houser | 83 | 91 | 85 | 89 | 3.83 | 4.10 | 3.86 | 4.07 | 7% | 14% | 11% | 10% | 0% | 0% | 0% | 0% | 87 | 3.97 | 10% | 0% |
| 3 Crash My Party | Luke Bryan | 82 | 89 | 89 | 82 | 3.79 | 4.07 | 4.11 | 3.77 | 24% | 28% | 25% | 27% | 0% | 0% | 0% | 0% | 86 | 3.93 | 26% | 0% |
| 4 Aw Naw | Chris Young | 78 | 92 | 85 | 85 | 3.71 | 4.21 | 4.00 | 3.93 | 17% | 10% | 7% | 20% | 3% | 0% | 4% | 0% | 85 | 3.96 | 14% | 2% |
| 5 Done | The Band Perry | 77 | 93 | 88 | 82 | 3.59 | 4.28 | 4.04 | 3.83 | 28% | 24% | 32% | 20% | 0% | 0% | 0% | 0% | 85 | 3.93 | 26% | 0% |
| 6 Parking Lot Party | Lee Brice | 84 | 86 | 88 | 83 | 3.83 | 3.97 | 4.00 | 3.80 | 28% | 21% | 18% | 30% | 0% | 0% | 0% | 0% | 85 | 3.90 | 24% | 0% |
| 7 Don't Ya | Brett Eldredge | 81 | 89 | 83 | 87 | 3.85 | 4.03 | 3.92 | 3.97 | 17% | 31% | 29% | 20% | 7% | 0% | 7% | 0% | 85 | 3.95 | 24% | 3% |
| 8 Get Your Shine On | Florida Georgia Line | 81 | 87 | 80 | 87 | 3.72 | 3.97 | 3.71 | 3.97 | 34% | 28% | 36% | 27% | 7% | 0% | 0% | 0% | 84 | 3.84 | 31% | 0% |
| 9 Night Train | Jason Aldean | 80 | 86 | 81 | 85 | 3.85 | 3.97 | 3.81 | 4.00 | 14% | 14% | 21% | 7% | 7% | 0% | 4% | 3% | 83 | 3.91 | 14% | 3% |
| 10 Mine Would Be You | Blake Shelton | 78 | 87 | 81 | 83 | 3.68 | 4.04 | 3.81 | 3.90 | 7% | 14% | 14% | 7% | 3% | 3% | 4% | 3% | 82 | 3.86 | 10% | 3% |
| 11 See You Again | Carrie Underwood | 77 | 87 | 83 | 81 | 3.59 | 4.00 | 3.82 | 3.77 | 34% | 24% | 39% | 20% | 0% | 0% | 0% | 0% | 82 | 3.79 | 29% | 0% |
| 12 Redneck Crazy | Tyler Farr | 78 | 83 | 79 | 81 | 3.74 | 3.83 | 3.81 | 3.77 | 21% | 28% | 29% | 20% | 7% | 0% | 7% | 0% | 80 | 3.79 | 24% | 3% |
| 13 Round Here | Florida Georgia Line | 77 | 83 | 75 | 85 | 3.55 | 3.89 | 3.56 | 3.87 | 14% | 14% | 21% | 7% | 0% | 3% | 4% | 0% | 80 | 3.72 | 14% | 2% |
| 14 Sunny and 75 | Joe Nichols | 79 | 80 | 77 | 82 | 3.75 | 3.79 | 3.73 | 3.80 | 10% | 17% | 18% | 10% | 3% | 3% | 7% | 0% | 80 | 3.77 | 14% | 3% |
| 15 Point At You | Justin Moore | 80 | 79 | 79 | 79 | 3.69 | 3.66 | 3.68 | 3.67 | 21% | 28% | 25% | 23% | 0% | 0% | 0% | 0% | 79 | 3.67 | 24% | 0% |
| 16 Southern Girl | Tim McGraw | 77 | 81 | 73 | 85 | 3.64 | 3.76 | 3.48 | 3.90 | 14% | 17% | 25% | 7% | 3% | 0% | 4% | 0% | 79 | 3.70 | 16% | 2% |
| 17 It Goes Like This | Thomas Rhett | 75 | 80 | 76 | 80 | 3.52 | 3.72 | 3.54 | 3.70 | 17% | 14% | 18% | 13% | 0% | 0% | 0% | 0% | 78 | 3.62 | 16% | 0% |
| 18 Carolina | Parmalee | 78 | 77 | 76 | 78 | 3.66 | 3.70 | 3.61 | 3.75 | 10% | 21% | 29% | 3% | 0% | 7% | 0% | 7% | 77 | 3.68 | 16% | 3% |
| 19 All Kinds Of Kinds | Miranda Lambert | 73 | 81 | 74 | 79 | 3.46 | 3.82 | 3.50 | 3.79 | 21% | 10% | 21% | 10% | 3% | 3% | 0% | 7% | 77 | 3.64 | 16% | 3% |
| 20 That's My Kind of Night | Luke Bryan | 71 | 81 | 74 | 78 | 3.44 | 3.76 | 3.62 | 3.60 | 28% | 24% | 21% | 30% | 7% | 0% | 7% | 0% | 76 | 3.61 | 26% | 3% |
| 21 Don't Let Me Be Lonely | The Band Perry | 74 | 76 | 77 | 73 | 3.45 | 3.87 | 3.72 | 3.56 | 17% | 10% | 14% | 13% | 0% | 21% | 11% | 10% | 75 | 3.63 | 14% | 10% |
| 22 Stay | Florida Georgia Line | 68 | 81 | 80 | 70 | 3.71 | 3.89 | 3.88 | 3.75 | 0% | 0% | 0% | 0% | 30% | 10% | 11% | 27% | 75 | 3.81 | 0% | 20% |
| 23 Sweet Annie | Zac Brown Band | 73 | 76 | 73 | 76 | 3.46 | 3.67 | 3.48 | 3.64 | 24% | 10% | 4% | 7% | 3% | 7% | 4% | 7% | 74 | 3.56 | 17% | 5% |
| 24 Red | Taylor Swift | 75 | 73 | 72 | 75 | 3.46 | 3.45 | 3.41 | 3.50 | 28% | 31% | 32% | 27% | 3% | 0% | 4% | 0% | 73 | 3.46 | 29% | 2% |
| 25 Radio | Darius Rucker | 75 | 71 | 71 | 75 | 3.54 | 3.73 | 3.61 | 3.63 | 17% | 10% | 25% | 3% | 3% | 24% | 18% | 10% | 73 | 3.62 | 14% | 14% |
| 26 Drunk Last Night | Eli Young Band | 71 | 71 | 71 | 71 | 3.50 | 3.73 | 3.61 | 3.60 | 17% | 0% | 11% | 7% | 10% | 24% | 18% | 17% | 71 | 3.60 | 9% | 17% |
| 27 We Were Us | Keith Urban | 72 | 68 | 69 | 72 | 3.38 | 3.61 | 3.52 | 3.45 | 28% | 3% | 21% | 10% | 0% | 21% | 18% | 3% | 71 | 3.48 | 16% | 10% |
| 28 Wasting All These Tears | Cassadee Pope | 71 | 68 | 73 | 67 | 3.39 | 3.44 | 3.56 | 3.29 | 24% | 17% | 25% | 17% | 3% | 14% | 11% | 7% | 70 | 3.42 | 21% | 9% |
| 29 Chillin' It | Cole Swindell | 69 | 66 | 65 | 71 | 3.42 | 3.57 | 3.43 | 3.54 | 17% | 3% | 18% | 3% | 10% | 28% | 25% | 13% | 68 | 3.49 | 10% | 19% |
| 30 Everything I Shouldn't Be ... | Thompson Square | 68 | 67 | 69 | 67 | 3.35 | 3.65 | 3.55 | 3.42 | 21% | 3% | 14% | 10% | 10% | 31% | 21% | 20% | 68 | 3.48 | 12% | 21% |
| 31 I Can't Change The World | Brad Paisley | 60 | 75 | 65 | 70 | 2.93 | 3.76 | 3.24 | 3.39 | 24% | 17% | 21% | 20% | 3% | 14% | 11% | 7% | 67 | 3.32 | 21% | 9% |
| 32 Everybody's Got Somebody ... | Hunter Hayes | 64 | 69 | 68 | 66 | 3.15 | 3.50 | 3.38 | 3.26 | 28% | 7% | 21% | 13% | 7% | 17% | 14% | 10% | 67 | 3.31 | 17% | 12% |
| 33 Friday Night | Eric Paslay | 63 | 68 | 64 | 67 | 3.25 | 3.89 | 3.71 | 3.40 | 10% | 10% | 11% | 10% | 17% | 38% | 39% | 17% | 66 | 3.52 | 10% | 28% |
| 34 Days of Gold | Jake Owen | 63 | 66 | 65 | 64 | 3.07 | 3.68 | 3.48 | 3.19 | 31% | 3% | 11% | 23% | 3% | 34% | 25% | 13% | 64 | 3.32 | 17% | 19% |
| 35 Whatever She's Got | David Nail | 56 | 69 | 66 | 60 | 3.00 | 3.71 | 3.43 | 3.29 | 10% | 0% | 0% | 9% | 30% | 30% | 22% | 36% | 63 | 3.36 | 5% | 30% |

FIGURE 6.30

A sample report radio stations use to make playlist adjustments based on listener Familiarity, Appeal and Fatigue of songs. Kelly Music Research conducts Current and Library Music Research for radio stations across the USA. For more information visit KellyMusic.com

Source: Courtesy of Kelly Music Research

Today it is common for stations to budget 5–10% of their annual income to research, and Christopher Porter believes it will probably increase. "As it evolves," he says, "it is likely that the marketplace will demand that more funds be allocated for research purposes. Research may not guarantee success, but it's not getting any easier to be successful without it." Research has been a part of radio broadcasting since its modest beginnings in the 1920s, and it appears that it will play an even greater role in the operations of stations as the new century deepens.

## CHAPTER HIGHLIGHTS

1. Beginning in the late 1920s, surveys were conducted to determine the most popular stations and programs with various audience groupings. Early surveys (and their methods) included C.E. Hooper Inc. (telephone), CAB (telephone), and Pulse (in-person). In 1968, RADAR (telephone to 6,000 households) began to provide information for networks. The leader among local market audience surveys until 2013 was Arbitron. That year the firm was purchased and rebranded as Nielsen Audio.

2. In 1963, the Broadcast Rating Council was established to monitor, audit, and accredit ratings companies. In 1982, it was renamed the Electronic Media Planning Council to reflect its involvement with cable television ratings. Renamed the Media Rating Council in 1997, it now represents Internet constituencies, as well as radio, TV, cable, and print.

3. Nielsen Audio measures listenership in the MSA, that is, the city or urban center, and the TSA, which covers the surrounding communities.

4. A station's primary listening locations are designated as the DMA.

5. The Nielsen Audio seven-day diary logs time tuned to a station; station call letters or program name; whether AM, FM, or satellite; where listening occurred; and the listener's age, gender, and area of residence.

6. From the late 1970s to the early 1990s, Birch/Scarborough gathered data by calling equal numbers of male and female listeners aged 12 and over. Clients were offered seven different report formats, including a computerized data retrieval system. The company went out of business on December 31, 1991.

7. With today's highly fragmented audiences, advertisers and agencies are less comfortable buying just ratings numbers and look for audience qualities. Programmers must consider not only the age and gender of the target audience but also their lifestyles, values, and behavior.

8. The Portable People Meter (PPM) is a cellphone–sized device that records radio audience listening patterns. Since its 2006 rollout the system is gradually displacing the seven-day paper diary.

9. Criticisms about underrepresented minority panelists in the early history of PPM measurement led to the formation of the PPM Coalition by industry representatives to improve media relationships with Arbitron.

10. Following its acquisition of Arbitron, Nielsen Audio announced intentions to increase PPM sample sizes and focus on improving efforts to recruit African-American and Hispanic panelists.

11. Criticisms leveled against the PPM for under-reporting listening led to the issuance of revised software in 2015.

12. Selecting music for airplay is part art, part science. Data provided by Nielsen's BDSradio service provide programmers with national- and market-based information for identifying listeners' song preferences.

13. Station in-house surveyors use telephone, computer, website, face-to-face, and mail methods.

14. Media buyers for agencies use station ratings to determine the most cost-effective buy for their clients. Two methods they use are the cost per rating point (CPP) and the cost per thousand (CPM).

15. Ratings estimates are a quantitative indicator of audience response to programming. Qualitative research outcomes about listener preferences (notably, recorded music) serve to inform the thinking of and the decisions made by programmers.

# SUGGESTED FURTHER READING

Balon, R.E., *Radio In the 90s*, NAB, Washington, D.C., 1990.

Bartos, R., *The Moving Target: What Every Marketer Should Know about Women*, The Free Press, New York, NY, 1982.

Berger, A.A., *Media and Communication Research Methods*, Sage, Beverly Hills, CA, 2008.

*Broadcast Advertising Reports*, Broadcast Advertising Research, New York, periodically.

*Broadcasting Yearbook*, Broadcasting Publishing, Washington, D.C., 1935 to 2010 (ceased publication).

Bryant, J., *Media Effects: Advances in Theory and Research*, 3rd edition, Routledge, New York, NY, 2008.

Buzzard, K., *Chains of Gold: Marketing the Ratings and Rating the Markets*, Scarecrow Press, Lanham, MD, 1990.

Buzzard, K., *Electronic Media Ratings*, Focal Press, Boston, MA, 1992.

Chappell, M.N. and Hooper, C.E., *Radio Audience Measurement*, Stephen Day Press, New York, NY, 1944.

Compaine, B. and Gomery, D. *Who Owns the Media?: Competition and Concentration in the Mass Media Industry*, 3rd edition, Lawrence Erlbaum Associates, Mahwah, NJ, 2000.

Duncan, J., *American Radio*, Author, Kalamazoo, MI, twice yearly.

Duncan, J., *Radio in the United States, 1976–82: A Statistical History*, Author, Kalamazoo, MI, 1983.

Eastman, S.T., *Research in Media Promotion*, LEA, Mahwah, NJ, 2000.

Electronic Industries Association, *Electronic Market Data Book*, EIA, Washington, D.C., annually.

Fletcher, J.E. (ed.), *Handbook of Radio and Television Broadcasting: Research Procedures in Audience, Programming, and Revenues*, Van Nostrand Reinhold, New York, NY, 1981.

Gunter, B., *Media Research Methods*, Sage, Beverly Hills, CA, 2000.

Jamieson, K.H. and Campbell, K.K., *The Interplay of Influence: Mass Media and Their Publics in News, Advertising, and Politics*, Wadsworth, Belmont, CA, 1983.

Jensen, K.B., *Handbook of Media and Communications Research*, Routledge, New York, NY, 2002.

Katz, H., *The Media Handbook: A Complete Guide to Advertising Media Selection, Planning, Research, and Buying*, 4th edition, Routledge, New York, NY, 2010.

Lazarsfeld, P.F. and Kendall, P., *Radio Listening in America*, Prentice Hall, Englewood Cliffs, NJ, 1948.

McDowell, W., *Troubleshooting Audience Research*, NAB, Washington, D.C., 2000.

National Association of Broadcasters, *Radio Financial Report*, NAB, Washington, D.C., 1955 to date, annually.

National Association of Broadcasters, *Audience Research Sourcebook*, NAB, Washington, D.C., 1991.

Nielsen, Portable People Meter 101 (online tutorial), www.arbitron.com/portable_people_meters/ppm_training.htm.

Park, D.W. and Pooley, J. (eds.), *The History of Media and Communication Research*, Peter Lang, New York, NY, 2008.

*Radio Facts*, Radio Advertising Bureau, New York, NY, published annually.

Shane, E., *Selling Electronic Media*, Focal Press, Boston, MA, 1999.

Webster, J.G., Phelan, P., and Lichty, L.W., *The Theory and Practice of Audience Research*, 3rd edition, Lawrence Erlbaum Associates, Mahwah, NJ, 2006.

Wimmer, R.D. and Dominick, J., *Mass Media Research: An Introduction*, 10th edition, Wadsworth, Belmont, CA, 2014.

## PROMOTIONS—PRACTICAL AND BIZARRE

The idea behind any promotion is to gain listeners. Over the years, stations have used a variety of methods, ranging from the conventional to the outlandish, to accomplish this goal. "If a promotion achieves top-of-the-mind awareness in the listener, it's a winner. Granted, some strange things have been done to accomplish this," admits Mississippi broadcaster Bob Lima. Today, radio stations use the Internet as a method to market themselves. Stations have elaborate websites with colorful graphics to catch the reader's attention, giveaways, and announcements of upcoming contests, concerts, and photos of winners of the most recent contests to encourage more listenership and participation. Additionally, stations have fully adopted social media technologies by encouraging listeners to friend the station on its Facebook page and follow the station on Twitter or Instagram. Stations will use whatever technology and platform needed to communicate with and potentially gain more listeners.

Promotions designed to captivate the interest of the radio audience have inspired some pretty bizarre schemes. In the 1950s, Dallas station KLIF placed overturned cars on freeways with a sign on their undersides announcing the arrival of a new deejay, Johnny Rabbitt. It would be hard to calculate the number of deejays who have lived atop flagpoles or in elevators for the sake of a rating point.

In the 1980s, the shenanigans continued. To gain the listening public's attention, a California deejay set a world record by sitting in every seat of a major league ballpark that held 65,000 spectators. In the process of the stunt, the publicity-hungry deejay injured his leg. However, he went on to accomplish his goal by garnering national attention for himself and his station. Another station offered to give away a mobile home to contestants who camped out the longest on a platform at the base of a billboard. The challenge turned into a battle of wills as three contestants spent months trying to outlast each other. In the end, one of the three was disqualified, and the station, in an effort to cease what had become more of an embarrassment than anything else, awarded the two holdouts recreational vehicles.

**FIGURE 7.1**
Stations promote their image
Source: Courtesy of Wolfpack Media LLC

Today, promotions have gotten edgier, especially on those stations featuring "shock jock" shows. Things can and do get out of hand when personalities go to the extreme to draw listeners' attention with on-air pranks and giveaways. Prior to migrating to satellite, Howard Stern held all manner of scatological promotions and contests, many centered around women removing their clothes, and Opie and Anthony asked listeners to have sex in public places. This ultimately got them removed from the air, thus proving there are limits to what a station can do to get attention from an audience. Of course, after a successful stint (or exile) on satellite radio, the duo was hired back by terrestrial radio—proving again that ratings matter most.

**FIGURE 7.2**
Although the *Opie and Anthony* show on WNEW-FM in New York garnered attention from local listeners for its promotion involving alleged sexual acts in public places, it also garnered unwanted attention from the FCC, which found the radio station contest in violation of obscenity and indecency regulations. It cost the radio station $357,000 in FCC fines and it cost Opie and Anthony their jobs

Source: Courtesy of *Radio World* and Paul McLane

## RADIOWORLD

NEWS & BUSINESS    TECH & GEAR    COLUMNS & VIEWS    GLOBAL    SHOW NEWS    R

# FCC Probes Church Sex

August 26, 2002

FCC Chairman Michael Powell stated he was "deeply disturbed" about the reports of an incident involving WNEW(FM) and a radio contest involving sex in public places, and has directed the agency to begin investigating the matter. A letter sent to WNEW owner Infinity Broadcasting asks several pointed questions, including the names of anyone involved in the contest and the nature of their responsibility. A transcript provided by the commission reads as if the sex was simulated, and not real. The FCC has asked Infinity if this is the case.
Infinity late last week yanked "Opie & Anthony" off the air and fired the jocks. WNEW GM Ken Stevens and PD Jeremy Coleman were suspended. The actions appeased the Catholic League, whose president, William Donohue, had earlier asked for the station's license to be revoked.

---

The tone and tenor of station promotions have certainly changed over the decades, notes Larry Miller:

> Although occurring in what now seems a gentler and kinder world, my personal favorite is the one about a station in LA in the early 1950s that sent out a "free Valhalla Oil credit card" to listeners. Well, there was no such oil company, but loyal listeners nevertheless spent a good deal of time searching for a Valhalla gas station. Everybody had a laugh.

Reporter Peg Harney offers testimony that the bizarre still occurs in radio promotions:

> As a publicity stunt and also to get people to use the local public library, a station in Ft. Worth, Texas, a couple years back announced it had hidden cash in small denominations in the fiction section. Approximately 800 people descended on the library and proceeded to pull books off the shelves looking for the money. The library had not been notified that the station was going to make the announcement, and it was totally taken by surprise. The librarian said that approximately 4,000 books were pulled from the shelves—some of them had pages torn out—and that people were climbing on the bookcases and making a tremendous mess. The station was forced to make a public apology, and it promised full financial restitution.

One of the most infamous examples of a promotion gone bad occurred when a station decided to air-drop dozens of turkeys to a waiting crowd of listeners in a neighborhood shopping center parking lot. Unfortunately, the station discovered too late that turkeys are not adept at flying at heights above 30 feet. Consequently, several cars were damaged and witnesses were traumatized as turkeys plunged to the ground. This promotion-turned-nightmare was fictionalized in an episode of the television sitcom *WKRP in Cincinnati*.

Even worse is when a death occurs as a result of a station's promotional stunt. In Sacramento, California, in 2007, at KDND, the station held a "Hold your Wee for a Wii" contest. It required contestants to drink as much water as possible without relieving themselves. A young mother of three children, for whom she was trying to win the Wii video game system, died after drinking two gallons of water. As a result of the death, 10 employees lost their jobs. *The Washington Post* reported, "The standard argument made by radio executives is that listeners who participate in stunts are adults and ought to take responsibility for their own actions." In 2009, a jury awarded the woman's family a $16.5 million judgment in a wrongful death lawsuit. In 2013, when the radio station's license renewal came up for review, legal challenges were filed with the FCC by community groups who remained outraged by the contestant's death. By 2017, Entercom License LLC, the owner of KDND, requested that the FCC dismiss

FIGURE 7.3A AND 7.3B
Radio stations will do whatever is necessary to attract listeners and appeal to their targeted demographic. This was a promotional event designed for female listeners

Source: Courtesy of Hot 89.9, Ottawa, Ontario

its license renewal application altogether, relinquishing control of the station. Joon Chun, of ChiefMarketer.com, says: "This lesson provides a sober reminder of how important it is to not ask people to do stupid things for promotions."

In an effort to increase listenership, in 2011, a Canadian radio station had a contest offering its listeners an opportunity to win a baby. LifeSiteNews.com reported the station's program director as saying:

> one in six people have trouble conceiving, and we know that our audience—we target females between the age of 25 and 54—is dealing with the issue of conceiving right now, and so we wanted to give them the opportunity to have a baby of their own.

The contest was designed to pay for in vitro fertilization (IVF).

In 2009, WRXL in Virginia held a contest called "Marriage Bailout 09," in which it gave listeners free divorces via an arrangement with a local attorney.

The list of glitches and botched promotions is seemingly endless. In the late 1960s, a station in central Massachusetts asked listeners to predict how long its air personality could ride a carousel at a local fair. The hardy airman's effort was cut short on day three when motion sickness got the best of him and he vomited on a crowd of spectators and newspaper photographers. A station in California came close to disaster when a promotion that challenged listeners to find buried treasure resulted in half the community being dug up by overzealous contestants. In Massachusetts, a station invited listeners to retrieve money-filled balloons dropped by helicopters into the surf, and contestants came close to drowning as the balloons floated out to sea.

These promotions did indeed capture the attention of the public, but in each case the station's image was somewhat tarnished. The axiom that any publicity, good or bad, is better than none at all can get a station into not only hot water but legal problems, contends station promotion director Chuck Davis: "It's great to get lots of exposure for the station, but if it makes the station look foolish, it can work against you."

The vast majority of radio contests and promotions are of a more practical nature and run without too many complications. Promotions that involve prizes, both large and small, spark audience interest, says Rick Peters, CEO of Bluewater Broadcasting:

> People love to win something or, at least, feel that they have a shot at winning a prize. That's basic to human nature, I believe. You really don't have to give away two city blocks, either. A listener usually is thrilled and delighted to win a pair of concert tickets.

Although numerous examples can be cited to support the view that big prizes get big audiences, there is also ample evidence that low-budget giveaways, involving t-shirts, albums, tickets, posters, dinners, and so forth, are very useful in building and maintaining audience interest. In fact, some surveys have revealed that smaller, more personalized prizes may work better for a station than the high-priced items. Concert tickets, electronic devices, and dinners for two rank among the most popular contest prizes, according to surveys. Cheaper items usually mean more numerous or frequent giveaways. *Inside Radio* reported:

> At the top of the list is a tangible value proposition to the listener, such as giving away concert tickets, gift cards, or other items of value. O'Reilly Auto Parts provides $25 and $50 gift cards and offers sale specials. Also frequently mentioned is the opportunity for listeners to meet their favorite personality, live entertainment or a sound system, activities and street visibility to draw passersby in.

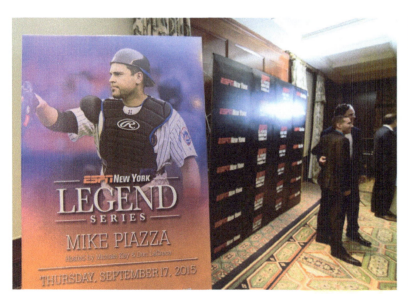

**FIGURE 7.4**

Attendees pose in front of the 98.7 FM ESPN, New York, "step and repeat" during the 2015 Legends Series featuring former New York Mets All-Star catcher Mike Piazza. Listeners were able to purchase tickets through Citi Private Pass, as well as win seats through an on-air contest. Attendees also included some of the advertisers

Source: Courtesy of 98.7 FM ESPN, New York

**FIGURE 7.5**

A tweet from the official 98.7 FM ESPN, New York, Twitter account promoting a chance to win a VIP Beer & Football experience sponsored by and held at the Brooklyn Brewery. The event was limited to winners and allowed winning listeners to meet and greet radio hosts Chris Canty and Anita Marks, as well as chat with them about football

Source: Courtesy of 98.7 FM ESPN, New York

The Internet and social media technologies have forced stations to place more of an emphasis on promotions and marketing for stations. Brian Foster, former Vice-President of NextMedia, which operates radio stations in eight states, says, "The number of options have grown at break-neck speed. While you used to compete against the station across the street, you now must battle against thousands of options with varying degree of personalization." Facebook and Twitter are commonplace on radio station websites. "Social media has become the new age billboard. Street presence is also critical, this would include fairs, concerts, etc.," says Foster.

## HOW TO WRITE A SOCIAL MEDIA POLICY FOR YOUR RADIO STATION

### Seth Resler

Every radio station needs a clear social media policy, especially given the high-profile nature of its air talent. The point of this policy is not to restrict your employees but to keep them from getting themselves into trouble. Social media is still relatively new, which is why we see so many public figures getting themselves fired by making social media faux pas. Don't rely on a vague "morals clause" in your airstaff contracts. This may give you the legal grounds to fire somebody after they make a mistake, but your goal is to prevent that mistake from happening in the first place. You need a social media policy.

**FIGURE 7.6**
Seth Resler

Here are some tips for creating a clear social media policy that will set expectations and keep everybody on your staff on the same page.

- *Get the right people involved.* When writing a social media policy, you should get all of the appropriate stakeholders involved in the process: management, human resources, even union representation if necessary.

- *Decide if your airstaff requires a separate policy.* While you should have social media policies in place that cover every member of your staff, there's good reason to write a slightly different policy for your airstaff. After all, they are public personalities in a way that your engineers or promotions staffers are not. In fact, you may want a different policy for your full-time airstaff and your part-time airstaff.

- *Spell out the scope of social networks you are covering.* Beyond the usual suspects, there are also a number of websites that include social features, for example blogs, blog comments, Reddit, YouTube comments, Yelp! reviews, Amazon reviews, etc. Anything posted to these websites by your airstaff is public and could reflect on your station. Does your policy apply to all of these or just some? It should be clear.

- *Decide if there are any networks you want to address specifically.* There are so many social networks, with new ones popping up all the time, that it doesn't make sense to address them all by name in your policy. However, you may want to specifically address some of the biggest networks, including Facebook, Twitter, and YouTube.

- *Draw a distinction between company social networks and personal social networks.* For example, your station may have a Twitter account and your afternoon drive jock may have a Twitter account. In general, you can probably be more protective of the company account, but that does not mean that jocks should have free rein with their personal networks.

- *Differentiate between reciprocal and nonreciprocal personal social networks.* Some networks, like LinkedIn, are reciprocal. In other words, both parties must approve of a relationship before it exists. Other networks are not. On Twitter, for example, anybody can follow you without needing your approval. This means that posts to Twitter have the potential to reach far more people than posts to LinkedIn. You may want to be more lax with reciprocal social networks than nonreciprocal social networks, because they more closely resemble private communication. However, anything posted online has the potential to spread.

- *Differentiate between Facebook profiles and Facebook pages.* Facebook allows users to create both reciprocal and nonreciprocal accounts. Profiles, which are meant to be used by individuals, are reciprocal. Pages, which are meant to be used by companies, organizations, and brands, are not reciprocal; anybody can follow them. Encourage your airstaff to keep a Facebook profile for personal use with people they know, and to create a Facebook page for their on-air persona. If they use their real name on the air, both accounts will have the same name, but your policy should govern their page with much more scrutiny.

- *Outline what you want people to do, not just what you don't want them to do*. You should expect members of your staff—particularly full-time on-air personalities—to post to station social networks a minimum number of times per day. You may also want to require a certain numbers of blogposts, or additional pieces of audio or video content each week.

- *Spell out the approval process*. Generally speaking, requiring approval of everything before it is posted to social media cripples your ability to engage with your audience. However, there may be certain topics, such as questions about contest rules, which should require approval. If so, make the approval process clear.

- *Outline a clear delegation process for social media accounts managed by multiple people*. For example, if you allow your station Facebook page to be managed by your full-time airstaff, and somebody posts a question about sales, make sure the policy spells out who that question should be referred to.

- *Require training*. In this day and age, every public personality should have basic social media skills. If there are people on your airstaff who do not, you should set up a training program to cover the basics.

- *Require periodic reviews*. While you do not need to review the social media posts of everyone on your staff, you should regularly review the posts of your full-time airstaff. Treat it the same as airchecking. This isn't just a time to make sure your staff isn't doing anything wrong but also to talk about how you can use social media even more effectively.

- *Outline the basic no-nos*. No cursing, no racism, no sexism, no homophobia, no pornography, no encouragement of illegal activity, etc. This is the easy part.

- *Require disclosure*. Your airstaff should clearly identify themselves when they post online and disclose their position at the radio station whenever they post anything related to the station or the industry. In other words, forbid anonymous trolling. Of course, some on-air personalities use stage names owing to concerns about safety or privacy. In these cases, the air talent should identify themselves by their on-air name.

- *Require transparency*. If your staff makes a mistake or misspeaks, they should acknowledge it and correct it as soon as possible.

- *Require honesty*.

- *Encourage timely responses*. If somebody posts a comment on the station blog or tweets to a certain jock, encourage them to do their best to reply in a timely manner. It helps to devise a system that makes it easy for air talent to do this. Social media management tools such as Hootsuite or Tweetdeck can help.

- *Discourage inciting remarks*. Posts can easily escalate into "flame wars" online. Make it clear that you expect your staff to be respectful at all times, and to do their best to stop things before they turn ugly.

- *Spell out the repercussions*. Make it clear how social media activity will be reviewed and judged, and what the procedure is if anything is found to be in violation of the station's guidelines.

- *Run it by a lawyer*. Make sure that your social media policy complies with any and all applicable laws.

Writing a social media policy can be intimidating if you are doing it from scratch. So don't. Go online and find the social media policy of another company and rewrite it to fit your needs. Here are some examples: IBM, Intel, Reuters, and Wal-Mart.

**Seth Resler** is a broadcasting veteran who, for over two decades, has worked behind both the mic and the programming desk in major markets, including New York City, Boston, Seattle, St. Louis, Providence, and San Jose. He left radio in 2006 to enter the world of online marketing. But he kept returning to the broadcasting industry, teaching radio stations how to apply the online marketing techniques being used by Silicon Valley companies. He writes a weekly column on AllAccess.com, offering Internet strategies for radio broadcasters. In 2015, Seth joined Jacobs Media Strategies as their Digital Consultant, helping radio stations combine all of their online tools into one overarching strategy.

## THE PROMOTION DIRECTOR'S/MANAGER'S JOB

Not all stations employ a full-time promotion director, but most stations designate someone to handle promotional responsibilities. At small outlets, the program director (PD) or even the general manager (GM) assumes promotional chores. Larger stations and station clusters with bigger operating budgets typically hire an individual or individuals to work exclusively in the area of promotion. "At major-market stations, you'll find a promotion department that includes a director and possibly assistants. In middle-sized markets, such as ours, the promotion responsibility is often designated to someone already involved in programming," says Bob Lima. Overall, the economy dictates the number of promotion positions available. When asked if today's job market is robust, Foster says, "No, budget realities have limited the growth of this particular segment inside of the radio stations."

Observed the late Ed Shane:

> Some promotion managers consider themselves "marketing directors." There are two levels of job responsibility for promotion people. Some are glorified "banner hangers," who make sure the grunt work is done at a station promotion or a live broadcast. Others are true department heads who exhibit leadership and vision within their operations.

Indeed the promotion director's responsibilities are manifold. Essential to the position are an understanding and knowledge of the station's audience. A background in research is important, contends Grube:

> Before you can initiate any kind of promotion you must know something about who you're trying to reach. This requires an ability to interpret various research data that you gather through in-house survey efforts or from outside audience research companies. You don't give away beach balls to 50-year-old men. Ideas must be confined to the cell group you're trying to attract.

Agreeing with Grube, Foster asserts knowing the radio station's audience is an essential part of the job. "They are the verb to the program director's noun. They are in charge of activating the vision and communicating with the station's P1 listeners (brand warriors)," says Foster about the relationship between the listeners and the promotion director.

Writing and conceptual skills are vital to the job of promotion director, says veteran radio executive Charlie Morriss:

> You prepare an awful lot of copy of all types. One moment you're composing press releases about programming changes, and the next you're writing a 30-second promo about the station's expanded news coverage or upcoming remote broadcast from a local mall. Knowledge of English grammar is a must. Bad writing reflects negatively on the station. The job also demands imagination and creativity. You have to be able to come up with an idea and bring it to fruition.

Chuck Davis agrees with Morriss and adds that, although the promotion person should be able to originate concepts, a certain number of ideas come from the trades, other stations, and consultants:

# JOB AD: PROMOTIONS DIRECTOR—ASHEVILLE NC

iHeartMedia Asheville has a rare opening for a Promotions Director in the beautiful Blue Ridge Mountains of Western North Carolina.

## Responsibilities

- Coordinates and attends client meetings with sellers and sales managers as needed to plan events and event logistics.
- Collaborates with multiple departments to create and execute **promotions** such as remotes, events, van hits and other street team activities from start to finish.
- Studying market conditions to determine the demand for company's services or products, and indicating the need for new products or services.
- Drives promotional vehicles.
- Performs basic office administrative functions and updates station website.
- Conducts on-site **promotions**, and handles clients and listeners.
- Sets up and runs audio and other types of equipment; hangs banners and other staging elements.
- Records events (i.e., photos, videos, audio and social media measures for station **promotions**).
- Sets up, breaks down and transports promotional event equipment as required.
- Prepares contest rules, waivers, and release forms for on-air, digital, social media and other contests.
- Supervises prize inventory and in-studio prize sheets as well as awarding of prizes at events.
- May coordinate and oversee on-site appearances, remotes and events.
- May be responsible for all winner prize fulfillment and release forms.
- Providing marketing advice to markets and stations.

The following responsibilities may be a separate role in larger markets. In smaller markets, it is normally combined with marketing management.

- Executes remote station promotional events and materials.
- Participates with station management in determining appropriate **promotions** for targeted demographic.
- Maintains station event calendar, writes copy for promotional spots, schedules live remotes from promotional events, prepares summaries of events, serves as primary coordinator for third-party tie-ins and supervises **promotions** coordinator and event staff.
- Ensures the provision of prizes, promotional materials, and event collateral. Ensures contest rules comply with FCC regulations.

## Qualifications

- Advanced skills in Microsoft Office, Photoshop and social media platforms
- Excellent organizational skills; ability to prioritize and effectively manage time
- High work standards and degree of attention to detail
- Problem-solving and decision-making
- Project management from start to finish; assumes responsibility & accountability for assignments and tasks
- Actively listens; clearly and effectively conveys information; demonstrates effective business writing skills; shows excellent grasp of grammar
- Exhibits good interpersonal skills; collaborates with others; maintains composure when faced with difficult situations and personalities
- Excellent driving record
- Physical ability to stand for multiple hours and lift or move 40-pound objects

## Work Experience

- 1–3 years' experience in outdoor **promotions** and/or marketing and/or customer service

## Education

- High school diploma; 4-year college degree preferred (emphasis in Communications, Advertising or Marketing)

**FIGURE 7.7**

A job ad for a promotions director gives an idea of the qualifications needed to do the job

Source: Courtesy of All Access Music Group Inc.

When this is the case, and it often is, you have to know how to adapt an idea to suit your own station. Of course, the promotion must reflect your location. Lifestyles vary almost by region. A promotion that's successful at a station in Louisiana may bear no relevance to a station with a similar format in Michigan. On the other hand, with some adjustments, it may work as effectively there. The creativity in this example exists in the adaptation.

Foster says the job of the promotion director has changed:

It has morphed. The "old school" promotion directors used to seek out opportunities and partnerships that allowed stations to promote their brand. However, with the complexity of today's marketplace this position has become more of a facilitator. We need to get back to being proactive and not reactive with this position.

Promotion directors must be versatile. A familiarity with graphic art is generally necessary, insofar as the promotion director will be involved in developing station logos and image IDs for advertising in the print media, on billboards, on social media, and websites. The promotion department also participates in the design and preparation of visuals for the sales area.

**FIGURE 7.8**
Cautionary words from a consultant
Source: Courtesy of Shane Media

### tactics: promotions

## A Promotions Report from Shane Media

## PROMOTIONAL PITFALLS

If you don't consider every detail when putting a promotion together, expect headaches. Here are common promotion mistakes encountered by the Promotion Marketing Association:

**Contradiction between the selling copy and the official rules.**

If your promo copy says "win a trip anywhere in America," and the rules say "continental U.S.," you're in trouble when the winner opts for Hawaii.

**The photo or illustration of the prize doesn't match the prize exactly.**

In a printed ad or Web promotion page, show the prize you intend to give away. Even a change of color (especially on a car) can cause a problem when the winner comes to claim the prize.

**Expenses are not explained.**

If you say "all expenses paid," the winner may expect a new wardrobe or to have the pets boarded while they take the prize trip. Name specific expenses you'll cover or set a dollar limit to avoid ambiguity.

**Over-estimating the value of a prize.**

Whatever you pay for the prize, there's always the possibility that the winner could get it cheaper. Airfare's a good example. A cross country trip at $3,000 could be had for $2,000 and the consumer might demand full value. Report a $3,000 prize to the I.R.S. and the winner claims $2,000, there's more trouble. Use a phrase like "full retail value."

**Using descriptive words without knowing the established meanings.**

"Luxury" and "deluxe" are travel industry words that set a standard for expectations. Don't give a stay at a "luxury" hotel and book a Day's Inn.

**Copy rules from someone else's contest or using last year's rules.**

There's always a minor detail that is unique to the situation. Check the law and whether it has changed since the last play of the contest.

**Allowing retailers to handle entries without guidance.**

A promotional partner needs to be as vigilant about security and abuse as you do. Provide detailed instructions on how to handle entry boxes and forms.

**Launching the promotion before you have the prizes.**

Secure the prize first and you never worry about a product that's behind on production, a retailer who fails to deliver, or a winner who shows up sooner than you expected.

# PROMOTION STRATEGY

## John Lund

Carefully scrutinize your on-air promotional activities, including contests, games, and giveaways. Listeners have even "more chances to win" once the Nielsen ratings sweep is under way and most radio stations are engaged in contesting. Give your promotions/contests a checkup to be absolutely certain they are functioning as designed. Reexamine each promotion's objective, design and execute according to the outline below:

I.   **Objective Phase**

   A.   Promotion is a tactical device that should:

      1.   have a positive impact on cume growth (when using outside media);

      2.   enhance the image of the radio station;

      3.   recycle listeners into other dayparts (to increase time spent listening);

      4.   it is beneficial if the promotion can also make the station revenue.

   B.   In addition, be certain the promotion conforms with:

      1.   the target demographic;

      2.   the radio station image;

      3.   the listening habits and lifestyle of the station's audience.

   C.   Examine the objectives of gaining cume and time spent listening

      1.   Are prizes significant enough for listeners to spend additional time listening?

      2.   The time that listeners stay tuned relates to the prize that is offered. Without an enormous prize, it may be unrealistic to expect many hours of continuous listening for a chance to win.

      3.   All programming (music, news, information, and talent presentation) must be fine-tuned to promote additional time spent listening.

      4.   Talents promote ahead benefits and provide genuine reasons for new and old cume to stay tuned.

      5.   Schedule live and recorded contest promos frequently enough to generate excitement and attain additional TSL from new cume.

      6.   Schedule well-produced promos that generate interest for new listeners.

      7.   After promoting ahead, talents deliver on their promise (as opposed to "delivering an empty box").

      8.   Talents convincingly sell the call letters or station name, positioning liners, and benefits of continued listening.

II.  **Design Phase**. The mechanics of the promotion are established in this phase. The following checklist provides necessary items to assure promotional success:

      1.   Contest rules are prepared and approved by legal counsel, and copies are available to listeners.

      2.   The contest has a definite start and end date.

      3.   The schedule of live and recorded promo announcements is created.

      4.   There is a precise format for talents who conduct the contest on air.

      5.   Winners' promos are regularly updated based on frequency of play.

**III. Execution Phase**. Talent execution is critical to the success of every on-air promotion. Consider the following suggestions to make every station promotion a big winner!

1. Talents relate contest information to the audience well (not merely read the copy).

2. A genuine level of enthusiasm is reflected.

3. Talents "sell" not just "tell" promotional benefits.

4. Talents conduct on-air contest procedure perfectly for the target demo.

5. Contest details and on-air execution do not sound overly chatty or congested with too many details.

6. Rules are simply conveyed in less than a minute.

7. Only "good-sounding" winners are on the air.

8. Contestants are not overly lambasted on air for incorrect answers.

9. Station name is frequently given as part of on-air conversations with contestants.

10. Talents promote ahead going into contest and provide genuine reasons for those not interested in the promotion to listen through.

11. Info such as winner's address or phone number never appear on-air.

12. On-air contest execution is limited to less than a minute.

13. Talents often mention when the next giveaway or contest is scheduled.

14. When only 15–20% of listeners express interest in contests, the remaining majority is not alienated because they like to play along.

Major promotions demand heavy on-air promotion:

1. Write-in promotions should be prepromoted for 10 to 14 days.

2. Use Nielsen reach and frequency calculations to determine promo frequency, or generalize as follows:

   • Recorded promos air every hour to 90-minutes.

   • Live liners air at least twice per hour.

   • As interest builds, supplement recorded promos with winner promos.

3. Maintain listener interest. Update liners every two days and promos twice a week.

4. Major promotions should be "the talk of the station." There should be a mention of the promotion in every stop set.

5. Minor promotions are often exclusive to a specific daypart, offer smaller prizes, and involve less commitment on the part of the radio station. Live liners and produced promos should be scheduled accordingly.

*And be sure your promotion always sounds fun, exciting and fresh!*

---

**John C. Lund** is President of Lund Media Group, the premier broadcast management and programming consulting firm in the United States and Canada. He has headed the company as President and Senior Executive Consultant since establishing the firm. A sister company, Lund Media Research, is a full service broadcast research firm that provides broadcasters with quantitative and qualitative perceptual research, focus group research, tracking studies, digital media research and analysis, and Internet research. Prior to establishing Lund Media, John Lund managed some of the highest rated broadcast stations in America, including WNBC and WNEW in New York, KLAC Los Angeles, WGAR Cleveland, KHOW Denver, and WISN Milwaukee. He next served as a Vice-President for America's largest media research firm, The Research Group, before going on to create Lund Media Group. John Lund is a frequent speaker at broadcast conventions and corporate meetings. Lund Media is located in Burlingame, California, near San Francisco.

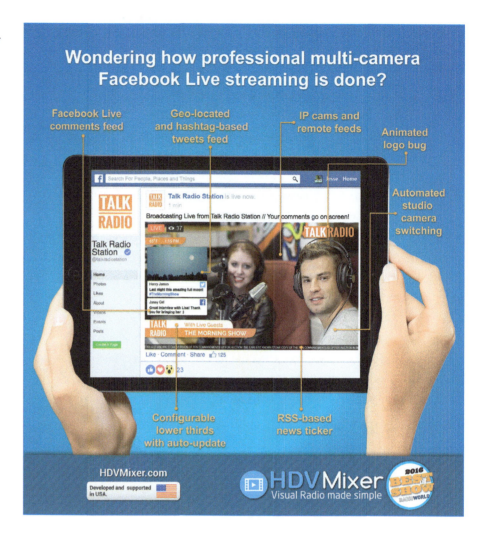

The promotion director's job should include an extreme comfort level with social media and how it is used to enhance engagement with the audience. Social media is the province of the promotion director because it extends the engagement of the station brand across new media platforms. Facebook creates conversation and connection between the station and its listeners, building excitement for a contest. Twitter allows instant updates on breaking news, contests, and promotional events.

The acquisition of prize materials through direct purchase and trades is another duty of the promotion person, who also may be called on to help coordinate sales co-op arrangements. "You work closely with the sales manager to arrange tie-ins with sponsors and station promotions," contends Morriss.

Like other radio station department heads, it is the promotion director's responsibility to ensure that the rules and regulations established by the FCC, relevant to the promotions area, are observed. This will be discussed later in the chapter, in the section "Promotions and the FCC."

Of course, it is important that a promotion director maintains a high level of communication with other station personnel, particularly the program director and sales manager, who are almost always an integral part of a promotion's execution and implementation. Everyone should be in the know about contests and promotions. Possessing the ability to work collaboratively with colleagues is another required skill in this position. "You must work well with a team but still be able to lead the station towards events and opportunities that will benefit the brand," asserts Foster.

# TYPES OF PROMOTIONS

There are two primary categories of station promotions: on-air and off-air. The on-air category will be examined first since it is the most prevalent form of radio promotion. Broadcasters already possess the best possible vehicle to reach listeners, and so it should come as no surprise that on-air promotion is the most common means of getting the word out on a station. The challenge confronting the promotion director is how to most effectively market the station so as to expand and retain listenership. To this end, a number of promotional devices are employed, beginning with the most obvious—station call letters. "The value of a good set of call letters is inestimable," says former station manager Richard Bremkamp, Jr. "A good example is the call letters of a station I once managed which have long been associated with the term 'rich' and all that it implies: 'Hartford's Rich Music Station—WRCH.'"

Call letters convey the personality of a station. For instance, try connecting these call letters with a format: WHOG, WNWS, WEZI, WODS, WJZZ, WIND, and WHTS. If you guessed country, news, easy listening, oldies, jazz, talk, and hits, you were correct. The preceding call letters not only identify their radio stations but also convey the nature or content of the programming offered.

Larry Miller adds:

Anything that can be made to spell "KISS" is always a favorite with listeners, starting with a KISS station in the Northwest back in the 1950s. Other similar calls include "Magic" for a soft AC, "Zoo" for a wild and crazy CHR or Hot AC, or "Rock" as in K-Rock. In Hawaii, calls that spell Hawaiian words have always been popular, such as K-POI. In the early 1970s, the ABC group of O&O FMs changed call letters to reflect "hip" or local culture with calls like KLOS in LA or KSFX in San Francisco or WRIF in Detroit or WPLJ (white port and lemon juice) in New York.

When stations do not possess call letters that create instant recognition, they often couple their frequency with a call letter or two, such as JB-105 (WPJBFM 105) or KISS-108 (WXKS-FM 108). This also improves the retention factor. Slogans are frequently a part of the on-air ID. "Music country—WSOC-FM, Charlotte," "A touch of class—WTEB-FM, New Bern," and "Texas best rock—KTXQ-FM, Fort Worth" are some examples. Slogans exemplify a station's image. When effective, they capture the mood and flavor of the station and leave a strong impression in the listener's mind. It is standard programming policy at many stations to announce the station's call letters and even its slogan each time a deejay opens the microphone. This is especially true during ratings sweeps, when survey companies ask listeners to identify the stations they tune into. Rick Peters observes:

If your calls stick in the mind of your audience, you've hit a home run. If they don't, you'll go scoreless in the book. You've got to carve them into the listener's gray matter and you start by making IDs and signatures that are as memorable as possible.

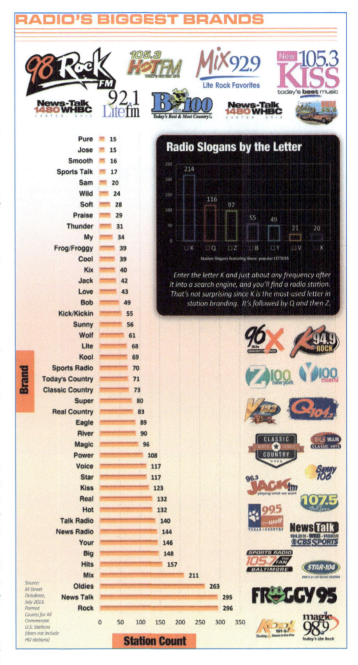

**FIGURE 7.11**
Slogans are used to brand and market the radio station

Source: Courtesy of *Inside Radio*

**FIGURE 7.12**
The slogan "the Buzz" is used on this station's vehicle
Source: Courtesy of WBTZ

**FIGURE 7.13**
The KISS-FM van
Source: Courtesy of SCS Unlimited and KISS-FM

Jay Williams, Jr., observes that call letters are being used less and less in the digital age:

> Stations identify themselves using their frequencies (92.5) today more than their call letters. This has become the case since the radio dial became digitized. The emphasis is now more numerical than alphabetical. Even the alphanumeric approach (Magic 92) has faded in favor of simply stating the station's frequency.

It is a common practice for stations to "bookend"—place call letters and/or frequencies before and after all breaks between music. For example, "WHJJ: Stay tuned for a complete look at local and national news at the top of the hour on WHJJ." Deejays also are told to graft the station call letters onto all bits of information: "92.9 Time," "102.5 Temperature," "102.5 Weather," and so on. There is a rule in radio that call letters can never be over-announced. The logic behind this is clear. The more a station tells its audience what it is tuned to, the more apt it is to remember, especially during diary-based rating periods. In markets measured by the Portable People Meter (PPM), constant repetition of call letters is not necessary because PPM is based on proximity of the meter carrier to a signal, not on call letter recall. Stations in the top 50 markets reduced call letter mentions and other talk elements in response to the technology.

On-air contests are another way to capture and hold the listener's attention. Contests must be easy to understand (are the rules and requirements of the contest easily understood by the listener?) and possess entertainment value (will nonparticipants be amused even though they are not actually involved?). A contest should engage the interest of all listeners, players and nonplayers alike.

A contest must be designed to enhance a station's overall sound or format. It must fit in, be compatible. Obviously, a mystery sound contest requiring the broadcast of loud or shrill noises would disrupt the tranquility and continuity of an easy listening station and result in tune-out.

Successful contests are timely and relevant to the lifestyle of the station's target audience, says Lima:

> A contest should offer prizes that truly connect with the listener. An awareness of the needs, desires, and fantasies of the listener will help guide a station. For example, giving away a refrigerator on a hot hit station would not really captivate the 16-year-old listener. This is obvious, of course. But the point I'm making is that the prizes that are up for grabs should be something the listener really wants to win, or you will have apathy.

The importance of creativity has already been stated. Contests that attract the most attention are often the ones that challenge the listener's imagination, contends Morriss:

**FIGURE 7.14**
The WTOP news van wrapped with WTOP call letters, frequency, website, and logo
Source: Courtesy of WTOP-FM

A contest should have style, should attempt to be different. You can give away what is perfectly suitable for your audience, but you can do it in a way that creates excitement and adds zest to the programming. The goal of any promotion is to set you apart from the other guy. Be daring within reason, but be daring.

On-air promotion is used to inform the audience of what a station has to offer: station personalities, programs, and special features and events. Rarely does a quarter-hour pass on any station that does not include a promo that highlights some aspect of programming:

- "Tune in to WXXX's *News at Noon* each weekday for a full hour of. . ."
- "Irv McKenna keeps *Nightalk* in the air midnight to six on the voice of the valley—WXXX. Yes, there's never a dull moment. . ."
- "Every Saturday night WXXX turns the clock back to the 1980s to bring you the best of the golden oldies. . ."
- "Hear the complete weather forecast on the hour and half-hour throughout the day and night on your total service station—WXXX. . ."

On-air promotion is a cost-efficient and effective means of building an audience when done correctly, says John Grube:

There are good on-air promotions and weak or ineffective on-air promotions. The latter can inflict a deep wound, but the former can put a station on the map. As broadcasters, the airtime is there at our disposal, but we sometimes forget just how potent an advertising tool we have.

Marketing expert Andrew Curran points to another area of promotion:

A stealth promotion might include members of the station database and is something that only the people eligible to win know is going on. For example, a station might announce a name three times a day for a chance to win $1,000. "We'd like to thank John Smith for listening to Classic Rock WXYZ." Then this person would have 20 minutes to call in and win and since only he can win, he's not competing with the whole city to get through on the phone. Plus, he feels important that he's eligible to win a special contest from the station. In the end, of course, a great promotion makes people want to tune in to the station.

FIGURE 7.15
Billboards catch the attention of commuters
Source: Courtesy of Rock 102

Radio stations employ off-air promotional techniques to reach people not tuned in. One traditional form is using billboards. Billboards are a popular form of outside promotion. To be effective, they must be both eye-catching and simple. Only so much can be stated on a billboard, since people are generally in a moving vehicle and have only a limited amount of time to absorb a message.

Placement of the billboard is also a key factor. To be effective, billboards must be located where they will reach a station's intended audience. Although an all-news station would avoid the use of a billboard facing a high school, a rock music outlet may prefer the location.

Bus cards are a good way to reach the public. Cities often have hundreds of buses on the streets each day. Billboard companies also use benches and transit shelters to get their client's message across to the population. Outside advertising is an effective and fairly cost-efficient way to promote a radio station, although certain billboards at heavy traffic locations can be extremely expensive to lease.

Newspapers with large circulations provide a great way to reach the population at large. They can also be very costly, although some stations are able to trade airtime for print space. Newspaper ads must be large enough to stand out and overcome the sea of advertisements that often share the same page.

Television is a costly but effective promotional tool for radio. A primary advantage that television offers is the chance to target the audience that the station is after. An enormous amount of information is available pertaining to television viewership. Thus, a station that wants to reach 18- to 24-year-olds is able to ascertain the programs and features that best draw that particular demographic.

The costs of producing or acquiring ready-made promos for television can run high, but most radio broadcasters value the opportunity to actually show the public what they can hear when they tune to

FIGURE 7.16A
A WTOP bus-back advertisement with DC Metro
Source: Courtesy of WTOP-FM

FIGURE 7.16B
Close-up of the advertisement

their station. WBZ-AM in Boston used local television extensively to promote its former morning personality Dave Maynard and its current sunrise news team. Ratings for the station have been consistently high, and management points to their television promotion as a contributing factor.

In 2000, the Pew Research Center found that just a little over half of the U.S. population used the Internet. By 2016, the study found that 88% of Americans used the Internet. Accordingly, it is no surprise that the Internet and social media are the most frequent means of off-air promotion for stations in the late 2010s, and this trend will likely continue into the 2020s. Listeners expect radio stations to have websites that contain all types of information including bios and photos of the on-air staff, contest rules, and links to social media such as Facebook and Twitter so that listeners can follow their favorite radio stations via new media technologies and their smartphones. *Inside Radio* reports:

> In addition to a significant on-air push, clients increasingly expect stations to promote appearances on Facebook, Twitter, and via their email database. But for stations doing dozens of appearances a week, that's not always feasible, so some clients negotiate social media up front. Appearance recaps, including photos, are also seen as essential. So is effective communication between the account executive, the promotion department and the talent. Some agencies set up pre-appearance conference calls. Others dispatch an event coordinator to the store to work with the station team.

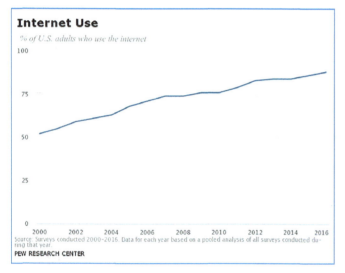

**Internet Use**
*% of U.S. adults who use the internet*

Source: Surveys conducted 2000–2016. Data for each year based on a pooled analysis of all surveys conducted during that year.
**PEW RESEARCH CENTER**

**FIGURE 7.19**

Internet adoption is high. Radio stations must utilize the Internet to communicate with listeners

Source: Courtesy of the Pew Internet and American Life Project Surveys

**FIGURE 7.20**

Mix 94.1 uses its webpage to promote the station using Facebook, Twitter, texting via smartphones, and other new media technologies

Source: Courtesy of NextMedia Group Inc.

# WHAT ARE THE GOALS OF YOUR RADIO STATION'S WEBSITE?

## Seth Resler

Your radio station has a website—but why? What is the website for? How does it fit into your radio station's overall strategy? What do you want listeners to do when they come to your website?

It's important for radio broadcasters to step back and think about these questions. If the best answers you can come up with are "because everybody has a website" or "because listeners expect it" or "because *branding*," then it's time to sit down and articulate some better responses.

What do you want listeners to do when they come to your website? Ultimately, you want listeners to do something that impacts the station's bottom line when they visit. With that in mind, here are some possible goals for your radio station's website:

1.  *Stream the station*. You probably want listeners to, y'know. . . listen. After all, when they stream the station through your website, that counts toward your Nielsen ratings, and your ratings directly impact the bottom line.

2.  *Sign up for the email list*. We no longer live in a world where advertisers just want to reach a lot of consumers; now they want to reach the *right* consumers. Digital outlets such as Facebook and Google have a ton of data that allow advertisers to target people precisely. To stay competitive, radio stations need to be gathering data on their listeners as well (and not just relying on the data they get from Nielsen).

    Data-gathering starts by capturing email addresses. Sometimes you'll be able to capture other information at the same time, sometimes you'll have to re-engage with listeners later to capture more data. But once you've got a listener's email address, your station is in a position to go back for more later. So one of the key goals of your website should be encouraging people to sign up for your radio station's email list.

3.  *Enter a contest*. Contests are a great way to capture listeners' data and build your station's email list. Contests can also be used to encourage listeners to create online content (photos, videos, etc.) that can be used to share on social media and attract more visitors to your station's website. Getting contest entries should be a key goal of your radio station's website.

4.  *Click on an ad*. If your radio station generates revenue by getting listeners to click on (or view) ads, then this should be one of the stated goals of your website.

5.  *Buy tickets to a station event*. Many radio stations generate revenue through events—both by selling tickets and sponsorships. The more people that attend the event, the more revenue the station can make. So ticket sales is a key goal of the station's website.

6.  *Buy station merchandise*. If your radio station generates revenue by selling t-shirts, hats, or lunch boxes, this should be one of the explicit goals of the website.

7.  *Download the station's mobile app*. If you have a mobile app that allows you to drive listening (and ratings) or generate revenue directly from the app, then the number of downloads can impact the station's bottom line. Use your website to encourage mobile app downloads.

8.  *Request advertising information*. Many radio stations overlook the fact that their website can generate sales leads. But if an email or a phone call from a potential client comes in via the website, it can be worth tens of thousands of dollars. One of the goals of your radio station's website should be to generate leads for the sales team.

A few notes on your station's website goals:

### A Website Can Have Multiple Goals . . .

There's no rule that says your website can only have one goal. There may be multiple things that you would like listeners to do when they come to the website.

### ... But Some Goals Are Worth More Than Others

All of your website's goals should ultimately impact the station's bottom line, but that doesn't mean they'll impact it equally. When you sell a concert ticket, the station may make $40 profit, while an advertising lead may generate $5,000 profit. Know the goals, but also know their value.

### Just Because You Can Measure Something, That Doesn't Mean It's a Goal

Notice what's not on the list of goals for your radio station's website: Facebook likes, retweets, pageviews, email open rates, etc. These are all good stats to track, and they can help inform your decisions as you try to increase your website goal conversions, but that doesn't mean they are important in and of themselves. They are a *means* to an end, not the end. Limit your explicit goals to the things that directly impact the station's bottom line, and don't get distracted by other data points.

### Everybody Should Agree on the Website's Goals

In every radio station that I've ever worked in, there has been tension between the programming department and the sales department. That's because the two departments have different goals: one is focused on ratings, the other on revenue. Most of the time, those two goals go hand in hand, but sometimes they don't, and that's when issues arise.

Don't make the same mistake with your digital strategy. Everybody—from the deejays to the digital team to the program director to the general manager—should agree on what the goals of the radio station's website are. If two people are looking at the same data and drawing different conclusions, you're setting your station up for internal strife.

### Review the Analytics Regularly

It's not enough to define the goals of your website; you also want to sit down regularly and see how well you're achieving those goals. I encourage radio stations to conduct a weekly website meeting to do this.

If your station hasn't taken the time to explicitly define the goals of its website, get the appropriate personnel together and do this. Once you've decided what they are, type them up and post them where everybody can see them. Your digital strategy will go farther if everybody is on the same page.

---

**Seth Resler** is a broadcasting veteran who, for over two decades, has worked behind both the mic and the programming desk in major markets, including New York City, Boston, Seattle, St. Louis, Providence, and San Jose. He left radio in 2006 to enter the world of online marketing but he kept returning to the broadcasting industry, teaching radio stations how to apply the online marketing techniques being used by Silicon Valley companies. He writes a weekly column on AllAccess.com, offering Internet strategies for radio broadcasters. In 2015, Seth joined Jacobs Media Strategies as their Digital Consultant, helping radio stations combine all of their online tools into one overarching strategy.

Stations give away thousands of items annually displaying station call letters and logos. Among the most common promotional items handed out by stations are posters, t-shirts, calendars, key chains, coffee mugs, music hit lists, book covers, pens, and car litter bags. The list is vast. Some stations still give away expensive items to build larger audiences.

Plastic card promotions have done well for many stations. Holders are entitled to a variety of benefits, including discounts at various stores and valuable prizes. The bearer is told to listen to the station for information on where to use the card. In addition, holders are eligible for special on-air drawings.

Another particularly effective way to increase a station's visibility is to sponsor special activities, such as fairs, sporting events, and theme dances, and to participate in parades and concerts. Hartford's big band station, WRCQ-AM, has received significant attention by presenting an annual music festival that has attracted more than 25,000 spectators each year, plus the notice of other media, including television and newspapers.

**FIGURE 7.21**
The brand-new Ford Mustang 98.7 FM ESPN, New York, and All American Ford were giving away during various Team 98.7 events from May to July of 2016. This client-sponsored giveaway was free to enter and the winner was chosen during the annual 98.7 ESPN Beach Bash

Source: Courtesy of 98.7 FM ESPN, New York

**FIGURE 7.22**
Team 98.7 FM ESPN, New York, promotions assistants prepare to interact with fans at a sponsored live broadcast of the Hahn & Humpty show at Millers Ale House in Paramus, New Jersey. Customers were given the opportunity to watch the Hahn & Humpty show live as well as enter to win a brand-new Mustang

Source: Courtesy of 98.7 FM ESPN, New York

**FIGURE 7.23**
WTOP advertises at Nats Park during a Washington Nationals baseball game

Source: Courtesy of WTOP-FM

**FIGURE 7.24**
Don La Greca, Michael Kay and Peter Rosenberg (left to right) during a client-sponsored live broadcast of *The Michael Kay Show* at a P.C. Richard. The event was free to the public and allowed fans to watch and listen to *The Michael Kay Show* simulcast on the YES Network

Source: Courtesy of 98.7 FM ESPN, New York

Personal appearances by station personalities and interaction with listeners by the radio personalities are always effective means to reach listeners while utilizing forms of off-air promotion. Remote broadcasts from malls, beaches, and the like also aid in getting the word of the station out to the public.

One last means of marketing a station is offered by Jay Williams, Jr., Co-Founder of DMR/Interactive and President of Broadcasting Unlimited:

Promotion and marketing have never been more critical. In the current economy, stations have to do everything they can to draw and hold an audience. Direct marketing through mail and/or by telephone is a very cost-effective way to target an audience and to keep a station in front of radio listeners, especially during rating periods. Telepromoting is becoming more prevalent. Directed or targeted marketing makes sense because stations must be more effective with what they have. The business of radio is changing. Audiences are fragmenting, brand loyalties are eroding. Mass marketing is losing its impact. Person-to-person or individualized marketing delivers tangible results.

The late Ed Shane concurred with Williams, adding:

> Direct marketing is the wave of the one-to-one future. Connections through Facebook, Twitter, and other social media allow stations easy access to listener ideas and feedback. Engagement through social media, when used effectively, will achieve the same result as direct mail, telemarketing, and database management.

**FIGURE 7.25**
WTOP scoreboard advertising at the Verizon Center during a Washington Capitals hockey game
Source: Courtesy of WTOP-FM

**FIGURE 7.26**
WTOP served as a media sponsor for the 2013 National Memorial Day Parade
Source: Courtesy of WTOP-FM

**FIGURE 7.27**
San Diego's The Mighty 1090 doing a live remote
Source: Courtesy of Broadcast Companies of America

**FIGURE 7.28**
Walrus 105.7 FM doing a live remote that gives listeners a chance to win
Source: Courtesy of Broadcast Companies of America

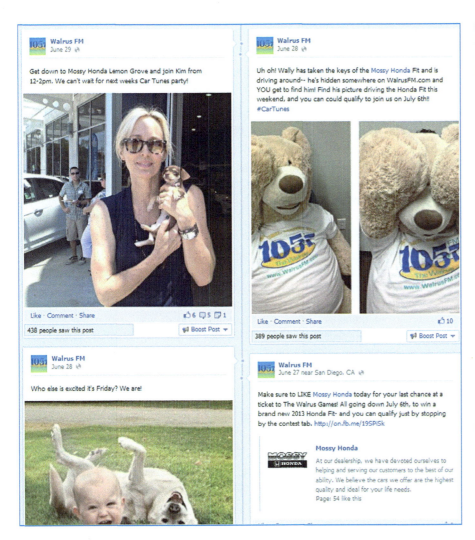

FIGURE 7.29
Social media such as Facebook is used to give listeners an opportunity to win prizes on the radio

Source: Courtesy of Broadcast Companies of America

FIGURE 7.30
A tweet from the official 98.7 ESPN Twitter account promoting the Ticket Tuesday sweepstakes executed during The Michael Kay Show. This contest cues listeners to call in and win tickets to NY sporting events

Source: Courtesy of 98.7 FM ESPN, New York

## FIND A PARADE AND JOIN

### Ed Shane

Promotion is an extension of your station's brand experience aimed at your target listener. It gets listeners directly involved with an activity or event that builds audience or enhances the image of your outlet and your advertiser's business.

As a programmer, I first ask the following question about any promotion: What are we trying to achieve? Reduced to the simplest terms, there are three goals:

1. Cume—building audience.

2. Time spent listening—holding onto audience.

3. Image—making the station memorable to the audience.

If the station is not trying to achieve at least one of the three, the promotion has no value.

The next question: Who's the target? The bottom line of any promotion is that it should be in sync with the needs and expectations of the audience. If the promotion doesn't resonate with your station's target listener, there'll be no benefit.

FIGURE 7.31
Ed Shane

The final question: What's the desired consumer response? Do we want them to listen? (I hope so. Too many promotions fail in this aspect.)

Note that none of this involves how many Twitter followers a station has collected or how many Facebook friends.

The same questions apply to promotions conducted via new media or social media as apply to old fashioned call-in-to-win promotions or live broadcasts from a retail location.

Twitter is a "news channel" that is perfect for calling attention to a new contest or promotion in an engaging, conversational way. Twitter allows for instant updates on contesting and promotional events. Facebook is a "conversation channel" that connects with listeners on what appears to be a personal level. It's also an easy way to get listener feedback on ideas. No social medium should be used on its own to drive a promotion unless it brings the strategy back to the three basic questions—especially the questions about driving new or extended listenership.

The hazard in concentrating too much on social media is that the station doesn't own its Facebook friends or its Twitter followers. Facebook and Twitter do. If they decide to change strategy, they can do what they want with your customers' information. Too many stations have used social media as a backstop against declining promotion budgets. Consolidation caused radio companies to reduce expenditures to make clusters more profitable. Often the promotion budget was among the first to disappear. This was exacerbated by the recession of 2008–2012, as stations further reduced the amounts spent on outreach advertising and on promotional activities alike. Even bumper stickers, once a mainstay of local promotional efforts, were no longer prolific.

In spite of the reductions in budgets, promotion is vital to radio as it connects with its communities.

If there's no money, find a parade and get in front of it. Make sure it's a parade your audience wants to join.

---

The late **Ed Shane** (1945–2015) served as CEO of the Houston-based Shane Media and was a programming and research advisor to radio in markets of all sizes.

## PROMOTIONS IN THE DIGITAL ERA

With a nearly 90% adoption rate among Americans, the Internet has had a profound impact on the way radio stations promote themselves in the late 2010s. The technological advances that have accompanied the Internet have made some promotional strategies antiquated while other, newer strategies have been found to be very effective. DMR/Interactive's senior Vice-President/Co-Founder Catherine Jung says, "For the most successful radio stations, the Internet has become a visual and interactive element of the brand. Many station sites now offer unique entertaining elements like videos, best-of podcasts, blogs and more." DMR/Interactive's Chief Executive Officer Tripp Eldredge adds:

It has also provided a powerful way to target current and new listeners. As a result, promotions that simply relied on 'be the nth caller' are giving way to digital registrations with instant-win components and frictionless sharing. That said, there continues to be a surprising amount of stations that have not evolved to the listener-centric, interactive approach. They tend to view the Internet as simply an extension to their transmitters.

Charlie Morgan, SVP/Market Manager of Emmis-New York, explains social media's role in branding and promotions from the management perspective. He says:

New Media/Social Media is definitely playing an important role in building brands and is a part of our station and talent's marketing efforts but it has not caused me to re-evaluate management or sales strategies. It is simply a way to augment and amplify the relationship with consumers.

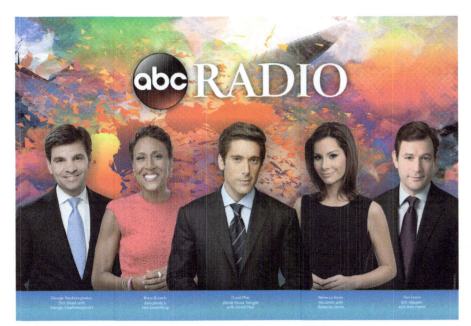

**FIGURE 7.32**
Stations promote their on-air talent as a way to draw in listeners
Source: © 2017 American Broadcasting Companies Inc.

Relying on the Internet and social media technologies has required stations to modify organizational structures at both single stations and clustered stations to technologically support the new promotional approaches. DMR's Chief Operating Officer, Andrew Curran, notes:

> Having unsuccessfully experimented with adding "webmaster" to the station engineer's duties, most have now evolved into a two-level model. The infrastructure and technology is developed and deployed via a corporate group. They set standards, evaluate technology, and implement the tools and best practices. At the local station level, there are usually a few people designated as the "digital team" whose primary responsibilities span from sales to programming to marketing. In a few large-operator cases, it's a completely separate group operating relatively separately from the local station.

Many social media promotions are used by stations to communicate with listeners effectively. Jung asserts, "Many have experimented with rewards programs, song research panels, text messaging, and mobile apps to extend their brands into these areas." Determining successful and effective Internet promotion strategies can be challenging owing to the uniqueness of the technology. "In fact," Eldredge says, "the challenge is defining and measuring success. Traditionally, the definition is related to ratings increases and revenue growth. Because there are now so many more variables, operators have a much more difficult time distilling out what components or tools are effective." Curran says,

> We guide clients with an overall philosophy of identifying and engaging across many touch points with who matters most to your format and station brand. With that in mind, technologies such as social media platforms and apps that provide fans with the opportunity to create and share content along with the ability to connect with each other fuel the most engagement and sharing activity.

Jung adds:

> Several clients of ours used the shared-participation gaming to create a bridge between traditional promotion and the social sphere. For example, the game of concentration was used to create a groundswell of participation and connection across social media, digital, and on-air. The shared participation of helping each other with the game created a deep and real connection between the participating listeners. The powerful outcome was that these listeners all credited the station with helping them create these amazing new relationships.

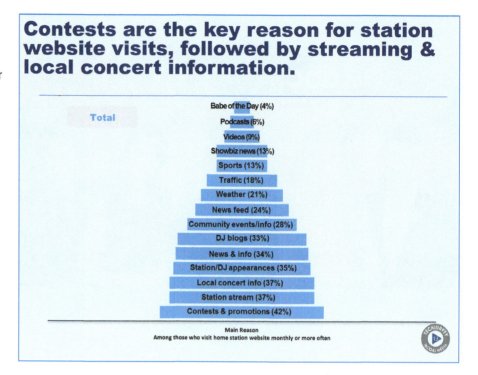

Contests are the key reason for station website visits, followed by streaming & local concert information.

Total

Babe of the Day (4%)
Podcasts (6%)
Videos (9%)
Showbiz news (13%)
Sports (13%)
Traffic (18%)
Weather (21%)
News feed (24%)
Community events/info (28%)
DJ blogs (33%)
News & info (34%)
Station/DJ appearances (35%)
Local concert info (37%)
Station stream (37%)
Contests & promotions (42%)

Main Reason
Among those who visit home station website monthly or more often

Smartphones are in the hands of nearly every consumer. It's important for radio stations to determine how to effectively target these consumers because not all demographics use all features of smartphones. For example, Jung observes,

> Part of the answer here depends on the format. For youthful formats like CHR and Hip Hop, texting and mobile is a large part of their focus with promotions. It's a smaller percentage, but growing for most other formats. Like everything, it's important to know your key listeners and how they engage with smartphones. What they would like to see. Now more than ever, it's important to be listener-centric.

For users of smartphones and social media technologies, the simple act of sharing content is important to consumers. Curran notes:

> On another level, many listeners who were not participating enjoyed watching the content and sharing created by those that were. This organic content generation provided a unique asset for the station and its listener community resulting in record-level sharing across the social networks, great content that could be repurposed on the air, and record ratings for the station.

As communication has become so much more interactive, with the listener/consumer (the old broadcasting, top-down model) increasingly becoming a participant/content provider, radio will best adapt to this change by empowering the listeners. Eldredge suggests:

> The more that station brands can empower the listeners to create, express, and share with other listeners, the more powerful the station brands can become. When listeners start to connect with other listeners through helping, creating, sharing, etc., they credit the station for that relationship-building. Stations that help listeners build relationships and enhance the relationships they already have will set themselves apart from the old-guard of "we broadcast, you listen." Similarly, programmers and air-talent that deeply understand their core listeners will naturally be able to respond and evolve their products and offerings more effectively. Knowing the life of the core consumer has never been more critical as you decide where to invest your limited time and money.

Employees working in the twenty-first-century radio station promotions department must not only be technologically savvy but also have a keen understanding of people and their use of technology. Eldredge asserts,

> A key skill is being able to know how to deeply understand the listeners, particularly the most important listeners of a station-brand. The ability to know tools and strategies to discover and synthesize listeners' tastes, activities, preferences, sharing patterns, etc. will set you apart because most stations and groups are simply employing tactics without setting a listener-centric strategy.

Curran adds, "In addition, promotions teams often work across the cluster, so you have to be able to understand and generate success across multiple formats."

## SALES PROMOTION

Promoting a station can be very costly, as much as half a million dollars annually in some metro markets. To help diminish the cost of station promotion, advertisers are often recruited. This way both the station and the sponsor stand to benefit. The station gains the financial wherewithal to execute certain promotions that it could not do on its own, and the participating advertiser gains valuable exposure by tying in with special station events. Stations can actually make money and promote themselves simultaneously if a client purchases a substantial spot schedule as part of a promotional package. Says Larry Miller, "An effective promotional campaign should try to include a sales component, in part to help allay the costs of advertising. If it's done right, it will bring in new business for the station."

There are abundant ways to involve advertisers in station promotion efforts. They run the gamut from placing advertisements and coupons on the station's website to joining the circus for the day, for example "WXXX brings the 'Greatest Show on Earth' to town this Friday night, and you go for half price just by mentioning the name of your favorite radio station—WXXX." The ultimate objective of a station/sponsor collaborative is to generate attention in a cost-efficient manner. If a few dollars are made for the station along the way, all the better.

As stated previously, the promotion director also works closely with the station's sales department in the preparation and design of sales promotion materials, which include items such as posters, coverage maps, ratings breakouts, flyers, station profiles, and much more.

A challenging economy and increased pressure from media other than radio has made advertiser participation in promotion vital. Consultant Ed Shane said that he regularly cautions his client stations to make sure advertiser involvement doesn't override the needs of the station: "We often lose 'ownership' of our promotions because our enthusiasm for getting a sponsorship clouds our view of the goals we set out in the first place. Promotions should be a win-win partnership."

## BUDGETING PROMOTIONS

Marketing expert Andrew Curran opens this section with his views on the challenges of finding resources to promote a station:

> In my experience, since revenue growth in radio has been relatively flat in recent years, marketing budgets are often the first thing to cut, especially in the third and fourth quarters of the year when a company needs to hit its financial numbers. In addition, it seems that stations seem to get the most marketing money when the ratings are down and instant results need to be delivered to get revenue up. Certainly this makes for some tense campaigns and often—if the promotion is successful and ratings go up—marketing dollars are moved to another station that is in need of help rather than allowing the original station to strengthen its position with additional marketing.

Obviously, cost projections are included in the planning of a promotion. The promotion director's budget may be substantial or all but nonexistent. Stations in small markets often have minuscule

budgets compared with their giant metro-market counterparts. But, then again, the need to promote in a one- or two-station market is generally not as great as it is in multi-station markets. To a degree, the promotion a station does is commensurate with the level of competition.

A typical promotion at an average-size station may involve the use of newspapers plus additional handout materials, such as stickers, posters, buttons, and an assortment of other items depending on the nature of the promotion. Television and billboards may also be utilized. Each of these items will require an expenditure unless some other provision has been made, such as a trade agreement in which airtime is swapped for goods or ad space.

The cost involved in promoting a contest often constitutes the primary expense. When WASH-FM in Washington, D.C., gave away $1 million, it spent $200,000 to purchase an annuity designed to pay the prize recipient $20,000 a year for 50 years. The station spent nearly an equal amount to promote the big giveaway. Most of the promotional cost resulted from a heavy use of local television. In the early 1980s, KHTZ-FM in Los Angeles spent more than $300,000 on billboards and television to advertise its dream-house giveaway. The total cost of the promotion approached half a million dollars. The price tag of the house was $122,000. Both of these high-priced contests accomplished their goals—increased ratings. In a metro market, one rating point can mean $1 million in ad revenue. "A promotion that contributes to a two- or three-point jump in the ratings is well worth the money spent on it," observes Rick Peters.

The promotion director works with the station manager in establishing the promotion budget. From there, it is the promotion director's job to allocate funds for the various contests and promotions that are run throughout the station's fiscal period. "The idea is to control the budget and not let it control you. Obviously computers have been a big help in this respect," states Marlin R. Taylor, who also contends that large sums of money need not be poured into promotions if a station is on target with its programming:

> In 1983, the Malrite organization came to New York and launched Z-100, a contemporary hit-formatted outlet, moving it from "worst to first" in a matter of months. They did a little advertising and gave away some money. I estimate that their giveaways totaled less dollars than some of their competitors spent on straight advertising. But the station's success was built on three key factors: product, service, and employee incentives. Indeed, they do have a quality product. Second, they are providing a service to their customers or listeners, and, third, the care and feeding of the air staff and support team are obvious at all times. You don't necessarily have to spend a fortune on promotion.

Larry Miller agrees:

> A really good promotion director can do effective promotions without spending a lot of money. First, utilize 'on air' promotions; second, trade out for stuff like contest prizes and newspaper advertising. You can do a lot for very little through a combined effort with programming.

Since promotion directors are frequently expected to arrange trade agreements with merchants as a way to diminish costs, a familiarity with and understanding of the station's rate structure is necessary. Trading airtime for use in promotions is less popular at highly rated stations that can demand top dollars for spots. Most stations, however, prefer to exchange available airtime for goods and services needed in a promotion, rather than pay cash.

**FIGURE 7.35**
The Federal Communication Commission takes violations of contest regulations very seriously and those violations can result in huge fines

Source: Courtesy of *Radio World* and Paul McLane

# TITLE 47: TELECOMMUNICATION

## Part 73—Radio Broadcast Services

*Subpart H—Rules Applicable to All Broadcast Stations*

§73.1216 Licensee-conducted contests

(a) A licensee that broadcasts or advertises information about a contest it conducts shall fully and accurately disclose the material terms of the contest, and shall conduct the contest substantially as announced or advertised over the air or on the Internet. No contest description shall be false, misleading or deceptive with respect to any material term.

(b) The disclosure of material terms shall be made by the station conducting the contest by either:
   (1) Periodic disclosures broadcast on the station; or
   (2) Written disclosures on the station's Internet Web site, the licensee's Web site, or if neither the individual station nor the licensee has its own Web site, any Internet Web site that is publicly accessible.

(c) In the case of disclosure under paragraph (b) (1) of this section, a reasonable number of periodic broadcast disclosures is sufficient. In the case of disclosure under paragraph (b)(2) of this section, the station shall:
   (1) Establish a conspicuous link or tab to material contest terms on the home page of the Internet Web site;
   (2) Announce over the air periodically the availability of material contest terms on the Web site and identify the Web site address where the terms are posted with information sufficient for a consumer to find such terms easily; and
   (3) Maintain material contest terms on the Web site for at least thirty days after the contest has concluded. Any changes to the material terms during the course of the contest must be fully disclosed on air within 24 hours of the change on the Web site and periodically thereafter or the fact that such changes have been made must be announced on air within 24 hours of the change, and periodically thereafter, and such announcements must direct participants to the written disclosures on the Web site. Material contest terms that are disclosed on an Internet Web site must be consistent in all substantive respects with those mentioned over the air.

NOTE 1 TO §73.1216: For the purposes of this section:
(a) A contest is a scheme in which a prize is offered or awarded, based upon chance, diligence, knowledge or skill, to members of the public.
(b) Material terms include those factors which define the operation of the contest and which affect participation therein. Although the material terms may vary widely depending upon the exact nature of the contest, they will generally include: How to enter or participate; eligibility restrictions; entry deadline dates; whether prizes can be won; when prizes can be won; the extent, nature and value of prizes; basis for valuation of prizes; time and means of selection of winners; and/or tie-breaking procedures.

NOTE 2 to §73.1216: In general, the time and manner of disclosure of the material terms of a contest are within the licensee's discretion. However, the obligation to disclose the material terms arises at the time the audience is first told how to enter or participate and continues thereafter.

Note 3 to §73.1216: This section is not applicable to licensee-conducted contests not broadcast OR advertised to the general public or to a substantial segment thereof, to contests in which the general public is not requested or permitted to participate, to the commercial advertisement of non-licensee-conducted contests, or to a contest conducted by a non-broadcast division of the licensee or by a non-broadcast company related to the licensee.

[80 FR 64361, Oct. 23, 2015]

**FIGURE 7.36**

The Federal Communications Commission has established legal regulations for all radio stations to follow when conducting contests and promotions

# PROMOTIONS AND THE FCC

Although the FCC has dropped most of its rules pertaining to contests and promotions, it does expect that they be conducted with propriety and good judgment. The basic obligation of broadcasters to operate in the public interest remains the primary consideration. Section 73.1216 of the FCC's rules and regulations (as published in the Code of Federal Regulations) outlines the dos and don'ts of contest presentations.

Stations are prohibited from running a contest in which contestants are required to pay in order to play. The FCC regards a lottery as any contest in which the elements of prize, chance, and consideration exist. In other words, contestants must not have to risk something to win.

Contests must not place participants in any danger or jeopardize property. Awarding prizes to the first five people who successfully scale a treacherous mountain or swim a channel filled with alligators certainly would be construed by the FCC as endangering the lives of those involved. Contestants have been injured and stations held liable more than once. The station in California that ran a treasure hunt resulting in considerable property damage incurred the wrath of the public, town officials, and the FCC. In a more tragic example of poor planning, a listener was killed during a "find the disc jockey" contest. The station was charged with negligence and sustained a substantial fine.

Stations are expected to disclose the material terms of all contests and promotions conducted. These include the following:

- entering procedures;
- eligibility requirements;
- deadlines;
- when or if prizes can be won;
- value of prizes;
- procedure for awarding prizes;
- tie-breaking procedures.

The public must not be misled concerning the nature of prizes. Specifics must be stated. Implying that a large boat is to be awarded when, in fact, a canoe is the actual prize would constitute misrepresentation, as would suggesting that an evening in the Kon Tiki Room of the local Holiday Inn is a great escape weekend to the exotic South Seas.

The FCC also stipulates that any changes in contest rules must be promptly conveyed to the public. It makes clear, too, that any rigging of contests, such as determining winners in advance, is a direct violation of the law and can result in a substantial penalty, or even license revocation.

## THE FCC HAS WRITTEN GOOD CONTEST RULES, NOW YOU SHOULD TOO

### Lauren Lynch Flick

The FCC's new Licensee-Conducted Contest Rule became effective on February 12, 2016. Under the new rule, a broadcast licensee conducting a contest still has the obligation to disclose the material terms of the contest "fully and accurately" and to conduct the contest substantially as announced. However, the new rule allows broadcasters to meet these requirements by posting the contest terms on their websites rather than reading them on-air. To take advantage of this new flexibility, broadcasters must:

- post the terms on the station's or licensee's website, or if neither the station nor the licensee has a website, on a free website that is available to the public 24/7, without registration;
- broadcast the website address with sufficient information for a consumer to find the terms easily, using simple instructions or natural language;

FIGURE 7.37
Lauren Lynch Flick

Source: Reprinted with permission courtesy of Pillsbury Winthrop Shaw Pittman LLP

- broadcast the website address periodically throughout the term of the contest;

- establish a conspicuous link or tab on the home page of the website that takes consumers to the contest terms;

- maintain the terms on the website for at least 30 days after the contest has ended and conspicuously mark those that are expired, including the date a winner was selected;

- on the rare occasions that a change in terms occurs during the contest, announce the changes on-air within 24 hours and periodically thereafter, and direct participants to the written terms on the website; and

- assure that the contest rules posted online conform to those announced on-air.

The effective date of the new rule was eagerly anticipated by broadcasters as the change grants them more flexibility in announcing contest terms, avoids long and complicated contest announcements on-air, and permits participants to review the rules at their leisure. However, in making the change, the FCC noted that "[a]s with all elements of contest-related announcements, the burden is on the broadcaster to inform the public, not on the public to discern the message."

Indeed, the law views the rules of a contest or sweepstakes to be a *contract* between the sponsor (station) and anyone who enters the contest, or even anyone who tries to enter and fails to do so successfully. If the sum total of your on-air contest rules are "be the 103rd caller after X song is played" and a vague "station policy" somewhere on the website that says you can only win once every 30 days, you have left a lot out of your "contract." For example, when a station ran a contest on-air like the one above and did not get many callers, the deejay simply awarded the prize to the last person to call in after hours of trying to attract more callers. The station was fined by the FCC because it did not run the contest substantially as advertised. Properly written contest rules should account for such situations, as well as other foreseeable developments, such as the phone lines going down after the trigger song has been played. A station with contest rules that don't address likely (or even unlikely) contest developments is inviting challenges from both contestants and regulators.

In that regard, stations should remember that the FCC is not the only regulator watching out for contest and sweepstakes violations. For example, some states' contest laws require that all announced prizes be awarded in order to prevent "bait and switch" contests. For stations giving away "time-sensitive" prizes such as concert tickets that have to be used on a specific date, the rules should address the situation where a winner is chosen but then turns down the prize or simply does not claim it because they cannot attend on the date specified. If the rules say that an alternate winner will be chosen after 10 days, there may not be enough time left before the concert to award the prize. The station with poorly written contest rules must then choose between violating the law by failing to award a prize, or violating the law by failing to conduct the contest in accordance with the announced rules. Badly drafted contest rules are a liability for any business, but are worse for broadcasters, as in addition to all of the state and federal laws governing contests, broadcasters are uniquely subject to the FCC's contest oversight as well.

Finally, while you might imagine that contest complaints come from those who lost the contest (and indeed they often do), many come from contest winners. While professional contestants who enter every contest will complain about the valuation placed on a prize for tax purposes, first-time winners are more likely to complain about having to sign a release to claim the prize, or, where the prize is large, having to provide the station with their social security number, appear in person, or attend a further event, such as the day when all the winners of keys must try them out in the grand prize car. These obligations need to be clear in the contest rules, not just to avoid liability but to ensure that the station is able to get the promotional value it anticipated from the contest. Contestants who demand anonymity and refuse to sign releases greatly undercut the promotional value of a big contest.

The bottom line is, now that the FCC will let you post your rules online for contestants and regulators to scrutinize, you need to ensure you have rules that can withstand scrutiny.

Lauren Lynch Flick is a Senior Counsel at Pillsbury Law Firm in Washington, D.C. Her main areas of focus include communications law and media and entertainment, and she advises broadcasters, marketers, mobile game companies, and other media entities on a broad range of regulatory issues.

She counsels clients regarding federal and state regulation of promotional sweepstakes, online gaming, consumer privacy, phone and text marketing, marketing to children, and broadcaster compliance with FCC regulations. Lauren assists clients involved in agency litigation and enforcement actions. She also handles complex commercial transactions in the media and communications industries including regulatory due diligence and structuring to insure compliance.

She was recognized by *Best Lawyers in America* in communications law (2018) and is a frequent contributor to Pillsbury's CommLawCenter and SocialGames Law blogs.

Lauren earned her J.D. from the Catholic University of America, Columbus School of Law, in 1990 and she earned a BA from Georgetown University in 1987.

**FIGURE 7.38**
Stations are expected to make contest rules clear to the public

Source: Courtesy of Shane Media

## WHAT TO INCLUDE IN "OFFICIAL RULES"

The official rules are a contract between the station as sponsor of the contest and the participant. There's no one way to draft official rules, but there are certain elements that most legal advisors recommend:

1. Methods of entry, including alternate methods, if necessary to avoid lottery "consideration."

2. Limitations on the number of entries, if applicable.

3. Prohibition of facsimile entries.

4. Method of determining winners.

5. Odds of winning.

6. Eligibility: age, residence, exclusion of employees and/or families of the station, sponsors, and other parties

7. Duration: the beginning and end dates for entry, when game pieces are available and when winner's lists will be available.

8. Limitation on liability.

9. Disclaimer of liability on lost, late, or misdirected mail or electronic entry.

10. "Void where prohibited" clause.

11. Responsibility for taxes on prizes.

12. Legal documents, as needed: Affidavit of eligibility and liability, permission to use name and images in publicity releases.

13. Unclaimed prizes. Not awarded, subject to "second chance" drawing, given to an alternate or runner-up, or other disposition.

14. Reservation of publicity rights.

15. Entries become the property of the station or sponsor.

16. Judges' decisions are final.

17. Disclaimer for printing or typographical errors that assures that no more than the advertised number of prizes will be awarded.

18. Minors clause, if needed, to restrict the game to those over 18.

19. Fraud/malfunction clause to allow station to disqualify anyone for tampering.

20. Availablility of the winner's list.

Although the FCC does not require that a station keep a contest file, most do. Maintaining all pertinent contest information, including signed prize receipts and releases by winners, can prevent problems should questions or a conflict arise later.

Stations that award prizes valued at $600 or more are expected by law to file a 1099-MISC form with the IRS. This is done strictly for reporting purposes, and stations incur no tax liability. However, failure to do so puts a station in conflict with the law.

## CHAPTER HIGHLIGHTS

1. To keep listeners interested and tuned in, stations actively promote their image and call letters. Small-market stations promote themselves to compete for audience with other forms of media. Major-market stations use promotion to differentiate themselves from competing stations.

2. Radio recognized the value of promotion early and used print media, remote broadcasts, and billboards to inform the public. Later, ratings surveys proved the importance of effective promotions. Today, radio stations use web pages and social media such as Facebook and Twitter to promote station activities, programming, and contests.

3. Greater competition because of the increasing number of stations and monthly audience surveys means today's stations must promote themselves continually.

4. The most successful (attracting listenership loyalty) promotions involve large cash or merchandise prizes.

5. A successful promotion director possesses knowledge and understanding of the station's audience; a background in research and marketing, writing, and conceptual skills; the ability to adapt existing concepts to a particular station; and a familiarity with graphic art. The promotion director is responsible for acquiring prizes through trade or purchase and for compliance with FCC regulations covering promotions.

6. On-air promotions are the most common method used to retain and expand listenership. Such devices as slogans linked to the call letters and contests are common.

7. To "bookend" call letters means to place them at the beginning and conclusion of each break. To "graft" call letters means to include them with all informational announcements.

8. Contests must have clear rules and must provide entertainment for players and nonplayers alike. Successful contests are compatible with the station's sound, offer prizes attractive to the target audience, and challenge the listener's imagination in order to win.

9. Off-air promotions are intended to attract new listeners. Popular approaches include billboards, bus cards, newspapers, television, discount cards, giveaway items embossed with call letters or logo, deejay personal appearances, special activity sponsorship, remote broadcasts, direct mail, and telemarketing. Station websites are promotional tools.

10. To offset the sometimes substantial cost of an off-air promotion, stations often collaborate with sponsors to share both the expenses and the attention gained.

11. FCC regulations governing promotions are contained in Section 73.1216. Basically, stations may not operate lotteries, endanger contestants, rig contests, or mislead listeners as to the nature of the prize.

## SUGGESTED FURTHER READING

Bergendorff, F.L., *Broadcast Advertising and Promotion: A Handbook for Students and Professionals*, Hastings House, New York, NY, 1983.

Dickey, L., *The Franchise: Building Radio Brands*, NAB, Washington, D.C., 1994.

Donnelly, W.J., *Planning Media: Strategy and Imagination*, Pearson Education, New York, NY, 1995.

Eastman, S.T., Klein, R.A., and Ferguson, D., *Media Promotion and Marketing for Broadcasting, Cable, and the Internet*, Focal Press, Burlington, MA, 2006.

Gompertz, R., *Promotion and Publicity Handbook for Broadcasters*, Tab, Blue Ridge Summit, PA, 1977.

Johnson, A., *The Radio Sponsorship and Promotions Handbook: Creative Ideas for Radio Campaigns*, Saland, New York, NY, 2007.

Macdonald, J., *The Handbook of Radio Publicity and Promotion*, Tab, Blue Ridge Summit, PA, 1970.

Matelsi, M., *Broadcast Programming and Promotion Work Text*, Focal Press, Boston, MA, 1989.

National Association of Broadcasters, *Best of the Best Promotions*, vol. 3, NAB, Washington, D.C., 1994.

National Association of Broadcasters, *Casinos, Lotteries, and Contests*, NAB, Washington, D.C., 2007.

Nickels, W., *Marketing Communications and Promotion*, 3rd edition, John Wiley & Sons, New York, NY, 1984.

Peck, W.A., *Radio Promotion Handbook*, Tab, Blue Ridge Summit, PA, 1968.

Ramsey, M., *Fresh Air: Marketing Gurus on Radio*, iUniverse, Lincoln, NE, 2005.

Rhoads, B.E., Bunzel, R., Snook, A., and McMan, W. (eds.), *Programming and Promotions*, Streamline Press, West Palm Beach, FL, 1995.

Roberts, T.E.F., *Practical Radio Promotions*, Focal Press, Boston, MA, 1992.

Savage, B., *Perry's Broadcast Promotion Sourcebook*, Perry, Oak Ridge, TN, 1982.

Shane, E., *Selling Electronic Media*, Focal Press, Boston, MA, 1999.

Stanley, R.E., *Promotions*, 2nd edition, Prentice Hall, Englewood Cliffs, NJ, 1982.

# APPENDIX 7A:

## ASSESSING THE IMPACT ON RADIO AND TELEVISION STATIONS OF THE FEDERAL TRADE COMMISSION'S RECENTLY REVISED GUIDANCE ON ENDORSEMENTS AND TESTIMONIALS

Source: Courtesy of Lauren Lynch Flick, Esq. Excerpt reprinted with permission Pillsbury Winthrop Shaw Pittman LLP

# Advisory

Communications                                    November 2009

## Assessing the Impact on Radio and Television Stations of the Federal Trade Commission's Recently Revised Guidance on Endorsements and Testimonials

by Lauren Lynch Flick

*On December 1, 2009, the FTC's newly-revised Guides on Endorsements and Testimonials will become effective. Broadcasters, including their on-air talent, need to know when a claim is an endorsement/testimonial, what on-air disclosures may be required, and what their obligations are to ensure that claims are truthful and not misleading. These endorsement/testimonial-related issues can arise in a variety of contexts, including when station personnel voice commercials, prepare copy for advertisers, engage in banter regarding a product or service, serve as a spokesperson for an advertiser, or provide content to their station websites.*

### Background

The Federal Trade Commission ("FTC") enforces certain federal laws promoting competition, including federal consumer protection laws prohibiting unfair and deceptive business practices. In that capacity, the FTC routinely investigates advertising to ensure that it is truthful and not deceptive. The FTC also publishes Guides which provide insight into the FTC's enforcement approach with respect to specific advertising practices. Broadcasters as a group have not traditionally encountered extensive direct regulation by the FTC because the FTC has most often focused on the advertiser, not the media disseminating the advertising message. However, broadcasters are subject to the FTC's jurisdiction, particularly when they or their employees are involved in the production and/or dissemination of endorsements for products or services. We previously provided our clients with an analysis of the FTC's recent revisions to its Guides on Endorsements and Testimonials.[1] This Advisory focuses more specifically on broadcasters' airing

[1] *See* Client Alert, FTC Updates Guidance on Endorsements and Testimonials in Advertising (October 15, 2009).

---

of endorsement material produced by third parties, endorsement material produced by the station, and endorsements featuring the station's own employees. For purposes of this Advisory, the terms "Endorsements" and "Testimonials" are treated as synonymous, since the FTC does not draw a distinction between them.

Endorsements and testimonials, especially by those well-known in a community, are recognized as having the potential to influence consumer perceptions of advertised products and services. The FTC's research concludes that the fact an endorser has received compensation for his or her statements or has a material relationship with the advertiser can affect the value consumers place on such an endorsement. Given the potential persuasiveness of endorsements, the FTC's regulations seek to assure that (1) the public is aware that the speaker is being compensated for the messages s/he is conveying about a product or service, and (2) the endorsement accurately reflects the characteristics of the product or service, including the generally expected result that the consumer will experience when using the product or service in the manner depicted. To achieve these goals, the FTC's Guides concerning endorsements assign specific disclosure requirements, as well as liability for the content of endorsements, to both the advertiser and the endorser. Broadcasters must be aware that if they receive compensation to directly convey positive messages about an advertiser's product or service, depending on the context, they may be considered endorsers and be liable under the FTC's regulations.[2]

The FTC's primary goal in revising the Guides, which were adopted in 1980, was to include examples that demonstrate how the FTC's established policies and practices apply to new media, such as blogs and other social media, which are increasingly influencing consumers' purchasing decisions. Nevertheless, many in the advertising community feel that the revisions go further, effectively establishing new standards of conduct under the existing law. In addition, many in the online community feel that the Guides unfairly establish standards for new media such as "bloggers" that are different from those for traditional media such as broadcasters. In stating their case, they draw comparisons between their activities and the practices of traditional media, noting that the Guides suggest a possibly higher standard for bloggers. The Federal Communications Commission ("FCC") has its own regulations regarding sponsorship identification and has raised concerns as to whether its regulations should be tightened to assure that the public is made aware when parties pay for broadcast content in an effort to influence the public. Thus, from both an FCC and FTC perspective, broadcasters are well advised to be proactive in complying with these governmental mandates.

## What Constitutes An Endorsement

The FTC defines an endorsement as:

> Any advertising message (including verbal statements, demonstrations, or depictions of the name, signature, likeness or other identifying personal characteristics of an individual or the name or seal of an organization) that consumers are likely to believe reflects the opinions, beliefs, findings, or experiences of a party other than the sponsoring advertiser, even if the views expressed by that party are identical to those of the sponsoring advertiser.[3]

[2] The FCC has long enforced its sponsorship identification rule requiring that whenever consideration is given in exchange for the broadcast of material, an over-the-air announcement be made stating that fact and identifying the sponsor. See Advisory, Paying the Piper: Avoiding Payola/Plugola Violations and Minimizing Liability (August 2009). The FCC has also been actively examining whether its sponsorship identification rule adequately achieves this public notification goal, particularly with regard to program material provided by third parties. Broadcasters must therefore be mindful of the changing state of the law at both the FCC and FTC when making an endorsement.

[3] 16 C.F.R. § 255.0(b) 2009.

This definition is little changed from the one that has been in place since 1980. The revision to the Guides makes clear that "the fundamental question is whether, viewed objectively, the relationship between the advertiser and the speaker is such that the speaker's statement can be considered 'sponsored' by the advertiser."[4] This focus on the audience's perception is important for broadcasters because advertisers increasingly seek to integrate their messages more seamlessly into programming, rather than relying on pre-produced "spot" commercials. Some of these efforts may lead the public to conclude that a message delivered by an identifiable station employee is a statement of the employee's true experience and beliefs about a product, when he or she may simply be reading advertising copy verbatim.

## Obligations When Making An Endorsement

Where an advertising message gives the impression that it reflects what the station employee personally believes or has experienced, rather than simply what the advertiser believes or has experienced, the endorser, the station employing the endorser, and the advertiser have an obligation to ensure that the public is aware of their relationship. They also have a duty to ensure that the message conveyed is accurate and that the claims made by the endorser can be substantiated.

### Disclosure

Whenever an endorsement is made in a context in which the public will not likely assume that consideration has been paid for the endorsement, a disclosure must be made to advise the public of that fact. The FTC recognizes that in certain circumstances, some persons are so famous (a "celebrity") that the public would naturally assume in traditional advertising contexts that the celebrity is being paid to give the endorsement and therefore no disclosure of that fact is necessary. However, if a celebrity's endorsement occurs outside the context of a traditional advertisement, disclosure may very well be required. Note that in either case, an endorsement has occurred. The only difference is whether the endorser's connection with the advertiser needs to be specifically disclosed.

To illustrate this situation, the FTC Guides provide the example of a celebrity who, during an interview on a television talk show program, discusses a recent surgical experience s/he has undergone. She makes positive statements about the experience and mentions the doctor/facility by name. The FTC states that the audience would likely assume that the celebrity received compensation for those statements if they were delivered in the context of a traditional commercial spot. However, because the statements occurred in the context of a talk show interview, a disclosure must be made.

The "celebrity" scenario poses a potential dilemma for stations. If their on-air personalities are viewed as "celebrities," then no separate disclosure of their relationship to an advertiser need be made when they endorse an advertiser's product or service on-air. However, as seen below, as an endorser, the on-air personality and the station employer have an obligation to make reasonable inquiry into the accuracy of the content of the endorsement and be satisfied that the claims are substantiated.

Keep in mind that the FCC's sponsorship identification rule already requires that disclosure be made when material being broadcast has been paid for or sponsored unless the sponsored nature of the content is obvious. The FCC's rule, however, does not extend to online or social media activities of on-air personalities. Here, the FTC believes that the likelihood that the public will not be aware of a relationship between a celebrity and an advertiser is greater and therefore requires disclosure. Thus, as broadcasters work with advertisers to develop innovative multi-platform advertising campaigns, they should consider whether the

[4] 74 Fed. Reg. 53124, 53126 (October 15, 2009).

listening/viewing audience will be able to recognize when the station or personality has received payment or something of value to convey the message, and craft appropriate disclosures.

## Accuracy

The advertiser is always liable for the accuracy of the information conveyed in its messages. Where a speaker endorses a product or service, s/he is also liable for the accuracy of the message conveyed.

In the context of an endorsement, the requirement of accuracy applies at two levels. First, the message must accurately convey the endorser's experience with a product or service. An endorser may not claim to use a product that s/he does not use, or to have achieved a result s/he has not achieved. For example, an endorser may not say that s/he lost a certain amount of weight using a product if s/he did not use the product or lose the stated amount of weight.

Second, the message must only convey information that can be substantiated. An advertiser may not make an advertising claim that it cannot support, and the advertiser will be held liable for inaccurate or misleading claims it makes. Importantly for broadcasters, a station employee endorser, and thus the station, will also be held liable for inaccurate or misleading claims that s/he makes on the advertiser's behalf. Thus, if the endorser or the station knows that a claim is incorrect, the employee may not repeat that claim in advertising. In the example the FTC gives, a celebrity is present during the taping of an infomercial for a roasting bag which is represented to reduce the time to cook a whole chicken to 30 minutes. The celebrity sees that the chickens used in the infomercial do not cook in the advertised time. The celebrity may not simply read the script provided and repeat the claim that s/he now knows to be inaccurate.

With respect to product representations that are not readily observable by the endorser, such as the savings that can be expected by switching to a particular brand of car insurance, the endorser must make "reasonable inquiries" of the advertiser as to the basis of the claim. If the endorser could be considered an "expert" with regard to the product being endorsed, the accuracy element requires that the person in fact be an expert with respect to that product and that the expert make reasonable inquiries into the claims being made in the advertisement. While the FTC does not provide guidance as to what it would deem a "reasonable" inquiry, it does note that such an endorsement cannot rely solely on letters from satisfied customers.

A very important aspect of the substantiation element contained in the revised Guides is that any claims the endorser makes about his or her experience with a product must either reflect the typical experience a consumer would expect to have using the product, or include a disclosure of what a typical consumer's experience would be. For example, if an on-air personality is paid to use a particular diet product and loses an atypical amount of weight using the product, s/he must include information about the amount of weight loss that would be typical when s/he is describing the experience of using the product. Similarly, if the personality received personal exercise training or started an extreme exercise regime at the same time as s/he began using the diet product, that "unique circumstances" fact must also be disclosed. The prior practice of simply including the disclaimer "Results Not Typical" is no longer acceptable as a safe harbor.

## Advertiser's Responsibilities

The Guides recognize that advertisers do not have full control over the statements of endorsers. Nevertheless, because the advertiser chooses to use this method of advertising, the FTC assigns responsibility to the advertiser, as well as to the endorser. The Guides state that advertisers should take steps to maintain control over the advertising message by providing the endorser with accurate and substantiated information to say about the product, monitor the endorser's statements, and correct any erroneous messages as soon as possible.

### Illustrative Examples for the Broadcaster

**Spots**

**Example 1:** A radio on-air personality states that a music countdown will resume after a commercial break, then plays a pre-recorded advertising message provided by the advertiser and voiced by someone other than the on-air personality. In this instance, it is clear that the statements made during the commercial break are those of the advertiser, not the on-air personality or station ownership/management. As a result, there is no endorsement by the station and no genuine potential for station liability, unless the station believes or has reason to know that the claims made are false or misleading.

**Example 2:** A radio on-air personality states that a music countdown will resume after a commercial break, then "live-reads" a scripted advertising message provided by the advertiser which makes positive claims about the gasoline mileage and performance of a particular automobile available at the advertiser's dealership. The announcer does not state or imply that s/he has personally seen or driven the car or that the views/opinions are his/hers. Again, this is during a commercial break, and the on-air personality will likely be perceived as only speaking in the place of the advertiser, not on the basis of his/her own beliefs and experiences. As a result, there is no endorsement and no genuine potential for station liability unless the station believes or has reason to know that the claims made are false or misleading.

**Example 3:** A radio on-air personality states that a music countdown will resume after a commercial break, then "live-reads" in a folksy way a scripted advertising message provided by the advertiser regarding the speed of relief from coughing provided by the advertiser's cough drop medication. In this case, given that the on-air personality uses his or her voice and it would not be unusual that the person would use the advertised product, there is an increased possibility that the audience would perceive such statements to reflect the on-air personality's own opinion or experience with the product, rather than the assertion of the advertiser. This example demonstrates the care that should be taken in drafting the content of advertising copy, as well as in carefully circumscribing "ad lib" comments by on-air personalities, to avoid the perception of an endorsement unless that is what is intended. In this particular example, while it may indeed be an endorsement, the fact that the announcement is occurring during an identified commercial break and the on-air personality is a local "celebrity" would support the position that specific disclosure of the advertiser relationship is unnecessary. However, keep in mind if treated as an endorsement, the endorser would have to undertake reasonable inquiry to verify any factual statements made.

**Example 4:** A radio on-air personality states that a music countdown will resume after a commercial break, then "live-reads" a scripted advertising message that the station's sales staff has drafted. Assuming the copy makes clear that the on-air personality is speaking in the place of the advertiser, not on the basis of his/her own beliefs and experiences, there is no endorsement. Note that this result is no different from the results in Examples 2 and 3, each of which depend on the exact language used in the spot. However, because the station staff has drafted the advertising copy, the station may have increased exposure to liability for false and misleading advertising. Accordingly, even though the on-air personality is not providing his/her endorsement, stations involved in drafting copy when producing a spot need to satisfy themselves that the claims made have been substantiated.

### Editorial Content

**Example 5:** A station reporter conducts a test of whether certain brand-name compact fluorescent light bulbs provide the energy and cost savings advertised, and thereafter reports on the test on-air, advising the audience that the light bulbs are an excellent energy and cost saving product.

This example is an "exception" to the normal definition of an endorsement. Where employees of traditional media, in the course of their assigned work, conduct and report such product reviews, the FTC does not consider them to be endorsing a product. The FTC also recognizes that with regard to traditional media, advertisers will routinely provide free or reduced price books and movies to reviewers, or sample products to consumer reporters. Accordingly, where the product used in the report was provided for free, and it is customary for the reporter to receive such free products without any particular obligation to review them or make positive public statements about them, there is no endorsement. The reporter does not have to disclose whether the product tested was purchased or received free of charge, and does not have to determine whether the experience with the product was typical. In this context, however, reporters frequently disclose whether they purchased the products themselves or received the products for free to help establish their independence and objectivity with their audience. Note that a blogger in the same circumstances would have to disclose the receipt of the free products or other relationship to the advertiser. This is one of the reasons bloggers assert that they are subject to a different standard than traditional media under the new Guides.

Note that even in traditional media, if a station receives compensation to air the reporter's story and to portray the product in a positive light, then a disclosure is required and the reporter/station will be accountable for the accuracy of the material aired.

### Banter

**Example 6:** A local eye surgeon performs, free of charge or at a discount, a vision enhancement procedure on a station's play-by-play sports announcer on the condition that the announcer make positive on-air mentions of the improvement in his/her eyesight. The doctor also purchases a number of traditional 30-second commercials from the station. During a lull in a game caused by an on-field dispute between a team coach and referees regarding a penalty call, the on-air announcer makes animated statements regarding the penalty and attributes his/her confidence in those conclusions to the vision enhancement procedure performed by the eye surgeon.

The announcer's statements about the vision enhancement procedure are an endorsement. Especially since they occur outside a typical advertising spot, the play-by-play announcer must disclose to the public that s/he has received the free/discounted vision enhancement procedure whenever s/he makes positive statements about the experience, doctor, or improvement in vision. In addition, the announcer is liable for the content of the endorsement. The endorsement must (a) reflect the announcer's true experience, (b) be accurate and substantiated, and (c) if the announcer's experience is not typical, provide information about the results a consumer could reasonably expect.

The doctor/advertiser must provide the announcer with correct information about the effectiveness of the procedure to convey to the public, and is required to monitor the announcer's statements to be sure that s/he in fact conveys both the disclosure and accurate information. Because the station's employee is making the endorsement in his/her employee capacity, the station has an independent obligation to ensure proper disclosure and accuracy by the announcer.

## Remote Broadcasts

**Example 7:** A station enters an agreement with a local restaurant owner and station advertiser to broadcast remotely from the grand opening of a new location of the restaurant. During the remote broadcast, the on-air personality repeatedly states that s/he is broadcasting from the new restaurant location and urges listeners to come to the restaurant to receive a free appetizer at the grand opening. The on-air personality states that s/he believes that the free appetizer is the best appetizer s/he has ever tasted. The on-air personality also interviews diners as they leave who state that the free appetizers are large and delicious. One of the diners leaving is the station's dining out/entertainment reporter who states that the restaurant has found a way to make food that is both delicious and under 500 calories per serving.

In this case, it is reasonably likely that the public would recognize that the restaurant and station have a material relationship and disclosure of that fact would then not be necessary. The on-air personality's statements regarding the free appetizer are an endorsement and must accurately reflect that s/he ate and liked the product, although the statement that it is "the best" is likely to be seen as mere puffery. The interviews with other diners leaving the restaurant are also puffery. The station's dining out/entertainment reporter, however, is likely to be regarded as an expert in the area of restaurant food. Therefore, any statements of fact made by the reporter, such as the restaurant's use of under 500 calories per serving portions would require the reporter to confirm that those under 500 calories per serving portions are indeed under 500 calories and that such portions are the rule, not the exception.

## Social Media

**Example 8:** The station encourages its on-air personalities to maintain pages on social media platforms such as Facebook and to send messages via Twitter to increase their popularity and on-air following. A station personality sends a "tweet" to his/her Twitter followers stating that s/he has just eaten a delicious meal at a certain restaurant.

The social media context is one of the main focuses of the FTC's revision to its Guides because the FTC is concerned that the public will not be able to recognize when information distributed in this manner is in fact an advertising message. Accordingly, if the on-air personality or station has agreed to make such positive statements in exchange for consideration, then a disclosure regarding that relationship must be made. Again, the personality's statement must fairly reflect his or her experience, i.e., that the food was enjoyable. Any other factual claims, such as the calorie content mentioned in Example 7 above, must also be substantiated. The advertiser must also monitor the mentions that are made regarding the restaurant to ensure that the disclosure and accuracy requirements are met. Note that in the context of a social medium that significantly limits the number of characters each message may contain, it may be difficult to provide the requisite disclosure. This should be taken into account before engaging in such a campaign.

**Example 9:** The station introduces a new program and host. The program debuts to low listener/viewership. Station personnel producing the program post comments on their personal blogs and social media pages commenting on the interesting, insightful, clever, and relevant discussions they have heard on the program and encouraging all their friends to tune in for the next episode of the program. This is an endorsement.

Station personnel have a material relationship with the program they are endorsing. They cannot pose as disinterested members of the listening/viewing public in order to generate interest in the program. They must disclose their relationship to the station.

These last two examples demonstrate the difficulty in separating employees' work and personal lives. Stations increasingly need to adopt social media policies and educate employees regarding their use to address these types of situations.

## Conclusion

Whether stations or their employees are making endorsements will be judged from the consumer's perspective and depends on the precise language of the message and the circumstances in which it is presented. As the above discussion indicates, these are complex legal waters to navigate. Broadcasters should consult legal counsel in creating appropriate policies and practices to minimize liability, as well as in promptly addressing incidents where an endorsement may create liability.

If you have any questions about the content of this advisory, please contact the Pillsbury attorney with whom you regularly work, or the author of this alert.

Lauren Lynch Flick (bio)
Washington, DC
+1.202.663.8166
lauren.lynch.flick@pillsburylaw.com

# CHAPTER 8

# Production

## A SPOT RETROSPECTIVE

The transition from analog to digital audio technology ushered radio into a new era in mixing and sound imaging. A typical radio station—whether it be broadcast, satellite, or Internet—produces thousands of commercials, public service announcements (PSAs), and station promotion messages (promos) annually. Additionally, stations will mix a vast array of positioning messages designed to create and reinforce stations' images with their audiences.

Radio insiders refer to commercial audio messages collectively as "spots." The term "spot" denotes a brief message, typically 60 seconds or less in duration, that contrasts its brevity with the approach utilized in the early days of the medium. In the 1920s, most paid announcements consisted of lengthy speeches on the virtues of a particular product or service. In the absence of suitable recording technologies, the general practice was to read the commercial script, known as "copy," live. Perhaps the most representative of the commercials of the period was one of the first ever to be broadcast, which lasted more than 10 minutes and was announced by a representative of a real estate firm from Queens, New York. Aired live over WEAF in 1922, by today's standards the message would sound more like a classroom lecture than a broadcast advertisement. Certainly, no snappy jingle or ear-catching sound effects accompanied the episodic announcement.

Most commercial messages resembled that lengthy real estate pitch until 1926. On Christmas Eve of that year, four singers introduced the radio jingle by gathering around the microphone to deliver a musical tribute to Wheaties cereal. It took several years, however, before singing commercials became commonplace. For the most part, commercial production during the medium's first decade was relatively mundane. The reason was twofold: the government had resisted the idea of blatant or direct commercialism from the start, which fostered a low-key approach to advertising, and the medium was just in the process of evolving and therefore lacked the technical and creative wherewithal to present a more sophisticated message.

Things changed by 1930, however. The austere, no-frills pitch, occasionally accompanied by a piano but more often done a cappella, was gradually replaced by the dialogue spot that used drama or comedy to sell its product. A great deal of imagination and creativity went into the writing and production of commercials, which were presented live throughout the 1930s. The production demands of some commercials equaled and even exceeded those of the programs they interrupted. Orchestras, actors, and lavishly constructed sound effects commonly were utilized to sell chocolate-flavored syrup or a muscle liniment. By the late 1930s, certain commercials had become as famous as the favorite programs of the day. Commercials had achieved the status of pop art.

Still, the early studios where talent labored to intone the sponsors' messages were primitive by today's standards. So-termed "production rooms" were technologically unsophisticated performance studios. Sound effects were mostly improvised show by show, commercial by commercial, in some cases using the actual objects with which sounds were identified. Glass was shattered, guns fired, and furniture overturned as the studio's on-air light flashed. Before World War II, few sound effects were available on records. It was just as rare for a station to broadcast prerecorded commercials, although acetate discs—

known as "electrical transcriptions" and usually abbreviated as an "e.t."—for turntable playback and magnetic wire recordings were used by certain major advertisers. The creation of vinyl discs in the 1940s inspired more widespread use of the e.t. for radio advertising purposes. Today, sound effects recordings are imported from CDs and downloaded from the Internet to be stored on computer hard drives.

The live spot was the mainstay at most stations into the 1950s, when two innovations brought about a greater reliance on the prerecorded message. Magnetic recording tape and 33⅓ rpm long-playing (LP) records revolutionized radio production methods. Recording tape brought about the greatest transformation and, ironically, was the product of Nazi scientists, who developed acetate recorders and tape for espionage purposes. The adoption of magnetic tape by radio stations was costlier and thus occurred at a slower pace than 33⅓ rpm disc use, which essentially required a turntable modification to accommodate playing the slower speed.

Throughout the 1950s, advertising agencies grew to rely on LPs. By 1960, magnetic tape recorders were a familiar piece of studio equipment. Initially, prerecorded spot announcements were played on air directly from reel-to-reel tape decks, similar or identical to the machines on which the messages had been recorded. While this technique was versatile it was also cumbersome—it required the deejay to manually thread the ribbon of magnetic tape through the guides of the playback deck and then shuttle the tape to locate the beginning of the recorded message and prepare it for playback. This practice, termed "cueing," was similar to the technique deejays utilized to prepare vinyl records on turntables for airplay. Stations relied more and more on prerecorded commercials following the introduction of the cartridge tape deck. "Cart machines" modernized control room procedures thanks to their ease of use. By enclosing the magnetic tape within a small, plastic cartridge, developers of the "cart machine" freed deejays from the burdens of loading, cueing, and unloading tape on unwieldy reel-to-reel decks. Self-cueing carts enabled deejays to play out short-form, recorded program elements with ease and rapidity. Commercial spots, PSAs, jingle IDs, sound effects, and other program features could be easily selected at random from the cart library and played (or "fired") on-air at the push of a button. Such rapid sequencing helped to quicken the pace, and revolutionized the sound of 1960s-era top 40 stations. Magnetic tape also fueled the development of automated radio by replacing the deejay with prerecorded programming served up to listeners via sequenced-playback reel-to-reel and cartridge tape machines. While "automated radio" endured much criticism for its lack of personality and spontaneity, it nonetheless did away with live announcements entirely and minimized the possibility for on-air mistakes to occur.

The *sound* of commercials became more sophisticated because practically any scenario one could imagine could be accomplished on tape. Perhaps no individual in the 1960s more effectively demonstrated the unique nature of radio as an advertising medium than did Stan Freberg. When, through skillful

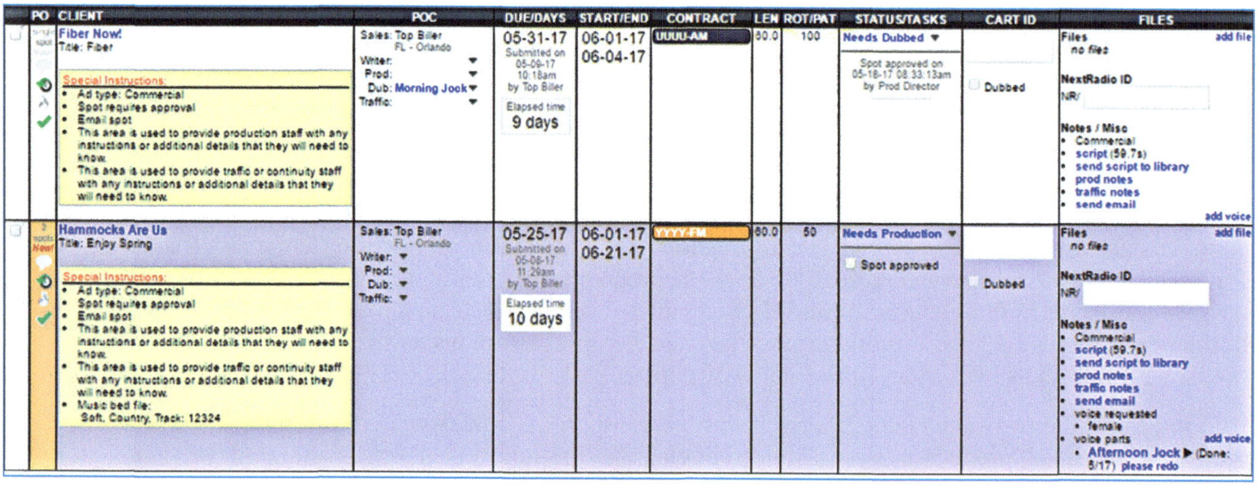

**FIGURE 8.1**

vCreative's vPPO cloud-based workflow system delivers detailed ad creation information from the sales department to the producer

Source: Courtesy vCreative Inc.

writing and the clever use of sound effects, Freberg transformed Lake Michigan into a basin of hot chocolate, dolloped with a 700-foot-high mountain of whipped cream, and crowned with a 10-ton maraschino cherry dropped from the sky by Royal Canadian Air Force planes, no one doubted the feat.

Today, the sounds of millions of skillfully prepared commercials trek through the ether and into the minds of practically every man, woman, and child in America. Good writing and inventive production are what make the medium so successful.

## FORMATTED SPOTS

In the 1950s the medium took to program *formatting* to survive and prosper. Today listeners are offered myriad sounds from which to choose; there is something for practically every taste. Stations concentrate their efforts on delivering a specific format, which may be defined as adult contemporary, country, classic rock, or any one of a dozen others. As you will recall from the discussion in Chapter 3, each format has its own distinctive sound, which is accomplished through a careful selection and arrangement of compatible program elements. To this end, commercials attempt to reflect a station's format. In the age of consolidation, says Larry Miller, "There is a tendency to do one-size-fits-all at the advertising agency level. In-house local retail may be more customized to fit the format." The need to match the

**FIGURE 8.2**

This catalog, issued quarterly, informs stations about public service campaigns and announcements available from the Ad Council

Source: Courtesy of the Ad Council

presentation styles of message and the music extends to prerecorded public service announcements (PSAs) produced and distributed by the Ad Council. This not-for-profit agency frequently develops public service campaigns utilizing format-specific production styles, content and talent.

## THE PRODUCTION ROOM

A radio station has two kinds of studios: on-air and production. Both share basic design features and have comparable equipment. Additionally, production studios are often arranged and configured to serve as back-ups in the event that technical difficulties render the on-air studio inoperable. In cluster operations where stations are colocated, there is often a single primary production facility.

In general, metro-market stations and clusters employ a full-time production person (known variously as production director, production manager, production chief, and more recently as chief imager or creative services director). This individual's primary duties are to record voice tracks and mix commercials and PSAs. Other duties involve maintaining the station's production libraries of background music "beds" and sound effects and mixing down promotional material and special programs, such as public affairs features, interviews, and documentaries.

Stations that do not have a slot for a full-time production person divide this work among the on-air staff. In this case, the program director often oversees production responsibilities, or a deejay may be assigned several hours of production duties each day and be called the production director.

At most medium and small outlets, on-air personnel take part in the production process. Production may include the simple transfer of an advertising agency spot into the station's computerized program

**FIGURE 8.3**

Audio mixing in a joint studio/control room

Source: Courtesy of Wheatstone

automation system, creating mixdowns ranging from a simple, instrumental music bed underneath a 30-second voicer to a complex, multielement mixdown of a 60-second two-voicer with sound effects and several bed transitions. Station production can run from the mundane to the exciting and challenging (for instance, mixing a commercial in such a way as to convey the message through a confluence of sounds).

Production directors in this digital age often are called imaging directors, and are recruited from the on-air ranks, having acquired the necessary studio dexterity and know-how to meet the demands of the position. In addition to the broad range of mixdown skills required by the job, a solid knowledge of editing techniques is essential. The production director is routinely called on to make gatekeeping decisions about content ranging from rudimentary replacements to performing more complex editing chores, such as the rearrangement of elements in a 60-second concert promo.

The production/Imaging director works closely with many people but perhaps most closely with the program director. The person responsible for production is expected to have a complete understanding of the station's programming philosophy and objective. This is necessary because commercials constitute an element of programming and therefore must complement the format execution, achieving compatibility with the music, the personalities, and the overall sound of the station. A production person must be able to determine when an incoming commercial clashes with the station's image. When a question exists as to the spot's content appropriateness or suitability, the program director will be called on to make the final judgment, because it is he or she who is ultimately responsible for what gets on the air. In the final analysis, station production is a product of programming. In most broadcast organizations, the production director answers to the program director. It is a logical arrangement given the relationship of the two areas.

The production/imaging director also works closely with the station copywriter. Their combined efforts can make or break a commercial. The copywriter conceives the concept and the producer brings it to fruition. The traffic department also is in close and constant contact with production, because one of its primary responsibilities is to see that copy gets processed and is made available in the on-air studio at the time when it is scheduled for broadcast.

Once again the extensive clustering of station facilities in the age of consolidation finds many production responsibilities centralized. By now many radio groups have established one production hub to mix the spots of their other outlets, especially when in the same market. Typically, this has resulted in the downsizing of individual station production staffs and the elimination of comprehensive mixdown studios at these sites.

## THE CONTROL ROOM

For ease of movement and accessibility, audio equipment in the on-air studio, termed the control room (CR), is commonly situated in a configuration consistent with the intended position of the person who operates the equipment. "Standing" arrangements help to promote and sustain deejay momentum and are commonly utilized at stations with high-energy formats. Alternately, studios designed for "seated" operation tend to put announcers into a more relaxed mood and elicit a subdued pace. The important role that well-designed, accessibly located studio furniture plays in contributing to a successful, creatively productive environment must be underscored.

Says David Holland, a designer with Omnirax Furniture Company:

Studio furniture is an integral part of any radio station with an impact that is financial, strategic, and personal. A clear idea of a studio's function will set the tone for decisions involving size of the space, shape of the furniture and equipment requirements. As the trend in equipment is clearly towards smaller and more powerful, the largest determinant of the size of the furniture is the number of people the studio needs to support. Careful consideration must be paid to relationships between board operators ("board ops") and talent, hosts and guests, screener and producer, etc. Both sound and sight lines must be maintained so that the studio functions as a cohesive whole. Proper attention to the design of the furniture affects everything from the sound over the airwaves and ergonomics of the working environment to the ease of installing and maintaining equipment.

**FIGURE 8.4**

*Terminator 2*-themed broadcast studio at Universal Orlando accommodates multiple guests

Source: Courtesy of the Telos Alliance

**FIGURE 8.5**

The studio for the *Free Beer & Hot Wings Morning Show* syndicated program features low-profile microphone support arms to ensure that talent can be viewed without obstruction on the video stream

Source: Courtesy of Steve McKiernan, executive producer, *The Free Beer & Hot Wings Morning Show*

**FIGURE 8.6**

Careful attention to furniture design, construction, and layout results in successful ergonomic interaction between talent and equipment

Source: Courtesy of ESPN and Omnirax Furniture Company

While the casual observer attaches significance to the aesthetic appeal of the studio layout, Holland explains the importance of understanding how station engineers interact with studio furniture. "Well-designed furniture," Holland states,

> pays careful attention to engineering requirements. At today's pace, equipment gets replaced sooner, talent may come and go—even ownership changes, but it is universally true that wire will still need to go everywhere to sustain the studio's operation. Engineers are at the heart of the station and furniture that supports their function will last for many years.

In-person visitors and webcam viewers alike must be favorably impressed with the layout and appearance of studios. Holland continues:

Studio furniture can and should reflect a station's personality and brand. It is a given that studio furniture must be rugged to accommodate a rotating corps of staff and guests in a 24/7 environment. But it is equally important that the furniture have an aesthetic and functional appeal to attract and impress talent, advertisers, and sponsors. Shape, materials, color, and hardware are some of the many elements that combine and interplay in successful furniture design. Functionally designed furniture supports the strategic goals of superior sound, ergonomics and engineering. And great looking furniture promotes personal pride of ownership and radio station morale.

The standard equipment found in radio studios includes microphones, an audio console (commonly referred to as the "board"), and computer audio playout systems loaded with program automation software (BE AudioVAULT FleX, RCS Zetta, or similar). Computer workstations in on-air studios are networked with production studio facilities. Video display monitors, CD playback decks, standalone audio editors, digital effects processors, telephone interfaces, and audio distribution/routing systems are also seen frequently in studios.

Designing the studio to support studio-cam video streaming has become an increasingly important consideration. Several companies market hardware and software solutions for video streaming, offering stations the opportunities for "opening the studio doors" to listeners. Despite the technological sophistication of the equipment, the production of the stream is becoming simpler and more user-friendly with the addition of features such as automated cameras and touch screen graphics production. "Networked" studios have simplified the task of adding visual content to the broadcast. Nonetheless, careful consideration about the design and layout of studios designated for video streaming should be given, focusing on maintaining sight lines between hosts and guests by minimizing any obstructions caused by the presence of studio equipment.

**FIGURE 8.7**

Multi-camera Facebook Live streaming using HDVMixer Visual Radio Solution by INSOFT (www.HDVMixer.com)

Source: Courtesy of INSOFT LLC

## AUDIO CONSOLE

The audio console is the centerpiece, the command center, the very heart of the radio station. *Radio* magazine lists approximately 30 manufacturers, of "consoles, mixers and control surfaces" in its *Buyers Guide Annual Resource Directory*. Although design characteristics and configurations vary, certain basic components and functions remain relatively constant. Consoles in all different sizes and shapes support the operations of stations ranging in size from the largest major-market group clusters to the smallest mom-and-pop AM daytimers. Characteristics and features common to all consoles include inputs that permit audio energy to enter the console and outputs through which audio energy is fed to other locations, VU or loudness meters that measure the amount or level of sound energy, pots (faders) that control gain (the quantity of audio energy), switches for designating the destinations of the audio signals, controls to adjust the volume of the studio monitor loudspeakers, and, occasionally, master gain pots for the purpose of controlling general output levels. Console designers continue to extend the use of digital technology for audio signal manipulation purposes. Today's modern approach is fueled by computerization and networking.

**FIGURE 8.8**
Marty Sacks

## CONSIDERATIONS FOR DESIGNING AN IP-AUDIO STUDIO

### Marty Sacks

Since the AES67 standard—an open standard for Audio over IP (Internet Protocol) interoperability—was ratified in 2013, the broadcast industry has experienced a dramatic change. Broadcasters now realize what the Telos Alliance learned way back in 2002 when we invented the first AoIP protocol for broadcast: IP-Audio studios save money, simplify workflows, reduce the amount of equipment you need, and eliminate massive amounts of wiring that used to be a fact of life in broadcast studios.

Without question, AoIP is the way of the future for broadcast audio. Therefore, when designing a new studio, you'll want your facility to have an IP infrastructure. No matter how small or large your studio is, it's important to think through the choices you're making in both equipment and in interoperability protocols available from different manufacturers. The decisions you make at this earliest stage in your studio's AoIP design will affect future capabilities in a profound way that you may not predict.

The AoIP protocol (ours is called Livewire+, which means Livewire + AES67) you choose will define a set of capabilities beyond the most basic audio interoperability made possible by AES67. For example, AES67 does not include Advertising/Discovery, GPIO (General Purpose I/O, also called 'tally' or contact closures), and Program Associated Data (PAD). Choose a baseline AoIP protocol that touts AES67 but does not add GPIO, and you may not be able to easily start and stop the equipment in your studio! For the announcer to be able to start the next song or commercial using the console buttons, GPIO must be supported by your protocol.

Additionally, some AoIP protocols are not fully AES67 compliant. Indeed, we hear the terms AES67 compliant and AES67 compatible thrown about a bit, often incorrectly. And while the two terms may sound the same, the difference between compliance and compatibility is huge. AES67, like all standards, can be minimally implemented. But when standards are minimally implemented, they minimally get the job done. It's possible to achieve a level of audio interoperability using AES67, yet still not fully comply with the standard. Simply put, compliance means that every single aspect of the AES67 standard is met. Compatible means some of the standard is complied with. There is a big difference.

One aspect of AES67, for example, calls for Unicast mode using SIP. This could be the exchange of audio between city pairs using AES67. Normally, city-to-city connections are created using a wide area network where the multicast streams normally found in IP-Audio Studio aren't likely to be supported. If your audio network's native AES67 protocol or your specific gear doesn't support Unicast, you might not be able to move audio back and forth without purchasing additional gear. A full implementation of AES67 is required at the protocol level and by the manufacturer of the gear you are purchasing to be assured of Unicast mode using SIP.

So why don't all AES67 protocols and/or manufacturers support Unicast mode using SIP? Because implementing it into the standard is fairly challenging. Despite the fact that it is hard work, we know from our experience with AoIP codecs that it's a capability that our customers want. Some manufacturers and protocols take the easy road and leave it out altogether. Those protocols and manufacturers are no longer AES67 compliant because they did not meet this part of the standard.

Unicast is just one instance of an AES67 standard that isn't complied with by all manufacturers and protocols. There are others. One AoIP protocol, for example, dynamically assigns IP addresses to its network-connected devices in AES67 mode. This is analogous to your mobile number changing every time you power up your smartphone! As you can imagine, this can wreak havoc with other devices intending to share audio on the network using AES67.

Unfortunately, there is no AES67 task force out there policing this, so it's a good idea to confirm that the gear and protocol you choose is fully AES67 *compliant* versus *compatible*.

Understanding the difference capabilities in AoIP protocols and how they implement AES67, will give you the best performance both now and in the future. And that future is very bright indeed, as more and more manufacturers jump on the AoIP bandwagon and begin incorporating AES67 into their products. For the broadcaster, this means greater efficiency, simpler installation, and reduced cost of building and maintaining your studio.

**Marty Sacks** is Vice-President of Sales, Support, and Marketing for the Telos Alliance.

All audio sources, ranging from studio microphones to automation program-playout systems to incoming remote broadcast pickup signals, are instantly routable and made available not only to any input fader on the studio console, but, equally importantly, to *any* studio's console that is connected to the local network. Equally important, the data that accompany the digital audio signal, such as the logic commands used to control device functions (e.g., audio playback start/stop control), must correspondingly route automatically from source to destination. Deejays can be assured that their personalized vocal presettings on microphone processors are automatically applied to the appropriate microphone regardless of the studio from which they operate. IP-audio-compliant equipment offers superior flexibility to show producers and on-air talent for managing audio control among grouped stations. Also it provides

**FIGURE 8.9**
This deejay is working "combo," performing the roles of "talent" and "board operator" simultaneously
Source: Courtesy of Wheatstone

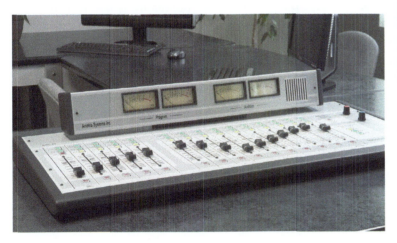

**FIGURE 8.10**
This control board features analog-scale VU meters
Source: Courtesy of Arrakis Systems

**FIGURE 8.11**
Unlike consoles equipped with mechanical-action faders, this compact mixer allows for audio signal adjustment by sliding a finger inside a grooved surface
Source: Courtesy Yellowtec

**FIGURE 8.12**
Studio equipped with turntables. Note the vinyl LP library, at left
Source: Courtesy of the Telos Alliance

significant layers of redundancy to assist station engineers in maintaining the integrity of operations whenever equipment failures occur or routine maintenance is performed. Some thoughts about console functionality, as viewed from the board operator ("board-op") perspective: The use of linear, or *slide*, faders is nearly universal in the modern console, although certain stations that rely on older equipment may have consoles equipped with rotary faders (pots). Slide fader popularity is due in part to the device's slim design. A clustered row of faders minimizes the arm-stretching gymnastics required of deejays to operate some of the old-school, rotary-pot control boards.

The *cue* or *preview* function of the console enables the deejay or board-op to privately monitor audio signals. The console brand Axia now uses the "Preview" terminology on consoles in place of "cue," and some other manufacturers do as well. Regardless of the term applied to this function, this console feature for privately monitoring audio signals consists of a low-power amplifier and loudspeaker/headphone arrangement. It enables board operators to hear sounds originating from digital automation systems, network-program feeds, and remote broadcasts without having to place them "on-air." Onboard intercom/talkback systems similarly permit the monitoring of audio signals originating externally from the studio without distributing them to other destinations. The setup and preparation of the sound sources facilitate their integration into the mix. Depending upon format, budget, and other considerations, consoles may be equipped with modules for controlling and monitoring telephone call-in shows and with circuitry for managing the equipment associated with profanity deletion.

The increasingly modular nature of console design is evidenced by equipment that is more technically sophisticated and customizable. A physical control surface, equipped with conventional faders and switches, is programmed to the specific needs of the studio via touch screen-accessible software. Among the advantages of this arrangement is that the console layout becomes less cluttered and more user-friendly for deejays. Operating parameters and features that are seldom used and/or infrequently modified nonetheless remain fully accessible through the software, thus preserving the console's technological flexibility while at the same time providing board operators with an uncluttered, ergonomic work surface. "Virtual" consoles, for instance, are gathering considerable attention and traction. Unlike a traditional audio control consoles, the virtual console relies on controlling the audio mix by means of apps and software. Personnel utilize flat-surface panels, tablets and/or smartphones to direct the audio flow via hardware that typically is located with the station's technical operations center (TOC).

**FIGURE 8.13**
Talent stations: The turret-style (left) and surface-mount (right) panels provide air talent with immediate access to a microphone cough switch, headphone volume control, and other studio monitoring functions

Source: Courtesy of Wheatstone

**FIGURE 8.14**
A countertop-recessed, fully customizable virtual console featuring IP networking

Source: Courtesy of Wheatstone

## COMPUTERS AND SOFTWARE

Computers are the soul of the audio studio—both on-air and production. Observes Vic Michaels:

> Studio computers would contain editing software, such as Pro Tools or Adobe Audition. The on-air computer would also contain automation software, such as Audio Vault. It would also possess Selector, which is needed to tell the Audio Vault system what to play. At my station, we have three computers in production: one is for Audio Vault automation, the second is for Selector music software, and the third is for editing on Pro Tools. All three are networked to the on-air computer. When one makes a commercial or records a song off a CD, it becomes an audio file that can be moved from computer to computer.

Computerization has all but eliminated the need for standalone audio playback devices in the control room. Songs, commercials, PSAs, promotional/imaging productions, and other show elements can be easily imported into the on-air automation system and then conveniently and randomly accessed at the time when they are needed for playout. Contrast this environment with the on-air studio of yesteryear, where the deejay frantically cued vinyl records on turntables and retrieved plastic tape cartridges ("carts") from storage racks for insertion into playback decks. Computerization frees the deejay of these cumbersome, repetitive tasks—time that can be better invested in improving show development and presentation.

The aforementioned AudioVAULT is one of several software systems that have proven worthy of standing up to the day-to-day rigors control room activity. Similar products—including Zetta, WideOrbit Automation for Radio, Dalet Radio Suite, Enco DAD, and others—merge audio production and program-playout functions, bringing to the table a host of on-screen features for simplifying operations while adding value to the presentation. Systems typically include on-screen displays of program logs that permit immediate addition, deletion, and rearrangement of songs, commercials, and other program elements. Virtual "cart decks" assist deejays by making short-duration audio files accessible for playback. Audio recorders make simple work of recording, editing, and playing back telephone call-ins. Web surfing during the course of a show is facilitated by systems' built-in browsers.

More recently, another category of software has found its way into station operations. Programs such as the Telos ProFiler and the OMT Technologies iMedialogger are replacing the cassette recording deck for "skimming" and program-archival purposes. "Skimmers" are dedicated to the sole function of documenting the on-air content and are typically configured to make recordings of broadcasts whenever microphones are open. Recording is initiated whenever a microphone is switched on; it ceases when the mic is turned off. "Skim" tapes thus provide program directors and other managers with accurate recordings of deejay performances, minus the time-consuming music and commercials. PDs are thus

**FIGURE 8.15**
RCS automated playout system Zetta. Colored "HotKeys" provide instant playback access to select audio files

Source: Courtesy of RCS

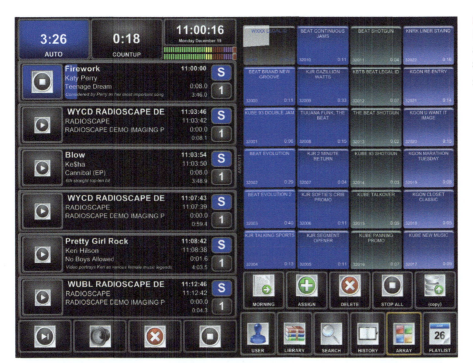

FIGURE 8.16
Enco's "DAD"—Digital Audio Delivery—automation software displays songs in sequential playback order

Source: Courtesy of Enco

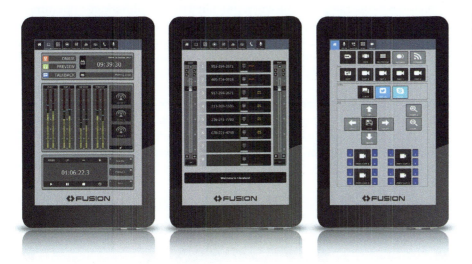

FIGURE 8.17
Tablet-based control surfaces maximize the workspace by virtualizing the monitoring and operating functions

Source: Courtesy of the Telos Alliance

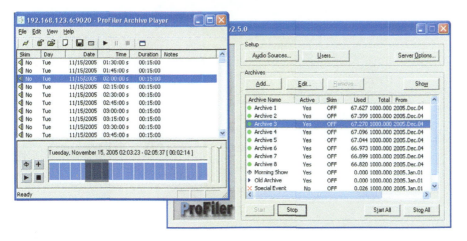

FIGURE 8.18
Air monitoring: skimming and logging functions performed by ProFiler

Source: Courtesy of the Telos Alliance

able to quickly and efficiently review the performances of on-air talent without having to navigate around the extraneous content. Today, this activity is easily performed on computers running program-archival software. In addition to managing the "skim" function, the software can operate in "log" mode, making simultaneous "skim" and continuous recordings that document the entire broadcast, second by second. The recorded audio files may be accessed readily and securely. Because the digital files can be accessed via the Internet, out-of-market personnel, including group PDs and programming consultants, can easily monitor station performance.

## VOICE-TRACKING

In the aftermath of station ownership consolidation and creation of studio clusters, radio corporations have found it cost-efficient to feed their stations prerecorded voices. These days it's likely that as much station announcing takes place out-of-market as it does within the local studio. Radio companies hire off-premise announcers to meet stations' voicing needs, so there is less and less origination of on-site deejay patter. Utilizing the voice-tracking technique, the deejay creates the illusion of real-time broadcasting, being present physically in the control room, announcing the songs, and playing the commercials. In reality, all voicing is prerecorded; the system correlates the voice recordings with the song playlist, commercials and other show features and delivers the mix to listeners. One announcer may be the voice of multiple stations, supplying each with deejay patter custom-created to the specific needs of each local market. Satellite feeds and the Internet-delivered audio populate local station airwaves with out-of-town voices.

Voice-tracking, conversely, may be performed just as readily by in-house announcers. When voice-tracking is done on station premises its use ramps up efficiency, providing more multitasking opportunities for station personnel. The need to be physically present in a studio solely for the purpose of delivering a 10-second talkover every 15 to 20 minutes is not necessarily productive or time-efficient. One result of voice-tracking proliferation has been a thinning in the ranks of announcers. Broadcast vet Jackie O'Brien observes:

> The field of radio broadcasting has changed tremendously over the past few years. Many positions have been lost due to the innovation of voice-tracking. While this may be a cost-efficient way to run a radio group, it has taken away the personality of the service. When I started in broadcasting, I felt the position was more than the sound of my own voice. There was a commitment made to service

**FIGURE 8.19**

Voice-tracking and other production activities are supported by this studio

Source: Courtesy of Entercom Radio Memphis

the public with news, information, and a little entertainment. This meant staying on through a snowstorm or covering local elections. It also meant talking the occasional lonely heart out of suicide. I've been at Metro Networks for four years. In that time, I've watched old positions I held in radio disappear to voice-tracking.

Critics charge that the practice has diminished the spontaneity and appeal of the on-air product. Further, the practice of recording comments in advance of their broadcast makes it difficult to deliver accurate time checks, weather forecasts, and other time-sensitive information. On the other hand, proponents of voice-tracking—notably station owners and management—cite the improved operator efficiencies that automation produces. Experienced talent can record (or *track*) a typical three-hour airshift in less than 30 minutes. Deejays are thus available for assignment to perform other station duties such as production and promotion. Tracking can assist owners in economizing on personnel salaries because fewer employees are required to staff the station.

It bears noting that automating the radio broadcast was first accomplished more than 50 years ago, and the arguments, both pro and con, presented in this discussion are just as viable today as when they were first asserted in the 1960s. Despite concern for the impact that voice-tracking has on the announcing profession and radio localism, more and more stations are using it, and the future would suggest that this practice—for better or for worse—will grow.

## STANDALONE RECORD/PLAY DECKS

As the evolution of audio technology progresses it is not uncommon even today to find control and production rooms sporting an intermixture of analog and digital record/playback decks. Few would argue that analog magnetic tape's time has passed. Nonetheless, certain stations find it convenient to maintain and support a working reel-to-reel or cartridge tape system, even if it's only to facilitate the digitization of legacy station archival recordings. Manufacturers experimented with several digital technologies in the 1990s seeking to find a viable replacement for the venerable analog cart machine. Equipment manufacturers introduced machines designed to write digital data files to removable storage media, including floppy disks, MiniDiscs, random access memory and, eventually, directly to hard disks. These next-generation "cart machines" appealed to producers. Station manager Vic Michaels observes,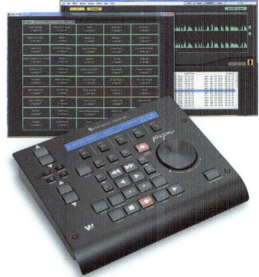
"They replaced the old-line carts, because they were faster, programmable, visual, digital, and competitively priced." Companies such as Sony, Tascam, Denon, and Otari manufactured the mini-disc machine. MD machines soon supplanted the traditional analog cart machine at most stations—and, almost as quickly, yielded the space to hard disk storage systems, along the way becoming yet another relic in the digital graveyard.

One free-standing digital playback device that has prevailed is the Instant Replay 2. This 360 Systems legacy device remains popular with deejays and show producers. Unlike most PC-based audio playout arrangements,

DigiCart/E Ethernet Audio™ Recorder

**FIGURE 8.20**
This successor to the analog cartridge tape recorder/reproducer offers instant playback access to 1,000 digital audio cuts

Source: Courtesy of 360 Systems

**FIGURE 8.21**
Snag a phone call, edit on the fly, and air it within minutes with the VoxPro6

Source: Courtesy of Wheatstone

the Instant Replay 2 is a dedicated-function unit. This easy-to-operate deck relies on physical-button transport control, providing operators with reaffirming, tactile responses during periods of time when hectic studio conditions demand split-second execution decisions. Digital standalone record/play decks—the VoxPro6 from Wheatstone is a good example—are also utilized for recording, editing, and playing back short-duration program elements, notably audio derived from telephone interfaces. The VoxPro6's proprietary "Gap-Buster" function is a useful utility for removing silence from audio tracks, thus improving the flow of recorded interviews and telephone conversations.

**FIGURE 8.22**
CD players continue to be used in some studios

Source: Courtesy of Denon

## COMPACT DISCS

Compact disc players entered the radio production studio in the 1980s. Although CD players have been largely displaced by PC-based playout systems, their value as a piece of production equipment has not entirely evaporated. Compact disc players revolutionized song playback in the 1980s, offering, among other features, far greater dynamic range reproduction than recorded vinyl or analog magnetic tape. CD audio reproduction has a characteristically lower signal-to-noise ratio than that of analog devices, resulting in a more pristine, less-distorted sound quality. CD playback decks also eliminated the need for physical contact with the media during cue-up, and erratic speed irregularities became virtually nonexistent. Because digital discs are specially coated, they are more resistant to damage than are vinyl discs although with improper handling they can be harmed. CD players are still useful in the production studio. They are a wonderful source for bed music (music that serves as background under voiced copy) and sound effects.

## AUDIO PROCESSING

"There are three domains of audio," says producer Ty Ford. "They are amplitude, frequency, and time." Some stations alter amplitude to create the illusion of being louder without actually changing the audio level. This is called compressing the signal. Production people use compressors to enhance loudness as well as to reduce or eliminate ambient noise, thus focusing on specifics of the mix. Audio signal compression (not to be confused with the similarly termed digital audio file data-compression technique) is often used as a method of getting listeners to take greater notice of a piece of production and as a remedy to certain problems.

Equalizers (EQs) manipulate the frequency domain of audio by boosting and/or reducing the pitch frequencies across the sound spectrum. EQs allow producers to correct problems such as boomy bass tones or high-pitched tinniness as well as to create sound parity between different elements of production. They are also useful in creating special effects. Equalization now can be accomplished onboard (within audio console circuitry) and outboard (either by a standalone hardware unit or within a software application such as Pro Tools or Audition). Most audio processors are time-domain devices. Outboard units, often referred to as "effects processors" or simply as "boxes," became popular production room fixtures in the 1980s and 1990s. Today, special effects are largely created within audio editing software and enhanced by plug-in options. Stations use digital processors to create a wide range of effects such as reverb, time/pitch alteration, and flanging.

Radio station producers have become increasingly interested in what audio processors are capable of offering their mixes. Today these boxes are familiar, often integral, items in production rooms. Their ability to enhance the production value of commercials, PSAs, promos, and features is inestimable. The use of samplers and synthesizers is common in radio production rooms too. A sample is a digital

**FIGURE 8.23**

This microphone processor is equipped with old-school vacuum tube technology to impart a distinctive signature of warmth and presence to the voice

Source: Courtesy of Aphex Audio and Freedman Electronics

**FIGURE 8.24**

Screens, screens everywhere: Multiple video monitors display important studio-operations parameters

Source: Courtesy of the Telos Alliance

recording of a small bit of sound. A sampler allows a production person to load a studio audio source (recorder, live mike) into its built-in microprocessor and then manipulate the digitized data with the aid of a synthesizer keyboard to create a multitude of effects. Samplers are wired to an audio console so that the sounds they produce may be integrated into a mixdown. They also are found in certain audio effects processors with musical instrument digital interface (MIDI).

## SIGNAL ROUTING

Patch panels essentially are analog signal routing devices that allow for items not directly wired into an audio console to become a part of a broadcast or production audio signal pathway. A patch panel consists of rows of jacks (receptacles) that have been wired to inputs and outputs connected to various external sources—studios, equipment, remote locations, network lines, and so forth. Routing switchers represent another method for distributing audio signals within and across studios. These standalone devices are usually centrally located and rack-mounted for easy access. Equipment input and output connections are accomplished easily by means of push-button selection. "Patch panels are still utilized,"

Vic Michaels says, but not as frequently as before. "Use is based on a station's needs. Digital consoles now have internal patch capabilities built right into the console so one can patch in certain effects or sources to any channel." "And, of course, with an IP-Audio network," broadcast technologist Clark Novak explains, "routing any output to any input system-wide can be easily accomplished in several different ways":

1. You can use a software application that has a graphic cross-point representation on screen that allows you to pick an input and output and route one to the other; this is common to both AoIP and older TDM routing switchers alike.

2. There are also hardware appliances that mount in-studio or TOC (technical operating center) racks that allow users to select from a list of inputs and outputs and switch them. Again, these are common to both TDM and AoIP routing systems.

3. Some systems allow the station engineer to build graphical interfaces, or "user panels," which can be displayed on a studio computer monitor. These panels typically have a preselected set of routing choices that allow the air talent to pick from a preapproved menu of routing operations.

**FIGURE 8.25**

Interconnections among consoles, processors, telephone systems, and monitors converge with Livewire networking technology

Source: Courtesy of the Telos Alliance

**FIGURE 8.26**

Adapt iOS and Android devices for newsgathering and podcasting with this compact plug-in mic

Source: Courtesy IK Multimedia US LLC

## MICROPHONES

Microphones are designed to pick up and convert sound wave energy into electrical impulses. Three basic design characteristics, called pickup patterns, determine the sensitivity and directionality of wave motion to which a microphone responds (see Figure 8.28). Omnidirectional microphones are sensitive to sound from all directions (360 degrees), whereas bidirectional microphones are most sensitive to sound originating from two, opposing directions (180 degrees). Bidirectional microphones thus are sensitive to sounds approaching it from its front and rear sides and are less sensitive to sounds reaching it from either side. The unidirectional microphone (and the related *cardioid* pattern, so-termed because of its slightly wider, heart-shaped pickup pattern) draws sound from only one path (90 degrees). Because of its highly directed field of receptivity, extraneous sounds that enter the microphone from the sides and the rear tend to be minimized or rejected. This feature has made the unidirectional microphone popular in both the control and production studios, where generally one

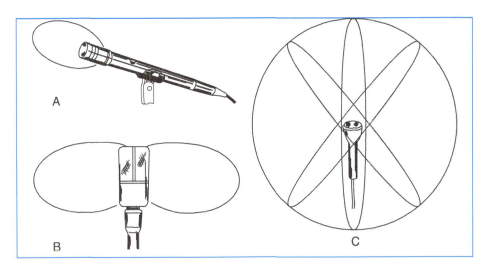

**FIGURE 8.27**
This newsgathering tool combines microphone and digital recorder into one handheld device. Interchangeable mic heads enable both omnidirectional and unidirectional sound capture

Source: Courtesy of Yellowtec

**FIGURE 8.29**
iOS and USB connectivity, five preset DSP (digital signal processing) modes and headphone monitoring makes the Shure MV51 large-diaphragm condenser microphone a podcaster favorite

person is at work at a time. Most studio consoles possess two or more microphone inputs so that additional microphones can be accommodated when the need arises to pick up the voices of additional persons.

Omnidirectional and bidirectional microphones are used less frequently today than in years past, as unidirectional mics are better-suited in most instances. Omnidirectional pickup is still appropriately utilized in interview situations, where two or more persons "share" one microphone.

Announcers must be aware of a microphone's directional features. Proper positioning in relation to a microphone is important: speaking outside the path of a microphone's pickup (a situation termed "off-mic") affects sound quality. At the same time, operating too close to a microphone without using proper breath control can result in distortions of the voice, known as popping and blasting. Keeping a hand's

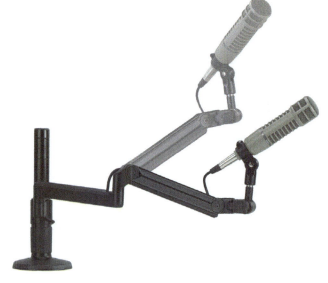

**FIGURE 8.30**

The RCA model 77DX ribbon microphone was a favorite of many deejays in the mid-twentieth century. Its design enhances low-frequency response, accentuating the resonance of the male voice

Source: Courtesy of Randal Crow and Chuck Bethea

**FIGURE 8.31**

Popular with announcers, the Shure SM7B is a classic cardioid dynamic mic noted for its clean and natural reproduction of speech

**FIGURE 8.32**

This mic boom features a table-hugging profile, elevating the arm just five inches off the table surface, to ensure clear sight lines between talent and studio video cameras. Pictured is the Electro-Voice RE20 dynamic cardioid microphone

Source: Courtesy of the O.C. White Company

length away from a microphone and "working" the mic slightly off the center axis of pickup will usually prevent this from occurring. Windscreens and blast filters may be attached to a microphone to help reduce distortion.

## TELEPHONES

The telephone instrument and the service that supports it have been essential tools for radio broadcasters since the medium's beginning and still are routinely utilized in both studio and remote applications. Due in part to a rise in the popularity of the talk program format and also in part to advancements in technology, studio telephone systems have become increasingly more sophisticated and complex. Decades ago the broadcast of a caller's voice was a technically unsophisticated arrangement: a simple electrical

**FIGURE 8.33**

Producers of talk shows utilize telephone hybrid equipment such as this six-line system

Source: Courtesy of the Telos Alliance

interface device inserted between a telephone desk set and an input fader on the control board was all that was needed. It was, however, a cumbersome arrangement that often left the deejay juggling the phone handset while trying to sustain other control room operations.

Today the phone-conversation broadcast is a streamlined operation, supported by digital circuitry and operating under computer control. Air talent no longer fumbles with the telephone receiver; incoming caller audio is directed into headphones while outbound studio conversation is picked up through studio microphones and relayed to callers. Sound fidelity is much improved and the increased naturalness of the reproduction has helped to minimize the unpleasant effect of "listener fatigue," the term for the psychoacoustic phenomenon that can result in listener tune-out.

## REMOTE PICKUP (RPU)

Remote broadcasts are a mainstay of radio stations regardless of market size. From coverage of professional sports contests to program origination from the county fair to the grand opening of the newest used-car dealership, broadcasters have been there, mics in hand, to describe the action and narrate the details for listeners.

In the previous millennium it was common for stations to have remote control room studios, either custom-constructed at the off-studio broadcast location or built into vehicles. Such accommodations put the magic of creating a radio broadcast on full display in front of spectators. The opportunities for listeners to be able to put a face to a voice, grab an autographed deejay photo, and participate in on-the-scene contests were attractive lures, and in many instances retail businesses were all too willing to pay for the privilege of hosting stations and their personalities.

As popular music formats transitioned from AM to FM in the 1970s and 1980s, competing stations recognized the difficulties of replicating the high-fidelity sonic quality of their studio broadcasts at remote broadcast sites. The diminished audio quality that originated from the remote venues was regarded as detrimental to a station's overall sound signature. Stations thus began dispatching talent to the remote locations with nothing more than their microphones, opting to retain music playback as a control room function. This approach preserved the audio fidelity of music reproduction. In more recent times, the desire of listeners to witness how radio broadcasts are engineered has waned. Audiences today are less interested than before in observing how a broadcast works—watching song playout on the ubiquitous personal computer, after all, is a procedure that is much the same in the home as it is in the station control room. As a result the activity has lost its allure.

That being said, the remote broadcast nonetheless remains a staple of many stations' schedules. Studio-to-remote site interconnection initially was accomplished using dedicated telephone circuits. During the 1960s, stations began using wireless VHF transceiving equipment to deliver audio. Transmitters manufactured by George Marti became ubiquitous instruments for remote broadcasting, and products bearing his name continue to be widely used for achieving short-hop (typically up to 30 miles) connection. Manufacturers of remote pickup equipment continue to embrace advances in technology, exploiting the capabilities of the Internet and cellular telephone networks. The result is a variety of products that are becoming ever more lightweight, portable, and feature-laden. A current generation

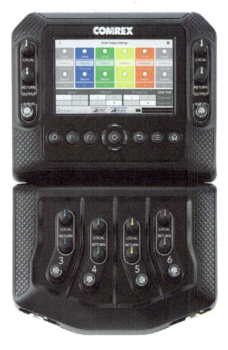

**FIGURE 8.36**
This compact codec accommodates two microphone- or line-level inputs. Shown with its optional clip-on mixer, which adds an additional four mc/line-level inputs

Source: Courtesy of Comrex

**FIGURE 8.37**
Report-IT turns your iPhone or Android smartphone into a pocket-sized, portable, 15kHz live IP-audio codec and ultra-slim, high-fidelity audio recorder

Source: Courtesy of Tieline

of portable RPUs combines the audio amplification and control features of a remote mixer with dedicated computer circuitry and modems, packaged in desktop and handheld configurations. High-fidelity audio and interruptible feedback (IFB) capabilities make possible the origination of remote broadcasts of technological sophistication and enhanced listenability.

Integrated services digital networks (ISDNs) are digital phone circuits that bring voices and other audio to studios with near-perfect sound quality. Because voice-tracking has become the means by which so many stations fill their airwaves, ISDN connections have become invaluable. As production director Matt Grasso observes,

> The day of the scratchy cell phone or muddy dedicated line is over. Your talent sounds like they are right in the studio. If they are at a club, not only can they talk, but they can broadcast the music they are playing there right over the air with the same quality you would get from a CD player in the main studio.

## DIGITAL EDITING

Old-school, physical tape splicing is a lost art, an editing technique that ranged in technological sophistication from effecting a simple paste-up repair to constructing a complicated rearrangement of sound elements. The practices of using a razor blade to cut and then applying adhesive tape to splice (reconnect) a plastic ribbon of magnetic audio tape is all but ancient history, having lost ground to "nondestructive," tapeless digital methods. It's a procedure that warrants mentioning solely because the authors of digital audio software co-opted some of yesteryear's terminology ("rewind," "fast-forward," "shuttle," etc.) into the designs of their programs.

Computers handle the bulk of editing in the production room. This tapeless approach involves loading audio into RAM or onto hard disk and making edits by means of observing the recording's audio waveform as displayed on a monitor and navigating the screen using a mouse, a keyboard or similar pointing device. Although digital editors initially represented a costly investment for stations, the widespread adoption of computerization helped to make systems affordable even to stations in the small markets. Editing today is easily accomplished with the assistance of software residing in the cloud, on program automation systems or dedicated workstations—even on smartphones!

## COPYWRITING

Poet Stephen Vincent Benet, who wrote for radio during its pre-TV heyday, called the medium "the theater of the mind." Indeed, the person who tunes in to radio usually gets no visual aids but must manufacture images on his or her own mind to accompany the words and sounds being broadcast. The station employee who prepares written material is called a copywriter. A copywriter's job consists primarily of writing commercials, promos, and PSAs, with the emphasis on the first of the three.

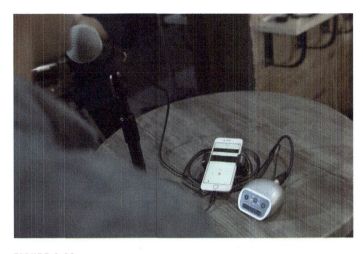

**FIGURE 8.38**

Plug your favorite low-impedance mic into the Shure MVi digital audio interface, connect it to your iOS or USB-enabled device and you're ready to begin recording your podcast

The job of the copywriter can be difficult. One criticism leveled against radio is "too many commercials." Perhaps the greatest challenge for the copywriter is to create commercials that engage listeners, not drive them away. Copywriter, author and educator Linda Conway Correll George offers this observation:

> By definition, radio is a frequency medium, reaching listeners with the same message multiple times. It is the repetition of lackluster, cookie-cutter approaches, however, that has led listeners to opt for fewer commercials, even though researchers concluded some time ago that cutting commercial loads doesn't increase program ratings. Realistically, purchasing air time is what pays the bills. And, according to a seasoned station traffic manager, imaginative, humorous, original, well-produced spots are what keep listeners listening. Even Millennials.

Not all stations employ a full-time copywriter. This is especially true in small markets, where economics dictate that account executives (AEs; the salespeople) write on behalf of their own advertisers' accounts. This is regrettable, according to George. Account executives, she contends, have as their priority the responsibility for "bringing home the bacon" by servicing the retail accounts (and thus elevating the profit margins). Nonetheless, circumstances occasionally dictate that AEs create their own copy. When confronting this situation, George says the AE has options:

Option 1: Attend a radio continuity workshop, if you can find one.

Option 2: Invite a radio commercial guru (from academe or the industry) to the station to teach a seminar on copywriting for radio to all the station's account executives.

Option 3: Buy a book on the subject.

Option 4: Listen to effective and award-winning spots. Google competition websites such as the Radio Mercury Awards, the Clio Awards, the Mobius Awards, the Silver Microphone Awards, the Summit International Awards. Google radio production company websites such as Dick Orkin Radio Ranch (www.radio-ranch.com). Listen. And learn.

Copywriters must possess a complete understanding of the unique nature of the medium, a familiarity with the audience for which the commercial message is intended, and knowledge of the product being promoted. As George puts it, the objective is to "hire a creative continuity writer who lives and breathes radio." A station's format will influence the style of writing in a commercial; thus, the copywriter also must be thoroughly acquainted with the station's particular programming approach. Commercials must be compatible with the station's sound. For instance, copy written for soft AC usually is more conservative in tone than that written for alternative rock stations, and so on.

Here's an example from WXXX "Home of the Hits":

> (SFX: Bed in) TJ's Rockhouse, Mart Street, Downtown Boise, presents Cleo and the gang rocking out every Friday and Saturday night. At TJ's there's never a cover or minimum, just a good time. Sunday Idaho's monarchs of rockabilly, Jobee Lane, raise the roof at TJ's. You better be ready to shake it, because nobody stands still when Jobee Lane rocks. Thursday is half-price night, and ladies always get their first drink free at Boise's number one club for fun and music. Take Main to Mark Street and look for the house that rocks, TJ's Rockhouse. (SFX: Stinger out)

And another example, this one's from WYYY "Soothing Sounds":

> Elegant dining is just a scenic ride away. (SFX: Bed in and under) The critically acclaimed Viscount (VY-count) Inn in Cedar Glenn offers guests an exquisite menu in a setting without equal. The Viscount's 18th-century charm will make your evening out one to remember. Jamison Longley of the *Wisconsin Register* gives the Viscount a four-star rating for service, cuisine, and atmosphere. The Viscount (SFX: Royal fanfare) will satisfy your royal tastes. Call 675–2180 for reservations. Take Route 17 north to the Viscount Inn, 31 Stony Lane, Cedar Glenn.

Some basic rules pertain to the mechanics of copy preparation. First, copy is word-processed and double-spaced for ease of reading. Next, left and right margins are set at one inch. Sound effects are noted in parentheses at that point in the copy where they are to occur. Proper punctuation and grammar are vital. A comma in the wrong place can throw off the meaning of an entire sentence. Be mindful, also, that commercials are designed to be heard and not read. Keep sentence structure as straightforward and uncomplicated as possible. Maintaining a conversational style will improve comprehension of the client's message.

**FIGURE 8.39**
Linda Conway
Correll George

## SKILLS AND PERSONAL CHARACTERISTICS OF A GOOD COPYWRITER

### Linda Conway Correll George

Ask copywriters what skills and personal characteristics they need to write effective copy, and the first trait they're likely to mention is curiosity. We're obsessively and compulsively driven to find out all we can about the products/services we sell, the people who buy them, and the media in which they're advertised. "Aha," you're saying to yourself. "I can just Google the Internet and find that out." You and 3.2 billion other Internet users!

The good news is that the information you're seeking is there. The bad news is that it's there for 3.2 billion other users to access, as well. So let's check your skill set.

1. Do you have the ability to dig deep and sniff out fresh information/facts? In addition to having a healthy supply of curiosity, copywriting expects you to be a good listener. And to hear, really hear what your target audience is saying. Both positive and negative.

2. Do you have the mental flexibility to turn a perceived negative into a positive? And to turn facts into benefits?

3. Good copywriters have extensive means of expression. The size of your vocabulary is important. But not the size of your words. Most copywriters don't write over their listeners' heads. But we do use variety of expression and colloquial language to connect with them.

4. Can you think visually? Although radio is not a visual medium, it is called "theater of the mind." One of the best writers of award-winning radio commercials is a Houston, Texas, art director—someone whose training and vocation focus on visual content.

5. Can you think aurally? Sound effects, music and different voices/deliveries can underscore and enrich the radio scripts we write, creating the character and atmosphere of locations/situations.

6. Good copywriters have a strong work ethic. We're expected to multitask. To meet deadlines. To stay focused. To polish and hone our efforts, creating scripts that are interesting to hear. And, at the same time, to maintain our passion for the craft and our sense of humor.

There are some caveats we follow:

7. *Caveat one.* We avoid clichés, overused phrases, and subjective generalities such as "famous," "amazing," etc.

8. *Caveat two.* We do not write advertising the way literature is written: there are no clauses. And no long, complicated sentences. We write the way we speak, using short, simple sentence construction. Even sentence fragments.

9. *Caveat three.* We do not make decisions for the listener: "You will be happy. . ."??? Maybe not.

10. *Caveat four.* We do not talk in exaggerated superlatives: "It's the finest money can buy". . ."the newest". . ."the smartest. . ."

11. *Caveat five.* We do not "ashcan," criticize, or belittle a competitor's product. Negativity rubs off on everybody.

One of the most professionally rewarding jobs I ever held in advertising was writing continuity—that is, commercials—for an FM radio station in western Massachusetts. I let my imagination and my scriptwriting run wild. One week, the Old Woman who lived in a Shoe was rounding up her brood to take them to a local shoe store, where they could find a variety of styles and sizes. Another week, an insurance competitor left inquiries unanswered and the phone ringing for 52 seconds; that's when listeners learned that our client not only answered insurance questions but also the phone.

The station's deejays, who had been long used to reading ordinary wall-to-wall commercial text with stock music tucked beneath the message, jumped at the opportunity to use their creativity, particularly their skill with distinctive voices, sound effects and production. Creating effective radio commercials takes imagination, writing/life experience, and an ear for the medium. Here are a few tips that will help you avoid the common mistakes rookie writers make.

12. INTERRUPT. Start by bringing station programming to a halt with an exaggerated voice or situation. A memorable sound effect or a challenging question. Use humor, despite the fact that advertising agency founder David Ogilvy, a revered and highly respected Hall of Fame copywriter, disparaged its use. And don't use slice of life: ordinary dialogue between two ordinary people is a slice of death:

    20-SOMETHING GIRL 1: "Do you want to go to the gym today?"

    20-SOMETHING GIRL 2: "Let's. There's this personal trainer I have a crush on!"

You've just turned listeners off. And wasted a minute of airtime and your client's money.

Observing the suggestions above, let's try the same dialogue again, but change the protagonists:

    GRANDMOTHER 1: "Do you want to go to the gym today?"

    GRANDMOTHER 2: "Let's. There's this personal trainer I have a crush on!"

Now add sound effects. Suddenly, listeners perk up.

13. COUNT the number of words. If it's a :60 spot, you'll need between 110 and 125 words, allowing time for production values; more if you want to set a fast and furious pace, fewer if it's leisurely (our normal speaking speed is approximately 2.5 words per second). For a :30 commercial, cut the numbers in half.

14. FOLLOW the caveats above.

15. REPEAT the client's name two to four times in your commercial.

16. ALWAYS use the pronoun "you." A radio commercial is an intimate one-on-one conversation between the listener and the medium.

17. SHOW, don't merely TELL. Use sound to create your location, your action, your emotions. Listeners will remember you.

18. LAYER your elements: Radio is a reminder medium. It's repetitive. If you don't add elements to refresh the ear (think SFX, humor, music, etc.,) listeners tune out way before your commercial ends.

That's about it. As you read this litany of writer attributes and directives, do you feel an affinity for the craft? Or, stated more clearly and simply, like a copywriter: After you finished the laundry list, did you like what you read? Then you might think about a career in our field.

---

**Linda Conway Correll George** began her advertising career as a copywriter at Young & Rubicam, New York. Following 13 years in the Big Apple, she moved to her farm and a continuity writer's job at a radio station in western Massachusetts, where she wrote her first award-winning radio commercial. Middle-management creative positions in major Texas markets, and more awards in national and international competitions followed, culminated in a VP/creative directorship in her native New England. She transitioned into academe in 1991, spending the next 22 years teaching advertising to students in Massachusetts, Missouri, Florida, Illinois, and India, and cheering them on to win more than 200 advertising awards. Her second book, *Creative Aerobics: Fueling Imagination in the 21st Century*, was published in 2017 by Sage Publishers.

**FIGURE 8.40**

From the remote broadcast location an operator can control the studio console via laptop with this virtual mixer software

Source: Courtesy of Wheatstone

Timing a piece of copy is relatively simple. There are a couple of methods: one involves counting words (see the box "Skills and Personal Characteristics of a Good Copywriter"). Another approach is to count the lines of copy. This method is based on the assumption that it takes, on average, three seconds to read one line of copy from margin to margin. Therefore, nine to 10 lines of copy would time out to around 30 seconds, and 18–20 lines would time out to one minute. Of course, production elements such as sound effects and beds must be included as part of the count and their timings deducted accordingly. For example, six seconds of sound effects in a 30-second commercial would shorten the amount of actual copy by two lines.

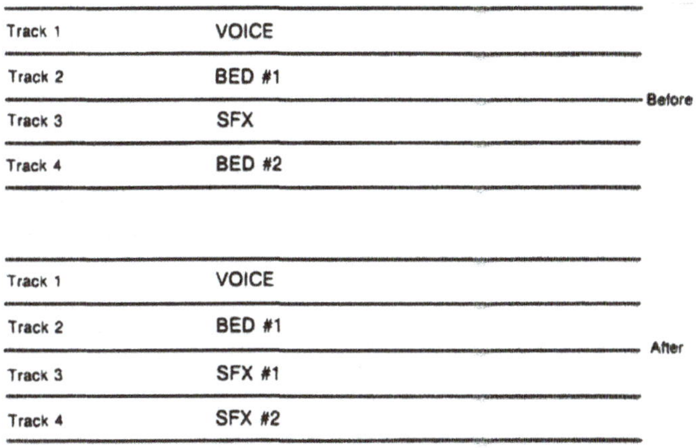

| Track 1 | VOICE | |
| Track 2 | BED #1 | |
| Track 3 | SFX | Before |
| Track 4 | BED #2 | |

| Track 1 | VOICE | |
| Track 2 | BED #1 | |
| Track 3 | SFX #1 | After |
| Track 4 | SFX #2 | |

**FIGURE 8.41**
Editing a multitrack involves adding or deleting tracks. Here BED 2 is replaced by SFX 2 on track 4

Because everything written in radio is intended to be read aloud, it is important that words with unusual or uncommon pronunciations be given special attention. Phonetic spelling is used to convey the way a word is pronounced. For instance: "Dinner at the Fo'c'sle (FOHK-sil) Restaurant in Laitone (LAY-ton) Shores is a sea adventure." Incorrect pronunciation has resulted in more than one canceled account. The copywriter must make certain that the announcer assigned to voice-track a commercial is fully aware of any particularities in the copy. In other words, when in doubt spell it out.

Excessive numbers and complex directions are to be avoided in radio copy. Numbers, such as an address or telephone number, should be repeated and directions should be as simple as possible. The use of landmarks ("across from city hall . . .") or reminders to search for the advertiser's website can reduce confusion. Listeners are seldom in a position to write down something at the exact moment they hear it. Copy should communicate, not confuse or frustrate.

Of course, the purpose of any piece of copy is to sell the client's product. Creativity plays an important role. The radio writer has the world of the imagination to work with and is limited only by the boundaries of his own.

## ANNOUNCING TIPS

Despite a dwindling in the radio announcer ranks caused by radio company consolidation and a proliferation in voice-tracking, thousands of men and women in this country still make their living before the microphone. In few other professions is the salary range so broad. A beginning announcer may make little more than minimum wage, whereas a seasoned professional in a major market may earn a salary in the six-figure range. Of course, competition for the metro-market station positions is keener, and expectations are higher. Radio personality Mike Morin says,

> You have to pay your dues in this profession. It's usually a long and winding road. It takes time to develop the on-air skills that the big stations want. It's hard work to become really good, but you can make an enormous amount of money, or at least a very comfortable income, when you do.

The duties of an announcer vary depending on the size or ranking of a station. In the small station, announcers generally fill news and/or production shifts as well. For example, a midday announcer at WXXX, who is on the air from 10 am until 3 pm, may be held responsible for the 4 and 5 pm. newscasts, plus any production that arises during that same period. Meanwhile, the larger station may require nothing more of its announcers than to record voiceovers. Of course, the preparation for an airshift at a major-market station can be very time-consuming.

An announcer must, above all else, possess the ability to effectively read copy aloud. Among other things, this involves proper enunciation and inflection, which are improved through practice. Legendary programmer Bill Towery contends that the more a person reads for personal enjoyment or enrichment, the easier it is to communicate orally:

I'd advise anyone who aspires to the microphone to read, read, read. The more the better. Announcing is oral interpretation of the printed page. You must first understand what is on the page before you can communicate it aloud. Bottom line here is that if you want to become an announcer, first become a reader.

Having a naturally resonant and pleasant-sounding voice certainly is an advantage. Voice quality still is very important in radio. The inclination toward the voice with a deeper register—for female announcers as well as male—has relaxed somewhat, in favor of announcers who can communicate effectively and persuasively in a natural, everyday tone. However, most voices possess considerable range and with training, practice, and experience even a person with a high-pitched voice can develop an appealing on-air sound. Forcing the voice into a lower register to achieve a deeper sound restricts volume, becomes muffled and can result in injury to the vocal cords. Achieving tonal warmth and expressiveness should be objectives. "Making the most of what you already have is a lot better than trying to be something you're not. Perfect yourself and be natural," advises Morin.

Relaxation is important. The voice simply is at its best when it is not strained. Moreover, announcing is enhanced by proper breathing, which is only possible when one is free of stress. Initially, being "on-mic" can be an intimidating experience, resulting in nervousness that can be debilitating. Here are some things announcers do to achieve a state of relaxation:

1. Read copy aloud before going on the air. Get the feel of it. This will automatically increase confidence, thus aiding in relaxation.

2. Take several deep breaths and slowly exhale while keeping your eyes closed.

3. Sit still for a couple of moments with your arms limp at your sides. Tune out. Let the dust settle. Conjure pleasant images. Allow yourself to drift a bit, and then slowly return to the job at hand.

4. Stand and slowly move your upper torso in a circular motion for a minute or so. Flex your shoulders and arms. Stretch luxuriously.

5. If possible, remain standing during your delivery. When seated, check your posture. Do not slump over as you announce. A curved diaphragm impedes breathing. Sit erect, but not stiffly.

6. Hum a few bars of your favorite song. The vibration helps relax the throat muscles and vocal chords.

7. Give yourself ample time to settle in before going on. Dashing into the studio at the last second will jar your focus and shake your composure.

**FIGURE 8.42**

A multitrack audio layout in Adobe Audition. Producers isolate individual audio elements into separate tracks to achieve greater control over the sound of the final mix

Source: Courtesy of Audra Wiant and Richard Withers

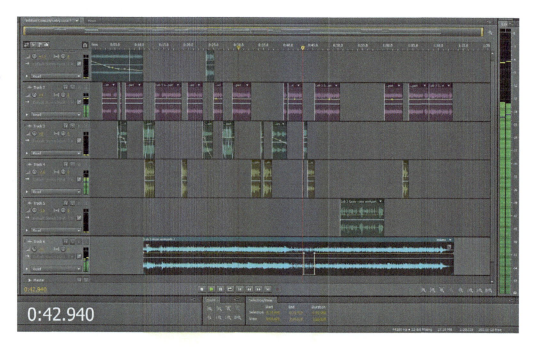

In most situations, an accent—regional or otherwise—is a handicap and should be eliminated. Contrary to the misperceptions, most radio announcers in the South do not have a drawl, and the majority of announcers in Boston put the "r" in the word "car." A noticeable or pronounced accent will almost always put the candidate for an announcer's job out of the running. Accents are not easy to eliminate, but with practice they can be overcome.

## THE SOUND LIBRARY

Music is used to enhance an advertiser's message—to make it more appealing, more listenable. The music used in a radio commercial is called a *bed* simply because it supports the voice. It is the platform on which the voice is set. A station may bed thousands of commercials over the course of a year. Music is an integral component of the production mixdown.

Today, sound libraries are almost always delivered via downloads. However, many stations still derive bed music from other sources. Demonstration CDs (demos) sent by recording companies to radio stations are a familiar source when used with appropriate copyright permissions, since few actually make it onto playlists and into on-air rotations. These CDs are particularly useful because the music is unfamiliar to the listening audience. Known tunes generally are avoided in the mixdown of spots because they tend to distract the listener from the copy. However, there are times when familiar tunes, supported by the appropriate copyright clearances, are used to back spots. Nightclubs often request that popular music be used in their commercials to convey a certain mood and ambiance. Movie soundtrack CDs are another good place to find beds because they often contain a variety of music, ranging from the bizarre to the conventional. They also are an excellent source for special audio effects, which can be used to great advantage in the right commercial. On-air CDs are screened for potential production use as well. Although several tracks may be placed in on-air rotation and thereby eliminated for use in the mixdown of commercials, some cuts will not be programmed and therefore will not be available for production purposes. Again, it bears repeating that legal permissions must be obtained before copyrighted recordings are utilized as commercial beds.

Syndicated bed music libraries are available at a price and are widely used at larger stations. The All Access Music Group online directory contains a complete listing of production companies offering bed music libraries. Additionally, a search of the Internet will yield lists of audio production sources. TM Studios in Dallas is an established and highly regarded source of production music and station imaging materials. According to TM's Greg Clancy,

> Stations need a variety of musical elements to support the position and image they wish to create. Clients may need production music to put behind a commercial for a local client. They may need pieces of music or sound effects to support a voiced "liner" that says the station name. Whatever their needs, we can help.

Creating a stylistic musical identity for a station poses a unique set of challenges to a jingle producer. At TM, Clancy says, the inspiration for a theme can come from "anywhere." He explains the jingle idea may originate in "the deep recesses of a composer's brain" or may be influenced by "styles that represent the current playlist of a particular station. Some programmers want the sound of the jingles to sound like the music played on the station, and some want the jingles to stand out from the format playlist by being completely different." The process begins with ideation:

> We typically start with a brief from the client, outlining structural and stylistic needs. He might have specific needs, such as requiring several themes to support his morning show. He might need traffic and news opens and beds . . . just depends on what the client wants. We also listen intently to how he wants the jingles to sound, and how he will use them. We typically create demos to make sure we are going down the correct path, then go into full instrumental production. The vocals are usually the last layers to be recorded, then mixing and mastering begin.

Music used for production purposes is cataloged so that it can be located and reused. Syndicated libraries come fully cataloged. When catalogs and sound files are stored side-by-side in a station computer

**FIGURE 8.43**
Instrumentalists perform their parts during a production music recording session

Source: Courtesy of TM Studios and WestwoodOne

**FIGURE 8.44**
Production studio for Bloomfield Hills Schools radio station The Biff 88.1 in Bloomfield Hills, MI

Source: Courtesy of Ronald C. Wittebols

database, producers can easily and readily identify, locate and integrate into a mix the appropriate track that can make the spot both memorable and effective. If a file exists for a bed that is not in current use and the bed is appropriate for a new account, then either a fresh file will be prepared or the new information will be added into the existing file.

No production studio is complete without a commercial sound effects library. Sound effects libraries can be purchased for as little as $100 or they can cost thousands. The quality (both in terms of authenticity and in fidelity) and selection of effects vary accordingly. Specially tailored audio effects also are available for imaging purposes, enabling stations to create unique sound signatures for promos and sweepers. Library prices can run into the thousands but the recordings can add a unique touch to a station's sound.

## CHAPTER HIGHLIGHTS

1. The first radio commercials aired in 1922.

2. Early commercials were live readings: no music, sound effects, or singing.

3. Dialogue spots, using drama and comedy to sell the product, became prominent in the 1930s. Elaborate sound effects, actors, and orchestras were employed.

4. With the introduction of magnetic recording tape and 33⅓ LPs in the 1950s, live commercial announcements were replaced by prerecorded messages.

5. The copy, delivery, and mixdown of commercials must be adapted to match the station's format to avoid audience tune-out.

6. The production director (imaging director) records voice tracks, mixes commercials, PSAs, and station imaging content. The director maintains the bed music and sound effects libraries, mixes promotional material and special programs, and performs editing chores.

7. At smaller stations the production responsibilities are assigned part-time to on-air personnel or the program director.

8. The production director usually answers to the program director and works closely with the copywriter and the traffic manager.

9. For ease of movement and accessibility, both on-air and production studio equipment are arranged in an ergonomic U-shape. The equipment and cabinetry can be configured to accommodate announcers who either are standing or seated.

10. The audio console (board) is the central piece of equipment. It consists of inputs, which permit audio energy to enter the console; outputs, through which audio energy is fed to other locations; VU meters, which measure the level of sound; pots (faders), which control the quantity (gain) of sound; monitor gains, which control in-studio volume; and master gains, which control general output levels.

11. When operating the console in cue or preview mode, the operator can listen privately to various audio sources without channeling them through an output directed to the audience.

12. Digital audio hardware such as the 360 Systems Instant Replay 2 and Wheatstone's VoxPro6 devices and automation software programs began to replace analog reel-to-reel and cartridge tape decks in the 1990s. They let producers digitally mix and archive extensive amounts of audio.

13. Compact disc players generally have been supplanted by computer-based audio playout systems although they remain useful in production rooms for providing quick access to music and sound effects recordings.

14. Audio processors, samplers, and MIDI enhance a radio production studio's product. Virtual processing effects are available in software such as Adobe Audition and Pro Tools, which have these features built in.

15. A patch panel is a signal routing device, consisting of inputs and outputs, for connecting the audio console with various external sources. Analog and digital technologies are utilized to manage signal routing, which occurs within the console as well as externally.

16. Microphones are designed with different pickup patterns to accommodate different functions: omnidirectional (all directions), bidirectional (two directions), and unidirectional (one direction).

17. Telephone technology has been central to the operation of radio stations since the beginning. Telephone equipment is especially important to the operation of talk-intensive formats.

18. Remote broadcasting is common and remains a widespread practice for news and sports coverage, and entertainment program origination. Wired and wireless telephone services are routinely utilized with remote pickup units (RPUs) to deliver audio signals to the main studio.

19. Audio editing ranges from simple repairs to complicated rearrangements of sound elements. The formerly popular razor-cut splicing approach to tape editing has been replaced by nondestructive computer and multitrack methods.

20. Digital audio workstations, which rely on computer technology and software (Pro Tools and Adobe Audition are very popular), are currently used in a vast number of radio production studios.

21. The station copywriter, who writes the commercials, promos, and PSAs, must be familiar with the intended audience and the product being sold. The station's format and programming approach influence the style of writing. Copy should be word-processed, double-spaced, and have one-inch margins. Sound effects are noted in parentheses, and phonetic spellings are provided for difficult words.

22. Aspiring announcers must be able to read copy aloud with proper inflection and enunciation. A naturally resonant and pleasant-sounding voice without a regional accent is an advantage.

23. The practice of voice-tracking is reducing the number of announcing jobs. More and more, local station announcing originates elsewhere, especially in cluster operations and when stations are a part of major station groups.

24. Every station maintains a sound library for use in spot mixdowns. Commercially produced sound effects, bed music collections, and unfamiliar cuts from CDs and the Internet (and even LPs) are common source materials. Digital equipment and computer workstations allow producers to create their own in-house effects.

## SUGGESTED FURTHER READING

Adams, M.H. and Massey, K., *Introduction to Radio: Production and Programming*, Brown and Benchmark, Madison, WI, 1995.

Alburger, J.R. and Hall, M., *The Art of Voice Acting*, Focal Press, Boston, MA, 2002.

Alten, S.R., *Audio in Media*, 8th edition, Wadsworth, Belmont, CA, 2007.

Alvear, J., *Web Developer.com Guide to Streaming Multimedia*, Wiley, New York, NY, 1998.

Baker, J., *Secrets of Voice-Over Success: Top Voice-Over Actors Reveal How They Did It*, 2nd edition, Sentient, Boulder, CO, 2009.

Ballou, G., *Handbook for Sound Engineers*, 3rd edition, Focal Press, Boston, MA, 2008.

Bartlett, B., *Stereo Microphone Techniques*, Focal Press, Boston, MA, 1991.

Campbell, T., *Wireless Writing in the Age of Marconi*, University of Minnesota Press, Minneapolis, MN, 2006.

Connelly, D. W. *Digital Radio Production*, 3rd edition, Waveland Press, Long Grove, IL.

Derry, R., *Audio Editing with Adobe Audition 2.0: Broadcast, Desktop and CD Audio Production*, Focal Press, Boston, MA, 2006.

Ford, T., *Advanced Audio Production Techniques*, Focal Press, Boston, MA, 1993.

Garrigus, S. R., *Sound Forge 8 Power!: The Official Guide*, Cengage Learning, Independence, KY, 2005.

Hausman, C., Messere, F. and Benoit, P., *Modern Radio and Audio Production: Programming and Performance*, 10th edition, Wadsworth, Belmont, CA, 2015.

Hilliard, R.L., *Writing for Television, Radio, and New Media (Broadcast and Production)*, 10th edition, Wadsworth, Boston, MA, 2011.

Hoffer, J., *Radio Production Techniques*, Tab, Blue Ridge Summit, PA, 1974.

Hyde, S.W., *Television and Radio Announcing*, 11th edition, Pearson, Boston, MA, 2008.

Kaempfer, R. and Swanson, J., *The Radio Producer's Handbook*, Allworth Press, New York, NY, 2004.

Keith, M.C., *Broadcast Voice Performance*, Focal Press, Boston, MA, 1989.

Keith, M.C., *Radio Production: Art and Science*, Focal Press, Boston, MA, 1990.

Labelle, B., *Background Noise: Perspectives on Sound Art*, Continuum, London, 2006.

Mack, S., *Hands-On Guide to Webcasting: Internet Event and AV Production*, Focal Press, Boston, MA, 2006.

McLeish, R., *Radio Production*, 5th edition, Focal Press, Boston, MA, 2005.

Mott, R.L., *Radio Sounds Effects*, McFarland Publishing, Jefferson, NC, 2005.

National Association of Broadcasters, *Guidelines for Radio Continuity*, NAB, Washington, D.C., 1982.

National Association of Broadcasters, *Guidelines for Radio Copywriting*, NAB, Washington, D.C., 1993.

Nisbet, A., *The Technique of the Sound Studio*, 4th edition, Focal Press, Boston, MA, 1979.

Nisbet, A., *The Use of Microphones*, 3rd edition, Focal Press, Boston, MA, 1989.

O'Donnell, L.B., Hausman, C., and Benoit, P. *Announcing: Broadcast Communicating Today*, 3rd edition, Wadsworth, Belmont, CA, 1996.

Oringel, R.S., *Audio Control Handbook*, 6th edition, Focal Press, Boston, MA, 1989.

Orlik, P.B., *Broadcast/Cable Copywriting*, 7th edition, Allyn & Bacon, Boston, MA, 2003.

Pohlmann, K.C., *Advanced Digital Audio*, SAMS, Indianapolis, IN, 1991.

Priestman, C., *Web Radio: Radio Production for Internet Streaming*, Focal Press, Boston, MA, 2002.

Rumsey, F., *Tapeless Sound Recording*, Focal Press, Boston, MA, 1990.

Rumsey, F., *Digital Audio Operation*, Focal Press, Boston, MA, 1991.

Sauls, S.J. and Stark, C.A., *Audio Production Worktext: Concepts, Techniques, and Equipment*, 7th edition, Focal Press, Burlington, MA, 2013.

Stephenson, A.R., Reese, D.E., and Beadle, M.E., *Broadcast Announcing Worktext*, 4th edition, Focal Press, Burlington, MA, 2013.

Watkinson, J., *Digital Audio and Compact Disc Technology*, 3rd edition, Focal Press, Boston, MA, 1995.

# CHAPTER 9

# Engineering

## CHARACTERISTICS OF AM AND FM STATIONS

AM and FM stations are located at different points in the electromagnetic spectrum: AM stations are assigned frequencies between 540 and 1700 kHz on the standard broadcast band, and FM stations are located between 88.1 and 107.9 MHz on the FM band.

Ten kilohertz (kHz) separate the carrier frequencies of AM stations and there are 200 kHz separations between FM station frequencies. FM broadcasters additionally are permitted to provide a secondary content delivery channel, termed a "subsidiary communications authority (SCA)" transmission, to subscribers on a small portion of their frequency allocations.

381

**FIGURE 9.1**

As seen from ground level, an FM transmitting antenna mounted at the top of a tower. Compare with Figure 9.5, which depicts the transmitting antenna from sky level

Source: Courtesy of Thomas A. White

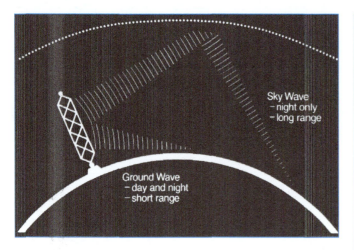

**FIGURE 9.2**

AM signal radiation

Source: From *FCC Broadcast Operator's Handbook*, Figure 3-2

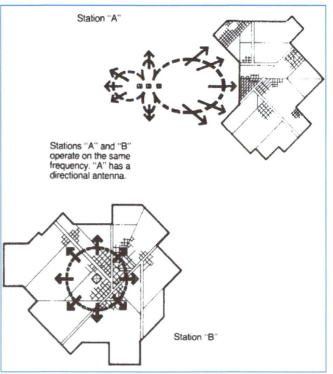

**FIGURE 9.3**

Nondirectional and directional antenna radiation

Source: From *FCC Broadcast Operator's Handbook*, Figure 7-2

The appeal of FM over AM during the years of its development in the 1950s and '60s was that the larger channel width provided FM listeners a better opportunity to fine-tune their favorite stations as well as to receive broadcasts in stereo. To achieve parity, AM broadcasters developed a way to transmit in stereo, and by 1990 hundreds were doing so. The fine-tuning edge still belongs to FM, because its sidebands (15 kHz) are three times wider than AM's (5 kHz).

FM transmission occurs at a much higher frequency (millions of cycle alternations, termed Hertz, per second) compared to AM (thousands of cycles per second). In operating at such a high frequency, FM is immune to the low-frequency energy emissions that plague AM. Although a car motor or an electric storm will generally interfere with AM reception, FM is static-free. Broadcast engineers have attempted to improve the quality of the AM band, but the basic nature of the lower frequency makes AM simply more prone to interference than FM. Broadcasters on the FM band see this as a key competitive advantage and referred to AM's ill-fated move in the 1980s to stereo as "stereo with static."

## Signal Propagation

The paths of AM and FM signals differ from one another. Ground waves create AM's primary service area as they travel across the earth's surface. High-power AM stations are able to reach listeners hundreds of miles away during the day. At night AM's signal is reflected by the atmosphere (ionosphere) back to earth's surface, thus creating a skywave that carries considerably farther, sometimes thousands of miles. Skywaves constitute AM's secondary service area.

In contrast to AM signal radiation, FM propagates its radio waves in a direct (line-of-sight) pattern. FM stations are not affected by evening changes arising from atmospheric cooling and generally do not carry as far as AM stations. A high-power FM station may reach listeners within an 80- to 100-mile radius because its signal weakens as it approaches the horizon. Because FM outlets radiate direct waves, antenna height becomes nearly as important as transmitter power. In general, the greater the height of an FM transmitting antenna, the farther the signal travels.

## Skywave Interference

The fact that AM station signals travel greater distances at night is a mixed blessing. Although some stations benefit from the expanded coverage area created by the skywave phenomenon, many do not. In fact, more than 2,000 radio stations around the country must cease operation near sunset, and thousands more must make substantial transmission-pattern adjustments to prevent interference. For example, many stations must decrease power after sunset to ensure noninterference with others on the same frequency: WXXX is a hypothetical, 5 kW AM station during the day, but at night it must drop to 1 kW. Another measure designed to prevent interference requires that certain stations direct their signals away from stations on the same frequency. Directional stations require two or more antennas to shape their pattern of radiation, whereas a nondirectional station that distributes its signal evenly in all directions needs only a single antenna. Because FM operates relatively free of atmospheric conditions, stations are not subject to the post-sunset operating constraints the FCC imposes on most AM outlets.

## Station Classifications

To guarantee the efficient use of the broadcast spectrum, the FCC established a classification system for both AM and FM stations. Under this system, the nation's 17,000-plus commercial, noncommercial and low-power radio outlets operate free of the debilitating interference that plagued broadcasters prior to passage of the Radio Act of 1927. According to the FCC:

The AM band frequencies are divided into three categories: Clear, Regional, and Local channels. The allowable classes depend on a station's frequency, in addition to other variables. On the Clear channels certain stations are specifically classified as Class A stations or as Class B stations. The other stations have their class determined by their frequency.

AM classifications are as follows:

- *Class A Station*. A Class A station is an unlimited time station (that is, it can broadcast 24 hours per day) that operates on a clear channel. The operating power shall not be less than 10 kilowatts (kW) or more than 50 kW.
- *Class B Station*. A Class B station is an unlimited time station. Class B stations are authorized to operate with a minimum power of 0.250 kW (250 watts) and a maximum power of 50 kW. (If a Class B station operates with less than 0.250 kW, the RMS must be equal to or greater than 141 mV/m at 1 km at the actual power.) If the station is authorized to operate in the expanded band (1610 to 1700 kHz), the maximum power is 10 kW.
- *Class C Station*. A Class C station is an unlimited time station that operates on a local channel. The power shall not be less than 0.25 kW nor more than 1 kW. Class C stations that are licensed to operate with 0.100 kW may continue to operate as licensed.
- *Class D Station*. A Class D station operates either daytime, limited time, or unlimited time with a nighttime power less than 0.250 kW and an equivalent RMS antenna field less than 141 mV/m at 1 km. Class D stations shall operate with daytime powers not less than 0.250 kW nor more than 50 kW. NOTE: If a station is an existing daytime-only station, its class will be Class D.

Part 73, Section 73.21 of the Code of Federal Regulations provides more details on AM station classifications.

FCC efforts to mitigate situations for certain stations that either were creating or affected by excessive interference resulted in the allocation of new AM band space. Termed the *expanded band*, the frequencies between 1610 and 1700 kHz were reallocated by the FCC for the purpose of allowing certain stations to migrate from the existing *standard band* to less-congested dial positions with lowered potential for electrical interference. During the period 1997–98 the FCC issued permits for *expanded band* operation to 65 stations.

| FM Station Class | Reference (Maximum) Facilities for Station Class (see 47 CFR Section 73.211) ERP (in kW) / HAAT (in meters) | FM Protected or Primary Service Contour | | Distance to Protected or Primary Service Contour (km) | Distance to 70 dBu (or 3.16 mV/m) City Grade or Principal Community Coverage Contour (see 47 CFR Section 73.315) (km) |
|---|---|---|---|---|---|
| | | dBu | mV/m | | |
| Class A | 6.0 kW / 100 meters | 60 dBu | 1.0 mV/m | 28.3 km | 16.2 km |
| Class B1 | 25.0 kW / 100 meters | 57 dBu | 0.71 mV/m | 44.7 km | 23.2 km |
| Class B | 50.0 kW / 150 meters | 54 dBu | 0.50 mV/m | 65.1 km | 32.6 km |
| Class C3 | 25.0 kW / 100 meters | 60 dBu | 1.0 mV/m | 39.1 km | 23.2 km |
| Class C2 | 50.0 kW / 150 meters | 60 dBu | 1.0 mV/m | 52.2 km | 32.6 km |
| Class C1 | 100.0 kW / 299 meters | 60 dBu | 1.0 mV/m | 72.3 km | 50.0 km |
| Class C0 (C-zero) | 100.0 kW / 450 meters | 60 dBu | 1.0 mV/m | 83.4 km | 59.0 km |
| Class C | 100.0 kW / 600 meters | 60 dBu | 1.0 mV/m | 91.8 km | 67.7 km |

**FIGURE 9.4**

FM station classes

Source: Courtesy of the Federal Communications Commission

**FIGURE 9.5**

An FM transmitting antenna, as viewed from its tower position 700 feet above ground. The antenna structure consists of 12 elements (bays) that enable the station to achieve an effective radiated power (ERP) of 100 kW

Source: Courtesy of Thomas A. White

**FIGURE 9.6**

FM transmitters of power capacities ranging from 3.5 to 40 kW

Source: Courtesy of Nautel

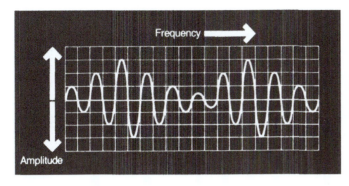

**FIGURE 9.7**
Amplitude modulated (AM) carrier
Source: From *FCC Broadcast Operator's Handbook*, Figure 5-2

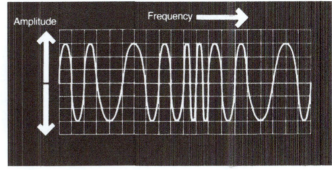

**FIGURE 9.8**
Frequency modulated (FM) carrier
Source: From *FCC Broadcast Operator's Handbook*, Figure 5-4.

In the 1980s the FCC reclassified the FM channels, introducing new classes of FM stations under its Docket 80–90 proceeding in an attempt to provide several hundred additional frequencies. More subclasses were added later. All antenna height designations refer to maximum *height above average terrain* (HAAT). They are as follows:

- *Class C*: These stations transmit with up to 100 kW of effective radiated power (ERP) from an antenna of no more than 600 meters in height.

- *Class C0*: These stations transmit with up to 100 kW of effective radiated power (ERP) from an antenna of no more than 450 meters in height.

- *Class C1*: Stations granted licenses to operate within this classification may be authorized to transmit up to 100 kW ERP with antennas not exceeding 299 meters. The maximum reach of stations in this class is about 50 miles.

- *Class C2*: The operating parameters of stations in Class C2 are close to Class Bs. The maximum power granted Class C2 outlets is 50 kW, and antennas may not exceed 150 meters. Class C2 stations reach approximately 35 miles.

- *Class C3*: These stations operate with shorter antenna height (100 meters) and with power that does not exceed 25 kW ERP. Class C3 signals extend approximately 24 miles.

- *Class B*: These stations operate with an antenna height of 150 meters and with power that does not exceed 50kW ERP. The reach of Class B signals is approximately 33 miles.

- *Class B1*: The maximum antenna height permitted for Class B1 stations (100 meters) is identical to Class As; however, Class B1s are higher-powered, and are permitted a maximum 25 kW ERP. Class B1 signals carry 25–30 miles.

- *Class A*: The maximum antenna height permitted for Class A stations is 100 meters. Class A stations are permitted a maximum 6 kW ERP. Class A signals carry approximately 16 miles.

Low-Power FM (LPFM) station classifications include the following:

- *Class L1*: 50–100 W ERP with a maximum antenna height of 30 meters.
- *Class L2*: 1–10 W ERP with a maximum antenna height of 30 meters.

At the time of this writing the FCC had been petitioned to create a new Class C4. The petition proposed allowing stations to operate with a maximum effective radiated power of 12,000 watts with a maximum antenna height of 328 feet. In recognition of the ongoing revisions made to FM classifications, readers are encouraged to consult Section 73.211 of the Code of Federal Regulations for the most current specifications.

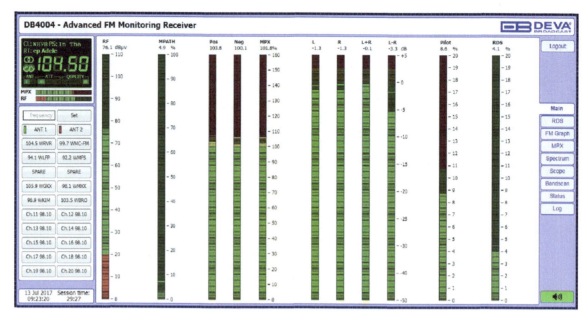

**FIGURE 9.9**
FM transmitter modulation percentages are displayed on this monitor

Source: Courtesy of Entercom Radio Memphis

**FIGURE 9.10**
Engineer refers to visual display prior to adjusting transmitter operating parameters

Source: Courtesy of Nautel

## FM Translators

An ancillary class of low-power FM transmitters, termed *translators* or *boosters* by the FCC serves to supplement the coverage of certain FM stations. The FCC authorized the use of translators in 1970 to extend the range of FM stations whose signal penetration was compromised by factors such as mountainous terrain. Generally, translators may not originate programming. Rather, they are intended for simultaneously rebroadcasting the programming of the originating FM station, although on a different frequency, in order to extend the signal to unserved areas. Commercial stations may rebroadcast only on the channels set aside for commercial broadcasting (92.1–107.9 mHz), whereas noncommercial stations are permitted to utilize any FM frequency ranging from 88.1 to 107.9 mHz. Translators are limited to 250 watts maximum of effective radiated power (ERP). Antenna height, another factor that determines signal coverage, varies according to specific conditions and circumstances.

# FM vs. AM: Technical Considerations

If electrical signals could be seen, they would look like the figures shown here. (Actually, they *can* be seen, on an instrument called an oscilloscope, which resembles a small television set.) If one were to whistle into a microphone with a pure low-frequency audio tone, the microphone would convert the voice into an electrical signal like Fig. 1.

Figure. 1. A pure audio tone converted into an electrical signal.

Figure. 2. A carrier wave produced by a radio transmitter.

An essential portion of a radio transmitter produces a much higher frequency electrical signal called the carrier wave like Fig. 2. To transmit intelligence, the radio transmitter must somehow superimpose the voice signal on the carrier wave, a process called modulation. (The radio receiver *demodulates*, or separates the desired audio signal from the carrier wave.)

Amplitude modulation or AM was the first type of modulation developed, early in the 20th century. When the amplitude or height of the carrier is changed in time with the audio signal, the result would look like Fig. 3

*TIME* ⟶

Figure 3. An amplitude modulated radio signal.

Figure 4. A frequency modulated radio signal, modulated by the same audio signal as in Fig. 3.

Instead of modulating the amplitude of the carrier, one can use the audio signal to change the *frequency* of the carrier, and that is frequency modulation. If the carrier were frequency modulated by the same audio signal as in Fig. 3, the result would look like Fig. 4. The frequency increases and decreases, but the amplitude of the modulated signal stays constant. The same intelligence has been transmitted. Of course a symphony concert with its multitude of sounds would produce a much more complicated looking waveform.

### Questions About AM vs. FM:

*Why is FM more static-free than AM?*

Static is caused by things like lightning discharges or electrical discharges from nearby motors or other electrical devices, and those discharges produce small bursts of radiated energy. The

AM receiver picks up the bursts of static along with the desired signal and adds them together. Static shows up as sharp vertical peaks (spikes) on the modulated waveform, and AM radios respond to them. However, in an FM receiver, the amplitude of the signal does not matter—only changes in frequency matter—so there is no static with FM.

*If it is better, why didn't people use FM in the early days of radio?*

AM was discovered first, and tends to be simpler. In the early days of radio, mathematicians thought they had "proved" that FM would not work as well as AM, but their analyses were oversimplified. E. H. Armstrong showed that if one used a sufficiently wide bandwidth, FM works just fine. For FM to work well, a much wider channel (bandwidth) is required than with an AM station. At the frequencies used in the AM broadcast band (roughly 550 to 1700 kilohertz) there is insufficient spectrum "space" to permit the wide channels needed for FM, but there is sufficient channel space available at the higher frequencies now used for FM (88 to 108 Megahertz). Another problem was that in the early days of radio, the vacuum tubes then available did not work well at the high frequencies where FM needed to operate. Another benefit of FM: the wider channels occupied by FM stations can accommodate modulation with wider frequency excursions than those from AM stations, so FM stations broadcast with much higher fidelity.

*Why can you sometimes hear far away stations on AM but not on FM?*

That has to do not with the difference between AM and FM, but rather *the different radio propagation conditions* in the AM band vs. the FM band. At the frequencies used in the AM broadcast band, signals can bounce off the ionosphere, especially at night, and be reflected back to earth at considerable distances from the transmitter, as shown in the figure below. But signals at the much higher frequencies used for FM generally do *not* bounce off the ionosphere, and so FM reception is limited to more or less a line-of-sight path.

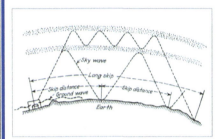

Figure 5. Charged particles in the ionosphere can reflect radio signals, which can then come back to earth quite some distance away from the transmitter.. These reflected signals often shows up at the frequencies used in the AM broadcast band, especially at night, but NOT at the much higher frequencies used for FM.

**FIGURE 9.11**
The difference between the two bands

Source: Courtesy of Brian Belanger, Radio and Television Museum

**FIGURE 9.12**
Devices pictured at the top use IP connections to deliver audio in a Studio/Transmitter Link (STL) array. Also pictured along the bottom are mixer-style encoders and smartphone apps for relaying audio from the remote site to studio-based receivers

Source: Courtesy of Tieline

In October 2015, the FCC announced details of its "AM Revitalization" initiative for breathing new life into the beleaguered AM band. In observing that a quarter-century had passed since the last effort to prop up the AM band occurred, FCC Media Bureau Chief Bill Lake wrote:

> AM radio has traditionally been the backbone of the broadcast service, and has time and again kept the public entertained and informed, as well as serving a vital role in times of emergency, disaster and severe weather. The Commission's goal is to assist AM broadcasters in the face of increasing technical challenges to their service, such as interference from electronic devices.

In an effort to advance its "fundamental goals of localism, competition and diversity in broadcast media," the FCC stated its intentions for widening the usage of FM translators by AM stations. Characteristically lower-powered AM stations licensed in Classes C and D immediately became eligible to apply for assistance by seeking permission to modify and/or relocate FM translators. Just six months after the announcement, applicants filed more than 600 requests to relocate FM translators. Media Bureau Chief Lake noted that the Commission acted on the applications expediently, granting permission to 80% of AM station licensees seeking this new lease on life. At the time of this writing the FCC had scheduled a window in summer 2017 for accepting additional translator applications from AM stations.

## DIGITAL AUDIO BROADCASTING (HD RADIO TECHNOLOGY)

The Federal Communication Commission decided in 2002 on a technology referred to as "in-band, on-channel" (IBOC) for digital AM and FM broadcasting. IBOC enables stations to operate in a "hybrid" mode, simultaneously transmitting over their existing frequency assignments both analog and digital signals. Digital manipulation codifies the analogous audio signal into data for broadcast. The reason for the transformation is simple: better and more-evolved sound. Broadcast stations employ digital technology in order to compete with audio alternatives, such as MP3 players, satellite radio, and mobile music services.

The advantage is that no additional frequency spectrum is required for implementing the digital signal. A unique feature of IBOC is its ability to support multiple transmission channels. Thus, while the main digital channel replicates the programming heard on the station's original analog primary channel, two additional digital FM channels are available for transmitting alternate program content.

In its decision the FCC approved iBiquity Digital Corporation as the sole provider of IBOC technology. iBiquity developed and branded its system as HD Radio and licensed its technology to broadcasters in the United States, Mexico, and other countries. In 2015 the audio technology company dts purchased iBiquity. One year later dts was acquired by Xperi Corporation.

**FIGURE 9.13**
Audio processor for FM and HD. By managing a broadcast signal's audio equalization, this device enhances a station's sound, making it clearer, louder and more sonically pleasant

Source: Courtesy of the Telos Alliance

The term "HD Radio" itself is *not* an abbreviation of the term "high-definition radio." Initially, iBiquity qualified the terminology, explaining on its website that "'HD Radio and the HD Radio logo are proprietary trademarks of iBiquity Digital Corporation. The 'HD' in HD Radio is part of iBiquity Digital's brand name for its advanced digital AM/FM system." Furthermore, the site informed readers, "It does not mean hybrid digital or high-definition digital; both of these are incorrect."

Although the present system of analog broadcasting essentially replicates sound waves (with inherent shortcomings), the digital broadcasting process converts sound waves into a low-bandwidth data bitstream. In digital, sound waves are sampled, and then are assigned numeric values (zeroes or ones) and become coded pulses. Simply put, in digital, sounds are mathematically quantified. Digital broadcasting is capable of achieving greater frequency response and dynamic range than is possible with analog transmission, notably AM. Thus, more audio information is conveyed to the listener, who hears more. Another positive feature from the broadcast operator's perspective is the fact that digital signals do not require as much power as analog signals do.

Because the technology is incompatible with existing AM/FM radios, listeners must acquire technology-compatible HD Radio receivers in order to access the digital signal. During the first decade of HD Radio broadcasting some observers expected the existing analog system of AM and FM broadcasting to become passé. This has yet to occur, and presently there are predictions that analog broadcasting will be around for a few more years. Speculators suggest also that, if digital becomes the preeminent broadcasting system, analog AM and FM stations will still be out there—that is, until the FCC no longer perceives them as providing a viable service. Press reports published in 2017 about the decreasing cost of HD radio transmitting equipment and the increasing number of HD radio-equipped car models suggests an improving future. In any event, the conversion to digital appears to be inevitable. Analog broadcasting will go the way of the turntable.

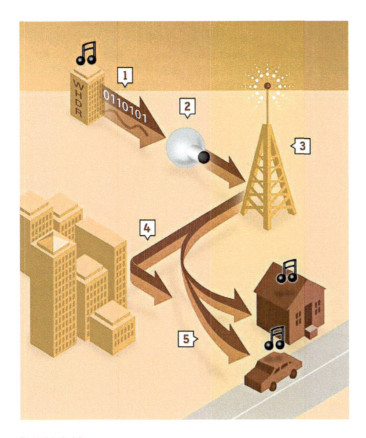

1. Analog and digital signals sent separately.
2. Signals combined prior to transmission.
3. Composite signal transmitted by station.
4. Multipath distortion only affects analog.
5. Signal compatible with both analog and digital radios—only digital radios receive multicast channels.

**FIGURE 9.14**
How HD Radio works

Source: © 2013 iBiquity Digital Corporation. Reproduced with permission from iBiquity

# SATELLITE AND INTERNET RADIO

## Satellite Radio

Satellite radio signals come from more than 22,000 miles out in space. Two companies, Sirius Satellite Radio and XM Satellite Radio, began operating in the early 2000s and merged in 2008. Initially XM Satellite Radio's initial transponders (two Boeing HS 702 satellites) were set aloft in a geostationary orbit, while Sirius Satellite Radio's first birds (three SS/L-1300 satellites) rotated in an elliptical pattern, ensuring that each satellite would spend around 16 hours over the United States. The web-based tracking service N2YO.com reports that SiriusXM currently has six active and reserve satellites in geostationary orbit.

**FIGURE 9.15**
Radio spectrum table

| | |
|---|---|
| VLF (Very Low Frequency) 30 kHz and below | – Maritime use |
| LF (Low-Frequency) 30 kHz to 300 kHz | – Aeronautical/maritime |
| MF (Medium Frequency) 300 kHz to 3000 kHz | – AM, amateur, distress, etc. |
| HF (High Frequency) 3 MHz to 30 MHz | – CB, fax, international, etc. |
| VHF (Very High Frequency) 30 MHz to 300 MHz | – FM, TV, satellite, etc. |
| UHF (Ultra High Frequency) 300 MHz to 3000 MHz | – TV, satellite, CB, DAB (proposed), etc. |
| SHF (Super High Frequency) 3 GHz to 30 GHz | – Satellite, radar, space, etc. |
| EHF (Extreme High Frequency) 30 GHz to 300 GHz | – Space, amateur, experimental, etc. |

Offering digital radio with sonic performance equivalent to CD sound reproduction, SiriusXM beams satellite radio signals to homes, cars, and portable receivers, serving more than 31 million subscribers. Satellite radio uses the S-band (2.3 GHz) for its digital audio radio service (DARS). Replacement satellites are kept ready for launch in the event of a satellite malfunction. Programming from ground stations is uplinked to the satellites and then relayed to terrestrial end users (subscribers). Receivers unscramble the incoming signals, consisting of approximately 140 channels of programming. In addition, the signals contain encoded data for displaying on receiver screens information about what is being broadcast (artist, song title, etc.). Ground repeaters are employed when needed to strengthen incoming satellite signals. According to former XM Satellite Chief Programmer Lee Abrams, the operation's technical department consists of four key areas: studios, hardware development, satellites and repeaters, and IT.

| Name | NORAD ID | Int'l Code | Launch date | Period [minutes] | Action |
|---|---|---|---|---|---|
| SIRIUS FM-6 | 39360 | 2013-058A | October 25, 2013 | 1436.1 | Track it |
| XM-5 | 37185 | 2010-053A | October 14, 2010 | 1436.1 | Track it |
| SIRIUS FM-5 | 35493 | 2009-034A | June 30, 2009 | 1436.1 | Track it |
| XM-3 | 28626 | 2005-008A | March 1, 2005 | 1436.1 | Track it |
| XM-1 | 26761 | 2001-018A | May 8, 2001 | 1436.1 | Track it |
| XM-2 | 26724 | 2001-012A | March 18, 2001 | 1436.1 | Track it |
| SIRIUS 3 | 26626 | 2000-077A | November 30, 2000 | 1436 | Track it |
| SIRIUS 2 | 26483 | 2000-051A | September 5, 2000 | 1436 | Track it |
| SIRIUS 1 | 26390 | 2000-035A | June 30, 2000 | 1436.1 | Track it |

**FIGURE 9.16**
Satellites have limited life expectancies. This table lists both original and replacement SiriusXM satellites

Source: Courtesy of www.n2yo.com

## Internet Radio

Broadcasts of radio programming have been available over the Internet since the 1990s. There are two types of Internet radio stations: those operated by broadcast stations and those that exist solely online. In the first category, stations typically simulcast their broadcast signals over the Internet. The second category of Internet stations is typically more eclectic in its programming offerings because the formatting constraints prevalent in broadcast radio do not exist in the independent outlets.

Thanks to the Internet, college radio is experiencing a surge of interest. Institutions can avoid the hurdle of obtaining FCC licensing and can establish Internet-only (I-O) stations at minimal expense. Backbone Networks Corporation is an example of a company that assists college broadcasters in navigating the technological waters of online radio. The company oversees the technical aspects of station streaming, thus enabling students and staff to focus their time and energies on program development. Paul Kamp, vice-president for business development and in-house counsel for Backbone, cites expense containment as the allure of online radio. He observes,

> Internet economics is helping to drive the shift toward Internet radio. A new station does not need to apply for an FCC license or purchase or lease time on a broadcast tower for broadcasting in a particular region. They only need to have the ability to generate and manage 168 hours of programming a week and all that it entails.

Unlike traditional terrestrial stations, whose reach and operating parameters are limited, technology imposes no geographical limitations in Internet radio.

However, in certain instances, broadcasters have proactively restricted access to their online streams, making access available only to listeners located within the station's terrestrial coverage area—a practice termed geofencing. Broadcasters adopted the practice as a means for minimizing expenses. Because geo-fencing limits the availability of streams to listeners within defined geographic areas the expense associated with streaming copyrighted music recordings can be reduced.

**FIGURE 9.17**

Compact, rack-mounted webcasting equipment processes, encodes, and streams digital audio

Source: Courtesy of the Telos Alliance

**FIGURE 9.18**

*Radio Wave*: bundled hardware/software equipment package for Internet radio stations. This system supports both live and fully automated (unattended) operation

Source: Courtesy of Radio Wave/Arrakis Systems

With Internet access, anyone almost anywhere can enjoy listening to Internet radio. An Internet station emanating from Dayton, Ohio, may be heard in Bangkok, Thailand, and tens of thousands of broadcasts are available. Kamp explains the magnitude of scale thus:

> The worldwide broadcast capability of Internet radio enables the broadcaster to broadcast to a targeted niche and still have a large audience. For example, you may only be able to reach one million listeners in the greater Dayton, Ohio, area with a Polka broadcast. Yet you can reach more than one billion people with an Internet radio station.

Unlike terrestrial and satellite radio, Internet radio has the capability of providing a full range of visual data, such as photos, text, video, and links. Interactive opportunities add further cachet to the medium's appeal. "As Internet radio grows outside of music radio and into other types of content," Kamp notes, formats such as "Talk, Public Radio, Sports and other specialized content that is created or owned by the station's Internet radio should find some substantial growth and provide some interesting programming."

**FIGURE 9.19**
Internet radio receiver features preset tuning selection

The process of distributing an Internet radio signal is not complex. Internet radio operations possess an encoding computer, which converts the audio into data packets that are routed to an end user's Internet-connected device. In the span of just more than a decade, Internet radio escaped its desktop computer tether. "In the early 1990s," Kamp explains, "you needed a computer with high speed Internet access to decode the streams in order to listen. Today the Internet is available on a myriad of devices like smartphones, tablets, and specialized Internet radio receivers made by traditional home audio manufacturers."

Broadcasters are turning to the Internet as a reliable and economical way to insert their stations into on-the-scene coverage of local community events. Remote broadcasting, according to Kamp, is easily accomplished because the Internet has lowered the barriers to entry:

> Internet or cloud-based solutions enable a very small remote system to be sent to the field instead of provisioning an ISDN line in the past. This frees the broadcasters from their studio, enabling them to go out into the community to broadcast events. This allows the broadcaster to get back to serving their community.

**FIGURE 9.20**
Randy Williams

## BEHIND THE SCENES: ENGINEERING A NATIONWIDE COLLEGIATE SPORTS NETWORK

### Randy Williams

Learfield Communications is a diverse company and respected industry leader in collegiate sports marketing, sponsorship rights, brand management and game-day productions for nearly 125 collegiate institutions, conferences and arenas across the United States. In addition, Learfield also provides its collegiate partners access to professional concessions and ticket sales; licensing and trademark consulting; digital and social platform expertise; and venue technology systems through its affiliated companies. Learfield's technical operations center (TOC) and game-day production facility is located in Jefferson City, Missouri; corporate headquarters and the senior- level management team is located in Dallas, Texas.

Through its multimedia rights agreements, Learfield creates, maintains, and grows a collegiate sports network of affiliated radio stations that broadcast many or all products offered. This can encompass NCAA football, basketball, women's basketball, volleyball, hockey, soccer, lacrosse, baseball, and softball games, as well as the related weekly one-hour coach's call-in show. Learfield will originate coverage of these events "live" from a local venue on or near the college/university campus and distribute the complete hosted product to all affiliated stations. Learfield partners with network television entities and local television stations for the "video" or television transmission side of the business, but handles all radio broadcasts internally.

A radio broadcast team consisting of a technical engineer and talent (play-by-play voice of the network and commentators) will arrive at the stadium/arena or local venue and set up the technical aspects of the broadcast. This crew will have a fully outfitted radio remote broadcast equipment package for interfacing with Learfield's TOC. Technology has evolved and improved over the years, but the main sources of connectivity between the local venue and the TOC continue to be through use of ISDN (integrated systems digital network), and IP (Internet protocol).

Both ISDN and IP connections require a "codec" device on each end: one at the live venue, and the other at the Learfield TOC. These devices are encoding/decoding units that convert audio signals into digital packets and transmit these data over a dedicated, high-quality telephone circuit. These circuits and codec devices allow two-way communication between TOC operators and talent at the stadium. Emergency backup systems are also installed, often over cellular or Wi-Fi devices in case of primary connection failures.

The remote crew at the venue will connect these ISDN/IP codecs and backup systems to a portable mixing console, wireless transmitters and receivers for roaming field reporters, headphone amplifiers, and crowd/effects microphones for capturing natural sounds to provide a full package of live event sound. The local venue engineer will mix all sources at the stadium/arena and transmit that audio to Learfield TOC over these ISDN and IP connections.

Learfield's TOC has a staff of engineers, producers, and board operators that manage and monitor all stadium/arena venue audio, and also insert network commercial content, production elements and automation cues for affiliated stations. This "complete broadcast product" is then distributed to all network affiliates either by satellite communication or by Internet stream (or both).

Learfield's engineering team operates a C-band digital satellite uplink for 35 of its "Power 5 Conference" college/university partnerships. Each affiliate will have a satellite receiver that is programmed and authorized only for the content they are contractually assigned to carry. The outputs of these satellite receivers are routed to a station's audio output for transmission over AM and FM frequencies. The other method of distribution is over Internet stream, which is utilized as both a backup to the satellite delivery system and also as a primary delivery method to 60+ collegiate partnerships.

Closed circuit broadband distribution (CCBD) is the Learfield-defined term describing distribution over the Internet to affiliate stations. A high-quality, dedicated Internet stream is encoded at Learfield's TOC in multiple formats ranging from "RTSP" to "HLS" to "ICECAST." Doing so allows broadcasters multiple choices for taking the broadcast feed in various methods or formats to best suit stations' needs. A URL address is assigned to a particular network feed, and is locked down with credential access that only the approved affiliate will possess. This step in the process, along with proprietary back-office software, will allow only the intended affiliate to access the audio stream and prevent the general public from accessing it. The affiliated station's operator will launch an audio player application installed on a studio computer, click on the appropriate URL, and the broadcast will start streaming "live" with minimal Internet delay directly from Learfield TOC.

Both satellite- and CCBD-delivered content is encoded for fully automated operation, and includes cues for stations to run a broadcast "unattended" with no intervention from a board operator at the affiliate station. In today's radio marketplace, where the need for more streamlined staffing to operate multiple stations simultaneously has become increasingly important, a fully automatable program service is highly desired.

---

**Randy Williams** is Chief Engineer at Learfield.

FIGURE 9.21
Learfield logo
Source: Courtesy of Learfield Communications LLC

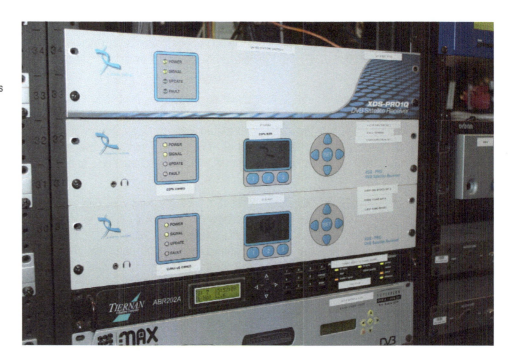

## BECOMING AN ENGINEER

Most station managers or chief engineers look for experience when hiring technical people. Formal training such as college ranks high but not as high as actual hands-on technical experience. Kevin McNamara, Director of Engineering at Beasley Broadcasting Group, states:

> A good electronics background is preferred, of course. This doesn't necessarily mean ten years of experience or an advanced degree in electronic engineering, but rather a person with a solid foundation in the fundamentals of radio electronics, perhaps derived from an interest in amateur radio, computers, or another hobby of a technical nature. This is a good starting point. Actually, it has been my experience that people with this kind of a background are more attuned to the nature of this business. You don't need a person with a physics degree from MIT, but what you do want is someone with a natural inclination for the technical side. Ideally speaking, you want to hire a person with a tech history as well as some formal in-class training.

Chief Engineer Jim Puriez concurs:

> A formal education in electronics is good, but not essential. In this business if you have the desire and natural interest, you can learn from the inside out. You don't find that many broadcast engineers with actual electronics degrees. Of course, most have taken basic electronics courses. Most are long on experience and have acquired their skills on the job. While a college degree is a nice credential, I think most managers hire tech people on the basis of experience more than anything else.

Entercom/Memphis Chief Engineer Skip Reynolds says the evolving nature of the business underscores the need for intelligent, skilled technologists. "Broadcasting as we know it is changing rapidly," he observes, "but the fact remains: radio is a one-to-many medium. That means there will still be transmitters, towers, studios for local origination, and remote facilities for local sporting events. That also means there are a lot of opportunities for engineers!" Reynolds adds,

> As you start out you may find the opportunity to specialize a bit, whether it be studio or transmitter maintenance, IT/computers or maybe producing sporting events. You probably will get to participate in larger projects like a studio rebuild or maybe installing a transmitter.

Equally important, in his opinion, is the need for engineers to achieve the delicate balance between work and home. Cultivating positive professional associations with co-workers is important, but it must be achieved without compromising the integrity of relationships with family or succumbing to personal sacrifice. "Above all," he says, "keep a cheerful and cooperative attitude. Prioritize your work. Be creative by finding better ways to accomplish a goal. Finally, pace yourself by allowing time for yourself and family."

Station Engineer Sid Schweiger also cites experience as the key criterion for gaining a broadcast engineer's position:

> When I'm in the market for a tech person, I'll check smaller market stations for someone interested in making the move to a larger station. This way, I've got someone with experience right from the start. The little station is a good place for the newcomer to gain experience.

*Radio World* Editor Paul McLane wrote about the dearth of young people entering the field and the need for specialists with various technical and computer skills: "Fluency never stops. People I respect say radio engineers should learn to think large, and that goes for digital audio and data training."

Numerous schools and colleges offer formal training in electronics and information technology (IT). The number shrinks somewhat when it comes to those institutions actually providing curricula in broadcast engineering. However, a number of technical schools do offer basic electronics courses applicable to broadcast operations. The Society of Broadcast Engineers (SBE) also provides valuable education and knowledge certification for engineering talent. Members of SBE chapters in markets across the US convene regularly, providing information and education for the novice technician and the advanced engineer alike. A good way to learn more about how to become a station engineer is by contacting a nearby chapter and arranging to attend a meeting. That's how Luke Lukefahr, IT Engineer for iHeartMedia/St. Louis, found entry into the industry. Lukefahr recalls:

> The Society of Broadcast Engineers has helped me immensely. When I attended my first meeting as a student in college I was able to meet a group of engineering professionals that worked in a market that I had only dreamed of working. Meeting so many different engineers allowed me to get my name out and show that even though I was young, I had a passion to learn as much as I could about broadcast engineering. By attending SBE meetings you not only get your name out, you have access to years of knowledge from a group of professional engineers. SBE also offers different educational programs and certifications which help engineers gain more knowledge about current and future broadcasting equipment.

For Lukefahr, SBE membership offers more than education:

> What really impressed me about the SBE is that it's like a family; the engineers that are members are not out for each other's jobs, they are just a group of people that are there to help. The iHeartMedia engineer that hired me is a member of the chapter where I attended my first meeting. During my first interview he said that he recognized my name. SBE gave me the chance to get my foot in the door. I still attend SBE meetings and I plan on becoming a certified broadcast networking technologist (CBNT).

While affirming his belief in the value of SBE membership, Lukefahr reflects on this early stage of his career, observing, "If I had to go back and change one thing I would have joined SBE during my freshman year of college because I would have become better-rounded in my knowledge of broadcast and IT equipment."

When deregulation occurred in August 1981, the FCC no longer required that broadcast engineers hold a first-class radiotelephone license. To receive the license, applicants were expected to pass an examination. An understanding of basic broadcast electronics and knowledge of the FCC rules and regulations pertaining to station technical operations were necessary to pass the lengthy examination. Today a station's chief engineer (also called chief operator) need possess only a restricted operator permit. Those who held first-class certification prior to license elimination now receive either a restricted operator permit or a general radiotelephone license at renewal time.

It is left to the discretion of the individual radio station to establish criteria regarding engineer credentials. Many do require a general radiotelephone license or certification from associations, such as the Society of Broadcast Engineers (SBE) or the National Association of Radio and Telecommunications Engineers (NARTE), as a preliminary means of establishing a prospective engineer's qualifications.

Communication skills rank highest on the list of personal qualities for station engineers, according to McNamara:

> The old stereotype of the station "tech-head" in white socks, chinos, and shirt-pocket pen holder weighed down by its inky contents is losing its validity. Today, more than ever, I think, the radio engineer must be able to communicate with members of the staff from the manager to the deejay. Good interpersonal skills are necessary. Things have become very sophisticated, and engineers play an integral role in the operation of a facility, perhaps more now than in the past. The field of broadcast engineering has become more competitive, too, with the elimination of many operating requirements.

**FIGURE 9.23**
Paul McLane

Source: Image courtesy of Teresa Castracane Photography

## ENGINEERING: CHALLENGING, REWARDING, IN DEMAND

### Paul McLane

Are you interested in a career in radio broadcasting technology?

Radio has been going through something of an existential crisis brought on by significant new competition and changes in how people consume audio. Broadcast engineering, too, has been challenged to ask itself fundamental questions. You might help reinvent the job category. Here are a few things you should know.

Radio broadcasting in the United States is a field chronically short of new tech talent. Organizations in both commercial and public radio need people skilled in electronics and RF transmission technology, particularly as older generations of engineers retire. Ralph Hogan, a past president of the Society of Broadcast Engineers, cited "the loss of retiring engineers from the industry at an alarming rate." This is an opportunity for you.

The skill set required has evolved to incorporate aspects of information technology, new media platform integration, radio data services and other sectors. Many—perhaps most—broadcast engineers do not hold traditional engineering degrees.

But, while radio employers can attract IT candidates with relative ease, they need people who can combine that mindset with a willingness to work in RF, mechanical structures and traditional electronics. So if you embrace a broad scope of technology, you will offer a potential employer a powerful combination.

Adrienne Wright, vice-president of technology for Emmis Communications, loves that an engineer's job involves such a range. "There is certainly still the traditional broadcast technologies, like antennas and transmitters that most people associate with radio," she said:

> However there are also IP-based appliances, servers, automation systems and routers that any "techie" would find interesting. All of the systems work together to create a product that millions of people listen to throughout the day in their cars, homes and even on their mobile devices. As radio technology evolves it also presents excellent opportunities for growth and development.

Why be a broadcast engineer? You'll play with technology and get paid for it. You can gratify your "problem-solver" itch. You'll work with large-scale systems and media platforms. You'll work with smart people (Adrienne Wright calls the Emmis engineering team "the most dedicated, knowledgeable group of people that I have ever worked with"). You'll learn about, and be challenged regularly by, new tech and approaches. You'll play a key role that companies find hard to fill, giving you an additional measure of job security.

Should you prove capable, you'll quickly earn enhanced responsibility. You may work independently or with little supervision. You may manage a capital expenditure budget and have the opportunity to build a studio, transmission facility, or network. You will have ample opportunity to "be the hero" should systems fail. If you learn to think strategically, you'll enjoy more access to organizational decision-makers than many employees do.

As a young man, Conrad Trautmann, Senior Vice-President, Technology and Operations at Cumulus Media, loved rock music and the station in his backyard that played it. When he realized that his love for electronics could be applied in the engineering department, he sought an internship there, launching a career. Now he oversees 450 stations in 90 cities and a radio network that broadcasts content via satellite to more than 8,000 radio stations. "I couldn't be prouder of the people who help run those stations and the fact that we are able to reach so many listeners through radio," he said.

> The content we produce on those stations is all available on the internet, which expands our reach beyond those 90 cities to anywhere in the world. The technology to transmit audio has continued to evolve and change the way people consume our content; and every day when I come to work there's something new to work on. Radio remains an exciting business, and there's always something new to learn.

You'll have the chance to help redefine what it means to be a broadcast engineer. Promising technologists have a particular opportunity to achieve as radio works to reinvent its role in the dashboard, living room, and smartphone, as well as integrate video content and social media strategies with their offerings. Your skills can be put to the test in many ways.

Are there downsides of radio engineering? Typical complaints include long hours, a broad range of skills to master, conditions that may be dangerous to the untrained, a lack of respect in some organizations and (ironically, given demand) a pay scale that is low relative to other technical fields.

Veteran engineer Tom Ray wrote on the Talkers.com website that many young people

> have no desire to be on call, to crawl around in swampy fields after hours, to service transmitters that can kill them, not to mention the fact that one can encounter a snake or other creepy crawly thing walking into the door of the transmitter building.

Yet these experiences can be part of the pleasure of it. Gary Kline, former Senior Vice-President of Engineering and IT for Cumulus Media and now owner of his own broadcast consulting practice, described the constant, "on-call" nature of the engineer's job—but he found that thrilling: "It's broadcasting and media and news and entertainment, and it is exciting. Along with that excitement and 24/7 atmosphere comes additional responsibility." He notes that there could be thousands, even millions of listeners to the systems you build. "Take New York City, for example. Build a studio in NYC and the audience is huge."

Not many educational institutions teach broadcast-specific implementations of RF, traditional electronics, IT infrastructure and network-based tools. It's OK to come into the field with a basis in one area and seek to build your skills through field experience and industry training.

Support for career development is improving. For example, the SBE offers an online "university," with courses in IP networking, streaming, FCC enforcement, audio processing, FM and AM systems, voice telco networks, RF safety and disaster recovery. A few state broadcast associations offer programs to encourage engineers; the Alabama Broadcasters Association is particularly active. The SBE has a well-respected certification program to help engineers demonstrate expertise.

The largest U.S. commercial radio company, iHeartMedia, employs more than 300 engineers. Several years ago it created an electrical engineering co-op program that offers college students an opportunity to expand their abilities with hands-on training with technologies and operations at iHeartMedia stations. Students alternate semesters working in the co-op system and then returning to school to pursue their degrees; a few qualify for scholarships.

The company separately created a market engineering development program, which offers employees one-on-one coaching, education and testing, along with special project experience—the goal is to advance participants quickly into market engineering manager roles. iHeartMedia Executive Vice-President of Engineering and Systems Integration Jeff Littlejohn has said the company wanted to make a strategic investment in the future of engineering: "We hope to attract and expose new talent to the ever-changing world of radio while also fostering the growth and development of our existing employees."

Conrad Trautmann of Cumulus recommends that you consider not just whether the job is a good fit for your skills but also whether the culture is positive and supportive. "We've created an internal talent network to give people a path to growth inside the company, and have made many transfers and promotions as a result," he says. "In engineering, we are committed to a stable infrastructure of our studios and transmitters and are making the investments needed to insure that."

In considering opportunities, also remember the newer entities that challenge the traditional definition of radio, whether it be satellite radio, Spotify, or the many companies that offer streaming or online content services. These firms may not rely on traditional over-the-air infrastructure, but they too hire technical candidates and are part of the expanding world of radio.

Some see today as a scary time in radio; others see exciting opportunity. Without question, however, the field offers professional opportunities to the student of electronics, the tinkerer, the technically savvy digital native. Resources are available to help a student develop industry-specific skills not found on the college curriculum.

---

**Paul McLane** is Editor in Chief of *Radio World*, the news source for radio managers and engineers, and editorial director of the Broadcast and Video Group of NewBay Media, overseeing publications *Radio* magazine, *TV Technology*, *Government Video* and the NAB Show *Daily News*. He was a journalist and news anchor for Delmarva Broadcasting Co. and held sales and marketing management positions with Radio Systems Inc. and Bradley Broadcast & Pro Audio. Contact him at pmclane@nbmedia.com.

**FIGURE 9.24**
*Radio World* is the go-to source of news for radio managers and engineers

Source: Courtesy of *Radio World*

# THE SOCIETY OF BROADCAST ENGINEERS

## Wayne Pecena

FIGURE 9.25
Wayne Pecena

The Society of Broadcast Engineers (SBE) was organized in 1964 and is the only member organization solely devoted to furthering and representing the interests of broadcast engineering and related media technology fields. The society represents over 5,000 members in more than 100 local chapters by offering a wide range of services and programs to the radio broadcast, TV broadcast, and media technology community, whether the member be a beginner or experienced professional.

The SBE certification program is one of the most visible programs offered by the Society, with more than 4,000 active certifications in place. Prior to the early 1980s, a Federal Communications Commission (FCC) first-class operators license was the benchmark for substantiating the knowledge and skill level of the broadcast engineer. In 1981, the FCC eliminated the requirement for a broadcast engineer to hold a first-class license. The responsibility for evaluating an engineer's skill and competence fell on the shoulders of the station license holder. Initiated in 1976, the SBE certification program was developed and has become the premier broadcast technology certification program in the industry. The SBE certification program seeks to raise the status of the broadcast and media technology professional by providing standards for professional competence. The program also seeks to encourage continuation of professional development through recognition of demonstrated knowledge, experience, and responsible conduct.

Annual compensation surveys conducted by SBE have shown that those holding SBE certifications receive higher annual median pay than those noncertified. Results of the SBE 2017 *Compensation Survey* demonstrated a 27% higher salary for radio technology professionals holding SBE certification.

That SBE National Certification Committee provides oversight and guidance to the SBE certification director, who carries out the program on a daily basis. Fifteen SBE certifications are available, ranging from the beginner operator level to the professional broadcast engineering level, with focus on both radio and TV fields. The certified radio operator (CRO), the certified broadcast technologist (CBT), the certified audio engineer (CEA), the certified senior radio engineer (CSRE), and the certified professional broadcast engineer (CPBE) are among the certification levels offered by the SBE. In addition, specialty endorsements are available in several fields that include AM directional specialist (AMD), 8-VSB specialist (8-VSB), and digital radio broadcast specialist (DRB). The certified broadcast network engineer (CBNE) designation is the latest certification offering and recognizes the importance and growth of information technology in the industry. Demonstration of technical knowledge through a structured testing program is the foundation of all levels of certification. The more advanced certification levels also have experience requirements.

Certifications are valid for a period of five years. Renewal of SBE certifications can be achieved through retesting or through documented participation in continuing education and professional development activities. Certification credit requirements vary based upon the class of certification. Credits are organized in several classes to ensure that well-rounded professional activities are attended and can be earned through participation in a wide variety of activities and events at the national, regional, and local levels. Activities such as attending recognized national conferences, attending regional SBE events, or attending local SBE chapter meetings qualify for certification credit. Credit can be earned by publishing a technical article, delivering a technical presentation, attending a manufacturer technical class, or participating in any SBE continuing education event, whether in-person or online.

Professional development programs are a cornerstone of services offered by the SBE. Programs available include more than 50 online webinars, 15 online SBE University classes, and in-person presentations offered throughout the country. The Ennes Workshop conducted each year during the National Association of Broadcasters (NAB) annual convention is one of the premier professional development offerings of the SBE in cooperation with NAB.

SBE, in cooperation with its Ennes Educational Foundation Trust, presents regional Ennes workshops, which are often sponsored by state broadcast associations or local SBE chapters. These workshops are conducted throughout the year at numerous locations. The Trust memorializes Harold E. Ennes, who authored more than 10 textbooks on broadcast engineering and communications. His work contributed immensely to the establishment of the SBE certification program. In addition to conducting workshops, the Ennes Educational Foundation Trust offers scholarships to deserving candidates who aspire to a career in the technical aspects of broadcasting.

SBE educational programs range from topics of interest to the beginner in the field as well as to those focused on furthering the knowledge of the seasoned broadcast or media technology professional. The three-day SBE leadership development course, held each summer, is a unique professional development program focused on preparing the technology professional for leadership and management roles in the industry.

Additional programs and opportunities offered to the SBE membership include legislative representation, the annual compensation survey, group insurance, frequency-coordination services, and online job-opportunity listing and résumé-posting services. The SBE Store offers a wide range of technology books at discount prices, certification preparation guides (SBE CertPreview), operator handbooks, and numerous SBE logo items. The SBE membership and certification lapel pins are popular items to recognize membership and one's SBE certification accomplishments.

The broadcast and media technology industry is rapidly changing. The migration of the broadcast technical plant to an informational technology–based infrastructure has been the most dominant technology shift. Many functions of the traditional broadcast plant can now be performed in the "cloud." The workforce profile is also changing as the broadcast professional is "graying." The SBE 2017 *Compensation Survey* indicated that 70% of survey respondents had between 36 and 40 years of experience and ranged in age from 59 to 64. Whereas this aging demographic might present a challenge for an employer who is seeking experienced technology professionals today, it also provides insight into future opportunities for younger persons to enter the industry.

Don't overlook future opportunities in the technology side of the business. Today, the SBE serves members in a wide range of technology fields ranging from the studio audio production operator to the chief engineer in the radio, TV, cable, and post-production media-related fields. SBE has provided over 50 years of service to these technology fields. It remains well positioned to continue offering services and programs focused on serving the broadcast and media technology communities for the next 50 years.

Consider joining the SBE. Student memberships at reduced pricing are available and student members are welcome to participate in local SBE chapters located across the U.S. The SBE website (www.sbe.org) provides a wealth of information regarding SBE programs and services. Stay in touch with the SBE through social media outlets Facebook, LinkedIn, and Twitter. The SBE national office is located in Indianapolis, Indiana, and may be contacted by email at executivedir@sbe.org, by telephone at 317–846–9000, or by mail at:

**FIGURE 9.26**
Society of Broadcast Engineers logo
Source: Courtesy of SBE

> Society of Broadcast Engineers Inc.
> 9102 North Meridian Street, Suite 150
> Indianapolis, IN 46260

**Wayne M. Pecena** is the Interim Director of Educational Broadcast Services at Texas A&M University and serves as the Director of Engineering for public broadcasting stations KAMU TV and FM. Pecena has over 40 years of broadcast engineering experience and holds BS and MS degrees from Texas A&M University. He is a fellow of the SBE and holds certified professional broadcast engineer and certified broadcast network engineer certifications with AMD, 8-VSB, and DRB specialty endorsements. Pecena serves as Secretary of the SBE Board of Directors and chairs the Education Committee. The Society recognized him as the 2012 SBE Educator of the Year; in 2014 he was named *Radio World* "Engineer of the Year." He is a frequent industry speaker on IP networking topics for broadcast and media technology professionals. Pecena began his career in broadcast engineering as a student technician in 1973 while attending Texas A&M University.

In the aftermath of deregulation the prospective engineer came under even closer scrutiny by station management. The day when a "1st phone" was enough to get an engineering job is gone. There is no direct "ticket" anymore. As in most other areas of radio, skill, experience, and training open the doors the widest.

The landscape of radio changed once again with passage of the Telecommunications Act of 1996. As a result station clusters abound. This means a chief engineer or director of a cluster's technical operation has formidable responsibilities. Instead of keeping one station on the air, this person may have as many as eight signals to watch over. In cluster operations, there may be several experienced engineers on site or one senior engineer who directs the duties of several techs and producers.

## THE EMERGENCY ALERT SYSTEM

Much has changed in the way broadcasters provide information to the public in times of threats to life and property. The Conelrad (for Control of Electromagnetic Radiation) system of public alerting came into existence following World War II as the nation and the world entered the nuclear age. Its 1963 successor, the Emergency Broadcast System (EBS), empowered the U.S. president to take control of electronic communications in the event of war or national emergency. A 1976 revision to the system endorsed its use during state and local emergencies, and in many parts of the U.S. activation of the EBS became commonplace during times of threatening weather. The role of EBS was thus enlarged so as to provide not just the president but also heads of state and local government with a protocol for communicating with the public in the event of a major emergency. By the 1990s, EBS too was viewed as outmoded. Rapid advancement and deployment of digital technologies underscored the need for a next-generation, automated warning system.

**FIGURE 9.27**

EAS receiver activity, as logged on receiver hardware

Source: Courtesy of Entercom Radio Memphis

**FIGURE 9.28**
This transmitter user-interface screen offers both local and remote site control capabilities, including the instrumentation and monitoring functions

Source: Courtesy of Nautel

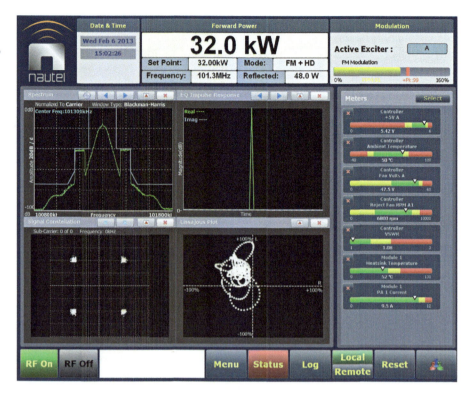

In response in 1994 the FCC announced the Emergency Alert System (EAS) as the successor to the EBS. Initially intended to layer the fundamental mission of the EBS over a modernized distribution system, today the FCC describes EAS on its website as:

> a national public warning system that requires broadcasters, cable television systems, wireless cable systems, satellite digital audio radio service (SDARS) providers, and direct broadcast satellite (DBS) providers to provide the communications capability to the President to address the American public during a national emergency. The system also may be used by state and local authorities to deliver important emergency information, such as AMBER alerts and weather information targeted to specific areas.

The FCC, in conjunction with the Federal Emergency Management Agency (FEMA) and the National Oceanic and Atmospheric Administration's National Weather Service (NWS), implements the EAS at the federal level. The president has sole responsibility for determining when the EAS will be activated at the national level, and has delegated this authority to the director of FEMA. National-level activation of the EAS, tests, and exercises falls under FEMA purview. The NWS develops emergency weather information to alert the public about imminent dangerous weather conditions. The FCC's role includes prescribing rules that establish technical standards for the EAS, procedures for EAS participants to follow in the event the EAS is activated, and EAS testing protocols. Additionally, the FCC ensures that the EAS state and local plans developed by industry conform to FCC EAS rules and regulations. The Federal Emergency Management Agency (FEMA) makes funds available to private and commercial stations designated to remain on the air before, during, and after an authentic emergency through the Broadcast Station Protection Plan. Broadcast facilities that cooperatively participate with FEMA in this arrangement are termed primary entry point (PEP) stations. According to the FEMA website:

> Primary Entry Point (PEP) stations are private or commercial radio broadcast stations that cooperatively participate with FEMA to provide emergency alert and warning information to the public before, during, and after incidents and disasters. The FEMA PEP stations also serve as the primary source of initial broadcast for a Presidential Emergency Alert Notification (EAN). PEP stations are equipped with back-up communications equipment and power generators designed to enable them to continue broadcasting

FIGURE 9.29
Rack-mountable LPFM transmitter
Source: Courtesy of Crown Broadcast IREC

information to the public during and after an event. The Integrated Public Alert and Warning System (IPAWS) Program Management Office (PMO) expanded the number of participating broadcast stations across the nation to directly cover over 90 percent of the U.S. population. PEP station expansion will help ensure that under all conditions the President of the United States can alert and warn the public.

EAS administrators continuously seek and embrace enhancements to the system, as well as any relevant innovations and revisions to procedures. A nationwide system test conducted in 2011 revealed weaknesses in the system, notably the fact that some stations were not within the reception range of a PEP station. A subsequent national test occurred in September 2016. On its website FEMA published a list of "key successes" derived from its assessment of the outcomes, including:

- A majority of stations reported a clean, clear, and easily understandable audio message.
- Some stations broadcasting in Spanish were able to select and play the Spanish language version of the test message.
- Use of the National Periodic Test event code allowed the test to occur without alarming the public
- The test elevated public awareness, providing important information on EAS within the landscape of public alert and warning.

Approximately 88% of participating stations nationwide successfully received and relayed the test message.

Another instance of innovation was FEMA's 2013 addition of Premiere Radio Networks as a PEP facility. Programming supplied by this iHeartmedia-owned subsidiary is estimated to reach more than 190 million listeners each week. In sum, EAS remains a system under scrutiny and evaluation as world events, such as 9/11, the hurricanes Harvey, Irma and Maria, and devastating tornadoes in Alabama, Missouri, and Oklahoma increase the need for an effective emergency alert system. In a related development, the U.S. Senate's 2017 passage of the Securing Access to Networks in Disasters (SANDy) Act confirmed "first informer" status on radio broadcasters. Dennis Wharton, the National Association of Broadcasters (NAB) Executive Vice-President of Communications, observed,

As Hurricanes Harvey and Irma have demonstrated, hometown radio and TV stations play a lifesaving role as 'first informers' during times of emergencies, and this legislation will provide local broadcasters with access to vital resources to stay on the air when disaster strikes.

At the time of press the "SANDy Act" was awaiting President Trump's signature.

The *EAS Operating Handbook* states in summary form the actions to be taken by personnel at EAS Participant facilities upon receipt of an EAN (Emergency Action Notification), an EAT (Emergency Action Termination), tests, or state and local area alerts. It is issued by the FCC and contains instructions for the above situations. The publication was last revised in 2017. Stations must maintain the *Handbook* at normal duty positions or EAS equipment locations when an operator is required to be on duty and it must be immediately available to staff responsible for authenticating messages and initiating actions (see 70 FR 71033, November 25, 2005).

**FIGURE 9.30**

AM and FM transmitter operating parameters are indicated by this software-based monitoring system. Sensors measure power levels, AM antenna radiating patterns, the integrity of FM transmission-line pressure, and the function of the tower light beacons. This product automatically notifies a station engineer by telephone if any parameter exceeds prescribed tolerances

Source: Courtesy of Entercom Radio Memphis

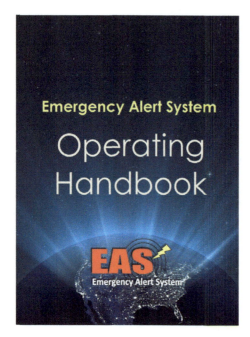

**FIGURE 9.31**

Cover of the 2017 *EAS Operating Handbook*

Source: Courtesy of the FCC; pdf download available at www.fcc.gov/general/eas-test-reporting-system

## AUTOMATION

The FCC's decision in the mid-1960s to require AM/FM operations in markets with populations of more than 100,000 to originate separate programming services 50% of the time provided significant impetus to efforts aimed at automating the radio broadcast. FM stations at this time generally were not profitable. As a result many combo stations, as they were called, had been simulcasting their AM programming over their FM signals to curtail programming expenses. Following more than two decades of the nonduplication prohibition, in the late 1980s the FCC eliminated many of the rules pertaining to this practice. Subsequently a number of stations resorted to simulcasting, this time as a means of coping with the realities of fierce competition and a declining AM market.

One typical response by stations to comply with the nonduplication rule yet keep expenses down was to automate their FM stations. Interestingly, automated FM broadcasts, which generally emphasized the presentation of large blocks of unannounced recordings in contrast to the constant deejay patter characteristic of many AM stations, actually helped the developing medium. FM stations began to assert their "personality," along the way attracting loyal devotees and attracting advertisers. By the late 1970s FM broadcasting, with its high-fidelity, stereophonic reproduction capabilities, surpassed AM in listenership.

Criss Onan, an active veteran of automation equipment sales and former broadcaster, recalls this time period as an era of reversal of fortunes. With the ascendancy of interest in FM, station owners veered from automation, returning their stations to live-talent operation in pursuit of increased revenues. AM stations, on the other hand, began what was to become a long path of descent, the result of audience defection. Onan recalls:

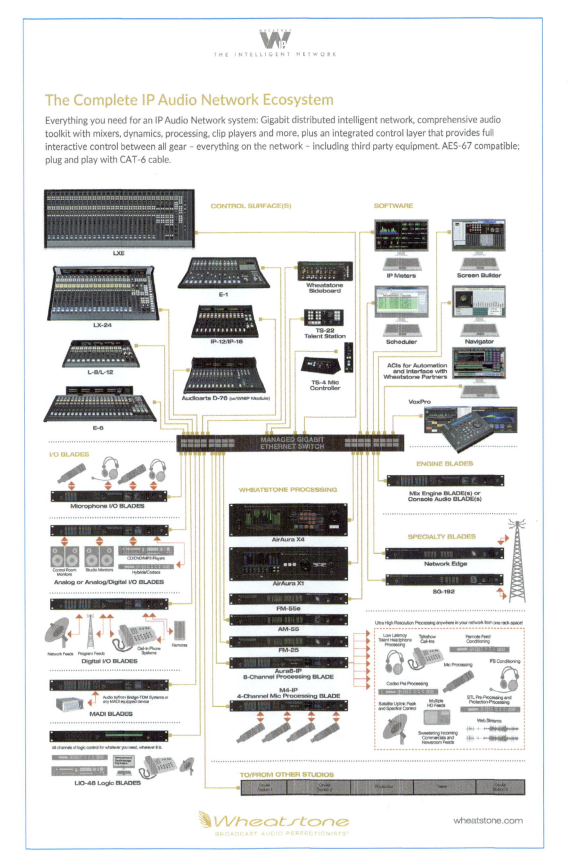

**FIGURE 9.32**

This protocol for networking studios provides flexibility for managing operations in station clusters

Source: Courtesy of Wheatstone

The declining listening to AM stations caused owners to investigate more cost-effective ways to produce programming. Programming services were created to utilize lowering satellite time rates to deliver 24/7 long-form music programming in several different formats. Although personal computers (PCs) were relatively expensive, station owners deployed them to insert local advertising spots in satellite program commercial breaks. The FCC's relaxation of ownership limits spurred increased sales of hard-drive automation systems. Being able to record an advertising spot once and have it instantly available in any studio for any station was much more efficient than having numerous tape decks with multiple tape copies of the same spot.

Prior to the arrival of PC-based automation, purchasing a tape-based, electromechanically operated system represented a substantial economic investment. Automation's appeal to owners, despite its hefty up-front expense, was economy: its use enabled managers to save money by cutting station staffing expenses. Onan cites the declining cost of PC-based systems as an instigator for the increase in automation utilization. "Today," he estimates, "almost all stations use hard drive-based automation systems." Another economic incentive that spurred interest in cost-reducing automation systems, Onan explains, was

the US economic recession in the late 2000s, which caused a significant advertising revenue reduction for most stations. Combined with high debt service from escalating station sale values, owners have aggressively consolidated station operations. This has caused a loss of jobs in the industry.

Owners embraced technology as a way to improve voice-talent productivity. "Voice-tracks in some dayparts on commonly owned stations in a market are now frequently recorded by the same talent," Onan observes. This mode of operation is not isolated solely to stations within a cluster. He continues, "Talent may also record voice tracks for the owner's other markets. Even independently contracted talent, producing content from home studios, is being used. This is possible using moderately fast Internet connections."

Automated stations, it must be observed, are not full walk-away operations. They employ operators as well as announcers and production people to oversee activities. The extent to which a station uses automation often directly influences its staffing needs. Obviously, a fully automated station will employ

**FIGURE 9.33**
New product designs undergo extensive testing in the Wheatstone Sound Lab
Source: Courtesy of Wheatstone

fewer programming people than a partially automated outlet. In the early days of PC automation, production of entertainment programming benefited from online connectivity; the Internet has similarly assisted in enhancing other station operations, which have since tapped into the web's capabilities for the convenience and versatility it offers. Criss Onan observes that program production was the first aspect of operations to be improved by the use of PC-based automation. Yet, this was merely the beginning of the revolution. He reflects on the changes to other aspects of station operation that have occurred:

> The production of advertising spots is being consolidated to regional centers by some owners as is the gathering, generation, and delivery of news. Scheduling of advertising spots and music is also being consolidated to regional centers or even national centers by owners. Stations in all size markets may be minimally staffed or entirely unstaffed during some dayparts such as overnights and weekends. Transmitter remote control systems automatically contact an on-call, designated operator if a parameter exceeds a specified tolerance.

What form will the next-generation automation system take? "In the future," Onan speculates, "scheduling and automation play-out functions may reside in the Internet 'cloud' hosted by service providers rather than provided by technical infrastructure at the radio station's site."

## CHAPTER HIGHLIGHTS

1. AM stations are assigned frequencies between 535 and 1705 kHz, with 10 kHz separations between frequencies. AM is disrupted by low-frequency emissions, can be blocked by irregular topography, and can travel hundreds of mile along surface level ground waves, or thousands of miles along nighttime sky waves.

2. Because AM station signals travel greater distances at night, to avoid skywave interference more than 2,000 stations around the country must cease operation near sunset. Thousands more must make substantial nighttime transmission adjustments (decrease power), and others (directional stations) must use two or more antennas to shape the pattern of their radiation.

3. FM stations are assigned frequencies between 88.1 and 107.9 MHz, with 200 kHz separations between frequencies. FM is static free, with direct waves (line-of-sight) carrying 80–100 miles. Both AM and FM stations are licensed for eight years as of this writing.

4. To guarantee efficient use of the broadcast spectrum and to minimize station-to-station interferences, the FCC established three classifications for AM stations and eight classifications for FM. Lower-classification stations are obligated to avoid interference with higher-classification stations. Recent FCC actions have created more subclassifications.

5. FM translators are low-powered transmitters used initially to extend the coverage of full-powered FM stations into hard-to-reach areas. More recently, translators assist AM stations to overcome coverage deficiencies and to enable AM daytimers to offer nighttime service.

6. Satellite radio employs both geosynchronous (XM) and elliptical (Sirius) orbits from more than 22,000 miles in space. When necessary, ground repeaters are used to strengthen signals.

7. The digital audio technology trademarked as HD Radio enhances the listening experience, offering superior frequency response and greater dynamic range. New spectrum space may be allocated to accommodate the digital service. Industry observers are divided in their opinions as to when HD Radio will supplant analog transmission.

**FIGURE 9.34**
An electro-mechanical controller sequenced the playback of analog reel-to-reel and cartridge tapes in this 1970s-era automation system
Source: Courtesy of Chuck Conrad, Chalk Hill Educational Media Inc.

8. Educational opportunities for prospective broadcast engineers include programs of instruction offered by colleges and universities, trade and technical schools and the Society of Broadcast Engineers (SBE).

9. A station's chief engineer (chief operator) needs experience with basic broadcast electronics and information technology, as well as a knowledge of the FCC regulations affecting the station's technical operation. The chief must install, maintain, and adjust equipment, and perform weekly inspections and calibrations. Other duties may include training techs, planning maintenance schedules, and handling a budget.

10. Program syndicators utilize Internet, ISDN, and satellite technologies to affiliated stations. In some instances the program content includes embedded automation-control information enabling affiliates to operate unattended.

11. The Emergency Alert System (EAS) (formerly the Emergency Broadcast System [EBS]), implemented after World War II, provides the president of the United States with a means of communicating with the public in an emergency. Over time, the role of the service has been expanded to include information about severe weather and, more recently, AMBER alerts. Stations must follow rigid instructions both during periodic tests of the system and during actual emergencies.

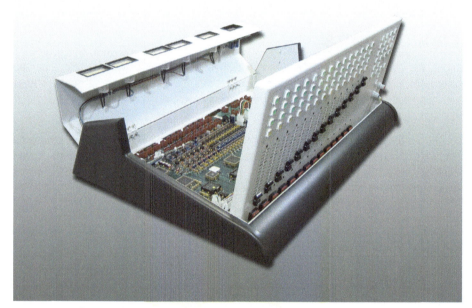

**FIGURE 9.35**
The engineer's view: a peek "under the hood" of a broadcast console
Source: Courtesy of Arrakis Systems

12. Many of today's commercial stations are fully or partially automated. Computer-assisted automation reduces staffing costs but requires investment in equipment. Automated programming elements are aired when metadata embedded with audio files issue commands to execute file playout. At many stations, satellite programming services use computers (at both uplink and downlink sites) to control station automation systems.

13. Direct satellite-fed stations need little equipment because programming originates at the syndicator's studios.

14. The FCC requires that a station's license and the permits of its operators be accessible in the station area.

# SUGGESTED FURTHER READING

Abel, J.D. and Ducey, R.V., *Gazing into the Crystal Ball: A Radio Station Manager's Technological Guide to the Future*, NAB, Washington, D.C., 1987.

Antebi, E., *The Electronic Epoch*, Van Nostrand Reinhold, New York, NY, 1982.

Butler, A., *Practical Tips for Choosing and Using Consulting and Contract Engineers*, NAB, Washington, D.C., 1994.

Cheney, M., *Tesla: Man out of Time*, Prentice Hall, Englewood Cliffs, NJ, 1983.

Considine, D.M. (ed.), *Van Nostrand's Scientific Encyclopedia*, Van Nostrand Reinhold, New York, NY, 1983.

Davidson, F.P., *Macro: A Clear Vision of How Science and Technology Will Shape Our Future*, William Morrow, New York, NY, 1983.

Ebersole, S., *Broadcast Technology Worktext*, Focal Press, Boston, MA, 1992.

Grant, A.E., *Communication Technology Update*, Focal Press, Boston, MA, 1995.

Hilliard, R.L., *FCC Primer*, Focal Press, Boston, MA, 1991.

Hoeg, W. and Lauterbach, T. (eds.), *Digital Broadcast Audio: Principles and Application of Digital Radio*, 2nd edition, Wiley, Hoboken, NJ, 2003.

Hong, S., *From Marconi's Black-Box to the Audion*, MIT Press, Cambridge, MA, 2001.

Mirabito, M. and Morgenstern, B., *The New Communication Technologies*, 2nd edition, Focal Press, Boston, MA, 1994.

Morton, D.L., Jr., *Sound Recording: The Life Story of a Technology*, Johns Hopkins University Press, Baltimore, MD, 2006.

National Association of Broadcasters, *Broadcast Engineering*, NAB, Washington, D.C., 2008.

Noll, E.M., *Broadcast Radio and Television Handbook*, 6th edition, Howard Sams, Indianapolis, IN, 1983.

Priestman, C., *Web Radio: Radio Production for Internet Streaming*, Focal Press, Boston, MA, 2005.

Reed, J.H., *Software Radio: A Modern Approach to Radio Engineering*, Prentice Hall, Englewood Cliffs, NJ, 2002.

Regal, B., *Radio: The Life Story of a Technology*, Greenwood, Westport, CT, 2005.

Reitz, J.R., *Foundations of Electromagnetic Theory*, Addison-Wesley, Reading, MA, 1960.

Roberts, R.S., *Dictionary of Audio, Radio, and Video*, Butterworths, Boston, MA, 1981.

Sarkar, T.K, Mailloux, R., Oliner, A.A., Salazar-Palma, M., and Sangupta, D.L., *History of Wireless*, Wiley-IEEE Press, Hoboken, NJ, 2006.

Starr, W., *Electrical Wiring and Design: A Practical Approach*, John Wiley & Sons, New York, NY, 1983.

Watkinson, J., *The Art of Digital Audio*, Focal Press, Boston, MA, 1992.

Wilson, D., *A Broadcast Engineering Tutorial for Non-Engineers*, NAB, Washington, D.C., 1999.

Wurtzler, S.J., *Electronic Sounds: Technological Change and the Rise of Corporate Mass Media*, Columbia University Press, New York, NY, 2007.

# CHAPTER 10

# Careers

## OVERVIEW

As heard over the radio airwaves of Kansas City on a recent Saturday morning . . .

*It's straight-up 8 o'clock, and it's time to plug in your ears to the hottest hour in radio: Generation Rap! Kansas City's number one teen talk show! Starring K.C.-area high school students. We're talking about major topics affecting today's generation. Now, get ready to build your mad skills, and speak your mind: It's Generation Rap!*

For 30 years and counting that's the greeting that kicks off Saturday morning for radio listeners across Kansas City. It's *Generation Rap*. Beamed over the 100,000-watt powerhouse signal of Hot 103 Jamz! KPRS, the show is topical, meaningful, and thoughtful. For many, it's simply an event the media refer to as *appointment listening*. Most importantly, *Generation Rap* is created, produced, and hosted by *teens*.

Viewed from a cultural media perspective, *Generation Rap* exemplifies the power and ability of radio to bring together neighborhood voices in open discussion of community issues. At the same time, the middle high- and high-schoolers who produce the show get an up-close and personal view of how radio broadcasting works.

Robyn King-Knight, an on-air radio personality on Hot 103 Jamz, is one of the *Generation Rap* mentors. *Generation Rap*, she explains, has origins at a legendary station noted as a Kansas City institution for public service broadcasting. "Carter Broadcast Group (licensee of Hot 103 Jamz! KPRS), she says, "has been on air since 1951" and for more than 60+ years the station has been "dedicated to giving the community a voice," allowing not only "teen voices to be heard but also the communities' voices, which was the intent on the creation of the show."

One of the principal benefits of participating with the show, she says, is that it opens doors to broadcasting careers for students. It's an activity that provides opportunities for participants to develop their skills in public speaking, writing, and production. "The radio station allows the students to take over the airwaves for an entire hour to discuss issues that they would probably never be able to simply discuss at home or at school and with a large listening audience."

Beyond their acquisition of these benefits, King-Knight observes that participants "learn software editing skills, host events around the city, and are invited as special guests to engagements. The skills students acquire from being in this prestigious group are endless to their future endeavors." King-Knight adds,

*The first-hand experience the teens get behind the microphone prepares them for careers in this industry. The teens have to keep the conversation going on air, which is difficult even for professionals at times. Many of the past students on Generation Rap have continued at Hot 103 Jamz. Nighttime deejay Taylor Made and Promotions crew member Nycko Vice have joined the team at the radio station where they started. Nycko Vice was a former host for Generation Rap and his enthusiastic voice on air has crossed over to helping in the promotion of the station. Taylor Made continues to give back by providing social media advice to students to promote Generation Rap. Another former host, Archie J, can be heard as Morning Co-Host and Producer of "The Susan Show" on WBNQ 101.5 in Bloomington, Illinois.*

She concludes by noting that many students

continue pursuing radio in college and many students work on their college radio station prior to graduation and moving into the industry. The students get a taste of radio personality life by becoming known in their schools and around the community. They also get to interview popular personalities and this makes them feel if they can interview a top artist or political figure then they can do anything. The confidence that is gained as a *Generation Rap* participant is invaluable.

**FIGURE 10.1**
Robyn King-Knight

Source: Photo Credit:
Royal Photography

## GENERATION RAP

### Robyn King-Knight

*Generation Rap* is a teen leadership radio program, aired at 8 am CT every Saturday since December 12, 1987, sponsored by Carter Broadcast Group on Hot 103 Jamz KPRS 103.3FM in Kansas City, Missouri. 2017 commemorated the thirtieth anniversary of *Generation Rap*. The show was originally conceived by Carl Boyd, Prim Carter Williams, and Jim "Grand Dad" Nunnelly. *Generation Rap* has received several national awards, including a literacy award from the Missouri State Teachers Association.

The *Generation Rap* show is produced by area middle-school and high-school teenagers who choose their own topics, host the show, and discuss the topic live and openly on KPRS. First, student producers are assigned a show topic and required to find guests to support the topic and an expert in the field to provide credibility. An outline of the show is also required that includes the questions that the student producers researched to ask of the show guest. A preproduction meeting is held during the week to allow the students and the guest to run through how the show will operate for the Saturday live show. Then on Saturday everyone arrives and the show goes live.

Although students are learning the knowledge for radio programing such as producer skills, speaking skills, broadcast writing skills, and communication skills, students from this program can use these vital skills in any profession of their choice after college. The show gives students opportunities to interview high-profile individuals such as social activists, sport figures, entertainers, and political figures. This also exposes students to these careers and past students have become some of the political and entertainers now being interviewed by current students. The show covers a vast array of topics from politics and health issues to entertainment and sports. *Generation Rap* is also a proponent for encouraging not only the students involved but also the listeners to pursue college by providing shows detailing how to apply to college or how to obtain college funding, broadcasting live from scholarship fairs.

As radio broadcasting and journalism has evolved over the years with the addition of social media there have been additions to the show. *Generation Rap* now has Twitter, Facebook, Instagram, and SoundCloud accounts to replay past shows. The students promote the show on these social media outlets to increase listenership and make listeners aware of the week's topics. Students also use the live feature on Facebook for listeners to view the behind-the-scenes aspect of the show.

In addition to the radio show, students learn software editing skills, host events around the city, and are invited as special guests to engagements. The skills students acquire from being in this prestigious group are endless to their future endeavors. Carter Broadcast Group provides an opportunity that instills valuable knowledge to the students involved in *Generation Rap*. The show has been strong for 30 years, assisting young people to achieve their dreams. I also thank *Generation Rap* for helping me see the passion I have for students' learning that sparked my educator profession. To another 30 years.

---

**Robyn King-Knight** is an on-air radio personality on Hot 103 Jamz with 20 years' experience in radio broadcasting. She graduated with a BA from the University of Missouri-Columbia, holds a Master of Arts in teaching from the University of Central Missouri, and is completing her doctoral degree. King-Knight held the position of Broadcast Vice-President for the Kansas City Association of Black Journalists (KCABJ) for 10 years. She teaches college and high school courses in English, media, and journalism, including yearbook, online, newspaper, broadcast, and photojournalism.

# RADIO AS A CAREER

Participating in a teen-produced show such as *Generation Rap* is just one of many ways for students to discover and learn about career possibilities in radio. Other high-school students take advantage of programs of instruction in radio broadcasting, and often get on-the-job training in laboratory stations, both online and terrestrial. Career days, in which station management invites high school and college stations to visit—and perhaps intern—at their facilities, also provide insight into the possibility of career pursuits.

Thus, the purpose of this chapter—appearing for the first time in *The Radio Station*—is twofold. The first purpose is to present information intended to inform readers about the various opportunities for employment the industry has to offer and help them decide where they want their place in this industry to be. The second is to provide a forum for the voices of several entry-level "high-achievers" to share stories about how they achieved early success in the profession.

## FARBER'S RULES

### Erica Farber

1. The best person does get the job. Be that person!

2. Do your homework. Learn about the company before your first interview and make sure it's a potential fit.

3. There are good bosses and bad bosses—look for best practices.

4. You will not always get what you want so do not complain. Ask for constructive feedback.

5. Stay out of office politics.

6. SHOW UP! Be on time and always be consistent!

7. Have a sense of humor. Don't take yourself too seriously.

8. Treat people the way you want to be treated.

9. Ask for what you want, and be specific.

10. Men and women process information differently: women revisit decisions; men decide and move on.

11. Work hard; don't just call it in.

12. Don't pretend if you don't know something. Ask questions; not knowing is not a weakness.

13. Don't be afraid to make mistakes—decisions and growth depend on them.

14. Friends vs. co-workers: Socialize with friends; work toward respect with co-workers.

15. Balance sheets are the lifeblood of business. Learn to read profit-and-loss statements. Learn to understand budgets.

16. Continue to learn—be open-minded.

17. Have a plan. Set goals and update constantly. Careers need planning; jobs don't.

18. Learn the difference between public and private: information shared online never goes away.

19. Use good phone etiquette. Phones are phones—leave messages. Check your own phone regularly.

20. Develop outside interests. It makes you a more interesting person.

21. Be trustworthy. If you are not trusted, you won't be respected.

22. Get involved. Make a difference. Involvement exposes you to people you wouldn't otherwise be exposed to.

23. Learn to handle stress: it will always be in your life.

24. Be true to yourself.

25. Never compromise your belief system.

Compiled and edited by Dr. William Dorman, Millersville University

---

**Erica Farber** is President and CEO of the Radio Advertising Bureau.

Sharply focused in its objective to educate Gen Z readers about preparing for their careers, this chapter showcases the voices of industry professionals working in their first, full-time positions in station programming, sales, promotion and engineering. Essayists speak about their career inspirations and examine the methods and strategies they employed in securing their positions. Their viewpoints offer personal anecdotes and expressions of opinion about the roles they play in four essential areas of station operations and are intended to offer firsthand insight into the business they've elected as their career choice. Each essayist concludes by noting that employment in the industry continues to reward them with personal satisfaction. It's a profession where creative, self-motivated individuals with talents for communication, persuasion, and technical ability find opportunities to blossom and thrive, and the experiences to be challenging and fulfilling. Recent entrants into the profession affirm a conclusion drawn by Nielsen Audio: the medium continues to be a vibrant and important medium for more than 92% of American teen and adult listeners. In an age where the number of listening choices and platforms are greater than at any time in history, AM/FM stations continue to demonstrate the ability to reinvent, innovate, and connect with listeners.

What might not be as well known is the variety of employment opportunities beyond that of the deejay that radio has to offer. "Behind-the-mic" positions in news and sports broadcasting continue to entice young people to pursue the profession. The need for talented, creative persons in the behind-the-scenes

**FIGURE 10.3**
Trevor Morgan accepts the National Association of Broadcasters' 2016 NAB Marconi Award for Rock Station of the Year on behalf of Zimmer Radio and Marketing Group and Classic Rock 96.7 KCMQ

Source: Courtesy of NAB and ZRMG

roles of show producers also are in this mix. Although not regarded as "on-air" positions, program, music, and news directors, sound board operators, and production assistants serve in vital capacities supporting the overall sound product of stations.

As a medium for delivering advertising messages, radio can be the career where business-minded students excel in station sales, marketing, and promotion departments. Increasingly, as stations embrace and exploit social media, the need for personnel to manage websites and oversee social media activities rises accordingly. The transition from analog to digital technologies has paved the way for employees educated in computer science and information technology.

**FIGURE 10.4**
Trevor Morgan

## PASSION

### Trevor Morgan

In a word, the thing that helped drive me to get my first broadcasting job was *passion*.

I was in my junior year of college when I found my passion for radio. I became obsessed with learning as much and I could about how radio works, and what it takes to be a great radio talent.

I started in the classroom by absorbing as much knowledge as I could on how to show prep, edit audio, write commercial copy, understand what ratings meant, and comprehend how radio worked as a business. I spent as much time as possible in the student radio station, taking as many shifts as I could, hopping onto others' talk shows, and even creating my own nerd-focused talk show.

Once I felt confident enough in my abilities, I went to find a part-time job at a commercial radio station. I found it at Pure Country C106.1 KWKZ in Cape Girardeau, Missouri. I had a weekend shift every other Saturday. Keep in mind, I hated country music. But my love for radio pushed me to keep at it. I even got permission to come in during the week when I could and observe the day-to-day operation of a radio station . . . for free!

As I finished my education I went home to St. Louis and got a production internship with Emmis Communications. There I was able to continue learning the ins and outs of the broadcast profession while making connections with people who could help me find my first job.

When the time came to start applying to radio stations and groups, I knew that it was competitive. If I wanted to get my first full-time radio gig I'd have to be willing to move wherever the job was. I was fortunate to find a job opening in Columbia, Missouri, at Zimmer Radio and Marketing Group and they took a chance by hiring me as a production assistant.

It has been over five years since I started at Zimmer Radio and being a radio professional has been even better than I had dreamed. I am now the Program Director and *Morning Show* co-host for Classic Rock 96.7 KCMQ. Along with the help of many at the station I've been a two-time finalist for the Radio Mercury Awards, and our station received the National Association of Broadcasters Marconi Award for Rock Station of the Year.

Passion has been what's driven me and it continues to drive me. I love this industry. I love that I can make listeners' days better. Even when the job requires me to do things I don't want to do, passion makes it easier.

In conclusion, my advice: Master as many skills as you can to make yourself valuable. Ask many questions and learn as much as you can. Keep a positive attitude. No one likes working with a cocky, arrogant downer. And make sure to create a compelling demo of your best work and share it.

Find your passion, and let it drive you.

---

**Trevor Morgan** is employed by Zimmer Radio and Marketing Group in Columbia, Missouri. He is Program Director of Classic Rock 96.7 KCMQ and the co-host of *The Morning Shag with Shags and Trevor*.

A good place to track trends and become more educated about emerging opportunities in radio can be found at the website of the National Association of Broadcasters (NAB) (www.nab.org). The NAB represents the interests of radio and TV broadcasters nationwide. As the principal industry advocate in Washington, D.C., the NAB works on the behalf of broadcasters to create awareness among policymakers. Its efforts help ensure that members of Congress and the Federal Communications Commission (FCC) are informed about issues of listener importance. The NAB Educational Foundation addresses the needs of broadcasters present and future, including its sponsorship of the annual Freedom of Speech Public Service Announcement (PSA) competition that provide scholarships for college students.

**FIGURE 10.5**
Brittney Quarles

## IT'S YOUR CAREER. TAKE CHARGE OF IT!

### Brittney Quarles

As I was growing up music was a backdrop to so many memorable moments in my life. I was hooked from birth and my first boom box. Yes, I am a Millennial who still knows the joy of boom boxes, CD Walkmans, and recording new songs from the radio to tape. I was in awe at the power of radio: how it shaped opinions, lives, and the culture. Naturally, it led me to want to know how it all worked. I am the local sales manager and internship coordinator at Radio One Inc. in Richmond, Virginia. It has been a quick, seven-year journey since my first internship (side note: internships are super important—find them early and submit multiple applications). Truth be told, I never thought about media sales. It was never discussed in my college broadcast courses, and no one I knew was in sales. I always thought I would be in programming. Sometimes you don't know which way your career will go, so be flexible when the opportunity comes.

Life hits you with some defining moments that seem like nothing but change everything. I accepted my first "real job" as a TV sales assistant at a national rep firm six months after my graduation, the same day Sallie Mae started calling (she still calls). I was commuting into Washington, D.C., having lunch in DuPont Circle, and networking at evening happy-hour events—truly "adulting." I didn't love the pay, but I did love the learning curve. One afternoon, about two years in, I walked into my boss's office to ask why I was not being trained for a junior account executive position. She said, "I heard you wanted to get back into radio, so I'm not wasting my time—I won't train you." Shortly afterward I resigned.

I had found my backbone; it was defining moment number one. I learned quickly that the industry is small, so don't burn a bridge (no matter how mad or right you may be). Find someone to be a champion for your talents, and be careful who you share your dreams with.

My next opportunity occurred at Radio One Inc. in Richmond, Virginia. Working for this company was specifically a dream for me. When I started at Radio One Inc. as an account executive my personal challenge was to get promoted within two years to sales management. You're probably thinking that "sales manager" (or anything with a "manager/director" title to it) sounds like fun, more money, somebody's boss, more perks. . . Yeah, but none of that was why I wanted to be in sales management. I was asked "are you sure" more times than I was asked "why do you want to be in management?" They asked me "Are you sure?" because of the stress, the potential to lose money, the level of responsibility, my age. . . It turns out some people genuinely cared about my well-being. I knew I wanted to be in management: to sit at different tables to try to effect change for my local team and our company as a whole. I never let anyone detour my vision; I created a case for myself and learned to ask for a role because I earned it, not because I "deserved" it (even if it's true). No one owes you anything! I also learned to maximize the moment—I had to take a leap! Defining moments two and three.

By now you may be wondering (hopefully) exactly what working in media sales entails. Fundamentally we are charged with keeping our local broadcast stations in business. It's "C.R.E.A.M." (Cash Rules Everything Around Me). You may think, "all day, boring, cold calling, being broke on 100% commission, and pushy sales terms similar to those associated with being a used-car salesman." But media sales has become more than "sales." We are now multimedia marketers who build campaigns to bring clients success via multiple platforms. We sell airtime, events, and sponsorships; we create large-scale activations;

and we build and promote custom content, digital, mobile, social solutions. The list goes on. And we still have fun!

Remember: no matter what path you take in this industry, your personal brand and work ethic will always be important. Something I tell a lot of new sales reps is this: hustle will beat talent when talent doesn't hustle. Don't quote me; I saw that on IG and loved it. But, honestly, don't just rely on talent. Challenge your best, take every opportunity you can get, lead by example and never stop learning! Pay attention to those defining moments in your life and trust the process.

**Brittney Quarles** is Local Sales Manager and Internship Coordinator at Radio One Inc. in Richmond, Virginia. She is responsible for recruiting and developing new talent, leading the local sales team, and increasing annual revenue. *Radio Ink* has recognized Quarles as an "African American Future Leader in Radio" and as one of the "Future Most Influential Women in Radio." She is a proud graduate of Howard University and holds memberships in the Junior League of Richmond and the Urban League Young Professionals. Quarles serves as a Member of the Board for the Central Virginia African American Chamber of Commerce.

A good entryway into understanding what the NAB is and the role it plays in informing and cultivating student interests is found online in its publication, *Careers in Radio*, 2nd edition. In it, author Liz Chuday devotes the first dozen pages to a comprehensive exploration of the numerous employment opportunities at stations. The list is organized along the typical station organizational structure model, with positions categorized by departmental position and accompanied by thumbnail job descriptions. The section "How To Succeed In Radio, From Those Who Have Been There, Done That" is particularly useful. Here, Chuday extends the discussion by providing advice and tips readers can follow when approaching station management for entry-level employment.

**FIGURE 10.6**
University students use hand signals to communicate between studios during a broadcast
Source: Courtesy of Studio École de France and the Telos Alliance

# JOBS AND SALARIES IN RADIO

Today, the radio industry continues to employ tens of thousands of persons. Yet, with all the downsizing in middle- and upper-level management positions that has occurred as a result of ownership consolidation and the continuing emergence of new and competitive audio media, this figure has eroded and likely will continue to do so in the coming years. In 2010, the U.S. Department of Labor reported that the industry profession of radio announcing was a source of nearly 62,000 jobs. That same year the Department predicted a 7% employment growth in the industry from 2010 to 2020. Joel Denver of the industry-observing website AllAccess.com speaks of the techniques for "climbing the ladder" in radio, yet questioned "whether there is still a ladder to climb." Jim Robertson, vice-president of Dix Communication, concurrs, adding, "Consolidation has affected employment for on air positions and promotion jobs due to staffing cutbacks. However, if graduates are willing to hit the streets selling, things are better."

Further, in 2015, the U.S. Department of Labor, in its Occupational Outlook Handbook, noted: "Employment of media and communication occupations is projected to grow 4 percent from 2014 to 2024, which will result in about 27,400 new jobs." The fast-changing media landscape and its transition from legacy AM/FM radio to a digital, multimedia industry means that demand for jobs will "stem from the need to create, edit, translate, and disseminate information through a variety of different platforms," according to the Labor Department.

Careers in radio are very exciting and rewarding, but can also be stressful. In 2017, commenting on the satisfaction that most who enter this profession experience, Fred Jacobs, President of Jacobs Media, said:

> And while income, stress, and environment are all elements that can make broadcasting tenuous at times, my assumption is that *job satisfaction* is what drives many of us to work those long hours. Whether you're playing Country music in afternoon drive in Tucson, hosting "Morning Edition" for the public radio station in Sacramento, or selling time for the Alternative station in Boston, chances are you're challenged, stimulated, and energized by what you're doing.

Jacobs added, "Many in radio get off on entertaining and informing audiences, serving communities, and building great brands. In the radio business, a single person, station, or team can make a big difference." If you possess these attributes, a career in radio may be for you.

Erica Farber, President and CEO of the Radio Advertising Bureau (RAB) cautions that selling is problematic for stations competing against new audio technologies. "We are not making sales calls. We don't know what to say," she admits. "We have to play catch-up a little bit." Nonetheless, she remains optimistic about radio's future. "I still feel very strongly [about the business] and see tremendous opportunity." Wisconsin broadcaster and PD Joe Calgaro laments the diminishing "farm system" for growing talent. "Those who work hard stand out from the pack and succeed," claims Mid-West Family Broadcasting's Susan Groves. The greatest chances for success, opines Kim Guthrie of Cox Media Group, belong to accomplished multitaskers. However, "if graduates are willing to hit the streets selling, things are better."

Fred Jacobs shares Farber's sentiments about a career in radio. In 2017, he conducted an informal survey via social media asking radio professionals about their job satisfaction and whether they had regrets about pursuing a radio career. Although there were some comments about disappointments along people's career, the overwhelming sentiment was that people would choose a career in radio again even despite the challenges. Jacobs found that "some radio vets—even through the tough times, the bad breaks, and the miserable bosses—say they never regret their decision to go into radio." Further, Jacobs says, "many commenters made a point to tell me just how much outright fun they've had throughout their years in radio."

A common misconception is that a radio station consists primarily of deejays, a place where few other job options are available. Wrong! Nothing could be farther from the truth. Granted, deejays comprise an important part of a station's staff, but many other employees are necessary to keep the station on the air. An average-size station in a medium market used to employ between 18 and 26 people, but

FIGURE 10.7
Engineer "rides gain" on deejay mic during a remote broadcast originating from the Bonnaroo Music and Arts Festival
Source: Courtesy of the Telos Alliance

today, owing to consolidation, fewer personnel may be employed when multiple stations form a cluster operation. Stations are usually organized along four major areas of operation: management, sales, programming, and engineering. Each area requires talented, energetic persons to occupy positions where a wide range of skills is needed. The previous chapters in this book bear this out. Proper training and education are necessary to secure a job at most stations, although broadcasters will train people to fill the less-demanding positions. Hundreds of schools and colleges offer courses in radio broadcasting, and most award certificates or degrees. As in most other fields today, the more credentials a job candidate possesses, the better he or she looks to a prospective employer.

Perhaps few other professions weigh practical, hands-on experience as heavily as radio does. This is especially true in the on-air area. On the programming side, it is the individual's sound that wins the job, not the degree. However, it is the formal training and education that usually contribute most directly to the quality of the sound that the program director is looking for when hiring. In reality, not all radio announcers have college degrees (the number is growing), but statistics have shown that those who do stand a better chance of moving into managerial positions.

## HAVE YOU CONSIDERED A CAREER IN ENGINEERING?

### Dominic Mendicino

In the fall of 2007, I would sit at my outdated and worn wooden desk adjacent to my terribly uncomfortable twin-size bed in my freshman dorm room at Columbia College Chicago, and wonder how to break into the audio engineering world as soon as I possibly could. In between classes, and prior to putting on my slightly tarnished Jimmy John's work hat every day, I stared at the list of Chicago recording studio names and phone numbers I created. I called each one of these studios twice a week, the first time I'd say, "Hi, are there any job openings available?" After a firm "NO," I waited a few days and called back asking if there were any internships available and got the same all too familiar response. At that time, all I wanted to do was sit behind an audio console in a recording studio.

A decade later, only a few blocks from where I sat diligently making those phone calls, I'm now a broadcast engineer at CBS Radio. The road I took to my current position was not a planned route by

FIGURE 10.8
Dominic Mendicino

any stretch of the imagination. In fact, I had no idea broadcast engineering was even an option as a career when I was in the classroom or freelancing as a recording engineer.

I finally did end up in a recording studio after a few months and a couple of large phone bills later. The recording studio I started at was on the northwest side of Chicago, called Medicine Man Recording Studio, and this is where it all started for me as a naïve, yet ambitious 18-year-old. I cut my teeth not only making records but ripping the studio apart and putting it back together again, constantly configuring and troubleshooting the systems.

With a firm grasp of the need to diversify my evolving skills, I continuously and ruthlessly sought out opportunities for all things audio engineering. My career has cast a wide net throughout the production world, and I have delved professionally into nearly every corner of the industry. I have traveled the world recording location audio for film, toured the country mixing monitors with pop recording artist Andy Grammer, and installed high-end commercial audio and video systems in some of the biggest venues in Chicago among many other odds and ends freelancing.

One area I hadn't been involved with yet, and always found intriguing, was radio broadcast. I have always had a fascination with the ability to get information to the masses, and the fact that hundreds of thousands of people are listening to the same song or voice at the exact same time absolutely amazes me. In fact, the main goal I pursued while sitting in the recording studio all those years was to one day hear a song over the airwaves that I had worked on.

With no connections to the radio industry, I scoured CBS Radio's job board every day for months and finally found an engineering position I was qualified and eventually hired for. At first, I was hired on as a part-time engineer focusing on remote broadcasts. I began utilizing every single skill I had learned in my previous experiences and very quickly became a strong asset to the company.

I successfully designed and built the systems in the live performance venues at CBS Radio Chicago, New York, Baltimore, and Washington D.C. The processes of building, running, and maintaining performance stages have been a big trend across our company. Each state-of-the-art venue is configured with live audio, recorded audio, full lighting, video, and camera switching systems. With my history in production, I also operate and mix in the Chicago live performance facility. We have had on average 100 performances a year in Chicago for the past four years, including rock artists such as Chris Cornell and pop artists such as Nick Jonas.

After proving myself with the build-outs of those rooms and being in the right place at the right time, I have officially made it into the broadcast engineer role at CBS Radio in Chicago. Again, a field I never really knew existed in college.

Relative to most engineers in radio I am—at age 28—one of the youngest in the industry. As the broadcast engineering population ages, it's only natural that a younger generation will soon take the reins. When I take a look around, it's difficult to see young engineers anywhere, let alone enough to close the gap the older generation is leaving behind. This may lead into an even more specialized field in the future with fewer engineers working on more and more sites.

Although not necessarily a profession taught in school, radio broadcast engineering is a very lucrative career, and will only increase in value as the demand for talent inevitably rises.

_____

**Dominic Mendicino** is a Broadcast Engineer for CBS Radio in Chicago.

Many station managers look for the college-educated person, particularly for the areas of news and sales. Thousands of communications degrees are conferred annually, thus providing the radio industry with a pool of highly educated job candidates. Today, college training is a plus (if not a necessity) when searching for employment in radio. The job application or résumé that lists practical experience in addition to formal training is most appealing. The majority of colleges with radio curricula have stations. These small, often low-powered outlets provide aspiring broadcasters with golden opportunities for gaining some much-needed on-air experience. Some of the nation's foremost broadcasters began their careers at college radio stations. Many of these same schools have internship programs that provide the student with the chance to get important on-the-job training at professional stations. Again, experience is the key, and it rates highly with the prospective employer. Small commercial stations often are willing to hire broadcast students to fill part-time and vacation slots. This constitutes professional experience and is an invaluable addition to the résumé.

Entry-level positions in radio seldom pay well. In fact, many small-market stations pay minimum wage. However, the experience gained at these small-budget operations more than makes up for the meager financial compensation. The first year or two in radio constitutes the dues-paying period, a time in which a person learns the ropes. The small radio station provides inexperienced people with the chance to become involved in all facets of the business. Rarely does a new employee perform only one function. For example, a person hired as a deejay will often prepare and deliver newscasts, will write and produce commercials, and may even sell airtime.

After an employee has advanced past the "dues-paying" stage, what are realistic salary expectations? The answers to that question, of course, depend upon which of the four station categories in which a person is employed.

Industry observer *Inside Radio* last reported salary information in 2014. As expected, the report revealed that compensation awarded to persons in sales and management tended to outpace earners who worked in programming- and engineering-related capacities. According to the national survey average-salary results, station managers, for instance, earned a salary of almost $125,000; sales directors' pay topped out at more than $175,000. The average salary earned by program directors was approximately $90,000, while station engineers were paid, on average, $70,000 annually.

| Occupation | Job Summary | 2016 Median Pay |
|---|---|---|
| Deejays/announcers | Announcers present music, news, and sports and may provide commentary or interview guests about these or other important topics. Some act as masters of ceremonies (emcees) or disc jockeys (deejays) at weddings, parties, or clubs. | $30,830 per year<br>$14.82 per hour |
| Broadcast and sound engineering technicians | Broadcast and sound engineering technicians set up, operate, and maintain the electrical equipment for radio programs, television broadcasts, concerts, sound recordings, and movies. | $42,550 per year<br>$20.46 per hour |
| Reporters, correspondents, and broadcast news analysts | Reporters, correspondents, and broadcast news analysts inform the public about news and events happening internationally, nationally, and locally. They report the news for newspapers, magazines, websites, television, and radio. | $38,870 per year<br>$18.69 per hour |
| Advertising sales agents/account executives | Advertising sales agents sell advertising space to businesses and individuals. They contact potential clients, make sales presentations, and maintain client accounts. Advertising sales agents work under pressure to meet sales quotas. They work in a range of industries, including advertising agencies, radio, television, and Internet publishing. | $50,380 per year<br>$24.22 per hour |

Source: Department of Labor Occupational Outlook Handbook

**FIGURE 10.9**
Kisha Hardwick

## DIGITAL: THE NEW SALES FRONTIER

### Kisha Hardwick

Digital sales. It's a term that is valued very highly in the advertisement world. Digital selling can assume many forms but it is up to the individual to determine how they wish to propel their career by selling it to its full potential. There is no textbook that addresses the right or wrong way to sell digital media. Unlike traditional media sales, the techniques of selling "digital" are rapidly changing, and the eager seller must keep up with the trends.

As a digital sales manager, my role has been to make sure that my team kept up with those trends and made sure they were selling it accurately. Now, I will warn you: leading radio account executives can be a bit challenging. Think about it: radio sellers typically have been in the sales industry for an average of between 10 and 15 years. They have seen many leaders and the "it" incentives change rapidly. Many are comfortable with selling only spot radio ads and think of digital as an "add-on" or "value-added" product. That's when a digital leader must rely on their knowledge to teach those account executives how a digital campaign can dynamically increase an advertiser's revenue.

There was one AE who would scowl every time I mentioned the word "digital." It was as if I was telling her the most horrendous story ever told. Her digital sales numbers were the lowest of the team and she had no desire at all to learn how to sell. Immediately I asked questions to determine where this animosity was coming from. Why the hate, lady? She finally told me that a previous digital leader was not as knowledgeable with the techniques of selling "digital" as they would like others to believe. This led the AE to lose one of her biggest accounts because our company couldn't deliver on the expectation set by the previous digital leader. Therefore, her reputation with this longtime client was ruined. So, after hearing all this, it made me understand why she might have had hard feelings when it came to discussing digital sales. But I didn't let her get off that easy. She was a talented seller and I knew she was more than capable of blasting those digital budgets! After our discussion, I put in place a plan to get her on track. It included weekly digital training and having her set more digital appointments, including with me. Once she started to understand the finer aspects of "digital," she began feeling comfortable with having those conversations with clients. Now her digital sales numbers are up and she's hitting both her spot and digital budgets.

I have led sales executives in both the radio and television industries. I would have to say I enjoyed leading my team at the radio station more than I did at the TV station. The best part about selling digital with radio is the ability to use "digital" to enhance the impact of a radio commercial. Follow me on this: A listener can hear a radio ad a bunch of times and will memorize a couple of phrases from it. What's the next thing they do? They Google it. The listener will Google a couple of brand phrases heard in the spot and will either click on the advertiser's pay-per-click (PPC) ad or have a similar banner ad served to them. Digital completes the brand recognition process for any radio campaign.

I have learned as a digital sales manager to make learning "digital" exciting for the sales team by conducting contests, sponsoring fun incentives, and other morale-building activities. Digital is meant to be the "fun" form of advertising. If the account executives enjoy learning about digital they'll have a better experience selling it!

---

**Kisha Hardwick** founded and operates the Atlanta-based digital marketing agency MediaGlo Digital Marketing. The firm assists businesses with services including website development, social media management, and more. She was previously employed with NBC 26 in Augusta, Georgia, Morris Communications, Raycom Media, and Cox Media Group.

Nowhere within the station structure do salary extremes swing as widely as do those of on-air personalities. *Billboard* magazine, a perennial observer of station programming activities, reports slightly more granular salary data than do other surveyors. For instance, morning show hosts earn annual salaries ranging from $100,000 in lesser markets to as much as $400,000 in the majors. Typical salaries for mid-size market performers range from $50,000 to $200,000, while talent in small markets can earn between $30,000 and $100,000 annually. The amount of compensation paid to major-market deejays that work in dayparts other than morning drive reportedly ranges from $70,000 to $150,000. For several years Bob Papper, Professor Emeritus at Hofstra University, has surveyed journalist salaries. The research outcomes, sponsored by the Radio Television Digital News Association (RTDNA), reveal an uptick in the amount of financial compensation afforded newsroom personnel. A statistic of note is the earning potential of web producers and editors. Median-salary statistics reveal that persons working in these relatively new and increasingly important positions earn as much as and perhaps more than their news-reporting associates.

To succeed in a business as unique as radio, a person must possess many qualities, not the least of which are determination, skill, and the ability to accept and benefit from constructive criticism. A career in radio is like no other, and the rewards, both personal and financial, can be exceptional. "It's a great business," says Lynn Christian, former Senior Vice-President of the Radio Advertising Bureau. "No two days are alike. I recommend it over other career opportunities." Corroboration of Christian's exuberance can be found in the results of the *Inside Radio* salary survey. There, respondents to the question, "If you 'had to do it all over again', would you choose a career in radio?" overwhelmingly affirmed their choice of profession, with 77% saying 'YES' and 23% saying 'NO.'"

**FIGURE 10.10**

Dual video displays enable the student deejay to monitor the scheduling of current and upcoming program elements

Source: Courtesy of Southeast Missouri State University

## GETTING INVOLVED: STUDENT ORGANIZATIONS

Many readers of this textbook are students enrolled in university courses, and many institutions incorporate laboratory radio station activities into the course curriculum. These stations serve valuable purposes as training grounds for on-air talent and managers, and have acquired reputations over the decades as fertile fields for seeding and growing new, innovative approaches to programming. Another opportunity for gaining experience, cultivating valuable business connections, and developing viewpoints consistent with those of industry professionals is to affiliate with a national student media organization.

Chapters of organizations catering to the specific interests and needs of prospective radio broadcasters have been established on high school and college campuses across the nation. Four well-known and respected organizations are the Broadcast Education Association (BEA), College Broadcasters, Incorporated (CBI), the Intercollegiate Broadcasting Society (IBS), and the National Broadcasting Society (NBS). These organizations share many attributes and objectives and generally seek to promote interest in broadcasting and multimedia among members and encourage the development of professional perspectives, attitudes, and behaviors.

Becoming a member and enthusiastically participating in local chapter activities and organization conventions can yield multiple benefits. Each conducts a national convention annually in a major media market. These popular and well-attended get-togethers provide invaluable networking opportunities with the industry's influential movers and shakers. Tours of media facilities are a part of many conventions' schedules. Several organizations also convene meetings at state and regional levels.

A popular activity in each organization is its media production competition. Students are awarded recognition of their exemplary performance skills across multiple categories of submissions. There's also an added bonus of recognition that results from having their production examples judged by media professionals. It's never too soon to begin creating name-awareness with the industry pros!

Membership structures vary. In some instances organizations offer individual student memberships while in other situations the structure is organized around a facility model that offers membership to all station staff.

This section presents the voices of leadership at four national student associations. Read about the organizations' missions and learn about the specific activities they conduct. Then consider carefully the benefits of membership. Find out if a chapter exists on campus. Chapters warmly reach out and embrace prospective members. If there is no on-campus organization chapter available, reach out to the national leadership. Representatives are glad to visit with prospects and discuss the many benefits of membership.

**FIGURE 10.11**
Heather Birks

### BEA STUDENT MEDIA CLUBS

#### Heather Birks

The Broadcast Education Association (BEA) is an international academic media organization, driving insights, excellence in media production, and career advancement for educators, students, and professionals. While BEA members share a diversity of interests involving all aspects of telecommunications and digital media, from the history of media to documentary production and on-air talent to audience measurement analytics, in recent years we have expanded our activities while still keeping a focus on preparing the next generation of media professionals. One of BEA's primary goals continues to be preparing college students to enter the radio and television business.

**FIGURE 10.12**
Broadcast Education Association logo
Source: Courtesy of BEA

In 2016 we launched the latest BEA student initiative: BEA Student Media Clubs (SMCs). The SMCs were developed to promote collaborative projects and discussions at colleges and universities, and assist and guide students by providing networking opportunities with the industry. To apply as a SMC your school must be a current BEA college/university member.

Since the SMCs are in their infancy now, we have been working with advisors to get the clubs active by sharing ideas and creating programs specifically for students involved in their school's SMC. BEA is in a unique position because of our connection to the industry. We are fortunate to partner with the National Association of Broadcasters (NAB) and the Radio Advertising Bureau (RAB) to manage the Radio Show Student Scholar Program. Since 2015, the Student Scholars Program has been offering college undergraduate and graduate students registration scholarships to attend the annual NAB convention each spring and the annual RAB Radio Show each fall.

Thanks to the support of 29 radio groups and associate businesses, students attend the Career Fair, a conference orientation featuring a series of special networking events, entertainment and educational content geared toward students. In addition, the scholars participate in the conference's management, content creation, sales, marketing, advertising, research, legal, technology, and young professional sessions. We are collaborating with RAB to introduce a mentor component into the program as well. Senior executives and staff of the supporting companies are all eager to closely work with the students to give them insight into the business during the actual radio show conference, but also to continue the dialogue after.

In addition to SMCs and the Radio Student Scholar Program, BEA provides close to $30,000 annually in academic scholarships to students and offers a creative competition called the Festival of Media Arts and several scholarly research competitions. In the near future we are planning a 48-hour film festival, offering a BEA Student Club of the Year Award, and a special orientation at BEA's annual Las Vegas convention for club student members, as well as their faculty advisor. We also offer complimentary registration for the club's faculty advisor, if 10 or more students attend BEA's convention, as a way to encourage and guide the student participation.

BEA's convention offers hands-on training sessions, research, and a series of sessions featuring professionals who talk about where the industry is headed and how to succeed. BEA is sensitive to the need to cultivate and foster opportunities for students and will continue to provide a platform to make those accessible and worthwhile.

---

**Heather Birks** has been the Executive Director of BEA, a media education association, since June 2006. She has created and developed strategic alliances with corporate and academic organizations, and worked with BEA's board to revitalize the association's annual convention, marketing and membership benefit efforts. Heather created a new format for BEA's annual convention to include focused workshops on production, documentary, scriptwriting, assessment, and research. She developed a series of academic and industry relationships to help educators promote research and get tools, techniques and contacts needed to teach future media professionals.

Heather came to BEA after working for more than 10 years at the National Association of Broadcasters (NAB)—the government relations department, membership and event planning for the television department, and finally to the NAB Education Foundation (NABEF). In the six years she worked at NABEF she helped build, manage and produce the Service to America Awards and helped launch and run the Broadcast Leadership Training Program, a 10-month executive MBA-style program for broadcasters interested in learning the art of assessing, acquiring, and running successful radio and television stations. In 1992 she graduated with a BA in Comparative Politics from Clark University in Worcester, Massachusetts.

**FIGURE 10.13**
Mark Maben

**FIGURE 10.14**
Warren Kozireski

## WHAT IS CBI?

### Mark Maben and Warren Kozireski

Radio started with a love of acronyms—CBS, BBC, MBS, and NBC. Today, many media outlets are known simply by their abbreviations—ABC, CBC, CNN, ESPN, FNC, HBO, MTV, PBS, PRI, and SBS. The ubiquitous use of abbreviations means we sometimes forget the original names of these media networks, channels, companies, and organizations. ESPN was originally shorthand for Entertainment and Sports Programming Networks, for example. In 2010, National Public Radio decided to change its name simply to its familiar and well-known initials NPR to reflect that it had become more than just "radio."

**FIGURE 10.15**
College Broadcasters Inc. logo
Source: Courtesy of CBI

Here's another abbreviation for you, and if you are reading this book it is one you need to know—CBI. It was initially short for College Broadcasters Inc., but today the organization is mostly known as CBI.

So, why should you know CBI? And what is CBI anyway?

In the simplest definition, CBI is a nonprofit membership organization of student-run electronic media outlets at universities, colleges, and high schools. The organization represents students involved in radio, TV, podcasting, webcasting, and other related media ventures. CBI works to advance the interests of student-run electronic media. You may think of CBI as college media's version of the National Association of Broadcasters (NAB).

CBI is, however, a much more dynamic organization than the simple explanation suggests. CBI exists to help students, their advisors, and their schools become better at what they do. Here are some of things that CBI offers:

*A community of support*: CBI has a variety of forums, such as social media and a thriving old-school listserv, where you can ask questions and get answers. CBI brings together students, advisors, professors, industry professionals, community radio volunteers, and others to talk about programming, staff management, station operations, promotions, audio and video editing, FCC issues, and much more. The CBI community helps one another by sharing information and crowdsourcing solutions to problems you may be facing at your media outlet. The odds are that someone from across the nation has experienced or is experiencing the same issue you are and can offer suggestions to help solve your problem.

*An annual convention*: CBI's National Student Electronic Media Convention (NSEMC) is America's only convention dedicated exclusively to the interests of student radio stations, TV/video outlets, webcasters, and convergent media. Each year the NSEMC attracts hundreds of students, advisors, faculty members, and industry professionals for three days of interactive sessions, workshops, exhibits, networking events, and more. Many sessions are led by award-winning media personalities, including NY Press Club, Emmy, Associated Press and Marconi award winners. The convention is another place where you can bring your challenges and find suggestions and solutions. It is also where you can make new friends and find mentors.

The NSEMC's location moves around the country to help maximize participation. The chances are that at least once every four years the convention will be in a convenient city for your station staff to travel to. The NSEMC also features a keynote address. Past keynote speakers include Dean McFlicker, vice-president and creative director of NBC Entertainment Marketing, 1010 WINS reporter and anchor Glenn Schuck, and CNN's Carol Costello.

*CBI has your back*: CBI has been on the forefront of advocacy that helps protect and preserve student-run electronic media. The organization has negotiated agreements that shield student stations from excessive webcasting fees and burdensome reporting, and CBI has been a strong voice against college radio station sales and regulations that would negatively impact student stations. CBI represents student radio interests when it comes to matters such as FCC ownership report requirements and performance rights royalties, with members appearing on Capitol Hill to testify on students' behalf. There is strength in numbers and CBI helps raise the voice of college radio and student electronic media so it is loud enough to be heard.

CBI has your back in other ways too. Providing advisor advocacy and offering teams to review station operations and governance is another way we support college electronic media. CBI's monthly *Radio World* columns raise awareness of student station interests and successes. CBI's early support of College Radio Day helped to establish this annual event as an important date on station calendars.

*National Student Production Awards*: Open to members and nonmembers, CBI's National Student Production Awards are among the most prestigious awards students can earn. Approximately 1,000 entries are received annually from individuals and media outlets competing for these coveted awards. If you've made some great audio or video, submit it for an award. If you win, it looks great on your résumé and Linkedin profile.

*Step into a leadership role*: CBI's board of directors includes a student representative position. Any student from a member media outlet who meets the eligibility requirements can run for this board position. It is a great way to further develop your leadership skills and learn how industry organizations operate from an insider's perspective. There are also committee positions and other volunteer opportunities within CBI where students, faculty, and professional staff can enhance their skills and experience.

No matter your career path, joining a professional membership organization can be essential to your professional development. Becoming involved with an organization like CBI while you are still a student is a good first step. Learning how to utilize and leverage the resources a professional association offers while still in college will position you to take full advantage of organizations such as AWC, CMMA, NFCB, NAHJ, PRPD, RAB, RTDNA, SBE, and SPJ. Ah, those abbreviations again!

---

**Mark Maben** is General Manager of Seton Hall University's WSOU-FM, the 2016 winner of the national Marconi Award for Noncommercial Station of the Year. A longtime broadcaster and educator, Maben's broadcasting career began in the early 1980s and he has worn just about every hat there is in radio, including building and running a station from construction permit to full operation.

**Warren Kozireski** is General Manager for 89.1 The Point/WBSU at the College at Brockport. WBSU has been honored by state or national organizations in various categories numerous times. Kozireski was awarded the State University of New York's highest honor, the Chancellor's Award for Excellence in Professional Service in 2002, and the "Joel Willer Award" by College Broadcasters Inc. in 2015, among other honors.

## INTERCOLLEGIATE BROADCASTING SYSTEM

### Chris Thomas

No matter what career field you ultimately end up choosing, you need to be a geek for it. A complete nerd. A total dweeb for all things that are your industry. It's cliché but one must eat, breathe . . . well, you get the idea. One way in which students interested in radio are able to accomplish this is to become involved in the Intercollegiate Broadcasting System (IBS). Since 1940, IBS has been educating our member schools, their students, faculty, and staff in areas such as FCC rules, programming, royalties, copyrights, engineering, and more. And, in addition to those benefits for member schools, IBS offers individual students many ways to get involved as well.

**FIGURE 10.16**
Intercollegiate Broadcasting System logo
Source: Courtesy of IBS

**FIGURE 10.17**
Chris Thomas

The easiest way to ensure people are aware of the energy and skill sets you will bring to the market is to network yourself (and then stay in touch with those you've connected with). At our annual IBS International Media Conference each spring in New York City you will make those connections. And not just with industry professionals either (of whom there are plenty on hand), but also with fellow students who are looking to do the same thing as you. Sure, you may consider them your competition for potential jobs, but ultimately everyone wants to succeed and those you network with now may just become your biggest advocates down the road. In addition to networking, our conference offers more than 100 sessions and multiple keynote speakers on all things media. If you can't make it to our national conference, don't worry: IBS holds several regional conferences each fall as well in cities such as Chicago, Boston, Miami, and Los Angeles.

Another key to success is to build up your résumé. Jobs and internships are the key components here, but everyone is going to have those things listed. What will make you stand out? You can distinguish yourself from the competition by winning awards for your high-quality work. The IBS College Media Awards program offers more than 65 categories spanning radio, video, social media, management, and more, so there is sure to be an area for your work. Just being named a finalist at the IBS College Media Awards means that your work is among the top 10% in the country. That alone carries a lot of credibility, even if you are not named the winner.

Finally, as a student looking to succeed in this field, everything needs to be at the top of your game, and IBS is here to help. At our conferences, we offer air check and résumé critiques, but, in between those times, our passionate volunteer board of directors has more than 300 years of combined experience in radio, television, and even print media, and we are always willing to offer advice, critiques, and more to those who are looking for a leg up.

For more information on the Intercollegiate Broadcasting System and all that it can do for you, please visit www.collegebroadcasters.us.

**Chris Thomas** is President of the Intercollegiate Broadcast System and the General Manager of WLTL Radio, La Grange, Illinois.

**FIGURE 10.18**
Jim Wilson

## NATIONAL BROADCASTING SOCIETY

### Jim Wilson

NBS-AERho, the National Electronic Media Association, is a dynamic connection of media professionals and aspiring students preparing to enter a competitive but rewarding career field. Its mission is to enhance the development of college students preparing for careers in electronic media industries. The organization connects students with practicing professionals; emphasizes industry ethics, diversity, and inclusiveness; and promotes opportunities for excellence in leadership, community service, and media production. With membership, students can benefit from local chapter activities, annual national conventions, and developing networking contacts for the future. In addition, the organization recognizes student and professional achievement. NBS-AERho gives students multiple opportunities to go beyond the classroom and gain a career advantage.

**FIGURE 10.19**
National Broadcasting Society—Alpha Epsilon Rho logo
Source: Courtesy of NBS-AERho

Founded in 1943 as Alpha Epsilon Rho-the National Radio Fraternity, the organization and its name have evolved with the electronic media industry. Focus has expanded to include television, cable, and satellite distribution of programming, internet communication, the transition to digital media and the growth of social media. More than 50,000 members have participated in chapters on college campuses across the United States. Student and professional membership over the years includes recognizable names such as Dick Clark, Judith Waller, Edward R. Murrow, Gordon Jump, Walter Cronkite, Bob Costas, and Al Roker, as well as thousands of successful professionals in all levels of the industry.

NBS-AERho has two components. NBS membership is open to collegiate students and professionals with an interest in electronic media. Alpha Epsilon Rho (AERho) is the honor society for electronic media students and is recognized by the Association of Collegiate Honor Societies. AERho members must meet the academic criteria established by the ACHS in order to qualify for membership.

Most of the membership participates through chapters established on college campuses. On the local level, students in NBS-AERho chapters engage in professional development experiences, network with local media professionals, participate in community service activities, and develop leadership skills. Students have the opportunity to participate in electronic media education programs during the course of the school year, enter a national media production contest, and attend the annual NBS-AERho national convention.

The National Undergraduate Student Electronic Media Competition is a valuable opportunity for college media students to submit their best work for review in a national competition. Industry professionals judge more than 50 categories of entries. Entrants receive professional feedback. Winners receive awards and national recognition.

The annual national convention is a highlight of membership, bringing together hundreds of electronic media students to a major media market. Industry leaders share media knowledge and insights as well as job search strategies. Students also benefit from networking opportunities and behind-the-scenes exposure to professional facilities in the host city. The national awards show recognizes student achievement both in the association and in the NBS-AERho competitions. Recent conventions have been held in New York, Hollywood, Atlanta, and Washington, D.C.

More information on NBS-AERho can be found on the organizational website at www.nbs-aerho.org.

---

What started out as a short fling in college radio led to an extended career in many facets of media. **Jim Wilson** worked as a disc jockey, sports announcer, news reporter, media salesman, producer, program director, general manager, program syndicator, and freelancer. Interspersed with his work in public and commercial media, Jim spent 25 years in higher education in teaching and administration. In 2000, he agreed to take a one-year appointment as the Executive Director of the National Broadcasting Society. He's still there today. The position provides an opportunity for him to enjoy his love of working with college students while helping open the door for them to enter the world of professional electronic media. However, his life wouldn't be complete without the support of his wife, Randi, two daughters and sons-in-law, three grandchildren, and many friends and colleagues.

Special-occasion events are another way for students to network and increase their knowledge. One notable activity that is growing in popularity and is capturing the attention of secondary school students is the annual High School Radio Day. Celebrated for the first time in May 2012, this occasion's purpose is expressed on its website (http://highschoolradioday.com). High School Radio Day, the site reports, is "A day dedicated to high school radio stations where students and advisors can celebrate the uniqueness of their program and make their community, their state, the whole country aware of what they do and how they do it." Five years later almost 80 terrestrial and online stations from 30 states joined in the celebration with events that ranged from a rear-view mirror look back on radio's rich cultural history to a forward-looking "young-ins" broadcast featuring recently appointed deejays in some of their earliest on-air appearances.

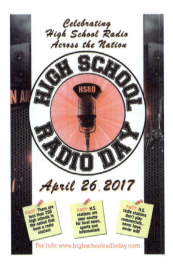

**FIGURE 10.20**
High School Radio Day logo

Source: Courtesy of www.highschool radioday.com

One notable supporter of HSRD is WBHF, "The Biff," operating at Bloomfield Hills High School in Bloomfield Hills, Michigan. Self-described "radio lover" Ron Wittebols serves "The Biff" as Manager and Technical Director. In an interview with *Radio World*, Wittebols observed the value and benefits that accrue to students who staff the award-winning station laboratory:

If you think about it, a high school radio station is the best "lab" class any school district could offer. Every discipline and theory to which a child is exposed during the school day can be practiced behind a broadcast console: speaking, writing, mathematics, team building, interpersonal expression, conflict resolution, marketing and sales, etc. It is an extension of the curricular philosophy of the Bloomfield Hills School District and an opportunity to put everything a student learns into play.

## TEENS ARE REDISCOVERING RADIO

### Ronald Wittebols

For years, industry experts have predicted the demise of the radio station, that newer generations prefer to receive audio and visual content via different platforms, and that there really is no way to win these ears back. The general consensus among these experts is to throw in the towel on traditional broadcast radio, embrace the change, and explore new platforms of content delivery.

Not so fast.

**FIGURE 10.21**
Ronald Wittebols, WBFH general manager. Pictured at left is retired "Biff" general manager Pete Bowers

Radio is the granddaddy of social media: a 100-year-old bullhorn that still works, still garners attention, and still commands respect among adults. Surprisingly, radio is enjoying a rediscovery among the younger set, especially on the campus of Bloomfield Hills High School, where preteens and teens are exploring and embracing the art of broadcasting at WBFH.

So why the renewed interest? Because radio is cool again. Although today's cutting-edge technology allows anyone with a smartphone to "go live" from any location, the younger set considers the equipment in a fully stocked broadcast studio to be "way cooler" and more interesting than a thin, sleek, new digital device with a touch screen. Yes, the smartphone is ubiquitous, coveted, and invaluable, but it's quickly being taken for granted.

An explanation of radio's newfound popularity may be that broadcasting seems to parallel the recent resurgence of vinyl records: everything old is new again. Perhaps the digital realm has left us devoid of static and whistling diodes, and the old-fashioned way of using transmission equipment to launch analog audio into the ether is more nostalgic. Maybe another explanation—as argued with vinyl discs—is that there exists a warmth and comfort in listening to a "magic talking box" versus an online streaming music service that offers no human voice. After all, radio is the most intimate medium.

The glass-walled WBFH studio with its prominent location inside Bloomfield Hills High School offers students the opportunity to see their friends and cohorts operating a broadcast console, microphones, audio equipment, and automation software. It's a hands-on operation. Instead of isolating people behind a wall of social media, the WBFH radio studio allows the talent to play to an audience of passersby. Radio slyly transforms youngsters from content consumers to content creators, especially when they ask, "Hey, can I put my friend on the air?" It's then when the bond between radio and teens is cemented. How cool is that? I got you on the radio!

The "live" remote always wins them over. The chance to be seen and heard high atop the grandstand at the football scrimmage, or the soccer battle or courtside at the basketball game is a big plus. (WBFH

FIGURE 10.22
Entrance to 88.1 "The Biff" studios and office

goes all-out with banners and headsets and hype.) Let's face it, broadcasting is show business, and what teen ego would pass up an opportunity to shine in front of a thousand parents, listeners, and classmates? You don't get that kind of attention speaking into a cell phone among the crowd in the stands.

Although it is true that radio today is being consumed on many different platforms, the purest form of producing radio broadcasting (microphone to transmitter) is still alive and thriving—and growing—among the younger set. The more things change, the more they stay the same.

**Ronald C. Wittebols** is Station Manager and Technical Director of WBFH Radio, a service of Bloomfield Hills Schools in Bloomfield Hills, Michigan.

## COLLEGE RADIO: LIFE-CHANGING YET UNDER-APPRECIATED

### Rob Quicke

College radio is the launching pad for many careers, not just those in broadcasting. In fact, research has been done into just how transformative participating in college radio is for students. So important is college radio as an outlet for self-expression that many students find their communications skills and their formation of self-identity are positively impacted by being involved with it. College radio literally gives a voice to the students who get behind the mic and have the guts to go on the air. There are generations of alumni who started in college radio and now work in different industries throughout the country but testify that college radio is a catalyst for self-development.

FIGURE 10.23
College Radio Day 2017 logo
Source: Courtesy of the College Radio Foundation

FIGURE 10.24
Rob Quicke

Yet college radio is often dismissed as a medium unto itself, and there are even those who believe it's nearly extinct. In an age of Internet music streaming, endless listening choices, and the subsequent fragmentation of audience, college radio is sometimes viewed as a thing of the past. I wanted to fight back against this misperception.

In December 2010, I watched a movie called *The Social Network* about the story of Facebook. I was tremendously inspired and wondered whether there was a singular idea that could unite and excite the college radio community in the same way that Facebook initially united the college community. The next day I woke up with the idea of College Radio Day (CRD). The idea seemed so obvious that I searched online to see if there was a precedent for a day of national unity for college radio, and I could not find any previous attempts to do so.

The idea percolated throughout the first half of 2011 and in May 2011 I launched the website (collegeradioday.com) and put the call out for college radio stations in America to join together for the event. The biggest fear was that no one would participate.

I knew we had my college station, WPSC at William Paterson University (where I am GM and Associate Professor), and my friend Peter Kreten, GM of WXAV at Saint Xavier University in Chicago, which was the only other station who had pledged to participate from day one. When I sent that first email out to as many college radio stations as possible, I could only hope that we could persuade 50 of them to join the event. What happened in the next four months is that 365 stations in America, Canada, and Jamaica signed up for the October 11 event!

Over the next five years we would grow so that we involved over 700 college radio stations in 43 different countries! In fact, so popular is CRD around the rest of the world that we now have World College Radio Day as the same event, but celebrated worldwide! For some countries, college radio is a relatively recent development—and in Europe and South America student radio stations are flourishing. Many of these stations speak different languages but essentially all make the same point: that college radio is one of the last remaining bastions of creative radio programming, free from the constrictions of having to be commercially viable, and a place where those involved in its programming believe passionately in its mission. College radio is still an important training ground for future professional broadcasters and I love how participating stations are free to celebrate CRD and WCRD by broadcasting whatever they want during the day, really unleashing their inventiveness and demonstrating their growing talents.

Our mission is simple: the aim of College Radio Day is to harness the combined listenership of hundreds of thousands of college radio listeners throughout the world and to celebrate the important contributions

**FIGURE 10.25**
College Radio Day delegation pictured in the White House Briefing Room

THE WHITE HOUSE

WASHINGTON

September 23, 2015

I am pleased to greet all those celebrating the 5th annual College Radio Day on October 2.

For over a century, radio airwaves have strengthened connections across America and around the globe. As a groundbreaking channel for broadcasting news, radio has helped tell the stories of our time and has changed how we see the world. And as a means of bringing people of all backgrounds together around voices and rhythms of distinct genres, eras, and origins, it has also played an essential role in shaping the sound of American and international music.

By keeping the legacy of college radio stations alive and strong, students on campuses from coast to coast experience the thrills of sharing and discovering media and creating stimulating programming. In doing so, they are lending their talents to a tradition that has been unfolding for generations and inspiring others to join in the work of shaping our future's course.

Wherever you're listening from, you have my very best wishes as you celebrate the unique contributions of college radio.

**FIGURE 10.26**
College Radio Day letter of recognition from President Barack Obama

of college radio by uniting for this one day. We encourage people who would not normally listen to college radio to do so on this day. More than ever, college radio is genuinely important because it provides local communities with music and programming that are unlikely to be heard anywhere else. Put simply, college radio is an important part of the media landscape because of its unique and fearless programming.

So I believe that CRD was an event that coincided with the need for college radio to make a collective statement that it was still around, and we challenged the media narrative that suggested college radio was doomed. Not so! College Radio Day was originally conceived as, and continues to be, a genuine celebration of college radio.

A landmark moment was being invited to the White House in 2015 and receiving a letter from President Obama that officially recognized and supported College Radio Day, and also further legitimated what we believe to be true about college radio:

> By keeping the legacy of college radio stations alive and strong, students on campuses from coast to coast experience the thrills of sharing and discovering media and creating stimulating programming. In doing so, they are lending their talents to a tradition that has been unfolding for generations and inspiring others to join in the work of shaping our future's course.
>
> President Obama, September 23, 2015

I couldn't agree more, and so the fight continues!

---

**Rob Quicke** is founder of College Radio Day and is also a tenured Associate Professor of Communication at William Paterson University, where he also serves as General Manager of WPSC 88.7 FM in Wayne, New Jersey.

# NATIONAL RADIO TALENT SYSTEM

The National Radio Talent System is a collegiate-level organization whose mission is to give students "a learning experience they could not get anywhere else." Gold-mine rich with a faculty consisting of some of the industry's top-shelf talent, the program continues to gain momentum and increase the number of venues that convene the state-wide Institutes. Founder and President Dan Vallie, a 40-year radio industry veteran, established the inaugural event at Appalachian State University for the purpose of attracting "intelligent and talented students with a positive attitude" and surround them during an intense, 10-day event with

radio professionals that teach them support and encourage a positive attitude that lets them know of the great opportunities in broadcasting and what an exciting time it is. The "professional faculty" from the industry that come and teach display the same attributes we want to see in young broadcasters entering the industry.

The 25 students accepted into each event emerge from the Institute prepared to excel in positions both on-air (personality, news, and sports) and revenue generation (sales, traffic, copywriting, and production).

**FIGURE 10.27**
Dan Vallie

## THE NATIONAL RADIO TALENT SYSTEM

### Dan Vallie

After decades of the industry talking about the need of a "talent farm system" or "talent incubator," we have finally done something about it. Up until now, there wasn't a "go-to" place to find young talent coming into the industry. Now, fortunately for today's aspiring young talent, there is.

The National Radio Talent System is a system of radio talent institutes on college campuses across America. It's the only program of its kind in the world. This is the campus to career connection most students need to get their careers started.

**FIGURE 10.28**
National Radio Talent System logo

It began officially in 2013 with the Kellar Radio Talent Institute as the inaugural institute, followed by the KBA WKU Radio Talent Institute at Western Kentucky University, the GAB Radio Talent Institute at the University of Georgia, Confer Radio Talent Institute at Bloomsburg University of Pennsylvania, Hubbard Radio Talent Institute at Central Washington University, the MBA Radio Talent Institute at Northwest Missouri State University, and the TAB Radio Talent Institute at the University of Tennessee, Knoxville, with additional institutes still being added.

Each Institute is 10 days long and is conducted on the university campus during the summer. All sessions are taught by almost 40 professional broadcasters, each in their own area of expertise. The broadcasters are from the state and region of the institute, but also come from across the country.

It is a total immersion in all things radio. The sessions address practically every aspect of the industry: on-air in music radio, sports, news, production, sales, programming, promotions/marketing, social media/digital, podcasting, engineering/IT, etc.

Students get that first job to get their career launched with iHeart, CBS, Entercom, Hubbard Radio, CNN, Cumulus, Beasley Media Group, and others. Some students go into related fields, including TV, NASCAR productions, and IMG Sports Network.

Students have to apply to be accepted and the number of students is limited to 25 per institute. They come from all over the state and region, in addition to students coming from the partner university. The institute students are college students or recent graduates, and can also include students who have recently graduated and are not yet working full-time in the industry. The institute looks for talented young people who have a developing passion for broadcasting.

Typical quotes from students include, "I would have never gotten into the business if it hadn't been for the Radio Talent Institute," "It changed my life," and "It's the best thing I did in my college career."

Students learn from the best in the business and describe the institute as "intense" and "fun." Most days include a social hour with broadcasters spending casual time getting to know the students and building relationships. Not only do the students learn what it takes to be successful in the industry, but at the end of the 10 days they have a professional network of 40 broadcasters.

The passion broadcasters have for the industry is well known; as many of them say, "The business gets in your blood." It shows, as well, in the many leading broadcasters who come and give their time to speak and teach to bring in young talent today who can be the leaders of our industry tomorrow, and it shows in the support from broadcasters who underwrite the institutes, with seven institutes springing up in the first four years of the National Radio Talent System, with more to come.

Radio aggressively embraces technology, as we should, and in doing so has become part of twenty-first-century technology and terminology as we approach the hundredth anniversary of broadcasting as an industry. But what has always made the difference, and will always make the difference, is people. That is proven again in the broadcasters, and the future broadcasters, of the National Radio Talent System as the industry thrives into this twenty-first century.

You can visit the National Radio Talent System and the radio talent institutes at NationalRadio TalentSystem.com.

---

**Dan Vallie** is a lifelong radio industry veteran, and the innovator and President of the National Radio Talent System, the only program of its kind in the world, designed to be a system of radio talent institutes on college campuses all across America, funded by individual broadcasters, broadcast groups, and organizations. Vallie founded Vallie Richards Donovan Consulting Inc., a premiere radio consulting firm, in 1988. He is also Practitioner in Residence at Appalachian State University.

## FROM AM TO FM TO XM: PARTING THOUGHTS FROM A SIX-DECADE PRO

### Marlin Taylor

Now that you've read the thoughts, suggestions, and stories of several individuals who found their way into meaningful roles within the radio industry, let me try to wrap up this information-packed book and leave you with a few bits of counsel as gleaned from my 60+ years in the working world, the bulk of which was spent in this industry with which I've had a love affair for the past 70 years!

**FIGURE 10.29**
Marlin Taylor

As I see it, and based on my own experience throughout these many years, your focus needs to be concentrated in these areas:

*Knowledge*: this might also be called intelligence . . . which the military calls G2. It begins with the reading of this book, so that you understand the inner workings of the radio station and our business. Next, it's reading the trade publications—most of which are now available online—not to just see who's got a new job and what opportunities might exist but to read reports and articles about industry developments, even audience ratings reports—a highlight position of my career came from reading the ratings for New York City and seeing which stations most needed help, then reaching out to the senior executive of its ownership with a to-the-point proposal based on how I believed I could bring them success.

And, from a military G2 aspect, never approach a station until you've thoroughly researched them, done some in-depth listening and carefully examined their website and Facebook page to gain insight as to how they operate and observe any weaknesses . . . so you can develop a sense of how you might "help them."

If, by this point, you are not feeling a deep-down passion—"fire in the belly"—for getting into the middle of this wonderful, crazy business, maybe you should be applying to the insurance company who's advertising for actuaries!

*Creativity and innovation*: These are generally considered separately, which they are, yet they are intrinsically linked. I define innovation as creativity in action! The entire business world has an urgent need to stimulate a greater flow of creative ideas ... and radio is right up there in having that need ... not just in programming, but in other aspects of the operation as well. For instance, radio's greatest need today is generating revenue through advertising sales. While selling may not be your "cup of tea," your creative genius could prove beneficial in creating ad campaigns that both entice the potential advertiser into trying your station ... plus inducing the listener to respond—after all, if the cash register doesn't ring, the client won't be satisfied.

Also, innovation isn't always a brand-new idea ... it can just as easily be a new twist on a well-worn concept that produces solid results ... in many cases at little expense.

*Perseverance*: If the passion is truly there and firmly fixed in your mind, commit to the long haul. And look to people who can be of positive influence and support ... while ignoring and avoiding the naysayers! When I was starting out following school, I didn't know what route my career would take ... all I really knew was that I wanted an opportunity to create programming that would bring joy to people's hearts and lives! I had reached my fourth stop, with a number of years having passed, before things began to fall into place and my career "found its groove."

These multiple points are brought home by the story of a sweet young lady named Mindy. I remember the day she arrived at XM Radio in May of 2001, having graduated from college in Florida only a day earlier.

She had developed a detailed concept for a children's show that she'd produce and host. Then, having done her homework, she knew that a company named XM Radio would be launching a satellite-delivered radio service in the fall of 2001, offering 100 channels of diversified programming, including one designed for children. Without question, this is where Mindy wanted to be ... and what she was proposing is exactly the kind of show programming guru Lee Abrams and his team needed and was looking for ... it was time for her to take action.

The *Absolutely Mindy Show* is still being heard on Sirius XM's "Kids Place Live" channel 16 years later!

Even though there are fewer positions available, I believe the opportunities are there for individuals who follow Mindy's lead and demonstrate how you can be an asset to the station or organization you wish to be employed by.

And, finally, never forget to:

- Step up! Take a risk! Be proactive!
- Live the "more" approach: do more, give more, and give your best, always!
- Commit to learn something new every day, no matter how small it may be.
- Never think or say "That's not my job!"

In sum, for anyone working in the field of mass communications, the first and foremost rule must be recognizing and delivering what's in the best interests and tastes of the listener/viewer/reader, as that is the reason for a radio or television station or publication to exist and the number one priority for achieving success!

---

**Marlin Taylor**'s 60-year career began when radio listening was still mostly on the AM band and concluded after he spent nearly 15 years in satellite radio, during which he created three channels to serve three distinct segments of the music-loving population. His full story is shared in his recently released self-written memoir titled *Radio ... My Love, My Passion*. For more information, visit his website, www.marlintaylor.com.

# CHAPTER HIGHLIGHTS

1. Radio broadcasting is a vibrant, evolving mass communication activity that attracts 92% of the U.S. listening audience of teens and adults each week. As a decades-old career option, it continues to attract talented and creative young adults into its workforce.

2. Introductory opportunities for becoming acquainted with the profession and earning hands-on experience are available in both secondary and higher education.

3. Although the position of deejay commands the most visibility, positions in the areas of productions, advertising sales, promotions, social media, and engineering/information technology offer equally viable career paths.

4. The National Association of Broadcasters (NAB) represents the interests of broadcasters from its headquarters in Washington, D.C. Its publication *Careers in Radio* examines the variety of employment possibilities available at stations.

5. The pace of growth in the radio announcing job market continues to edge slowly upwards, its pace dampened by the rise in popularity of alternative listening platforms.

6. Employment downsizing is the result of ownership consolidation. An emerging trend is for employers to task their staffs with increased responsibilities, underscored with higher performance expectations.

7. While hands-on experience remains much-desired by employers, increasing emphasis is being placed on the value of applicants' college educations. Internships are popular activities for acquiring on-the-job training.

8. Entry-level salaries generally are meager but the profession offers opportunities for significant earnings increase by those personnel who advance to larger markets. Earnings potential varies most widely for those employed as hosts of morning shows.

9. Determination, skill, and the ability to accept and benefit from constructive criticism are three desirable personal attributes of radio professionals.

10. BEA, CBI, IBS, and NBS are four national organizations open to membership for college students interested in pursuing radio broadcasting careers. Types of membership and opportunities for members vary by organization. Each organization sponsors a national student media production competition.

11. High School Radio Day and College Radio Day are two recently established events that sponsor annual celebrations of radio broadcasting activities in secondary and higher education.

12. The National Radio Talent System offers college students in several states opportunities to convene with industry professionals in an intense, 10-day retreat setting.

13. Radio broadcasting, like many industries, needs creative and innovative personnel. Creativity and innovation are intrinsically linked, according to veteran broadcaster Marlin Taylor. He defines "innovation" as "creativity in action."

# SUGGESTED FURTHER READING

ABC News Internship Program, http://abcnews.go.com/Site/page?id=3069947.

ABC Radio Careers, http://abcradio.com/careers.

*All Access* Music Group Job Market, www.allaccess.com/forum/viewforum.php?f=9.

Associated Press Careers, www.ap.org/careers.

Beasley Media Group Job Archives, http://bbgi.com/careers.

Broady, J., *ON-AIR: The Guidebook to Starting A Career As A Radio Personality*, BVI, San Bernadino, CA, 2007.

Capitol Broadcasting Company, Careers, www.capitolbroadcasting.com/careers.

Careers at Cumulus Media, www.cumulus.com/careers.

Careers at Entercom, www.entercom.com/career_gateway#.WdChVHRJmpo.

Careers at iHeartMedia, http://iheartmediacareers.com/Pages/default.aspx.

Careers at NPR, www.npr.org/series/750004/careers.

CBS Radio Career Center, http://cbsradio.com/careers.

Chuday, L., *NAB's Guide to Careers in Radio*, 2nd edition. National Association of Broadcasters, Washington, D.C., 2008, www.broadcastcareerlink.com/documents/NABRadioCareers.pdf.

Cox Media Group Careers, https://jobs.coxmediagroup.com/category/broadcast-jobs/1646/11228/1.

Emmis Careers, www.emmis.com/emmis-careers.

Entercom Career Center, http://entercom.com/careers/.

Fox News Careers, http://careers.foxnews.com.

Hearst Career Sites, www.hearst.com/careers.

Hubbard Radio Careers, http://corporate.hubbardradio.com/careers.

iHeartMedia Jobs, http://iheartmedia.jobs.

*Inside Radio* Classified Ads, www.insideradio.com/classifieds/job.

Lerner, M. and Blumenfeld, M.J., *Careers with a Radio Station (An Early Career Book)*, Lerner, Minneapolis, MN, 1983.

Pandora Careers: Current Openings, www.pandora.com/careers/all.

Public Media Employment Opportunities, www.cpb.org/jobline.

*Radio Ink* Job Listings, https://radioink.com/category/jobs.

Salem Media Group Careers, https://rn22.ultipro.com/SAL1004/JobBoard/ListJobs.aspx?__VT=ExtCan.

Schneider, C., *Starting Your Career in Broadcasting: Working On and Off the Air in Radio and Television*, Skyhorse, New York, NY, 2007.

Scripps Careers, www.scripps.com/careers.

Townsquare Media Careers, www.townsquaremedia.com/careers/openings.

Urban One Careers, https://urban1.com.

WNYC Jobs, www.wnyc.org/careers.

Working at SiriusXM, www.siriusxm.com/careers.

# Glossary

**AAA** Adult album alternative format, also known as "Triple-A."

**AAC** Advanced audio coding, used for digital audio.

**ABC** American Broadcasting Company, network.

**AC** Adult contemporary format.

**Account executive** Station or agency salesperson.

**Active audience (actives)** Listeners who call radio stations to make requests and comments or in response to contests and promotions.

**Active listeners** The number of distinct registered users, including subscribers, who have requested audio from a streaming service's servers within the trailing 30 days to the end of the final calendar month of the reporting period.

**Actuality** Actual recording of news event or person(s) involved.

**Ad Council** National clearinghouse for public service announcements.

**Adjacencies** Commercials strategically placed next to a feature.

**Ad-lib** Improvisation; unrehearsed and spontaneous comments.

**Affidavit** Statement attesting to the airing of a spot schedule.

**Aircheck** Recording of live broadcast.

**All Access** An online trade publication produced by the All Access Music Group.

**Alternate Broadcast Inspection Program (ABIP)** A collaboration between the FCC and state broadcast associations in which the station goes through a mock inspection modeled after the one conducted by FCC field inspectors.

**AM** Amplitude modulation, a method of signal transmission using the standard broadcast band with frequencies between 535 and 1705 kHz.

**AMAX** Enhanced AM receiver developed by the NAB.

**AMBER alert** America's Missing: Broadcast Emergency Response.

**Analog** Continuous variation in quantity of sound waves and current.

**Announcement** Commercial (spot) or public service message of varying length.

**AoIP** Audio over Internet protocol.

**AOR** Album-oriented rock radio format.

**AP** Associated Press, a wire and audio news service.

**App** Abbreviation for a software application used on mobile devices.

**Arbitron** Audience measurement service to determine the number of listeners tuned to area stations. It was sold to Nielsen and rebranded as Nielsen Audio.

**ASCAP** American Society of Composers, Authors, and Publishers, a music licensing service.

**Attenuate** Reduce signal; decrease levels or output.

**Audio** Sound, modulation.

**Audio Ad Center** A CBS Radio digital platform designed for advertisers to purchase online audio advertising.

**Audio animator** Term used by satellite radio denoting a production person.

**Audition tape** Telescoped recording showcasing talents of air person.

**Auditorium test** Research method involving large-room survey of panelists about song preferences.

**Automation** Equipment system designed to play prepackaged programming.

**AWRT** American Women in Radio and Television.

**Baby boomers** Born 1945 to 1964.

**Back announce** Recap of preceding music selections.

**Barter** Exchange of airtime for programming or goods.

**BEA** Broadcast Education Association.

**Bed** Music behind voice in commercial.

**Blasting** Excessive volume resulting in distortion.

**Blend** Merging of complementary sound elements.

**Blog** Internet journal or diary page of personality or talk host.

**BM** Beautiful music radio format.

**BMI** Broadcast Music Incorporated, a music licensing service.

**Board op** Control board operator.

**Book** Term used to describe rating survey document; the "Bible."

**Branding** Establishing station identity and value.

**Bridge** Sound used between program elements.

**BTA** Best-time-available, also run-of-station (ROS); commercials logged at available times.

**Bumper** Music played to intro segments on talk programs and features.

**Call letters** Assigned station identification, beginning with "W" east of the Mississippi and "K" to the west.

**Call-out** Music research conducted by calling panelists to play song snippets and document responses. See **hook**.

**CCC** Clear Channel Communications.

**CFR** *Code of Federal Regulations*.

**CHR** Contemporary hit radio format.

**Churn** The percentage rate at which users of a given online audio service leave that service from one time period to the next time period.

**Classic hits** Radio format; preferable to the descriptor "oldies" in some usages.

**Clear Channel** FCC-designated AM service classification for stations authorized to serve wide areas at high power.

**Clock** Diagram indicating sequence or order of programming ingredients aired during one hour.

**Clustering** Combining the operations of several stations, resulting in a cluster.

**Codec** Audio encoding and decoding equipment.

**Cold** Background fade on last line of copy; descriptive term for denoting the manner in which a song (or other recording) ends.

**Combo** Announcer with engineering duties; AM/FM operation.

**Commercial** Paid advertising announcement; spot.

**Compact disc (CD)** Digital recording using laser beam to decode surface.

**Compression** (1) Manipulation of audio dynamic range for the purpose of managing amplitude; (2) manipulation of digital audio files utilizing a bit-reduction technique for the purpose of decreasing file size.

**Console** Audio mixer (board) consisting of inputs, outputs, switches, meters, and pots.

**Consolidation** See **clustering**.

**Consultant** Station advisor or counselor; "radio doctor."

**Control room** Center of broadcast operations from which programming originates; air studio.

**Cool out** Gradual fade of bed music at conclusion of spot.

**Co-op** Arrangement between retailer and manufacturer for the purpose of sharing radio advertising expenses, so-called because of its "cooperative" feature.

**Copy** Advertising message; continuity; commercial script.

**CPB** Corporation for Public Broadcasting.

**C-QUAM** Compatible–Quadrature Amplitude Modulation, which bridged the gap between AM stereo and HD Radio.

**CRB** Copyright Review Board.

**CRM** Customer relationship management.

**CRMC** Certified radio marketing consultant.

**Crossover** A recorded song that appeals to two different audiences and is chosen for airplay by programmers in two or more formats.

**Crossfade** Fade-out of one element while introducing another.

**Cue** Signal for the start of action; to prepare a device to play a recorded audio element using a console's on-board loudspeaker to monitor the signal.

**Cume** The average number of persons listening to a particular station for at least five minutes during a 15-minute period.

**DAB** Digital audio broadcasting.

**DARS** Digital Audio Radio Service.

**Dayparts** Periods or segments of broadcast day: for example, 6 am to 10 am, 10 am to 3 pm, 3 pm to 7 pm.

**Daytimer** AM station required to sign on the air at or after local sunrise and leave the air at or near sunset.

**Dead air** Silence where sound usually should be; absence of programming.

**Deejay** Host of radio music program; announcer; disc jockey.

**Demographics** Audience statistical data pertaining to age, sex, race, income, and so forth.

**Digital** Conversion of analog waveform to numerical code.

**Direct broadcast satellite (DBS)** Powerful communications satellite that beams programming to receiving dishes at earth stations.

**Directional** Station transmitting signal in a preordained pattern so as to protect against interference other stations on similar or identical frequency.

**Distortion** Audio garble.

**DMA** Designated market area.

**DMX** Digital music satellite service.

**Dolby** Noise reduction system.

**Donut spot** Commercial in which copy is inserted between segments of music.

**DOS** Director of sales.

**Double billing** Illegal station billing practice in which client is charged twice.

**Downloading** Gathering audio or video from the Internet for local storage.

**Downsizing** Reducing staff by combining functions and departments.

**Drivetime** Radio's primetime: 6 am to 10 am and 3 pm to 7 pm.

**DST** Differential survey treatment.

**Dub** Copy of recording; duplicate (dupe).

**EAN/EAT** Emergency Alert Notification/Emergency Alert Termination (via EAS).

**Eastlan** Audience measurement service specializing in smaller markets using telephone-recall methodology.

**EBS/EAS** Emergency Broadcast System/Emergency Alert System.

**Edit** To alter composition of recorded material; splice.

**ENG** Electronic newsgathering.

**Engagement** The ability of programming to make listeners act upon something that was promoted.

**Equalization** Manipulation of frequency spectrum, also known as "EQ."

**Erase** Elimination of recording from storage medium.

**ERP** (1) Effective radiated power; (2) tape head configuration: erase, record, playback.

**Ethnic** Programming for minority group audiences.

**Facebook** An online social networking site created in 2004 by Harvard student Mark Zuckerberg.

**Fact sheet** List of pertinent information on a sponsor.

**Fade** To slowly lower or raise volume level; descriptive term for denoting the manner in which a song (or other recording) ends.

**FCC** Federal Communications Commission, the government regulatory body with authority over radio operations.

**Feedback** Recycling of audio signal; reamplification.

**Fidelity** Relative comparison between original sound and its mediated reproduction.

**Fixed position** Spot routinely logged at a specified time.

**Flight** Advertising air schedule.

**FM** Frequency modulation; method of signal transmission using 88 to 108 mHz band.

**Format** Type of programming a station offers; arrangement of material, formula.

**Frequency** Number of cycle-per-second excursions of an electrical sine wave.

**Full service** Format featuring a balance of music, personality and information elements. See **MOR**.

**Gain** Volume; amplification.

**Generation** Dub; dupe.

**Gen X** Born 1965 to 1976.

**Gen Z** Born 1996 to present.

**Geo-fencing** the practice of restricting the availability of online station streams to specified geographic areas.

**Grid** Rate card structure based on supply and demand.

**Ground wave** AM signal traveling the earth's surface; primary signal.

**HD** dts-trademarked term denoting advanced digital AM-FM broadcasting.

**HD2, HD3** HD Radio frequency side-channels.

**Headphones** Speakers mounted on ears; headsets, cans.

**Hertz (Hz)** Cycles per second; unit of electromagnetic frequency.

**HLT** Highly leveraged transaction.

**Hook** The catchiest or most memorable portion of a song; a snippet used in conducting music research of listener preferences.

**Hot** Over modulated.

**Hot clock** Wheel diagram indicating when particular music selections are to be aired.

**Hype** Exaggerated presentation; high intensity, punched.

**IBEW** International Brotherhood of Electrical Workers; union.

**IBOC** In-band, on-channel.

**ID** Station identification required by law to be broadcast as close to the top of the hour as possible; station break. Announcement wording consists of FCC-assigned call letters followed by city of license.

**iHeartRadio** A computer and smartphone application that allows for online audio listening owned by iHeartMedia Inc.

**Imager** Audio production person; an imaging director.

**Input** Terminal receiving incoming audio signal.

*Inside Radio* An online trade publication examining all aspects of the radio industry.

**Institutional** Message promoting general image.

**I-O** Internet-only radio station.

**iPad** A type of portable tablet computer.

**IPAWS** Integrated Public Alert and Warning System.

**iPod** A type of portable media player.

**IRT** Internet radio tuner.

**ISDN** Integrated services digital network.

**IT** Information technology.

**ITU** International Telecommunications Union, the world broadcasting regulatory agency.

**iTunes** A computer and smartphone application that allows for online audio listening by Apple.

**Jack** Plug for patching sound sources; patch-cord, socket, input.

**Jack format** Programming emulating iPod sound mix.

**Jingle** Musical commercial or promo; signature, logo.

**Jock** See **deejay**.

**JRAM** *Journal of Radio and Audio Media.*

**KDKA** First radio station to offer regularly scheduled broadcasts (1920).

**Kilohertz (kHz)** One thousand cycles per second; AM frequency measurement, kilocycles.

**K-Love** Contemporary Christian music service operated by the not-for-profit Educational Media Foundation.

**Level** Amount of volume units; audio measurement.

**Licensee** Individual or company holding license issued by the FCC for broadcast purposes.

**Line** Connection used for transmission of audio; phone circuit.

**Line-of-sight** Path of FM signal; FM propagation.

**Liner** Recorded vocal promo used to ensure adherence to a station image. See **sweeper**.

**Liner card** Written on-air promo used to ensure adherence to station image; prepared ad-libs.

**Listener fatigue** Undesirable psychoacoustic phenomenon resulting from extended exposure to lower-fidelity, distorted sound reproduction.

**Live copy** Material read over air, not prerecorded.

**Live tag** Postscript to taped message.

**LMA** Local marketing (or management) agreement.

**Local channels** Class D AM stations found at high end of band: 1200 to 1600 kHz.

**LP** Long-play phonograph record.

**LPFM** Low-power FM.

**Make-good** Replacement spot for scheduled commercial that was not broadcast..

**Market** Area served by a broadcast facility; DMA.

**Master** Original recording.

**Master control** See **control room**.

**Megahertz (mHz)** Million cycles per second; FM frequency measurement, megacycles.

**Mergers** Consolidation or combining of assets and resources.

**Millennials** Born 1977 to 1995.

**Mini-disc machines** Digital cart decks employing floppy disc technology for audio reproduction and archiving.

**MIDI** Musical Instrument Digital Interface.

**MIS** Manager of information systems.

**MIW** Mentoring and Inspiring Women in Radio.

**Mixdown** Integration of sound elements to create desired effect; production.

**MMD** Mobile multimedia device.

**MMS** Mobile music services.

**Mobile device** A small handheld device with a computer screen that has most of the capabilities of a standard computer.

**Monitor** Studio speaker; aircheck.

**Mono** Single or full-track sound; monaural, monophonic.

**MOR** Middle-of-the-road radio format.

**Morning** Drive radio's primetime daypart: 6 am to 10 am.

**MP3** Digital audio file format.

**MRC** Media Ratings Council.

**MSA** Metro survey area; geographic division in radio survey.

**Multitasking** Performing several duties.

**Multitracking** Recording sound-on-sound; overdubbing, stacking tracks.

**Music sweep** Multiple selections played back-to-back without interruption; music segue.

**NAB** National Association of Broadcasters.

**NABET-CWA** National Association of Broadcast Employees and Technicians-Communications Workers of America.

**NABOB** National Association of Black Owned Broadcasters.

**NAEB** National Association of Educational Broadcasters.

**Narrowcasting** Directed programming; targeting specific audience demographic.

**NBC** National Broadcasting Company; network.

**Network** Broadcast entity providing programming to affiliates: NBC, CBS, ABC.

**Network feed** Programs sent via telephone lines, the Internet and satellites to affiliate stations.

**New media** Digital technology that allows consumers to access information anytime and anywhere.

**News block** Extended news broadcast.

**Nielsen** Parent company of Nielsen Audio.

**Nielsen Audio** Formerly Arbitron.

**NPR** Formerly National Public Radio.

**NRSC** National Radio Systems Committee.

**NTR** Nontraditional revenue.

**O&Os** Network- or group-owned and operated stations.

**OES** Optimum effective scheduling.

**Off-mike** Speech or other sound occurring outside a microphone's pickup pattern.

**Out-cue** Last words in a line of recorded copy.

**Output** Transmission of audio or power from one location to another; transfer terminal.

**Overdubbing** See **multitracking**.

**Overmodulate** Exceed standard or prescribed audio levels: pinning VU needle.

**P1, P2, P3** Nielsen Audio scale of a station's time spent listening (TSL).

**Packaged** Canned programming; syndicated, prerecorded, taped.

**Pandora** A computer and smartphone application that allows for online audio listening.

**Passives (passive audience)** Listeners who do not call stations in response to contests or promotions or to make requests or comments.

**Patch** Circuit connector; cord, cable.

**Patch panel** Jack board for connecting audio sources: remotes, studios, equipment; patch bay.

**PBS** Public Broadcasting System.

**PEP** (Emergency Alert System) primary entry point (station).

**Playback** Reproduction of recorded sound.

**Playlist** Roster of music for airing.

**Playout** Sequenced reproduction of program elements by software-based automation equipment.

**Plug** (1) To promote; (2) audio connector.

**Podcast** Online archived/posted audio available for downloading or streaming.

**Popping** Break-up of audio due to gusting or blowing into mic; blasting.

**Portable People Meter (PPM)** Nielsen Audio's proprietary electronic audience measurement device.

**Positioner** Brief statement used on-air to define a station's position in a market.

**Pot** Potentiometer; volume control knob, gain control, fader, attenuator.

**Preview** To privately audition or monitor an audio source. See **cue**.

**Production** See **mixdown**.

**Production room** Studio dedicated to the purpose of creating recorded program material and commercials, usually for subsequent broadcast.

**Promax** Broadcast Promotion and Marketing Executives Association.

**Promo** Live or recorded announcement featuring details about an upcoming program to elicit listenership.

**PSA** Public service announcement; noncommercial message.

**Psychographics** Research term dealing with listener personality, such as attitude, behavior, values, opinions, and beliefs.

**Public inspection file** Certain documentation related to the station's license, which stations are required by the FCC to maintain.

**Punch** Emphasize; stress.

**R&R** (now-defunct) *Radio & Records* magazine.

**RAB** Radio Advertising Bureau.

**Rack** Prepare or set up for play or record: "rack it up;" equipment container.

**RADAR** Radio's All Dimension Audience Research; nationwide measurement service by Nielsen Audio.

*RAIN* *Radio and Internet Newsletter.*

**Rate card** Radio station statement of advertising fees and terms; rarely used today.

**Rating** Estimated audience tuned to a station; size of listenership, ranking.

**RDS/RBDS** Technology that enables AM and FM stations to send data to "smart" receivers, allowing them to perform several automatic functions.

**Recut** Retake; rerecord, remix.

**Remote** Broadcast originating away from station control room.

**Reverb** Multiple relections of sound waves; akin to echo.

**Ride gain** Monitor level; observe VU meter display.

**Rip 'n' read** Airing copy unaltered from newswire service.

**RPU** Remote Pick-Up.

**RSS** Really simple syndication

**RTDNA** Radio Television Digital News Association.

**Run-of-station (ROS)** See **BTA**.

**SAG-AFTRA** Screen Actors Guild-American Federation of Television and Radio Artists.

**Satellite** Orbiting device for relaying audio from one earth station to another; DBS, Comsat, Satcom.

**SBE** Society of Broadcast Engineers.

**SCA** Subsidiary Communication Authorization; subcarrier FM.

**Secondary service area** AM skywave listening area.

**Segue** Uninterrupted flow of recorded material; continuous.

**SESAC** Society of European Stage Authors and Composers, a music licensing service.

**SFX** Abbreviation for a sound effect.

**Share** Percentage of station's listenership compared to competition; piece of audience pie.

**Side-channel** An additional HD channel or frequency.

**Signal** Sound transmission; RF.

**Signature theme** Logo, jingle, ID.

**Simulcast** Simultaneous broadcast over two or more frequencies.

**SiriusXM** Satellite radio service; subscriber-based audio program source.

**Skim** To record a deejay performance or a recording of same.

**Smartphone** A mobile phone with advanced computing capabilities.

**Smooth jazz** Radio format emphasizing elements of jazz and pop music.

**Sound imager** Audio producer, animator.

**Spec spot** Specially tailored commercial used as a sales tool to help sell an account.

**Sponsor** Advertiser; client, account, underwriter.

**Spot set** Group or cluster of announcements; stop set.

**Spotify** A computer and smartphone application that allows for online audio listening.

**Spots** Commercials; paid announcements.

**Station** Broadcast facility given specific frequency by FCC.

**Station identification** See **ID**.

**Station log** Document containing specific operating information as outlined in Section 73.1820 of the FCC *Rules and Regulations*.

**Station rep** Company acting on behalf of local stations to national advertising agencies.

**Stereo** Multichannel sound; two program channels.

**Stickiness** A measure of user online audio engagement which answers the question "how likely is a user to return to the service day after day?"

**Stinger** Music or sound effect finale preceded by last line of copy; button, punctuation.

**STL** Studio–transmitter link.

**Straight copy** Announcement employing unaffected, non-gimmicky approach; institutional.

**Streaming** Delivering media content in real time via the Internet.

**Streams** The individual media contents being delivered via the Internet.

**Stringer** Field or on-scene reporter.

**Subliminal** Advertising or programming not consciously perceived; below-normal range of awareness, background.

**Sustain** Descriptive term for denoting the manner in which a song (or other recording) ends.

**Sweeper** Transitional recorded jingle between program elements used to ensure adherence to a station image. See **liner**.

**Syndicator** Producer of purchasable program material.

**Tablet** A mobile, handheld computer.

**Tag** See **live tag**.

**Tagging device** Allows listener to buy songs they hear on radio.

**Talent** Radio performer; announcer, deejay, newscaster.

**Talk** Conversation and interview radio format.

**TAP** Total audience plan; spot package divided between specific dayparts: AAA, AA, A.

**TDGA** Traffic Directors Guild of America.

**Telescoping** Time-reducing compression technique applied to audio to achieve a desired length; technique used in audition tapes and concert promos, editing.

**TFN** Till further notice; without specific kill date.

**Timeshift** Listening to a broadcast program that is convenient to the consumer rather than the moment at which it was created.

**Trade-out** Exchange of station airtime for goods or services.

**Traffic** Station department responsible for scheduling sponsor announcements.

**Translator** Low-power FM transmitter used to (1) extend the coverage of full-power FM stations into areas of otherwise problematic reception and (2) assist daytime AM stations in extending service into the nighttime.

**Transmit to broadcast** Propagate signal; air.

**TSA** Total survey area; geographic area in radio survey.

**Turnover** The number of times the audience turns over within a given daypart.

**Twitter** An online social networking site, created in 2006, that allows individuals to microblog using 280 characters or less.

**UC** Urban contemporary format.

**UHF** Ultra-high frequency.

**Underwriter** See **sponsor**.

**UNESCO** United Nations Educational, Scientific and Cultural Organization.

**Unidirectional mic** Microphone designed to favor sound pick-up from a single direction; cardioid, studio mic.

**UPI** United Press International, a news service.

**VOA** Voice of America.

**Voiceover** Talk over sound.

**Voicer** Voice of news reporter.

**Voice-tracking** Prerecorded deejay comments inserted into broadcasts at prescribed times under software-automation control.

**Volume** Quantity of sound; audio level.

**Volume control** See **pot**.

**VT** Voice track.

**VU** Meter gauge measuring units of audio.

**WARC** World Administrative Radio Conference, an international meeting charged with assigning spectrum space.

**Web radio** Online radio station.

**Website** Internet site.

**WestwoodOne** Radio programming network and syndicator.

**Wheel** See **clock**.

**Wi-Fi** Wireless Internet access.

**Windscreen** Microphone filter used to prevent popping and distortion arising from air movement across diaphragm.

**Wireless telegraphy** Early radio used to transmit Morse code.

**Wrap** Open and close voicers in actuality.

# Index